Activities Keep Me Going & Going

Volume A

Body of Knowledge

A guidebook for activity professionals, who plan,
direct and evaluate activities
with older persons.

by

Jennifer L. Krupa, ACC

Mary E. Miller, ACC

Charles W. Peckham, ACC

Arline B. Peckham, BA

Volume A
2ND Printing 2011

Copyright 2011 by Otterbein Homes

Inquires should be addressed to:

Otterbein Homes
Attn.: Charles Peckham, Sr.
585 North St. Rt. 741
Lebanon, Ohio 45036
513-932-7218
Fax: 513-932-932-5159

International No. 978-0-931990-08-3

Printed and bound by
Thomson-Shore, Inc.
Dexter, Michigan

This book is dedicated to all of the activity professionals who designed
the original Modular Education Program for Activity Professionals I and II (Basic
and Advanced Courses) and the Modular Education Program for
Activity Professionals 2nd Edition, as well as activity professionals in
community-based settings and long-term care.

Preface

"It would be dreadful for us to increase the duration of life without doing something to make life worthwhile," wrote a resident in a long-term care facility.

Medical technology has made the extension of the life span a reality. Today, people often outlive the prediction made on actuarial charts. Technical advances, new drugs and surgical techniques as well as an emphasis on wellness and healthy life styles have added years to life for multitudes of older adults. An older person living at home or in a long-term care facility may not be appreciative of an extended life, if that life is boring, or if there is little interaction with others, or if, because of health problems, they are limited in activities that were once enjoyable..

Older adults living in long-term care facilities have 5-13 hours per day of leisure time. A resident may have 6–10 hours of sleep, 3–6 hours of activities of daily living and 1–3 hours of treatment per day. Some residents nap more than one hour per day. A person living alone at home may have about the same amount of leisure time but may have fewer contacts with people. If a person is receiving home health service, he/she has contact with other persons but there may be little or no activity other than activities of daily living, depending upon family, friends or the agency providing the services.

Persons living at home, in assisted-living facilities, retirement communities, in long-term care facilities or members of Senior Centers and Adult Day Services need activities. A lack of stimulation, activity and interaction can lead to boredom and depression, which can then lead to other health problems. Individual, one-to-one and group activities have been the focus of agencies, organizations and facilities providing care and/or services for older adults. Opportunities for involvement in community activities sponsored by recreation non-profit organizations, i.e., YMCA, YWCA, church groups, senior centers, travel organizations, and hospital programs for older adults, etc., continue to increase. Wellness programs have increased since the 1980's. Volunteer opportunities and accessible transportation have provided older adults an opportunity to continue their involvement in the community.

The activity profession has had tremendous growth over the last 40 years. Activities are provided for older adults in a variety of settings in the community, in long-term care and specialized facilities/programs for specific populations, e.g., residents with dementia including Alzheimer's disease.

Activities are anything that a person does that is not medical treatment. Individual activities can be reading, writing, watching television, listening to music, gardening, needlework, people watching, feeding birds, petting an animal—something a person does by himself/herself. A one-to-one activity is an activity that is done with one other person, such as talking on the phone, playing a game of checkers, conversation, working on a puzzle, dining out, shopping, going for a ride, or vacationing. It may also be playing horseshoes, playing tennis, or praying with someone. Group activities can be small or large. The activity can be structured: leader-directed or spontaneous, planned or unplanned. Parties, picnics, celebrations, socials, and entertainment are usually large groups; group games, discussions, cards, etc. are generally small-group activities.

Three people may be interested in the same activity but participate differently. An example would be gardening. One person likes to select, plant/sow a garden; another person is involved in the local garden club; the third person may be involved in selling the fruits of his/her labor.

An activities program is a formal program. It is planned and structured to meet the participants' needs (physical, cognitive, emotional, social, spiritual, creative/ expressive, work/service and leisure), interests, preferences, abilities and limitations. In long-term-care facilities and in some community-based programs, the program may be based on physician orders.

Activity gives meaning to life, adds life to years, and may make the difference between the will to engage or disengage. It was the positive statement of a resident of Otterbein Lebanon Retirement Community "Activities keep me going!" that became the title of the first book printed in 1982 (*Activities Keep Me Going*: A Guidebook for Activity Personnel Who Plan, Direct, and Evaluate Activities with Older Persons, authored by Charles W. Peckham and
Arline B. Peckham).

The role of activities in the life of an older person continues to receive attention from physicians, health care and social-service providers, local, state and federal government agencies, family members and volunteers. As of July 1, 1995 activities in long-term-care were no longer the sole responsibility of activity professionals, but an interdisciplinary responsibility. In the new June 2006 new interpretive guidelines for activities, emphasis is place on interdisciplinary approach to resident centered care. (Federal Regulation 483.15 Quality of Life, Tag Number: F248).

This book is dedicated to activity professionals who have the awesome tasks of assessing participants, planning, developing, coordinating, implementing and evaluating programs for older adults as well as some younger persons in the community and in long term care facilities; educating staff, recruiting, training, supervising and evaluating volunteers; employing, supervising, appraising staff performance; working with families; and continuously trying to improve the quality of services and life of older persons for whom activities and services are provided.

In this totally reworked *"Activities Keep Me Going & Going,"* the Modular Education Program for Activity Professionals (MEPAP, 2nd Edition) provided the outline for this 2011 edition. The authors are indebted to the NCCAP Education Re-engineering Committee for the outline. We appreciate their detailed and voluminous work.

The approach taken in writing this book was that of using the Core Content and Key Concepts of the MEPAP 2nd edition.

Acknowledgments

The authors gratefully acknowledge the support and assistance of the following without whose help this volume would not have been possible:

Otterbein Homes' Board of Trustees and corporate leadership, who became partners in publishing this book, Don Gilmore and John Stephenson.

Jennifer Krupa, who contributed to this volume by reviewing, updating, editing and adding pertinent information. Lorain County Community College, students of the MEPAP classes, The Northeast Association of Activity Professionals who contributed to portions of the book.

Mary E. Miller & Associates, who contributed a major amount of information to create Volume A, 1st Edition, and Jennifer Tuertscher who did some word processing. Home Care Pharmacy, an Omnicare Company, who provided a Drug List.

Charles and Arline Peckham, who wrote portions of Volume A and reviewed, edited, organized and directed the publishing of this book.

Charles Taylor, Executive Director of the National Association of Activity Professionals and the Board, who gave us permission to use NAAP's definition of Activity Services, Standards of Practice and Code of Ethics.

Cindy Bradshaw, Administrator of the National Certification Council for Activity Professionals, along with Kathy Hughes, Chairperson of NCCAP, have been very supportive.

Cindy Bradshaw, who gave the authors permission to use the MEPAP outline as well as the NCCAP Code of Ethics and Standards of Practice.

The members of the MEPAP Re-engineering Committee, who prepared the 2004 outline for educational activity professionals – Cindy Bradshaw, ACC, Anne D'Antonio-Nocera, ACC, LNHA and Kathy Hughes, ACC.

Laura Woods, a skilled computer operator, who organized the information creating an attractive and readable text and did a yeoman's job preparing the copy on a PDF file for the printer.

James Recob and Betty Lyden, residents of Otterbein Lebanon, who reviewed portions of the manuscript.

The numerous sources unknown to the authors from whom ideas have come. (Note: In all cases where the original source of an idea or activity was known, credit has been given.) The authors assume responsibility for any errors that may have found their way into this volume.

CONTENTS

CHAPTER 1

ACTIVITY SERVICE PRACTICE SETTINGS

CHAPTER 2

COLLOQUY

CHAPTER 3

PROFESSIONAL FRAMEWORK

CHAPTER 4

GOVERNMENTAL AND SOCIAL SYSTEMS

CHAPTER 5

ADVOCACY: IN THE PUBLIC ARENA

CHAPTER 6

THE BEHAVIORAL SCIENCES

CHAPTER 7

ADULT CLIENT POPULATION

CHAPTER 8

PROFESSIONAL APPROACH TO CARE

CHAPTER 9

CARE PLANNING PRACTICES

CHAPTER 10

CARE GIVING PRACTICES

CHAPTER 11

ACTIVITY SERVICES: SYSTEM OF DESIGN, DEVELOPMENT AND EVALUATION

.Chapter 1

Activity Service Practice Settings

Welcome to the professional field of Activities, a growing profession. The activity profession is eclectic in terms of professional backgrounds (education, training and experience). This is changing with the national movement of the National Certification Council for Activity Professional (NCCAP) to provide specific training for all activity professionals by certified instructors effective January 1, 2007, leading to voluntary national certification with NCCAP and meeting the federal requirements for qualified activity professionals in nursing homes or professional standards for other service settings.

Definitions of Activity Service

In 1974, the federal government established the first regulations requiring an activities program in nursing homes. The term "Activities Coordinator" was used to define the person responsible for the activities program. The term "Activities" versus recreation was used to broaden the scope of services to include religious activities and services other than recreation.

- "Activities" refer to any endeavor, other than routine ADLs, in which a resident participates that is, intended to enhance her/his sense of well being and to promote or enhance physical, cognitive, and emotional health. These include, but are not limited to, activities that promote self-esteem, pleasure, comfort, education, creativity, success, and independence.

Introduction:

The activity profession, the clients we serve, the settings in which services are provided, and the services we provide have changed over the course of time. To meet the ever-changing needs of our clients and to reflect these changes, the Definition of Activity Services has been revised.

Activity professionals may provide some, many, or all of these services to the clients within their chosen setting. The extent to which services are provided is directly related to the setting in which the activity professional works.

Activity Services: An Activity professional's first priority is to deliver programs to clients that focus on physical, cognitive, social, spiritual, and recreational activities.

Additionally, as part of the interdisciplinary team, activity professionals:

- work closely with rehabilitation professionals to design individual interventions to help clients maintain and/or regain use of extremities, speech, and the ability to read and write.
- adapt services and approaches to meet the needs of clients with dementia disorders.
- assist the professional team with client behavior management.
- assist in the transition from life in the community to life in the facility, and facilitate community integration.
- help keep the clients and families connected through family events, newsletters, the Internet, and regular correspondence.
- encourage social interaction and help clients make new friends.
- help clients maintain or help establish strong intergenerational bonds.
- teach new skills such as using a computer to play games to keep in touch with the client's loved ones through e-mail, or to provide new activities of interest.
- are good listeners, able to ascertain their client's needs, and offer support when coping with difficult situations?
- work closely with clergy to provide spiritual opportunities within the facility, encourage continued involvement with the client's church, and provide religious materials.
- assist with promoting good nutrition and hydration.

- offer support and encouragement with pain management.
- help the clients die with dignity and provide support to the family through this difficult time; help facilitate the grieving process, and take an active role in providing palliative care.

History of Care & Services for the Elderly

"Knowing roots and history helps in understanding the present."

History of Activities Programming

In early writings programming for older adults was referred to as "recreation" for the aged, "recreation" for the ill and handicapped, "recreation" in nursing homes, "therapeutic recreation" for the aged, "therapeutic recreation" in nursing homes, "programming for seniors," "senior centers," "golden age clubs," etc. Today, the terms "activities," "activities programming," *"activity therapy(ies)" (when provided by certified/registered Art Therapist, Horticulture Therapist, Music Therapist, Occupational Therapist, Poetry Therapist, Recreation Therapist)"* "recreation," *"recreation therapy"*, "therapeutic recreation" and "therapeutic activities" are being used most frequently. The term used by agencies and organizations regarding programming for older adults is dependent upon the specific population of older adults being served, the place where services are being provided, the purpose, mission, philosophy, goals and objectives of the agency/organization, source(s) of funding, and standards regulating the agency or organization (government, voluntary/ regulatory agencies, professional standards *including national certification and/or state licensure),* and policies and procedures).

Seventeenth Century

The Poor House

The Poorhouse concept was derived from the Elizabethan poor laws. The New England Puritan settlers had been aware of their mother country's concept of poor relief. The 1601 Elizabethan poor laws established a system of local government and local responsibility for the poor. Overseers of each parish levied taxes on property. The tax money was used to provide relief for the poor. There was a division between neighbors and strangers. Families and the community were responsible, but not responsible for people who were not a part of the family or community.

According to the English and American poor laws, only permanent residents were to be assisted. Others needing assistance were shipped to their country of origin.

The poor laws supported the deserving poor not the undeserving poor. People truly in need (the old, the blind, the widow, the lame and the impotent) received restricted aid. The able bodied poor who were capable of working were excluded from aid. During early colonial time, the needy people received assistance from their local community. The young were to be supported by parents and grandparents and older parents were to be supported by their adult children. Poor people without families had to appeal to public authorities for assistance.

The care of the aging members of society in the early history of humankind fell to the family members. Families lived in tribal or communal groups. Elderly persons were cared for by the blood relatives or others in the tribal society. Aged members became the responsibility of the family. Some cultures expected families to care for their own. There were no community systems to care for those outside of the family unit. In time families began to become marginally separated from the tribe.

In the colonial period county farms were established to care for older persons who had no family support. These persons were often call "inmates" and were expected to contribute to the workload and were assigned tasks according to their ability. These tasks (activities) served to keep them occupied for periods of time and helped with the work.

As the geographic areas were divided into counties, many county homes were developed on operating farms where much of the food was raised. These were often referred to as "poor farms" and were considered a haven for those who were down and out. As time passed some of these county homes became nursing homes. Federal and State funds provided for the poor and ill and those isolated from family and friends. Such facilities later became designated for nursing or long-term care and were operated by the county. In many counties in the North Central areas of the United Stated the former county homes have been closed and the buildings used for other county services.

Following the Civil War homes were established to care for the orphans and widows of soldiers as well as those alienated from family or those who had, through disease, accidents, mental illness, war, etc. lost their family or community support system. This involved persons of any age, but many were the older person who needed help.

Government Sponsored Homes

In early colonial history there are accounts of facilities being built for persons of any age who had little or no family support.

Particularly when the male member of the family was deceased, the family was left vulnerable. The widow could attempt to maintain the household through domestic efforts such as spinning, sewing, cooking, etc., or could look for a potential second marriage. When fathers and mothers both died, family or friends took the children.

As a last resort there was a government agency sometimes referred to as a poor farm for the children, the disabled, or the elderly who had no other source of support. Activities were minimal.

These government facilities were often owned, managed, and supported by the local legal entity such as the county. Such facilities were administered by the county. At a later time Aid for Dependent Children and Aid for Aging provided options for these persons with special needs.

In the 1940's and 1950's many counties gradually phased out government-sponsored facilities. Other counties maintained the facilities but cared largely for the elderly.

Eighteenth and Nineteenth Centuries

In the eighteenth and nineteenth centuries humane treatment of the insane was fostered. Schools for the deaf opened in Paris in 1760. A school for the blind was opened in Paris twenty-five years later. In 1817 the first school for the deaf in the United States

opened in Hartford, Connecticut. The Deaf-Mute College opened in 1864 in Washington, DC. In 1917 it was renamed Gallaudet College after Thomas Hopkins Gallaudet, a teacher of the deaf and mute. Between 1829 and 1832 schools for the blind were founded in New York, Pennsylvania and Massachusetts. Massachusetts is credited with having the first school for the mentally retarded by a state act in 1848.

In the early 1800's psychiatrists prescribed physical exercise, reading, handicrafts and music for patients. The first psychiatrist, Dr. Benjamin Rush, advocated in 1821 that the Pennsylvania hospital use homely tasks (activities) for therapeutic effect (i.e., domestic tasks such as spinning and weaving, and games—checkers, chess, listening to the violin or flute, and taking trips into the community). History shows other hospitals using activities for therapeutic effects (Asylum of New York Hospital, 1821; McLean Hospital, Massachusetts, 1822, Friends' Asylum, Frankfort, Pennsylvania, 1830).

Florence Nightingale's Notes on nursing (1873) stressed variety (activities) for the patient. She used pets for the chronically ill. Recreation was provided for soldiers. She found music to have good effect on patients. Stringed and wind instruments were recommended. She advised visitors of appropriate and inappropriate topics of conversation and she recommended that babies be brought in to visit patients. Utilization of activities as treatment continued to be used and expanded in the treatment of the mentally ill in psychiatric hospitals. Recreation programs in hospitals were developed after WWII, starting in VA hospitals and then in Rehabilitation Hospitals and in some nursing homes.

Twentieth Century

In the early 1900's older adults lived with and were cared for by their families as there were three or four generations living in the same household. Persons considered to be elderly were not as old as persons living today. Life expectancy was about 50 years. Conversation, music, singing, games, reading and holiday celebrations were the activities in which an older family member could participate. Older family members were stimulated by the sounds of voices, music and singing as well as from the smells of fruits and pastries being cooked and baked.

If someone did not have a family or could not be cared for at home, he/she went to the poorhouse, almshouse, or asylum, which were considered the places of last resort. In these settings food, shelter and some medical care was provided. Church groups began to visit the "old folks' homes." Volunteers from different groups first provided friendly visiting and then holiday refreshments. Volunteerism grew and other services were developed (e.g., religious services, entertainment, bingo and letter writing.).

The 1929 Old Age Assistance Act offered alternatives to institutionalization in most states. The Social Security Act of 1935, a work-related program, provided Social Security benefits for older people. After age 65 people became eligible for Social Security benefits, which continue to assist people in remaining in their homes and having money for living and health care, as they grew older.

Planning and building new hospitals was made possible by the Hill-Burton Act (1946). The Act was extended in the 1950s as chronic illness became a national problem, e.g., TB Hospitals.

In 1959 the Heyman Commission of New York City reviewed health services in the city. Recreation in nursing homes was found to be inadequate. As a result, a stipulation requiring recreation personnel was included in the new code in 1963. Other states also had licensing laws in the 1950's that required recreation programs, i.e., California, Connecticut, etc.

Almshouse

The first institution for the poor, built in Boston in 1664 was called an Almshouse. Many almshouses were developed through out the country over time. An influx of immigrants from all over the world came to the United States between 1820 and 1860; most of the people were Irish and German. In many cities, one third of the population was foreign born.

Rest Homes

In the mid-1900s Rest Homes were developed. They were often started by a nurse or healthcare worker who would take an older person with deteriorating conditions into their homes and subsequently they were equipped to provide shelter, food and care for two or three persons. These homes were unregulated and sometimes provided less than adequate care. Caretakers were overworked and under paid. The residents or their families were responsible for paying the services and care. In some cases the state provided minimum payments to the care providers. However, because of the lack of standards and regulations the services and care that were provided was not consistent, some adequate and others poor.

Diversity of Activity Service Settings

The commonality among all activity professionals is their interest and work with older adults (age 55 and older) in the community and in different institutional settings caring for older adults. Today, activity professionals work in a variety of settings including, senior centers/clubs, multipurpose centers, senior focal point, community care, board and care, adult activity day services, assisted living, intermediate care, skilled nursing, rehabilitation, sub acute care, specialty facilities (Alzheimer's, multiple sclerosis, bariatric care (obesity treatment) and retirement facilities as well as hospitals with skilled nursing, geropsychiatry or other specialized units.

An activity professional can start in an entry level position and progress up the ladder to new and exciting positions as an employee of an agency providing services for older adults or move to another agency for older adults. Other roles include teaching in an educational institution or being a self employed entrepreneur as an activity specialist, activity consultant, educator/trainer, writer, designer of activity supplies and equipment or marketer of activities supplies and equipment.

Today, trained, nationally certified activity professionals and recreation therapists have a wide variety of settings in which to practice. Activity professionals working in settings serving older adults encounter clients with many different diseases, diagnosis, disabilities, chronic pain, special diets, recovery from acute illness, or different stages of terminal illness. No matter what setting, the activity professional or the recreation therapist must provide meaningful activities based on a client's individual needs, abilities, desires, interests and preference while being aware of his/her disabilities and limitations.

History of Activities in Treatment

In ancient civilization man danced, sang, played music and games, juggled, and participated in sports and festivals. Priests in Egypt established elaborate temples as retreats for the sick. Rituals were meant to appease the gods. Patients walked in beautiful gardens, took excursions on the Nile, danced, listened to concerts and observed comic representations.

Medicine was considered a non-religious art among the Greeks. Temples were built to treat the ill. Epidaurus, the most famous temple, had several facilities including a theater, library, stadium and a sanatorium to house parties. Religious activities were held in the temples. Annual events included poetry and miming contests. Athletic contests were held every four years. In ancient Greece, Pythagoras emphasized the use of music, gymnastics and dancing for treatment of mental disorders.

The Greek physician Bithynia supported humane treatment of the mentally ill. People were taken out of dark cells and provided sunshine and exercise. The philosophy of humane treatment returned to primitive levels with the fall of the Roman Empire. The Christian Church became the leader and the new Europe developed. Hippocrates taught that illness and disabilities were to be studied as natural phenomena. The Islamic hospitals treated people, particularly the mentally ill, with kindness. Fountains were used in fever wards; chapels, lecture halls and libraries, and a dispensary staffed by both men and women were a part of Cairo's Mansur Hospital. Employees recited the Koran. Musicians assisted patients to sleep. Storytellers were used for distractions. Money was given to discharged patients to tide them over while they recovered.

Activity Service for Clients' Growth & Development in Later Life

The Medicare Act of 1965 authorized care in long-term care facilities. Many extended care facilities were built. Recreational areas were usually centrally located in a room separate from the dining room. In some cases the dining room was to be used for dining and recreation.

In 1974 the Rules and Regulations for the Medicare Act (1965) mandated for the first time the provision of patient activities in skilled nursing and intermediate care facilities. The standards included weekend activities in skilled nursing facilities and if the activity coordinator was not qualified, he/she was required to have consultations from a qualified person. The regulations and interpretive guidelines provided national regulatory standards for programming, individualized care plans, space, supplies, equipment and visiting hours.

The regulations and interpretive guidelines were changed several times from 1974 to 1992. The interpretive guidelines, not the regulations were again changed in 1995 and 2006.

Professional Role of the Activity Practitioner

In 1975 a self-advocating resident, Michael Smith, of Colorado sued the State of Colorado for not assuring the provision of quality care in nursing homes in his state. He won his case. He sued the then Secretary of Health and Human Services, Margaret Heckler, for failing to assure that every state conduct an adequate survey and enforce regulations that promoted quality of care for all residents in nursing homes.

In 1983, the Health Care Financing Administration (HCFA) now known as Centers for Medicare/Medicaid services (CMS) requested the Institute of Medicine (IOM) to provide an in-depth study of long-term care. The findings showed substandard care in over one-third of the nation's nursing homes. The IOM made recommendations that the revision of the survey system be patient outcome-driven, the federal requirements and enforcement system is revised and that there be a single set of conditions for both Medicare and Medicaid.

In the OBRA'87 (Omnibus Budget Reconciliation Act) the Quality of Life Regulations included regulations regarding activities and qualifications of activity professionals. The final regulations that became effective July 1, 1995 had new interpretive guidelines for activities. More emphasis was placed on individual resident's needs, interests and preferences as well as all staff being involved in the provision of activities. This was the first time that emphasis was placed on a team approach to activities as a part of a resident's quality of life as defined by the resident.

Continuum of Health Care Services

Retirement Communities

Churches of various denominations and fraternal organizations, such as Masons and Unions, saw a need in the post Civil War period and established homes which cared for both children and older persons. By the 1950's Aid for Dependent Children provided relatively well for the children. Some of the facilities then turned their attention to care for the persons who were developmentally disabled.

Other care communities—with the number of older persons continuing to increase—became retirement communities and served only older persons. Often these facilities were planned as continuing care retirement communities (CCRC).

This change was accelerated with the enactment of the Medicaid and Medicare programs in 1965. Church and fraternal groups who had not created a retirement community began in the 1960's to provide such facilities.

Consequently, along with the rapid growth of nursing homes, there was a profound increase in retirement communities. Today such communities provide houses or apartments for the independent elderly as well as residential care, personal care, and/or assisted living units. Most of the communities also provide nursing care with many participating in the Medicaid and Medicare programs.

Retirement communities may also provide home health care, adult day care services and special care units e.g. Alzheimer's and dementia units.

The national association for these facilities and services is the American Association of Homes and Services for the Aging (AAHSA). Continuing care retirement communities are major players in providing a wide range of care and services for older persons.

One of the features of a retirement community is an array of activities including trip/tours/vacations, creative and performing arts, cards and games, socialization, celebrations, special events, fitness, gardening, educational programs and wellness programs as well as independent activities. Many retirement communities offer religious services. Some facilities have golf courses (or nearby courses), swimming pools (indoor/outdoor), fishing, tennis courts, shuffleboard courts, horseshoe pits and other recreational/sport areas as well as quiet areas in which to enjoy nature and its beauty.

Senior Centers

The first community center devoted entirely to older adults was started by the New York City Department of Welfare in 1944. Prior to this, older adults were involved in organized recreation in multi-generational service agencies. In the 1950's, municipal recreation departments started recreation programs for older adults; thus, the focus was on recreation.

Not all senior centers are owned and operated by municipal recreation departments. Some are funded through other local, state, and/or federal funding and private donations. Membership fees are required for some centers, but not for all.

Congress passed the Older Americans Act in 1965. The act has been amended several times. President George Herbert Walker Bush signed the Older Americans Act Amendments of 1992 (Public Law 102-375) on September 30, 1992.

Title III of the act provides funding of services for frail, older individuals, supportive services; congregate nutrition services; home-delivered nutrition services, school-based meals for volunteers and older individuals, and multi-generational programs, in-home service, preventive health service and supportive activities for caretakers who provide in-home services to frail older individuals.

There has been a tremendous growth of multipurpose centers from the 1960's to the present. In 1961 the estimated 218 senior centers in the United States grew to 1058 senior centers by the late 1960's. Depending upon community needs and available funding these multipurpose centers offer health, psycho-social services, nutrition, exercise center, computer access and recreation services. Some offer outreach programs. Nutrition centers offer social and recreation programs.

Title IV of the Older Americans Act provides funds for training, research and discretionary projects or programs (including purposes of education and training projects, grants and contracts, multidisciplinary centers of gerontology, demonstration projects, special projects in comprehensive long-term care, ombudsman and advocacy demonstration projects for multi-generational activities, neighborhood senior care program, senior transportation, demonstration program grants, resource center for Native American elders, demonstration programs for older individuals with developmental disabilities, and career preparation for the field of aging).

Creative art therapies (art therapy, dance and movement therapy, and music therapy) and therapeutic recreation were included in the 1992 Amendments. This will provide new dimensions of services in the future.

In the 1990 Edition of Senior Center Standards and Self-Assessment Workbook, Guidelines for practice by the National Council of the Aging, Inc., referred to Senior Centers as being focal points.

The 1999 edition of the National Senior Center Self-Assessment and National Accreditation Manual's definition of a Senior Center is:

"A senior center is a community focal point where older adults come together for services and activities that reflect their experience and skills, respond to their diverse needs and interests, enhance their dignity, support their independence, and encourage their involvement in and with the center and the community.

As part of a comprehensive community strategy to meet the needs of older adults, senior centers offer services and activities within the center and link participants with resources offered by other agencies. Center programs consist of a variety of individual and group services and activities.

The center also serves as a resource for the entire community for information on aging, support for family caregivers, training professional and lay leaders and students, and for development of innovative approaches to addressing aging issues."

Senior center programs consist of a variety of individual and group services and activities. These services and activities include:

- Health and wellness programming;
- Arts and humanities programming;
- Intergenerational programming;
- Information and referral services;
- Social and community action opportunities;
- Transportation services;
- Volunteer opportunities
- Educational opportunities
- Financial and benefits assistance;
- Meal programs.

Senior centers also serve as a resource for the entire community for information on aging, support for family caregivers, training professional and lay leaders and students, and for developing innovative approaches to addressing aging issues.

In the glossary, the terms "activities" and "services" are not listed. However the term "program" is defined as:

"Activities and services offered by the senior center. Activities generally are for the purpose of personal enrichment and include recreation, arts and crafts, socialization, education and cultural enrichment, and leadership and training opportunities. Services are aimed at meeting individual needs in such areas as health, nutrition, information and assistance, counseling. Services are aimed at meeting individual needs in such areas as health, nutrition, information and assistance, counseling and income supplementation."

Here, the purpose of activities is stated as related to personal enrichment and includes a variety of categories versus specific activities that were once listed under recreation e.g. arts and crafts, games, music, drama, singing and dancing, e.g. exercise, and computers, trips and tours, etc. The focus is on the outcome for the individual participant—meeting his/her individual needs and interests.

Senior Housing

The statement," I want to die in my own home", is commonly heard from older adults who do not want to move from their present home. Most often the statement is followed by, "I don't want to go to a nursing home; I want to die here." This is possible for a healthy person. One with infirmities who cannot keep up with daily personal care needs assistance in their own home. Cooking, making the bed, cleaning, etc., with the help of an outside agency, home health organization or employment of a person(s) to take over the necessary tasks so that the person can remain in his/her own home. Long Term Care Insurance may provide the needed financial support within the guidelines of the Long Term Care policy.

If needed, a home can be reconstructed to be accessible, allowing a person to remain independent. Home and Garden TV has shown how a bathroom that was redesigned so that a couple could function easily with a two sink counter top. The design of the sink and the cabinet below, allowed the husband, who uses a wheel chair, to use the full width, length and depth of the sink from his wheel chair. By opening the lower cabinet recessed doors, he could wheel himself in the open space, which allowed him to freely use the sink. The bathroom was also reconstructed to allow the husband easy access to the shower. All the changes in the bathroom were esthetic as well as functional. Unless one knew about the changes, the bathroom looked like it was void of accessible features, which the couple wanted.

Older adults may opt for downsizing and living in a smaller home or apartment within a specific community. They are still responsible for the maintenance of their personal home, whether they do it themselves or hire someone to do it. Living in an apartment complex, allows a person to care for his/her personal space but not be responsible for major inside or outside upkeep. An apartment complex may have a designated area for tenants to garden or they may have a small area outside their ground floor apartment or a patio that can be used for container gardens.

Real estate advertisements often advertise a small home as being a starter home, retirement home or for downsizing. Other types of housing for independent living may be advertised by builders, owners of independent living communities as well as real estate companies.

Activity professionals are not usually employed to develop and implement programs for people living in independent housing. Independent homeowners may or may not develop their own neighborhood get together or other activities. They may be mostly involved in individual and/or family activities. They may be involved in the community special events, ongoing activities/services, educational programs and/or participating in Senior Citizen Centers, YMCA, or Recreation Centers providing services.

Older adults may prefer a specific type of independent living communities or continuous retirement community that is religious, cultural or gender based.

Lisa Leff, of The Associated Press, wrote a story titled, "Not your traditional retirement housing" relating to gay and lesbian retirement communities. Ms. Leff states, "As the generation of gay men and lesbians who came out of the 1950 and 1970's reaches retirement age, about a dozen specialized senior developments across the country are either operating or in the works.

In such senior –heavy locales as California, Arizona and Florida as well as less traditionally gay-friendly places like North Carolina and Texas, builders have found a market in a segment of the gay population that worries getting old will mean going back to the closet.

People select a retirement community for several reasons including living with people of like minds and interests. Golfers may select a golfing retirement community whereas skiers would prefer a retirement community in an area where they can continue to ski. A retirement community for gays and lesbians allows people to be with people like themselves without fear and where they can feel safe in their older years.

Controversy abounds about the concept of gay and lesbian communities. Some people like it others do not. Some people in the retirement field oppose the idea of separate communities. Should society be forced to accept gay and lesbians in retirement communities or should separate communities be developed in the first place.

An activity professional working in a gay and lesbian community needs to understand the dynamics and culture of gays and lesbians and treat them individually with respect.

The trend to build independent residential communities for older adult, e.g. age 50 and older, who want a hassle free life style and perhaps specific recreational amenities (indoor/outdoor pool, exercise facility, golf course, walking/hiking areas, boating, fishing, swimming, skiing, park like setting, will continue as baby boomers want more free time to be involved in their favorite activities without having to travel a distance.

An activity professional may be employed part time or full time by an association of an independent residential community to plan and conduct activities per their preferences including trips. An activity professional may be more of a concierge providing information on community events, arrange tickets for social, cultural, educational activities or for making restaurant reservations, arranging transportation, group vacation trips, or planning parties and holiday and cultural celebrations for the residential community.

Maintenance Free Homes

Independent older adults may want to continue to live independently without the hassle of caring for their homes, e.g. replacing the roof, cleaning gutters, mowing the grass, shoveling snow, fixing the doors/windows, thus they can purchase or rent maintenance free type housing.

Maintenance free homes can include condominiums, patio homes, villas, townhouses or other facilities specifically for older adults or persons with disabilities. A person may own their home and land or may own their home but not the land (landominium).

This type of housing is for independent older adults who do not want to be responsible for the maintenance of their home and outside areas. In addition to the mortgage or rental fee there is a maintenance fee established by the owner or members of the complex. People living in these types of homes sign a

contract related to the maintenance fees and services. In some communities there is a resident organization that determines the fees and oversees the care of the buildings and outside areas. The maintenance fees usually cover any mechanical problems, plumbing, lighting, flooring, etc as well as outside maintenance including grass cutting and/or snow removal.

Maintenance free homes may be a separate complex in a community or a part of a Continuing Care Retirement Community. It is anticipated that maintenance free housing will continue as baby boomers want to spend less time in taking care of their home and more time for leisure.

Older adults may choose independent housing in their present community or surrounding area, or a specific state/region offering a preferred climate with opportunities for preferred leisure activities or to be near family. The northern snowbirds may want to retire in the south where it is warmer, just for the warmth or to participate in their preferred warm weather activities.

Upscale Homes

Some baby boomers as well as present older adults prefer to transition to a larger more spacious, glamorous home with updated kitchen, baths, laundry with the latest fixtures, appliances, flooring, walls, ceilings, lighting etc. with separate space for visiting children and grandchildren. Outdoor space maybe centered on preferred activities including an outdoor kitchen.

Adult Day Services

Adult day care was started in psychiatric hospitals. The Soviet Union started the first day hospital in 1942. Patients lived at home while receiving intensive therapy on an outpatient basis. Between the years 1945 and 1949 day hospitals were developed at the Adams House in Boston, the Menninger Clinic in Topeka, Kansas and the Yale Psychiatric Clinic in Massachusetts. There was much development of psychiatric day hospitals or day treatment programs in the 1960's with the Community Mental Health Movement. Private and not-for-profit programs were opened. Criteria for participation focused on a psychiatric diagnosis, ability to live in the community, willingness to participate in the program and physician referral.

England is credited with developing the first day hospitals for adults with disabilities, many of whom where older adults. Dr. Lionel Cosin, the "father of adult day care," opened the first adult day hospital in 1950. Medical, rehabilitation, social service, transportation and meal services were provided.

Dr. Cosin's model was implemented at the Cherry State Hospital in Goldsboro, North Carolina in the late 1960's. In 1971, Dr. Cosin was again instrumental in increasing the interest of adult day care as a component of a continuum of long-term care service in the United States, when he presented his program to the Senate Special Committee on Aging. In 1972 Hawaii became the first state to have regulations for adult day care.

In 1974, Medicaid funds became available to states for adult day care. By 1986, there were approximately 1200 adult day care centers in the United States. There is great diversity among adult day care centers. The intensity of care and staffing differ, depending upon the purpose, goals, objectives, funding sources, geographical location and needs of adults and older adults in the community. Some centers are freestanding, while others may be a part of a social agency, long-term care facility, hospital or even a business corporation, i.e., adult day care center for relatives of employees. Services of day care can include medical, nursing, rehabilitation, psychosocial activities, therapeutic activities, therapeutic recreation, transportation, meals and support services.

Activities programs in adult day care vary depending upon the needs, interest, preferences, abilities and limitations of the participants, amount of indoor and outdoor space, staffing, transportation and budget. In many adult day care programs there are two to five activities going on simultaneously. Some activities may be individual, one-to-one or group activities. The program always includes rest periods. There is much emphasis on socialization, cognitive and physical activities.

Activities include but are not limited to cognitive activities using short- and long-term memory (current events, discussions, word games, reading, writing, etc.), creative activities (art, crafts, needlework, cooking, baking, flower arranging, poetry, movement/dance), expressive activities (creative writing, journals, life-review, reminiscing, discussions, music, dance/movement), physical activities (exercise, walk programs, adapted sports, yoga, relaxation exercises, etc.), social activities (conversation, parties, picnics, celebrations, socials, special events, cards, games, trips and tours, dining out, shopping), spiritual (prayer, Bible study and other religious activities as appropriate) and leisure activities of choice.

Standards and Guidelines for Adult Day Care by the National Institute on Adult Day Care defines adult day care as:

> **"A community-based group program designed to meet the needs of functionally impaired adults through an individual plan of care. It is a structured, comprehensive program**

> **that provides a variety of health, social and related-support services in a protective setting during any part of a day but less than 24-hour care.**

> **Individuals who participate in adult day care attend on a planned basis during specific hours. Adult day care assists its participants to remain in the community, enabling families and other caregivers to continue caring for an impaired member at home."**

The focus of adult day care is on an individualized plan of care. Nursing homes have an individualized plan of care for residents, but the plans differ in that 24-hour care is provided. Adult day care provides services for less than 24 hours. Senior centers do not have individualized plans of care, although they may have individual program plans and provide socialization, recreation, health, education, transportation and meals much like a day care center.

The terms "therapeutic activities," "purposeful activities," "activities," "activity programming," "planned activities," "group daily activities," "monthly calendar of activities," and "activities schedule" are used in the **National Adult Day Service Association (NADSA)** Standard and Guidelines for adult day care. "Therapeutic Activities" is listed among the eight essential core services. The other services are Personal Care, Nursing, Social Services, Nutrition, Transportation, Emergency Plan and Education.

The standards state:

> **"Therapeutic Activities"**

> **The activity plan shall be an integral part of the total plan of care for the individual. The planning of activities shall reflect professional understanding of needs and abilities of the participants.**

> **Activities shall emphasize the individual participant's strengths and abilities rather than impairments and shall contribute to participant feelings of competency and accomplishment."**

Purposeful activities are described as meeting the participants' interrelated needs and interests (social, intellectual, cultural, economic, emotional, physical and spiritual). A holistic approach is emphasized to promote personal growth and enhance the self-image and/or to improve or maintain the functional level of participants. Activities offered relate to opportunities for personal outcomes, i.e., maintaining life-long skills, improving physical and emotional well-being, improving capacity for independent functioning, developing interpersonal relationships, participating in activities of interest, learning new skills and gaining knowledge, challenging potential abilities, developing creative capacities, exposure to community events, cultural enrichment, and having fun and experiencing enjoyment.

Factors to be considered in activities programming include consideration of individual differences in health status, lifestyle, ethnicity, religious affiliation, values, experiences, needs, interests, abilities and skills. Activities may include individualized activities, small and large group activities, active and spectator participation, intergenerational experiences, involvement in community activities and events, service to individuals and to the program, outdoor activities as appropriate and opportunities to voluntarily perform services for individuals and the program, and community groups and organizations. Participants may choose or not choose to participate in activities. The activities schedule is coordinated with other staff and services of the center. The monthly calendar is posted in a visible place and can be distributed to family/caregivers and others. Group daily activities are posted. Simultaneously, alternative activities need to be planned.

CARF Standards

Adult Day Services can voluntarily select for a fee to be accredited by CARF (The Commission on Accreditation of Rehabilitation Facilities, Inc.) in accordance with the 2010 Adult Day Services Standards Manual with Survey Preparation Questions.

An Adult Day Service can be accredited for three years. If the Adult Day Service does not meeting CARF standards it may be accredited for one year, receive a provisional accreditation or be denied accreditation.

In the glossary of the 2010 Adult Day Services Standards Manual with Survey Preparation Questions, the following definitions are stated:

"**Activity:** The execution of a task or action by an individual."(This definition is from the World Health Organization, *International Classification of Function, Disability and Health [UCF]*.)

"**Activity limitations**: Difficulties an individual may have in executing activities." (This definition is from the World Health Organization's *International Classification of Function, Disability and Health [ICF]*.)

Assisted Living Facilities

Assisted Living

Assisted Living facilities became popular in the late 80's and early 90's. Many of today's assisted living facilities are specialized facilities caring for persons with Dementia, Alzheimer's type.

An assisted living facilities or community is a step between independent living and a nursing home. Residents in assisted living need help with daily living activities (bathing, dressing, meals, housekeeping) but do not need nursing home care. The monthly rental contract identifies the services provide by the facility. Additional services may be provided for a fee by the assisted living facility or an outside agency.

Activity professionals are employed full and part time to meet the needs, interests, and preferences of

residents within their abilities. Activity professionals may use a variety of techniques for stimulation, motivation and resident participation in individual, family, one-to-one and group activities, intergenerational activities, inside or outside the facility and in the community.

Specialized Assisted Living:

Some assisted living facilities specialize in the care and services for people with Dementia, Alzheimer's type or other dementias. The goal is to provide care and services that assist in maintaining the residents' abilities. Establishing a level system of programming provides successful activity outcomes. Residents in the early state of Dementia, Alzheimer's type, are usually able to make simple decisions about activities, where as at the later stage of the disease, residents are dependent upon staff for stimulation, i.e. sensory stimulation, and to initiate socialization.

Assisted living is new nomenclature for an array of services. Assisted living facilities provide care and services with the emphasis upon personal choice in a homelike setting. Some of the main features are private bath, temperature control, private space, lockable doors and kitchenette.

While this type of unit has been around for a long time, the emphasis on autonomy for the person to enjoy a homelike atmosphere, where care and services are brought to the person rather than taking the person to another area for assistance, is new for some providers.

Under this new philosophy of independence and personal choice, older programs such as rest home, adult care, congregate living, personal care and custodial care are now being modified to meet this new demand.

The term assisted living (AL) was used first as a marketing title. It implied assistance with the activities of daily living (ADSL), which may be described as personal care services. The emphasis is on giving the resident as many choices as possible and encouraging the resident to manage and do as much as possible for him/herself. Staff in the assisted living facility assist the residents as much as possible in their own units and encourage as much self-sufficiency as possible. This philosophy and type of care and services help to keep the resident from prematurely going to the nursing care area.

Assisted living is being defined, developed and legalized across the country. Some Northern European countries have used this model for years.

Activities in assisted living facilities focus on residents maintaining their independence, involving residents in planning, preparing, developing and implementing programs as much as possible, and planned structured programs in the facility and in the community. Lending programs are made available to residents, such as: books, magazines, inspirational reading, portable VCR and monitor, and CD/DVD, recorders, CDs and computers. Programs focusing on wellness may have exercise facility/ equipment and pool, walking areas and educational programs with a focus on health and wellness.

Programs usually include art/crafts, exercise, cards and games, entertainment, classes, trips, shopping, socials and other activities of interest. Often trips and tours are combined with services in the community and/or with programs for residents who reside in independent living units. Religious programs are conducted in the facility and often residents are encouraged to participate in church services in the community with transportation being provided by the facility, the local church or the family.

Group activities are the primary focus with some one-to-one activities being provided by activity professionals and volunteers. One-to-one activities are encouraged among peers.

Programming can be somewhat difficult as older persons living in assisted living want to remain independent and may not be willing to try new activities or to get to know other residents. Another problem is that residents may begin to show cognitive deficits but will not admit to needing assistance in remembering days, dates and times of programs. A person may forget or argue that he/she did not sign up for an activity/program or outing. The activity professional is challenged to meet the residents' changing needs (physical, cognitive, emotional and social).

Home Care

Home care may be needed for persons living independently or in assisted living facilities. Services can be arranged by a social worker in a hospital, nursing home or rehabilitation facility before a person is discharged. A person or family member can independently contact a community home health agency to arrange for medical and or personal care services. Long-term care insurance may pay for these services per the guidelines of the policy or services can be provided on a fee-for-service basis.

Professional caregivers (R.Ns, L.P.N.s, and certified nursing assistants) often advertise their services identifying the types of services they provide.
Non professionals may advertise their personal care services including activities, e.g. being a companion, taking a person shopping or doing the shopping, light housekeeping, transportation to doctors, therapy or other medical needs and willingness to take someone to church, special events (community, cultural, sport, etc.) or senior center.

Home health care is increasingly becoming a service of the 21st century. With home health care (medical, assistance with Activities of Daily Living (ADL), homemaking tasks, etc.) older adults are able to remain in their homes. All professionals involved with a client provide various degrees of socialization. Assistance is provided as needed for individual activities (turning radio, TV, CD/DVD player, talking book on/off; providing reading materials; setting up a puzzle or cards for solitaire; placing a CD/DVD in a player; placing a phone in reach, etc.).

There have been a variety of programs throughout the United States that provide in-home recreation. Activity professionals have developed independent businesses to provide in-home activities on a fee-for-service basis

As the need for home health care increases so will the need for in-home activities. Reimbursement for services will be the key factor. Activity professionals will be needed to cross-train home health aids or to train others to provide activities and socialization.

Both now and in the future, with advanced technology and a computer-literate society, older adults will utilize a computer for cognitive stimulation and interacting with others via the Internet.

Hospice

Hospices began in England in 1904 and in the United States in 1972. Hospice provides medical and psychosocial services for persons who are dying. Activity professionals working in long-term-care facilities with a hospice unit or hospice services provide activities much like they do for other residents in long-term care. Individual, one-to-one, family and group activities are provided. The activities program is individualized. In the beginning, a resident may wish and be able to participate in a small-group activity or attend a large-group religious and/or entertainment program. In time, as the person declines and prepares for death, he/she may withdraw from peer social activity, wanting to be with family, selected friends and/or staff, or to be alone.

One-to-one activities may center on life review, reminiscing, talking with or about the family, current events and/or specific topics of interests. Games, puzzles, crafts and other action-oriented activities may be of interest. In time the person may withdraw from the activities that require physical, cognitive and emotional energy, and focus on individual spirituality.

A person may prefer quiet individual activities such as: watching TV, listening to the radio, listening to music, listening to relaxation and/or inspirational tapes, praying, reading, writing, etc. The person may or may not want much interaction with others but may appreciate having someone to be with him/her in silence—for comfort.

The activity professional may play a key role in the end stage of a person's life, providing the proper supplies and equipment, supporting the person through listening or prayer, and being there for quiet meaningful moments.

Special Care Units

The implementation of special-care units for residents with Alzheimer's disease/dementia has increased tremendously since the mid 1980's. Today there are special care units within long-term-care facilities and freestanding facilities. Assisted living units for residents with early-stage Alzheimer's disease are increasing, thus meeting a different need in the community.

Activity professionals have played an important role in specialized units since their inception. In the early development of these units, the activity professional provided the majority of the activities. In the late 1980's the activity professional's role changed to assessing residents, developing activity care plans as a part of an interdisciplinary care plan, and training direct care staff to implement the care plans by providing a variety of activities.

Activities in special-care units include individual, one-to-one and group activities. Activities are based on cognitive ability levels as well as the resident's needs, interests, preferences and physical, emotional and social abilities and limitations. Some residents are able to participate successfully in integrated activities with residents with high-cognitive-functioning abilities.

Individual activities may include reading, looking at picture books, writing, drawing, painting, coloring, walking, puttering, manipulating objects, folding towels and/or clothing, home-making tasks (sweeping, cleaning tables, dusting), people watching, caring for a doll or stuffed animal, watching an action oriented video, listening to music and any other activity of interest.

Small groups are the norm. They may be 15 to 45 minutes in length depending upon the resident's interests and attention span. The lower the cognitive functioning level of residents the smaller the groups need to be so that there is sufficient time for interaction, cueing and redirection. Group activities include sensory stimulation, reminiscing, discussions, word games, table games, matching games, bingo or some type of adapted bingo, Bible study or stories, church, reading stories and/or poems, music, singing, dancing, arts/crafts, simple drama, exercise, adapted sports, outdoor activities, trips, dining out, shopping, etc.

An activity professional may be a supervisor of the activities program providing some activities in addition to the activities provided by the direct-care staff. Another role for the activity professional is that of a consultant to the unit manager and direct care staff.

Increasingly, activity professionals are becoming directors or assistant directors of special care units in the community and in long term care facilities. As a director of the unit/program, the former activity professional is responsible for the total operation, staffing and programming for the unit. It is a 24-hour responsibility.

Hospital-Based Skilled Nursing Units

Since the 1990's there has been a surge of short-term care, hospital-based skilled nursing units for older adults. The length of stay varies with a range of 1-30 days. Often the average is less than two weeks. The skilled-care units are under the same regulations as long-term-care facilities; however the length of stay is short versus long as in a long-term-care facility.

The resident's focus is on going home. They place the value of their time on therapy and treatment, sleep/rest, visiting with family and friends, and individual activities i.e. reading, watching TV or video, listening to the radio or music. Socialization is done during group dining, therapy, with family and friends, and in structured or impromptu groups.

The activities program focuses on providing supplies and equipment to continue independent individual activities (TV/VCR monitor, video, cassette recorder and choice of tapes, choice of reading materials, puzzles such as word search, fill-in-the-blank, jigsaw and pull-apart books of jokes/riddles, art/crafts, needlework, solitaire or other activities of choice).

One-to-one activities are with family/friends, activity professionals and volunteers. Pastoral care provides one-to-one counseling, prayer, communion, and blessings. Religious services may be televised.

Small group activities are usually held in the dining/lounge area. Group activities change week-to-week depending upon the resident population. One week there may be several card players. The next week there may be none.

In some facilities the activity/dining room becomes the hub for residents to gather before/after therapy and meals. Thus some residents may be involved in an individual activity, while others are engaged in a one-to-one activity with a peer, volunteer or visitor, or are involved in a group activity independently or with the activity professional or volunteer.

Admissions and discharges are fast-paced in a hospital-based skilled-care unit. The activity professional may spend a considerable amount of time assessing individual residents and planning for discharge. Residents may need leisure education, time to adjust to using adaptive equipment and techniques for leisure activities, and time to learn about accessible community resources. An activity professional may lead leisure awareness groups or may have to work with residents individually.

Sub Acute Units in Long Term Care Facilities

Sub acute units in long-term-care facilities are much like the skilled-nursing units in hospitals. The length of stay is short. Some residents go back home, other go to facilities where they can function at their highest-level i.e. assisted-living, long term-care. The resident's focus is on therapy and he/she will often state a lack of interest in getting involved with others or in activities because of the expected short-term stay.

Programming is much the same as hospital based skilled-care units. Emphasis is on individual, one-to-one and then group activity. Individual ministers, priests and rabbis may provide individual pastoral care in addition to that of volunteer clergy or laypersons.

The philosophy of the program may include group dining and socialization; thus, group activities and programs are conducted prior to meals or immediately after meals to allow residents to conserve their energy. Families are included in group activities and special family activities (celebrations, parties, carry-in dinners, special events, etc.).

Residents may participate in integrated programs in a centralized area with residents in long-term care, e.g. music, singing, parties, picnics, entertainment and religious activities. If it is known that a resident is to reside in the nursing home after discharge from the sub acute unit, the activity professional may gradually introduce the resident to activities that are provided for long-term-care residents.

The activities program is constantly changing to meet the individual needs, interests, preferences, abilities and limitations of residents. Planning a week ahead versus a month ahead, except for special events, allows activity professionals the opportunity to provide appropriate programming daily.

Residential Homes and Senior Housing

Activity professionals work in a variety of settings that offer care and/or services to older adults and persons with disabilities. It is important for the activity professional to understand the internal working environments of the service setting on the continuum of care as well as the setting's business structure.

The types of service settings include but are not limited to:

Apartments:

Some apartment complexes are for all ages, others are for older adults or persons with disabilities that need accessible housing without personal assistance for Activities of Daily Living, transportation, etc.
An activity professional may be employed to develop and implement activity programs for all ages, including children, teenagers, and adults as well as family activities, intergenerational, age specific (pre-school, school age, teens, young adults, or exclusive programming for older adults). An adult or an older adult apartment complex may have a Club type (fee or non fee) based program for participation or the use of the activity areas (Club house, pool, patio). The activity professional may be responsible in overseeing club members being responsible for offering activities. There may be other apartment complexes owned by the same corporation. An activity professional may be responsible for overseeing the development of programs for designed complexes in a state, in several states or region(s). The activity professional would be required to travel (possibly including overnight) to oversee the development, implementation and evaluation of the activity or recreation programs offered in his/her designated complexes.

Continuing Care Retirement Community (CCRC)

A Continuing Care Retirement Community offers a variety of levels of care from independent living to assisted living, nursing home (skilled care, intermediate care, rehabilitation, respite,). Some CCRCs offer specialty units in assisted living or nursing home for people with Dementia, Alzheimer's type.

The majority of CCRCs are religious based, i.e. Catholic, Methodist, and Baptist, etc., while the community is based on one denomination, they are open to potential residents of all faiths or non-believers. A catholic or Jewish Community would focus on their religious beliefs and practices as well as provide protestant services for others. Full or part time priests, rabbis and ministers are employed to meet the religious/spiritual needs of residents.

Nursing Facilities

Nursing Homes:

Nursing homes provide a variety of care and services for residents, who have physical, cognitive, mental, and/or behavior problems and who need 24 hr. medical supervision. Skilled care nursing facilities may have specialized units for residents who need special care, i.e., dialysis, wound care, or specific diagnosis such as multiple sclerosis, dementia, bariatric care.

A nursing home may be a specialty rehabilitation facility offering rehabilitation services on a short or long-term basis. The emphasis of care is on rehabilitation.

 Skilled Care:

Skilled care facilities provide a registered nurse (R.N.) 24 hours per day and sufficient nursing staff in accordance with federal and state laws. An R.N. provides treatments and procedures in accordance with their state licensure. A Licensed Practical Nurse (L.P.N.), who is also licensed by the state, provides care and services within their licensure law. State tested nursing assistants provide care and services for which they are trained under the supervision of an R.N. or assigned L.P.N. Certified Nursing Assistants (CNA) also provide direct care and services for residents under the supervision of the Director of Nursing an R.N. or assigned R.N or L.PN.

A registered dietician assesses, plans individual resident's diet based on their personal history, diagnosis, tests and lab reports, preferences and abilities, i.e. ability to feed self, swallow liquids/food without choking. The dietitian also plans the daily menu and oversees the dietary manager, safety and quality control of the dietary department.

Rehabilitation services (physical therapy, occupational therapy, speech therapy) are provided by the facility's rehabilitation staff or through contractual service with an agency.

Recreation Therapy may be a part of the Rehabilitation Department or as another therapy combined with activities. The Recreation Therapist provides different treatment and services than an activity professional. Recreational therapists must be nationally certified, registered or licensed. A resident must have a physician's order for Recreation Therapy whereas a general order, i.e. resident may participate in activities of choice, may have alcoholic beverage, may go on outings, is given for activity services. Sometimes a specific physician's order is given for activities (Involve in exercise and walking program 30 min., 3-5 times a week).

Skilled nursing facilities are required to have a "qualified" activity director who meets some of the qualifications of a qualified activity professional, under the federal regulations 483.15 (f) Activities, tagF249. The activity director with or without the assistance of other activity professionals, depending upon the size of the facility and residents needs, plans, develops, implements, evaluates the activities program and makes changes as needed. The interpretive guidelines for tag 248 emphasize team approaches to activities.

Social Service is provided by a licensed social worker in accordance with federal and state regulations. The social worker provides care and services for individual residents, education and support for family members, significant others or guardians, contacts community organizations for referral and or services, e.g. community support group, appointments such as dental, ophthalmologist, community mental health services, etc., obtaining clothing and personal items if resident has no one to provide these items, overseeing resident funds and making arrangements for Medicaid or Medicare payment for individual resident care and services allowed by state and federal laws.

Rehabilitation services are provided by the following professions: occupational therapy, physical therapy, and speech therapy. Physical and occupational therapy assistants administer therapy under the direct supervision of a licensed or registered physical or occupational therapist.

Intermediate Care Facilities

Intermediate care facilities provide nursing services 24 hours a day but are not required to have an R.N. 24 hours a day as residents do not require skilled care provided by an R.N. Other clinical services provided in skilled care facilities include but are not limited to a dietitian, activities professional and social worker. If a resident needs rehabilitation services, arrangements are made with a local rehabilitation organization.

Respite Care

Short-term respite care is provided for residents who may need additional 24-hour medical supervision after a hospital stay before they can return to assisted or independent living.

A care giver may need a rest from the responsibility of caring for someone 24 hours a day or want to go Out of town or take a vacation or have some other need or responsibility that would prevent him/her from caring for someone for a specific time period. With a physician's assessment and orders, a person can receive respite care on a fee-for-service basis, long-term care insurance plan or medical insurance if it is covered by the person's medical insurance plan.

Short Stay and Special Care Units

Sub Acute Care is provided for someone who has an acute illness, e.g., a life-threatening infection, or is recovering from an injury, fractured pelvis, head injury, but not ready to return to assisted or independent living.

Sub acute care in a nursing facility is less expensive than a hospital because a nursing home does not have all the overhead expenses, e.g. X- ray, pharmacology, emergency, obstetric, surgery, departments, etc. that are a part of a hospital's expenses.

Activity professionals work with residents in sub acute care as a specialty unit, providing individualized programming and coordinating with other activities in the facility, i.e., special events, group activities. Acute care patients may be tired from their disease, disability, or treatments and have little energy for participation in activities. Additionally, activity professional has to be very cognizant of infection control, and physical activity and how it affects the resident.

Adapting Care and Services to Fit Work Settings and the Clients Served

A major task of the activity professional is to plan activities that focus on the physical, psycho or social, cultural and spiritual wellbeing whether through one on one, individual, or group activities. Such activities need to be adapted to the needs of the residents, or clients. These services need be a part of the resident's individual, daily schedule and be integrated with other services whether in the home, community or long term care facility. The activity professional will show compassion and seek to confer healing and restoration.

The facility and or environment can enhance or restrict the setting in which activities are conducted. The ultimate test is whether the residents or clients are being served in ways that meet their wants as well as their needs. Remember, the resident or client is the reason.

Legal and Business Entities

All reputable facilities or agencies are incorporated as a legal provider of care and services. Incorporation is a legal process that takes place in the state. In order to conduct business the organization needs an IRS (Internal Revenue Service) number, which is secured by completing forms and submitting them to IRS indicating the nature of the organization and the services to be provided.

Some new approaches to assisted living and nursing care residents/clients will be assisted or cared for in a homelike environment. Activity professionals will need to be prepared to serve in these various settings sometimes referred to as "greenhouse" cares for approximately ten residents/clients.

Activity professionals, regardless of the setting or environment, should maintain a consistent philosophy of professional approach and follow the standards and protocol of the profession as well as local, state and federal regulations.

There are two main incorporation entities, profit and non-profit plus government facilities. Profit facilities or agencies are seeking to make a profit while delivering meaningful care and services. Non-profit facilities are often sponsored by churches, community and other groups set up to provide the service without making a profit for owners or share holders. So those entities do not pay some taxes, i.e. corporate taxes, yet pay other taxes such as sales taxes on items sold in independent living facilities or to friends. In a continuing care community the independent facilities pay property taxes in some states. Any surplus of income is to be used to further assist the mission of the organization and some reserves for emergency use.

Mission Statement

In most facilities and agencies a mission statement is developed to set forth in a concise sentence or two the purpose or mission of the organization. The governing body such as a Board of Directors or the owner(s) adopts the mission statement often in conjunction with strategic planning, to focus on their reason for being. At times there are Vision Statements that follow which reveal the reason, objectives and goals of the organization on the one hand focusing on the care and service for the elderly and disabled and the other hand managing the organization with integrity and fiscal responsibility.

The activity professional learns this mission statement and seeks to embody the mission in the activity program along with the other departments of the agency/facility. Services and health care are developed on a continuum starting in the home, senior centers, adult day services, services in independent housing and apartments. The right place depends on the client/resident's wishes and needs.

Organizational Structure
"Good employee relations encourage a high level of productivity."

"Employees need to know the structure of the organization and their roles, responsibilities and to whom they are accountable."

Organizational Chart

An organizational chart is a point of reference. It indicates the hierarchy of communication and responsibility. It provides a formal structure for the organization.

Line-Staff Organization

The line-staff organizational chart indicates the lines of authority and responsibility. In most organizations using a line-staff organizational chart, the professional activity manager is on the same horizontal line as other department managers. He/she is responsible to the administrator and responsible for the activity staff, and sometimes the pastoral care staff and volunteers. In some organizations there is a professional volunteer manager and a pastoral care manager; thus, these services would not be under the auspices of the professional activity manager.

In the drawing above, the administrator is responsible to the board of directors. The administrator is also responsible for the non-clinical as well as clinical departments, including the activities department.

The activities director is responsible to the administrator and responsible for the activity department, and volunteers.

The dotted lines show lines of communication, but not of authority or supervision. Thus the dotted line from the activities consultant to the administrator and the director of activities indicate with whom the consultant has direct communication. This is not to say that the consultant does not communicate with other managers and staff in the organization.

In this hierarchy, activity staff communicates with the director of the department. The director communicates with the administrator. If there is a problem within the department that cannot be resolved, the activity staff can request a meeting with the director of activities and the administrator.

The organizational chart coordinates with job descriptions. All job descriptions need to identify the supervisor of the employee by job title, not by personal name.

Organizational Chart

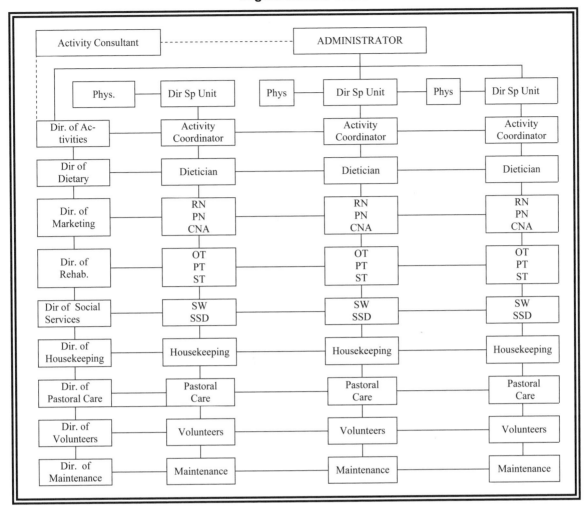

Matrix Management

In a matrix management system, specialization of different services is emphasized. There is a director for each service and staff for each service is provided by professional departments. The philosophy of services for each specialty may be similar but different. Quality care is the ultimate goal but it is achieved through different specialized services emphasizing interdisciplinary teams.

Examples of specialized services in a long-term-care facility would be five distinct specialized programs:
1. Dementia Unit
2. Skilled Nursing Care Unit
3. Gero-Mental Health Unit
4. AIDS Unit
5. Rehabilitation Unit

Each program would have a director. Staffing and staffing patterns would differ because of the care needed. Philosophy of care, delivery of care, treatment, length of stay, participation patterns in activities, family involvement, documentation, etc., would all differ. The scope and outcome of activity programs and services would differ for each service.

The professional activity manager would be responsible for recruiting, hiring, training, supervising, and appraising an employee's performance in coordination with the director of each of the specialty programs. Activity professionals assigned to a specific specialty program would function, as team members of the unit and at the same time are members of the activity department.

Matrix Models

Dual Supervision

Activity professionals assigned to specific programs need to be trained to understand the philosophy, care and services of the specialty unit. Additionally, he/she would need training on the disease/diagnosis of residents for the assigned unit. The number of activity professionals and hours of work would also differ for each unit.

It is difficult for an activity professional to be supervised by two professionals, the professional activity manager and the director of the unit. It takes good communication, coordination and delineation of responsibilities for matrix management to work. The professional activity manager must be knowledgeable of all the specialty services and must support all activity professionals on his/her assigned unit.

Consultant Model

In the consultant model, department managers are consultants versus supervisors. They consult with the unit managers, teams assigned to the unit and staff in their specialty area. They do not have any authority regarding personnel, programming, documentation, etc.

In this model the activity professional assigned to a specialty unit works as a team member and is responsible to the director of the unit. The activity professional and the director of the unit confer with the department manager in a consultative capacity. The consultant does not have supervisory responsibility. The consultant may be involved in recruiting, hiring, training and evaluating activity professionals, but is not responsible for day-to-day supervision. If there is a problem the department manager can be requested to assist in defining a perceived problem and making recommendations for a solution.

The activity professional works more independently in this model, yet he\she has the availability of the expertise of the consultant. The consultant may be a full-time or part-time employee of the organization or facility. A consultant may be employed as an independent consultant through contractual services (fee-for-service basis). The consultant's roles and responsibilities may be similar yet different for each specialty unit, depending upon the needs of each unit.

Formal Authority

In any organization there is a legal entity, which had the formal authority to establish its mission, vision and structure. Authority is established in a Board of Directors or trustees or by the owner(s) or government entity. Administrative authority starts at the top with the president, Chief Executive Officer, Executive Director, or an administrator. The Board or owner employs this person. This top person makes the key decisions based upon the policies and instruction of the Board or owners. The Chief Executive officer oversees the department heads and is often referred to as the Administrative Staff. They are the key persons in the chain of command. The department heads along with the CEO develop and follow administrative policies and procedures. Department heads supervise or direct the supervisors who in turn direct the hands-on staff.

In activities if there is more than one activity professional, one is designated as director and this person has the overall responsibility for planning, directing, executing and evaluating the activity program. The ultimate focus is on the resident(s) or client(s).

Chain of Command

Command means to have authority, control, order and mandate. The person who has that has the highest position in top of the chain in the facility or agency. Titles given include chief executive officer (CEO), chief financial officer (CFO), executive director, administrator or similar designations.

The CEO selects department directors of heads who are specialists in the various areas of care and services such as activities, dietary, nursing, housekeeping, social worker, maintenance, etc. These persons serve as subordinate to the CEO and are the leaders on the second level of the chain of command. Each department has various line staff that carry out the direct care services. They are workers on the third level of authority and are responsible to the department director. In some departments there may be another level of supervisors i.e. the shift leader. Activity professionals in facilities or agencies with more than one staff person will have one or more assistants who take orders from the activity director. Usually the person in charge has more education and experience. The key to a successful organization is to have qualified workers who are dedicated and committed to the residents/clients, have open communication and accept the chain of command.

Division of Work

Organizations divide the various services into departments, i.e. nursing facilities usually have the following departments: nursing, activities, social service, housekeeping, maintenance. The departments have defined work areas, and roles but need to maintain good working relationships with other departments. The CEO of each facility or agency needs to structure the organization to create a warm compassionate, cooperative environment for all of the employees so that this spirit of satisfaction and goodwill will affect the resident/client.

In program or activity departments with more than one staff person the CEO or supervisor determines which activity person is in charge. That professional becomes the overall director of the activity program. In larger facilities or agencies there can be a number of activity staff persons. While they all work together as a team, each will be assigned specific roles and/or specific areas where they are responsible to carry out compassionate, significant and appropriate activities.

Some activity professionals will have special skills, e.g. play musical instruments, sing, paint, etc. For special occasions this person will be called upon to lead a group in music or may share talent in celebrating a birthday in other areas of the facility. Activity professionals assist each other in providing the best programs and services possible. So while the division of work is necessary, the activity department should function as a team and work closely with the other department employees. Such teamwork will benefit the residents/clients.

Organizational Behavior

An organization is made up of a group of persons that systemize their individual roles for a specific purpose. An organizational chart is developed to show the chain of command and defines the hierarchy of leadership. Each level of leadership has an authority figure that orders and directs responsibilities or tasks. In the job description, amenability is set forth to confirm who the boss is. The person accepting that position is expected to behave ethically and fulfill the job according to the defined role.

Good behavior can lead to team building or bad behavior can lead to the creation of a dysfunctional team. Clear communication between the various levels of authority is essential. Organizations providing services for the elderly and disabled usually have departments which are assigned specific functions. When there is good communication and cooperation between departments the delivery of services will be enhanced. Activity professionals need to relate closely with nursing, social service, housekeeping and dietary staff. The residents/clients will benefit by such cooperation and teamwork. A successful organization serving residents/clients will focus on what is best for those being served.

Human organizations develop a culture and identity based upon the original developers and is changed or modified by those who follow. Formal rules are set forth and informal rules develop. Each organization has a philosophy, a territory, a vocabulary, history and culture and they have clusters of sub-organizations. Some leaders in these organizations share honors and influence while other leaders see successes as their own achievement.

The facility or agency has to develop an organizational structure to carry out the functions and services such as plans, goals, and working relationships. Successful organizations providing services for older persons must develop a chart of organization that shows the line of authority and the skills and expectations needed to fulfill certain roles.

Supervisors should use that authority in an effective way, on the one hand to give orders and directives that are clear and appropriate, and on the other hand such supervision should be supportive and not commanding or demeaning

Distribution of the work in an activity department should be fair. Activity professionals should accept their assigned roles and carry out the planned programs in a compassionate and effective manner. If the activity person feels he/she is being treated unfairly, he/she needs to speak to the supervisor or the department head. Bad mouthing others can affect morale in all departments of the facility. Negative persons hurt the morale and will negatively affect the program. Remember, the resident/client will also be affected.

Accountability

Persons are employed because of their personality, education and experience. Once they are assigned a role they are responsible and accountable for carrying out that role. Employees are responsible for the outcome of their work as well as for their behavior. CEOs and department heads should praise employees who are outstanding workers. Special recognition should be given at appropriate time. However, employees who are not committed to providing average or high level of care should answer to their supervisor and/or department head. They may need to move to a different job.

Private space, such as in the supervisor's office should be used to speak with an activity professional that is not performing up to par. This may occur at the annual evaluation session or by special appointment in case of a particular incident or need.

An effective activity department will recognize the importance of each member of the team being accountable. The accountable activity professional will strive to do his/her best.

Responsibility

The primary responsibility starts with the person in charge: CEO, Executive Director, or Administrator. The CEO is responsible to develop and amend administrative policies and procedures which the Board or owner(s) has approved.

Responsibility begins with the establishment of an administrative chart which gives order and design to delegating appropriate authority to the various levels of employees. The CEO is responsible for hiring the supervisory level staff and working with the human resource person to advertise, interview, check references and hire new employees. Department heads working with the human resource person may have the authority to hire their personnel.

The activity department head is responsible for developing a job description and clarifying the duties to be performed. In cases where the applicant does not appear to be able or does not seem suitable to assume the responsibility, or for any other reason, the activity director makes the decision to decline the applicant.

Responsibility is a must throughout the organization. Each employee, including the activity professional must carry his/her responsibility in fulfilling the assigned duties. Effective organizations have dedicated and responsible employees.

Activity Department heads will interpret to new employees the policies and procedures of the company as well as the department, share regulatory requirements and department services, discuss safety factors, infection control and ethical practices.

Summary

Activities have been used for healing since ancient civilization. Throughout the years, activities have played a major or minor role in the provision of services for older adults. The focus of the 1990's and into the 21st century is empowerment of older adults to continue life interests and activities with adaptations as needed. Recognition of activities as a part of a quality of life will continue to expand in the community and in residential and long-term-care settings.

In the early treatment of people, music and singing were provided and may add to the quality of life. Galen used music and poetry for people who were disturbed and violent. Music was used to relieve pain. He believed that games relaxed the mind and body. The Greeks believed that people needed a balance of physical exercise and intellectual activities. To prevent social disorganization, the Romans used the circus and other spectator types of activities.

The diversity and history of activity service settings is enlightening for activity professionals. The history expands over several centuries and continues to grow as needs of older adults change. Today's activity professionals will lead the way for tomorrow's changes in the provision of activity services.

In any service setting, it is important to know: (1) the mission of an organization (2) organization structure (3) formal authority (4) the chain of command, (5) division of work (6) organizational behavior (7) accountability and (8) responsibilities. Trained activity professionals have the opportunity to work in a variety of service settings during their tenure of being an activity professional. This opportunity can continue through retirement. Retired activity professionals may continue to work part-time in their last service setting or in a new service setting.

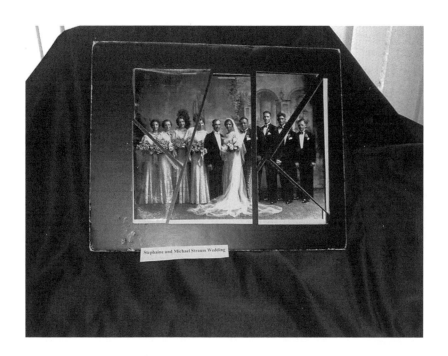

Person Centered Puzzle made from a copy of the resident's wedding picture.   J. Krupa

Chapter 2

Colloquy

"Communication can be verbal or non-verbal."

An activity professional is a leader, no matter what position he or she holds. An activity professional responsible for conducting an activity is a leader of the group. The activity professional hired to manage the activities services is a leader of the activity services staff, a team player and may be a leader for a specific committee(s) within the organization and in the community. All activity leaders need to be good communicators with the people they serve, answer to, or interact with on a daily or less frequent basis.

An activity professional manager must be confident, assertive and responsible in communicating with those above, below or latterly in the organizational structure. Good communication is essential to being an effective leader/manager.

An activity professional in a management position is responsible for reporting to his/her supervisor, the administration and sometimes the board of directors. The activity professional manager is responsible for communicating with staff so that: (1) residents needs, interests and preferences are met, (2) the mission and goals of the organization and department are implemented (3) an interdisciplinary approach to care and services is emphasized, (4) all staff are kept up to date on current issues regarding residents and the facility (5) activity staff, facility staff and administration receive in-service training and (6) the activity service department evaluations of programs, services, and staff are utilized for quality assurance and improvement.

Active Listening

"Learning Occurs When One is Actively Listening"

Activity professionals need to be effective listeners. When communicating with another person, the activity professional must focus attention entirely on what the person is saying and on his/her non-verbal communication (expressions, gestures, posture, etc.; maintaining eye contact and showing interest by nodding, expressing empathy, asking questions, gesturing relating to what was heard, and/or being silent, and/or summarizing. Additional effective listening responses include clarifying, probing, interpreting, confronting (if needed), informing and perception checking.

Listen for feelings, emotions, facts, sentiments, meaning and reactions. It is important to understand the person's perception of a problem/situation as well as his/her actual experience or perception of an experience. Two people may have the same experience but their perception of the experience may differ.

Barriers

Communication barriers can include: not being present, becoming judgmental, giving advice that was not solicited, being opinionated, being defensive, showing disapproval, interrupting and making value judgments. Topic jumping reduces the consistency and quality of communication. Offensive language, inappropriate use of words and misinformation can be detrimental to communication. Asking "why" - type questions may make a person feel defensive. Not allowing sufficient time for processing information and/or answering questions has a negative effect on communication. Accents, articulation, and rate of speech may also have a negative impact on communication.

Personal experiences, values, beliefs, perceptions, attitudes, and judgment can shade what is heard. Activity professionals need to constantly be aware of communication barriers and to minimize them.

Verbal Communication

Quality and tone of voice, inflection, articulation, speed, vocabulary and emotional feelings all have an impact on verbal communication. Communication is not only what is said but also how it is said and how it is perceived.

Responder Skills

"Listening can be an act of loving"

Activity professionals need to speak to participants in a vocabulary that they understand. Words have different meanings in different parts of the country. A "machine" may mean "an automobile"; "a poke" can be a bag, etc. A participant may not speak English; thus, the activity professional needs to learn basic words of the participant's language, e.g., German, Spanish, to be able to communicate.

Professional language is essential when communicating with team members. Activity professionals need to know basic medical, regulatory, organization and business terms. One facility may call a meeting in which all clinical departments meet to discuss an individual resident's needs, care, progress and goals, a Care Plan Meeting. Whereas another facility may refer to the same process as an IDT (interdisciplinary team) meeting.

An activity department's "staff meeting" may include in-service training, whereas, another activity department may have two separate meeting to accomplish the same tasks. One meeting to discuss the department's goals, progress, share new information, planning, identifying responsibilities, time lines, etc. An in-service training meeting focuses on the topic of the in-service.

Non-Verbal Communication

"Faces mirror the soul"

Non-verbal communication includes eye contact, facial/hand gestures (smile, frowns, waving of hand, pointing, etc.), movement of head, body, arms/legs, proper distancing, posturing (leaning forward/backward, standing/sitting tall). Non-verbal communication needs to be congruent with verbal communication.

Adaptations

Adaptations may be needed to communicate with persons (residents, participants, staff, volunteers, families etc.) with visual, auditory and/or cognitive impairments.

Visual Disabilities

In communicating with a person with visual impairments, the activity professional uses descriptive words that help a person see what is being said or described, e.g. 12" pink vase. Using directional words such as up/down, right/left, front/back, over/under, center, and around can assist a person in understanding directions. The "Clock Method" may also be used to describe location during an activity; the red paint is at 1:00 on your pallet.

Hearing Disabilities

Lowering the tone of voice can assist a person with a hearing deficit to hear spoken words. Amplification may be needed to increase volume to foster the ability to hear. Facing a person and speaking slowly allows another person to lip-read. If a person wears a hearing aid, be sure the battery and the hearing aid are working. A person wearing a hearing aid may find it difficult to communicate in a noisy environment, e.g. a party.

A person who is unable to hear and read lips may be able to communicate with a picture board. Activity professionals can make picture boards representing different activities, e.g. bingo, church, bowling, crafts, music, etc. Pictures from activity catalogs can be use to make an activity picture board. Electronic equipment (such as a talking board) enables some participants to communicate effectively. Speech pathologists can recommend different types of communication aids for participants with communication deficits.

Physical Disabilities

In speaking to a participant using a wheelchair, sit and speak on his/her eye level. When speaking to a person in bed, try to find the position in which the person is most comfortable talking, i.e., sitting up with the activity professional sitting, standing or lying on one side with activity professional sitting.

Eye contact is important, as is the ability to hear one another.

Activity professionals need to be aware of the physical energy that is used by some participants in their attempts to speak. Short interactions may be satisfying and not too taxing.

Cognitive Disabilities

In working with participants with cognitive deficits, the activity professional must address the person by name to get his/her attention before initiating communication. Often times repeating their name will keep them on the task at hand. Remain calm and speak slowly and clearly. Provide ample time for a person to respond. Repeat questions or directions as needed and repeat as originally stated. A person who is confused often forgets what you said rather than not understanding you. Use gestures to assist the person in understanding the spoken word. Ask simple open-ended questions. When asking a choice-type question, give two choices versus three or four. If a person is unable to answer simple open-ended questions, ask yes/no questions. Observe nonverbal responses for residents who are unable to give a verbal response to questions. Redirect a person as needed. Use cueing and gesturing.

A person who is confused cannot respond to reality orientation, try validation therapy. Past time may be present time for the participant. Do not argue with a resident who is confused. Inform the person that you do not understand what he/she is trying to say. A person may not be able to identify a need but may ask a question related to a need, e.g., "Do you have an out house?" The person is trying to say that he/she has to go to the restroom. A participant may be able to communicate needs/feelings through a stuffed animal or doll by saying what the animal or doll needs or asking for assistance with the doll or stuffed animal. Observing non-verbal patterns and gestures when a person has a mild degree of confusion will assist an activity professional in knowing what specific gesturing means when the person is no longer able to verbalize. Participants who are confused may call an item by a totally unrelated name. They may refer to their sweater as "happy"; this would be valuable to know upon admission.

Psychiatric Disabilities

A person with a psychiatric problem may or may not have a communication problem. A communication problem may be related to thought disorder or reaction to medication (such as slurred speech). Remain calm, set limits (as needed), and be specific, clear and firm if a person is upset. It is often helpful to take the person to a quiet area to talk. This will avoid distraction. Use reality orientation as appropriate when working with a person who is confused. If a person hallucinates, attempt to orient him/her to reality, e.g. if a participant states that he sees bugs on the wall, the activity professional's response could be, "You see bugs on the wall but I don't see bugs on the wall." Avoid stating negative feelings. In expressing displeasure, focus on the person's behavior and not on the person. Be considerate and respectful. Be sure the participant understands. Rephrase questions and comments as needed.

Cultural Difference in Communication
"Communication is understanding another"

It is important to understand cultural and ethnic diversity among participants, families, volunteers, staff, administration and the community at large. Webster's Ninth New College Dictionary defines cultural and ethic as:

Cultural: "… the customary beliefs, social forms, and material traits of a racial, religious, or social group."

Ethnic: "… of or relating to large groups of people classed according to racial, national, tribal, religious, linguistic, or cultural origin or background."

A non-English speaking person may or may not be able to read English. A volunteer may be needed to assist with obtaining information from a resident to complete his/her activity assessment. The section containing the identification of the resident's interests and preferences could be written in the resident's language so that the resident could complete the assessment. A volunteer, peer or family member who speaks the resident's language as well as English, may have to interpret the resident's written responses. Pictures of activities on 3"x 5" cards can be used for the resident to select activities of interests or printed pictures with space to check off activities of interest is another way for a resident to identify interests.

Learning basic words of a specific language is helpful in communicating with residents, staff as well as others who do not speak English. There are a variety of foreign language books, tapes, videos, and CD's on the market. Experience, trial and error is part of the learning process of communicating with people who do not speak English.

Life Dialog Communication

"One cannot unspeak a word"

Activity professionals need to know when and what types of questions need to be used with residents for assessment, conversation, discussion, reminiscing, life review, etc. Professional questions can be eye openers, perceived as threats or a means to elicit information

It is imperative to know and understand the different types of questions and when to use which ones. Yes/no questions are the least threatening types of questions. Open-ended questions provide specific responses beyond the yes/no. A choice question allows for one of two or multiple choices. Feeling-type questions offer an opportunity for a person to express his/her feelings. Opinion and "WHY" type questions are the most threatening type of questions. "Why" type questions are often negative but can elicit clear responses.

Examples:

Yes/No
Resident: Would you like to sit by the window?
Staff: Can you attend the Community Harvest? meeting on Tuesday, at 2:00 P.M.

Open Ended:
Resident: What did you watch on TV last night?
Staff: What new activities do you think we need to add to the activity calendar for Unit B?

Choice:
Resident: What color ribbon to do you want for the trim, red or blue?
Staff: What computer activity are you more interested in teaching: introduction to computer, how to use the Internet, or how to e-mail?

Feeling:
Resident: How do you feel about the changes in the new monthly newsletter?
Staff: What are your feelings about expanding the evening entertainment program?

Opinion:
Resident: What do you think the president should do regarding the war in Iraq?
Staff: How could we improve communication? with the nursing assistants?

WHY:
Resident: Why didn't you attend the evening activity last night?
Staff: Why weren't the craft supplies put away?
         After this morning's program?

Memory:

In communicating with participants, the activity professional must know their memory function. Some will use short-term and long-term memory. Others will use only long-term memory. Reality orientation requires short-term memory whereas validation therapy is focused on long-term and remote memory. A participant may be able to correctly respond to a reminiscing question, but unable to answer the question "What day is today?" or "Today is what day?"

Information Sharing Culture

"Our social group gives us meaning"

Activity professionals need to be prepared to attend and participate in meetings, conferences and training. Often there is follow up communication, which needs to be timely and accurate.

Activity professional managers are responsible for assisting staff with their professional development through in-service training and continuing education. In-service training is provided within the organization whereas continuing education is provided outside the organization by a professional organization (local, state, national), or a professional individual in the community

The activity professional providing an in-service must do so in an effective learning environment with open communication and established objectives for learning. The learner needs to know what is to be learned as well as why something needs to be learned. Adults have different learning styles, some are visual and need visual aids; others are more auditory and learn through listening others learn by doing. It is important for the presenter to know and incorporate the preferred learning style of participants in preparing learning opportunities and materials. In today's world, adults like to be entertained as they learn. Videos, meaningful comical stories, jokes, cartoons, inspirational poems, stories, quotations, puzzles, fill in the blank questions, quizzes with multiple choice answers, drawings, games, challenges, reflection, feedback, etc. are typical methods to get and hold a learner's attention. Teaching easier skills before more complex skills and teaching sub skills before practicing complex skills facilitates learning and appropriate application. Often learning is a process of going from A to B so that C is understood.

Communication is a two-way process of sending and receiving information. Activity professionals need to be able to communicate effectively with residents/participants, staff, administration, volunteers, families, vendors, and community contacts. This involves verbal and nonverbal interpersonal communication as well as written communication. It is essential to get a person's attention before attempting communication.

An activity professional is constantly communicating as a part of his /her job. Thus he/she needs to have effective communication skills. Interpersonal communication skills are developed over a lifetime. William D. Hitt. States: "The key to effective interpersonal communication is authentic dialogue. dialogue means open communication with the intention of establishing a living mutual relation. It includes both speaking and listening; it includes both the expression of thought and the expression of feelings. It is a mutual sharing between one self and another self."

In "The Leader-Manager Guidelines for Action", Hitt gives ten (10) guidelines for effective interpersonal communication:

1. Express your thoughts clearly.

   First organize your thoughts, think before you speak, select the appropriate words that best communicate your thoughts, speak in the language of the listener and strive for clarity.

2. Be willing to express your feelings.

   People want to know where you are coming from – tell them. Express feelings with responsibility.

3. Put yourself in the place of the other person.

   Empathy is being sensitive and able to see something through another person's eyes.

4. Be "truly" present.

   Give the person you are talking to your undivided attention.

5. Be a good listener.

   Use active listening skills. Listen so that you understand, ask questions to clarify, paraphrase key points, and check your perception.

6. Postpone evaluation.

   Wait until you have heard everything before making an evaluation.

7. Avoid becoming hostile when another person's view differs from your own.

   Learn how a person's point of view came about, what it means and why the person supports his/her point of view. Try to incorporate these points of view into your own thinking and giving credit to the person who generated the idea.

8. Be willing to change your convictions as new truths are uncovered.

   Have an open mind. Hear and try to understand other people's point of views. With new insight, you may change your own point of view.

9. Be willing to confront.

   Conflict is a part of life. It needs to be guided and channeled. Be willing to confront with views different from yours so that you have an authentic dialogue.

10. Think win-win.

In a confrontation with an adversary, work towards a positive outcome to achieve objectives and emerge as winners.

Professional communication skills are developed through training, experience and mentoring. Communication needs to be clear, honest and appropriate to the setting/topic.

(William D. Hitt) *Used with permission.*

Building Community and Workplace Collegiality

"Team work is caring and sharing"

Activity professionals must be aware of how their communication affects others and strive for collegiality. Working in a pleasing and supportive environment is motivating. A good morning, recognizing others by name and a sincere smile adds friendliness to the environment. Recognizing other's good word or work builds self-esteem and support.

A mentor is helpful in learning and understanding the politics and communication within the organization. No organization is prefect. There will be times of disagreements, arguments and negative reactions.

Argumentation

"The description is in the mind of the describer"

In discussing disagreements, the voice and views of all persons involved need to be heard, respected and confirmed. Keeping to the facts of disagreement and not letting negative personal feelings enter into the discussion fosters open communication. That is not to say that voicing feelings as to why someone feels as they do related to the topic of discussion, is not a part of the dialogue. Jumping to conclusions negates compromise. New views and ideas can open another person's perception and opinion. Trusting interpersonal relationships facilitate the augmentation to a win-win situation

Negotiation

"Negotiation is the path to a solution"

Life is a process of negotiations learned in early childhood. Some of the same tools a child uses to negotiate something wanted are utilized in the work place. It is a give and take situation, keeping in mind what is best for the people and services involved. Residents may want to negotiate a new time for a specific activity that affects the work schedule of staff. Thus the negotiation process involves many people, time frames and adherence to the organization's mission, goals, policies and procedures. Negotiation is not always a simple process and takes time to achieve the results.

Conflict Management

"Compromise is the art of management"

Conflict management can be stimulating, challenging and energizing or seen as a negative, down hill spiral experience with no positive outcome. Activity professionals need to keep a positive attitude even during adversary times and experiences. There is more energy when one is positive than negative in dealing with a situation. It also relieves stress and negative personal self-talk. One can learn from others how their attitude, verbalization and non-verbal behaviors affect their input into a discussion. Confrontation needs to be individualized, respectful and supportive. The focus needs to be kept on what is best for the residents, as ultimately all decisions affect the resident directly or indirectly.

43

Differences in Coping Styles

"Various coping styles should be respected"

How one deals with conflict will vary depending on a number of factors. It is important to know and understand your own personal coping styles and how they affect a situation or other people. Calm people open to criticism can hear what is being said versus speculating on the meaning. The information can be internalized with a positive resolve. Anger can be expressed through words, actions and deeds. Some people cope by being non-committal, using avoidance, smoothing over the situation as if it will go away. Others will forcefully express themselves with words and/or actions, i.e. people who bang on a table to make a point, blaming others, not taking responsibility, feeling victimized, voicing self pity, avoiding risks, rejection and mistakes, still others want to be rescued and taken care of, feeling belittled, berated, unloved, unwanted or other indications that their self esteem has be injured. Other negative coping can include turning to food or drink etc. Activity professional managers need to understand people's individualized coping skills and assist them in transferring negative feelings and actions to be more positive about themselves as well as others in the organization. Coping styles are learned behaviors and can change over time. The way one copes affects his mind, body and spirit. Effective coping skills are essential for healthy living and functioning well in an organization.

Written Communication

"Some things are not done until they are written"

Hitt, in his 1988 book, "The Leader-Manager Guidelines for Action" gives the following ten (10) guidelines for effective writing:

1. Write in the language of the reader

    Hitt recommends that before you write something, focus on the reader and reflect on his/her education, experience and interests and then write accordingly.

2. Focus on the key ideas.

    The length of a written communication is not as important as to focus on one main idea even if the topic has secondary or tertiary ideas. Organize the content of the written document to support the idea or topic.

3. Organize your material in a coherent manner.

    Hitt states" Readers will understand your material better if it is organized in "chunks". Hitt recommends limiting the number of chunks or major points to three or four.

    Outlining the material before writing will provide a logical flow from one idea to the next.

4. Choose a style and stick to it.

    An organization may have policies and procedures that dictate the format for writing business and clinical communication, including e-mail. Hitt states "Style includes choice of words, sentences, and paragraph format." It should be appropriate to the situation and parties involved." The most important thing is to choose an appropriate style and stay with it.

5. Make the paragraph the basic unit of composition.

    Each paragraph should emphasize one idea, starting with the first sentence. Transition sentences lead to the following paragraphs until the communication is completed.

6. Use definite, specific, concrete language.

    Be specific and to the point using words that are clearly understood.

7. Use the active voice rather than the passive voice.

8. Use short words rather than long words.

   Clinical and technical words may be long; thus cannot be shortened.

9. Omit needless words.

10. Apply the basic rules of grammar properly.

    (William D. Hitt) *Used with permission.*

Participant Communication

Large print needs to be used for all participant-related-communication, i.e. posters, announcement, newsletters, activity schedules, etc. Any communication that is posted needs to be at eye level for persons who use a wheelchair. Color contrast is also important. Black print on white paper or white print on black paper is easy to read. Color contrast can be detrimental when it is difficult to see the print, i.e. words printed in pink on white paper.

Professional Communication

Activity professionals are responsible for a variety of written clinical and non clinical communication including but not limited to: activity documentation, (assessment, care plans, participation records, progress notes, incidental notes), activity schedules, letters, memos, thank you notes, information in newsletters, posters, invitations, e-mail, fax, minutes of meetings, in-service training report/records, health and safety reports, plans of action related to regulatory deficiencies, proposals, quality assurance reports and other reports, etc.

All professional communication needs to be clear and concise. Grammar, punctuation, sentence structure and spelling need to be correct. Correct terminology is important. The person(s) to whom one is communicating must be considered so that he/she understands the communication.

Letters and Thank-You Notes

Letterhead stationary is used for formal typed letters. Thank-you notes may be typed on letterhead stationary or hand-written on agency/facility blank note cards. The protocol for typed or handwritten thank you notes is determined by the agency/facility. Participants can write thank you notes on behalf of other participants, agency/facility as appropriate.

Signature

An activity professional uses his/her legal signature and certification initials on letters, thank-you notes and reports. Initials are used after the activity professional's typed name on a memo versus a signature.

A first name or initials can be used for informal, interdepartmental communication, as long as no one else has the same name or initials. There may be several Kristins' but only one Kristin Smith. So each Kristin would use the initial of their first and last name, i.e., K.S. versus K.

Newsletters and Announcements

All newsletters and announcements need to be professionally designed and written. The graphics, content and printing reflect on the agency/organization. Drafts of all public communication need to be reviewed and approved by administration prior to mailing/distribution.

A newsletter can serve one or several purposes. It can be an internal or external, as well as a monthly, quarterly, and/or annual publication. The purpose, readership and budget will affect the content. An internal newsletter may be only for participants, or for both participants and staff. In a long-term care facility the newsletter may be used for multiple purposes, i.e. informing residents, staff, families, physicians, referral agencies, vendors and the general public about events, happenings, and changes in the facility.

If an activity calendar is part of a newsletter, it needs to be identical to the activity calendar/schedules posted in the agency/facility. It is wise to add the disclaimer statement, "Subject to change," to the calendar.

45

Press Releases

Press releases to newspaper, radio and television stations must be newsworthy. The release needs to capture the attention of the reader. The five basic questions of who, what, when, where and why need to be answered in paragraph or outline format.

Each press release needs to identify a contact person, telephone number and the best time to call. The media do not have infinite time to make calls in attempt to reach a contact person. Secretaries and/or switchboard operators need to be informed when a call from the media is expected, and whether or not the activity professional can be paged to take a phone call or if another person will take the call.

Copies of photos need to be sent with a photo release by the person or representative whose photo is being used. All names need to be checked for correct spelling.

An activity professional can call the media for assistance in writing a press release. Reading information in newspapers submitted by other agencies/organization is one means of learning about content. Closely observing news about activity programs or other happenings is another way to become familiar with what is considered newsworthy.

Maintaining Records of Communication

Keeping a copy of all communication for future reference is helpful, but it does not have to be kept forever. Developing a policy for the length of time communication will be kept is recommended. Communication may be kept by subject ("Memos"), projects ("Mother's Day Celebration"), calendar year ("2006 Letters") or any other method that facilitates location of the item when needed.

Keeping a record of computer files for all written communication reduces the amount of information that has to be stored in a file cabinet. An activity professional needs to decide when a computer-generated communication needs to have a hard copy on file and when it is sufficient to have it on a back-up system.

"People First" Terminology

In talking or writing about participants with disabilities use "People First" language. Place the person before the disability, i.e. refer to a person as "a person with a disability versus a disabled person". Refrain from using a disability term when referring to a person, i.e. an "Alzheimer's person" versus "a person with Alzheimer's". In referring to people who use a wheelchair, it is proper to state "a person who uses a wheelchair" or a "wheelchair user."

Chapter 3

Professional Framework

"Trustworthy is the Standard for Practicing Professionals"

Origin and History of the Activity Profession

Early Volunteers and Professionals

Volunteers paved the way for social, recreation and activities programs in senior centers, clubs and nursing homes. In 1870 the first senior center opened in Boston. Seventy years later a senior center opened in 1943 in New York. In 1947 San Francisco opened a senior center, and Philadelphia opened a center for older adults. From these early beginnings, senior centers have continued to grow and be staffed with recreation professionals, therapeutic recreation professionals, social workers, gerontology specialists and other professionals. It was mostly social workers and recreation professionals along with volunteers that provided the leadership in organizing, developing and implementing social/recreational programs for older adults in the community in the 1950's and 1960's.

In 1959 Mayor Wagner of New York City set up the Heyman Commission to review health services in the city. The lack of recreation in nursing homes was one of the findings. As a result a new code for personnel went into effect in 1963, including recreation personnel.

The forerunners of states or cities requiring recreation in homes for the aged and nursing homes were California (homes for the aged and nursing homes); Connecticut (homes for the aged); New York (homes for the aged); and New York City (nursing homes). It was not until 1974 that the federal government required activities programs in intermediate and skilled nursing facilities. These regulations have been changed over the years, with the most significant changes resulting from OBRA'87 (Omnibus Budget Reconciliation Act). The implementation of the revised regulations was in April 1992. The final regulations became effective July 1, 1995. The most recent change of interpretive guidelines for surveys was June 1, 2006.

The first adult day care in the U.S. was developed in 1958 when a three-year project in a day hospital rehabilitation began in Schenectady, New York. Twelve programs were started in the 1960's and the number grew to 20 in the 1970's. In the 1980's there were over 1,200 programs. As these programs grew, so did the need for therapeutic recreation and activity personnel.

With the enactment of the Office of Economic Opportunity (the Johnson Administration's War on Poverty Program), the Medicare Act (1965), and the Older American's Act (1965), programs, training and services for older adults in the community and in long term care facilities evolved. The 1960's were a time for change for older adults. The 1970's saw the emergence of activity coordinators.

Activity Coordinator

The term "activity coordinator" was developed to define the role and responsibilities of a person responsible for patient activity programming in nursing homes, under the 1974 federal regulations for intermediate and skilled nursing homes. The term "activities" versus the former term "recreation" was used to broaden the scope of services to include religious activities and services other than recreation. A variety of job titles emerged, i.e., Activity Director, Activity Coordinator, and Activity Assistant. Each title included the term "activity/activities." These job titles were later used in other settings, e.g., community agencies, adult day care. The roles and responsibilities under these job titles are defined in job descriptions.

Activity Professionals

With the increase of activity coordinators working in a variety of settings (nursing homes, retirement centers, assisted-living facilities, community-based programs, etc.) came the development and birth of the term "activity professionals," as state associations began developing activity professional associations. The main impetus for the term came in 1981 with the development of a national organization, The National Association of Activity Professionals (NAAP). The term was further strengthened by the 1986 development of the National Certification Council for Activity Professionals (NCCAP). The familiar term "activity coordinator" (actually a job title) that had originated in the 1974 regulations for nursing homes was changed to the broader term "activity professional." Effective April, 1992 the federal regulations and interpretive guidelines include "activity professional" under the listing of qualifications of a "qualified" person to direct the activities program for skilled nursing facilities (Sniffs) and nursing facilities (NF's) receiving reimbursement under Medicare or Medicaid.

Therapeutic Recreation Specialist

During the period of the 1960's to the 1980's, other professional organizations were developed. The National Therapeutic Recreation Society was formed in 1965 and the American Therapeutic Recreation Association was formed in 1984. These two professional organizations are for therapeutic recreation professionals, some of whom work with older adults in a variety of settings. Nationally, therapeutic recreation specialists are certified by the National Council for Therapeutic Recreation Certification (NCTRC) as a certified therapeutic recreation specialist (CTRS).

Therapeutic recreation specialists working with older adults are often members of the American Therapeutic Recreation Association and/or the National Therapeutic Recreation Society, as well as the National Association of Activity Professionals. In addition to being a certified therapeutic recreation specialist (CTRS), they can be certified by NCCAP as an activity director certified (ADC) or as an activity consultant certified (ACC)

Other Specialists

Other specialists, i.e., art therapist, dance/movement therapist, drama therapist, horticultural therapists, music therapist, occupational therapist, poetry therapist, etc., who work with older adults also belong to NAAP and are certified through NCCAP, while being members of their specific professional organizations and being certified or registered by their respective certification or registration organizations. Other professionals with training and experience in education, social work, business, nursing, ministry, etc. have also become activity professionals.

The Activity Education Movement: History and Significance

In the 60's there were a few training programs to prepare personnel to work in activities or therapeutic recreation. Colorado Activity directors offered their first educational training course in 1963

On July 1, 1965, the Therapeutic Recreation Project for the Aged (TRA project), funded by the Office of Economic Opportunity (President Johnson's "War on Poverty") was started in Cincinnati, OH. This unique project was two fold:

1. to provide training and employment for young adults (age 16-21 years) and older adults (age 60 and over)
2. to provide therapeutic recreation services to older residents in sheltered care institutions in the Greater Cincinnati area.

Within a 22-month period the project staff of 76 (71%were over 60 years of age) had served over 1,050 older residents (average age of 76) in 18 institutions. The average age of residents in institutions in the 60's was much younger than residents of today.

When the demonstration TRA project was completed in 1967 over 100 persons had been trained and programs had been developed in 21 institutions. Training in Cincinnati continued. In 1972 the University of Cincinnati was the first college in the state to offer a college-credited course for Activity Coordinators.

36-Hour Course

The development of the 36-Hour Course for activity coordinators in nursing homes was the first national movement to train activity professionals. In 1972, the U.S. Department of Health, Education and Welfare contracted with the American Nursing Homes Association to develop and conduct a nationwide three-phased Activity Coordinator Training Project. The training project was in preparation for the first regulations requiring activity coordinators in nursing homes (effective in 1974). There were not enough occupational therapists or therapeutic recreation specialists to fill the new required positions; thus, training programs for people to work as activity coordinators were needed.

Six or more key people in each state (representing the state nursing home association, therapeutic recreation, occupational therapy, social work, administration, nursing and other related professions) were asked to serve on state planning committees. Regional training programs for multiple states were held. State planning committees attended a two-day orientation program on developing a 36-hour training program for activities coordinators on a statewide basis. Some of the people involved in this early training endeavor are still very active in the activity profession today at the local, state and/or national level.

Phase I of the training project was for states to develop their own requirements for training of activity coordinators. State coordi-

nating agencies were identified. Some were state health departments; others were state nursing home professional organizations. The intent was for states to develop requirements, using the 36-hour training as a guide. It was not intended that the 36-hour training would become the required/accepted training for activity coordinators in nursing homes, as more hours were needed. However, the 36-hour training became the norm. Some states did require more hours.

The state planning committees under the auspices of the state-coordinating agency had the task of identifying and training teachers/consultants to develop and conduct the training programs for activity coordinators at the local level. Some states like Ohio immediately proceeded with the task. Other states for a variety of reasons did not proceed with this task for several years.

Phase II was the development of training teams of professionals to teach the required training programs. Professionals included, but were not limited to, therapeutic recreation specialists, recreation professionals, nurses, occupational therapists, social workers, administrators, etc., to teach the required training program. The teaching teams' responsibility was to set up and teach the training program for activity coordinators at the local level.

Phase III was the provision of training for persons interested in becoming activity coordinators in nursing homes. Some training programs were offered at a centralized location in the state, i.e., states with small numbers of nursing homes, others were offered at multiple training sites.

People with a wide variety of backgrounds (Girl Scout leaders, Bible study leaders, homemakers, nursing aids, young people right out of high school, secretaries, teachers, artists, musicians, volunteers, and people with a wide variety of activity interests/skills such as arts and crafts, games, music, dancing, nature and needlework) were trained. All had an interest in working with older adults in nursing homes and using their training and skills to develop activity programs. Some of the training programs started in 1972, with many more being initiated in 1974 when the federal regulations required activity coordinators for intermediate and skilled nursing care facilities.

Principles of Professionalism

"Unforgiving destroys relationship as well as oneself"

A professional in any field is a trained, competent person who lives up to the profession's standards, code of ethics, abides by city, state, federal regulations; is licensed, registered (if applicable) and/or certified by a recognized certifying agency for the profession. A professional joins and is involved in professional organizations, demonstrates ethical conduct, dresses appropriately for the profession and job responsibilities; continues to learn and grow through experience, mentoring, and further education. A professional is respected and feels qualified to be a member of a profession. Individual professionals feel a kin to other professionals in the field at professional meetings, conferences and educational programs. There is an indescribable feeling when a professional is looked upon as being a professional by another person in the same or different profession.

Roles of the Activity Professional

"Reaching out in love"

The roles of an activity professional vary, depending upon:

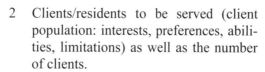

1. Specific service setting (apartment complex, senior center, adult day service, retirement community, assisted living facility, nursing home).

2   Clients/residents to be served (client population: interests, preferences, abilities, limitations) as well as the number of clients.

3. History and longevity of facility or organization. The role in a new facility/organization would differ from a service setting that has been in existence for some period of time and needs continuation or reorganization of services, change in staffing, etc.

4. Job description.

5. Staffing (qualifications and competencies, number of staff, hours of work, etc.)

6. The roles of activity professionals in the various service settings, i.e., apartment complex, assisted living, nursing homes, continuing care communities (CCC) were explained in Chapter One, Activity Service Practice Settings. Additionally, activity professionals with advanced education and experience can be educators/trainers, activity consultants as well as mentors.

7. Volunteers.

8. Geographical location (area of the country, city or suburb, weather, etc.)

9. Available space (indoor and outdoor).

10. Available transportation.

11. Safety.

12. Regulations (city, state, federal), voluntary standards (JCAHO, CARF).

13. Budget.

Educator/Trainer

An educator/trainer provides training for new and experienced activity professionals, conducts workshops, provides in-service training, gives speeches, develops educational materials and supports the development of the field through education and training. An example is the 180 hr. Modular Education Program for Activity Professionals (MEPAP) 2nd Edition. Instructors must be trained and certified by the National Certification Council for Activity Professionals (NCCAP) to teach the course. In some states the activity professional educator must have a degree or advanced degree to teach the 180 Hr. MEPAP 2nd Edition in a college or university.

Activity Consultants

Activity consultants work as independent activity consultants or as a corporate consultant for an organization, a non-profit or for profit organization. They work with a variety of clients and service settings. Their role is defined in a job description. Activity consultants are internal or external change agents. The internal consultant is an employee of an organization who provides consultation services for clients within the organization. The external consultant is free to work with a variety of clients. The internal consultant has a job description; where as the external private consultant responsibilities is part of the consultant's contract for contractual services. The consultant and client agree upon a contract by which the consult provides needed services. Contracts differ deepening upon the need of the service setting.

Mentor

An activity professional can be a mentor to other activity professionals in the same or different service settings, as well as to other professionals and non-professionals.

A mentor is an experienced person, a professional who advises/coaches another person. A protégé is a person who receives guidance and direction from a mentor Mentoring is like coaching another individual related to professional responsibilities, learning how to function successfully in the selected service, getting along with other professionals, understanding the history, philosophy and mission of the service setting, supporting professional development through education, training, experience and continuing professional development throughout one's career.

Continuing Professional Development
"One learns little while speaking"

An activity professional's education does not stop upon receipt of a degree, certificate of completion of the MEPAP 2nd Edition (180 hours of education and 180 hours of practical experience) or national certification by the National Certification Council for Activity Professionals. Developing a professional development plan for continued professional growth and development is an effective way to establish professional goals and plans for meeting the goals. A professional development plan may include learning a specific skill, acquiring more information on a specific topic, in-service training, attending a professional education program, e.g., a local, state, regional or national professional workshop or conference, reading specific professional material, researching information at the library or internet, preparing and providing an in-service or continuing education program, observing activity services in similar or different service settings, being involved in professional organizations, utilizing leadership skills or being involved in service setting committees. It is said that an activity professional's work is never done; the same is true regarding professional development. The activity profession is dynamic and continually growing. Every activity professional must keep up to date and be self-motivated to utilized new knowledge and skills for the benefit of those they serve.

Benefits of Collegiality
"Trust comes from open, honest sharing"

Getting along with other people in the same or different departments in the selected service setting fosters a friendly environment. Activity professionals are dependent upon other professionals to implement a team approach to activity services and programs. Good verbal and written communication skills are essential for fostering a team approach. It is easy to communicate with a professional who is aware of other people's needs, feelings, responsibilities and time restraints. Social graces such as calling people by name, saying please and thank you, encourages another person to respond and think highly of the person who initiated the interaction. An activity professional must always present him or herself in a professional cordial manner in every interaction with clients/residents, peers, supervisors, mangers and administrators.

Contributing Talent and Time to the Activity Profession as a Means of Personal Growth
"Allow time for giving and receiving ideas"

Activity professionals have a professional responsibility to share their time and talents with other professionals through involvement in professional organizations. The growth of any profession is dependent upon individual professionals giving of themselves to better the profession. An activity professional may assist the profession by serving on committees, taking a volunteer leadership role in a professional organization, researching needed information, conducting or responding to surveys pertaining to the profession, advocating for the profession verbally or in writing, supporting the profession and professionals with sincere recognition, being aware of happenings that may have a negative affect on the profession and professionals.

Providing in-service training and continuing education for other professionals, e.g., administrators, nurses, social worker, dietary personnel, housekeeping and maintenance personnel, volunteers and families allows the activity professional an opportunity to think about the activity profession and share its purpose and goals with others. In the process, the activity professional increases his/her perception of the field, role and responsibilities as well as changes that affect the persons served.

NAAP Standards of Practice

The activity profession, like other professions, operates by following the profession's standard of practice. The standards are guidelines for practice. Each activity professional is responsible for following the profession's standards. Often the standards are written as responsibilities in a job description.

Activity Professionals need to be aware of the NAAP Standards of Practice as well as state and federal regulations. If a regulation changes, the activity professional would still go by professional standards. Whatever standard of Practice or state or federal regulation is more stringent, the activity professional would adhere to it. Activity policies and procedure may need to be change to reflect the standard or practice or regulation. See Appendix L for the NAAP Standards of practice.

Certified activity professional are responsible for reading, knowing and following the

NCCAP code of ethics. In the NCCAP Code of Ethics under Section I, Resolving Ethical Issues, it states, "If it is found that a Certified Activity Professional is not adhering to the NCCAP Code of Ethics--- through written reports, through "doctored" documents, etc, -- the certification will be rescinded or denied..:"

A certified activity professional who looses certification would no longer be able to use the certification initials after his or her name and would need to inform the administrator of the lost of certification. If national certification was a criterion for employment, the person would be dismissed. See Appendix H, for National Certification Council for Activity Professionals Code of Ethics.

STANDARDS OF PRACTICE

GENERAL STANDARDS OF PRACTICE

PROVISION OF ACTIVITY SERVICES

1. ACTIVITY ASSESSMENT/PROFILE:
The Activity Professional shall conduct an activity assessment/profile for each client/resident to determine his/her activity needs, interest, preferences, and abilities.

2. ACTIVITY PLAN:
The Activity Professional shall develop an individual, interdisciplinary activity plan with each client/resident. The activity plan shall be based on the resident's/client's activity assessment/ profile and shall be designed to enable each resident/client to achieve and/or maintain his/her highest level of well being.

3. IMPLEMENTATION OF ACTIVITY PLAN:
The Activity Professional shall direct the activity plan and shall involve the interdisciplinary team in the implementation of the individualized therapeutic interventions.

4. EVALUATION OF THE ACTIVITY PLAN:
The Activity Professional shall continuously evaluate and document the resident's/client's response to each activity. The revision of the activity plan shall be based on the resident's/client's response to the therapeutic interventions.

5. ACTIVITY PROGRAM:
The Activity Professional shall be resident/client centered and enable the resident/client to maximize his/her potential in the activity program.

MANAGEMENT OF ACTIVITY SERVICES

6. STAFF CREDENTIALS/EDUCATION:
The Activity Department shall establish a plan to ensure each activity employee is qualified to perform his/her assigned tasks, maintains appropriate credentials, and is provided with opportunities for professional development.

7. PLAN OF OPERATION:
The Activity Department shall have written policies and procedures based on the National Association of Activity Professionals (NAAP) Standards of Practice and Scope of Practice; regulatory requirements; facility/corporate requirements, and the standards established by accrediting agencies.

8. RESOURCE UTILIZATION:
The Activity Department shall develop and maintain a plan for identifying, acquiring, and utilizing resources to achieve the department's goals.

9. QUALITY IMPROVEMENT/PROGRAM EVALUATION:
The Activity Department shall develop and implement a systematic and ongoing plan to evaluate the quality, effectiveness, and integrity of the activity services.

10. ETHICAL CONDUCT:
The Activity Professional shall adhere to the NAAP *Code of Ethics*.Adopted by the Membership of NAAP, November 2001, Sevierville, Tennessee. Copyrighted. Use only with permission. *Used by permission.*

NAAP Code of Ethics

A code of ethics refers to the expected behavior of a professional. Each professional field, i.e., physicians, lawyers, bankers, etc., have their own code of ethics specific to their profession. Activity professionals adhere to the NAAP (National Association of Activity Professionals) Code of Ethics.

Certified activity professional are responsible for reading, knowing and following the NCCAP code of ethics. In the NCCAP Code of Ethics under Section I, Resolving Ethical Issues, it states, "If it is found that a Certified Activity Professional is not adhering to the NCCAP Code of Ethics--- through written reports, through "doctored" documents, etc, --the certification will be rescinded or denied..:"

A certified activity professional who looses certification would no longer be able to use the certification initials after his or her name and would need to inform the administrator of the lost of certification. If national certification was a criterion for employment, the person would be dismissed. See Appendix H, for National Certification Council for Activity Professionals Code of Ethics.

Code of Ethics for Activity

Professionals

Preamble:

The National Association of Activity Professionals and its members are dedicated to providing activity services and programs, which meet the unique needs and interests of the individuals we serve. Principles:

I. **Conduct**

The Activity Professional shall maintain high standards of personal conduct and professional integrity on the jobsite at all times. The Activity Professional shall treat colleagues with professional courtesy and ensure that credit is given to others for use of their ideas, materials, and programs.

II. **Dignity/Rights**

The Activity Professional shall treat the client/resident with regard towards personal dignity at all times. The Activity Professional shall respect and protect the rights -- civil, legal and human -- of the clients/residents at all times. The Activity Professional shall work through appropriate channels to protect the rights of clients/residents and report abuse and exploitation.

III. **Confidentiality**

The Activity Professional shall treat any information about clients/residents as confidential. Information that must be shared with other staff and volunteers in the course of care shall be exchanged in a professional manner.

IV. **Empowerment**

The Activity Professional shall enable clients/residents to participate in the planning and implementation of their care, as well as making independent medical, legal, and financial decision.

V. **Participation**

The Activity Professional shall enable clients/residents to maximize their potential in activity participation through adaptation, cues/prompts, protection from undue interruption, and assistance in rescheduling of other events that may interfere with the client's/resident's ability to participate in activities of their choice.

VI. **Record Keeping**

The Activity Professional shall maintain client/resident records in an accurate, confidential, and timely manner. The Activity Professional shall follow facility policies and procedures in the formatting of such records. In the absence of facility policy the appropriate state and/or federal guidelines shall be followed.

VII. **Professional**

The Activity Professional shall participate in continuing education opportunities, strive for professional competence, ensure accurate resumes, and differentiate between personal comments/actions and official NAAP positions.

VIII. **Supervisory**

The Activity Professional shall treat persons being supervised with dignity and respect, protect their rights, and provide accurate and fair evaluations.

IX. **Communication**

The Activity Professional shall strive to maintain open channels of communication with administration, other departments, families, and clients/residents.

X. **Provision of Services**

The Activity Professional shall provide programs -- regardless of race, religion (or absence thereof), ethnic origin, social or marital status, sex or sexual orientation, age, health status, or payment source -- which assist the client/resident in achieving and maintaining the highest practicable level of physical, intellectual, psychosocial, emotional, and spiritual well-being.

XI. **Legal**

The Activity Professional shall comply with all applicable federal, state and local laws regarding the provision of services.

Adopted by the Board of Trustees, April 1996, Orlando, Florida
Copyrighted. To be used only with permission. Used by permission.

National Certification

NCCAP Code of Ethics

Preamble

The National Certification Council for Activity Professionals (NCCAP) is a professional certification organization committed to promoting quality of life for persons receiving services from professionals certified with this organization. All certified Activity Professionals are expected to adhere to the standards listed herein addition to general principles of ethical conduct endorsed by all health-related disciplines.

These ethical standards are intended to clarify to present and future certified members and to those served by them, the nature of the ethical responsibilities held in common.
As the code of ethics of this organization, this document establishes principles that define the

ethical behavior of certified members. All members of the National Certification Council for Activity Professionals are required to adhere to the Code of Ethics.

The following declaration establishes principles that define the ethical behavior of certified members and is called the Code of Ethics of the NCCAP. The Code of Ethics will serve as the basis for processing ethical complaints initiated against members of the organization.

A. Professional Responsibility

All certified Professionals have a responsibility to read, understand and follow the professional's Code of Ethics and Standards of Practice. They are expected to adhere to these standards in their professional practice to maintain their certification.

B. General Standards

1. The certified member influences the development of the profession through continually endeavoring to improve professional practices, by teaching, through service, by advocacy and leadership.
2. The certified member recognizes that professional growth is continuous.
3. The certified member recognizes the need for continuing education to ensure competent services.
4. The certified member gathers data on the effectiveness of their practice and is guided by their findings.
5. The certified member neither claims nor implies professional qualifications exceeding those possessed.
6. The certified member recognizes the extent of their competence and provides only those services for which they are qualified by training or experience.
7. The certified member accepts employment only for positions for which he/she is qualified by education, training, and appropriate professional experience.

C. Resident/Client Relationship Standards

1. The certified member guards the rights and individual dignity of the resident/client and promotes their welfare whether in a group or individually.
2. The certified member does not condone or engage in discrimination based on age, color, culture, disability, ethnic group, gender, race, religion, sexual orientation, marital status, or socioeconomic status.
3. The certified member does not bring personal issues to the resident/client relationship.

4. The certified member shall advocate on behalf of the resident/client to receive accurate activity services.
5. The certified member must ensure that residents/clients of various functional ability levels have equal access to activity services and they are provided to them accurately in the context of the service setting.
6. The certified member must ensure that every resident/client in a given setting receive activity services if they desire them.
7. The certified member respects their resident/client's right to privacy and provides for the maintenance of client confidentially in discourse and in records. In group work, the certified member must set a standard of confidentially regarding group participants' disclosures.

D. Professional Relationship Standards

1. The certified member shall respect the agency offering quality of life by supporting administration and being an effective team member.
2. The certified member has a responsibility to the institution in which s/he performs service to maintain the highest standard of professional conduct and services to their clients. The acceptance of employment implies that the certified member is in agreement with their general policies and objectives, and therefore, provides services that are in accordance with them. If the certified member finds that the institutional policy and service systems hamper resident/client potential and/or prevents access to service, the certified member must seek to cause the employer to change such policy and/or systems. Failing to effectuate change after extensive efforts, the certified member should seriously consider terminating the affiliation.

3. Ethical behavior among professional associates, both certified and non-certified, is expected at all times.
4. The certified member must seek professional review and evaluation on a regular basis.
5. The certified member must establish interpersonal relations and working agreements with other department personnel and define relationships, responsibilities and accountability in regard to their common residents/clients.
6. The certified member who supervises activity staff must be responsible for in-service development of activity staff, must inform their staff of department ethics and core values and program goals, and provide staff with practices that guarantee the rights and welfare of each resident/client who receives their services.
7. The certified member who supervises activity staff must be just and fair with staff, give credit when it is due and give counsel when work performance is below standard.

E. Educational Standards

1. The certified member shall successfully complete academic and continuing education sessions in order to better understand the residents/clients and how activity services enhance their well-being.
2. The certified member shall continue to complete educational sessions both academic and continuing education, in order to keep abreast of quality activity programming, as evidenced by appropriate and timely recertification through NCCAP.
3. The certified member shall report accurately and fairly the educational sessions attended and the credit received.
4. The certified member shall refuse to participate in falsification of any educational documents.

5. The certified member shall seek competency rather than to fulfill minimum requirements.

F. Experiential Standards

1. The certified member shall learn activity programming through supervised experience in conducting activities in the various gerontological settings.
2. The certified member shall meet federal and state regulations regarding standards to be a certified and qualified director of an activity program before marketing him/herself as a professional in the provision of activities programming.
3. The certified member shall be a high quality provider of activities that enhances the lives of residents/clients.
4. The certified member will avoid any falsification or misrepresentation of one's employment record.
5. The certified member shall function at the highest practical level of one's ability and skills to the benefit of the residents/clients.

G. Professional Preparation Standards

The certified member who trains has particular ethical responsibilities that go beyond that of the certified member who does not train other activity professionals.

1. The certified member who is responsible for training other Activity Professionals must be guided by the Standards for Professional Preparation of Activity Professionals.
2. The certified member who trains must emphasize and support the uniqueness of the activity profession, rather than teach the orientation of other professions whose members may give services in the activity realm, regardless of the certified member's personal college work. The certified member responsible for education programs must be skilled as a teacher and practitioner.

3. The certified member who has been approved as a MEPAP instructor must follow the Program Administration Guidelines in all aspects, or ensure that their sponsoring agency follows them.

4. The certified member who has been approved as a MEPAP instructor and who conducts the MEPAP training must be in compliance with the current Teacher Administrative Manual.

5. The certified member who is the primary instructor of the MEPAP must assure that academic study and supervised practice (practicum) are integrated, and have clearly stated policies regarding the responsibilities of the supervisor and the student for the field work and their responsibilities to the institution where the supervised work is taking place.

6. The certified member who has been approved as a MEPAP instructor must orient students to program expectations and requirements for successful completion.

7. The certified member who has been approved as a MEPAP instructor must evaluate students informally and formally through testing.

8. The certified member who has been approved as a MEPAP instructor must encourage students to value the ideals of service through leadership and advocacy for their residents/clients in their places of employment.

9. The certified member who has been approved as a MEPAP instructor must persuade students of the need for continuous education to ensure competent service and professional growth throughout his/her career. They must ensure students learn that to influence the development of the profession they must make continuous efforts to improve their own professional practices.

10. The certified member who has been approved as a MEPAP instructor must make students aware of their ethical responsibilities and of the standards of the profession.

11. The certified member who has been approved as a MEPAP instructor must make students aware of their responsibilities to advocate for their residents/clients in the local, state and national arenas.

H. Consulting Standards

The certified member who provides consulting services to define and solve work-related problems or potential work-related problems with an activity professional or their work system has unique ethical responsibilities that go beyond that of the certified member who does not consult with other activity professionals.

1. The certified member, acting as a consultant, must have a high degree of self-awareness of his or her own values, knowledge, skills, limitations, and personal needs when entering a relationship that involves human and/or organizational change.

2. The focus of the consulting relationship must be on issues to be resolved and not on the person or persons presenting the issues.

3. The certified member in the consulting relationship and the person(s) consulted with must agree upon the problem definition, ensuring goals and the predicted results of interventions.

4. The certified member in the consulting relationship must encourage growth, coping, and self-direction in the person consulted with. The certified member consultant must not become a decision maker for the person consulted with or create a dependency on the consultant.

I. Resolving Ethical Issues

Certified Professionals are responsible for understanding and following this Code of Ethics. Lack of knowledge or misunderstanding of an ethical responsibility is not a defense against a charge of unethical conduct. If it is found that a

Certified Activity Professional is not adhering to the NCCAP Code of Ethics --- through written reports, through "doctored" documents, etc, --- the certification will be rescinded or denied. The mechanism for review in such instances will be through the Certification Review Committee, the Executive Director, and finally the Appeals Committee.

Adopted by the NCCAP Board of Directors – September 22, 1990.

Revised by the NCCAP Board of Directors ---- April 29, 2003. Used with permission

Professional Certification

Every profession has some type of voluntary or required certification, registration or license to practice. Certification and registration is usually provided by a state   or national certifying or registration organization. Licensure is state mandated. State licensure board approves applicants prior to permitting them to take the state licensing exam.   Some certification organizations, i.e., National Certification of Therapeutic Recreation Council (NCTRC) require all new applicants to pass a test. Certified Therapeutic Recreation Specialists can take a test in lieu of submitting acceptable continuing education credits or not having the required professional experience over the past 5 years for recertification

Professional certification indicates that a professional has met established criteria to be certified. Professional certification is a means for the general public and the people served, to know that a professional has training and experience and is certified to provide professional services. Having a certification certificate provides evidence of meeting regulatory standards for being a qualified activity professional. It assists administrators, directors of activity services and human resource personnel in making a decision regarding employing an applicant for a new or vacant position.

It is the responsibility of a qualified activity professional to seek certification through NCCAP (National Certification Council for Activity Professionals and keep certification up to date. Displaying certification (professional achievement) informs others that one is certified; thus, qualified to provide activity services. Certified Therapeutic Recreation Specialist and other activity orient therapist (art therapist, music therapist, drama, dance therapist, poetry therapist, occupational therapist, and horticulture therapist) can apply for NCCAP Certification. However, a certified activity professional can not apply for certification from another organization unless she meets the standards for certification or registration from the specific organization. A Therapeutic Recreation Specialist can apply for certification with NCCAP but a person who has completed the ME-PAP2nd Edition would not be qualified to apply for Therapeutic recreation Specialist certification. Certification as a CTRS is more stringent than being a certified Activity Professional at one of the levels of certification.

Activity professional shall follow the professional practice of using their certification initials, i.e., ADC (Activity Director Certified), after their signature on professional documents, i.e., *Sally Smith, ADC* to inform all readers of the professional's credentials.
See Appendix H for the National Certification Council for Activity Professionals Certification Standards (NCCAP) and Application. It is advisable to check with NCCAP to see if the standards listed in Appendix have changed.

NCCAP Code of Ethics

The National Certification Council for Activity Professionals (NCCAP) is one of the certifying bodies recognized by Federal law and incorporated in many state regulations. NCCAP is the ONLY national organization that exclusively certifies activity professionals who work with the elderly.

Benefits of being a Certified Activity Professional:

- **Enhanced professional recognition and development**
- **Collaboration at the national level with other long-term health care agencies**
- **Four newsletters annually**
- **Inclusion in the national registry of Certified Activity Professionals**

NCCAP Certification Standards

NCCAP certifies on three levels:
- **Activity Assistant Certified – AAC**
- **Activity Director Certified – ADC**
- **Activity Consultant Certified – ACC**

Each of these levels has differing TRACKS to help you obtain your certification.

Each of these TRACKS has a minimum of three qualifying components:
- Academic Education and the Modular Education Program for Activity Professionals
- Activity Experience
- Continuing Education
- Consulting Experience (ACC) level only)

Activity Assistant Certified (AAC)

Track 1
- 30 college semester credits (must include English and 1 other required coursework area)
- 2000 hours within the past 5 years
- 20 clock hours (Body of Knowledge) within the past 5 years.

Track 2
- High school diploma or GED and 6 college credits that must include English and 1 other required coursework area

- 4000 hours within the past 5 years
- 20 clock hours (Body of Knowledge) within the past 5 years.

Track 3
- Modular Education Course for Activity Professionals, Part 1. (Core Contents of 1-11 of the MEPAP 2nd Edition)
- 2000 Hours within the past 5 years
- 20 clock hours within the past 5 years

Activity Assistant Provisionally Certified- AAPC

The Activity Assistant Provisionally Certified is one who is working towards the requirements to meet NCCAP standards for AAC certification.

- Completion of the MEPAP
- (Part I Core Content I-11)
- 50 volunteer hours (can be the practical/or other volunteer hours)
- 20 CE's (can include honors classes, AP classes may be accepted)

The rationale; the activity profession needs to promote itself to the younger generation. The high school students that are attending the ME-PAP classes would be encouraged to continue on in the profession if they become credentialed in this manner. The first step in pursuing a career in activity professionalism. Then the student would either pursue the AAC or the ADPC, upon completion of their high school experience, by obtaining their diploma, additional experience hours (the AAC) or completion of the MEPAP part 2 and additional experience hours and CE's (for the ADPC).

*This was suggested by the instructors and accepted by the NCCAP Board spring 2008

Activity Director Certified (ADC)

Track 1
- Bachelor's Degree (must include English, and 7 other coursework areas)
- 4000 hours of activity experience within the past 5 years

- 30 clock hours (Body of Knowledge) within the past 5 years
- Modular Education Program for Activity Professionals (MEPAP)

Track 2
- Associate Degree (must include English and 5 other coursework areas)
- 6000 hours within the past 5 years
- 30 clock hours (Body of Knowledge) within the past 5 years
- Modular Education Program for Activity Professionals

Track 3
- 60 college semester credits (must include English and 5 other coursework areas)
- 6000 hours within the past 5 years
- 30 clock hours (Body of Knowledge) within the past 5 years
- Modular Education Program for Activity Professionals

Track 4
- MEPAP Part I (Core Contents 1-11)
- MEPAP Part II (Core Contents 12-19)
- 12 semester college credits (in addition to 1 & 2) must include English and 1 other coursework area

One who meets NCCAP standards to assist with supervision in carrying out an activity program.
- 6000 hours activity experience within the past 5 years
- 30 clock hours (Body of Knowledge) within the past 5 years

Activity Director Provisionally Certified (ADPC)

The Activity Director Provisionally Certified is one who is working toward requirements to meet the NCCAP standards for the ADC certification. It is provisional for 6 years and nonrenewable after that time. To maintain the provisional certification must be renewed every 2 years during the 6 years with 30 clock hours. By the end of the 6 year period, all components

must have been met to be ADC Track 4 (or meet ADC certification standards from Track 1, 2, or 3). The ADPC must meet 3 of the 5 standards in ADC Track 4.

Activity Consultant Certified (ACC)

One who meets NCCAP standards to be a consultant for an activity program, staff or department.

Track 1
- Master's Degree (must include English and 7 other coursework areas)
- 2000 hours activity experience within the past 5 years
- 40 clock hours (Body of Knowledge) within the past 5 years
- 200 hours of activity consulting experience
- Modular Education Program for Activity Professionals

Track 2
- Bachelor's Degree (must include English and 7 other coursework areas)
- 4000 hours within the past 5 years
- 40 clock hours (Body of Knowledge) within the past 5 years
- 200 hours of activity consulting experience within the past 5 years
- Modular Education Program for Activity Professionals

Track 3
- Bachelor's Degree (must include English and 7 other coursework areas)
- 4000 hours activity experience within the past 5 years
- 40 clock hours (Body of Knowledge) within the past 5 years
- (Arranged with Track 3 Consultant Review Committee)
- Modular Education Program for Activity Professionals

The candidate for certification will complete an independent study program with The Professional Activity Manager and Consultant published in 1996. Successfully completing this book and a project is the consulting experience for this track.

General Standards Information

Academic Education

May derive from a wide variety of curriculums: Social Work, Recreation, Education, and Business Degrees. These are a few of the educational backgrounds that represent our certified members.

Activity Experience

Activity work experience (within the past 5 years) with elderly populations, where at least 50% are 55+ years of age. Some volunteer work with the elderly may be applied.

Continuing Education

Current education (within the past 5 years): workshops, seminars and college courses that keep the activity professional abreast of present trends. NCCAP's Body of Knowledge contains 27 areas of education with many sub-headings that are applicable.

Consulting Experience

May include: advising a group, working one to one, teaching a class, conducting workshops, publishing professionals articles, supervising student and/or managing 5 or more activity staff persons (see standards for specific information).

Fees
The cost of being certified initially ranges from $55 to $75 depending upon the level.

Specialty Tracks to Certification Process

Effective January 1, 2009, NCCAP certified individuals can apply to have a specialization designation by adding 10 hours of continuing education specific to that specialization as follows: ADC, for example, a specialization in assisted living, would be ADC/ALF. A specialization in memory care would be ADC/MC. A specialization in adult day programs would be ADC/ADA specialization in educating would be ADC/EDU, AC would be AAC/AL.

Every profession has some type of certification, registration or license to practice. A state or national certifying or registration organization usually provides certification and registration. Licensure is state mandated. State licensure board approves applicants prior to permitting them to take the state-licensing test. Some certification organizations, i.e., National Certification of Therapeutic Recreation Council (NCTRC), require all new applicants to pass a test. Certified Therapeutic Recreation Specialists can take a test in lieu of submitting acceptable continuing education credits or not having the required professional experience over the past 5 years for recertification, e.g., a person not able to work because of some type of illness, injury or who prefers not to work while raising a family or continuing advance academic education full time. The test taken for recertification is the same as the one taken by new certification applicants. If a person does meet standards for certification or recertification, he or she cannot be certified.

It is the responsibility of a qualified activity professional to seek certification through the NCCAP (National Certification Council for Activity Professionals) and keep certification up to date. Displaying certification (professional achievement) informs others that one is certified, thus, qualified to provide activity services. Certified Therapeutic Recreation Specialist and other activity-oriented therapist (art therapist, music therapist, drama therapist, poetry therapist, occupational therapist, horticulture therapist) can apply for NCCAP certification.

Activity professionals use their certification, i.e., ADC, Activity Director Certified after their signature on professional documents, e.g., *Sally Smith, ADC* to inform all readers, of the professional's credentials.

Why Become NCCAP Certified

Cindy Bradshaw, ACC, Executive Director of NCCAP, gives the following seven reasons of "Why Become NCCAP Certified?"

1. Federal Law, OBRA, (F249) states that an activity department must be directed by a qualified professional. One of the ways to become qualified is to become a Certified Activity Professional

2. NCCAP certification is recognized by CMS (Centers for Medicare & Medicaid Services) formerly called (HCFA) Health Care Financing Administration as an organization that certifies activity professionals who work specifically with the elderly.

3. NCCAP certification assures administrators and surveyors that you have met certain professional standards to become certified.

4. Many administrators will only hire activity professionals who are already certified.

5. Some administrators offer a higher salary to a certified professional.

6. Become NCCAP certified so others will know that you are nationally qualified and giving quality activity service to residents/clients.

7. Become certified to elevate the credibility of YOUR Profession!!!"

Other certification organizations:

Activity professionals with an educational background in another activity oriented field can be certified by NCCAP in addition to their other certification; however, activity professionals cannot be certified, registered or licensed by another certification, registration or licensure organization unless he or she meets the standards of other organizations. Susan E. Lanza organized a chart to show the various organizations and what is required for a professional in the organization to be certified, registered or licensed. The requirements are considerably higher than NCCAP's standards. NCCAP has consistently raised the bar for certification.

Training Requirement of Other Activity Professionals

Often new activity professionals are confused by other activity oriented professionals and terminology. A brief history of Activity Therapy will explain how the term Activity Therapy was developed and why some departments are called Activity Therapy Department verse Activity or Activities Department.

In many psychiatric hospitals with specialty units for older adults and psychiatric day program, a variety of activity therapists representing different specialty areas, i.e., art therapy, music therapy, dance therapy, drama therapy,

poetry therapy, horticulture therapy, occupational, and music therapy, therapeutic recreation provide different therapies. In the early 60's during the community mental health movement, the term activity therapist was used to represent all personnel who provided activities in state psychiatric hospitals and some private psychiatric hospitals. The professional department was called Activity Therapy department. Each staff member was referred to as an activity therapist. Name tags listed the person's name followed by the initials of their specialty credentials (certification, registration, licensure), i.e., art therapist, (ATR) occupational therapist (OTRL), music therapist (RMT), therapeutic recreation or recreation therapy, (CTRS).

An Activity Therapy department included generalist. An activity therapist generalist did not have any specific training. State educational requirements were often quite low. A person did not have to have a H.S. diploma or GED to be an activity therapist generalist. Many of the activity therapist generalists were trained on the job. An activity therapist generalist would have no credential initials behind their name of their name tag.

Some nursing homes in the early 70's picked up the title of activity therapist without hiring actual activity therapist specialist, or music programs were referred to as music therapy when no credentialed music therapist was providing the program.

Today, there are facilities with activity therapy departments with activity therapy specialist and trained activity professionals. Job descriptions define their role and responsibilities. Participation in the various activity therapies provided by therapists is by referral, i.e., a physician's order and a team's recommendation. Activity therapist may provide co treatment for individuals and small groups.

Activity therapy specialist may work in other departments other than the activity department such as rehabilitation. Some activity therapist may provide part time contractual services; others may work on a fee for service basis, charging a fee for their service for people willing and able to pay.

Activity professionals need to be aware of the requirements of each activity therapy specialist, which are more stringent than the required training, experience and continuing education for nationally certified activity professionals. Professional requirements for the different therapies continue to change as they have for activity professionals. Some therapies require the passing of a national exam in addition to internship or supervised clinical experience. Information about the various activity therapies can be obtained on line or from the professional organization listed in Appendix G.

Research and Activity History

Knowing the history of activities assists the activity professional in understanding what preceded the activity profession and how the activity professional continues to use and/or, modify successful activities for people with various limitations/disabilities.

Virginia Frye and Carol Peters (1972), therapeutic recreation (TR) educators are credited as well as other TR educators in researching and documenting how activity was used in a variety of health and community settings. Some local and state activity organizations have researched and documented the development and expansion of activities in a variety of service settings.

Research of documented information on activities has continuously shown how activities have been used for treatment, relaxation, recreation, maintaining or improving cognitive, physical, social skills, as well as promoting wellness. Activity professional continue to learn about successful programs and techniques through reading research written by activity or other professionals in professional journals, books and news letters and sometimes from research based articles in popular magazines. Activity professionals can be a part of research studies conducted by professionals in the community, state/national organizations as well as colleges and universities.

In chapter 2, a brief History of Activities Programming is provided under the topic heading "Activity Service Practice Settings" and the History of Activities in Treatment is stated under the topic Diversity of Activity service Settings. In the History of Activities in Treatment, music, games, exercise walking, excursions (outings) etc. were, part of an individual's total treatment. Psychiatric care in the 1800's included exercise reading, handicrafts and music. Florence Nightingale stressed a variety of activities for patients including pets, music, visitors as well as babies.

Today, older adult participants and residents enjoy the same types of activities with a more modern focus. Music preferences will continue to change as the baby boomers receive services in the community or long term care. There has been a tremendous change in arts and crafts with emphasis on the enjoyment of "doing" for some people and a creative outcome for others. The supplies and equipment available for arts and crafts and new projects has steadily increased over the years.

Pets, including Pet Therapy, facility owned pet(s) as well as volunteers sharing their pets during visits continue to be affective. The Eden Alternative includes pets in the human habitat philosophy. Some independent and assisted living facilities allow residents to have their own small pet, live with them. They are responsible for caring for their own pet.

Bingo, a game of chance, has continued to thrive in the community with competition from other games of chance, i.e. scratch or rip off tickets, lottery tickets and state approved gambling games. While some participants may still want to play bingo, others may prefer to purchase lottery or scratch/rip off tickets and/or go to places where they can legally gamble.

Florence Nightingale recommended that babies be brought to the hospital for visiting. Many older adults enjoy having baby visitors of family, friends, staff as well as volunteers. Programs may include baby contests and baby games, and twin fashion shows or watching babies interact with toys, stuffed animals or dolls. Some retirement communities, assisted living facilities and nursing homes have a child day care center in which the older adults can go to watch the children, rock them or play with them. Often the child day care center in integrated into the activities program

In the early 70's most long term care settings offered what was called **A, B, C Programming** (Arts and crafts, Bingo and Church). Programming was very limited so was trained activity professionals, available supplies, equipment and budget. As more people became trained, more activities were offered, budgets were increased, so that more supplies and equipment could be obtained.

Today's activity professionals are creating new programs that will be a part of the next generation of activity professional's repertoire, as individuals utilize their creativity, knowledge and skills. What new programs will be developed as a result of older adults being interested in high tech equipment, games, educational programs and other programs? What new programs will be developed based on today's international, national, regional and state events? What new programs will be developed based on the change in the weather, economy, transportation, education, nutrition, sports (including adapted sports), fitness, fashion, home decorating, gardening, hi tech, books and publications and wellness?

Today's activity professionals are making history, creating a legacy for tomorrow's activity professionals and participants.

Research Defined

The 2006 edition of Webster's Dictionary & Thesaurus for Home, School and Office defines research as "a careful search or investigation: systematic investigation towards increasing the sum of knowledge…"

It is important for activity professionals to know and understand research directly or indirectly related to the profession. The activity profession is young. Much of what is known and practiced is based on research by others who preceded the activity profession as it is known today. Occupation Therapy, Music

Therapy, Therapeutic Recreation are some of the activity oriented professions that preceded the activity profession. Research in these professions led the way to understanding how activity can have a positive affect of older adults living in the community and in health care facilities.

In 1986, the Committee on Nursing Home Regulation had completed an extensive search on the origins of regulations in long-term care. This research identified a lack of standards and poor care in the 50's. The report also addressed the fact that the 1935 Social Security Act provided government assistance for the elderly poor but did not provide for residents in institutional settings. As a result of this action, the private sector of nursing home was developed. This committee identified that the first survey of nursing homes was in 1954 after changes were made to the Social Security Act to provide government funds for nursing home care.

In 1986, the Committee on Nursing Home Regulation reported:

- A lack of standards of care and that care provided in the 50's as far back as 1956 was poor.
- In 1959, overwhelming substandard conditions were identified in the Special Subcommittee on Problems of the Aged and Aging. As a result, in 1963 guidelines were drafted, and issued, called the Nursing Home Standards Guide. In 1965, with the advent of Medicare and Medicaid, standards were broader but implementation was difficult.
- President Nixon passed many enforcement guidelines that were to streamline and correct the system. This included the specific training standards for staff in nursing homes.
- In 1974, the regulations for the nursing home survey process changed to address the different ways facilities met standards. Also in 1974 the first skilled nursing facility (SNF) regulations were implemented.

- In 1976, regulations for intermediate care facilities were implemented. In 1990, the guidelines for intermediate care facilities were eliminated and replaced with nursing facility guidelines. In 1993, the American Health Care Association defined nursing facility as facilities other than hospitals which provide nursing care maintenance and personal care to individuals unable to care for themselves due to health problems.

- In 1984, a group of residents in Colorado nursing home successfully sued the owners of their facility as well as the government, i.e. Medicaid for disregard of their rights, substandard care, and acting as a body that failed to properly monitor their problems.

Initially the case was won, but then was appealed and reversed. However this case made a tremendous impact on how nursing homes were to be surveyed in the future. After a couple of survey monitoring changes, the Omnibus Reconciliation Act (OBRA) survey, still enforced with changes over the years, was implemented. The OBRA survey emphasizes resident outcomes, quality of life and quality of care. The activities regulation and interpretive guidelines are found under the regulation Quality of Life.

This brief history based on the research by the Committee on Nursing Home Regulation helps activity professionals understand how the US has changed regulations to improve quality of life and quality of care in nursing homes.

As they say- "We have come a long way since the 50's in providing care and services in nursing home including activities.

The Ethics in Research

In research, the following definitions are used for"

1. Validity – means that evidence is grounded on facts that will withstand examination and criticism- the evidence is convincing and conclusive
2. Reliability- means the evidence has integrity, is dependable, trustworthy, and truthful

The results of research are used to:

1. Confirm the accuracy or support of a particular intervention, service, program or product.
2. Develop new safety measures, interventions, programs, products and services.

Unethical altering of findings can lead to physical, intellectual, emotional harm as well as misuse of funds.

Resources for Contemporary Research Related to Activity Services include but are not limited to the following publications:

1. Activities, Adaptation and Aging focuses on research by professionals in the field as well as health and psychosocial professionals. The results of studies often confirm or recommend specific activities, interventions, techniques or further research.

2. The Provider Magazine a free monthly publication for long term on providing care and services for the older adults in assisted living and health care facilities.

In the December, 2005 issue of Provider, the following four articles provide valuable information for activity professionals:

1. "Defining Quality, What do residents, families, and employees really want?"
2. News Currents, "Social Activities Promote Sleep; Study Looks at Patients with Dementia."
3. Lourde, Kathleen, "Alzheimer's Patients Respond to Cognitive Techniques"
4. "Facility Creates Onsite TV Channel" Channel"

Creative Forecasting is a monthly activity publication that reports research findings, new activities, poems, arts and crafts, ideas, and an overview of new publications, new products and services.

See Appendix G– Activity Resources.

Activity professionals can research clinical journals for articles that impact the provision of activities directly or indirectly. Clinical journals (medical, nursing, social work, art therapy, music therapy, occupational therapy, rehabilitation, physical therapy, therapeutic recreation etc.) can be found in public libraries, colleges and universities. Clinical research can often be found on the Internet by topic, author, sponsoring or funding agency.

Stages of the Research Process

"When learning stops, one vegetates"

Research is a systematic study of an area of knowledge that the researcher wants to explore. One may begin with a strong desire to research a special area of current knowledge, to push back the frontier of knowledge. Research in education seeks to explore a special subject that may provide additional knowledge that will help in understanding why some situations develop and reveal ways of dealing with the problem. Research is important to test current facts or principles. After the concern has been determined the next stage is to study the current sources on the subject. This is followed by determining the best way to carry out the research, e.g., Study the literature on the subject. A major concern is focusing on how time and resources allow the research to be done and establish a budget with sources of funds available.

Activity professionals could develop a research project to determine the best group activity that reaches the most residents/clients, or perhaps the place where certain activities have been done. Is this the best time and place? Does this research project amplify the mission and vision of the facility or agency?

The final stage is to evaluate the results, then choose the best alternative for implementing the findings. Recognize that new information contributes to the activity profession's body of knowledge. Research is needed to validate the activity program.

Defining the Research Problem

"Beyond understanding is mystery"

Once the general area of interest and concern has been determined the next step is to define the problem within the range that is doable. The problem can be too comprehensive to be investigated in the time frame available. Or the problem can be too narrow and too small so the results will be compromised.

The findings should have a meaningful purpose once the research has been done. Another caution suggests that if others have done the research it is questionable whether more research is necessary. Check available resources and the delivery of activity programming. With the shrinking availability of the health care dollars, at the same time the boomer moves into the ranks of the elderly, research is needed. The best ways to meet this problem needs to be found. Designing the method of research is important. Will the investigation discover any new knowledge? Will it have any importance to the field in which the research is being done? Activity professionals should look to their area of service and seek to solve problems that would help the staff to improve. Mental health counseling, geriatric nursing practices, such as physical therapists, gerontologists, occupational therapists, recreational therapist, social services and others are doing research which needs to be studied. Does taking residents/clients who have dementia for rides make them more confused within a 24-48 hour period or does it have a calming effect? There may be difference in residents going on morning, afternoon or evening rides.

Activity professionals can seek the assistance of other professionals in designing a formal research study. Graduate students in local colleges and universities are often looking for a research topic related to their field of study and may be willing to assist in designing, developing and conducting needed research. The college or university will have policies and procedures related to ethical research. The service organization will need to develop research policies and procedures including the voluntary involvement of participants. Safety and confidentiality are essential in any research study involving participants.

Research, can be as simple as looking up a topic on the Internet or library or asking other professionals what they do to get a consensus.

Research should help to deliver activities that are more meaningfully. The residents/clients are the reason.

Methods of Data Collection

Methods of data collecting will vary depending upon the type of problem that one seeks to investigate. If it is a problem of the make-up of the residents/clients population one could review the personal histories of the resident or client, collecting the numbers who are native in the United States, those with a second language and those who have no family, etc. One can search the books and periodicals that are published giving information on special concerns of a given population. In a word, search the sources to find the information one needs.

Data needs to be collected in a controlled manner so the outcome will be valid and reliable. Sloppy investigation will yield little in the way of valid useful findings.

Activity professionals who are seeking to do research on a certain concern may need some help from a mentor, staff person, or teacher to help design and collect appropriate data. Care should be taken to make sure that the research plan is sound and that the findings will be valid and reliable. Research can help activity professionals to improve the delivery of activities.

The method of data collection is dependent upon the type of study that is to be done. Methods can include but not be limited to:

1. interviews
2. observation
3. record review
4. surveys
5. case studies

Validity

Validity means that evidence is grounded on facts that will withstand examination and criticism – the evidence is convincing and conclusive.

Reliability

Reliability means that the research has integrity, is dependable, trustworthy and truthful.

Usability

Usability means that the instructions for the research are easy to understand.

Ethics

Ethics is a moral standard of conduct and behavior. Civilized societies develop a code of ethics, which is the moral standard for that group of citizens. Once this standard has been set either by law or custom, persons in that society are expected to live up to that standard. Ethics involves professional behavior to report research findings accurately, timely without any falsification to make the findings appear what they are not.

Standards vary from society to society, i.e., how men or women are expected to conform to the standards of the society in which the person lives.

Ethics is the guide to moral judgment and behavior. Persons who break the code of ethics may be shunned or imprisoned.

Activity professionals need to conduct themselves according to the moral and ethical standards of the facility or agency, The National Association of Activity Professionals (NAAP), the National Certification Council for Activity Professionals as well as the general society in which they serve. Professionals and religious persons are expected to be above reproach. Questionable behavior would be a moral and ethical violation, i.e., hugging all residents/clients whether they want to be hugged or not. One resident said to the person who had just hugged her, "Don't ever do that again." Alert activity professionals will follow the customs and moral standards of the facility. Ethical behavior is a requirement for activity professionals.

Summary

The activity profession has grown tremendously since the 1974 federal regulations requiring activity coordinators in long-term care facilities (skilled nursing facilities and intermediate care facilities). The term "activity professional" developed over time. The main impetus for the term was the development of the National Association for Activity Professionals (1981). The term was strengthened by the development of the National Certification Council for Activity Professionals in 1986 and the April 1992 federal regulations (The Long Term Care Survey, Rules and Regulations).

Activity professionals come from a wide variety of backgrounds. Some professional are trained in specific fields (art therapy, music therapy, horticulture therapy, therapeutic recreation, etc.). Each specialty has its own certification or registration organization. Activity professionals may be former teachers, social workers, nurses, or other professionals or people without formal education in a specific field, who have had paid or volunteer experience in activities and working with older persons.

Qualifications of activity professionals are established by government agencies, national organizations, and/or the place of employment. National certification is increasingly becoming a requirement for employment.

Chapter 4

Governmental and Social Systems

Regulations

"Regulations are continuously changing"

Early 1900's

Three and four generations of families lived under one roof and took care of their elderly relatives. Activities included church and family-oriented activities, e.g., attending church, family gatherings, conversation, holiday preparation and celebrations, singing and games. When confined to bed or room, an older person was kept informed of daily family activities, entertained by the sounds of family singing, stimulated by the smells from the kitchen and sounds from outside.

The "poor house" or "asylum" was places of last resort for older persons who could not be cared for by families or for older persons who had no families. There were no planned activities. Church groups began to visit people in the "old-folks' homes." Friendly visitors provided refreshments primarily during the holidays. In time, volunteers brought in other community groups for entertainment, bingo, religious services, letter writing, and conversation.

1929   OAAA

The Old-Age Assistance Act offered alternatives to institutionalization in most states.

1935   SSA

The Social Security Act (SSA), a work related program, provides social security benefits for older people. Income is based on earnings sub-ject to pre-retirement tax. Self-employed people are eligible for retirement benefits provided they had a designated minimum amount of income per year. Individuals who may not have worked but are dependent on someone, e.g., spouse, also received benefits. The law established the criteria for payment, to which it was to be paid, and the amount.

1946   H-B Act (Facilities)

Congress passed the Hill-Burton Act, an amendment to the Hospital Survey and Construction Act of 1944. The purpose of the Hill-Burton Act was to assist states in determining needs as well as planning and building facilities. New facilities in conjunction with existing facilities were to provide adequate hospitals, clinics and similar services.

1950's

Chronic illness became a national problem. Congress broadened and extended the Hill-Burton Act several times so that more hospitals and other health care facilities could be built, e.g., nursing facilities, TB Hospitals.

Volunteerism continued to grow. Volunteers paved the way for recognition of the need for planned programs of activities and for someone to direct and conduct them.

Licensing

1959

"recreation" [handwritten]

Mayor Wagner of New York City set up the Heyman Commission to review health services in the city. Recreation was recognized as one of the inadequacies. In 1963 a new code included recreation personnel.

Other states had laws for licensure for nursing homes and homes for the aged that included requirements for a recreation program. California required recreation as a part of licensure for homes for the aged and nursing homes whereas, Connecticut and New York required recreation in the licensure requirements for Homes for the Aged, and New York City required it for nursing homes.

Keogh Retirement Plan

1963

Keogh Plan (HR10) is a tax deferred retirement saving plan for self-employed individuals. This plan has provided a much needed option for the self-employed persons who need to save for retirement. There is a maximum amount that can be contributed each year. (Internet)

Medicare & Medicaid

1965

The Medicare Act authorized care in long term care facilities for patients who were hospitalized for at least three consecutive days, who needed skilled-nursing care, and who were to be admitted to a Medicare certified facility within 14 days of their discharge from the hospital. Medicare required regular evaluation and a maximum of a 90-day stay in a Medicare certified facility. In the late 1960's and in the 1970's, there was tremendous growth of extended care facilities—some in hospitals, but mostly in free-standing facilities. Over the years the regulations changed.

The Medicare program (Title XVII) is divided into two parts: Part A – Hospital Insurance and Part B – Medical Insurance. There are no additional fees for Part A for all who are eligible for Medicare. Part B requires a monthly fee, which is deducted from the monthly Social Security check. Individuals who are eligible for Medicare, but who are earning more than is allowed for Social Security benefits, pay a monthly fee to the Health Care Financing Administration.

Medicaid provided for persons whose resources were expended. With the continued increase in health care costs, more persons need Medicaid which is paid by Federal and State funds.

1974   1st Activities [handwritten]

The 1974 Rules and Regulations for the Medicare Act were the first federal regulations to mandate the provision of patient activities in long term care facilities; skilled-nursing facilities and intermediate care facilities. Standards included having a qualified person to direct the activities program, an individual plan for each resident as a part of the overall plan of care, programming (including weekend activities in skilled nursing care facilities), space, supplies and equipment, as well as visiting hours. In skilled care facilities the activities coordinator required consultation from a qualified person if he/she was not qualified.

Quality of Care

1975 *advocacy + surveying*

Michael Smith, a self-advocating resident in a Colorado nursing home, filed suit against the State of Colorado for not assuring the provision of quality care in nursing homes in his state. He won the case and continued his advocacy for better quality of care nationally. He sued the then Secretary of Health and Human Services, Margaret Heckler, for failing to assure that every state conducted adequate surveys and enforced regulations that promoted quality of care for all residents in nursing homes.

Individual Retirement Account (IRA)

1978

Individual Retirement Accounts were authorized by Congress late in 1978. (Internet) The employer withholds dollars from the employees' pay. In a traditional IRA this incomes is not taxed until the person withdraws the money. There is a penalty if withdrawn before the person is 59 ½. At the age of 70 ½ a percentage of the value must be withdrawn annually. These dollars are invested in a variety of investments, often determined by the IRA owner. Both the principle and earnings are taxed when received.

1983

The Health Care Financing Administration (HCFA) requested the Institute of Medicine (IOM) to provide an in-depth study of long-term care. The results of the study were released in 1986. Over one-third of the nation's homes provided substandard care according to the findings. As a result, IOM made three major recommendations: (1) revision of the survey system to be patient-outcome-driven; (2) revision of the federal requirements and enforcement system, and (3) a single set of conditions for both Medicare and Medicaid.

Survey Process

1986

Changes in the survey process took place in 1986 when the HCFA developed the Patient Assessment of Care Survey System (PAC). The focus was no longer on the review of staff qualifications, policies and procedures, and process rather; the focus became outcome of care. Surveyors observed residents and care provided, interviewed residents, family, staff and volunteers, and reviewed residents' medical records to be sure they were congruent and that residents were receiving quality care. While better than the process surveys, the new regulations still did not ensure quality resident care.

Congress passed the Omnibus Budget Reconciliation Act (OBRA '87) as a follow-up to the IOM report in December 1987. The requirements for long-term-care, surveys, and en forcement system became effective October 1, 1990. The final OBRA regulations and interpretive guidelines became effective in April 1992.

1987

Three major changes took place:

October 1987 HCFA published new conditions of participation, including some of the IOM recommendations.

November 1987 HCCA published a proposed Survey and Enforcement System.

December 1987 Congress followed up on the IOM report by passing the Omnibus Budget Reconciliation Act (OBRA '87). OBRA mandated a new survey process, enforcement procedures and regulations.

Accurate Care & Services

1990

On October 1, 1990 OBRA '87 "Requirements for Long-Term Care" survey and enforcement system became effective. All Medicare and Medicaid skilled nursing facilities and nursing facilities are surveyed under the OBRA regulations. The focus of surveys is based on outcomes of care and service for individual residents.

OBRA Survey

This new process was based on outcomes for each resident. All Medicare and/or Medicaid certified facilities, skilled nursing facilities or nursing facilities are surveyed under the OBRA regulations.

Quality of Life

1992

In April 1992 the final OBRA regulations and interpretive guidelines, written in a holistic approach, became effective. The Quality of Life requirements specified the qualifications of the director, delineated the expectations of the activity program, as well as required activity documentation.

Resident Rights

1995

Full OBRA

The final OBRA enforcement regulation of June 1995 became effective on July 1, 1995. Other changes effective July 1, 1995 include numerous interpretive guidelines and the survey process.

The focus of the new survey process is on the quality of life for individual residents.

The following regulations directly or indirectly affect the activities department's responsibilities and services:

483.10	*Residents Rights*
483.13	*Resident Behavior and Facility Practices (restraints, abuse)*
483.15	*Quality of Life (includes activities)*
483.20	*Resident Assessment (includes activity pursuits)*
483.25	*Quality of Care (implementation of residents' plans of care)*
483.30	*Nursing Service*
483.35	*Dietary Service*
483.40	*Physician Services*
483.45	*Specialized Rehabilitative Services (activity services need to know and coordinate with rehabilitation services)*
483.55	*Dental Services*
483.60	*Pharmacy Services*
483.65	*Infection Control*
483.70	*Physical Environment (includes activity space, supplies and equipment)*
483.75	*Administration (includes clinical records)*

Quality of Life (Check with administrator or the director of nursing to be sure that this regulation is still current.)

74

Roth Retirement Account

1997

The Roth IRA was authorized by Congress in the taxpayer relief act of 1997 (Internet). While it follows some of the regulations of the traditional IRA the Roth has major differences. The contribution going into a Roth Retirement Account is paid from after tax dollars. However, there will be no taxes levied on the funds when they are withdrawn. The amount contributed each year is limited and Roth has a more liberal withdrawal plan.

Keogh, traditional IRAs and Roth IRAs are set up to encourage persons to save for retirement. These funds are designed to grow and provide retirement income in addition to Social Security and other personal savings.

Quality of Life

(Check with the administrator or the director of nursing to be sure that this regulation is still current.)

Activities

Revised 2006

The guidelines for surveys were changed **not** the 1995 regulation for activities F248). The qualifications of an activity professional remained the same as the 1995 regulations (F249) with a minimum of revisions in structure so that the regulation is clearer.

Interpretive guideline for 483.15 (f) (1)

The facility must provide for an ongoing program of activities designed to meet, in accordance with the comprehensive assessment, the interests and the physical, mental and psychosocial well-being of each resident.
Intent 483.15 (f) (1) Activities

The intent of this requirement is that:
·The facility identifies each resident's interests and needs; and

·The facility involves the resident in an ongoing program of activities that is designed to appeal to his or her interests and to enhance the resident's highest practicable level of physical, mental and psychosocial well-being.

The federal regulation # 483.15 (f) (1) Activities new interpretive guidelines (effective June 1, 2006) for tag F248 give the following definition of Activities:

- "Activities" refer to any endeavor, other than routine ADLs, in which a resident participates that is intended to enhance her/his sense of well-being and to promote or enhance physical, cognitive, and emotional health. These include, but are not limited to, activities that promote self-esteem, pleasure, comfort, education, creativity, success, and independence.

  NOTE: ADL-related activities, such as manicures/pedicures, hair styling, and makeovers, may be considered part of the activities program.

- "One-to-One Programming" refers to programming provided to residents who will not, or cannot, effectively plan their own activity pursuits, or residents needing specialized or extended programs to enhance their overall daily routine and activity pursuit needs.

- "Person Appropriate" refers to the idea that each resident has a personal identity and history that involves more than just their medical illnesses or functional impairments. Activities should be relevant to the specific needs, interests, culture, background, etc. of the individual for whom they are developed.

- "Program of Activities" includes a combination of large and small group, one-to-one, and self-directed activities;

and a system that supports the development, implementation, and evaluation of the activities provided to the residents in the facility.[1]

Survey Procedures and Probes: §483.15.(f) (1)

Investigative Protocol: Activities

Objective:

To determine if the facility has provided an ongoing program of activities designed to accommodate the individual resident's interest and help enhance her/his physical, mental and psychosocial well-being, according to her/his comprehensive resident assessment.

Use:

Use this procedure for each sampled resident to determine through interview, observation and record review whether the facility is in compliance with the regulation.

Procedures:

Briefly review the comprehensive assessment and interdisciplinary care plan to guide observations to be made.

1. Observations

Observe during various shifts in order to determine if staff is consistently implementing those portions of the comprehensive plan of care related to activities. Determine if staff takes into account the residents food preferences and restrictions that involve food, and provide ADL assistance and adaptive equipment as needed during activities programs. For a resident with personal assistive devices such as glasses or hearing aides, determine if these devices are in place, glasses are clean and assistive devices are functional.

For a resident whose care plan includes group activities, observe if staff informs the resident of activities schedule and provide timely transportation, if needed, for the resident to attend in-facility activities and help the resident access transportation to out-of- facility and community activities.

Determine whether the facility provides activities that are compatible with the resident's known interests, needs, abilities and preferences. If the resident is in group activity programs, note if the resident is attempting to leave, or is expressing displeasure with, sleeping through, an activity program. If so, determine if staff attempt to identify the reason the resident is attempting to leave, and if they addressed the resident's needs. Determine whether the group activity has been adapted for the resident as needed and whether it is "person appropriate."

Note: If you observe an activity that you believe would be age inappropriate for most residents, investigate further to determine the reason the resident and the staff selected this activity. The National Alzheimer's Association has changed from endorsing the idea of "age appropriate" activities to promoting "person-appropriate" activities. In general, surveyors should not expect to see the facility providing dolls or stuffed animals for most residents but some resident are attached to these items and should be able to continue having them available if they prefer.

Regarding group activities in common areas, determine if the activities are occurring in rooms that have sufficient space, light, ventilation, equipment and supplies. Sufficient space includes enough space for residents to participate in the activity and space for a resident to enter and leave the room without having to move several other residents. Determine if the room is sufficiently free of extraneous noise, such as environmental noises from mechanical equipment and staff interruptions

For a resident who is involved in individual activities in her/his room, observe if staff has provided needed assistance, equipment and supplies. Observe if the room has light and space for the resident to complete the activity.

Qualified Professional F tag 249

(2) The activities program must be directed by a qualified professional who:

    (i)   Is a qualified therapeutic recreation specialist or an activities professional who:

        (A)   Is licensed or registered, if applicable, by the state in which practicing; and

        (B)   Is eligible for certification as a therapeutic recreation specialist or as an activities professional by a recognized accrediting body on or after October 1, 1990; or

    (ii)   Has 2 years of experience in a social or recreational program within the last 5 years, 1 of which was full-time in a patient activities program in a health care setting; and

    (iii)   Is a qualified occupational therapist or occupational therapy assistant; or

    (iv)   Has completed a training course approved by the State.

Note: State rules may be stricter which must be followed.

Interpretive Guidelines: §483.15 (f) (2)

A "recognized accrediting body" refers to those organizations or associations recognized as such by certified therapeutic recreation specialists or certified activity professionals or registered occupational therapists.

Survey Procedures and Probes: §483.15 (f) (2)

If there are problems with provision of activities, determine if these services are provided by qualified staff.

A copy of the Long Term Care Survey and any updated information can be obtained from the American Health Care Association, Washington, DC 20005 and the National Technical Information Services, Springfield, VA.

Interpretive Guidelines: §483.15 (f) (2) (revised 2006)

§483.15 (f) Activities

§483.15 (f) (1) The facility must provide for an ongoing program of activities designed to meet, in accordance with the comprehensive assessment, the interests and the physical, mental, and psychosocial well-being of each resident.

Certification

INTENT: §483.15(f) (1) Activities

The intent of this requirement is that:

- The facility identifies each resident's interests and needs; and
- The facility involves the resident in an ongoing program of activities that is

- designed to appeal to his or her interests and to enhance the resident's highest practicable level of physical, mental, and psychosocial well-being.

Refer to Appendix H.

OBRA 87
Omnibus Budget Reconciliation Act in 1987

Congress passed the Omnibus Budget Reconciliation Act in April 1992. This act sets the minimum standards of care and rights for persons living in certified nursing facilities in the United States. Congress sometimes bundles a number of bills together including budget, into one large bill. This 1987 Omnibus Budget Reconciliation Act included the Federal Nursing Home Reform Act along with other bills which were rolled into one omnibus bill to ensure final passage.

These minimum Federal Health Care Regulations for nursing homes are requirements for nursing facilities and regulatory agencies. These minimum standards are a baseline for the Long Term Care surveyors and ombudsmen to follow and ensure the wellbeing, happiness and fulfillment of the residents. All Medicare and Medicaid providers are required to meet these standards. State inspectors now go beyond spending time with staff and records. In addition they are to have conversation with residents and families as well as observe dining, medication, administration and activities. OBRA has provided regulations for comprehensive care of the residents in Long Term Care facilities throughout the nation and has improved the care and treatment of the residents.

In long term care, an ongoing program of activities refers to the provision of activities in accordance with and based upon an individual resident's comprehensive assessment. The Institute of Medicine (IOM)'s 1986 report, "Improving the Quality of Care in Nursing Homes," became the basis for the "Nursing Home Reform" part of OBRA '87 and the current OBRA long term care regulations. The IOM Report identified the need for residents in nursing homes to receive care and/or services to maximize their highest practicable quality of life. However, defining "quality of life" has been difficult, as it is subjective for each person. Thus, it is important for the facility to conduct an individualized assessment of each resident to provide additional opportunities to help enhance a resident's self-esteem and dignity.

Research findings and the observations of positive resident outcomes confirm that activities are an integral component of residents' lives. Residents have indicated that daily life and involvement should be meaningful. Activities are meaningful when they reflect a person's interests and lifestyle are enjoyable to the person, help the person to feel useful, and provide a sense of belonging.[2] (Alzheimer Association)

Institute of Medicine

The Federal Government created the National Academy of Sciences for the purpose of advising the Government on scientific and technological matters. The Institute of Medicine (IOM) was developed by the Academy as a non-governmental organization. While the IOM does not receive direct federal appropriations various federal agencies provide the IOM funds for their specific studies. Most of the studies are done for federal agencies; however other interests may sponsor a research project.

The Institute of Medicine has a unique role of assembling unpaid volunteer experts to study and report to an independent body. This is to assure that a rigorous and independent effort is made to study various health issues. The findings are based on evidence and reported by independent experts. The research is paid for by government agencies. Non-governmental sponsors seeking a specific study fund the research but the final report is made by members of the IOM and without influence of the sponsors.

Employed personnel conduct the research of various concerns and issues. The outcome is discussed and evaluated prior to the writing of the final report by the IOM experts. Following is a list of some of the studies that the IOM has made:

Quality of Health Care

Patient Care Records
Care at End of Life
Dental Education
Disability Study Design
Health Insurance
Medicine and Ethics
Research on Cancer and Heart
Managed Care Organizations
Medicare and Medicaid
Improving the Quality of Long-Term Care
Health Care Programs and Policies
Immunization Safety Review

Racial and Ethnic Disparities in Health Care
Measuring and Monitoring Disabilities
Government Role in Improving Health Care
Vaccination Program Implementation
Transforming Health Care Quality
Exploring Complementary and Alternative
    Medicine
Review Centers for Disease Control
Electronic Health Record System
Improving Palliative Care
Strategic Health Care Visioning
Health Care for Mental and Substance
    Abuse Patients
Preventing Medication Errors

Residents' Views on Activities

Activities are relevant and valuable to residents' quality of life. In a large-scale study commissioned by CMS, 160 residents in 40 nursing homes were interviewed about what quality of life meant to them. The study found that residents "overwhelmingly assigned priority to dignity, although they labeled this concern in many ways." The researchers determined that the two main components of dignity, in the words of these residents, were "independence" and "positive self-image." Residents listed, under the categories of independence and positive self-image, the elements of "choice of activities" and "activities that amount to something," such as those that produce or teach something; activities using skills from residents' former work; religious activities; and activities that contribute to the nursing home.

The report stated that "Residents not only discussed particular activities that gave them a sense of purpose but also indicated that a lack of appropriate activities contributes to having no sense of purpose." "Residents rarely mentioned participating in activities as a way to just 'keep busy' or just to socialize. The relevance of the activities to the residents' lives must be considered." According to the study, residents wanted a variety of activities, including those that are not childish, require thinking (such as word games), are gender-specific, produce something useful, relate to previous work of residents, allow for socializing with visitors and participating in community events, and are physically active. The study found that the above concepts were relevant to both interviewable and non-interviewable residents. Researchers observed that non-interviewable residents appeared "happier" and "less agitated" in home with many planned activities for them.

Non-traditional Approaches to Activities

The nation's first Greenhouse homes were opened in Tupelo, Mississippi in the spring of 2003. These small homes would be real homes in appearance and function. Life and continued growth is the goal. Residents have private rooms and a bath, yet are a part of a family of 8-12 persons. The atmosphere is that of a home rather than an institution.

Surveyors need to be aware that some facilities may take a non-traditional approach to activities. In neighborhoods/households, all staff may be trained as nurse aides and are responsible to provide activities, and activities may resemble those of a private home.[3] (Thomas, W.H.) Residents, staff, and families may interact in ways that reflect daily life, instead of in formal activities programs. Residents may be more involved in the ongoing activities in their living area, such as care-planned approaches including chores, preparing foods, meeting with other residents to choose spontaneous activities, and leading an activity. It has been reported that, "some culture changed homes might not have a traditional activities calendar, and instead focus on community life to include activities. Instead of an "activities director," some homes have a Community Life Coordinator, a Community Developer, or other title for the individual directing the activities program.[4] (Bowman, C.S.)

For more information on activities in homes changing to a resident-directed culture, the following websites are available as resources: www.pioneernetwork.net; www.culturechangenow.com; www.qualitypartnersri.org (click on nursing homes); and www.edenalt.com.

ASSESSMENT

The information gathered through the assessment process should be used to develop the activities component of the comprehensive care plan. The ongoing program of activities should match the skills, abilities, needs, and preferences of each resident within the demands of the activity and the characteristics of the physical, social and cultural environments.[5] (Glantz, C.G.)

In order to develop individualized care planning goals and approaches, the facility should obtain sufficient, detailed information (even if the Activities RAP is not triggered) to determine what activities the resident prefers and what adaptations, if any, are needed.[6] **The facility may use, but need not duplicate, information from other sources**, such as the RAI, including the

RAPs, assessments by other disciplines, observation, and resident and family interviews. Other sources of relevant information include the resident's lifelong interests, spirituality, life roles, goals, strengths, needs and activity pursuit patterns and preferences.[7] (Gantz, C.G. & Richman, N.) This assessment should be completed by or under the supervision of a qualified professional (see F249 for definition of qualified professional).

NOTE: Some residents may be independently capable of pursuing their own activities without intervention from the facility. This information should be noted in the assessment and identified in the plan of care.

CARE PLANNING

Care planning involves identification of the resident's interests, preferences, and abilities; and any issues, concerns, problems, or needs affecting the resident's involvement/engagement in activities.[8] (Hellen, C.) In addition to the activities component of the comprehensive care plan, information may also be found in a separate activity plan, on a CNA flow sheet, in a progress note, etc. Activity goals related to the comprehensive care plan should be based on measurable objectives and focused on desired outcomes, e.g., engagement in an activity that matches the resident's ability, maintaining attention to the activity for a specified period of time, expressing satisfaction with the activity verbally or non-verbally, not merely on attendance at a certain number of activities per week.

NOTE: For residents with no discernable response, service provision is still expected and may include one-to-one activities such as talking to the resident, reading to the resident about prior interests, or applying lotion while stroking the resident's hands or feet.

Activities can occur at any time, are not limited to formal activities being provided only by activities staff, and can include activities provided by other facility staff, volunteers, visitors, residents, and family members. All relevant de-

RAP
RAI

partments should collaborate to develop and implement an individualized activities program for each resident.

Some medications, such as diuretics, or conditions such as pain, incontinence, etc. may affect the resident's participation in activities. Therefore, additional steps may be needed to facilitate the resident's participation in activities, such as:

> If not contraindicated, timing the administration of medications, to the extent possible, to avoid interfering with the resident's ability to participate or remain at a scheduled activity; or

> If not contraindicated, modifying the administration time of pain medication to allow the medication to take effect prior to an activity the resident enjoys.

The care plan should also identify the discipline(s) that will carry out the approaches. For example:

> Notifying residents of preferred activities;

> Transporting residents who need assistance to and from activities (including indoor, outdoor, and outings);

> Providing needed functional assistance (such as toileting and eating assistance); and

> Providing needed supplies or adaptations, such as obtaining and returning audio books, setting up adaptive equipment, etc.

TR PT ST OT

Concepts the facility should have considered in the development of the activities component of the resident's comprehensive care plan include the following, as applicable to the resident:

- A continuation of life roles, consistent with resident preferences and functional capacity, e.g., to continue work or hobbies such as cooking, table setting, repairing small appliances[9]; (American Occupational Therapy Association)

OT

- Encouraging and supporting the development of new interests, hobbies, and skills, e.g., training on using the Internet;

- Connecting with the community, such as places of worship, veterans' groups, volunteer groups, support groups, wellness groups, athletic or educational connections (via outings or invitations to outside groups to visit the facility).

The facility may need to consider accommodations in schedules, supplies and timing in order to optimize a resident's ability to participate in an activity of choice. Examples of accommodations may include, but are not limited to:

- Altering a therapy or a bath/ shower schedule to make it possible for a resident to attend a desired activity that occurs at the same time as the therapy session or bath;

- Assisting residents, as needed, to get to and participate in desired activities, e.g., dressing, toileting, transportation;

- Providing supplies, e.g., books/ magazines, music, craft projects, cards, sorting materials for activities, and assistance when needed, for residents' use, e.g., during weekends, nights, holidays, evenings, or when the activities staff are unavailable; and

☐ mag's
☐ books
☐ music
☐ cards
☐ materials
☐ list off hrs

- Providing a late breakfast to allow a resident to continue a lifelong pattern of attending religious services before eating.

Fridays-Jews
Sundays
Saturdays? Christians
Muslims?

Interventions

The concept of individualized intervention has evolved over the years. Many activity professionals have abandoned generic interventions such as "reality orientation" and large-group activities that include residents with different levels of strengths and needs. In their place,

no more reality orientation

individualized interventions have been developed based upon the assessment of the resident's history, preferences, strengths, and needs. These interventions have changed from the idea of "age-appropriate" activities to promoting "person-appropriate" activities. For example, one person may care for a doll or stroke a stuffed animal, another person may be inclined to reminisce about dolls or stuffed animals they once had, while someone else may enjoy petting a dog but will not be interested in inanimate objects. The surveyor observing these interventions should determine if the facility selected them in response to the resident's history and preferences. Many activities can be adapted in various ways to accommodate the resident's change in functioning due to physical or cognitive limitations.

Some Possible Adaptations that May be Made by the Facility[10, 11] (Henderson, A., Cermak, S., Castner, W., Murray, E., Tromley, C. & Tickle-Gegnen, L., Pedretti, L.W.)

When evaluating the provision of activities, it is important for the surveyor to identify whether the resident has conditions and/or issues for which staff should have provided adaptations. Examples of adaptations for specific conditions include, but are not limited to the following:

For the resident with visual impairments: higher levels of lighting without glare; magnifying glasses, light-filtering lenses, telescopic glasses; use of "clock method" to describe where items are located; description of sizes, shapes, colors; large print items including playing cards, newsprint, books; audio books;

- For the resident with hearing impairments; small group activities; placement of resident near speaker/activity leader; use of amplifiers or headphones; decreased background noise; written instructions; use of gestures or sign language to enhance verbal communication; adapted TV (closed captioning, magnified screen, earphones);

- For the resident who has physical limitations, the use of adaptive equipment, proper seating and positioning, placement of supplies and materials[12] (Christenson, M.A.) (based on clinical assessment and referral as appropriate) to enhance:

  o Visual interaction and to compensate for loss of visual field (hemianopsia);

  o Upper extremity function and range of motion (reach);

  o Hand dexterity, e.g., adapted size of items such as larger handles for cooking and woodworking equipment, built-up paintbrush handles, large needles for crocheting;

  o The ability to manipulate an item based upon the item's weight, such as lighter weight for residents with muscle weakness[13]; (Coppard, B.M., Higgins & Harvey, K.D.)

  For the resident who has the use of only one hand: holders for kitchen items, magazines/books, playing cards; items, e.g., art work, bingo card, nail file taped to the table; c-clamp or suction vise to hold wood for sanding;

- For the resident with cognitive impairment: task segmentation and simplification; programs using retained long-term memory, rather than short-term memory; length of activities based on attention span; settings that recreate past experiences or increase/decrease stimulation; smaller groups without interruption; one-to-one activities;

NOTE: The length, duration, and content of specific one-to-one activities are determined by the specific needs of the individual resident, such as several short interventions (rather than a few longer activities) if someone has extremely low tolerance or if there are behavioral issues.

Examples of one-to-one activities may include any of the following:

- o Sensory stimulation or cognitive therapy, e.g., touch/ visual/auditory stimulation, reminiscence, or validation therapy such as special stimulus rooms or equipment; alerting/upbeat music and using alerting aromas or providing fabrics or other materials of varying textures;

- o Social engagement, e.g., directed conversation, initiating a resident to resident conversation, pleasure walk or coffee visit;

- o Spiritual support, nurturing, e.g., daily devotion, Bible reading, or prayer with or for resident per religious requests/desires;

- o Creative, task-oriented activities, e.g., music or pet activities/therapy, letter writing, word puzzles; or

- o Support of self-directed activity, e.g., delivering of library books, craft material to rooms, setting up talking book service.

- For the resident with a language barrier: translation tools; translators; or publications and/or audio/video materials in the resident's language;

palliative

- For residents who are terminally ill: life review; quality time with chosen relatives, friends, staff, and/or other residents; spiritual support;

touch; massage; music; and/or reading to the resident;[8] (Hellen , C.)

NOTE: Some residents may prefer to spend their time alone and introspectively. Their refusal of activities does not necessarily constitute noncompliance.

- For the resident with pain: spiritual support, relaxation programs, music, massage, aromatherapy, pet therapy/pet visits, and/or touch;

- For the resident who prefers to stay in her/his own room or is unable to leave her/his room: in-room visits by staff/other residents/volunteers with similar interests/hobbies; touch and sensory activities such as massage or aromatherapy; access to art/craft materials, cards, games, reading materials; access to technology of interest (computer, DVD, hand held video games, preferred radio programs/stations, audio books); and/or visits from spiritual counselors;[14] (Glantz, C.G. & Richman, N.)

- For the resident with varying sleep patterns, activities are available during awake time. Some facilities use a variety of options when activities staff are not available for a particular resident: nursing staff reads a newspaper with resident; dietary staff makes finger foods available; CNA works puzzle with the resident; maintenance staff take the resident on night rounds; and/or early morning delivery of coffee/juice to residents;

- For the resident who has recently moved-in: welcoming activities and/or orientation activities;

- For the short-stay resident: "a la carte activities" are available, such as books, magazines, cards, word puzzles, newspapers, CDs, movies, and handheld games; interesting/contemporary group activities are offered, such as dominoes, bridge, Pinochle, poker, video games, movies, and travelogues; and/or individual activities designed to match the goals of therapy, such as jigsaw puzzles to enhance fine motor skills;

- For the younger resident: individual and group music offerings that fit the resident's taste and era; magazines, books and movies that fit the resident's taste and era; computer and Internet access; and/or contemporary group activities, such as video games, and the opportunity to play musical instruments, card and board games, and sports; and

- For residents from diverse ethnic or cultural backgrounds: special events that include meals, decorations, celebrations, or music; visits from spiritual leaders and other individuals of the same ethnic background; printed materials (newspapers, magazines) about the resident's culture; and/or opportunities for the resident and family to share information about their culture with other residents/families, and staff.

Activity Approaches for Residents with Behavioral Symptoms[15, 7]
(Day, K. & Calkins, M.P.) (Glantz, C.G. & Richman, N.)

When the surveyor is evaluating the activities provided to a resident who has behavioral symptoms, they may observe that many behaviors take place at about the same time every day, e.g., before lunch or mid-afternoon. The facility may have identified a resident's pattern of behavior symptoms and may offer activity interventions, whenever possible, prior to the behavior occurring. Once a behavior escalates, activities may be less effective or may even cause further stress to the resident (some behaviors may be appropriate reactions to feelings of discomfort, pain or embarrassment, such as aggressive behaviors exhibited by some residents with dementia during bathing[16]). (Barrick, A.L., Rader, J., Hoeffer, B. & Sloane, P.) Examples of activities-related interventions that a facility may provide to try to minimize distressed behavior may include, but are not limited to the following:

For the resident who is constantly walking:

- Providing a space and environmental cues that encourage physical exercise, decrease exit behavior and reduce extraneous stimulation (such as seating areas spaced along a walking path or garden; a setting in which the resident may manipulate objects; or a room with a calming atmosphere, for example, using music, light, and rocking chairs);

- Providing aroma(s)/aromatherapy that is/are pleasing and calming to the resident; and

- Validating the resident's feelings and words; engaging the resident in conversation about who or what they are seeking; and using one-to-one activities, such as reading to the resident or looking at familiar pictures and photo albums.

For the resident who engages in name-calling, hitting, kicking, yelling, biting, sexual behavior, or compulsive behavior:

- Providing a calm, non-rushed environment, with structured, familiar activities such as folding, sorting, and matching; using one-to-one activities or small group activities that comfort the resident, such as their preferred music, walking quietly with the staff, a family member, or a friend; eating a favorite snack; looking at familiar pictures;

- Engaging in exercise and movement activities; and

- Exchanging self-stimulatory activity for a more socially-appropriate activity that uses the hands, if in a public space.

For the resident who disrupts group activities with behaviors such as talking loudly and being demanding, or the resident who has catastrophic reactions such as uncontrolled crying or anger, or the resident who is sensitive to too much stimulation:

- Offering activities in which the resident can succeed, that are broken into simple steps, that involve small groups or are one-to-one activities such as using the computer, that are short and repetitive, and that are stopped if the resident becomes overwhelmed (reducing excessive noise such as from the television);

- Involving in familiar occupation-related activities, (Resident, if they desire, can do paid or volunteer work and the type of work would be included in the resident's plan of care, such as working outside the facility, sorting supplies, delivering resident mail, passing juice and snacks, refer to F169, Work);

- Involving in physical activities such as walking, exercise or dancing, games or projects requiring strategy, planning, and concentration, such as model building, and creative programs such as music, art, dance or physically resistive activities, such as kneading clay, hammering, scrubbing, sanding, using a punching bag, using stretch bands, or lifting weights; and

- Slow exercises, e.g., slow tapping, clapping or drumming); rocking or swinging motions (including a rocking chair).

For the resident who goes through others' belongings:

- Using normalizing activities such as stacking canned food onto shelves, folding laundry; offering sorting activities, e.g., sorting socks, ties or buttons; involving in organizing tasks, e.g., putting activity supplies away; providing rummage areas in plain sight, such as a dresser; and

- Using non-entry cues, such as "Do not disturb" signs or removable sashes, at the doors of other residents' rooms; providing locks to secure other resident's belongings (if requested).

For the resident who has withdrawn from previous activity interests/customary routines and isolates self in room/bed most of the day:

- Providing activities just before or after meal time and where the meal is being served (out of the room);

- Providing in-room volunteer visits, music, or videos of choice;

- Encouraging volunteer-type work that begins in the room and needs to be completed outside of the room, or a small group activity in the resident's room, if the resident agrees; working on failure-free activities, such as simple structured crafts or other activity with a friend; having the resident assist another person;

- Inviting to special events with a trusted peer or family/friend;

- Engaging in activities that give the resident a sense of value, e.g., intergenerational activities that emphasize the resident's oral history knowledge;

- Inviting resident to participate on facility committees;

- Inviting the resident outdoors; and

- Involving in gross motor exercises, e.g., aerobics, light weight training to increase energy and uplift mood.

Some residents will seek excessive attention from staff, and/or peers, at social programs, small group activities, service projects.

For the resident who lacks awareness of personal safety, such as putting foreign objects in her/his mouth or who is self-destructive and tries to harm self by cutting or hitting self, head banging, or causing other injuries to self:

- Observing closely during activities, taking precautions with materials (e.g., avoiding sharp objects and small items that can be put into the mouth);

- Involving in smaller groups or one-to-one activities that use the hands, e.g., folding towels, putting together PVC tubing;

- Focusing attention on activities that are emotionally soothing, such as listening to music or talking about personal strengths and skills, followed by participation in related activities; and

- Focusing attention on physical activities, such as exercise.

For the resident who has delusional and hallucinatory behavior that is stressful to her/him:

- Focusing the resident on activities that decrease stress and increase awareness of actual surroundings, such as familiar activities and physical activities; offering verbal reassurance, especially in terms of keeping the resident safe; and acknowledging that the resident's experience is real to her/him.

The outcome for the resident, the decrease or elimination of the behavior, either validates the activity intervention or suggests the need for a new approach.

INTENT: (F249) §483.15(f) (2)
Activities Director

The intent of this regulation is to ensure that the activities program is directed by a qualified professional.

Definitions

"Recognized accrediting body" refers to those organizations that certify, register, or license therapeutic recreation specialists, activity professionals, or occupational therapists.

Activity Director Responsibilities

An activity director is responsible for directing the development, implementation, supervision and ongoing evaluation of the activities program. This includes the completion and/or directing/delegating the completion of the activities component of the comprehensive assessment; and contributing to and/or directing/delegating the contribution to the comprehensive care plan goals and approaches that are individualized to match the skills, abilities, and interests/preferences of each resident.

Directing the activity program includes scheduling of activities, both individual and groups, implementing and /or delegating the implementation of the programs, monitoring the response and/or reviewing/evaluating the response to the programs to determine if the activities meet the assessed needs of the resident, and making revisions as necessary. NOTE: Review the qualifications of the activities director if there are concerns with the facility's compliance with the activities requirement.

A person is a qualified professional under this regulator tag if they meet any one of the qualifications listed under 483.15 (f) (2).

Determination of Compliance (Task 6, Appendix P)

Synopsis of Regulation (F249)

This requirement stipulates that the facility's program of activities be directed by a qualified professional.

Criteria for Compliance

The facility is in compliance with this requirement if they:

- Have employed a qualified professional to provide direction in the development and implementation of activities in accordance with resident needs and goals, and the director:

- Has completed or delegated the completion of the activities component of the comprehensive assessment;

- Contributed or directed the contribution to the comprehensive care plan of activity goals and approaches that are individualized to match the skills, abilities, and interests/ preferences of each resident;

- Has monitored and evaluated the resident's response to activities and revised the approaches as appropriate; and

- Has developed, implemented, supervised, and evaluated the activities program.

If not, cite at F249.

Noncompliance for F249

Tag F249 is a tag that is absolute, which means the facility, must have a qualified activities professional to direct the provision of activities to the residents. Thus, it is cited if the facility is non-compliant with the regulation whether or not there have been any negative outcomes to residents.

Noncompliance for F249 may include (but is not limited to) one or more of the following, including:

- Lack of a qualified activity director; or

- Lack of providing direction for the provision of an activity program.

V. Deficiency Categorization (Part V, Appendix P)

Once the team has completed its investigation, reviewed the regulatory requirements, and determined that noncompliance exists the team must determine the severity of each deficiency, based on the resultant effect or potential for harm to the resident. The key elements for severity determination for F249 are as follows:

1. Presence of harm/negative outcome(s) or potential for negative outcomes due to a lack of an activities director or failure of the director to oversee, implement and/or provide activities programming.

   - Lack of the activity director's involvement in coordinating/directing activities; or

   - Lack of a qualified activity director.

2. Degree of harm (actual or potential related to the noncompliance).

3. Identify how the facility practices caused, resulted in, allowed or contributed to the actual or potential for harm:

   - If harm has occurred, determine level of harm; and

   - If harm has not yet occurred, determine the potential for discomfort to occur to the resident.

4. The immediacy of correction required.

   Determine whether the noncompliance requires immediate correction in order to prevent serious injury, harm, impairment, or death to one or more residents.

Severity Level 4 Considerations: Immediate Jeopardy to Resident Health or Safety

Immediate jeopardy is not likely to be issued as it is unlikely that noncompliance with F249 could place a resident or residents into a situation with potential to sustain serious harm, injury, or death.

Severity Level 3 Considerations: Actual Harm that is not Immediate Jeopardy

Level 3 indicates noncompliance that results in actual harm, and may include, but is not limited to the resident's inability to maintain and/or reach his/her highest practicable well-being. In order to cite actual harm at this tag, the surveyor must be able to identify a relationship between noncompliance cited at Tag F248 Activities) And failure of the provision and/or direction of the activity program by the activity director. For Severity Level 3, both of the following must be present:

1. Findings of noncompliance at Severity Level 3 at Tag F248; and
2. There is no activity director; or the facility failed to assure the activity director has responsible for directing the activity program in the assessment, development, implementation, and/or revision of an individualized activity program for an individual resident; and/or the activity director failed to assure that the facility's activity program was implemented.

    NOTE: If Severity Level 3 (actual harm that is not immediate jeopardy) has been ruled out based upon the evidence, then evaluate as to whether Level 2 (no actual harm with the potential for more than minimal harm) exists.

Severity Level 2 Considerations: No Actual Harm with Potential for more than Minimal Harm that is not Immediate Jeopardy

Level 2 indicates noncompliance that results in a resident outcome of no more than minimal discomfort and/or has the potential to compromise the resident's ability to maintain or reach his or her highest practicable level of well being. The potential exists for greater harm to occur if interventions are not provided. In order to cite Level 2 at Tag F249, the surveyor must be able to identify a relationship between noncompliance cited at Level 2 at Tag F248 (Activities) and failure of the provision and/or direction of activity program by the activity director. For Severity Level 2 at Tag 249, both of the following must be present:

1. Findings of noncompliance at Severity Level 2 at Tag 248; and
2. There is no activity director; or the facility failed to involve the activity director in the assessment, development, implementation, and/or revision of an individualized activity program for an individual resident; and/or the activity director failed to assure that the facility's activity program was implemented.

Severity Level 1 Considerations: No Actual Harm with Potential for Minimal Harm.

In order to cite Level 1, no actual harm with potential for minimal harm at this tag, the surveyor must be able to identify that:

There is no activity director and/or the activity director is not qualified, however:

- Tag F248 was not cited; The activity systems associated with the responsibilities of the activity director are in place;

- There has been a relatively short duration of time without an activity director; and

- The facility is actively seeking a qualified activity director.

Changes

Laws, rules and regulations will continue to be updated to meet the changing needs of residents in long term care. It is anticipated that residents of the future will be older, more ill, and have more cognitive impairments than today's residents as well as younger residents, i.e., baby boomers, from diversified socio-economic backgrounds. People are living longer, many of whom have long term care insurance and are able to stay at home with support and care from families, community agencies and community programs, e.g., adult day care programs; thus, older people are not entering nursing homes at an early of an age as was the practice in the 1950's through the 1980's. Laws and rules and regulations need to be changed to care for the needs of changing desires of the elderly.

Laws, Rules and Regulations

City, county, state and the federal government pass laws. A federal law encompasses all 50 states, whereas, a city, county or state law is only for that particular jurisdiction. State laws can be enacted as a mandate of a federal law. City and county laws may be the results of state mandates.

Once a law is passed, rules and regulations are written. Interpretive guidelines are then developed to ensure that the regulations are followed. Laws, rules, regulations and interpretive guidelines can be amended at any time. The effective date of laws and regulations are usually announced far in advance of implementation: however, in an emergency, a law can be placed in effect immediately or within 45 days. Laws can also be phased in over a period of time, e.g., 1-3 years. Their effective dates can be changed at any time.

Licensure and Certification

A long-term-care facility is **licensed** to operate and **is certified** to receive federal funds for operation and services (Medicare and/or Medicaid). A facility must comply with state, county and/or city regulations to be licensed. For certification, a facility must meet the federal "Conditions of Participation" to receive direct Medicare or Medicaid funding through the state.

Non-compliance results in being denied a license and/or certification. If licensure is denied, or not renewed, the facility cannot operate. If certification is denied, federal funds for operation and services are not granted. A licensed facility whose certification is denied can still operate with restrictions including being responsible for the care of Medicaid residents (even though there would not be reimbursement), transferring residents to other facilities and only accepting private-pay residents until their certification is renewed. The loss of revenue per resident per day can be fatal.

Long-term-care facilities and surveying agencies can be thought of as a partnership. The facility submits an application and a fee for licensure to the appropriate state, county or city department that licenses long-term-care facilities. A licensed facility can then formally request certification to receive federal funds (Medicare/Medicaid) for the residents who are eligible to participate in these two programs.

The agencies/organizations responsible for licensure and/or certification survey the facility for compliance with regulatory standards. Licensure and certification is granted for a specified period of time if the facility complies with the regulations. After receiving the initial license and certification, facilities are surveyed on a regular basis (determined by law) for continued compliance with laws, rules, regulations, and changes if any.

Trained surveyors – usually nurses, dieticians, social workers and sanitarians – conduct the licensing and certification surveys. The unannounced survey is conducted over a period of days in accordance with regulatory policy and procedures. If a licensed and certified facility does not comply with the laws, it can lose its license and certification.

A complaint to the licensing and certification agency can result in a surveyor following up on the complaint with an unannounced visit to the facility to check the validity and seriousness of the complaint. Most of the time the complaint can be resolved. Other times it may be serious enough to warrant a full survey. If residents are in immediate danger, a facility can be shut down in 24 hours. If residents are not in immediate danger, the facility will be given a designated time frame to correct deficiency, e.g., 3-5 days. Facilities can go through an appeal process. Depending upon the severity of the deficiencies, a facility can be fined. A specified amount per bed per day will be charged until the deficiency is corrected.

Activity professionals need to be knowledgeable of all laws related to their services, including licensing and certification. Most long-term-care facilities are licensed by the state and certified by the federal government. However, licensing could be under the jurisdiction of the county or city. Ohio is one example of a state having two different government licensing departments. The Ohio Department of Health licenses all long-term-care facilities outside the city of Cincinnati; and the Cincinnati Department of Health is the licensing agency for all long-term-care facilities within the boundaries of the city of Cincinnati.

State laws differ. One state may require that personal care homes be licensed, whereas, this may not be required for another state. It is important to know what is required and the difference between state and federal regulations. If a state law is more stringent than a federal law, the surveyor will survey based on the more stringent law. If a facility's policies are more stringent than state or federal laws, surveyor will use these as the standards for compliance.

Voluntary Regulatory Agencies

CARF (Commission on Accreditation of Rehabilitation Facilities) and JCAHO (Joint Commission on Accreditation of Health Care Organizations) are two organizations that have established standards for voluntary accreditation. Participation in their certification process is voluntary. Voluntary, hospitals and freestanding health care facilities are highly acclaimed when they have accreditation from CARF and/or JCAHO. Long-term-care facilities can also be certified if they meet the criteria of one or both of these organizations. The CARF and JCAHO standards are different from governmental regulations. Thus a licensed long-term-care facility can be certified to receive Medicare and Medicaid funds and also be certified, under different standards, by CARF and/or JCAHO.

Other Laws and Regulations

1992 The Older Americans Act Amendments

Congress initially passed the Older Americans Act in 1965. The 1961 White House Conference on Aging influenced some of the contents of the act. The act has been amended several times with the White House Conferences on Aging having an impact on each of the amended documents. The purpose of the act was to help older persons by providing funding for services, training and research in all states. These activities were to be coordinated through the Administration on Aging. The Area Agencies on Aging were to oversee the expenditure of funds.

On September 30, 1992, President George H.W. Bush signed the Older Americans Act Amendments of 1992 (Public Law 102-375). This act was to amend the Older Americans Act of 1965 to: (1) authorize appropriations for fiscal years 1992 through 1995, (2) authorize a 1993 National Conference on Aging, (3) amend the Native Americans Programs Act of 1974 to authorize appropriations for fiscal years 1992 through 1995 and (4) for other purposes.

The Older Americans Act Amendment of 1992 has eight title sections. Listed below are the eight titles with some of the services related or possibly related directly or indirectly to activities and/or programming for older adults listed after each title. For more information contact the Area Agency on Aging.

Title I Objectives and Definitions (including definitions of art, dance and music therapy).

Title II In 1992 the Amendment focused on Law & History of key changes related to elder rights and legal assistance of older Americans.

Title III State and Community Programs of Aging includes in-home services for frail, older individuals; supportive services; congregate nutrition services; home delivered nutrition services; school-based meals for volunteers, older individuals, and multi-generational programs; in-home service, preventive health services, and supportive activities for caretakers who provide in-home services to frail, older individuals.

Title IV Training, Research and Discretionary Projects and Programs includes purposes of education and training projects, grants and contracts, multidisciplinary centers of gerontology, demonstration projects, special projects in comprehensive long-term-care, ombudsman and advocacy demonstration projects for multi-generational activities, neighborhood senior care programs, senior transportation demonstration program grants, resource center for Native American elders, demonstration programs for lone individuals with developmental disabilities, and career preparation for the field of aging.

Title V Community Service Employment for Older Americans includes older American community employment program, coordination, interagency cooperation, equitable distribution of assistance, and treatment or assistance provided under the Older American Community Service Employment Act.

Title VI Grants for Native Americans includes distribution of funds among tribal organizations, application by organizations serving Native Hawaiians, and distribution of funds among organizations.

Title VII Vulnerable Older Rights Protection Activities includes allotments for vulnerable elder right-protection activities; ombudsman programs; programs for prevention of elder abuse, neglect and exploitation; outreach; counseling; and assistance programs.

Title VIII Amendments to Other Laws; Related Matters.

> **Subtitle A** Long Term Health Care Workers
>
> **Subtitle B** National School Lunch Act (meals provided through adult day-care centers).

> **Subtitle C** Native American Programs
>
> **Subtitle D** White House Conference on Aging

1990/1992
The Americans with Disabilities Act

The Americans with Disabilities Act (Public Law 101-336 enacted July 26, 1990) is referred to as ADA. The Act provides comprehensive civil rights protection to individuals with disabilities in the areas of employment, public accommodations, state and local government services, and telecommunications. The ADA contains the following titles and brief explanation:

Title I Employment
(Effective July 26, 1992)

An employer of 25 or more people is prohibited from discriminating on the basis of disability against a qualified individual with a disability in any aspect of employment. Employers need to analyze job roles and functions and identify abilities and skills needed to do the job. An employer must make reasonable accommodation for a person who meets the educational skill and abilities to perform the tasks of a specific job. Reasonable accommodations include, but are not limited to, removing architectural barriers in the work place, providing auxiliary aids or services, reassignment of non-essential tasks, changing the individual's work schedule, permitting supplemental unpaid leave, or reassignment of an employee to a vacant position.

Enforcement: File complaint with Equal Employment Opportunity Commission

Title IIA Government Services
(Effective January 26, 1992)

State or local government service means every program, service and activity of such entity. All departments and entities of state or local government are prohibited from discriminating on the basis of disability in the provision of services against a person who, with or without a reasonable accommodation, meets essential eligibility requirement to receive special service(s).

Enforcement: There are three routes:

First Complaint: Municipality or state for internal resolution

Second Complaint: U.S. Department of Justice or designated federal agency

Third Complaint: Federal court lawsuit

Title IIB Public Transit
(Effective August 26, 1992)

Public transit includes rapid-rail system, Para-transit system, fixed-route system and demand-responsive systems. State or local government, which operates these transit systems, cannot discriminate on the bases of disability in providing these services. Some of the regulations will be phased in over a period of time (key rail stations must be accessible by July 26, 2020 and one car per train by July 26, 1995).

Enforcement: File complaint with the U.S. Department of Transportation or a lawsuit in federal court.

Title III Public Accommodations
(Effective January 26, 1992)

All new construction must be accessible to and usable by individuals with disabilities. Private, non-profit organizations or businesses which provide services, goods or facilities for the public are prohibited from discriminating on the basis of disability in the provision of these public accommodations. Reasonable accommodations must be provided for individuals with disabilities who meet the essential eligibility requirements for public accommodations by the organization or business. Reasonable accommodations include, but are not limited to, the removal of architectural or communication barriers, provision of auxiliary aids or services, and changing rules or practices. When structural change is needed for the removal of a barrier, it must be readily achievable or an alternative method of accommodations must be considered.

Enforcement: File complaint with the U.S. Department of Justice or lawsuit in federal court.

Title IV Telecommunications
(Effective July 26, 1993)

All telephone companies must provide tele-communication relay services for people with hearing and/or speech impairments.

Enforcement: File complaint with the Federal Communications Commission.

2000 HIPAA

Health Insurance Portability and Accountability Act of 1996

History:

Congress passed Public Law No. 104-191, called the "Health Insurance Portability and Accountability Act" (HIPAA) on August 21, 1996. The Department of Health and Human Services (HHS), under the leadership of HHS Secretary Tommy G. Thompson was given the responsibility to develop the regulations for HIPAA. The final version of the HIPAA regulations was issued in December, 2000 and became effective April 12, 2001. Part of the regulations included a two (2) year grace period. Thus, the HIPAA regulations did not go into effect until April 14, 2003.

Prior to HIPAA, there were no federal privacy standards to protect a person's medical records and other health care information provided to health care plans, doctors, hospitals, and other health care providers. State laws that are more stringent supersede HIPAA.

Periodically the Department of Health and Human Services will propose changes or issue updates, explanations and clarification. A period of public comment follows any proposed change. During the period of public comment, proposed change(s) can be modified or withdrawn. After the public comment period, change(s) may be put into effect by a specified date. A standard can be modified only once in a 12 month period.

Purpose:

The purpose of the Health Insurance Portability and Accountability act of 1996 (HIPAA) was to: (1) improve portability and continuity of health insurance coverage in the group and individual markets, (2) to combat waste, fraud, and abuse in health insurance and health care delivery, (3) to promote the use of medical savings account, to improve access to long-term-care services and coverage, and (4) to simplify the administration of health insurance.

HIPAA Provisions:

A person generally should be able to see and obtain copies of his/her medical records, as well as request correction(s) if he/she identifies an error or mistake.

1. Health Care Providers must notify their patients of their rights and any potential use of their personal medical information.
2. Personal Health Information (PHI) may not be used for purposes not related to health care. Providers of health care may use or share only the minimum amount of protected information needed for a particular purpose.
3. Covered entities must obtain permission from an individual for specific authorization disclosing patient information for marketing purposes.
4. Electronic transaction is encouraged. HIPAA requires new safe guards to protect the confidentiality and security of health information. The final HIPAA regulations cover health plans, health care clearing houses, and health care providers who conduct certain financial and administrative electronic transactions, i.e. enrollment, billing and eligibility verification.

Definitions: (Not all inclusive from Public Law 104-191 August 21, 1996 Health Insurance Portability and Accountability Act of 1996):

"Health Care Clearing House: means or private entity that processes or facil processing of non-standard data elements or health information into standard data elements.

Health Plan: means an individual or group plan that provides, or pays the cost of medical care.

Health Care Provider: means a provider of medical or other health services…and any other person furnishing health care services or supplies.

Health Information: means any information, whether oral or recorded in any form or medium, that –

(A) is created or received by a health care provider, health plan, public health authority, employer, life insurer, school or university, or health care clearinghouse; and
(B) is related to the past, present, or future, physical or mental health or condition of an individual, the provision of healthcare to an individual, or the past, present, or future payments for the provision of health care to an individual.

Individually Identifiable Health Information: means any information, including demographic information collected from an individual, that –

(A) is created or received by a healthcare provider, health plan, employer, or healthcare clearinghouse; and
(B) is related to the past, present, or future physical or mental health or condition of an individual, the provision of health care to an individual, or the past, present, or future, payments for the provision of health care to an individual, and
(i)   identifies the individual; or
(ii) with respect to which there is a reasonable basis to believe that the information can be used to identify the individual.

Enforcement:

"Enforcement activities will focus on obtaining voluntary compliance through technical assistance. The process will be primarily **complaint** driven and will consist of progressive steps that will provide opportunities to demonstrate compliance or submit a corrective action plan. A HIPAA **complaint** may result in an investigation.

The Centers of Medicare and Medicaid Services (CMS) will be responsible for enforcing the transacting and code, set standards that are part of the administration simplification provisions of the Health Insurance Portability and Accountability Act.

1. CMS will continue to enforce the insurance portability requirement of HIPAA.
2. The HHS (Health and Human Service Office for Civil Rights (OCR) will enforce the HIPAA privacy standards.
3. A new office is being created. The office will have a single mission of
4. Bringing together CMS's responsibilities under HIPAA, including enforcement.

Civil Money Penalties

Violation of the law can result in a fine, not more than $100,000 and imprisonment, not more than ten (10) years. The law's specific fines and years of imprisonment depend upon the severity of an offense.

2003

Feeding Assistant

Purpose: To provide more residents with assistance in eating and drinking and to reduce the incidence of unplanned weight lost and dehydration.

Definition: "Paid feeding assistant means an individual who meet the requirements specified in §483.35 (h) (2) of this chapter and who is paid to feed residents by a facility, or who is used under an arrangement with another agency or organization."

Requirements:

The Feeding Assistant rule permits, under certain conditions, long-term-care facilities to use paid feeding assistants to supplement the feeding services provided by nurse aides. All states must have approved training programs for feeding assistants, using federal requirements as minimum standards. Feeding assistants:

1. Must have successfully completed a State-approved training program, prior to feeding residents.

2. Must work under the supervision of a registered nurse (RN) or a licensed practical nurse (LPN).

The federal law requires a paid feeding assistant to have a minimum of 8 hours of training in the following areas:

1. Feeding techniques
2. Assistance with feeding and hydration
3. Communication and interpersonal skills
4. Appropriate responses to resident behavior
5. Safety and emergency procedures, including the Heimlich maneuver.
6. Infection control
7. Residents Rights
8. Recognizing changes in residents that are inconsistent with their normal behavior and the importance of reporting those changes to the supervisory nurse.

Implications:

Activity Professionals can be trained feeding assistants. Activity Professionals with the proper training will be able to feed residents during parties and other types of social functions. It will also allow other trained professionals to feed during meals, parties, socials and special events, thus freeing up the activity professional to do other tasks.

Activity Professionals need to be aware of an interdisciplinary approach to feeding and at the same time be realistic as to how much time can be provided for feeding without jeopardizing the activity program.

Definitions:

CMS – Centers for Medicare & Medicaid Services

HCFA – Health Care Financing Administration

IOM – Institute of Medicine

OBRA '87 – Omnibus Budget Reconciliation Act

CMS (Centers for Medicare & Medicaid Services)

These centers are established by the United States Government to process the medical claims for those persons who are covered by this national insurance program. Physicians and medical facilities send claims to these centers for payment.

Summary

Regulations and/or interpretive guidelines will continue to change. Activity professionals are responsible for keeping abreast of changes as well as any changes related to the actual survey process. Activity professionals can keep up to date with changes through belonging to activity professional organizations and attending continuing education programs related to regulations, interpretive guidelines as well as changes in the survey process.

Activity professionals must also keep abreast of other regulations that impact care and services, as well as safe use of products (supplies and equipment). Changes in activity policies and procedures may be needed to reflect the changes in regulations or new regulations.

Activity professionals must also keep abreast other regulation that impact care and services, as well as safe use of products (supplies and equipment). Changes in activity policies and procedures may be needed to reflect the changes in regulations or new regulations.

Training of activity professionals has increased from a minimum of 36 clock hours of training in 1974 to two NAAP/NCCAP 90-hour courses requiring a 90-hour practicum for each course in 1994. In time, states may require increased training and national certification. In 2004, NCCAP adopted the MEPAP 2nd Edition, which includes 180 clock hours of academic education as well as 180 hours of practicum.

Requirements for national activity professional certification have changed over the years and will continue to change. Requirements will become more stringent in the areas of academic education, experience and continuing education.

Involvement in professional organizations is one means of keeping up to date with the profession. Attending professional conferences provides opportunities for personal and professional growth.

Reading and learning from research related to activities, care, services, new techniques or new products assist the activity professional in learning and providing new care and service.

Being an activity professional is a challenging and rewarding career. With the aging of America, as well as other countries, employment opportunities will continue to grow. Activity professionals will need to be ready to meet the challenges ahead.

Chapter 5

Advocacy: In the Public Arena

"Policies provide the structure for public services"

Introduction

Advocacy means to act, speak, or write in support of an issue. In the public arena the issues or concerns can be local, state, national or international. Activity professionals have a stake in issues that relate to the current generation of older or disabled adults as well as the boomer generation, especially the needs for health care. Being an advocate is every citizen's business in a democracy. Input by concerned advocates is important to township and city councils, state assemblies, U.S. Congress and United Nations.

To be an effective advocate one has to support those who share a common concern by attending open sessions, testifying before a committee, writing letters to appropriate persons, supporting causes with money contributions and voting. The United States laws are passed and altered by interested citizens who are advocates. As the population changes, laws need to change to address the new realities, i.e., elderly and disabled wanting to stay in their own homes Advocates raise the issues and support various solutions to the specific issues, i.e., adequate funding for medical needs. Advocates look at what is and compare it with what should be.

Identifying Issues Which Genuinely Need Advocacy

Some of the issues that need to be addressed for the frail and vulnerable members of our society include adequate income, personal services, health care, housing, transportation, etc.

Income: How much is a livable income? There is a great deal of difference between high cost areas like New York City vs. living in a small rural town. What is fair? Social Security has been in place since the late 1930's, however, there was no inflationary increase for the first 30 years. So the purchasing power for senior citizens was reduced each year by inflation. In the early 1970's an inflation factor was added so that Social Security keeps pace with cost of living. Many advocates were needed to complete this change. Many pensions on the other hand do not have an inflation factor built in to their pension plan.

Health Care: The federal government and state are experiencing Medicaid costs that are budget breakers. Caps have been put on medicine reimbursements. Advocacy is needed to address future health care needs for the total population including care for the elderly and disabled.

Affordable Housing for Senior and Disabled: Through the Housing Department of the Federal Government special housing facilities have been built and the rent is subsidized.

Transportation: Elderly persons who are unable to go shopping, to medical appointments and outings need transportation provided. Activity professionals can advocate for this service.

Aging and Inequality

"Perception can distort reality"

As persons age they have different patterns and life styles. While we are created equal in that we are human beings, we are unequal in the innate quality of our being such as different statures, intellect, education, talent, social environment, family structure, as well as racial or ethnic background.

Choices each person makes are a major factor that determines whether the inequality spread becomes larger or smaller, e.g., stay in school or drop out. Each person makes choices that enhance their lives, just maintain life, or lead to dismal conditions, e.g., homelessness.

The elderly and disabled are in part a product of those choices, e.g., smoking has caused older persons to have poor health and in some cases, an early death. Others may have poor health because the genes they inherited have caused health issues. Disabilities are sometimes caused by accidents – some are due to carelessness while others are caused by outside forces, e.g., weather or road conditions.

As advocates our task is to find ways to provide financial resources, housing, transportation and other services that the elderly and disabled need. Activity professionals as compassionate care givers can help by advocating for the aging and disabled at the local, state, regional and/or federal level.

Understanding Current Policy Debates

"Policies provide the structure of human activity"

Current policy debates include Social Security for the boomer generation, funding for Medicare and Medicaid, minimum wages, health services, etc. Like any debate there are advocates on at least two sides, as well as many points of view.

In a democracy all citizens can and should participate in the debate and seek positive system changes.

Regarding Social Security some of the current ideas include solving future funding, raising salary levels on which wage earners pay Social Security, raising the age for full retirement to age 70, cutting the benefits to the recipients and investing some of the tax money in the stock market. When Social Security began in 1935 there were many paying in for each person receiving Social Security income. In 2007 there are three wage earners for each recipient. However, when the majority of the boomers are retired there will be only two wage earners for each recipient.

Medicare faces the same problem because the finances come from an employment tax. Medicaid, however, comes from general tax dollars. Taxes are raised to pay for Medicaid. There is a movement to keep the aging and disabled in their own homes or apartments and provide in-home services such as personal care (bathing, etc.) homemaker, cleaning and meals on wheels. This is a major cultural change. Activity professionals will need to be informed about these issues and get involved in advocating for the elderly and disabled.

The Policies of Aging

"As ordinary persons one can be an extra ordinary channel"

Policies are principles, statements and plans that guide government, companies, communities and clubs. These statements are set forth to guide the organization in providing care and services. Various entities including local, state, and national policies provide for the aged and disabled. Services that are provided include protection, income, health care, housing, transportation, etc. Elderly and disabled may live in federally funded housing with the rent based upon a percentage of income, i.e., 30%. The government picks up the remaining portion of the cost. This program was developed through advocacy aimed at protecting the elderly and disabled from being homeless.

This elderly and low income policy has been in place since the great depression in the 1930's. Older Americans are benefiting from policies that were established when there was a great need.

Health care is another major policy for the elderly and disabled. Many of the residents/clients are currently benefiting because some advocates saw a need and pushed to establish the policies.

Activity professionals should be sensitive to the residents/clients who are benefiting from these policies for aging and disabled.

The Economics of Aging
"Economics should provide for basic needs"

Economics in the broadest sense is providing for the material needs of older and disabled persons. The basics of economics on a personal level are income and expenditures. In government there must be sufficient revenue to provide the goods and services for the persons in the respective territory. Most of the revenue for government comes from taxes. Community groups raise revenue by projects gifts and businesses raise revenue through sale of products or services.

An older person's resources are dependent upon income and expenses, saving or spending patterns. In cases where persons have the same income, one may accumulate savings and resources while another may have a life style of spending whatever he/she gets. Since we live in a democracy where persons can choose job roles, places to live, life styles, child rearing patterns, etc., some residents who have had advantages and opportunities have accumulated adequate funds so they can provide for themselves as they age. Others who are limited by ability, by bad choices or bad luck may come to retirement and not be able to cover their cost of living. Activity professionals need to consider their future needs in the choices they make.

Advocating in the Public Arena
"There can be no achievement without action"

One of the major issues that all citizens face is how much time and energy they will spend to advocate in the various public arenas. Sometimes one can be active in getting a tax levee passed to provide for older and disabled persons to stay in their own homes. This means networking with county or city leadership, being on a task force to advocate for the passing of tax issues or supporting the effort by gifts of money, time and skills. Such efforts can help older persons receive services in their own homes.

At the state level it may call for joining a political party, or a caucus group to advocate for a change in state law or regulations. In some cases, it may be the best choice to advocate for the state issue to be voted down. At the national level often one works through their elected senator or representative or by attending group sessions to design a position to be taken or sent to the legislature, e.g., proposals to the White House Conferences in the years they are held. Activity professionals can play an important role in influencing the legislature to pass legislation that meets needs of older and disabled persons.

Advocacy involvement can include but not be limited to:
1. Signing petitions,
2. Submitting statements supporting or opposing change in legislature
3. Initiating a proposal for change, new services, needed support
4. Writing to legislatures regarding supporting local, state, or national activity professional organizations
5. Involving participants in advocacy involvement

Advocating as an Individual

"Spirit energy release by one can be absorbed by another"

At times it becomes prudent for an individual to advocate for a given issue. One may feel very strongly about an issue, contact one of the political entities and lobby by phone, letter or email directly to the legislative member. This can happen on a local, state or national level. Learning to know the representative or decision maker on a personal basis helps to strengthen ones influence. Supporting candidates monetarily as they run for office is important. Each individual can make a difference by helping in a campaign.

The legislator, commissioner, judgeship needs help and assistance as they run for office. Also after the election many elected officials, especially at the state and national level have offices or places to meet interested citizens during the year. Voters need to share their concerns with their legislators. Activity professionals can influence the elected official in regard to issues that affect the elderly and disabled as well as themselves. One does not always need a group to affect the outcome of legislation.

Advocating as a Group

"We can't versus we will try"

Group advocates can sometimes present a stronger voice if the group can meet together and study the issues then come to a consensus. Once the issue has been thoroughly discussed both the pros and cons, the conclusion can be communicated to the legislator. It is helpful if the key elements can be set forth in summary or influential fashion. These groups can be party members or a mixture of party members on both sides of the isle along with independent voters. Sometimes the broader the representation the more weight the arguments will carry. The reasoning should be sound, backed up with research and statistics and set forth in a clear and convincing manner. This serves to make the advocacy more persuasive.

Activity professionals might join an existing group or start a group if they see a particular issue that needs to be discussed. At times it may be appropriate to include the residents/clients in the effort.

Federal Policy Making

"Positive attitudes can bring about positive change"

Advocating influencing federal policy takes connecting with United States Senators and the congressional representative, especially in the district where you live and vote. After all, the senators and representatives are depending upon voters to support them in the elections. Sometimes one can invite these elected officials to come to your facility to meet and see residents. This is particularly true if you have independent or alert assisted living residents/clients who have an issue they would like to discuss.

In cases of a special celebration of a resident's 100th birthday, candidates are often willing to make a visit. The United States president will send a special certificate to persons reaching an advanced age, if notified. Cultivating the relationship of the political leaders on the national scene can be significant. Occasionally a CEO may go to Washington D.C. to see their representative. Activity professionals can take the initiative to make this contact. Relationship is a two-way street. You need to show an interest in your representatives and they will usually respond positively. If you have this kind of contact you can phone, write a letter or email a person to indicate how you feel about a particular issue.

State Policy Making

"Motivate state officials in making positive policies"

State policy making is done largely through the governor or your own district senator and representative. There are times when one contacts a state legislator in another district but for the most part lobbying or advocacy occurs through the representative in ones own district. You are one of their constituents. They know as a voter you can make a difference the next time they come up for a vote.

State issues such as taxes, social concerns and issues that impact your county or region can be a concern. Such concerns are important when they will impact you, your family and the residents/clients with whom you work. Activity professionals can invite these elected representatives to your facility or agency when you have a special occasion such as a ground breaking, dedication, celebrate a resident's achievement or age celebration. Many times these state representatives live in an area nearby and will make a special effort to attend such special occasions.

Local Policy Making

"True community is caring for others"

Local policy making is somewhat easier because the policy makers live in your neighborhood or town. One may see the local county commissioners and other local elected officials at the grocery store, shopping center or community event. Either working through a group or contacting the politicians individually will probably occur more often. County commissioners have weekly meetings and one can attend, observe or request to speak regarding a special issue. Again the elected officials tend to be open to voter's ideas. The policies that are local are more specific. Activity professionals can make contact with local officials and invite them to attend some of the events at the facility/agency so they will have knowledge of what is going on. One can influence policy when one has cultivated the friendship of the local political leaders.

Federal Register

Federal means that a group of states have formed a compact to create a union of states and have agreed to subordinate some of their governmental power to that central authority. Register means to record the events and actions of a given body. Actions of the federal legislation are recorded and records of the actions are preserved. The legislative actions include the laws that are passed. Congressional committee reports are registered and preserved for future reference. When the federal laws are passed they are given an act number and the year in which the law was passed. For example the first Older Americans Act was passed by congress and signed by the president in 1965. The Older American Act has been revised in 1973, 1978, and 1981. These revisions include new provisions, e.g., resident rights, federally mandated minimal entitlements for residents in long term care facilities including the right to privacy and choice of physicians.

Activity professionals should be aware of the residents' rights in the Old Americans Act, as well as Medicare and Medicaid to name a few of the items in the federal register.

Proposed Rule

Laws that are passed and signed are written in very general terms, so rules are needed to provide interpretation of the law for implementation. The departments in which the law falls establishes rules which give guidance to those persons to refine the application of the law. These are called rules and regulations. In order to make sure the law is interpreted correctly, there is a period for reviewing the rules. During this period legislators and federal administrators may allow opportunity for interested persons to influence how the final rules and/or regs are written. The amount of time can be a matter of months until consensus is reached by those who have the authority to finalize the rule.

Activity professionals have been represented through the national Association of Activity Professionals (NAAP) in influencing the rules relating to activities in long term care facilities. Contact with the National Health Department continues with representatives from the NAAP Board. NAAP members can influence the Board representative by being a member of NAAP and contacting the Board.

Public Comment Period

When the law has been passed and the outline of the law developed and the rules and regs have been set, there is a time for public comment. This is a time providing opportunity for companies, states, communities, local entities and individuals affected by the law and the rules to make their comments. These comments help the rule makers to modify the rules if necessary. Entities that are most affected by the law and regs are the ones who spent time and energy to analyze how these regs will affect their business, manufacturing or services.

The regs are written by department staff persons who have knowledge of what regs, if any, are being replaced, expanded, or modified. In cases of law and regs addressing a new concern input from practitioners is very important to determine whether it is workable, flexible and interpretable so that intent of the legislation can be fulfilled. Activity professionals have had input through NAAP and NCCAP in regard to activities being questioned

Community Action Projects

"Motivate and participate in community efforts"

In the mid 1960's the War on Poverty was set in motion. A major component was establishing Community Action organizations through the United States. Regions were defined and a regional staff was put in place to work with the states in developing single or multiple county Community Action organizations. Projects were established by these organizations to address unmet human needs. These programs included help for the low income, disabled, handicapped, children, youth, families, the elderly and persons in society who were suffering from various health conditions and problems. The first task was to define the needs through research, focus groups and inquiries. Some of the findings were the need for education for preschool children from low income families, more adequate housing, money for heating and cooling, meals on wheels, help in appropriate ways to apply for a job, family counseling, and other needs.

Unique to Cincinnati, OH, the TRA (Therapeutic Recreation for the Aged) Project provided training for over one hundred low income people ages 16-21and over 60 years of age and developed therapeutic recreation programs in twenty one institutions. Many of the trained people went on to become activity directors and assistants when the 1974 federal regulation required activities in nursing homes. One person retired from activities at age 83, she had begun her new career at age 62. Projects were addressed through Community Action organizations. Activity professionals can become aware of the Community Action programs in their area and support those programs.

Advocacy on Line

Since the computer has come into most homes in America and persons become familiar with on line services, one can become an advocate through on line. Going on line and checking the area of interest can lead to information about what is being proposed, what laws have been passed and what regs have been set forth or are being considered.

Through the internet the activity professional can find information that is available. If one finds a proposal that they either support or oppose he/she can advocate his/her point of view. The internet has become a major source for information. Through chat rooms one can register feelings and suggestions.

Advocacy in the Workplace

"Seek the best for each team member"

After an activity professional has been employed for a time and sees the need for a change in work place, one can begin by making suggestions for change. The activity professional who is director of the department can, in consultation with the CEO or supervisor, express his/her interest in making changes. If the boss agrees, changes can then be made. If there is a need for resident/client input then, through the resident council or a representative committee, the change may be discussed with them. When a consensus is achieved the issue may be taken to the CEO or resident council for ratification of the decision. Activity professionals amenable to the activity director may propose their ideas to the director. If the department manager agrees the change does not substantially affect the residents/clients or facility policies it can be implemented. However the department director may want to get approval from the CEO or the resident council. Systematic changes often take time because system changes may affect residents/clients as well as other employees. However any changes that can be made to serve the residents/clients more effectively or economically should be worked through the chain of command to benefit those being served.

Summary

Activity professionals have an opportunity and responsibility to advocate for care and services for the people they serve. They can be an advocate for participants/residents in the service setting in which they work, or for all older adults and people with disabilities.

An activity professional can be an individual or group advocate with as much involvement as he/she wishes. It is important that an activity professional does not get caught up in advocacy that it consumes all of his/her time, having a negative effect on their family, work and/or personal wellness.

Chapter 6

The Behavioral Sciences

"Everyone is someone"

Life Course Perspective

"Hope is the future"

Life course is how one experiences a timetable of life events and society looks upon how a person chooses his /her life course. In American society there is an unwritten rule of expectations regarding how and when a young adult progresses through adulthood and into being an older adult.

Today, young adults have far more variables in selecting their life events versus young adults of previous generations. The choices made in early life affect the future of an individual. A woman who has children in her 20s may be a young grandmother whereas a woman who has children in her 40s is considered an older mother. The age of a parent affects their later life events, i.e., work, career, income, savings, housing, family responsibilities, child education etc. A young couple would not have the financial income to raise a family like an older couple who have saved for a family.

A woman or man may put off education in order to raise a family; thus, seek higher education after the children are raised, which would affect the amount of income that could be earned as well as retirement savings.

Looking back over the years shows how the life course perspective is changed. One could look at the life course perspective of family members and friends compared to their own perspective. The following examples give some changes in life perspectives since WWII.

After WWII, late 1940s, males were expected to have a job, go to college or trade school, marry, have a family, support the family, and pay into social security for retirement. Depending upon his job and income the male may have had the luxury of having an additional retirement plan. A male would be loyal and work for the same company all his life and at the end be rewarded with a gold watch. The females place was in the home, cooking, cleaning, caring for family and being supportive to her husband. Some women went to college, nursing school, or secretarial school to support themselves while single and then decided whether or not to work after marriage. Some women had no choice but to work to augment the husband's salary.

In the 1950s many women were corporate wives and were an integral part of keeping their husband personally groomed for his job, e.g., purchasing their clothing, having their clothes cleaned, shirts starched and ironed, mending as needed. Wives would pack husbands suitcases if their job required traveling. Sometimes wives were expected to travel with their husbands and make arrangements for childcare during the traveling period. Non-corporate wives were responsible for laundering husbands uniforms, keeping them in good repair, housekeeping, child care, having dinner ready at designated times and serving family meals daily.

In the 1960s more women sought education beyond high school, e.g., college, nursing school, skill training and were expected to work in their chosen field. Some women married during or right after college or their field of advanced education. Some women dropped out of school, married and had children and then went back to complete their education and work.

In the 1970's through today, more women sought education beyond high school and continued to work while raising a family. A two-person income allowed for larger homes, two or more cars, second homes, more conveniences, family vacations, a variety of lessons for children, involvement of children in sports and other after school activities, in home businesses, and other amenities.

Women have entered professions, the trades, businesses, and non-traditional occupations. They have become clergy, worked in TV newsrooms, served in the military and have been more involved in political careers

Some men chose armed force services following high school or college; then seek advanced degrees. Men involved in learning a trade, continue using their skills throughout their working years, often for more than one employer. Men are more involved with household tasks, raising children and supporting wives in their work.

While some wives stay home to raise the family, some men do the same, giving up their careers for awhile and then returning to work

The changes over the years of male and female roles have altered the life course perspective. Today's youth have no boundaries when they become adults as to what they will do after high school (school, job, marriage, family, retirement). Some will work and be able to save for early retirement and then develop a second career. Others will retire early and have enough retirement savings to lead a life of luxury. Still others will work until they are eligible for Social Security. Men and women will both be eligible for social security depending upon the amount of time they have worked and the amount of money they contributed to Social Security While there is skepticism about the future of Social Security, young adults are advised to pay into their own retirement plans, throughout their years of work...

Life Course Phase

Demographic events change the life course, i.e., birth and death. Demographic changes effects different cohorts. Middle age, a phase of life course, has been changed. Middle age was not considered different from adult life.

Women in the nineteenth century had many children, starting in there twenties and continuing until they were nearly forty years old. These women were responsible for childbearing tasks for forty or more years, age 20-60 years. Their years of 40-60 continued to be consumed with raising children. They spent 90% of their lives raising children. Couples reached 60 years of age before their children were grown. Often couples would become grandparents while raising their young children. With low life expectancy, couples may have had only a few years before being widowed.

In contrast to the 20th century, couples in the 1970s had smaller families, e.g., two children spaced two years apart and spent only 40% of their life with child rearing responsibilities. Children left home by the time the parents were

in their 40s. This gave the parents twenty years to be together without children.

Increased life expectancy and the changing patterns of child bearing created what was thought to be middle age, a separate phase of life course. Sociologists see a restructuring of middle age. It is not the same for everyone. Around age 35, people experience the early phase of middle age where they have personal and social responsibilities. Child rearing may include school age children as well as adolescents or early adulthood offspring. Mothers may be returning to part time or full time work or school. Some people may retire early while others prefer to continue their work beyond retirement age. During the late middle age, children are increasingly caring for their older parents with fewer siblings to assist. Middle age responsibilities often include double responsibility, caring for aging parents as well as children and/or grandchildren. This is often referred to as the sandwich generation. Middle age adults can identify with their parents and vise versa.

As people age they are more aware that life is finite and that death is very real. A 20 year old is not fully aware of this. Middle age brings responsibility as well as understanding of life and growth.

Life Span
"Time is more than hours or minutes, it has content, meaning &purpose"

Life span is the greatest number of years a person can live. Man's life span has been noted to be about 125 years. There is more public recognition of people turning 100 years old. Modern medicine and healthy living has allowed people to live longer. In the future there will be more centenarians (100 year olds).

Age Grades
"The art of aging is a practical art"

Age grades are a way of grouping people by status using age as a social category. Males ranked in a hierarchical order by their age group in some societies are an example of a society's generational principle for life course organization. Each group such as warriors (young men) and elders (older men) has specific roles.

Social gerontologists have divided older adults into the following three categories by chronological age as they represent different developmental stages of aging.

65-74	Young old
74-84	Old or middle age old
85 & over	Old old or old old age

Age Norms

Act your age, summarizes the term, age norms. Age norms are informal standards indicating the appropriate age and behavior for various life events, e.g. marriage, children, retirement. Age norms are general and will vary by sub groups in society.

Cohort Experience

Persons born in the early 1900s have experienced a lifetime of changes and adaptation. The automobile has become the primary mode of transportation. Radio and TV are a source of enjoyment, entertainment and education. Antibiotics and psychotropic drugs have become commonly used drugs, as have other drugs associated with diseases that affect adults and older adults. Automation, credit cards, computers and home shopping via Internet are a few examples of modern technology to which people have become accustomed. Change has come about because of World Wars I and II, the Korea, Vietnam, and Persian Gulf Crisis and Desert Storm as well as Iraq, environmental concerns, health-related concerns and research, new laws, the economy, and technology. The industrial revolution brought about change in the work force and the economy. Women entered the work force and their roles in life continued to change. Families have become more mobile. Older family members have had to be self-reliant or depend upon friends, neighbors and/or community agencies for help and services.

Today, an older person may refer to him/herself with reverence as being a **senior** citizen with privileges and responsibilities. Reduced rates on meals, transportation, entertainment, travel and education are appreciated, as they offset fixed incomes. Sharing knowledge, skills, and talents with families, friends and the community is a fulfilling experience. Most older people are concerned with the communities that they helped to build. They take an active role in voting and learning about the issues that affect their personal and family lives and the country. Older people can continue to learn and grow. Some seek basic education that they did not have an opportunity to complete. Others become or continue to be involved in higher education, skill classes and new technology.

A person 65-67 years of age, depending of the birth year, is eligible for retirement with full Social Security benefits. Today with downsiz-ing of companies, people are being given the opportunity to retire early, at 50–64 years of age with full private pensions or a high percentage of their private pension. Some people prefer not to retire until their 70s or 80s providing they are in good health; capable of doing their job and employers have work for them.

People who have retired from the work force are called retirees. When companies, e.g., fast food chains advertise for part time work they often use the term "retirees" when they want to employ an older, experienced person. Thus the retired person can be gainfully employed, yet refer to him/herself or have others refer to him or her as a retiree with respect and admiration.

Crowded Nest
"Reaching out in love"

The crowded nest is a rather new phenomenon. Some young people remain at home longer than previous generations rather than seek independent living. The crowded nest is when young people leave home, return home, single or married, with or without children, creating an environment where more people are living in the same amount of space than before the family member left home. Parents may have created a new life style or living arrangements after a young family member left. Now they all have to adjust to new living arrangements. This can be challenging for every one. The person returning home wants independence, as do the parents. The parents may have chronic illness or disabilities and not have the energy and patience they once had to deal with the change of the family arrangement.

Empty Nest

Parents feel the empty nest when the last family member, a son or daughter leaves the home for school, job, marriage, etc. Normal family routine is disrupted. Responsibility has shifted from the children to each other. This calls for an adjustment. The parents may have 20 or more years without their children living with them, creating feelings of loneliness, depression, separation, anxiety, worry or a feeling of independence and personal growth. A couple may feel the need to downsize their living arrangements; thus seek new housing.

Longitudinal Research

Gerontologists conduct two types of research. One is longitudinal research involving the same group of people over a long period of time. The other type of research is cross sectional, which compares people from the different cohorts.

Example of longitudinal research is:

1. Health and Retirement Survey

Thirteen thousand individuals born between 1931 and 1941 were interviewed in 1991 (first interview). The first results showed that Hispanics of pre-retirement age had low levels of health insurance. In the future the studies will be able to show the affect of how low health insurance affects their health in the future. The study will also show how increased divorce rates will affect individual's life style as well as income.

Social gerontologist Vern Bengtson and his colleagues at the University of Southern California initiated a study in 1971 of 300 three-generation families to study how attitudes, values, and traits were transferred from one generation to the other. Surveys were collected from these same families for a quarter of a century with new surveys being conducted every three (3) years. One outcome debunked the myth of a gradual weakening of families. Researches found that family solidarity remained continuous over the life course.

Research also found that daughters had more contact with aging parents than sons. Widowhood created more parent child contact while middle class children have less contact with parents.

This research has been expanded to four generations and the results have been reported to a government panel responsible for making decisions regarding family policies. One of the outcomes based on the study was the development of intergenerational programs.

Sandwich Generation

A sandwich generation has evolved in recent years. Today, there are increasing numbers of adults and older adults responsible for children and grandchildren, while simultaneously being responsible for parents and/or older relatives or significant others. Thus, the person is sandwiched between different generations of responsibility. As one advances in years, he/she may find him/herself providing direction, support, and/or care and financial assistance to older family member(s) while simultaneously being responsible for his/her own children.

Cumulative Disadvantage

"The pain and suffering of one causes pain for others"

Life course framework is the study of aging related to the interaction of historical events, individual decisions and opportunities and the early life experiences in determining later life outcomes. Quadagno (2005) cites the theory of cumulative disadvantage and highlights the influence of earlier life experiences on the quality of life in old age. If one is advantaged in early life, he/she has more opportunity for education, good job, and high salary and to save for retirement. A disadvantaged youth will most likely not have the same life opportunities and will experience inequality in old age.

In the 65-year-old cohort there is increasing diversity between members, which creates greater inequality. A person with an advantaged life may be leading a life of financial security and luxury whereas a person that experienced a disadvantaged life may experience poverty, poor health and lack of support and socialization.

Two types of cumulative disadvantage over the life course are: (1) gender inequality and (2) racial inequality.

Gender inequality is mostly related to women. A woman's economic status was affected when she assumed the traditional role of staying home, doing the housework and being responsible for caring for children or parents. When a woman decides to quit work or work part time while caring for children and/or parents she is not able to earn and save what she could have, if she had continued to work full time. A woman experiences returning to work at a lower pay level than if she had continued working.

Women also experience receiving substantially lower wages than men with the same education and experience. Gender inequality continues into retirement. Women are penalized for their non-working years when they raised their family. They were less able to save money in individual retirement account, pension plans and Social Security; thus, they have less personal money for retirement. Today, young women who follow the male life course model have more opportunity for advancing in their career, earning higher wages and saving more for retirement.

Historically, **racial inequality** was greater prior to the Civil Rights Act of 1965. African American men and women who were paid low wages, offered part time work and experienced high rates of unemployment ultimately experienced life course sequences, i.e. low income from private pensions and Social Security. While there is still racial inequality because of changes in the labor market and racial discrimination in employment and still less opportunity for pension and social security earnings; it is anticipated that racial inequality should decline in the future among the elderly if higher income employment opportunities are reached.

Social Clock
"Old is someone else"

Jill Quadagno, (2005), refers to the social clock as "being a prescriptive time table for major life events." The social clock influences when people marry, have children and retire as well as how people feel entering a new life phase. They may not be ready to be grandparents, feeling that they are too young and don't have support of peers their age. In a study by Bernice Neugarten and her team of researches, found that people who were aware of their social clocks and had clear expectations about their timing of events that precipitated the transition from being a teenager to being an adult, including finishing school, marrying and for males beginning work. Neugarten and her associates concluded that men and women were aware of whether they were on or off time for major life events according to their social clock.

Quadagno (2005) writes," Many of Neugarten's measures seem biased in ways that no longer reflect societal norms. This is especially true in regard to gender issues. Neugarten's research was based on the implicit assumption that "men were the breadwinners and women the family caregivers." Women's accomplishments of raising their families were completed before middle age; whereas, middle age men were in their prime of life, holding their top jobs and greatest responsibility. These assumptions no longer hold as there are more than 70% of women in the workforce. Today, middle age adults are going to school to complete or continue their education, changing careers or continuing and advancing in their careers.

Summary

Every one has a life course, a timetable of life events. Society has a way of looking at the way a person chooses his/her life course. In America there is an unwritten rule as to when in a person's life, a life event should take place, i.e. completion of school, job, marriage and family, retirement etc. When a person does not follow the norm, he or she is looked upon as being different which may or may not be acceptable to other people.

Middle age around age 35 is not the same for every one. One person may have recently married and started a family while another person is experience empty nest or being responsible for grandchildren. Another person may be starting college or specialized or moving up the professional ranks or changing career.

Society has become more aware of life span, the greatest number of years a person can live. *The Today Show* announces people names and show their picture on national TV when they be come 100 years old or more. Age grades are a way of grouping people by status as a social category where as age norms are informal rules indicating the appropriate behavior at different ages. "Act your age" is often heard from and elder when a younger member of society is not acting in what is perceived to be appropriate for the person's age.

People go through life with a variety of cohort experience. A group of people of different ages experience the same event at the same time ,i.e., war, changes in housing, life style, art, music, politics, local, state, regional or national happenings, i.e. disasters, political events, educational changes, styles, sports, transportation, shopping etc. People born and raised in the 50's experience many changes as a group, cohort that is not being experienced by people born in the 90's. Cohorts who started work in the 20's expected to work their entire life for the same company and receive a gold watch at their retirement celebration. They had no intention of working where as today, many retires work part time to supplement their retirement income and/or because they like and want to work. It may be in a different field, but they are doing it because it is their choice.

Adults can experience the crowded nest when children return home with or without their own children and every one in the home has to adjust to more people living in the same amount of space as prior to the child returning home.

The emptiness is experienced when children move away from home. The normal family routine is disrupted; the home feels empty with the child being gone and parents are no longer responsible for the child. The parents experience new time together that may not have been planned. They may have 20 or more years without the responsibility of caring for children. This experience can create negative feelings of separation, anxiety, worry that their children are OK, depression, not needed or they can experi-

ence this time as personal growth and do things that they did not have time to do before. The couple or living spouse may want to down size and seek new living arrangements.

Social research assists us in understanding the social changes in society and how it affects the present and next generation. A longitudinal research study is over a long period of time with the same people and across sectional research compares people of different cohorts.

The sandwich generation has evolved in recent years. Some adults are responsible for their family as well as for a parent, sibling, aunt/uncle or grandparent. The person for whom they are responsible other than their family may live with them or in another residency. The sandwich generation must make personal sacrifices, i.e. put off education, purchasing a new home etc. so that they can concentrate of providing for the person of the older generation as well as their family.

Cumulative disadvantage affect a person in old age. If a person is advantage in early life, he/she has more opportunity for education, good job, high salary and able to save for retirement. A disadvantaged youth will not have the same life opportunities and will experience inequality in old age. Two disadvantages over the life course are gender inequality and racial inequality.

Gender inequality is mostly related to women. A woman has to make a decision to be a stay at home mom and reduce income and savings for retirement or continue to work and not have as much time as she prefers with the family.

Racial inequality was greater prior to the Civil Right Act of 1965. Both African American men and women were paid lower salaries, offered part time verses full time work, and experienced high rates of unemployment. It is anticipated that racial inequality should decline in the future among the elderly, men and women, if life course employment opportunities are reached. Today's African American children, have more. opportunities for education and employment than previous generations. They will have more responsibility and earnings to continue development of employment opportunities for future generations.

A social clock is specific time tables for major life events, i.e., when people marry, have children, grandchildren, and retire as well as how people feel entering a new life phase. They may feel too young to be grandparents and don't have the support of peer their age. A couple may whish to retire young and plan an active retirement and find that their peers are non supportive because they cannot do the same.

Bernice Neugarten, a well known sociologist and her team, found that people where aware of their social clock and had clear expectations of the timing of life events that precipitated the transition from being a teenager to an adult, including completing school, marrying and for males beginning work Neugarten and her associates concluded that men and women were aware of whether they were on or off their major life events according to their social clock.

Neugarten's measures appear biased in ways that no longer reflect societal norms. This is especially true concerning gender issues. Neugarten's research was based on implicit assumption that men were the breadwinner and women were the family care givers. Women completed their role for family care giver by middle age and men were in their prime of life holding their top job. These assumptions no longer hold true as 70% of the women are in he workforce. Today's middle age adult have a wide variety of opportunities to continue their education, change careers or continuing and advancing in their careers. Some women work because they want to and are able to see that family needs are met. Other women, i.e. have to work to supplement the husband's salary or because they are a single parent and breadwinner.

Chapter 7

Adult Client Population

"Youth is a product of nature and nurture while age is a product of chance and choice."

Gerontology is the scientific study of the biological, psychological and social aspects of aging.

Social Gerontology

"As human beings, we are basically alike with differences"

Social gerontology is a subfield of gerontology. Social gerontology emphasis is on the social rather than the biological or physical aspects of aging. Quadangno (2005) gives the following definitions for the terms: gerontology and social gerontology:

"Aging is a normal, universal process which begins at birth and continues until death. Aging includes the physical, intellectual, emotional, social and spiritual growth and development of a person as a unique human being."   (Bernice Neugarten)

Chronological Age

"All humans experience degrees of suffering and pain"

Chronological age is used to identify a specific group of people in a study. Age 65 is considered old in the United States because that is when people become eligible for Social Security. However, age 65 for retirement has changed. People born in 1940 had to be 65years and 6 months to receive Social Security. The age requirement for social security continues to increase until people will have to be 67 years of age according to the current law to receive their Social Security benefits.

Age 50 is the minimum one may join AARP (American Association of Retired Persons), the largest senior citizen organization in the United States. Senior Centers have age markers starting at 50. This has been reduced from 60 to entice more members. It has also created age diversification among members and participation in activities. The younger senior members want and participate in different programs from older participants in their 80s – 90s. Younger participants may be active with families, neighbors, and the community, able to drive, and wanting more educational and wellness related opportunities versus older members wanting and needing more social programs.

Using chronological age for studies can be a problem as not all 65 plus year olds are in the same health, social network, support, income bracket or interests and preferences; thus, chronological age is a poor indicator of old age. One person may be young at 85 and another old at 50. Politicians, actors, actresses, doctors, lawyers, and men and women of other walks of life continue their profession late in life or until they die whereas other people give up work their passion at an earlier age. Social gerontologists have found that 65 year old people have little in common with 85 year olds and 20 year old people have little in common with 40 year olds when relating to interests and experience. A contemporary example of interests and experience is the use of home computers. The majority of older adults age 85 and over have no interest in learning how to use a computer; whereas, people age 65 are more interested and may use them for keeping in contact with family and friends, banking, researching topics of interest, writing their life histories, etc. In the 1980's some computer companies started promoting computer lessons for the people 50 years of age and older knowing that this population, including college graduates did not have exposure to computer use.

Functional Age

"Aging changes call for letting go"

A person's functional age (the age at which one operates) may differ greatly from his or her chronological age. One person may continue to work and be active in civic, community and church affairs and remain independent at age 85, while another person of the same age is very frail and dependent upon others to meet his personal needs. Physical appearance may also determine functional age, e.g., gray hair, wrinkles, and a physical feature associated with old age such as baldness, male's bushy eyebrows and elongated muscles, etc.

Family Life Cycle

As infants we are born into families and are totally dependent upon parents to love and care for us. In mid-life we assume the parent-worker role and other family members become dependent upon us. Then in the advancing years persons who live long enough once again become dependent upon others. The residents in long-term-care facilities are going through this final stage of the life cycle. The activity professional can understand why many residents fight to remain independent for as long as possible.

Role Reversal

As persons age and become frail and incapacitated, the adult children often have to assume the parent role. This is referred to as role-reversal, for the parent becomes dependent upon the children to manage personal affairs. This can be a very traumatic experience for a resident who is forced to admit that he/she is no longer able to independently handle personal and financial affairs. While the activity professional does not normally become involved in this transition, a resident's attitude and level of participation in activities may be affected when the transition occurs.

Role Changes

Role changes occur frequently between couples. One is more able and provides care, support and services. Then a sudden change occurs in the "well one's" condition and the so called less able one is forced to render support. This kind of drastic change can interrupt participation in activities. When role changes occur the activity professional maintains contact, with love and support, and waits until a new pattern emerges where participation again is possible. Sometimes through the team care-plan session or direct contact with a counselor or administrator the activity professional solicits help for residents going through role changes.

Demography of Aging

"It's not the number of years but the quality of those years"

America is an aging Society. It has evolved from a young society to an aged one. The 60 million Americans age 55 and older is expected to almost double between 2007 and 2030 to 107.6 million. When the baby boomers reach retirement, Americans age 55 and older will make up 31% of the population. Another 12% of the population with be 65 years or over.

The average Life expectancy for women and men in the US has increased. Women are expected to live 79 years and men 72 years.

Life expectancy for people who reach 65 today is an additional 17.9 years (16.3 for males and 19.2 for females). Forty (40) % of adults age 65 are likely to live to be 90 by 2050.

The 85 years and older population, continues to be the fastest growing population. It is expected that this population will reach 5.7 million in 2010 and possibly 18.2 million by 2050. This 85 year and older population seeks more sheltered care verses living at home.

In 1996, the elderly population consisted of:

Whites	83.0 %
Blacks	8.1 %
Asian and Pacific Islanders	2.3%
Hispanics	4.5 %

It is expected by 2030 there will be less white older adults and more black, Asian and Pacific Islanders and Hispanics

Education has increased with age. In 1997 66 % of older adults completed high school. It is expected that 24 % of older adults will have a bachelor's degree by 2030. Future activity professionals will be providing activity services for a large number of people with a bachelor's degree than today. This will change some of today's programming to meet tomorrow's better education participants.

As the aging population change so will activities and services in long term care. There has been a decline of the white population using long term care services and an increase of the black population using and surpassing the white population using long term care services.

Human Wellness

"One can focus on wellness or illness"

Human wellness is individualized. Wellness is more than the opposite of illness. Human wellness can be achieved at any age. Today there is more focus on wellness through education, prevention, nutrition, exercise, intellectual, physical and social programs in the community, on TV, CD's, computer, internet, e-mail and increased opportunities to communicate by cell and digital phones.

Wellness includes six aspects: (1) physical (2) intellectual (3) social (4) emotional (5) vocational and (6) spiritual. Personal knowledge, motivation and participation determine one's overall wellness.

Social gerontologists have categorized functional aging into three categories related to wellness: (1) well, (2) somewhat impaired and (3) frail.

The well elderly are involved with family and community responsibilities. They may continue their employment or seek new employment opportunities. They are also involved in social and leisure activities including volunteering.

The somewhat impaired elderly is another stage of life, called the transitional stage. They begin to experience chronic ailments and need assistance from others, family, friend, or community agencies. They may need specific assistance with personal care, shopping, cleaning and transportation so that they can participate in life experiences. A person may need assistance with activities of daily living, cooking, cleaning, shopping but be able to socialize with family and friends and/or with transportation, go to the doctors, senior center or other senior programs and church, as well as travel.

The frail elderly are more dependent upon others for their daily activities because of their physical or mental deterioration. The frail elderly are dependent upon their family or institutions to meet their daily needs. The frail elderly are more susceptible to infection, falls, and general physical, mental social decline because of their impaired organ function and systems.

Universal Health Needs

"Families need to be related by love as well as blood"

Universal health needs includes, a healthy life style, and health behavior. People have choices and options regarding their life and how they choose to live it. Health behaviors can contribute to good health or adversely affect health.

Health is the absence of disease, as well as physical, mental and social well being. One's health is based on one's health life style. Individuals are responsible for their own health, with consultation from the medical profession.

Universal health needs include but are not limited to:

A. Good nutrition and hydration
B. Adequate sleep and rest
C. Weight control
D. Release of Stress
E. Physical Activity
F. Anger Control
G. Infection Control:
   a) Hand washing
   b) Staying away from others when ill
   c) Staying away from people who have infectious disease or following infection disease procedures

d) Storing, preparing and serving food properly
H. Safety
   a. Handling sharp items properly
   b. Using proper mechanics when pushing a wheelchair or Geri chair, lifting or moving items
   c. Driving safely
   d. Wearing helmets as needed for activity
   e. Wearing protective clothing when needed
   f. Following directions when handling hazardous materials or waste.
   g. Ear protection from noise
   h. Eye protection as needed
   i. Using prescribed medications as directed.
   j. Warming up prior to exercising
   k. Seeking medical treatment when needed
I. Prevention:

   a. Regular medical and dental exams
   b. Health screenings (breast exam, mammography)
   c. Flu shots
   d. Pneumonia shot
   e. Sun screen
   f. Vaccinations
   g. No drugs
   h. Drinking responsibly

   i. Knowing family health history and potential for disease or specific diagnosis

Health is not just an aging concern. Good health starts early in life. Today there is more emphasis on personal responsibility for individual health care. There is more health education via TV, newspapers, community health forums, support groups and in schools. Restaurants have begun advertising that they do not use trans fats in their food. These types of public announcements assist in educating the public. Pharmaceutical companies advertise their products and what they are used for as well as the possible side affects. Americans are more aware of the content of foods and are more educated in terms of what to look for regarding their individual health. There has been an increase of articles in professional journals and magazines on sleep, stress, hydration, weight control, exercise/physical activity, and sun exposure, use of helmets for cycling, motor cycle riding, and sports. There has also been an abundance of information of what foods to eat and exercise to prevent chronic diseases, i.e., osteoporosis, heart and lung disease as well as good mental health.

Safety and prevention has been stressed by medical personnel, researchers, wellness professionals and others. Individuals are responsible for their health throughout life. The universal health needs affects every generation and individuals as they progress through life. Taking heed to what is known about health, safety and prevention can have a positive impact on tomorrow's older adults.

Theories of Psychological and Physical Aging

Gerontology is the study of aging. A variety of theories have been developed to try to explain the underlying causes of aging. Some focus on the physical aspects (biological theories); others focus on the psychological and social aspects (psychosocial theories). For orientation purposes, a brief introduction to some theories is being presented.

Biological Theories

Genetic theory: A person is programmed from birth. Genes inherited from parents are the major factors in the aging process. The theory holds that everyone has a biological clock. Cells grow and divide as programmed. Environmental factors may affect one's life span but not outweigh the genetic factor. Looking at family traits on both sides of families, one can see similarities, e.g., height, body build, hair color, graying early or late in life, age at death, etc. The DNA (deoxyribonucleic acid) controls the formation of essential information required by a cell. The information is transferred and transcribed by a second molecule, RNA (ribonucleic acid) to another location in the cell, where the assembly of proteins occurs.

Mutation theory: Possible mutations or mistakes in the genes caused by environmental factors affect the aging process. Carcinogenic substances can cause mutations of genes.

Wear and tear theory: Over-use of cells, molecules and biological structures gradually wear the body down and cause destruction. The wear and tear of critical molecules will lead to damage that is not reparable.

Error theory: Errors involved in the transmission of information from the DNA through the RNA to the final protein cause the death of a cell. The RNA molecules are continuously being formed; whereas the DNA remains stable. Thus, it is thought that the accumulation of many errors may be the cause of the death of the cell.

Cross-link theory: Molecules develop links either between parts of a specific molecule or between molecules. These cross-links in changes (chemical and physical) affect how the molecule will function in the body. The collagen in connective tissue is most affected. This is seen in decreased elasticity in the skin, blood vessels, muscles and other tissues in the body.

Autoimmune theory: The immune system protects the body against foreign bodies (microorganisms and mutant cells, e.g., cancer cells. The immune system generates antibodies that react with the proteins of the cells and attack foreign cells. Antibodies de-crease with age after adolescence. With the reduction of antibodies, the immune system may not be able to recognize normal versus mutated cells. Auto-immune diseases increase and show increased incidents in older adults.

Neuroendocrine theories: There is a general decline in the endocrine system in the adult years, i.e., cessation of menses around the age of 50. The endocrine system includes the thymus gland (this which controls immunity) and the thyroid gland (which controls metabolism). The pancreas does not respond as quickly to a rise in blood sugar in an older person as it does in a younger person. The onset of adult diabetes is more common among older persons. The endocrine system keeps the body balanced (homeostasis), seeing that the body temperature is neither too high nor too low, and keeps acid, salts and water in their normal range. The decline in the neuroendocrine system is a cause of the aging process.

None of these cellular or physiological theories can stand alone. The physical aspect of aging along with the psychological aspects of aging must be considered when trying to determine the aging process.

Psychological Theories

Three theories related to aging and activities are the activity theory, disengagement theory and continuity theory. These theories are based on life satisfaction in older adult years. The way one sees and feels satisfaction is very individualized. What may be satisfying to one person is not to another. These theories can assist the activity professional in recognizing and understanding the activity involvement of older persons.

Activity theory: This theory holds that most older persons are happiest when they are engaged in some kind of rewarding and satisfying activity. In the activity theory a person must be active to be happy. New interests replace work and old activities. New friends replace those who have moved or are deceased. Older adults who fit into the activity theory of aging can be seen active in senior center activities and programs, involved in independent individual activities, and/or committed to causes and concerns, education, travel, clubs and organizations other than senior citizen centers.

Senior Centers provide opportunities to for older adults to remain active with the same or new peers. A member or guest can be involved in as much or as little activity as he/she chooses.

Residents in a retirement home may be very active in group activity, e.g., trips as well as community causes and work. They have the time, interest, knowledge and skills or are willing to learn whatever it takes to get a task done. In long term care facilities, one may be 100% more active than when living at home if the activities are enjoyable, convenient, and provide an opportunity to meet new people and keep one's mind off the aches and pains. Residents are eager to participate. They say that activities keep them active, give them a reason to get out of bed (something for which to look forward) and a reason for being.

Participants in day-care centers have opportunities to remain active in a variety of activities mostly during the day. Some day-care centers for older adults have weekend and evening activities. The programs are structured yet flexible as in long term care facilities.

Disengagement theory: One of the first psychological theories was the theory of disengagement which held that as a person ages he/she tends to voluntarily withdraw from activity and social patterns. In a large measure this is a self-inflicted, energy-saving system. On the other hand, to some extent, society causes older persons to withdraw through encouraged or forced retirement at a certain age. Research indicates that older persons do disengage to different degrees and at different rates. The exception would be the person who maintains an active role until meeting a sudden death. But in general, for the very old person, a degree of disengagement takes place as the person loses agility and energy. Activity professionals need to plan activities that will limit the use of activity energy for the frail and ill.

Continuity theory: This theory maintains that older persons tend to carry into retirement and aging the same activities and lifestyle they have maintained throughout the middle years. An assessment of participants' social history, lifestyle, interests and involvement in activities (individual, family, one-to-one, group [small and large]), present abilities and limitations are important. Adaptations may have to be made and accepted by the individual to continue meaningful activities, e.g., for reading, reading large-print material or listening to a Talking Book. A retired farmer may enjoy a small vegetable or flower garden. A homemaker may be interested in baking pies for a fund-raiser.

Some people feel secure and content to continue activities exactly as they have done them in middle years. Others are willing to consider learning or trying a new method of doing an activity. In all activity settings (senior center, adult day care, retirement homes, assisted living and in long term care facilities), participants may be extrinsically motivated to try something new related to previous activity, as they see others involved.

Activity professionals need to respect participants' needs, wants and wishes, while trying to keep them up-to-date with activities through exposure, demonstrations, discussion classes, etc. To do this, the activity professional has to stay abreast of activities, techniques, supplies, resources and the changing needs of participants.

Motivation Theory:

Abraham Maslow, a psychologist, developed a hierarchy (pyramid) of needs that influence motivation. The two lower needs, physociological and safety and security must be met before the three higher needs can be achieved.

Psychological needs include hunger, thirst, rest/sleep, sex and shelter. One must fulfill these needs to survive. Safety needs include security, stability, law and order, and freedom from fear. Love and belonging needs are met by relating to friends, lovers, and children. If the need is not fulfilled, one experiences loneliness. The need for self-esteem emerges when love and belonging needs are met. This includes self-respect and respect for and from others. The final need, self actualization, is met by becoming all that one is capable of becoming.

The self-actualized person has a realistic perception of self and others. He/she knows his/her strengths and limitations and is able to see others and events realistically. The person is able to be spontaneous.

A person who is self-actualized has his/her own values and does not accept everything just because others are doing it. The person is able to problem-solve, and to set and accomplish goals. He/she can detach from others without feeling lonely, likes being alone, and enjoys privacy. Independence and self-motivation are other traits of a self-actualized person. The beauty of nature, life, children, art, music, etc. is appreciated. The self-actualized person has good interpersonal relationships, is free to express love for others, can show affection, sympathy, kindness and patience, and is tolerant of others. He/she is able to laugh at him/herself. Creativity is expressed. One is able to support and accept social change in an effective manner while supporting his/her culture.

Erickson's Eight Stages of Life

Eric Erickson developed a theory involving eight stages of life. His theory is that we develop our personality by the way we resolve the stages in our life. There are two ends of the spectrum: positive and negative. We can be in the middle of the spectrum or change positions depending on our life situation and how we choose to resolve it.

1. *Trust vs. Mistrust.* When a baby cries and someone cares for the baby's needs, a sense of trust begins to develop. Mistrust is developed if the baby is not loved and cared for. The positive outcome is hope.

2. *Autonomy vs. Shame/Doubt.* Children begin to want to help themselves. If they are encouraged, they are apt to develop a sense of autonomy. If they are put down it results in shame or doubt. The positive outcomes are Willpower and Self-Control.

3. *Initiative vs. Guilt.* A child begins to differentiate between right and wrong. The positive outcomes are Direction and Purpose.

4. *Industry vs. Inferiority.* If a person is encouraged and his/her work and effort are noticed, it will stimulate industry. Otherwise, inferiority will occur. The positive outcome is Competence.

5. *Identity vs. Identity Confusion.* This is a time for role-playing and challenging authority. There is a need to set some limits so that the child will know what is expected. If no limits are set, it can cause identity confusion. The positive outcomes are Devotion and Fidelity.

6. *Intimacy vs. Isolation.* This is the time that meaningful relationships are developed. The negative spectrum would be isolation, and the unwillingness to share self with other people. The positive outcomes are Affiliation and Love.

7. *Generativity vs. Stagnation.* This is the time for high productivity including promotions in one's career. There is constant movement, a time to give something of one to leave to the world. The opposite is stagnation, a willingness to stay in the same job, do the same things, have the same routine, and get into a rut. The positive outcomes are Production and Care.

8. *Integrity vs. Despair/Disgust.* This is a time to look back at life and evaluate accomplishment but still see opportunity for more accomplishments. If a person enters old age with the attitude, "I did accomplish something in my life," he/she should be able to adjust. The opposite is despair/disgust. One expresses anger, fear of death, or makes statements that life was no good – a waste and feels depressed. The positive outcomes are Renunciation and Wisdom.

9. *Middle age:* forty to sixty years.

10. *Old age* or senescence: sixty years to death. One must solve problems during each stage before progressing to the next stage. Poor adjustment and immaturity results from failure.

Old age is a period of change (physical, mental, emotional, social and spiritual) and adaptation. Everyone's dream is to live a happy and successful life.

Erickson's Eight Stages of Human Life

Period of Life	Opening Issues for Each Stage	Positive Outcome
Infancy	Basic trust versus mistrust	Hope
Childhood	Autonomy versus shame and doubt	Willpower & Self-Control
Pre-school	Initiative versus guilt	Direction and Purpose
School Age	Industry versus inferiority	Competence
Adolescence	Identity versus identity Confusion	Devotion and Fidelity
Young Adulthood	Intimacy versus isolation	Affiliation and Love
Adulthood	Generativity versus Stagnation	Production and care (self absorption)
Later Adulthood	Integrity versus despair (and disgust)	Renunciation and Wisdom

Havighurst's Developmental Tasks

Havighurst's developmental tasks include:

1. Babyhood and Early Childhood
2. Late Childhood
3. Adolescence
4. Early Adulthood
5 Middle Age
6. Old Age

Developmental tasks are tasks that occur at certain times during one's life. Successful completion of one task leads to happiness and success in the next task. Failure to achieve a task can lead to a person feeling unhappy, not being accepted by society and having difficulty with later tasks. The task of old age is primarily adjustment. One has to adjust to decreased physical strength and health, retirement and reduced income, and death of spouse. One has to affiliate with peers of the same age group and establish satisfying living arrangements. As one grows older he/she must adapt to new social roles.

Life-Span Theory

One's life span is subdivided into stages of life. Each stage has its own developmental and behavioral characteristics. Today, life span is subdivided into the following ten stages:

1. Prenatal period: conception to birth
2. Infancy: birth to the end of the second week
3. Babyhood: end of the second week to end of the second year
4. Early childhood: two to six years
5. Late childhood: six to ten or twelve years
6. Puberty or preadolescence: ten or twelve to thirteen or fourteen years
7. Adolescence: thirteen or fourteen to eighteen years
8. Early adulthood: eighteen to forty years
9. Middle age: forty to sixty years
10. Old age or senescence: sixty years to death
    One must solve problems during each stage before progressing to the next stage. Poor adjustment and immaturity result from failure.

Old age is a period of change (physical, mental, emotional, social and spiritual) and adaptation. Everyone's dream is to live a happy and successful life.

Organ Systems: Function, Changes with Aging

"Atrophy is the price one pays for inactivity"

Skin, Hair and Nail Changes

Skin becomes dry, less elastic, wrinkled, and more prone to bruising and tearing with age. Sweat glands decrease in number and function. The sebaceous glands decrease in activity and less oil is produced. Age spots appear particularly on areas of the body that are exposed to sunlight. Facial lines occur in the 20's. They are caused by habitual expressions. The lines become more pronounced particularly around the eyes, nose and mouth. Facial lines are also related to inherited genes. Smoking and exposure to the sun can increase the aging process. Application of moisturizer or hand creams often softens the skin. Increased water intake can assist with hydration.

Hair loses pigmentation and changes to gray or white. It becomes thinner, a characteristic more predominant in men than in women. It is also drier and may lose luster. There is often an increase of hair in the nose and ears particularly in men. Application of a conditioner to the hair will soften the hair and can make it easier to manage.

Nails grow slower, become more dry and brittle and lose their luster.

Musculoskeletal System

Muscle strength peaks at about 30 years of age. Muscles lose their mass and strength slowly until the 50's and then drops rapidly. The speed with which nerve messages are transmitted typically slows down. Ability to exert muscles declines and reaction time is slower. Use of muscles in moderation through physician-approved exercise can assist in maintaining strength and delay the slowing of reaction time. Muscle tissue turns to fat. It is common during middle age for males to gain an inch or more around the waist, and for women to gain in the hips. Women also gain inches in their abdomen and upper arms.

118

Bones become thinner and more brittle with age. Bone loss in the spine and thinning of the disks between the vertebrae cause one to lose one to three inches of height between the ages of 35 and 85. Broken bones heal slower. Exercise, walking and other weight-bearing activities assist in building strength of bones at any age by increasing calcium. Before being involved in any kind of exercise, older persons should consult with their physician.

Joints become stiff as the cartilage in the joints is reduced. Range-of-motion exercises help keep joints functioning. A physician should be consulted as to the type and/or amount of exercise that is needed before a person becomes involved in an exercise program. The wrong exercise or amount of exercise could cause harm in either healthy or diseased joints.

Immune System
The thalamus gland shrinks by the time one reaches adolescence. The immune system starts to weaken around the age of 30. This makes the 30 year adult and particularly older adults more susceptible to illness/infection. The white blood cells that fight off illness-production (bacteria and viruses) are not as effective as they once were. Viruses, flu, pneumonia and other infectious diseases can be life-threatening to older adults. Flu shots are recommended for most older people. Avoiding contact with people who have the flu or a cold can reduce the risk of catching it. Rest and involvement in low-energy activities (watching TV, listening to the radio, reading) can assist with the healing process.

Gastrointestinal System
Teeth have thinner enamel and are more brittle but are not normally lost as one ages. Many older people born in the late 1800's and early 1900's wear dentures and partial plates. They did not have the preventive care and highly technical dentistry that is practiced today. As one ages, salivary activity decreases and oral mucosa is drier. Taste buds are reduced. Esophageal mobility decreases. Gastric acids and enzymes are reduced. The stomach takes longer to empty. The liver becomes smaller and has less storage capacity. There are lesser amounts of pancreatic enzymes. Insulin secretion may be altered. The intestinal muscles become weaker and peristalsis is slower.

What one eats and the ability to chew and swallow affect one's digestive system. Because the stomach produces less of the acid that aids the digestive process as one ages, it may cause discomforts of gas, heavy feeling after eating, or loose stools. Older people grew up having learned to eat related to the four food groups that were thought to be equally nutritious. Today, people of all ages have to learn the USDA's new Food Guide Pyramid to daily food choices. The pyramid shows very clearly which foods should be eaten most and least. Diet, exercise, rest and stress reduction are appropriate means for healthy digestion.

Cardiovascular System
Plaque builds up in the inside of the blood vessels which makes them more rigid. The heart tends to enlarge with age and its ability to contract decreases. Valves become thick and rigid. The left ventricle thickens and the aorta and aortic branches dilate. The carotid arteries may be less efficient. Tachycardia is not tolerated as well. Vasomotor tone decreases and the vagal tone increases. Heredity, high-fat diets and lack of exercise have adverse effects on the circulatory system. A physician should be consulted before one engages in any type of exercise, e.g., aerobic, yoga, walking, sports.

Respiratory System

Lungs become increasingly rigid and their ability to expand and contract is decreased. This causes the less efficient exchange of oxygen and carbon dioxide through the alveolar membranes (tiny sacs in the lungs where the gaseous interchange of oxygen and carbon dioxide occurs). The alveoli are decreased in number, become less elastic and possess fewer capillaries. The diaphragm and thorax weaken. Thoracic expansion is reduced. Inspiratory reserve volume decreases and respiratory reserve volume increases. Cough efficiency is reduced. Sometimes the blood flow to various organs is decreased. Thus, there is decreased oxygen to the organs which causes damage. A physician should be consulted prior to involvement in deep breathing exercise and/or other exercise.

Reproductive System
Menopause (the cessation of the menstrual cycle) begins around 50 years of age. For some women, it can start in the 40s or late 50s. The vulva vascularity decreases along with elasticity and subcutaneous fat. The labia flatten. Pubic hair is lost. The vaginal epithelium becomes thinner and less vascular. Vaginal se-

cretions are more alkaline and of lesser amounts. The cervix and uterus decrease in size. The fallopian tubes and ovaries atrophy. Both ovulation and estrogen production cease. Breast tissue atrophies. The mammary tissue is replaced by fat. With the reduction of estrogen and other female hormones, some women experience vaginal dryness and painful intercourse. Hormone replacement therapy or use of a vaginal lubricant can remedy the problem.

Male testes decrease in size and firmness. It takes longer for the male to have an erection, and ejaculations are slower and less forceful. Both sperm and testosterone continue to be produced. Enlargement of the prostrate gland is very prevalent. While there is gradual decline in reproductive functioning in men at a late age, the changes vary greatly among men.

Most older adults are able to lead active and sexually satisfying sex lives. Longer resting periods may be needed between orgasms. Lubrication in women may take longer and orgasms may be shorter and less intense.

Urinary System

The bladder muscles become weaker and bladder capacity decreases. There are fewer nephrons, renal filtration is slower, the renal threshold for glucose is higher and tubular re-absorption is altered. Older people can experience urgency, incontinence and/or stress incontinence, an involuntary loss of urine, e.g., from laughing, sneezing, coughing, exercising. This is caused by pressure placed on the pelvic muscles, which have become weakened. Stress incontinence may restrict an older person from engaging in a favorite activity or being around other people for fear of incontinence and odor.

Neurological System

The weight of the brain decreases and neurons are reduced in number. An older person needs more time to respond and to react, but sensory function is not reduced. Instructions for an activity may need to be given more slowly and be repeated. Recall of information involving short term, long-term and/or remote memory may take longer, i.e., reality orientation questions, trivia questions, reminiscing. Knowing a person's predominant sense, i.e., auditory or visual, helps to facilitate memory and recall. One person may retain or remember something if he/she sees it, while another person may do better if he/she hears the information. Reaction time may be slower when one is involved in physical, i.e., the gross motor movement of exercise sports, lifting, bending, etc., as well as the fine-motor movement in picking up and using small objects for crafts and games, etc., creative, cognitive, and affective activities. Safety is a concern when an older person with decreased sensory awareness is engaged in activities involving contact with cold or heat, i.e., cooking, baking, crafts, outdoor activities, walking, gardening, etc.

Normal physical changes of aging are gradual. Acceptance, adjustment and adaptation to the change can be upsetting to some and taken in stride by others.

They Didn't Know Me

There was a body on my frame
Which in my youth, went with my name,
But then the body changed its lines.
While name remained with youngish times.
Some hair and teeth have gone astray;
A slower pace has come to stay.
And stronger glasses on my nose
Have let me see my little toes.
This makes it difficult to say
That I'm the same as yesterday.
With time and life's propensities
I'm stuck with new identities.

Mildred Crane
Resident, Otterbein Lebanon

Common Disorders and Diseases

"Often it is easy to overlook the good"

Chronic Conditions

Older people may have one or more chronic conditions. The four major chronic conditions are arthritis, hypertension, hearing impairment and heart disease. Other chronic conditions seen in older people are orthopedic impairments, cataracts, sinusitis, diabetes and tinnitus. New medical treatment (medication, therapy, surgery, repair and/or replacement of body parts), diet, rest, and change in lifestyles can help a person cope with his/her chronic conditions. Independence in activities of daily living (ADL) such as eating, bathing, dressing, transferring and toileting, can be maintained through the use of assistive/adaptive devices and equipment. Canes, walkers and wheelchairs provide assistance and independence in ambulation. Visual and hearing aids/devices also help one to remain independent. Home health service can assist with bathing, dressing, feeding, homemaking tasks, etc. to allow older people with illness and disabilities related to chronic illness to remain in their homes versus being placed in a nursing home.

Activity Involvement

Involvement in an activity may be affected by physical, cognitive, emotional and social factors. Cognition may be impaired affecting memory (short-term and long-term memory), intellectual abilities, concentration, attention span, or the ability to read, write or do math, organize, plan or problem-solve. Physically a person may have pain, fatigue, edema, paresis, paralysis, limited range of motion, limited movement, sensory impairment, inability to speak, incontinence, or physical reactions to medication. Emotionally a person may react with denial, fear, anger or depression. He/she may be unable to accept the disease(s) or disability, be unwilling to take medication or receive treatment, or become very dependent (learned helplessness). Body image may be altered. Socially, one may withdraw from family, friends and activities. Family and friends may withdraw from the person because of being unable to accept the person affected by the chronic condition and limitations.

Physical Problems

AIDS: AIDS (Acquired Immune Deficiency Syndrome) is caused by HIV (Human Immunodeficiency Virus). The AIDS virus destroys the body's immune system, thus damaging the system's ability to fight off other diseases. A person with AIDS can develop a variety of life-threatening illnesses and disabilities, eventually leading to death.

Research has shown that HIV is present in blood and/or in vaginal fluids or semen of the person infected with the virus. The virus can be transmitted through having sex with a person who is affected and using or sharing or sticking one's self with a needle or syringe that had been previously used by or for a person who was infected with HIV. People have been infected through blood transfusion; however, this risk has almost been eliminated since the testing of blood supply that began in 1985. Babies can become infected during their fetal development, at birth or through breast-feeding.

The AIDS virus enters the body through the blood stream. It attacks the white blood cells. A person infected with AIDS may be symptom free but is able to infect others. AIDS Related Complex (ARC) is less serious than AIDS. When the AIDS virus destroys the immune system, other germs and cancers cause "opportunistic" diseases. Some of the diseases include Pneumocystis Carinile (Pneumonia and Tuberculosis) and Cancer (Kapose's Sarcoma evidenced by multiple purplish blotches and bumps on the skin). The AIDS virus can attack the nervous system causing brain damage and psychological problems (change in feelings and mood). Dementia is a common problem.

Persons with AIDS need to be protected from other people with colds, flu or chicken pox. They have difficulty fighting off these types of infections.

While AIDS is not an older adult disease, it can affect a person at any age. Depending upon the age of onset, i.e., middle age, older adult an older person can develop AIDS in later life.

Arthritis: There are over 100 forms of arthritis. The most common are rheumatoid, osteoarthritis and gout. Arthritis cannot be prevented or cured. However, modern medicine can relieve pain in most cases. Depending upon the health of the individual and the type and severity of the disease, treatment may include rest/relaxation, exercise, weight-control, diet, use of heat or cold, therapy, surgery, medication, joint protection and self help aids.

Gout: Usually a big toe suddenly becomes swollen and extremely painful. A person may not be able to walk without an assistive device. Gout is more prevalent in men than in women.

Lupus: Women of child bearing age are most affected by this type of arthritis. Many body tissues become inflamed and damaged—mostly the skin, joints and internal organs.

Osteoarthritis: Usually this affects the joints in the neck, back, shoulder, elbow, wrist, fingers, hips, knees and feet. It can be very painful. Pain may come and go. The intensity of the pain can vary from moderate to severe

Rheumatoid: This is more common in women than men. It usually affects the joints of the hands, wrists and feet, but it can affect any moveable joint. Joints swell and pain is experienced on both sides of the body. It can be crippling. Especially common is morning stiffness.

Cardiovascular Disease: Heart and vascular diseases increase with age. The risk for heart disease is affected by heredity. Men are more at risk than women to develop heart disease and blood vessel disease. The death rate for blacks due to cardiovascular disease is higher than for whites. Diet, exercise, rest/relaxation, no smoking, medication, or surgery, if needed, can be the prescribed treatment for the various cardiovascular diseases.

Arrhythmias: Irregular heart-beats are called arrhythmias or dysrhythmia. It occurs when the heart's natural pacemaker (electrical signals) develops an abnormal rate or rhythm, when the normal pathway is interrupted, or when another part of the heart takes over as the pacemaker. This causes the heart to pump less efficiently.

Two problems associated with irregular heart beats are:

Bradycardia: This is caused by excessive slowing of the heart-beat. It may cause light-headedness, dizziness, near-fainting or fainting spells. A pacemaker can be implanted to correct the **slow** heart beat.

Tachycardia: This is caused by rapid heart-beat. It may cause rapid heart action, palpitations, light-headedness, dizziness, near fainting or fainting. The rhythm may be regular or irregular.

Ventricular tachycardia is a life threatening rapid heart-beat in the ventricles.

Ventricular fibrillation occurs when the lower chambers of the heart are quivering and the heart cannot pump any blood. A person immediately collapses and sudden death follows if medical assistance is not immediately provided. Electrical shock can convert ventricular tachycardia and ventricular fibrillation into a normal rhythm if recognized in time. These conditions can be controlled through medication. A fibulator (an electrical implant device) can be implanted to control rhythm.

Angina: When the coronary arteries (the blood vessels that bring oxygen and nutrients to the heart) are blocked, pain may result. The pain is often described as a dull ache, a heavy full feeling, tightness or squeezing, or a burning sensation in the middle of the chest behind the breast bone. Discomfort in one or both arms, neck and jaw can also occur. Pain is usually felt during exercise, but then goes away in a few minutes after the activity that brought it on is stopped. When there is severe narrowing of the artery and a person experiences angina when at rest, he/she may be at risk for a heart attack.

Atherosclerosis: There is a normal hardening of the arteries as one grows older. Atherosclerosis is a slow, progressive disease. It can start in childhood or progress rapidly in the 30's, or for some people it doesn't become threatening until the 50's or 60's. The disease is caused by a build-up of plaque, which can partially or totally block the flow of blood through an artery. The plaque can cause bleeding (hemorrhage) on the plaque or formation of a blood clot (thrombus) on the plaque's surface. Either of these can block an artery and cause a stroke or heart attack.

Congestive Heart Failure: When the heart muscle is damaged or overworked, the heart lacks the strength to keep the blood circulating normally throughout the body. When the blood flow from the heart is slow, it causes the blood in the veins returning blood to the heart to back up, causing congestion in the tissues. Symptoms include edema (swelling) of the legs and ankles and sometimes other body parts. Shortness of breath can occur when fluid collects in the lungs and interferes with breathing. The kidneys are also affected. They are unable to get rid of water and sodium (salt), which increases edema.

Heart Attack: A heart attack is caused when the blood flow to the heart muscle (myocardium) through the coronary arteries is severely reduced or stopped. This is called a myocardial infarction (MI). The coronary arteries can be blocked by an obstruction, i.e., build up of plaque (Atherosclerosis) or a blood clot. When a blood clot is lodged in the coronary artery, it is called a coronary thrombosis or coronary occlusion. When the blood supply to the heart is cut off drastically or for a long period of time the heart muscle cells suffer irreversible injury and die. Death or disability can result, depending upon the damage to the heart muscle. Spasms in the coronary artery cause the artery to narrow, and blood flow to the heart decreases or can stop. Spasms can occur in normal blood vessels as well as diseased vessels (atherosclerosis). A heart attack may result from a severe spasm.

High Blood Pressure: As people grow older their blood pressure rises. Blood pressure changes depending upon activity, emotional state and rest. Blood pressure is measured in the arteries. There are two pressures. One is systolic; the other is diastolic. Systolic pressure is the pressure in the arteries when the heart contracts; where as, diastolic pressure is the pressure when the heart is at rest and fills between beats. Blood pressure is read in millimeters of mercury (MMHg). There are two numbers. The top number is systolic pressure; the bottom number is the diastolic pressure. Blood pressure varies among individuals. High blood pressure exists when the reading is 140/90 or greater for both numbers. Additional testing may be needed to see if blood pressure is consistently high.

If high blood pressure is not lowered, it can lead to a stroke, heart attack, or other medical problems. High blood pressure can be controlled by diet, i.e., low-salt, weight-control, exercise, no smoking, change of lifestyle, reduced stress and medication.

Stroke: Blood clots or a hemorrhage in the blood vessels cause strokes. Clots formed in a diseased heart can break off and move through larger blood vessels, and then get wedged in smaller arteries in the brain. Brain cells die when the brain is deprived of the needed oxygen and nutrients. Dead brain cells are not replaced; thus, the part of the body controlled by these nerve cells can't function.

Symptoms of a stroke include but are not limited to weakness or paralysis of a part or parts of the body, difficulty in seeing, inability to speak or difficulty in speaking, disorientation, disturbance in thought patterns, memory, change of behavioral patterns, etc. These symptoms can be temporary or permanent. If they are temporary, the episode is a TIA (transient ischemic attack). The TIA can last five minutes to 24 hours. Usually TIAs are warning signs of a stroke.

The effect of the stroke is dependent upon type and severity. Brain damage can affect the senses, language, ability to speak and understand speech, thought process, memory, and behavioral patterns. A person may lose sight in one eye or a part of one or both eyes and lose feeling on one side of the body. When this happens, the person may be unaware of this side of the body. This is referred to as neglect, i.e., right- or left-side neglect. They may not see objects (food, furniture) or print on the damaged side of the body. A person may not eat food on one side of the plate because he does not see it. He/she may not be able to dress both sides of the body, or may bump into walls or furniture on the neglected side.

Perception of everyday objects may be changed as a result of a person's inability to see, touch, move and think. Recognition of familiar objects may be difficult. Objects may look closer or farther away as a result of visual deficits. This then can cause falls, spills and/or burns. Aphasia may be the result of a stroke. A person may not be able to express him/herself verbally, understand others or be able to read and/or write.

Aphasia is seen most when there has been damage to the right side of the body.

Dysarthria is the inability to properly use the muscles that are involved in talking (tongue, palate and lips); thus, speech can be slow, slurred and not understood. Chewing and swallowing may also be a problem. If the person lacks feeling on one or both sides of the mouth, he/she is at risk of choking. A stroke can affect the person's cognitive ability to think and to plan and carry out tasks—even simple tasks. A person may not know how to start a task, or the sequence for doing the tasks, or may forget how to do simple tasks that he/she has done routinely for years. Both hemispheres of the brain control different functions of the body. If the left side of the brain is damaged, it affects the right side of the body, i.e., paralyzed right side, and/or speech/ language, memory and performance deficits and changes behavioral style to one that is slow and cautious. If the right side of the brain is damaged, it can cause paralysis on the left side of the body as well as deficits related to spatial, perceptual, memory and language deficits. Behavioral style may be quick and impulsive.

These are four types of strokes:

Cerebral Thrombosis is the most common type of stroke. It is caused when a blood clot (thrombus) forms and blocks an artery. This type of stroke usually occurs at night or first thing in the morning, when the blood pressure is low. It is often preceded by a TIA (transient ischemic attack), or a mini-stroke.

Cerebral Embolism results when a wandering clot (embolus) or some other particle forms in a blood vessel away from the brain, usually in the heart. The clot blocks an artery leading to the brain or in the brain. The most common cause of this type of emboli is blood clots formed during atrial fibrillation. The blood pools and clots in the atria, as a result of blood not being pumped out completely when the heart beats, because the atria quivers instead of beating effectively.

Subarachnoid Hemorrhage is caused by a rupture of a blood vessel on the surface of the brain. It bleeds into the space between the brain and the scull, but not into the brain.

Cerebral Hemorrhage is the result of a defective artery in the brain that bursts. The blood floods the surrounding tissue. A hemorrhage can be caused by an aneurysm bursting or a head injury. An aneurysm is a balloon-shaped, blood-filled pouch that projects from the weak spots in an artery wall. The amount of bleeding from a hemorrhage determines the severity of the cerebral hemorrhage. People can die from a cerebral hemorrhage because of increased pressure to the brain. People who live may recover better than a person who had a stroke caused by a blood clot. In the latter, the clot-injured brain cells can not rejuvenate. With a hemorrhage a part of the brain is compressed. As the person recovers, the pressure gradually diminishes. The brain may return to its normal state.

Cancer: Many cancers occur in people 50 years of age or older. The most common types in women are cancer of the breast, lung, uterus, colon or rectum.

Cancer of the prostate, rectum and lungs are the major cancers affecting men. Skin cancer is more prevalent among people with light skin and people who are exposed to the sun for extended periods of time.

Chronic Obstructive Pulmonary Disease (COPD): This is a group of diseases that include asthma, bronchitis, emphysema and bronchiectasis. The common factor in all the diseases is recurrent obstructive airflow.

Asthma (Bronchial Asthma) causes the airways to narrow as a reaction to non-specific factors such as respiratory infections, colds, emotions, fumes, exposure to chemicals, cold air and exercise. The bronchiole is obstructed on expiration. This can be caused by muscle spasm, edema of the mucosa, and thick secretions.

Atopic (Extrinsic) Asthma is caused by external agents, pollens, dust, mold spores, foods and insecticides. Exposure to allergens causes an attack.

Nonatopic (Intrinsic) Asthma means that the specific cause cannot be identified. It can be precipitated by a variety of situations such as a cold, upper respiratory infection and sometimes exercise.

Bronchiectasis develops over a period of time. It is caused by recurring inflammatory and infectious disease (pneumonia and chronic bronchitis type of cough) which affects the elasticity and muscle response of the bronchial walls. This is an irreversible condition.

Chronic Bronchitis is excessive mucus secretion in the bronchial tree, which causes chronic and recurrent productive cough.

Emphysema destroys the cilia under the mucus lining. It causes destruction of the alveolar air sacks in the walls of the lungs, creating large inefficient air spaces. The lungs lose their elasticity. It is difficult to breathe in fresh oxygen and to expel foreign matter (pollen, dust, chemical irritants, etc.). This affects the heart, as it has to work harder to pump blood —limited in oxygen—throughout the system. Exhalation is impaired, but inhalation is not obstructed.

Constipation: Older persons may experience a decrease in the frequency of bowel movements and difficulty in the passage of stool. This is a problem, but not a disease. Causes can include lack of fiber, fluid, exercise (decreased muscle tone), misuse of laxatives, some drugs (antidepressants, antacids containing aluminum or calcium, antihistamines, anti-Parkinson and diuretics) and ignoring the natural urge to defecate. Constipation can also be caused by a blockage or abnormalities in the digestive system.

Diabetes: There are two types of diabetes; insulin-dependent diabetes and non-insulin-dependent diabetes. The latter was previously referred to as adult-onset diabetes. Diabetes mellitus is a disorder. The body cannot convert foods into the energy needed for daily activity. Sugar and starches are changed to glucose. Control of glucose in the body breaks down. Glucose builds up to dangerous levels which causes symptoms and damages body organs. A diabetic coma can be caused when the glucose level becomes too high. Unconsciousness can result when the glucose level is too low (hypoglycemia). Diabetes can have long-term complications such as blindness, heart disease, gangrene, kidney failure, stroke and nerve damage.

Type I: Insulin-Dependent Diabetes: This form of diabetes, which is more severe, usually starts in childhood or adolescence. However, the onset can happen at any age. Insulin is required along with a controlled diet and exercise.

Type II: Non-Insulin-Dependent Diabetes. In this form of diabetes, glucose can be controlled by diet, exercise and weight-control.

Hearing: Adults over 65 may have some degree of hearing loss. Impaired hearing affects communication and socialization. People may become suspicious of others whom they think are mumbling and not speaking up loud enough to be heard. Hearing loss can be caused by environmental noise over a long period of time, build-up of fluid or ear wax, infection, abnormal bone growth, vascular accidents (stroke), heredity and/or normal age-related changes. A person who appears confused, uncooperative or not responsive may have a hearing impairment. Depending upon the cause and severity of the hearing impairment, some people can use a hearing aid, learn to read lips, or use sign language.

Central Deafness: This type of deafness is caused by damage to the nerve centers in the brain. The person is not able to understand language, even though sounds are heard. A hearing aid may be helpful.

Conductive Deafness: The mechanical movement in the inner or middle ear is impaired or blocked causing the inability of sound waves to travel properly through the ear. The person with this type of hearing impairment may feel that his/her voice is louder than normal and that voices and sounds from other sources seem muffled.

Presbycusis: This type of hearing impairment is sometimes referred to as old-age hearing. It is an inability to hear high-pitch tones, e.g., female voice, music).

Fibromyalgia is a rather new diagnosis that has affected adults of all ages.

Multiple Sclerosis (MS): This disease usually occurs between the ages of 20 and 40. It is due to the loss of myelin (the material that covers and insulates nerves). The myelin can be lost in any nerve in any part of the body. MS usually occurs in attacks. Each attack leaves a little more damage than the previous one. Some people will have remissions, in which there are no signs or symptoms of MS. Symptoms and severity are individualized. The first symptoms may be a tingling or temporary weakness of a body part after bathing. Other symptoms can include blurred vision, difficulty with speech, lack of bladder control, and unsteadiness in walking. In severe cases, persons may not be able to walk, feed themselves, hold their head up, maintain balance in a wheelchair, or project their voices to be heard in normal tones.

Osteoporosis: This systemic condition causes a reduction of bone mass or density, i.e., a thinning of the bones. Thus the bones are fragile and very susceptible to fractures. It is most common in post-menopausal women because of the loss of hormones. The wrists, hips and spine are the most common fracture sites. Vertebrae weakened by osteoporosis can cause spinal curvature, a forward curvature of the upper back. With the curvature is a loss of height. Treatment includes hormone replacement, exercise and calcium. Safety is important to prevent falls and fractures.

Vision: The four leading causes of loss of vision among older persons are cataracts, diabetic retinopathy, glaucoma and macular degeneration.

Cataracts: Behind the black pupil and color iris of the eye is a clear lens that focuses light into the eye. This lens becomes cloudy or opaque (cataract) as one ages. Depending upon the density and size of the cataract, there may be no vision loss or there may be a severe loss. The cataract may need to be removed when there is substantial loss of vision. Surgical removal of the cataract can restore vision for most people. It is 90% successful. After the removal of the cataract, focusing power is replaced by either an intraocular lens inserted in the eye during surgery, a contact lens that is worn on the comer (front of the eyes) or prescribed eyeglasses.

Diabetic Retinopathy: Diabetes can cause inadequate insulin production, which then damages the small blood vessels that nourish the retina. The blood vessels can leak, causing distorted vision. Blood can get into the center of the eye, causing severe loss of vision. Laser treatment can be used to seal off or reduce abnormal blood vessels. Potentially, this can reduce vision loss.

Glaucoma: Loss of vision can occur when there is pressure built up in the eye, due to faulty draining of normal eye fluids. Glaucoma occurs in people over 40 years of age. Glaucoma can be treated with prescribed eye drops, oral medication, laser treatment and surgery.

Macular Degeneration: This is the leading cause of severe vision loss of persons over 65 years of age. The macula (a special part of the retina) which is responsible for central vision loses its ability to function. Macular degeneration can cause an inability to recognize faces and read fine print. Vertical lines may be distorted. A person may see a dark spot in their vision. While central vision is impaired, peripheral vision is intact. Laser treatment can help some people. Most people benefit from using some type of magnification device.

The Special Senses

"Communicating through touch"

Sensory Perception

The **senses** tend to decline, with changes in the ability to see, hear, smell, taste and touch. Some changes begin to take place in the '40s, while others may not occur until the '70s or '80s.

Visual acuity changes markedly after age 40 or 50, limiting ability to accommodate to objects near and far. With pupils decreasing in size, allowing less light to enter, and lenses becoming more opaque, bifocals may be needed. The narrowing of the visual field results in a decrease in peripheral vision, and bright lights are required to see. Night-time vision is difficult. Glare can be disturbing. Older persons may need glasses or magnifying glasses for reading and close work, e.g., needlework, more light for any tasks, and/or a night light. Shields or sunglasses may be needed to reduce glare. Night time vision may be difficult. An older person may fear going out at night. A night light can diminish the fear of falling during the night. Some older persons will accept visual changes and be willing to try adaptive equipment to continue their leisure interests. Others prefer to give up the activity. Talking Books (widely distributed by The Library for the Blind and other organizations) are enjoyed by many people who are unable to read books or magazines. People unable to read the daily newspaper can listen to it being read by a volunteer through Radio Reading Service.

While this service is not as broad a service as the Talking Books, it is available in many major cities in the USA.

Hearing declines a little each year beginning in the mid-teens. The most noticeable gradual change occurs after age 50. High-frequency tones become more difficult to hear (presbycusis). When communicating with an older person, use a normal tone of voice, talk slowly, enunciate clearly and allow time for a person to respond. Many people talking at once and background noises (including music) may interfere with the ability to hear. Messages sent over an intercom may be distorted and hard to understand. Persons with hearing aids may withdraw from large group activities because they cannot hear over the background noise. Some type of amplification for one-to-one conversation and/or small and large groups can facilitate enjoyment of a visit or an activity requiring the ability to hear. A variety of amplification equipment is available through Radio Shack and other companies specializing in augmentative communication.

Taste buds (especially sweet and salt) decline slowly. After age 70 there is a more rapid decrease, making it difficult to distinguish tastes and causing food to seem flat and unappetizing. Teeth may be missing. A person may have to wear dentures. This may cause some chewing problems. Older people may want their food more highly seasoned. Chances are they will prefer a diet similar to the one they have always had. However, health problems often limit what a person may eat, causing dissatisfaction.

New food, snacks and beverages are continually being produced. Manufacturers identify the content of the food or beverage produced; assisting the buyer in knowing what is in the item. Some people enjoy trying new foods. Socials, parties, pot-luck dinners, holiday and seasonal celebrations, and special events are natural times to introduce people of all ages to new foods and/or beverages. Small sample bites of a new item are often appealing.

Smell declines as a result of destructive changes from a lifetime of upper respiratory infections, viruses, environmental toxins, etc. The lessened ability to smell affects one's ability to taste. Inability to smell can be dangerous. Body odors can be offensive and have a negative affect on socialization. The fear of having a body odor can also limit one's involvement in activities with others.

Touch diminishes, as does sensitivity to pain with age. An older person may not be able to feel to pick up or use small lightweight objects such as thread and needle for sewing. A person may be at risk if unable to distinguish hot from cold. This could have an adverse effect when a person is cooking, bathing, cleaning, or involved in outdoor activity.

Dementia and Alzheimer's Disease
"Love isn't love until it is shared"

Dementia is caused by specific disease or pathology. It is characterized by loss of intellectual abilities that interfere with functioning (roles, responsibilities, activities of daily living, and social functioning). Some conditions can be stabilized, some can be reversed and others cannot. Dementia is caused by a specific brain disease and/or by a lack of adequate blood flow to the brain (multiinfarct dementia).

Alzheimer's disease is a disease that causes dementia, first named in 1907 by Dr. Alois Alzheimer. It causes malfunction and death of nerve cells. Specific diagnostic traits of Alzheimer's are amyloidal plaques and neurofibrillary tangles which are abnormal deposit of dead and dying cells and twisted protein fragments inside nerve cells. This is causes a decrease in brain chemicals such as acetylcholine which is the chemical bridge between nerve cell. There is currently no prevention or cure for Alzheimer's disease.

Alzheimer's disease is the most common cause of dementia and is most often a disease of older persons usually diagnosed after age sixty. It is estimated that over four million persons in the United States suffer from Alzheimer's (2007). Like other dementia a person with Alzheimer's is characterized as having memory loss and deterioration of memory function. At first Alzheimer's may be mistaken as normal memory loss in older persons. As time goes on the person with Alzheimer's will not only have memory loss but planning and thinking becomes increasingly difficult. Later the ability to perform the normal activities of daily living declines until the person needs full care.

Creutz-Deldt-Jacob Disease is caused by a slow-acting virus, although there is a genetic component. It is characterized by global mental impairment and general apathy and confusion. Mad cow disease.

Dementia with Lewy Bodies (DLB) is one of the most common types of dementia. Symptoms include drowsiness, lethargy, staring into space and disorganized speech. Persons affected by this disease may have visual hallucinations, as well as loss of spontaneous movement and depression. The disease is caused by a build-up of lewy bodies which are an accumulation of bits of alpha-synuclein protein. These nuclei of neurons are found in areas of the brain that control particular aspects of memory and motor control. Researchers don't know why this alpha-synuclein accumulates into lewy bodies.

There is a link between lewy bodies and Parkinson's disease since both diseases are related to "synucleinapathies" of multiple systems. Lewy bodies are often found in Parkinson's as well as Alzheimer's so diagnosis is difficult to pinpoint. Some medications may assist to control some psychotic or motor symptoms. Like Alzheimer's and Parkinson's, Dementia with Lewy Bodies is a neurodegenerative disorder that progressively causes a deterioration of the intellect and motor skills. Average survival time is about eight years.

Fronto-temporal Dementia (also know as Pick's Disease) is caused by the shrinking of key parts of the brain due to damage and loss of nerve cells and their connectors. Fronto-temporal Dementia shrinkage of the brain is similar to Alzheimer's, Creutz-Deldt-Jacob, Lewy Bodies and Huntington disease. The shrinking pattern is different in each of these diseases and yet persons suffering from these diseases can show similar symptoms.

Fronto-temporal dementia involves a disturbance of behavior and personality. Patients change their character and become uninhibited and restless. This results in anti-social attitudes and action. Often patients with this disease will limit their range of behavior to repetitive and ritualistic activity. They lack insight into their illness and adopt an uncaring and unsympathetic attitude toward friends and family. In the later stages the patient becomes apathetical and less talkative. Physically the patient gradually wastes away and has problems swallowing and breathing. This is Motor Neuron Disease which can develop in young adults and often runs in families. The duration of the disease can last for a number of years.

Parkinson's disease: This disease starts about the age of 50 or 60. It is a progressive, degenerative disease which is individualized. The first symptoms include a rhythmic shaking of the hands and/or head and a "pill-rolling" rubbing of the thumb and forefinger. These movements stop when a person is involved in an activity, but return when the activity ceases. As the disease progresses, a person may have difficulty starting movement, changing position and talking. The face becomes mask-like (flat) with little expression and decreased eye-blinking. Posturing is a forward flexion of the trunk. Muscles become weak and rigid. The person walks with a shuffling gait. Dementia is gradual, with initial forgetfulness, episodes of minor confusion and depression, followed by irritability, paranoia, visual hallucination,

and social isolation. Dysphasia (the inability to swallow) may occur as the disease progresses. Scaly and dry skin appears around the eyebrows and ears. A person may have problems with urinary retention, urgency or hesitation in micturition, gastric retention and constipation.

Vascular Dementia can be determined by autopsies. Up to 20% of patients with dementia are victims of this disease. Multi-Infract Dementia (MID) is one type of Vascular Dementia which is caused by multiple strokes that affect the brain. MID is caused by blood clots in the brain leading to the death of brain tissue. High blood pressure and diabetes which cause MID are treatable.

Most often the onset of Multi-Infract dementia occurs between the ages of 60 to 75. Poor cognitive and motor function, psychiatric problems, inappropriate social behavior, memory loss, migraines, depression, incontinence and hallucinations are symptoms of Multi-Infract dementia.

Symptoms of vascular dementia vary according to the severity of the strokes, but include:

- Memory loss
- Confusion
- Forgetfulness
- Poor concentration
- Inability to copy with simple daily activities
- Inability to follow simple instructions
- Laughing or crying inappropriately
- Behavioral changes
- Impaired social skills
- Eating problems
- A shuffling or jerky gait
- Incontinence and/or lack of bowel control
- dementia

Binswanger's Dementia is an uncommon subtype of multi-infract dementia which affects the deep hemispheric white matter of the brain. Binswanger's is a neurological disease that affects the frontal lobes of the brain. Binswanger dementia is linked with hypertension and severe atherosclerosis. Symptoms are intellectual impairment, personality changes, mood swings and memory loss which become progressively worse.

Effects of Pharmaceuticals

"Medication is a daily activity"

Medications

Medications are prescribed by doctors or physician assistants to treat disease and/or alleviate pain, itching, and discomfort, to affect mood state, to induce sleep, etc. Older persons often take multiple prescribed medications for acute and chronic illnesses, as well as over-the-counter drugs. Medications may be prescribed to alleviate adverse side effects from specific medications. Sometimes a person has to learn to live with side effects of a life-saving medication.

Problems

One of the problems for the elderly is that they may have several physicians prescribing medications for specific diseases. They may or may not have a family physician overseeing their total health care and medication regimen.

An older person may not know body parts (particularly internal organs) and/or understand body systems. Medications may be identified by color or by the times they are taken versus the names of the medication. The purpose of medications may not be fully understood. The necessity of taking milk, water, or food with medications or not eating specific foods with certain medications may not be understood or followed.

Forgetfulness can affect the frequency and amount of medications taken. Impaired vision and/or the inability to open medications can result in noncompliance with a medication therapy. Uncomfortable side effects or feeling better are often the reasons given for stopping prescribed medications without first consulting a physician.

An older person may not understand how medications are absorbed in the body. Medications are discontinued if they don't work fast enough or if the initial normal side effects are too unpleasant or uncomfortable. The need to allow the body time to adjust to medications or withdrawal from them may not be understood. Older people have a right to refuse medication. However, they may not want to learn how the medication can help them. Another problem is that an older person may not understand the rationale for medications.

Drug Therapy in the Elderly

"Drugs help to balance the body chemistry"

I.   Factors affecting drug action in the body

A.   Absorption
1.   To have an effect in the body, the drug must first break into smaller particles and dissolve in gastric juices. Only after dissolving can the drug be absorbed into the bloodstream. Once absorbed, the drug is distributed to other parts of the body. Some factors of absorption are affected by the aging process.

B.   Distribution
1.   Occurs when the drug moves from the bloodstream to various fluids and tissues within the body. Some factors affecting distribution which are related to the aging process are:
    a.   decreased plasma protein
    b.   increased proportion of body fat (longer effects from certain drugs)
    c.   less body water

C.   Metabolism and Excretion
1.   Most drugs are metabolized in the liver and excreted by the kidneys. However, elimination occurs by other routes such as perspiration or saliva. Factors affecting metabolism and excretion are liver and kidney function. The rate at which a drug is metabolized varies with each individual. Hepatic (liver) function and renal (kidney) function normally decline with age.

D.   Age
1.   The elderly usually need lower doses and longer dosage intervals because hepatic func-

tion and renal function generally decrease with age.

E. Multiple Drug Therapy and Disease State

1. Other factors can interfere with the drug's ability to exert full therapeutic effect. The most common symptoms/signs of adverse drug reaction in the elderly are:
    a. confusion
    b. constipation
    c. depression
    d. extra pyramidal symptoms
    e. falls
    f. incontinence
    g. memory loss
    h. restlessness

Adverse Effects of Medication

Medications can have adverse physical and psychological effects. Physically a person may feel tired, weak, drowsy and/or dizzy. Other physical symptoms can include dry mouth, blurred vision, elevated or lowered blood pressure, headaches, ringing in the ears, dehydration, bloating, nausea, stomach irritation, ulcers, diarrhea, constipation, urinary retention or incontinence, increased or decreased heart rate, electrolyte imbalance and loss of appetite.

Psychological effects can include hallucinations, mood swings, depression, agitation, paradoxical excitement and change in affect. Psychoactive medications can cause extra pyramidal effects in varying degrees. Extra pyramidal effects are characterized by involuntary movements of the head, face, mouth, neck, and/or tongue. Other effects include stiffness of arms and legs, changes in gait pattern and disturbance in posture.

Importance of Knowing About Medications

Activity professionals need to be aware of medications that participants/residents are taking, as medication can affect a person's participation in activity. The side effects may deter participation.

A person may refuse to participate in an activity if he/she is experiencing one or more adverse physiological and/or psychological effects.

In community settings and in health care settings, the activity professional may be the first person to see changes in a participant that may be potential side effects of medication. This change needs to be discussed with the participant as well as with nurses in a health-care setting. Side effects are often displayed one to two hours after medication is taken. Many medications are taken before or after meals. Some activities are conducted one to three hours after meals. The activity professional may be the first person to see a change in a participant.

Activity professional needs to know food restrictions related to medications for planning food-related activities. Dairy products (milk, ice cream, cheese) may not be allowed. This would necessitate having substitute foods at a party, ice cream social, coffee hour, wine and cheese party or picnic, and/or not offering milk-based puddings for sensory stimulation.

In community settings, activity professionals need to be aware of medications in case of an emergency. Paramedics need to know a person's medication and to relate this information to other health care professionals if the ill or injured person is not able to give the information. In long-term-care facilities activity professionals need to carry a list of medications for each resident on outings. This is for emergency purposes. Time does not always allow a call to the facility in an emergency to get a list of medications for paramedics or emergency-room staff. It is also important to have a list of medications to which a person is allergic or sensitive.

Resources for Knowing about Medications

Activity professionals are not trained in pharmacology, yet need to know basic information to communicate with participants/residents, physicians, nurses and other health-care team-members.
All health-care organizations have books on medication. The most popular is the *Physician's Desk Reference* that is updated annually. There are a variety of nurses' books on drugs and medication. Local book stores and public libraries have books on drugs and medications for non-medical persons. Pharmaceutical companies provide literature on the drugs that they manufacture and distribute. Pharmacists can provide computerized patient education information on specific drugs. The information sheets identify the name of a drug, what it is used for, how the medication is to be taken, potential side effects, precautions, and drug interaction information if pertinent.

Physicians, pharmacists and nurses are good resources for answering questions. Local health/disease related organizations offer education classes that include information on medication, such as the Diabetes Association or the Heart Association. A local pharmacist can provide in-service and continuing education programs in facilities and in the community. Courses on pharmacology are offered at colleges and universities; however, there usually are required academic prerequisites.

Medication Education

Education programs on medicine for older adults can be a part of a community-based or long-term care program. Education classes can be on medication in general or focus on specific medications.

Medication education is very much a part of a wellness model of programming. Speakers, video, skits, printed material, and homework assignments can all be a part of a medication education program. Programs can be singular, a series or on-going.

Pharmacists, physicians, nurses from local hospitals, health-care agencies and pharmaceutical companies often provide free educational services. Most speakers prefer one month to three months notice. Programs of 45 to 60 minutes can be planned weekly, bi-weekly, monthly, or quarterly depending upon the need and interests of participants.

See Appendix F for Drug List.

Psychosocial Challenges to Older Adults' Wellbeing

"All humans experience isolation and alienation as well as moments of jubilation and celebration"

Cognitive

Brain cells begin to decline by age 20, but normal intelligence does not decline until the 80's. The brain has two hemispheres (left and right). Each sphere is responsible for different functions:

>   ***Left Brain*** involves language, reading, writing, arithmetic, some types of logical thinking, organization, and movement/sensation on the right side of the body.

>   ***Right Brain*** involves emotional control, creativity, music, processing of non-verbal materials such as pictures, higher mathematics and movement/sensation on the left side of the body.

Intelligence is one's ability to learn or understand reason, apply knowledge, and to think abstractly. There are two types of intelligence:

>   ***Crystallized intelligence*** includes the skills, abilities and understanding gained through instruction and observation in school and personal experience. It increases throughout a life span, because it is based on cumulative learning. Crystallized intelligence compensates for the loss of fluid intelligence.

>   ***Fluid intelligence*** is the adaptability and capacity to perceive things and integrate them mentally. It is the ability to shift from the familiar to the unfamiliar patterns, and visual motor flexibility. Fluid intelligence increases from infancy through adolescence. It levels off during adulthood and there is a steady decline in middle age and late adulthood.

Memory is the retention and retrieval of new material. It includes short-term memory, long-term memory and remote memory. Memory loss is not a part of the normal aging process. It is experienced more through a disease process.

>   ***Short-term memory*** is the ability to recall information from a few seconds to a few weeks immediately after it has been received

>   ***Long-term memory*** is the storage of important information. It can be stored through a variety of learning and living experiences.

>   ***Remote memory*** is reliving the past. Once something is stored, it can be retrieved. It may take an older person more time to process and retrieve the information.

Learning includes the ability/capacity to learn. Performance is the ability to put forth what was learned. Older people can continue to learn. Motivation, cautiousness and meaningfulness of the tasks are all a part of the learning process. Older people need more time to process information, and instruction needs to be slower than for younger people. Memorization and rehearsing materials are two methods of learning. Organization of materials into topics and subheadings is another method of learning.

Personality

Personality is the sum total of an individual. It is the complex characteristics that distinguish one person from another, including organization, beliefs, behavior, habits and perceptions. Personality remains stable throughout adulthood. A person becomes more unique with age. A person becomes more of who he/she is and is clearer about what it is he/she wants, likes or dislikes. Slight changes may be seen in older adults as abilities and energy declines. The person with the outgoing personality will still be outgoing but not as demonstrative. There may be a slight turning inward as one becomes more cautious and experiences the slowing down of physical and sensory functioning.

Socialization

Socialization is the interaction and interdependent relationships with people. It is a learned pattern of behavior which can remain constant or change over a lifetime. Socialization is related to personality, motivation and opportunities to be involved with others. Some older persons prefer limited social involvement outside the family, while others prefer and seek relationships outside the family circle. Childhood friends can remain close throughout the life span. Friendships developed with neighbors, or through work, church, community groups, etc. can be the most important relationships for some older persons. Acquaintances may be many but true friends may be few.

Factors Affecting Socialization

At any stage of development, there are many factors that affect socialization. First, the individual sets the stage for what he/she prefers concerning with whom he/she wishes to socialize. Some people prefer to be alone and are happy. Others are alone and are unhappy. One individual may be at ease initiating a conversation while another is at ease in responding to a greeting or conversation. Friendships are often developed around interests (art, music, dancing, sports, church, gardening, travel, etc.), work, involvement with family/school/community activities, and causes. Socioeconomic status, values, philosophy of life, religious preferences and practices, the area in which one lives (geographical location), weather, transportation, and physical/emotional health all affect socialization. Roles change over a lifetime. One is born a son or daughter and acquires a family role of sister, brother, grandchild, aunt, uncle, cousin, etc. Upon marriage one becomes a spouse, mother, father, grandparent and great grandparent. Through death of a spouse, one becomes a widow or widower. Responsibilities also change with roles. As an adult, one may be responsible for elderly parents/relatives, while simultaneously being responsible for adult children and grandchildren. In older adulthood, one may become dependent upon younger members of the family for support, care, homemaking, yard maintenance tasks, transportation, etc. When there is no family to which to turn for support/assistance, a significant other becomes the prime provider. Often this person is a distant relative, a member of the extended family, or a friend.

Successful Adaptations to Aging

"Aging is a process of moving from awareness to acceptance, from action to adaptation"

An older adult can experience one or more chronic conditions, physical and/or psychosocial problems. The onset of problems may occur before or after age 65. Some older adults accept and cope with disabilities and losses; others may become helpless and feel powerless.

Losses and Adaptations
The normal process of living involves development, losses, change, adjustments and adaptations throughout the life span. Losses appear more prevalent in older adulthood. Whether losses are physical, cognitive, social or financial, they have an emotional effect on a person. Some people cope better than others, depending upon their attitude, previous coping experiences, health, finances, spiritual beliefs and support systems.

Normal physical changes and losses require acceptance and adjustment. Losses due to illness, disease and disabilities often require greater adjustment and coping ability. Financial loss, such as living on a fixed income, determines how an older person will utilize his/her resources to meet physical needs (food, clothing, shelter, health and dental care), social needs (involvement with family and friends, giving of gifts, entertaining, local and long distance telephoning, transportation), cognitive needs (stimulation, learning, creativity), spiritual needs (involvement in church and religious services, groups and activities), emotional needs (involvement with others, expression of feelings) and leisure interests.

Loss of work role and responsibilities can greatly affect one's feelings of self-worth and self-esteem. Years of being productive and in the work force provide structure, feelings of success, accomplishments and pride in caring for one's self and family, as well as socialization. Some people look forward to retirement; others would prefer to continue to work for any variety of reasons, most importantly economic. Women who have not worked outside the home have to adjust to a spouse being at home all the time versus just during nonworking hours.

In adult and middle age, parents experience the natural progression and independence of their children. They have to adjust to their adult children no longer needing them to meet their basic needs. They also have to adjust to the role of being an in-law and a grandparent. Sometimes, they may have to adjust to their adult child moving back home with or without children. Retired older adults may lose their freedom (time, space, responsibility, utilization of financial resources, socialization, etc.) as the needs in the family change. They may become responsible for support and care of an older relative or close friend, and/or children and grandchildren. Loss of family, relatives and friends through death is usually experienced more in older age than during a person's younger years. Sometimes these losses are experienced one right after another without adequate time for grieving and acceptance of the loss. These losses can affect the person socially and emotionally as well as financially.

Losses, changes in abilities, increased disabilities, illness and change in marital status and family relationships as well as friends, decrease opportunities for socialization. These changes and challenges affect how persons think and feel about themselves. One person may be positively challenged whereas another may become depressed, helpless and feel powerless.

Relationship between Physical and Psychosocial Functions

"We can't change our birthday but can change our behavior"

The weight of the brain decreases and neurons are reduced in number. An older person needs more time to respond and to react, but sensory function is not reduced. Instructions for an activity may need to be given more slowly and be repeated. Recall of information involving short-term, long-term and/or remote memory may take longer, i.e., reality orientation questions, trivia questions, reminiscing. Knowing a person's predominant sense, i.e., auditory or visual helps to facilitate memory and recall. One person may retain or remember something if he/she sees it, while another person may do better if he/she hears the information. Reaction time may be slower when one is involved in physical, i.e., the gross motor movement of exercise, sports, lifting, bending, etc., as well as the fine-motor movement in picking up and using small objects for crafts and games, etc., creative, cognitive, and affective activities. Safety is a concern when an older person with decreased sensory awareness is engaged in activities involving contact with cold or heat, i.e., cooking, baking, crafts, outdoor activities, walking, gardening, etc.

Normal physical changes of aging are gradual. Acceptance, adjustment and adaptation to the change can be upsetting to some and taken in stride by others.

Common Psychological Disorders – Symptoms and Interventions

"A positive attitude assists in accepting physical and psychosocial changes"

Psychosocial Problems

Affective Disorders are characterized by a disturbance in mood and feelings. These disorders have symptoms of mania (elation), depression or both. Major affective disorders are diagnosed when the full syndrome of a manic or depressive episode is present.

Bipolar Disorder (Manic-Depressive Disorder) is characterized by a manic stage with an elevated mood and excessive mental and physical activity. Symptoms include hyperactivity boundless energy, little need for sleep, rapid change of thoughts, distractibility, impulsiveness, and increased grandiose ideas about self, power, abilities, participating in many activities/projects but not finishing projects, dangerous activities (reckless driving, investments, purchases with or without financial ability), irritability and impatience, and the person can be potentially assaultive when limits are set. The manic stage is usually short, i.e., up to two weeks, followed by depression.

Major Depression is characterize by dysphonic (depressed) mood and disinterest in activities and pleasure. Symptoms include loss of energy, weight, appetite, interest and pleasure in usual activities (including sex), psychomotor agitation or retardation, sleeping problems, feelings of low self-esteem, worthlessness, dependency and difficulty in thinking. Older adults may have memory loss and/or disorientation.

Cyclothymiacs Disorder is not as severe as a major depression or manic disorder. The disorder is cyclic with periods of elation and depression as well as months of normal effect. The duration is usually two or more years.

Dysthymic Disorder (Depressive Personality Disorder) has characteristics similar to major depression. Psychotic symptoms and mood swings are not present. The condition continues over time, with no clear onset. A person may show other symptoms such as a sense of emptiness, dissatisfaction with life, irritability and/or concern with suicide.

Anxiety Disorders are characterized by fear or avoidance that prevent social functioning and curtails intimate relationships and/or work. Symptoms include sweating, dizziness, diarrhea, upset stomach, dryness in the mouth, hyperventilation (shallow breathing), pains in the chest, lump in the throat, choking, frequent urination (with no physical cause), inability to concentrate, recurring thoughts that are not dispelled by logic, rigidity and difficulty in making changes.

Anxiety States (Neurosis) occurs without a specific trigger. Fear can center on one or more things/situations such as dying, losing control, inability to do something, having a specific disease or disability or becoming insane.

Obsessive-Compulsive Disorders are characterized by having an obsession and a compulsion. Obsession is a frequent focus on issues such as losing control, a body part or function, fear (e.g., fear of germs), or total focus on a specific interest (trains). Compulsive behavior is ritualistic behavior, e.g., excessive hand washing, continual dusting and cleaning, repetitive checking of switches being off or other ritualistic behavior, to reduce anxiety although it serves no real purpose. The person is unable to control thoughts and behavior.

Phobic Disorders are related to irrational fears of circumstances (riding in an elevator, being in a crowded room, riding in a car), or objects (insects, animals). The fear is much greater than the actual danger and interferes with functioning. The person who is afraid of crowds won't go out of house or room, if living in an institution.

Chemical Dependency is a chronic disease that is incurable, progressive and fatal in nature. It is a dependency upon mood-altering chemical including alcohol. One becomes preoccupied with drug or alcohol usage, has increased tolerance to the drug or alcohol, changes his/her life style to accommodate usage and experiences harmful consequences from usage. The disease affects a person physically, mentally, emotionally, socially and spiritually. Drug addiction (marijuana, cocaine, heroine) is seen more in young and middle-age people. Older adults can become dependent on prescription and/or over-the-counter drugs. Some over-the-counter drugs contain alcohol that may be habit-forming.

Older patients in hospitals or in outpatient treatment may be taking antipsychotic, antidepressant, antianxiety or pain-relieving medication. The effect of drugs in older persons is different from younger people. Older persons may abuse prescriptive medication to feel good, better, etc. and ultimately can become dependent.

Alcohol is the first drug of choice among older people. Alcoholism among the elderly is described as being early-onset or late-onset. Early-onset is when the dependency on alcohol occurred prior to retirement. In late-onset, the dependency occurs after retirement. An older social drinker may become dependent on alcohol when he/she experiences one or more losses (job, spouse, family members, friends, income, home, independence, health, body part or function, etc.). In the late-onset as well as the early-onset thus, the person finds life and its problems too big for coping and turns to alcohol for relief.

Older people process alcohol more slowly than younger people. This can cause intoxication from mild drinking. Alcohol can have potentially dangerous effects when combined with medication. A person may not read the warning label or not adhere to the warning on prescription and over-the-counter-drugs causing unintentional personal harm.

Delirium usually starts rapidly and lasts for a brief duration. It is characterized by rapid decrease in mental functioning (orientation, memory, thought process), sleep-disturbance and ability to cope with the environment. In older persons, it can be caused by alcoholism; medications; nutrition; depression or acute emotional stress; cardio-vascular, vascular, and/or pulmonary conditions; post trauma or surgical reactions, fevers, tumors, and metabolic imbalances.

Dementia Abuse Statistics
Source the National Ombudsman Report 2003

19,000 reported cases of abuse to Alzheimer's residents by gross neglect

83,000 reported cases of reported cases of dignity, respect and staff attitude

2200 reported cases of wandering and elopement

This is due to lack of education which causes staff not to have sensitivity and burnout

Education is lacking in most Long-term Care Facilities. Most facility in-services are 20-30 minutes long and in most cases nightshift watch videos and as a Consultant one often witnessed staff talking, sleeping and even using cell phones. Most successful in-services have live interaction with instructors.

Twenty-six states require dementia training for those who work with older adults.

Depression has many causes and appears in different degrees of intensity and duration. Depression can be a dominate problem or one of many problems related to a specific diagnosis and/or disability, situation or circumstance. Depression can range from a short period of feeling down in the dumps to severe depression. A let down from the excitement over a family/holiday celebration, feeling sad over the loss of a possession (broken or stolen) or feeling blue/down for no apparent reason are examples of temporary depression, in which recovery occurs in a short period of time (hour, day, week).

Older persons experience a variety of losses over time (family, friend, roles, responsibilities, home, income, abilities, etc.) People are normally saddened by these losses and go through a grief process that includes a period of depression. When the grieving process has been worked through, a person is able to go on with life. If the person gets stuck in the depressive phase, the sadness and dejection may intensify over time leading to greater depression—an affective disorder of major depression.

Emotional symptoms of depression include anxiety; crying; feelings of helplessness; hopelessness; rejection of any positive comments; disinterest in appearance, hygiene, home, or environment; environment; wanting to be in a darkened room; self-centeredness and lack of concern for others; anger; hostility; and suicidal ideas. Physically a person may have a lack or increase of appetite, weight loss or gain, sleep disturbance (inability to sleep or excessive sleep), somatic complaints (aches and pains) or the inability to perform basic activities of daily living because of a perceived physical limitation. Cognitive behaviors can include a change in the thought process, memory, orientation, obsessive thoughts/ideas, limited verbalization, slowed speech, and negative statement about self ("I can't") or about others. Socially, a person who is depressed withdraws from people, relationships and activity.

Helplessness is the discomfort of not having a need fulfilled, feeling anxious and being unable to act (physically, mentally, emotionally, socially) to relieve the discomfort. It is the inability to mobilize energy to effect a change.

Learned Helplessness is a state where a person perceives events as being uncontrollable. The person may respond by being passive, depressed, anxious, or unable to be successful. An older person may exhibit learned helplessness when a spouse dies, and he/she feels that he/she can't take care of him/herself. After having a stroke or another type of disability, a person may want to be waited on versus wanting to try to learn to use adaptive techniques for eating, bathing, grooming, dressing or ambulation. When the struggle is perceived as being too great, the person gives up.

Powerlessness is a perceived lack of control over a situation or immediate event. The degree of powerlessness can be affected by the importance of a desired goal/outcome, the person's expectation and perception of being in control, or belief that his/her actions will make a difference in the final outcome.

An older person may feel powerless over a health, housing, family, financial or other problem and let someone else assume power and/or responsibility. Voting for an elected officer may be perceived as the individual's vote not counting, so the person doesn't vote. Feeling that death is the ultimate stage of life, one may not want to follow a diet, take medication, or be involved in medical treatment, because he/she is old and is going to die anyway. The feeling of powerlessness may have been a part of a person's entire life. It can also be a new perception for an older person who has experienced significant losses.

The onset of problems may occur before or after age 65. Some older adults accept and cope with disabilities and losses; others may become helpless and feel powerless.

Needs, Tasks & Intervention for Dealing with Loss

There are many normal changes in the biological process of the body as one ages. Because changes are individualized, they can happen to different people at different ages. Only a few of the most prevalent changes will be discussed here.

Universal Needs
- Need to belong
- Need to love and be loved.
- Need to be useful
- Need to be respected
- Need to be responsible
- Need to make choices

The need to belong starts with the family unit and expands to other groups throughout life. Membership in churches, clubs, organizations, and involvement in school, work, and the community provide a sense of belonging. Being a graduate of the class of 1945 (for example) gives one an identity with peers of the same class. Being an employee of a specific business or organization also satisfies the need to belong (to a work force). Some older adults fulfill their belonging needs in later life by becoming members of a senior center and/or new groups related to specific interests and hobbies.

Love also starts with family and expands to others throughout life. One learns to trust parents or significant others at an early age, and this sense of love grows. Intimate relationships are developed. It is not enough to love others; one also needs to feel loved. People express their love physically, emotionally and socially. A willingness to go out of one's way to help another can be both an expression of brotherly love and emotionally uplifting. The words "I love you" are an expression of one's love for another. Acceptance and return of this expression fulfills both individuals' needs. (This is not to imply that the words "I love you" need to be spoken to feel love for another or be loved by another.) Expressions of love are in many forms such as acts of kindness and helping others, remembrance of birthdays/significant holidays with cards/gifts, a telephone call/letter to inquire how someone is, spending time with another person, sharing a meal with someone and/or accepting someone unconditionally.

Older adults show their love in a variety of ways for different generations of family members. Being a grandparent and having time to share with grandchildren and great-grandchildren can create special bonds. Imparting values, family history and support of younger generations is a means of sharing love. Preparing and leaving a legacy—whether it is material or nonmaterial—is a form of love for others and future generations. Feeling useful gives one a sense of pride. Time and talents are utilized to varying extents. Words or deeds of appreciation, while welcomed, are not needed to feel "useful." Only the person who actually gives of him/herself can feel useful. It is an inner indescribably satisfying feeling of doing something for someone or for a cause. Older adults have a variety of abilities, skills, experiences and time to share with others. This could be helping within the family, neighborhood, or community, or volunteering in agencies, organizations and facilities.

Respect is earned. A child learns to respect parents or significant others as well as how it feels to be respected. This respect grows and is extended to others. Addressing a person by name of his/her preference, role, social and/or professional status is one form of respect. Another aspect is what and how something is said to another, being aware of another's feelings, rights and preferences as well as role and position in society. Respect is something one feels and gives to another. Older adults are referred to with respect as mother, father, grandma, grandpa, Mr., Mrs., or Ms. A person may be respected for his/her kind deeds, knowledge, skills and abilities within the family and/or community. A retired person may be referred to with respect from former co-workers and peers.

Learning to take responsibility starts at an early age. Putting away one's toys is learning to take responsibility for care of possessions. Learning to be responsible for one's actions and consequences is a lifelong learning experience. Responsibility includes caring for oneself and the health and safety of others, caring for one's own possessions and the possessions of others, using talents and skills to make a living and help others, respecting rights and laws, and accepting consequences for irresponsible behavior.

As one ages responsibilities remain the same, yet change. There is the responsibility of caring for family and friends, accomplishing work-related tasks, making a living, and caring for one's health, home and possessions. There is also the responsibility of planning for retirement and making arrangements for disposal of personal property after death. The latter responsibility includes making a will, informing family of health-related decisions, e.g., living will, arrangements for funeral (preferences), financial arrangements for burial, and informing family or significant others of wishes related to disbursement of personal property. Opportunities to make choices in daily living, work, leisure and religion provides a sense of control, mastery and independence. Individual choices facilitate personal expression, interests, preferences, direction and goals. An individual is often characterized by choices in clothing, housing, speech, expression of feelings, education, role and societal status, leisure and religious pursuits, etc. Opportunities to make choices related to change is accepted by some and rejected by others, which results in dynamic inter-relationships in the family, at home, at work and in the community. Older adults have many opportunities to make choices in later life. These choices include housing and living arrangements, financial expenditure, use of leisure time, involvement with family, friends and the community, religion, politics, work, i.e., new career, part-time work and volunteer work. Human needs must be recognized in all activity settings. Activities provide a means for meeting needs. There are opportunities to belong to groups, feel loved and share love, feel useful and respected, take responsibility and make choices.

Needs of Residents in Long Term Care

In addition to the universal needs, residents in long term care facilities have other specific needs including the following:

1. Need to adjust to illness, disease and/or disability.
2. Need to adjust to losses related to entering a long-term-care facility (family, friends, home, routine, community, etc.).
3. Need to adjust to living in a new environment and community, the community being the people living, working, volunteering and visiting within the facility as well as the broader community (the public community). Residents capable of going on outings with family, staff or volunteer have more opportunity to become familiar with the public community which may be different from where they used to live, i.e., different neighborhood, area of the city, or state.

4. Need to become acquainted with residents and staff, and to develop trust relationships.
5. Need opportunities to be independent and make decisions when capable and to continue former lifestyle as much as possible.
6. Need activities to relieve boredom, loneliness, depression and withdrawal, and to promote a positive attitude and self-confidence.
7. Need activities to continue former interests, develop new interests, have something in which to look forward; to promote wellness (physical, mental, emotional and social well-being); foster continuation of religious practices as well as involvement in the community (i.e., attending church in the community, shopping and attending social activities, etc.) and with the family.
8. Need activities which are adapted to the residents' needs, interests, preferences and functional abilities, to emphasize what they can do rather than what they cannot do.

Palliative & Hospice Care

"We are called to show compassion"

What is Palliative or Hospice Care?

Palliative care is given to patients/residents who are suffering from chronic and serious illness. Palliative care provides much the same care as hospice. The major difference is hospice care is determined by the doctor who does the diagnosis – the patient/resident has up to six months to live while palliative care has no time frame. These programs have been provided for more than 30 years.

Both hospice and palliative care seek to lessen the pain and discomfort for dying persons. Persons are supported with love and care. Basic needs, such as physical, spiritual, emotional and mental, at the end of life are being met by treating and comforting the patient resident. The patient/resident should be as free of pain and distress as possible. Family members are greatly relieved when they see their loved one relatively free of pain.

Comfort treatment is the primary goal in palliative and hospice care in the last months of a patient/resident's life. These comfort measures may be offered in various settings: hospital, nursing facility, assisted living, or home. The focus is to improve, to the degree possible, the quality of life for the dying person.

Care Givers

Hospice and other palliative caregivers are trained professionals who develop special skills to care for the dying. Teams are made up of two or more of the following caregivers: doctor, nurse, social worker, chaplain, home health aide, family members, and volunteers as well as others. Hospitals, hospice and other programs organize persons with a special philosophy of love and care as well as develop rules and regulations that guide the caregivers. These caregivers comfort and support more than a million dying Americans every year.

Who Can Receive Palliative Care?

Anyone who is seriously ill and is judged to be in the end of life state may receive palliative care. Hospice limits care to those determined by the doctor to be within six months of death. Palliative care patients/residents may receive treatment and curative care while hospice provides medicines and treatments aimed at providing comfort and support.

Who are the Payers?

Medicare and Medicaid will cover those who are eligible for some treatments and medications in palliative care. Medicare pays all charges for hospice care while in most, but not all, states Medicaid will cover the hospice charges. Some private insurance policies will pay for some treatment and medicines for palliative care while most private insurances pay for hospice care. In palliative care payments are based on services that the patient/resident receives. In hospice care covered by Medicare and Medicaid the providers are paid with a package deal. Palliative and hospice care provide treatment and comfort that assist patients/residents in receiving treatment and tender loving care at the end of life.

Life Story is a simple assessment that is used before dementia accelerates. The information is used in a palliative care setting and is clearly posted for staff use. The information allows the more personal approach to the resident and also humanizes for the staff. (See sample on next page.)

Life Story

My name is_____. I like to be called_____.

I was born on_____ in _____. I am from a family of_____.

My parent's names were_____.

Education: _____

Cultural/ethnic background _____ Language _____

My occupations were _____.

I was married to _____ and have _____ children,

I was married on_____, place of Marriage_____.

I have _____ grandchildren

Grandchildren names_____

Some of my favorite hobbies\ interests\travels included:

_____

_____

Some of the things I like to talk about include:

_____

_____

Military service_____ and Volunteer service_____

Some of my accomplishments are:

_____

Some of my favorite rituals are: (reading the morning paper, shower before bed)

_____

Some of my favorite music is _____

Other things you should know about me include:

_____

_____

Death & Dying

"Residents/clients are moving from independence to dependence and death"

Dying is the process of moving toward death. In a sense humans go through a dying process each time there is a major separation—saying goodbye for a time, selling sentimental possessions, and loss of family members or friends, are experiences of dying. As people age the chances for losses and separation increase. In a large measure aging is a dying process, which prepares persons as well as families and friends for death.

One can experience the dying process at any age. It is most eminent when one has a terminal illness, which is more prevalent among older people. When talking about death, people express a desire to die at night in their sleep (free of pain and suffering), at home and in their own bed.

Dr. Elizabeth Kubler-Ross, a psychiatrist, has contributed much to the understanding of death and dying through her research and writings. She identified five stages of dying. Since her early writings, much has been written on the subject.

The five stages of dying identified by Dr.Kubler-Ross are not meant to be interpreted as a smooth, simple process of going through one stage and then on to the next. The process is individualized. One may struggle in one stage more than another. A person can bounce back and forth among the stages. Time is also a factor. A lingering terminal illness may allow more time to ultimately accept death. A short illness may not allow sufficient time to experience all or most of the stages. Some people cope with dying by fighting against the odds. Others would rather not discuss or think about it. Still others may come to acceptance easily because of their philosophy of life, coping ability, physical energy, illness/disability, support system(s) and/or other factors.

Five Stages of Death and Dying

Denial: Temporary Shock! A person may not believe that he/she has a terminal illness ("It can't be." "Tell me it isn't so." "I can't die."). They want medical tests rechecked ("My test results must have gotten mixed up with someone else's,") or a second opinion is demanded. Denial is also seen when a person is reluctant to discuss his/her illness with medical staff, family and or friends. Persons may also isolate themselves from others, so as to not have to face reality.

Anger: Verbal and non-verbal forms of anger and aggression are expressed. Anger can be displaced. One may take his/her anger out on the medical staff, family, friends, dog, etc. A person may become overly demanding, self-centered, highly complaintive, or verbally and/or physically aggressive, or may refuse care and treatment. Anger can also be toward God ("How could He do this to me?", "He let me down." "What did I do to deserve this?").

Bargaining: A wish or a plea for an extension of time is desired. The wish may be to attend a son's or daughter's graduation/wedding, go on a planned vacation, complete a special project, or live long enough to see a grandchild that is to be born. Sometimes the pleas are made with the doctor or other medical staff, but most frequently it is made in silence with God ("God, please let me live long enough to____." "If you let me live, I promise that I will ____.")

Depression: Verbal expression of sadness, crying, self-isolation, refusal to eat or drink, disinterest in personal appearance, prolonged periods of sleep not induced by illness or medication are all signs/symptoms of depression. The depression can be related to losses, financial burdens, separation from loved ones, concern for family, friends, or a business/job, not being able to celebrate a holiday in the usual fashion, not being able to send a child to college, etc. A person may not want to discuss his/her feelings and may have self-inflicted death wishes ("If I'm going to die, I'll kill myself." "I can't take it any longer." "You would be better off without me.").

Acceptance: A person may verbally express acceptance ("I'm ready when the Lord wants me." "I'm tired and ready to go."). Expressions of love, gratitude, desires after death (care of family member, property, disposal of possessions, funeral preferences, etc.) may be shared. As a person with a terminal illness grows weaker, a smaller circle of visitors may be desired as well as shorter visiting periods, with or without verbal communication. To have one's hand held in silence may be all that is wanted.

A person having gone through all the emotions of the previous four stages may look different. While thin and tired, the person may have a relaxed facial expression, decreased body movement, shallow breathing, yet feel peaceful having accepted that he/she is going to die. It is at this stage that families and friends find it difficult to cope. The dying person has accepted his/her death, but others can't bear thoughts of losing him/her. This can make it difficult to talk about. The dying person may focus on helping the other accept his/her impending death.

Death

Death can be defined as the final moment of separation, or death can be defined as cessation of heart beat and the stopping of the bodily functions. Death is a part of living. However, it is climactic and final. Some people prepare for death as they age, take responsibility to make out a will, talk with family and friends about their wishes upon their death, attend to legal matters, arrange for funeral and burial services, organize papers, give property (family heirlooms, mementos, photo albums, furniture, clothing, jewelry, etc.) to family and friends, as well as give or make arrangements for others to have land, home, car(s), etc. upon their death. For some older people, it is difficult to talk about or to plan for their own death.

Individual reactions to death will vary depending in a large measure on the death traumas the person has experienced. If a person is not prepared or has not experienced the sudden tragic loss of a loved one, the trauma can be devastating. On the other hand, if the person has worked through his/her feelings about death, the trauma may be very mild. Reading, discussing and preparing for death helps one to understand and prepare for the acceptance of death for themselves as well as family and friends.

Grief

When death occurs, grief is experienced because of the broken relationship and loss. Since grief can be experienced by degrees, some people grieve dramatically while others grieve mildly. The suffering is related to the amount of preparation and to the degree of loss, as well as to the strength of a support system which can fill the void.

The skill of handling grief is a learned skill like many other human experiences. Older persons have usually developed the skill of handling grief since they have had many grief experiences. While the hurt and pain are still fully realized, the older person knows from experience that one has to go on and build one's life around faith and the relational resources that remain.

Grief Process

The grief process is experienced with any loss (person, job, home, money, pet, etc.). The grieving process differs with each individual and for what is lost. The grieving process being presented is related to the death of a person; however, the process can be applied to other losses, but perhaps not to the same extent or intensity, depending upon the loss.

First State: Shock—disbelief that a loved one has died. One may feel numb, unable to go on with normal routine and tasks momentarily for a short period of time. Statements such as, "I can't believe…" "Tell me it isn't so." "Are you sure?" "How could that happen?" "No, no, no!!!" A person may be bewildered, confused and unable to respond or may remain silent.

Second state: Emotional Release—crying. Some people cry openly in public; others cry in private. Over a life time, one may have learned that he/she has to be "strong" and not show emotion, no matter how bad it hurts. Men often have more difficulty showing emotion than women, because of their upbringing and cultural orientation.

Third State: Depression, loneliness, withdrawing, and feeling isolated—one may develop an "I don't care anymore" attitude toward life. A person may withdraw from family, friends, routines, activities, eating, bathing and other aspects of life that once were important. He/she may feel life is not worth the struggle.

A strong death wish may result. If this death wish becomes dominant and intense, the person may become suicidal. When the psychological pain becomes too severe, the person may wish to escape this extreme hurt and need professional help.

Fourth Stage: Physical Symptoms—colds, gastrointestinal distress, aches, pains, inability to sleep or eat. Symptoms of chronic disease/illness may be exacerbated. Survivors may experience symptoms suffered by their deceased loved one. A general feeling of not feeling "good" may prevail.

Fifth Stage: Panic—inability to concentrate except on the loss of the loved one may be experienced. Dreams may be disturbing. Fear may overwhelm and debilitate. A person may not be able to function, thus becoming dependent on others.

Sixth Stage: Guilt and Regrets—Feeling that one did not do something or was not as loving, available, or caring as he/she should have been, no matter what the situation, can be very distressing. Statements such as "I wish I had...," "If only I had...," "Maybe if I had...," 'I shouldn't have...," may be expressed in private or to others when talking about the deceased. Guilt can be expressed about anything or everything concerning the deceased person.

Seventh Stage: Anger and Hostility—Anger can be expressed toward the deceased person "why did he/she have to..." "Look what I'm left with!" "If he/she had.... he/she wouldn't be dead today." Anger can be projected towards a professional, boss, relative or a friend. They are to blame. "If they would only have...," "Why didn't he/she/they/..?" Anger can be displayed when least expected. A person may be angry over the loss of a loved one and take it out on someone or a pet close to him and not realize the intensity of the anger expressed. Some people become angry and hostile toward God. They may lose faith and trust in God and give up any spiritual/religious beliefs and practices.

Eighth Stage: Inability to Return to Usual Activities—a person may have found a comfort level in grieving and be unable to move on, as it is too difficult to face the world again alone. A person may stay home. Answering the phone may be more comfortable than taking the initiative to initiate a phone call. Having visitors is appreciated but to ask someone to visit may be too difficult. A dependent person often has more difficulty in making changes than does a person who has a sense of independence.

Ninth State: Hope Begins to Return—Things "seem" to be better. There is a ray of heartfelt sunshine versus gloom and despair. Thoughts and feelings are placed in perspective. One is still very much aware of the pain, hurt and loss of the deceased; however, adaptation and adjustment become easier. One is ready to make changes and get on with life.

Tenth and Final State: Adjustment to Reality—Life is different. There are new challenges and opportunities ahead. One learns that he/she can live a meaningful life, including sharing humor, laughter and love. The grieving process can also be a personal growth process. Having accomplished the grieving process does not mean that the person will not miss the loved one, nor have days of sadness or moments of loss and tears when least expected. A situation, reading a story, or seeing something can trigger a memory of the deceased. Birthdays, holidays, seasonal activities and get-togethers with family and friends may be difficult the first few times. Talking about the deceased loved one before, during and after the social facilitates the adjustment process.

Older persons have a lifetime of loving, living, dying, coping and preparing. They have developed skills in the area of facing death and losses over their lifetime. The way they handle death and grief serves as a model for younger generations.

Professionals working with older adults need to work through their own feelings about death. It is through this process and knowledge about one's feelings about death that the professional can assist others who are experiencing the dying or grief process. Love, support and hope can help us cope with death whether it is our own death or the death of those whom we love and for whom we provide services.

Summary

Biologically, people are different. In growing older a person can be happy being active (replacing work, old activities and replacing friends who have moved or died), continuing interests and activities from middle age, or disengaging. As people develop they go through several stages of life. Each stage brings new challenges. Successful completion of tasks and stages brings satisfaction.

The normal process of aging is gradual. Acceptance, adjustment and adaptation to the change(s) can be upsetting to some and taken in stride by others. Chronic conditions associated with aging are treated with the latest medications and treatments. Wellness verses illness needs to be promoted so that people with chronic conditions see themselves as being able to do things verses seeing themselves as helpless and powerless. Adults also experience psycho-social challenges as they grow older. Family, friends, peers die, children move away from home, leaving a person with a smaller social world or no socialization. Some people are willing to seek and make new friends; others prefer to keep to themselves, often feeling lonely and depressed. The final stage of life is death. Some people prepare themselves and inform family and/or friends of their wishes. They accept death as a part of living. All older adults experience grief over the lost of a spouse, child, parent, sibling or job, home, driving, physical abilities, a pet, etc. People are unique and experience grief in similar but different ways. There is no time table for acceptance of a lost.

Activity professionals need to work through their own feelings about death so that they can help others. It is natural for an activity professional to grieve over the lost of a client, but not to the extent that it interferes with family or professional responsibilities. Grieving for some clients may be momentary whereas others may be for a week, month, year (s) depending upon the amount of time the activity professional and client knew each other and the extent of their involvement.. Each client leaves a little of themselves with the activity professional when he/she dies. An activity professional may need to seek professional counseling to deal with grief related to a client or just may need time to adjust to the change in his/her professional life.

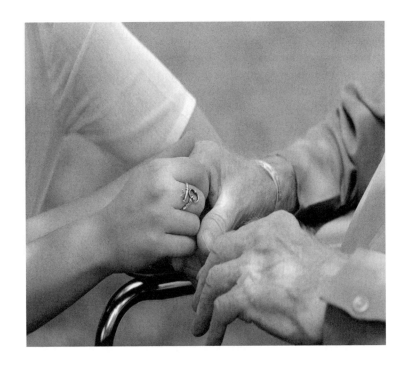

Chapter 8

Professional Approach to Care

"Giving and sharing ideas can be awesome"

Self Care and Wellness as the Basis for Effective Practice

An activity professional's job is exciting, challenging and fulfilling. Wanting to help others help themselves and to maintain or improve the quality of life of older adults is an awesome role and responsibility. Barton, Grudzen and Zielske (2003) recommend using the term, service, rather than helping others. They stated that the concept of help implies that the helper is superior to the person being helped and that the person being helped is indebted to the helper. Whereas, the word, service, denotes that people are equals. Residents in long term care receive assistance for a fee and staff provides the service. This same concept can be applied to other organizations where the participants pay a fee (personal, through insurance, Medicaid or Medicare) such as senior centers, adult day service centers, assisted living, etc.

In order to value and provide services to others, activity professional need to take care of themselves. To give all of oneself to the people you serve can be physically, mentally, emotionally and spiritually draining. Not keeping a balanced life style is harmful. When one is physically, mentally, emotionally, spiritually drained, he/she cannot be creative, caring or responsive to the people being served. When things go wrong, one sees the situation as hopeless or may feel helpless. With good health and a positive attitude, problems become challenges and creative problem solving is accomplished. Poor health can have a negative affect on attitude and performance.

Activity professional need to ask themselves if they are taking care of themselves; do they enjoy their work and responsibilities; are they in the field because they want to serve, thinking they have to satisfy someone else's ideas.

You may be a new or experienced activity professional and have decided that field is not for you. That is OK. You will need to explore why you chose the field, what you like and don't like about it and identify your skills and limitations. This self evaluation will assist in determining if work in another health or human service field is right for you. Given some time and self exploration, you may decide you like what you do but not where you work or your peers. What can be changed or is it more appropriate that you find employment elsewhere?

Support System:

Human life is dependent upon a support system. As children we are dependent upon our parents and other adults. As we mature we become more self-sufficient while still needing assistance from others.

Activity professionals need the support of family, peers, residents and their families, administration and the community, as well as professional and certification organizations.

Spouse or Significant Other

The activity professional's role is very diversified-long days, evenings, weekends, on-site, offsite, small group, large group, one-to-one, etc. Moving from one activity to another calls for a high level of energy. Schedules vary, patterns are disrupted, and routine is pushed aside. During work time the resident's/participant's interests and needs come first.

This means that the spouse or significant other is left out of the priority loop. Sometimes it means they are expected to do extra household duties, shop for essentials, and assist with special projects. Spouses and significant others who are supportive and committed to being helpful make the activity professional's role much easier and satisfying.

Children

Some activity professionals have preschool and/or elementary children in their households. It is hoped that family members or agencies can provide care while the activity professional is providing activities for residents/participants. Good care of the younger generation is very important in providing appropriate and satisfying support. Activity professionals may have adolescents who need their personal time and support. While family comes first part of the time, work has priority at other times.

Administrative Support

Activity professionals need strong administrative support. Gone are the days when administrators hired persons with little or no training just to fill a required position in activities. More and more ads seeking activity professionals are requiring certification, training and experience. The activity profession is maturing. Administrators who value activity professionals will support the activity professional. The administrator will show respect, appreciation and overt support. Where this occurs, adequate compensation, fringe benefits and bonuses will follow.

Facility Co-Worker Support

Activity professionals are team members who work with others. They plan, coordinate and cooperate with all co-workers, professionals and non-professionals. In planning the various activities they are sensitive as to the effect activities have on nursing, dietary, housekeeping, social services, etc. Consideration of the roles of co-workers keeps the lines of communication and cooperation open and responsive. Effective activity professionals are good team members. They offer support; thus, they receive support as well.

Activity Staff

In larger agencies there will be more than one activity professional. As a rule, each is assigned an area or special activities to carry out. It is important that activity professionals support each other and work together in developing an effective program. Activity professionals become a close-knit group who are supportive of each other. They cover for each other during times of illness, bereavement leave, vacations, etc. All activity professionals need to be committed team members.

Resident Family Support

In planning many of the special activities with residents/participants, activity professionals need to work with family members. This is especially true of celebrations such as birthdays, anniversaries or other significant events in the residents'/participants' lives. Calling family members and enlisting family ideas and support can make the event more meaningful for the resident/participant. Sometimes family members with special skills will help in programs honoring their loved ones. At times they can be enlisted to help in future activities. Family members can be supportive of the activities program and staff.

Family Council

A family council can sponsor resident/family activities with a minimum of support and coordination by the activity professional. Members of family council may provide food, decorations and paid programs, e.g., entertainment. Coordination with activity professionals would include date, time, place, ordering of food/decorations, music, paying for entertainment, setting up the space, setting up the activity, and clean-up.

Resident Council

Members of the resident council provide input into the governing of a facility or agency. Residents provide support of activity professionals by voicing their choices, concerns and recommendations for activities. Residents' evaluation of activities such as a special event assists the activity professional in his/her effort to continuously try to improve the activities program. Minutes of resident council meetings provide a record of residents' suggestions, concerns and evaluations. A review of the record reinforces accomplishments, increasing the activity professional's self-esteem and personal/professional satisfaction.

Ombudsman

The local and state ombudsmen are advocates for the residents. They can also be advocates for staff and administration. An ombudsman can support residents' preferences and recommendations when there is little or no administrative support for an activity professional to implement appropriate recommendations.

Activity professionals can seek ombudsman support when residents recommend activities that are not realistic but insist on their implementation. Ombudsman support can be requested when an individual resident and/or family is not able to resolve a conflict related to the activities program. Activity professionals can contact their local or state ombudsman when there is a question related to residents' rights or quality of life issues. The ombudsman is an important, supportive community resource that is often under-utilized.

Consultant

A consultant can provide advice, counseling, training, support and resources. A corporate consultant provides consultation for facilities and agencies owned or managed by the corporation. A private consultant contracts with a variety of agencies and facilities. Activity professionals can seek assistance from their corporate consultant (if they have one) or request administrative approval to contract with a private consultant. Consultation may be one-time, short-term or long-term. The professional relationship between an activity professional (client) and consultant is one of trust. The role of a consultant can be varied; however, the basic role is to help the client help him/her self. Client independence is the primary goal.

Under OBRA regulations (483.75 Administration (h)),"If a facility does not employ a qualified professional person to furnish a specific service to be provided by the facility, the facility must have that service furnished to residents by a person or agency outside the facility under an arrangement." An inexperienced untrained activity professional may work with a consultant until such time that he/she is qualified by state and/or federal law.

Professional Peers

Networking and knowing other professionals is a great resource for support. Activity professionals understand one another and are willing to listen and share expertise, resources and experience. The activity profession is a sharing profession. Activity professionals are willing to assist one another. Each is just a phone call away. A new activity professional can call activity professionals in the local area to introduce himself/herself, find out about local organizations and/or other opportunities to meet local professionals, and learn about resources and training opportunities. Visiting other facilities provides activity professionals opportunities to see and learn about new activities, systems and resources.

Professional Organizations

Local and Regional Associations

In many areas, local and regional activity associations have provided a network of professionals who are interested and committed to helping one another. This becomes a major support group where problems and concerns are shared and possible solutions suggested. Belonging to these groups can be very helpful.

State Associations

Almost every state has a state activity professional association in place. The major focus of state associations is to provide educational conferences and disseminate information of common interest. State associations are a major source of support and assistance.

National Associations

The National Association of Activity Professionals (NAAP) has been organized to influence legislation, share information and provide a national network for activity professionals. Belonging to and supporting the association helps activity professionals to have an impact on the care and services of older persons. The National Certification Council of Activity Professionals (NCCAP) has developed a certification standard which can provide support and assistance to activity professionals in the field.

Bio-psycho Social Model of Care

"Activities can stimulate mind, body and soul"

The bio-psycho social model of care treats the whole person. This can be applied to the activity professional as well as to clients. Bio refers to the physical aspect of care; psycho refers to the mental, emotional, spiritual aspects of care and social, to the social aspect of care.

All people are individuals, thus similar but different from one another. Activity professionals need to be in touch with themselves and be aware of their bio-psycho-social needs. Awareness may be evident but a plan to meet one's needs may not be valued; thus the activity professional may attempt unknowingly to meet their needs through work, which can be toxic to the activity professional, the people being served, as well as other professionals in the work place.

An activity professional may feel he/she gets enough exercise at work, transporting residents to and from

146

activities, leading exercise groups, walking long distances in the workplace. But is this really enough? Has a recent physical indicated high blood pressure, high cholesterol, diabetes, being over weight and/or other negative findings that could be decreased through a regular exercise routine off the job? Are mental or emotional problems interfering with work, i.e., preoccupation, worrying about someone or something, feeling stressed out, etc.? Are feelings of social inadequacy, not feeling accepted or respected, affecting interactions with clients, peers and/or management?

Activity professionals, like other health and human service professionals must take care of themselves to prevent fatigue, burnout, impatience, negative interactions and poor services.

Clients must be treated as individuals. Activity professionals can apply a person-centered approach, developed in the 1990's versus a task-centered approach to their care and services. Hopefully, a person-centered approach is the organization's model of care and services. If it is not, the activity professional can utilize the approach and perhaps influence the other disciplines. Activity professionals have demonstrated a person-centered approach over the years, even though the term was not developed until the 90s.

It takes time to get to know a client's social history, likes, dislikes, abilities, limitations, interests, prefer-

ences, what makes them happy or sad, how they prefer to be treated, e.g., do not awaken until noon, do not go to specific activities, etc. A person in severe pain may feel some relief after interacting with someone or participating in an activity of choice. During interaction, it is not what is said, it is how something is said that can have a positive or negative affect. Knowing a client's cognitive and hearing ability is imperative, when trying to communicate. Social interaction with peers assists a new client in adjusting to the new setting, accepting losses, making new friends and feeling accepted and worthwhile.

A very outgoing bubbly activity professional may not be accepted by a quiet reserved client; thus, the activity professional must be aware of how his /her personality affects a client. A quiet reserved activity professional may not show enough enthusiasm to spark a client's interest in participating in an activity.

The activity professional's total being affects his/her job performance and relationship with clients. First there has to be trust to establish a relationship. An activity professional needs to feel and express trust with clients. The client must feel that information is confidential, privacy is respected and communication is open. The activity professional must be sensitive to diversity and does not abuse his/her power as a care giver.

Cultural Patterns of Communication

"Communication occurs when there is understanding"

It is important to know and understand all participants' culture, ethnic/religious backgrounds, dominant traditions and celebrations, in order to respect them and implement appropriate services, programs and activities. Participants from different ethnic and religious backgrounds may have knowledge and experience in celebrating traditional holidays and special events, e.g., Christmas, Thanksgiving, and Halloween and not be offended if these events are celebrated. However, it is important to recognize differences even if it is only one person, .e.g. celebrating Hanukkah with a resident of Jewish faith, on a one to-one basis, with family or with other participants who are of other faiths. It can be a time for a person of Jewish faith to explain his/her beliefs and rituals

for a specific religious holiday and for others to experience foods and beverages associated with the holiday.

In recent years, the celebration of Halloween in some social or health care organizations has been replaced with fall celebration (decorations, food, outings, games, poetry, art, etc.). This is more environmental and seasonal not affecting the religious or cultural backgrounds of participants. There may be enjoyment in seeing children dressed in costumes and giving them surprises but not being involved in other types of Halloween celebrations. This type of event could be any time of the year; however it is most meaningful to children and parents, who wish to participate, on or near the annual Halloween celebration.

Participants, family members and friends of participants with the same religious/cultural background can assist activity professionals in understanding their traditions and celebrations. They can assist in planning and implementing programs, celebration, and specific activities. Groups in the community can be contacted for assistance, such as ethnic groups (colleges and universities) community groups (public library may have names of contact people for groups) and churches, synagogues or religious organizations.

Some Catholics may be willing to attend an interdenominational service but not receive communion unless a priest is leading the service. People of Jewish faith are either Orthodox Conservative or Reformed Jews with different beliefs and practices. Orthodox Jews may not want to attend a Sabbath service conducted by a Reformed Rabbi and vise versa. Muslims read from the Book of Koran versus the Christian Bible. The days of worship vary, Friday for Muslins, Saturday for Jews and Sunday is primarily the day of worship for the Christians.

In the US, an event related to one cultural or religious group may be celebrated in one part of the country and not in others, i.e., St. Patrick's Day is celebrated with a televised New York City parade. It is an Irish custom to eat a corn beef and cabbage meal, eat soda bread, and drink green beer. German feasts are celebrated with a variety of German meals, beer and a variety of desserts, i.e., cream puffs.

A potential participant may have painful memories, even if a long time ago, related to a specific holiday and does not want to celebrate with others. Recognizing the person's pain/hurt and not inviting them to a celebration may be the most kind and considerate thing to do. Allowing the person to voice his/her feelings and experiences on a one- to-one basis may communicate to the participant that the activity professional respects the participant and recognizes his/her grief.

Non Verbal Communication

Cultural patterns of communication include non verbal communication, e.g., gestures, facial expressions. An activity professional may feel at ease in giving other people hugs; however not everyone likes to be hugged. Permission needs to be granted prior to hugging a participant. A handshake is more of a universal gesture. An activity professional can extend a hand and a participant can choose whether or not to accept a hand shake. A high five is rather new and used more among men than women. The high five is often associated with sports or initial male greetings with a younger person. Touching such as tapping one on the shoulder to imply congratulations, recognition for having accomplished something, may not be accepted in some cultures. It is important to know acceptable non verbal cultural communications for positive interactions with participants of various cultures. This can be explained to other participants so that they respect all peers.

Communication

Communication is a two-way process of sending and receiving information. Activity professionals need to be able to communicate effectively with residents/participants, staff, administration, volunteers, families, vendors, and community contacts. This involves verbal and nonverbal interpersonal communication as well as written communication. It is essential to get a person's attention before attempting verbal communication.

Verbal Communication

Quality and tone of voice, inflection, articulation, speed, vocabulary and emotional feelings all have an impact on verbal communication. Communication is not only what is said but how it is said and how it is perceived.

Questions

Activity professionals need to know when and what types of questions need to be used for assessment, conversation, discussion, reminiscing, life review, etc. Yes/no questions are the least threatening types of questions. Open-ended questions provide specific responses beyond the yes/no. Feeling-type questions are the most threatening type of question.

Memory

In communicating with participants, the activity professional must know their memory function. Some will use short-term and long-term memory. Others will use only long-term memory. Reality orientation requires short-term memory whereas validation therapy is focused on long-term and remote memory. A participant may be able to correctly respond to a reminiscing question, but unable to answer the question "What day is today?" or "Today is what day?"

Vocabulary

Activity professionals need to speak to participants in a vocabulary that they understand. Words have different meanings in different parts of the country. A "machine" may mean "an automobile"; "a poke" can be a bag, etc. A participant may not speak English; thus, the activity professional needs to learn basic words of the participant's language, e.g., German, to be able to communicate.

Non-verbal communication includes eye contact, facial/hand gestures (smile, frowns, waving of hand, pointing, etc.), movement of head, body, arms/legs, proper distancing, posturing (leaning forward/backward, standing/sitting tall). Non-verbal communication needs to be congruent with verbal communication.

Hearing Meta Messages

"Listen for hidden messages"

Meta message is the underlying meaning of what a person says (Barton, Grudzen, and Zieldke, 2004). These authors say that often a real message is unconsciously cloaked in a cover story. A resident in a long term care facility may say, "I want to go home." Metamessage: "I don't feel cared for here." Staff can explore what is wrong or why the person feels she/he wants to leave. Communicating with a resident in a way that the resident understands helps the resident emotionally and spiritually and may facilitate a more positive attitude and satisfaction.

A parent may hear a metamessage from a school age child, i.e., "I don't want to go to school." The parent explores the reason, physical, mental, emotional, or social, and finds out that the child has not studied for a test or completed a project that is due, or that the child was called names by a peer and does not want to face him/her today.

Barriers to Effective Communication with Clients

"Prejudgments can become barriers in communication"

Communication barriers can include being judgmental, giving advice that was not solicited, being opinionated, being defensive, showing disapproval, interrupting and making value judgments. Topic-jumping reduces the consistency and quality of communication. Offensive language, inappropriate use of words and misinformation can be detrimental to communication. Asking "why" - type questions may make a person feel defensive. Not allowing sufficient time for processing information and/or answering questions has a negative effect on communication. Accents, articulation, and rate of speech also have a negative impact on communication.

Personal experiences, values, beliefs, perceptions, attitudes, and judgment can shade what is heard. Activity professionals need constantly to be aware of communication barriers and to minimize them.

Sensory Modalities

"Our senses are gateways to experience"

Adaptations may be needed to communicate with persons with visual, auditory, and /or cognitive impairments.

Visual Disabilities

In communicating with a person with visual impairments, the activity professional uses descriptive words that help a person see what is being said or described, e.g., 12" pink vase. Using directional words such as up/down, right/left, front/back, over/under, center, and around can assist a person in understanding directions.

Hearing Impairment

Lowering the tone of voice can assist a person with a hearing deficit to hear spoken words. Amplification may be needed to increase volume to foster the ability to hear. Facing a person and speaking slowly allow another person to lip-read. If a person wears a hearing aid, be sure the battery and the hearing aid are working. A person wearing a hearing aid may find it difficult to communicate in a noisy environment, e.g., a party.

A person who is unable to hear and read lips may be able to communicate with a picture board. Activity professionals can make picture boards representing different activities, e.g., bingo, church, bowling, crafts, music, etc. Pictures from activity catalogs can be used to make an activity picture board. Electronic equipment (such as a talking board) enables some participants to communicate effectively. Speech pathologists can recommend different types of communication aids for participants with communication deficits.

Physical Disabilities

In speaking to a participant using a wheelchair, sit and speak on his/her eye level. When speaking to a person in bed, try to find the position in which the person is most comfortable talking, i.e., sitting up with the activity professional sitting or standing, or lying on one side with activity professional sitting. Eye contact is important, as is the ability to hear one another. Activity professionals need to be aware of the physical energy that is used by some participants in their attempts to speak. Short interactions may be satisfying and not too taxing.

Cognitive Disabilities

In working with participants with cognitive deficits, the activity professional must address the person by name to get his/her attention before initiating communication. Remain calm and speak slowly and clearly. Provide time for a person to respond. Repeat or rephrase a question as needed.

Use gestures to assist the person in understanding the spoken word. Ask simple open ended questions.

When asking a choice-type question, give two choices versus three or four. If a person is unable to answer simple open-ended questions, ask yes/no questions. Observe nonverbal responses for residents who are unable to give a verbal response to questions. Redirect a person as needed. Use cueing and gesturing.

If a person who is confused does not respond to reality orientation, try validation. Past time may be present time for the participant. Do not argue with a resident who is confused. Inform the person that you do not understand what he/she is trying to say. A person may not be able to identify a need but may ask a question related to a need, e.g., "Do you have an out house?" The person is trying to say that he/she has to go to the restroom. A participant may be able to communicate needs/feelings through a stuffed animal or doll by saying what the animal or doll needs or asking for assistance with the doll or stuffed animal. Observing non-verbal patterns and gestures when a person has a mild degree of confusion will assist an activity professional in knowing what specific gesturing means when the person is no longer able to verbalize.

Psychiatric Disabilities

A person with a psychiatric problem may or may not have a communication problem. A communication problem may be related to thought disorder or reaction to medication (such as slurred speech). Remain calm, set limits (as needed), and be specific, clear and firm if a person is upset. Take the person to a quiet area to talk. Use reality orientation if the person is confused. If a person hallucinates, attempt to orient him/her to reality, e.g., if a participant states that he sees bugs on the wall, the activity professional's response could be, "You see bugs on the wall but I don't see bugs on the wall." Avoid stating negative feelings. In expressing displeasure, focus on the person's behavior and not on the person. Be considerate and respectful. Be sure the participant understands. Rephrase questions and comments as needed.

Value of Listening
"Learning occurs when one is actively listening"

Activity professionals need to be effective listeners. When communicating with another person, the activity professional must focus attention entirely on what the person is saying and on his/her non-verbal communication (expressions, gestures, posture, etc.). Maintain eye contact and show interest by nodding, expressing empathy, asking questions, gesturing relating to what was heard, and/or being silent, and/or summarizing. Additional effective listening responses include clarifying, probing, interpreting, confronting (if needed), informing and perception-checking. Listen for feelings, emotions, facts, sentiments, meaning and reactions. It is important to understand the person's perception of a problem/situation as well as his/her actual experience or perception of an experience. Two people may have the same experience but their perception of the experience may differ.

The Face of Dignity

"Respect the dignity of others"

The authors, Barton, Grudzen and Zielske, of Vital Connections in *Long-Term Care Spiritual Resources for Staff and Residents* (2003) define dignity as a sense of personal worth and value.

Activity professionals and other professionals must treat participants with respect and recognize their individuality. This includes but is not limited to: addressing the person by his/her preferred name, Mr., Mrs., Ms., Dr., first name, and nick name prior to becoming a participant. Accepting a person's limitations and making adaptations without calling attention to a limitation is helpful and respectful.

Welcoming a new participant is essential in any health or human service organization. It gives the new person recognition and an opportunity to affirm the recognition. Welcoming the new participant in an activity or recognizing him/her after absence of participation shows support and respect.

A welcome committee or a buddy program can be invaluable in helping a new participant feel welcomed.

A member of the welcome committee or a buddy can introduce the new person to peers; explain procedures for specific activities or interests and/or offer to converse and get to know the person.

During the initial interview and completion of the activity assessment, the activity professional can inform the new participant of available activities related to his/her interests and preferences as well as the possibility of developing other activities of interest. This gives the new participant the feeling of being recognized and respected

Appropriate recognition, praising and asking for input into some topic fosters the feeling of being valued. Encouraging the participant to share his/her experiences and accomplishments with peers and staff emphasizes self worth. Telling one's life story or part of a life story is an opportunity for life review and feeling good about experiences. Coming to terms with negative experiences assists with self esteem and self worth.

Circle of Support

"Humans are born to help others"

Quadagno (2005) defines a social support system as "the network of relatives, friends, and organizations that provide both emotional support, such as making the individual feel loved or comforted, and instrumental support, which refers to help in managing activities of daily living." Throughout life some old friends remain permanent, others come and go. New friends may become the most supportive. In health care facilities, participants may have their own set of peer friends and do not have a need for new friends. Yet the new participant has a need to feel accepted and part of the peer group. It is not uncommon for staff to have a better or more intimate relationship with some participants than others related to simi-

larities, i.e., both being from the same neighborhood, church, community organization, worked or had family members who worked at the same place of employment, knows the same people, speak the same language, have the same interests, etc. This type of interpersonal relationship is acceptable providing it does not harm relationships with other participants, i.e., that they feel they are not equal to the person who is receiving or appears to be receiving more attention.

Family support may come to full circle over the life time of an individual. The parents and/or grandparents who played a significant role in a child's life may now be the primary focus and care of the child as an adult.

An activity professional may develop an intimate relationship with a participant and is loved and supported by the participant.

Autonomy

"Respect the residents' autonomy"

Autonomy is the right to self governance. A participant has the right to vote and determine his/her wishes related to advance directives, a living will and durable power of attorney for health care. A living will identifies the person's wishes for health care if he/she is unable to make health care decisions. The person designated as the durable power of attorney for health care has the authority and power to oversee the financial aspects of a person's care.

Activity professionals need to be aware of participants advance directives and have a procedure to obtain them if a participant is in need of health care while he/she is away from the organization, i.e. outing. It is advisable to carry a list of participant's names, i.e., first name and last initial or last name and first initial (for privacy) with advance directives listed, e.g., do not resuscitate. An activity professional can be an advocate for the resident's advance directives being implemented during care conferences, when he/she is with the person away from the organization or through one-to-one or group discussion on advance directives when a person initiates the topic.

The activity professional may be asked to have advance directives and to keep some type of written communication as to who to contact for the advance directives in case of illness, accident or injury.

The Need for Connection

"Listening is giving"

Al human beings need an opportunity to socialize and feel connected to others throughout life. In old age, this may be more of a challenge for: (1) people living on fixed incomes, and not having the finances for socialization, i.e., not having money for transportation for social events, (2) people who experience chronic illnesses, and (3) people who have ADL limitations (self care limitations, e.g., dressing, eating, bathing, toileting, transferring from between bed and chair or wheel chair and toilet, and/or IADLs instrumental activities of daily living limitations such as the inability to prepare own meals, do laundry, take medication appropriately, go shopping, manage money or use the telephone.

Today, many older people do not understand technology related to credit card, paying a bill by phone, or not understanding the procedures to make a doctor's appointment when instructed to follow a variety of steps, e.g., press one (1) if you want to make or change an appointment, press two (2) if you want to leave a message for the doctor, etc. Most often there is a list of numbers to dial and a person can become anxious about which number to press or remember the instructions. They need some one to help them, e.g., family member, friend, volunteer, paid professional. Through meeting needs, a person stays connected with others.

Involvement in senior centers, adult day services, or other community groups for the aged or intergenerational groups and experiences a person meets new people and widens his/her circle of friends and associates. New friends and acquaintances may replace family and former close friends who are unable to keep in touch or provide assistance as needed.

The activity professional can assist participants in making new friends with peers over time. Some people may be resistive to making new friends for fear of losing them. This needs to be discussed with the person's health care team and possible psychological referral to deal with loses.

Continuous Care Retirement Communities (CCRC) offer a variety of structures and unstructured activities in which resident can meet peers, make new friends and form friendship networks. Meal time provides residents an opportunity to sit with designated or preferred peer and converse; thus getting to know and support one another. Informal small groups and friendships may be developed by married couples, single men and/or women who become friends or mixed groups who become friends related to a specific interest. It is the personal integration of individual residents or participants in health or community setting that enhances their quality of life and reduces isolation.

Passing on the Spirit of Life
"Prayers should express our deepest needs and fondest hopes"

All creatures that have a nervous system including birds, animals and humans have a spirit. That is why cats, dogs, horses, etc. relate to the human spirit and make good pets. The physiological bodies with a nervous system provide the body for the spirit. It is the spirit – the mind and hearts – that represent the highest level of being.

As humans our minds, emotions, passions and hearts are the areas of humankind that make the difference in what one becomes. This is the spirit – the spirit of a person makes the difference. Our spirits guide our choices. Choosing the positive or the negative make for good or evil, better or worse and helping or hurting.

Ones beliefs make a difference, e.g., the atheist does not believe in a greater spirit, the Agnostic is not sure whether there is a higher power or not, while the religious person believes in a higher power – God, Allah, Great Spirit, Lord, Jesus, etc.

Passing It On

According to surveys more than 90% of Americans believe in a higher power and most would call the higher power, God. God is the ultimate spirit. The United States was established by leaders, many of whom were Christian. A Chaplain was and still is called upon to open the houses of Congress with prayer.

Prayer is the act of communicating with God. Many Americans pray daily (one or more times); others pray periodically and still others pray when facing a crisis. Prayer can be very important to many residents/clients in the facilities or agencies in which activity professionals serve.

As older persons face illnesses, accidents and death there is often a strong desire for prayer and support. Through prayer one can pass on the spirit of life. Christians, Muslims and some Jews in death believe the spirit is released from the physical body and is freed to enter the spirit world. The place in the Christian faith is called heaven. This is where they believe they will reside with God forever and ever. Activity professionals who have meaningful faith can pass it on.

In a number of facilities or agencies there is a chaplain who ministers to the spiritual needs of the residents/clients. Sometimes the chaplain is a full time, paid position, at other times the residents are served by a local clergy person who calls on individuals or holds religious services for the residents/clients who want to attend. Activity professionals may be asked to assist in arranging and helping residents to attend. As the residents/clients move toward death they often seek spiritual council and support. Many who believe in the afterlife are looking forward to being released from a worn-out body. For those persons, death is a welcome release and an event to celebrate. Their spiritual legacy lives on in family and friends who knew and loved them. The activity professional frequently becomes spiritually connected to the dying resident. The spirit of that person is passed on through the activity professional, family, friends and other staff persons.

Models of Care

In this chapter the Bi-psycho-social model of care is presented. This is only one model. There are a variety of service models through which activity services are provided in a health care setting. Some of the models being presented are new, others are old. A combination of models can be used. In selecting a model, four (4) criteria can be used: (1) the mission of the organization, (2) size of the facility and available space for programming, (3) the number of staff, activity and others and (4) the training and expertise of staff in understanding and implementing a specific model.

Person Centered Model of Care:

The Philosophy of Person Centered Care in Dementia

Person Centered Care is not about forms, lists, reporting and extra work. Person centered care respects the dignity and completeness of each older adult. Each person is recognized, not the disease. A person's unique background is also recognized and communicated to all staff often through the use of an assessment tool called the life story. The life story is information gathered early in the disease or from the family to provide the staff with the resident's background. This information can help the resident feel at ease during care and helps the staff to feel more connected to the resident. The person's right to autonomy and the right to say no are respected. Cultural differences, ethnic background, choices and preferences are all respected by the staff. The philosophy embraces the unique qualities and life story of the person. Included are the person's remaining skills and abilities as well as the opportunity to support the person as a member of a community and make a connection. As consumers become more knowledgeable, they require facilities that provide more choices and autonomy. Today's research on current workforce trends indicate that aides are looking for more "relational" work environments that foster positive relationships for staff and residents. Facilities using the person centered care approach have found that they are providing more meaningful care, comfort, companionship and safety. Staff supports the person to be successful and maintain independence in decisions and activities of daily living, even if it is quicker for the staff to do it.

Principles and Values of Person Centered Care

Assuming the person has the ability:
- Every person has strengths, gifts, and contributions to offer.
- Every person has hopes, dreams and desires.
- Each person is the primary authorities on his or her life.
- Every person has the ability to express preferences and to make choices.
- A person's choices and preferences shall always be considered.
- Person centered care is a continuing process of:
  - Listening
  - Trying things
  - Seeing how they work
  - Changing things as needed

We discover the hopes, dreams and desires of older adults by asking and listening.
Some of the hopes, dreams and desires of older adults are:
- Go to church
- Visit my husband's grave
- Eat out sometimes
- See my grandkids
- Eat the foods I like
- Sit at a computer again

Ten Points to Listening

1. Believe that the person has something to give and is of value
2. Help people discover their gifts
3. Listen with an open mind
4. Listen to dreams and visions, not just to what is in the present
5. Listen without hurrying
6. Listen to fears and pain
7. Listen with no intent to fix or control anyone
8. Listen for words that actions may not reveal
9. Listen to recognize opportunities
10. Knowing that things take time

(Beerman, Pat)

We must listen in new ways for the non-verbal older adult:
- What makes the person happy or sad?
- What comforts the person?
- What triggers difficult behavior?
- Share our knowledge with others.
- Ask those who know the person best.

It is best to think of person centered care as an attitude not a procedure.

Culture Change

"Cultural changes call for activity changes"

Culture change in long term care is an ongoing transformation based on person directed values that restore control to older adults, their families and their care givers. This transformation includes changing core values, choices regarding the organization of time and space, relationships, language, rules, objectives used in every day life, contact with nature and rituals.

A transformation in a health care facility may look dramatically different from the living, working, and care giving environments today. Residents living in a culture change home truly direct their own care and make choices about how they spend their time. The direct care workers in these organizations are highly involved in decisions that are relevant to their jobs and the people they care for. The residents, their families, and the workers are a part of a thriving, independent community.

Culture change is not just for nursing homes. The philosophy can be applicable to any situation where elders or people with disabilities are engaged in a care giving connection. These individuals risk losing control over their lives to whatever part of the health care system they are involved in. The culture change transformation turns institutions into real homes. Progressive providers have found ways to invite clients and workers onto their board of directors. Included are direct care-givers on the training team who have reorganized scheduling systems to ensure the residents develop consistent care giving relationships with the direct care givers. Other progressive providers are holding community focus groups to poll the community on what they would like to see in a long term care environment. Remember these are your future residents.

Culture change is also found in the hospital environment. It is called the Planetree Model. Founded in San Francisco in 1978, Planetree is a non-profit organization dedicated to personalizing and demystifying the healthcare experience and creating patient-centered care in healing environments. The Planetree model empowers patients and families through information and education and encourages "healing partnerships" with care-givers. Symbolized by the sycamore tree (plane tree) under which Hippocrates taught medicine, Planetree's holistic approach encompasses healing in all dimensions.

Bathing is a good example of change in practice based on a person's directed values. In the traditional nursing home, baths are offered two days a week, a new resident just moving in may inherit the prior resident's bath schedule regardless of her preference or customary routine. This one change, to be done effectively, causes many systems in the home to need to change. Facility policy and procedures have to be re-written, care plans improved, long standing shift routines changed, nursing assistants need to become empowered to listen and to respond to resident needs. Nurses need to be educated on the new bathing techniques and person directed thinking so that they can support the nursing assistants in their changed roles. The way staff performance is evaluated and new staff orientation must change to reflect the culture change philosophy.

Progressive providers engaged in culture change are experiencing positive outcomes. Employee workmen's compensation in less, staff turnover decreased 30-40 percent, no agency workers are used, and some homes have a waiting list for interested employees. Significant improvements are found in resident, employee and family satisfaction. Reduction in depression and use of medications to treat depression and behavior are noted. Involvement with the outside community including children, schools, clubs, faith based organizations and town government increased. Culture change will make facilities more Baby Boomer Friendly.

Eden Alternative

The Eden Alternative is a not-for-profit organization developed by Dr. William Thomas in 1991, a model for cultural change within nursing facilities, dedicated to improving the experience of aging and disability around the world. It is a powerful tool for improving quality of life and for recapturing a meaningful work life. The Eden Alternative shows us how to transform a nursing home to provide an opportunity to give meaningful care to other living things, animals and plants. Designing an environment with variety and spontaneity can succeed where pills and therapies fail. The Mission of Dr. Thomas is "it's better to live in a garden… improving the lives of the elderly and their caregivers by transforming the communities in which they live and work". The Eden Alternative's vision is the elimination of loneliness, helplessness and boredom which often plaques nursing homes. Dr. Thomas has expanded his vision to include the Green House model which creates small intentional communities for a group of elders and staff. It is a place that focuses on life, and its heart is found in the relationships that flourish there. A radical departure from traditional skilled nursing homes and assisted living facilities, the Green House model alters facility size, interior design, staffing patterns, and methods of delivering skilled professional services. Its primary purpose is to serve as a place where elders can receive assistance and support with activities of daily living and clinical care, without the assistance and care becoming the focus of their existence. The Green House is intended to de-institutionalize long-term care by eliminating large nursing facilities and creating habilitative social settings.

Medical Model

The Medical Model is the traditional illness centered approach to treatment. The treatment focus is on the disease not the person. The medical doctor and his recommended treatments carried out by other health care professionals are the driving force of care and services. This is seen in hospital short term care settings, rehabilitation settings and other clinical settings. A physician's order for Therapeutic Recreation or Activities may be broad in scope and often given at the request of the Therapeutic Recreation or Activity professional. At times, there may be differences about care between acute medicine and rehabilitation medicine. A cure phase is the ultimate goal of acute medicine and then referral to Rehabilitation medicine; whereas Rehabilitation medicine prefers to treat the whole person, by restoring functions through integration with all phases of care. Therapeutic Recreation and Activity professions may offer diversional activities. Therapeutic Recreation personnel may offer Leisure Awareness, Leisure Education, Community Integration, Social Interaction Skills and therapeutic groups which may or may not be co-lead with another member of the Rehabilitation team.

Wellness Model

In a Wellness model the person is seen as a whole person, physically, mentally, emotionally, socially and spiritually. Even though a person has a disease or disability, the treatment emphasis is on wellness. Treatment focuses on strengths as well as limitations not just on illness, disability or limitations.

A comparison of the Medical- clinical Model and the Wellness Model is to think of them both on a continuum with the Medical-clinical Model being at one end and the Wellness Model being at the other end. Austin (1982) believes that therapeutic recreation personnel and activity professionals should be concerned with clients along the entire spectrum.

A holistic medicine based on treatment plans, is similar to the Wellness Model.

The highest level of wellness, mind, body and spirit, is sought based on capabilities. An activity professional working within the wellness model can work with restorative nursing to increase functional ability through physical and cognitive activities (exercise, games), helping a resident to understand how involvement in activities can help him cope with his illness or disability as well as develop new skills or utilize adaptive equipment or techniques that can be used after discharge.

Long –Term Care Model

The Long-Term Care Model has developed over the past thirty (30) years. Today, it includes Residents Rights, Quality of Life and Quality of Care issues as a part of the planning process, which includes individual independent activities, one-to-one activities involving staff, volunteers, families, friends and peers, group activities in and out of the facility and in the community. One program does not fit all. Programming is based on assessed needs, abilities, interests, preferences and limitations.

Today there are many specialized units within Long Term Care facilities such as Alzheimer's/Dementia Units, Behavior Units, MS (Multiple Sclerosis) Units, Sub Acute Care units, Rehabilitation Units, Dialysis Units, Wound Care Units, Bariatric (obesity) Care Units, Hospice Units as well as other special care units. Activity professionals are usually assigned to one of these specialty units to work with the other team members in providing an interdisciplinary approach to activity services. The activities provided for resident on an Alzheimer's unit would be very different from activities provided for residents in a Bariatric Unit. Residents with Alzheimer's disease would have different cognitive abilities and may also have physical limitation due to chronic illness or cognitive impairment. Residents on a Bariatric, MS, or Rehabilitation unit have more physical limitations and less cognitive impairment. The age of residents in each specialty unit may differ; thus their interest and preferences differ. Younger residents may enjoy electronic hand-held games or using the computer where as residents with Alzheimer's disease tends to respond to activities requiring long-term memory.

Centralized versus Decentralized Programming:

In the early 70's when activities became a part of federal regulations for nursing homes, activity professionals usually only had one area in the total facility for programming and that was the dining room. It was here that programming took place. Activity professionals had to plan the time for activities around the meal and housekeeping schedules. A part of the planning process was to allow sufficient time to transport residents to the dining room for activities. This could take 30 or more minutes depending upon the size of the facility, the lay out, i.e., single floor or multiple floors, the number of elevators and whether or not residents were up and ready to go to activities. In the early 70's most nursing homes did not have a specific area for activities and there was usually no or little space to conduct activities in separate areas.

Homes built in the late 60's included a small activity room, a large entry area and dining room. Today, most nursing homes have several social areas, possibly an activity room and use of the dining room for programming. In large facilities, there may be a dining/activity area on each unit or floor. Decentralized programming was created in the 80's as more facilities had dining/activity areas on each unit/floor. The emphasis was on "taking the program to the people versus the people to the program." The decentralized programs allowed for more time for programming as transportation time was reduced. Activity professionals could plan smaller group activities to meet the needs, abilities, interest preferences and limitations of residents living on the particular floor/unit. There was and still are some centralized activities, e.g., parties, church, entertainment, etc.

Today's modern facilities are built with well planned space for activities of each unit/floor. Activity staffing includes one or more persons assigned to each floor; thus, they are responsible for the activity program on their assigned floor/unit. This has increased the amount of programming offered in a facility and better meets the needs of the participants, especially residents in specialty units. A person centered Wellness Model or restorative model can be developed within the decentralized model of programming.

Restorative Model

The Restorative Model is usually referred to as restorative nursing. New residents may have ADL limitations and would benefit from a restorative nursing program. Residents in restorative nursing programs may demonstrate the need for more intense therapy (occupational therapy, physical therapy, speech therapy, respiratory therapy, psychological therapy). People who complete rehabilitation are often referred to restorative nursing in a long-term care facility to continue to gain skills or to maintain skills.

MDS 2.0 User's Manual gives the following definition for: "Rehabilitation/Restorative Care – Included are nursing interventions that assist or promote the resident's ability to attain his or her maximum functional potential. This item does not include procedures or techniques carried out by or under the direction of a qualified therapist, as identified item P1b. In addition, to be included in this section, a rehabilitation or restorative practice must meet all of the following additional criteria:

- Measurable objectives and interventions must be documented in the care plan and in the clinical record.

- Evidence of periodic evaluation by licensed nurse must be present in the clinical record.

- Nurse assistants/aides must be trained in the techniques that promote resident involvement in the activity.

- These activities are carried out or supervised by members of the nursing staff. Sometimes under licensed nurse supervision, other staff and volunteers will be assigned to work with specific residents.

  This category does not include exercise groups with more than four residents per supervising helper or caregiver."

A physician's order is not required for restorative nursing care. Restorative care is counted on a 15 minute basis either one-to-one or a small group of four (4) people per supervising helper or caregiver.

The MDS 2.0 User's Manual (2004) states: "Skill practice in such activities as walking and mobility, dressing and grooming, eating and swallowing, transferring, amputation care and communication can improve or maintain function in physical abilities and ADLs and prevent further impairment.

Activity and therapeutic recreation professionals can work with the restorative nurse coordinator in developing small groups of four people for restorative programs. Restorative nurse assistants can assist with larger groups of residents so that there is one professional per every 4 residents in the restorative program. Walking programs, grooming programs (make up); communication programs, cooking programs, emphasizing ingesting nutrition and hydration by mouth are examples of restorative programs.

Therapeutic Recreation Model:

The Therapeutic Recreation Service Model developed by Peterson and Gunn (1984) is a client centered model related to the resident's amount of leisure involvement and focuses on three areas of services that address specific needs: (1) treatment, (2) leisure education, and (3) recreation participation. Peterson and Gunn recommended that activity and recreational personnel only focus on one of the three service categories.

Peterson and Gunn (1984) described the treatment category as "some specific planned process to bring about desired positive change in behavior or pathology." A therapeutic recreation specialist or activity professional uses the treatment category to address the behavioral area of functioning (physical, mental, emotional, and social functioning) usually in a highly controlled setting within the medical model. Sometimes a therapeutic recreation therapist co-leads groups or co-treats participants. A person in speech therapy may apply what has been learned in speech therapy during an outing where it is required to give a verbal order for a meal and beverage. The therapeutic recreation specialist can give an evaluation of the person's ability to use his speech in a public setting as well as other skills the speech therapist wants evaluated. An occupational therapist (OT) may have been working with a resident to increase his dressing skills. The therapeutic recreation specialist or activity professional would observe the person putting on his coat/hat, gloves, etc. and report back to the OT on the resident's ability to dress him/herself independently, with some assist or with total assist.

Leisure education is an educational model where the therapeutic recreation specialist or activity professional is an instructor or counselor helping the participant to learn new skills or provide information. The concept of play, which is considered a core behavior, is the basis of leisure education. Leisure education addresses four areas (1) leisure awareness, (2) social interaction skills, (3) leisure skill development and (4) leisure resources.

Recreation participation is a structured program that fosters enjoyment, fun, and self expression, within an organized delivery system. The participant must have certain skills and abilities to participate in order to have an enjoyable experience. A person may have learned how to bowl and keep score and utilizes these skills when bowling with others. Whether the person wins or loses, he enjoys the activity and socialization with bowling peers.

Peterson and Gunn (1984) recommend using the term/concept Leisure Life Style in Long Term care because of the participant's increased length of stay. A part of adjustment to Long Term care is developing a leisure life style. Some residents will be totally dependent upon staff for participation in an activity of choice. Other residents will be independent in selecting and participating in individual, one-to-one and/or group activities.

Therapeutic Milieu Model:

A therapeutic Milieu Model is different from Milieu Therapy technique. The therapeutic Milieu Model was first used in psychiatric hospitals. It is effective to use with geriatric residents who have psychiatric problems. In the therapeutic milieu model, residents participate in activities and assume personal control for participating in diversional activities as well as other activities.

Lanza (1997), states: "the goals for the activity professional in the therapeutic milieu model are to assist clients in reestablishing their emotional health through increasing functioning and skill development, arranging and encouraging participation in diversional programs, and allowing for client participation in the entire planning and treatment process. Because discharge is part of the expected process, activity planning includes opportunities to participate in appropriate life skills and exposure to community life."

Therapeutic Techniques

"Therapeutic techniques and intervention need to be individualized"

Therapeutic techniques and interventions can be effective for older adults. The techniques used most frequently are Milieu Therapy, Reality Orientation, Remotivation, Reminiscing and Validation Therapy. First, an older adult needs to be assessed as to his/her abilities, limitations and potential for benefiting from a specific therapeutic technique. Secondly, techniques need to be analyzed to determine the abilities and skills an older adult needs for the technique to be successful.

Milieu Therapy

Milieu therapy includes all the action and interaction in the environment which can have a positive effect on the older adult. The action in the environment includes the physical plant, e.g., layout of the agency/organization, physical arrangement of rooms and furniture, colors, lighting, heating/cooling, ventilation, flooring, wall-covering [paint/wallpaper], window covering [drapes, shades, blinds], decorations, noise and odor control.

Interaction includes all the interaction between staff, participants, family, friends and volunteers. Participants are affected by relationships. Friendly, caring staff assists participants in adjusting to a new program, organization or facility, as well as helping them feel at ease. Congenial interactions among peers, fosters caring for one another. Knowing limits helps participants feel safe and secure.

An organization is like a family. People get along well together when there is peace and harmony. If there is a problem with management, supervision or employees, it can have a negative effect on participants. This is much like the effects of a dysfunctional family. Residents who have disagreements and conflicts with peers and/or staff often disrupt the milieu, making it unpleasant for others. It is important to identify and correct the causes of conflict, disagreements and anger for a happy and healthy environment.

Activities programs play a large part is establishing a therapeutic milieu. Through a wide variety of activities and programs, participants can be empowered to utilize their skills and to learn new ones. Interests can be fostered. Friendships can be developed. Feelings can be expressed in an acceptable manner. Abilities and limitations can be accepted. Adapta-tions can be made for greater involvement, participation and enjoyment. Participants can continue to live with dignity and respect.

Milieu therapy can include reality orientation, remotivation or validation therapy. It is important to know the focus, and who can potentially benefit from each technique.

Reality Orientation

Reality orientation (RO) is orientation to person, time, place, and expectation. It has been used in hospitals for many years. Following surgery, patients are oriented by staff as they awaken from anesthesia. Patients in psychiatric hospitals are oriented to reality as an intervention for someone who does not know where he/she is, what day, date or year it is, who he/she is, or who others are (family members, friends, staff)—related to a specific diagnosis, e.g., psychosis, medication, and/or unfamiliar environment.

History of Reality Orientation

The Veterans' Administration Hospital in Tuscaloosa, Alabama is credited with developing reality orientation programs in the 1960's for veterans who were confused and disoriented related to brain damage from strokes and other diagnoses. The VA Hospital trained professionals, paraprofessionals and lay people to conduct 24 hour RO and RO classes in community settings and nursing homes. Reality orientation was considered a part of Milieu Therapy.

The Tuscaloosa program was designed by Dr. James Folsom and Lucille Taulbee. Dr. Folsom had developed earlier programs at the Topeka, Kansas, Veterans' Administration Hospital. The RO program grew out of a former program, Attitude Therapy, which Dr. Folsom had developed at the Mental Health Institute in Mt. Pleasant, Iowa.

Today, reality orientation is used with individuals living at home; patients in hospitals, residents in assisted-living facilities, personal-care facilities and nursing homes; those who participate in adult-day service programs and senior centers; and those in a variety of community programs, e.g., mental-health programs. Reality orientation can be used to maintain a person's orientation or to assist someone in regaining orientation. Simple reminders for an alert, cognitively-non-impaired older adult may be all that is needed, i.e., reminder of the day, date, and/or year. A person with significant cognitive impairment, i.e., dementia, Alzheimer's type may only be able to comprehend his/her name. Thus, consistently calling a person by a familiar name (Hattie, Mrs. Jones, Dr. Willmer) reinforces the person's orientation to himself or herself. Recovery or partial recovery of loss of short-term memory related to anesthesia, head injury, stroke, trauma, medication, fever, stresses, losses, change of environment, etc., may be regained through continuous use of reality orientation (person, place, time).

24-Hour Reality Orientation

Twenty-four-hour reality orientation is a team approach. Everyone who comes in contact with the older adult provides RO (orientation to person, time, place, expectation).

Greeting and calling someone by name and introduction to self and/or others foster orientation to person, "Hello, Mrs. Jones, I'm Julia Smith. I would like you to meet my friend, Harriet Andres." It is important to address a person by his preferred name, i.e., first or last name, or nickname. A nickname should only be used when preferred by the person.

Orientation to person, also includes knowing the names of family members, relatives, friends and staff, i.e., in an agency or institutional setting. Older adults in programs or agencies or those residing in a long-term care facility need time to learn staffs' names and positions. Staff needs to reinforce their names so that the older adult knows them by name or at least recognizes them, and knows who to ask for assistance. Family members may need to introduce themselves if their loved one does not know or recognize them. A person may not know a staff member or volunteer by name, but may recognize them by what they wear (uniform or street clothing). Name badges in large print can assist the older adult to remember and call a staff person or volunteer by name.

A person forgetting the day and/or date or wanting to know the time may ask another person for the information, i.e., "What day it?" "What time is it?" "What is today's date?" Someone unaware of the day, date or time may not be able to ask questions, thus is dependent on others for providing the information daily on a consistent basis. Orientation to time of day can be included in daily contact ("Good morning," "Good afternoon," "Good evening," "Good night"). Include the day or date ("Today is Tuesday." "Today is February 14th, Valentine's Day." "Today is March 1, 2010."). Direction and/or expectation can be provided with orientation to time ("It is five o'clock. It's time to eat dinner."). An older adult may not know what is expected unless reminded. "Mrs. Jones, you have a dental appointment today at 3:00 P.M.".

Orientation to place includes the name of the place (person's own home, agency/facility [retirement home, assisted living, nursing home]) and familiarization with names and location of rooms/areas, entrances and exits. Knowing physical boundaries inside and outside of the home and/or agency/facility is important for orientation as well as safety.

Otterbein Home

Today is:

The Date:

The Year is:

The Weather is:

(Optional)   **The Next Meal is:**

(Optional)   **The Next Activity is:**

(Optional)   **The Holiday is:**

A structured environment is important for reality orientation. Clocks, calendars, and reality orientation boards are visual reminders of day, date, year, and time of day. Current newspapers, magazines, radio, and TV provide orientation to time and events (local, state, national and international). Signs and room numbers provide orientation to surroundings in agencies and facilities. Posters announcing events, activity schedules, and decorations assist in knowing what is going on as well as the season or holiday.

Residents in long-term-care facilities need to be oriented to all their surroundings (room, bathroom, shower room, dining room, activity room, lounges, therapy room, nurses' station, etc.). Color coded units, room numbers on walls next to doors, paintings, and pictures and/or decorative items on walls can facilitate orientation to the environment.

Reality Orientation Classes

Structured RO classes in rehabilitation and long-term care settings can assist in the facilitation of RO when combined with 24-hour reality orientation. Participants meet five days per week in small groups for 30 to 45 minutes. The group is led by an instructor. Classes are structured, using orientation and repetition. The same routine is followed for each session. Participants are greeted. The leader and participants introduce themselves. If a participant is unable to introduce him/herself, the leader does it for him or her. The session begins by reading the RO board, identifying the name of the organization/ facility, day, date, year, weather, and sometimes the next meal, activity and holiday.

> The leader may ask a participant to read the board. Participants can be asked questions related to information provided, with or without the use of the RO board to assess and reinforce learning and recognition and recall of items (short-term memory). The leader may use other techniques such as flip charts prepared with questions or information partially filled in. Participants are asked to fill in the blank spaces (verbally or in writing). Cards (3"x 5") can be pre-printed with orientation information. Participants can be asked to select the correct day, date and year, or to select cards and put them in sequence for the day and date, year to foster recognition and organization.

Large-face clocks can be used for telling time and to identity what is done at a specific time. The leader turning the hands of the clock to 12:00 may ask, "What do you do at 12:00 (noon)?"

The leader must be committed to leading the group. Consistency is imperative for participants to learn and remember orientation information, with or without the assistance of cues or visual aids. Learning aids can either be purchased or made, i.e., RO boards, clocks, calendars, etc. Creating new materials assists the leader in maintaining interest, and potentially prevents participants from becoming bored. Materials can include pictures of activities for recognition and identification of time related to what time a specific activity is done, i.e., breakfast, lunch, dinner, church, bingo, and other activities. Pictures of season or holidays to paint or fill in with magic markers or crayons (medium of participant's choice) can reinforce what is being learned/relearned. Making a monthly calendar is a practical and useful item for participants to use daily. Participants can be instructed to cross off the previous day, so that they have a simple way of knowing what day it is by looking at their calendar. A calendar can be made on 8 1/2" X 14" paper with a drawing representing the month or season on the top half of the paper and the calendar form on the bottom. Color can be added to the drawing. Participants can fill in the calendar month and dates following a preprinted calendar.

Object identification and sensory stimulation are often added to the group when participants are able to handle more information. Some facilities have developed a basic and an advanced RO group. The basic group focuses on orientation to person, time and place; whereas the advanced group offers more activities, i.e., sensory-stimulation, object recognition, simple recognition/recall games, etc.

Use of Reality Orientation

Today, reality orientation is provided at the beginning of activities. Participants are greeted with the day and date and the name of the activity. Staff and volunteers are introduced before the activity begins ("Good morning; today is Wednesday, July 30, 2010.) I am Sally Hunter, Activity Assistant. Mrs. Jones, our new volunteer, will be assisting us with crafts today. I would like you to introduce yourselves," etc.) Reality orientation can be incorporated within an activity, i.e., talking about the day, date, what is happening in the news and weather, new information about the facility, activities, changes, etc.

Use of Reality Orientation with Older Adults with Severe Cognitive Impairment

The primary focus of reality orientation is on assisting someone to maintain or regain orientation. Reality orientation is also used as a kind, considerate technique with persons who do not have the ability to remember something for a short period of time, in order to help them maintain their dignity. The focus is on the moment, not for a longer term effect. Staff introducing themselves by name may save a person the embarrassment of not being able to call the person by name or to read his/her name badge. Helping a person find his/her room by pointing to a specific picture outside the room or a room number reduces anxiety for the moment. When the person leaves the area, he/she will be dependent upon staff for assistance in using the same technique for finding his/her room again. Giving simple instructions assists the person in knowing what is expected, i.e., "Mrs. Butles, roll the ball." "Eat your ice cream." "Put on your glasses, etc." Thus reality orientation is often a part of cueing and redirection.

When a person's cognitive abilities have severely declined, continuously addressing the person by name reinforces who he/she is. Each person who comes in contact with the participant needs to introduce him/herself. The participant will not remember who the person said he/she is, but will feel the kindness and respect. Orientation to name is used in conjunction with validation therapy for participants who are considered to be old-old and time-confused. Validation is explained at the end of this chapter.

Summary

Reality orientation can be used for its initially intended purpose—orientation to person, time, place, for older adults with some mild to moderate short-term-memory loss. It can be incorporated into the total philosophy of care. Staff and caregivers must recognize when it should be used to achieve goals with long-lasting effect and when it is to be used for the moment to protect and foster an older person's dignity.

Remotivation

"Reaching into the past to motivate for the present"

Remotivation is a structured group technique. The focus of the technique is for participants to regain interest in their lives and surroundings. Through discussions it is hoped that participants will renew interests and return to activities that once were meaningful prior to their illness/disability. A trained group leader follows a structured five-step format to discuss pre-planned topics. Props (visual aids and objects) are used to enhance the discussion. Group members interact with the leader and between participants.

There are two types of remotivation groups: basic and advanced. In the basic groups, topics of an objective nature are discussed. In these remotivation groups, the group leader follows a five step structured program. Controversial topics such as religion, politics and sex are avoided; these topics can be discussed in advanced remotivation groups. Participants must complete a basic remotivation group prior to being asked to participate in an advanced remotivation group.

Trained remotivation leaders and other team members select six to fifteen potential participants. Remotivation is explained to the selected participants. They are then asked to participate in a basic remotivation group. Only participants willing to participate are accepted into the group. Meetings are held once a week for twelve weeks or two times a week for six weeks. Sessions are approximately 45 minutes in length.

History of Remotivation

Remotivation was started in 1949 by Dorothy Hoskins Smith, an English teacher. Initially she developed a public-speaking class for psychiatric patients at the VA Hospital in Northampton, Massachusetts. She became interested in working with regressed, withdrawn and catatonic patients. Poetry was used to bring patients into contact with reality and then she worked on redeveloping patients' communication skills.

Remotivation was developed as a highly-structured group technique to be used with severely regressed persons with psychiatric illness. In 1956, the Mental Health Association of Southeastern Pennsylvania and the Smith Kline & French Laboratories provided a grant for Mrs. Smith to set up remotivation classes at the Philadelphia State Hospital. Two hundred nurses and attendants were trained to use remotivation on their wards. Trained instructors provided training throughout the United States. In 1960, regional training centers were established by the American Psychiatric Association. The National Remotivation Technique Organization (NRTO) was organized in 1971.

The Philadelphia State Hospital provided 30-hour training courses in Basic and Advanced Remotivation in the 1970's. Professionals working in a variety of settings (not just psychiatric hospitals) around the country received training in Basic and Advanced Remotivation. The number of these trained instructors continued to expand and remotivation was implemented in a variety of settings, not just psychiatric hospitals and day treatment centers. Remotivation groups were formed in agencies/organizations serving clients with mental retardation and/or physical disabilities. Senior centers, nursing homes and adult day service centers also began to use remotivation successfully.

Original Goals and Objectives

The original goals for remotivation were:

(1) Deinstitutionalization of persons in psychiatric hospitals, through decision-making and relating to reality

(2) Prevention of regression and maintenance of functioning of older adults in nursing homes

The objectives were:

(1) Orientation to reality

(2) Self-expression through verbalization and socialization

(3) Maintaining or regaining cognitive abilities

Having accomplished these objectives, it was believed that the participants would have enhanced self-esteem and self-worth.

Remotivation Group

Remotivation is a structured group meeting, not a class. The group meets one to three times per week for 30 to 45 minutes for a total of twelve sessions. It is a closed group. Only participants selected and willing to participate in the group are allowed to attend. Once a specific group is started, no new participants can join. This is to maintain the cohesiveness of the group. When the group completes twelve sessions, participants can continue in an advanced group or be discharged from the group. New groups are formed as needed.

Participants

Participants are selected by the trained remotivation leader and other team members. Usually, six to fifteen participants are selected. The purpose of the group is explained to potential participants. They are then asked to join the groups. Their right to refuse to join is respected.

Selection of participants will depend upon the setting, abilities and limitations of the participants. Criteria for referral (selecting members for a group) is based on limitations, e.g., being withdrawn, unmotivated. Criteria for participating in the group are based on abilities, i.e., ability to interact, hear, speak, no preoccupation or hallucinations, and willingness to participate. The group needs to be made up of some participants who are verbal so that verbal interaction within the group can be facilitated. Criteria for termination from the group are completion of twelve remotivation sessions, inability or unwillingness to remain in the group, or discharge from the facility or termination from the organization.

Remotivation Technique

The remotivation leader selects a specific topic. The next task is to develop a plan for using the topic following the five steps for a remotivation session. This is a structured written plan which includes specific questions to be asked, poetry related to the topic, and objects to be identified and explored.

Five Steps for Remotivation:

1. Climate of Acceptance

The remotivation leader sets a warm, welcoming and pleasant climate. Individual participants are welcomed by name as they enter the room or the group seating. The leader shakes participants' hands and touches their hand or shoulder to make social contact. A positive comment to each person assists in helping participants feel valued and wanted in the group. The group leader introduces him/her self. This can be done individually with group members as they are welcomed, or to the group before everyone is welcomed individually.

2. A Bridge to Reality

The remotivation leader may use "bounce" questions to get everyone to focus on the topic. Bounce questions usually go from general to specific questions leading to the topic.

Example - *Bounce Questions*

What types of churches were in the neighborhood or city where you grew up?

What did the churches look like, i.e. red brick, stone, white, etc.?

What was at the top of the church or roof? (A steeple.)

What is in the steeple? (Bell)

When was the bell rung?

These questions help the participants transfer thoughts from whatever they were thinking about, to the selected topic, "Bells."

A poem about bells could be read. A picture of a steeple with a bell could be shown. Information in the paper could be read. Participants share in the reading of materials.

3. *Exploring the World We Live In*

In this step the topic is explored in depth. The leader uses prepared questions to facilitate the structured discussion. All participants are included in the discussion to facilitate their involvement; the remotivation leader may use indirect questions to the group as a whole or may direct specific questions to individuals. Visual and auditory aids are very helpful. Items to see, touch, explore and/or identify as to similarities and differences provide a multisensory experience.

In discussing bells, the remotivation leader may use samples of actual bells made from different materials, i.e., metal, glass, brass, plastic, paper, pewter, silver, copper, etc., pictures of bells from books, magazines, greeting cards, decorations (wedding bell, Christmas bell, etc.), maps of where bells are made, short interesting stories about bells, a short video on bells, or any other type of prop to enhance the discussion.

The preplanned questions could relate to different types of bells, use of bells, or experiences with bells.

4. *Exploring the Work of the World*

Originally this step was for patients in psychiatric hospitals to explore possible jobs that they might want to consider upon release from the hospital. Today, it can be used with older adults to talk about past accomplishments. It can also be a catalyst for discussing changes and the work of the world today. Step # 4 can also be omitted from the discussion.

5. *Climate of Appreciation*
At the end of the session, the remotivation leader summarizes the discussion. Individual participants are recognized for their specific contribution. All group members are thanked for their attendance and involvement. The remotivation leader then announces the next meeting and welcomes everyone to attend.

After the discussion, food and/or beverages may be served to foster socialization and group cohesiveness. It is not necessary to provide food; however, the authors highly recommend that food be served, i.e., coffee/tea/pop and a snack.

Originally remotivation was developed for regressed psychiatric patients. Today the technique can be used with older adults who are withdrawn and uninvolved in activities and with others who where involved in activities at one time (i.e., prior to present illness or disability). The structured steps and use of props can enhance group discussion and awaken memories and interests. Step #1 (Climate of Acceptance) and Step #5 (Climate of Appreciation) can be used in most activity groups.

Resocialization

"Resocialize through the sharing of love"

Resocialization is a group technique using both discussion and involvement in activities to increase socialization (verbal and nonverbal). Through the process, relationships develop which can pave the way to friendships. Resocialization can foster renewed interests in former activities or the development of new interests in activities. Resocialization groups have evolved over the years. They have structure but are less formal than remotivation. The leader is a facilitator, not an instructor.

Resocialization Groups
Resocialization groups are small (three to twelve people). These groups are generally for older adults who are new to a long-term-care facility, or who have become isolated from others due to cognitive, emotional or physical decline related to an illness or disability. The group meets one to three times per week. Usually the same group members meet; however, if a person terminates from the group, another person can take his/her place.

The group leader introduces him/herself and requests group members to introduce themselves. Name tags, written in large print, can be used to assist participants in addressing each other by name and/or remembering names. A participant may be asked to distribute name tags, giving that person a role and an opportunity to learn names and faces.

Food and a beverage are generally served before or during the group meeting as a part of the socialization process. Topics for discussion can be chosen before the meeting related to group interests/concerns, i.e., family; relationships; adjustment to aging, chronic illness or disability; values and experiences; and reminiscing. A topic can be continued. Simple get-acquainted games can be played, e.g., ice-breakers. Non-threatening social games involving interaction with peers, e.g., Ungame, Life Stories, Penny Ante, can also be played for increased socialization.

As the group advances and individuals become more comfortable, other activities can be tried, i.e., word games, cards, board games, and physical games such as ring toss, bowling, or basketball where individuals can receive support from peers. Creative activities (art, crafts, poetry, movement, dance, simple drama) can foster interaction and increase self-esteem and the esteem of peers.

When a participant achieves the goals for participating in the group, he/she usually is ready to participate in other structured small- or large-group activities. Termination from the group may be difficult for some participants. They may need a little extra reassurance regarding participating in the regularly-scheduled activities program.

Resocialization groups are designed to assist an older person to socialize with peers. The ultimate goal is independent socialization and involvement in activities of former interests or new activities of choice.

Socialization

"It takes at least two persons to socialize"

People by nature are social. Everyone has a need to belong (to a family, circle of friends, church, etc.). The purpose of socialization groups in agencies and facilities is to facilitate socialization among peers. It is a means for people to get to know and care for one another and potentially become friends. Socialization groups can be open or closed, formal or informal. Criteria for participation in the group may include participants new to a program or facility, residents in facilities who do not have visitors, participants who have not established relationships with peers but are willing to meet others, and participants who are not comfortable in initiating conversation.

Socialization groups can be developed for participants with different levels of social, cognitive, physical and emotional functioning abilities. Participants in a high-level group would be more involved in the planning process. Participants who have cognitive impairments can be involved in planning, even though they may forget what they planned from week to week. The leader reminds the group of what they had planned. Participants with mood/behavioral deficits may be able to function well in a supportive group of peers or may need a separate group which is highly structured. Mood and behavior may change

as a result of participating in a socialization group as participants feel accepted and valued.

Socialization Groups

Socialization groups like resocialization groups are small groups of three to ten people. Groups meet once a week for 45 to 60 minutes. Emphasis is on interaction between peers. Refreshments are provided as part of the total socialization experience. Participants are involved in planning group meetings, including refreshments. Groups can be open or closed, formal or informal.

The group leader is a facilitator. Initially the group leader plans the group meetings. When group members become comfortable, the leader involves the participants in planning meetings. This empowers participants to make decisions and fosters interaction and awareness of individual peers' likes and dislikes.

Activities can include interactive games, craft projects, service projects, discussion, reminiscing or whatever is of interest to the participants. Socialization can be facilitated through sharing of supplies, working on a group project, sharing of accomplishments, reminiscing or actively participating in a discussion. Non-threatening games such as The Ungame, Life Stories, and Penny Ante provide opportunities for group members to share, get to know one another better, laugh and have fun.

Group members can have roles and responsibilities, i.e., hostess, set-up, clean-up, passing out supplies, keeping score in games, etc. If discussion is used, participants can select the topic at the meeting or in advance for the next meeting. Thus, they are empowered to make decisions.

Participants sit around a table for the group meetings. The leader introduces him/herself, welcomes participants and states the purpose of the group. This is followed by group members introducing themselves, often with a handshake. Ice-breakers can also be used for introductions.

The group leader starts the socialization group by introducing a discussion topic or an activity. The purpose of an activity is explained. Participants may be asked to assist with passing out supplies.

Refreshments are served during or after the meeting, depending upon the focus of the meeting. Initially, group members may feel more at ease if refreshments are served first. The group leader, knowing the participants, has to decide when to serve food. If participants are only motivated by food, it may be not be effective to serve food first.

During the process of the group meeting, participants are praised for their involvement by both the leader and their peers. Individual recognition is given by the leader to the participants by calling them by name, asking questions, commenting on their ideas/experiences/feelings, and pointing out what peers have in common.

At the conclusion of the group meeting, the group leader thanks members for their participation either individually or as a group. Participants can be asked if they have any questions or comments about the group meeting.

The next meeting is discussed, allowing participants to make suggestions. The group leader always needs to prepare options for the next meeting, in case participants cannot think of what they want to do. The focus of the next session is identified. The group leader concludes the meeting with a positive comment, poem, or thought for the day related to interacting with others. Group members exchange good byes with a handshake or hug.

Summary:

Socialization groups assist participants in their adjustment to new settings and community living. Members of the groups grow individually and with one another as they participate in a variety of interactive activities. Food and/or a beverage are a part of the group meeting. The group leader is a facilitator; however, group members can assume roles and responsibilities. This can increase self-esteem as well as socialization. Activities involving interaction facilitate socialization through sharing supplies, working on a group project, involvement in group games, sharing accomplishments, discussions and reminiscing.

Validation Therapy

"Validation is important for the disoriented"

Validation therapy is a technique used with disoriented, old-old adults. It validates every person as a unique individual. The purpose of validation therapy is to assist a person to regain his/her sense of dignity and self-worth, and to resolve feelings related to conflicts in life. Observation of body language is important in recognizing the different stages of disorientation. Empathy is used to build trust. The goal is to maintain communication (verbal and nonverbal) to reduce anxiety. When a person is not able to verbalize, communication is at the emotional level.

History of Validation Therapy

The theory of validation therapy was developed by Naomi Feil, ACSW, at Monteflore Home for the Aged in Cleveland, Ohio. Naomi began working with disoriented old-old people in 1963. Her initial goal was to help the severely disoriented old-old with a variety of diagnoses, to face reality and to relate to each other in a group. By 1966, she found that trying to help disoriented old-old to face reality was unrealistic. In a group, she found that exploring feelings and reminiscing helped group members to respond to one another. She noted that music stimulated group cohesion and feelings of well-being.

From her experience, she dropped reality orientation in 1967 and developed validation. Ms. Feil states:

"I learned Validation from people with whom I worked. I learned they have wisdom to survive by returning to the past." 1989

There are two principles underlying validation therapy:

1. Early emotional learning stays with a person in the old-old stage of development, even though cognitive abilities decline. A person can emotionally experience the hurts, guilt and conflicts of early life (infancy and childhood) during the late stage of life (85 years and older). A person emotionally remembers the touch and caring voice of mother, as well as the hurts. Childhood memories are seen and heard. They are seen with their "minds eye." The past emotions that are felt at present are real to the person; thus, these feelings become facts to them.

2. The last stage of development for the old-old adult is vegetation versus resolution, according to Feil. This is based on Erik Erikson's Life Stages in which he defines the last stage of life as "ego integrity versus despair." The person who achieves this stage of development has accepted life and has resolved conflicts in life (ego integrity).

   When the person has not achieved ego integrity by the old-old stage, he/she will not be able to accept losses (physical, emotional) and has feelings of despair. If past conflicts cannot be resolved, a person vegetates until death.

According to Feil, there are four stages of disorientation: **(1)** *malorientation,* **(2)** *time-confusion,* **(3)** *repetitive motion* and **(4)** *vegetation.* Each stage has specific physical and emotional characteristics and feelings that are experienced.

Stage One: Malorientation

The maloriented person holds onto past ways (socially-prescribed rules) of dealing with life. He/she denies feelings. Conflicts are expressed in disguised forms. People and objects become symbols for persons and experiences in the past. Anger toward a parent or sibling that was never resolved may be negatively expressed to someone who reminds the maloriented person of a person in the past. They need someone to trust, to be a parent to validate them, so that they can express old feelings as if they were the present. Integrity is the goal, thus avoiding vegetation.

Some of the emotional characteristics of malorientation (stage one) are repeating unresolved conflicts of the past while holding on to present reality; wanting to be understood and to understand; having a sense of humor; playing games with rules, confabulating (making up stories) to deny confusion; denying feelings and resisting change; blaming others; becoming furious with others who do not use self-control; and holding on to personal possessions tightly, i.e., purse, papers, sweater, hat, cane.

Physically, the maloriented person can see, hear, speak and move. His/her stance is rigid. Arms are folded, and finger and hands are often pointed. Movement in space is definite, precise and sustained. Eyes are clear and focused. Body muscles, face and lips are tight. The jaw often juts out. The voice is harsh, whining and shrill.

Cognitively, these persons are able to read, write, use dictionary words, and figure math. They have ability for rational thinking. They can also achieve insight into the reasons behind behaviors.

Socially, the maloriented person resents intimacy and invasion into his/her personal space. He/she does not like to be touched.

Stage Two: Time-Confusion

When a person who is maloriented is no longer able to deny his/her losses and unable to hold onto reality, he/she enters stage two: time-confusion. He/she can't conform to social rules and societal dress codes. Fantasy begins. In this stage, present reality is substituted for early memories. The use of symbols increases to represent people and experiences of the past. Language also changes.

The emotional characteristics of a person in stage two are several: expression of feelings (not facts); energy is focused on resolving past conflicts to trigger feelings of pleasure and usefulness; demanding immediate satisfaction of basic needs (food, love, sex); loss of sense of humor; personal feelings identify time, (not clock time); deserves to be loved (since food is love, wants food immediately after eating, and may continue to focus on wanting food); is aware of genuineness versus superficiality of others; and responds positively to eye contact and nurturing, genuine, loving relationships.

Cognitive decline includes immediately forgetting names, dates and faces from the present; short attention span; irrational thinking, not remembering facts; loss of metaphoric thinking; inability to categorize (people, objects); inability to compare (a doll is a baby); inability to recall recent events but has excellent recall for past events that foster strong feelings; does not listen to people in present time; loss of awareness of self and others; thinks in vivid images; clearly hears sounds from the past; can be poetic and creative in trying to explain item from the past (words need to be carefully deciphered to understand what the person is trying to say); uses unique word forms from early memories; expects others to understand their unique language; uses pronouns with specific references ("She" could be mother, aunt, sister, teacher, wife, self or place.); does not give pertinent facts to be understood; increasingly uses symbols (representing people, and events of the past); and uses melodies (humming) and rhythms (rocking, tapping and body movements) as a substitution for words. Even though there are many cognitive limitations, people with time-confusion have the wisdom to resolve conflicts.

A person with time-confusion is unable to write, figure math or play games with rules. However, he/she usually still can read.

Physically the tight muscles in stage one loosens. Movement is graceful. Body posture changes to a shuffling gait with shoulders slumped forward and neck down. Breathing is slow and sustained. Hand gestures that were once pointed now match gestures (often questioning-type gestures). Speech is slow and the voice-tone is low. It is seldom harsh or whiny as in stage one.

Validation helps to reduce stress in a person who is experiencing time-confusion. It also provides moments of rational thinking and reduces the need to return to past-time. A nurturing relationship and interactions, sharing of feelings and validation often prevent a person from withdrawing to stage three.

Stage Three: Repetitive Motion

If a person is unable to resolve his/her feelings through a nurturing relationship, he/she often declines further into pre-language sounds and movements for self-nurturing. He/she tries to resolve the past by using body parts to represent people of the past.

In stage three, there is further cognitive loss. There is increased loss of sense of self and body in space. Outside stimuli is shut out. The ability as well as the desire, to think is lost. The person remembers early experiences. Ability to read, write a sentence and play games by rules is lost. He/she may be unable to talk in sentences but is still able to sing. Attention span is short. Concentration is focused on one person or object at a time. While expression of feelings is not verbally, persons in stage three have the wisdom to express feelings non-verbally to resolve conflict in the past (relationships, experiences, etc.).

Physically, the need for speech is lost due to disuse. Sensory abilities decline (seeing and hearing) as does the ability to walk well. Incontinency is the norm. The person may have energy for dancing and singing, but little energy for talking or thinking. Movement is graceful, but the person is unaware of movement. Eyes are closed or not focused. Repetitive movements are the result of feelings and body movements becoming intertwined.

Socially and emotionally, a person is resigned to isolation and self-stimulation. Crying may be frequent. Constant repetitive movements and sounds provide pleasure, relieve boredom, control anxiety, help resolve feelings, and reassure existence. A sense of humor is lost. Need-satisfaction is wanted immediately. An inability to wait is displayed. Physical repetitive movements have an emotional cause. A person who is emotionally hungry may eat anything. Angry feelings toward someone in the past may be expressed through banging. The pounding may lesson as feelings are expressed. Anguished pacing increases.

A person in stage three can respond to a combination of close contact, eye contact, nurturing touch, and voice-tones. Repetitive movements can be matched to show empathy when words are lost.

Stage Four: Vegetation

In this stage, a person gives up. There is no longer the desire to resolve the needs and conflicts of the past. The person shuts out the outside world and may live in a state of vegetation for a long time, even years.

Cognitive abilities decline to the point that the person in stage four does not recognize family or friends seen every day. Fantasies are no longer expressed in words or body movement. Recognizable symbols are no longer used.

Emotionally, the person does not respond to eye contact, touch or voice-tone. He/she does not try to express feelings or resolve unfinished past contacts.

Physical changes include sleeping or sitting with eyes closed most of the time. When eyes are open, they are dull—not focused—staring and unseeing. Muscles are loose, but do not show expression. Movement is slower, i.e., half-time movement. Murmurs are very weak and usually one sound. However, they are rare.

There is little evidence of response to validation. However, people in the vegetation stage need recognition, touch and nurturing, even though therapeutic gains may not be evident.

It is hoped that a disoriented, old-old person will not decline to the vegetation stage of life.

Summary

Validation is a technique of working with the disoriented old-old. Four stages of disorientation have been developed. A disoriented, old-old person can be assisted in the process of resolving past needs and conflicts. A variety of therapeutic techniques can be utilized including personal recognition, a nurturing relationship, eye contact, touch and mirroring. The goal is intervention to prevent a person from giving up and vegetating.

Validation can be used for a one-to-one relationship or in groups. The Feil method explains the process for one-to-one relationships and how to form validation groups.

Naomi Feil, an international speaker, presents validation therapy workshops through a variety of continuing-education-sponsoring organizations. Information on training can be obtained from Validation Therapy, Cleveland, Ohio.

Sensory Stimulation

"Sensory stimulation can be fun, fantastic and fulfilling"

Sensory stimulation can be used as a group, one-to-one or individual technique. The technique is used with older adults with cognitive impairments who have difficulty relating to and responding to their environment. In addition to cognitive impairments a person may also have reduced opportunities for stimulation related to physical, emotional and/or social disabilities/limitations. The focus of sensory stimulation is to increase awareness and response to the environment. This is done by stimulating the five senses (visual [sight], auditory [sound], tactile [touch], gustatory [taste], and olfactory [smell]). In sensory-stimulation groups, participants sit around a table except when participating in a physical activity such as ball-toss or bean-bag toss.

Sensory-Stimulation Groups

Sensory-stimulation groups are structured by the leader. The planned group can include all five senses and kinesthetic experiences (movement/exercise) or focus on one or two senses, depending upon the abilities and responses from the participants. A person with loss of central vision would not benefit from a visual activity. A person with sensor neural hearing impairment would not be able to hear most sounds. Cueing and redirection are often used along with sensory stimuli.

In long-term-care facilities, sensory stimulation groups are scheduled three to seven times per week for 30 to 45 minutes. Groups consist of three to ten people, depending upon the ability levels of participants (the lower the cognitive-functioning ability level, the smaller the group). For residents with very low-cognitive-functioning abilities, groups scheduled for late morning and afternoon work well, as residents are rested from the night before or from an afternoon nap. When possible it is best to conduct the sensory groups in lounges or day rooms on units versus an activity room far away from the unit. This reduces resident anxiety and fear of leaving the familiar space of the unit. Another space to use is the dining room immediately prior to meals, as this room is familiar to residents.

Scheduling sensory groups at pre-meal time in the dining room or in therapeutic dining rooms can be effective. Usually residents with low-cognitive-functioning abilities are taken to the dining room 30 or more minutes before the noon and evening meal. Sensory stimulation can be conducted around tables or in an open area where residents can be seated in a circle. One or more nursing assistants or rehabilitation aids (with training in sensory stimulation) could be scheduled to assist or conduct sensory-stimulation groups. The structure and activity for sensory groups in a dining room would differ from a sensory group conducted in a smaller space with no interruptions.

It is best to have participants sit in a circle or around a table where they can see each other. If simple bending/stretching exercise, ball toss, or other adaptive sports are to be used, participants need space in which to move. Simple stretching of upper extremities and deep breathing can be done while sitting around a table.

Criteria for referral and participation in sensory groups can include moderate to severe impairment on standardized cognitive-functioning tests, e.g., a score of five to ten errors on the Short Portable Mental Status Questionnaire (SPMSQ), ability to remain upright or in a semi-reclining position, i.e., Geri recliner, limited verbalization or non-verbalization, repetitive movement/ stimulation, i.e., continuously touching self or objects, rubbing, patting, pounding table/chair], ability to respond to stimuli, i.e., eye contact, smile, gesture, withdrawal from stimuli, change of body movement or breathing pattern, and ability to participate in a group, with or without cueing and/or redirection.

The structure for a sensory-stimulation group for older adults who have moderately impaired cognitive functioning abilities would start with a welcome, introduction with shaking of hands, and orientation to day, date, year and group. Simple exercise (range of motion, stretching, bending, breathing) to music would follow. The five senses would then be stimulated around a theme.

A theme could relate to a season, holiday, object, or interest of participants. For an apple theme, an apple pie could be placed in an oven or microwave oven so that the scent is distinguishable when participants enter the room. An electric potpourri with apple-scented oil could also be used. Fresh apples of different colors could be placed on a table for immediate viewing. Pictures of apples, an apple orchard, or apple products in magazines, seed catalogs and advertisements could be shown. Participants could use the movement of picking apples and placing them in a basket as a part of their exercise for kinesthetic awareness. Singing songs or listening to songs about apples ("Don't Sit under the Apple Tree") and reminiscing about apples would provide auditory stimulation (sound). Apple scratch-and-sniff papers could be used for smell. Apples could be given to participants to touch, smell and eat, thus stimulating the sense of touch, smell and taste. Cooled, hot apple pie could be served for taste. Diets and swallowing precautions need to be followed when providing food. Simple identification questions could be asked, or simply talking and reminiscing could be a part of the total group experience.

When sensory groups are conducted for residents with very low-cognitive-functioning abilities, the leader most often uses a one-to-one technique with each one in the group. While one person is being individually stimulated, the others can watch or listen to the action and interaction. Over a period of time working with the same residents, the leader will discover to which sense(s) the resident responds best and can build upon successful experience. When presented with an object (large ball, stuffed animal, doll) some residents will respond by holding the object while others will push the object away. One person may prefer large objects; another may respond to small objects. Picture books of babies, children, flowers, pets/animals, and food or other objects provide visual stimulation of both color and object.

Music/movement and singing provide kinesthetic experience and auditory stimulation. Spices, scratch-and-sniff scents, perfume or after-shave lotion on a cotton ball or live flowers stimulates the sense of smell. A beverage and/or snack stimulate taste.

One-To-One Sensory Stimulation

A person with severe loss of cognitive, physical, and social functioning can still be stimulated. He or she may not be able to see or may have a hearing impairment but is usually able to smell and feel being touched.

When presenting an item to smell, the activity professional tells the resident what is being presented for him/her to smell. Place the object beneath the nose and slowly pass it under the nostrils. Often a person will open his/her mouth and thrust the tongue forward in response to the stimulation. Movement of the nostrils may be seen. An adverse reaction is movement of the head away from the stimuli.

Objects can be placed in a person's hand(s) or next to the face, hand or arm. If needed, the person's hand can be guided over an object as it is explained (name, color, size, texture, and possible experiences the person had with the object). Objects of different textures, e.g., cotton ball, feather, fabric, mitten, etc., can be stroked on the back of the person's hand, the inner or outer arm, or the neck or cheek. A soothing unrushed voice provides calmness in addition to the stimulus.

Music, singing, playing recorded familiar sounds (horn, animals, bell, music boxes, etc.) provide auditory stimulation. Before the activity professional presents the stimulation, the participant needs to be informed of what is to be heard. After the stimulation has been presented, the activity professional can comment on the stimulation. Holding the participant's hand lightly and moving to the rhythm of the music/song adds a kinesthetic experience. If the person's hand/arms are contracted, stroking the person to the rhythm of the music provides tactile stimulation in addition to the auditory stimulation.

Taste can be stimulated through a variety of beverages and foods, in keeping with diets and swallowing ability. Informing a resident what is to be tasted and having him/her smell the items stimulates both smell and taste. Beverage and food items can be related to seasons, holidays, flavors and personal preferences.

Visual stimulation can be accomplished by showing and explaining objects, or pictures, or picture books on a specific topic, e.g., dogs, cats, horses, animated objects, e.g., walking/barking dogs, provide an interesting stimulus to watch and hear if sound is part of the object.

Individual Stimulation

Residents with low-cognitive-functioning abilities are often dependent upon family and staff for stimulation. Residents receive the benefit of team members and families working closely together. Favorite music can be played. Mobiles, pictures, objects on walls and tables, photo albums, and picture books provide visual stimulation. Stuffed animals, dolls or other objects to hold provide both tactile stimulation and comfort. Short videos on animals or children (and sometimes animated cartoons) can be effective stimuli. Viewing videos made by families may be a source of comfort for a person. Daily use of powders, perfumes, perfumed soaps, shaving and after shave lotions, or cologne are pleasurable tactile and olfactory sensations.

Staff needs to be aware of the environment in which a resident lives. Is it pleasurable and conducive to stimulating the senses?

Summary

Sensory stimulation can be used with persons with different levels of cognitive impairments. It can be used for one-to-one, individual and group stimulation. Participant response will differ, related to abilities, interests and preferences. The activity professional needs to be creative in deciding what material to use. Observation of responses is very important. New stimuli can be selected once the activity professional knows the participant's response to various types of stimulation.

Treatment Modalities and Team Approach to Quality Care
"Collaboration facilitates a team approach"

Older adults with physical or psychological impairment have a wide variety of opportunities for physical rehabilitation and psychological treatment in hospitals, rehabilitation centers, sub-acute units, long-term-care facilities and community-based services. Treatment is provided by an occupational therapist, physical therapist, speech pathologist, respiratory therapist, massage therapist, psychiatrist, psychologist, recreation therapist, art therapist, dance/movement therapist, drama therapist, horticulture therapist, music therapist, or poetry therapist. Restorative care is provided by trained restorative aides.

All evaluations and treatments must be ordered by a physician. Individual therapists decide on the evaluation and treatment procedures for an individual in relation to the older adult's diagnosis, presenting symptoms, functional abilities, goals and willingness to participate in treatment. Certified occupational therapy assistants (COTA) work under the supervision of an occupational therapist. Physical therapy assistants (PTA) work under the supervision of a licensed physical therapist. Restorative aides work with a rehabilitation nurse or a nurse trained in restorative nursing.

Treatment can be individual or by group depending upon the need and treatment modality being used.

Individualized treatment may be short-or long-term. In sub acute and rehabilitation units there is a heavy emphasis on therapy with the goal of an older adult returning to his/her highest level of functioning. The ultimate goal may be independent living, independent living with some community services, e.g., assistance with bathing and meal preparation, or placement in an assisted living facility or long-term-care facility. Treatment initiated in a hospital setting may be followed up by the same or different therapists in a home or institutional setting, i.e., assisted living, long-term-care facility.

Collaboration with Therapists

"Gratitude is the grease in human relations"

Activity professionals need to collaborate with therapists providing treatment for residents. It is important to know how to actively augment therapy through activities, as well as when a resident needs rest to regain energy for therapy. Residents/participants need to be educated on the importance of activity participation in relation to their diagnosis, disease process, functional abilities and maintenance/enhancement of abilities gained through therapy. This individual educational process can start during and/or after therapy.

There are a variety of ways in which activity professionals and therapists collaborate. Specific groups, i.e., meal-preparation, community-reintegration, etc, may be co-lead by therapists and activity professionals. Therapeutic programs may be developed using a level system. Criteria are established for each level, and either a therapist and/or an activity professional are responsible for specific levels. A person involved in physical therapy may graduate to a restorative type of exercise program and progress to a maintenance type of exercise program. A physical therapist would provide the initial evaluation and treatment, and assist and supervise other team members in conducting their assigned exercise programs. This type of coordinated programming is most beneficial to the resident. It also provides a coordinated process that can be understood by all professionals involved in the care of a resident/participant, while helping family members understand why a resident/participant is participating in different programs.

Activity professionals need to learn as much as possible about the different types of therapies and how they can collaborate their efforts with therapists. Collaboration will vary in different settings. However, with the increase of managed care and emphasis on rehabilitation and other types of specialty care, activity professionals will increasingly be working with other therapists.

Activity professionals need to be open-minded and ready to collaborate with therapists for the best interests of and quality of life for residents. The following examples of collaboration between therapists and activity professionals are not all-inclusive. However, they will provide a stepping stone for thinking about and understanding collaboration.

Occupational Therapists (OT

Occupational therapists are certified and licensed to practice in most states. Certified occupational therapy assistants are also licensed in accordance with state regulations. In long-term-care facilities an occupational therapist may work full-time or part-time as an employee or on a contractual basis. Thus the amount of time that an occupational therapist is available for collaboration with activity professionals will be dependent upon the need for O.T. services in the specific setting.

O.T.s evaluates cognitive, physical, emotional and social functioning through a variety of standardized assessments, observations, interviews and record reviews. Treatment can vary from one to several goals. Individual interventions also vary depending upon the resident's/patient's needs abilities and willingness to participate in treatment.

Occupational therapists can provide training for activity professionals to better understand occupational therapy and to support residents' involvement in it. If an activity professional is not working with an occupational therapist, he/she can seek informal training/observation at a local hospital, rehabilitation center or other long-term-care facility.

Occupational therapy focuses on the upper body parts such as range of motion, muscle strengthening of arms and relaxation, coordination, i.e., eye/hand, eye/mouth, splinting, activities of daily living (eating, bathing, dressing, toileting, etc.) and instrumental activities of daily living (meal preparation, cleaning, using the phone, traveling, grocery shopping, financial management, etc.), use of adaptive equipment and assistive devices, adapting activities, conservation of energy, task segmentation, positioning, stress management, coping skills, life skills, sensory integration, self-esteem and socialization. An occupational therapist may work with a resident/patient in a work-hardening program so that he/she can return to work. An O.T. may evaluate a resident's/patient's home for accessibility and make recommendations for changes in the home for easier access and conservation of the person's physical energy.

An occupational therapist can assist an activity professional in determining appropriate activities to augment occupational therapy in coordination with a resident's interests, preferences and functional abilities. Assistance may be needed in adapting activities, obtaining adaptive equipment for leisure pursuits, understanding how to communicate and/or motivate a resident to participate in activities (individual, one-to-one and group). A resident may be working on a project in O.T. and need reminders or assistance to work on assignments between O.T. sessions. The activity professional would need to know the goal for the resident as well as specific techniques to use or not to use during his/her involvement with a resident. Observation and feedback to an O.T. on a resident's behavior, abilities and motivation is important, for the O.T. in his/her assessment of the resident's total progress.

Activity professionals may co-lead a group with an occupational therapist. Trans-disciplinary groups may involve multiple professionals. This allows multiple leadership for the group, thus providing increased one-to-one attention/supervision. It can also increase the number of times a group can be provided. It prevents canceling a group when there is only one person available to conduct a specific group and he/she is absent.

An occupational therapist may not be directly involved in the provision of treatment but may supervise treatment provided by a certified occupational therapy assistant. The O.T. can assist the COTA and the activity professional in their collaboration of efforts and services.

Physical Therapists (PT)

Physical therapists and physical therapy assistants (PTA) are licensed in accordance with state regulations. Physical therapy can include active and as-

sisted exercise, balance training, ambulation, massage, range of motion, muscle strengthening/relaxation, pain management, muscle stimulation, etc. Computerized assessment can be used to measure function, strength, energy, etc. Reassessments can be used for comparison. New technology allows residents to see their progress on a computer monitor or print-out. This can reinforce their understanding and involvement in P.T.

Physical therapists can provide training for activity professionals in lifting and transfer in case of an emergency, safety in working with residents with physical disabilities, types and purposes of different types of canes/walkers/wheelchairs/ orthotics/ prostheses and different types of P.T. treatment. If an activity professional is not working with a physical therapist, he/she can seek informal training at a local hospital or rehabilitation center.

The most frequent collaboration of PTs and activity professionals is exercise, physical activity and community integration. Exercise programs can be graded so that residents with similar needs and abilities are involved in specific programs. A physical therapist can assist an activity professional in adapting physical activities for specific residents and reinforcing their involvement in physical activities. An activity professional needs to know when to motivate a resident to walk to an activity and when it is best to escort a resident in a wheelchair for short and/or long distances.

An activity professional may collaborate with a physical therapist and a recreation therapist in community reintegration programs (use of public transportation, shopping, going to places of business and/or interest - church, senior center, volunteer sites, etc, and learning about accessible community buildings, restaurants, places of entertainment), as well as barriers to community reintegration.

Speech Pathologist, B.S.

Speech pathologists are licensed as required by state regulations. They provide evaluation and treatment relating to cognition, language, speech, communication and swallowing. Speech pathologists teach residents how to use augmentative communication devices, e.g., computers, switch plates, voice activators, amplifiers, etc.

Training can be provided for activity professionals in understanding language, communication, the swallowing process and symptoms of potential swallowing problems, and use of augmentative communication, as well as understanding treatment provided by a speech pathologist. Activity professionals can learn specific techniques for communicating with residents with language, speech and communication problems. A speech pathologist can recommend games and other activities to assist a resident in regaining or maintaining language, speech and communication skills.

Activity professionals can collaborate with speech pathologists in following their recommendations for communicating with individual residents, assisting with practice assignments, involving residents in a variety of activities that require different types of cognitive, speech and language skills and providing the speech pathologist with feedback on the resident's use of functional speech and language skills and/or use of argumentative communication. On an outing to a restaurant, a resident could demonstrate his/her cognitive, language, speech and communication skills by reading a menu and ordering with or without assistance. Observation of interaction with others during the outing would be another means of assessing a resident's progress with speech therapy that is important for the speech pathologist to know.

Respiratory Therapist (RT)

Respiratory therapists are also licensed in accordance with state laws. They provide assessment and treatment for persons with pulmonary problems, i.e., Chronic Obstructive Pulmonary Disease (COPD), neuromuscular disease, neuro-skeletal trauma and complex medical problems. Respiratory treatment includes resident/family education, exercise, oxygen, suctioning, airway management, weaning a potential resident from a ventilator, psychological intervention, and follow-up care. Respiratory therapists utilize a team approach to respiratory care involving physical therapists, occupational therapists, speech pathologists, nurses, recreation therapists, psychologists and/or psychiatrists in respiratory programs in hospitals, rehabilitation centers and in long-term-care facilities.

Activity professionals need to understand respiratory diseases and diagnoses as well as the total effect that a respiratory disability has on a resident's physical, cognitive, emotional, social, and spiritual functioning. Additionally activity professionals need sufficient information on how to communicate and interact with persons who are ventilator-dependent and those who are being weaned from a ventilator.

Respiratory therapists can assist activity professionals in designing activity programs to best meet the resident's functional abilities, interests and preferences. Communication and conservation of energy may necessitate non-verbal or limited verbal and physical activities. Sensory activities involving the use of smell may need to be modified or eliminated. Specific breathing exercise as a part of an exercise program can facilitate breathing. The activity professional needs to know with whom to emphasize inhaling versus exhaling. Blowing bubbles, using a pinwheel and/or a kazoo may be effective for one resident and harmful to another.

Activity professionals can seek the assistance of a respiratory therapist in establishing an individual and one-to-one activity program for residents who will not or cannot participate in group activities. Respiratory therapists can also support family involvement with a resident in activities, e.g., provision of supplies/equipment for individual activities and/or involvement in one-to-one and group activities as appropriate.

Psychologist, B.A. or M.A.

Psychologists are licensed in accordance with state law. They work with individual residents as well as with groups. Psychologists utilize a variety of standardized assessments, comprehensive interviews and observations to assess residents. Treatment includes resident education, psychotherapy, counseling, stress management, group therapy, support groups, and family education and therapy.

A psychologist can help an activity professional gain an understanding of the psychosocial issues, concerns and the individual resident's dynamics related to aging, illness, disabilities, placement, motivation, etc. A psychologist who works with groups can provide training and assistance in developing group protocols and understanding group dynamics.

Activity professionals collaborate with psychologists in supporting behavior-modification programs for individual residents, involving residents in specific activities recommended by a psychologist in keeping with a resident's interest, preferences and abilities, and/or scheduling group therapy or support groups led by a psychologist. Activity professionals need to give feedback to a psychologist on a resident's expression of feelings, interaction with peers, staff, family and/or volunteers. Motivation and involvement in activities is important for the psychologist to evaluate the resident's total psychosocial functioning.

Psychiatrist, M.D., Ph.D.

Information on a resident's interaction, motivation and participation in activities (individual, one-to-one and/or group), behaviors, responses and outcomes is important for a psychiatrist for an initial evaluation of a resident during treatment and for follow-up sessions. Responses to medication are very important. Responses may be seen in activities before other staff sees the initial effect because residents are often involved in activities when medication starts to take effect.

Suicidal precautions, behavior-management programs, dietary restrictions related to medications and orders for involvement in specific types of activities need to be followed. Most residents receiving psychiatric care see their psychiatrist at his/her office versus in the long-term-care facility. Thus, the activity professional can report information in writing about a specific resident to the psychiatrist which is sent along with other information or through nursing telephone conversations with the psychiatrist. Regardless of the style of communication, it is important for the activity professional to communicate with psychiatrists.

Recreation Therapist, B.A. or B.S.

Recreation therapists (RT) can be certified nationally as certified therapeutic recreation specialists (CTRS). Some states require licensure. The terms "recreation therapist" and "therapeutic recreation specialist" are used interchangeably. In rehabilitation settings, professionals are most frequently called recreation therapists as they are a part of the rehabilitation team. In long-term care the professional is called a recreation therapist or a therapeutic recreation specialist.

Recreation therapists utilize a variety of activities much like an activity professional does for similar or different outcomes. Recreation therapists utilize informal and standardized assessments. Treatment can include aquatics, exercise, sports and other physical activities, cognitive, creative/expressive and social activities, relaxation techniques, stress management, leisure education, leisure integration, community reintegration, social/ leisure skills, instrumental activity of daily living skills, reality orientation, remo-

tivation, validation, support groups, discharge planning and family education.

In long-term care facilities the recreation therapist and activity professional may co-lead specific activities and/or conduct similar activities for specific residents for different outcomes. The recreation therapist can assist the activity professional with the assessment of residents, activity analysis, program design/planning/development/ evaluation, individual and group techniques to use with residents, training in understanding lifestyles, leisure needs, motivation and adaptations.

In long-term-care facilities with rehabilitation and/or sub acute units, the recreation therapist works with residents on these units and the activity professional works with residents on other units. The activity professional and recreation therapist collaborate with transitional programs for residents in the rehabilitation and sub-acute units who will be transferred to other units in the long-term-care facility. Other collaboration can include having residents in rehabilitation and sub acute units attend leisure and spiritual activities conducted by activity professionals.

The roles, responsibilities and opportunities for collaboration differ in all settings employing recreation therapists and activity professionals. Staffing is considerably different—with usually one recreation therapist for a small rehabilitation and/or sub-acute unit and multiple activity professionals for all other units. The responsibility for evening and weekend leisure activities may or may not be a shared responsibility depending upon the philosophy, treatment program and staffing in the rehabilitation and sub-acute units.

Physician, M.D. or D.O.

Activity professionals may or may not work directly with physicians. However, they collaborate with physicians by following physician orders and giving feedback to physicians in care conferences, through nurses and therapists, and through activity documentation. Questions and concerns can be related to physicians through nursing if a physician is unavailable for personal contact when he/she is in the facility, i.e., hours other than when the activity professional works or when the activity professional's is involved in programming. Direct contact does not have to limit the activity professional's collaboration with physicians.

Nursing, B.S. degree, RN or LPN

Nurses are either licensed practical nurses or registered nurses licensed by the state. Nurses assess a resident upon admission and develop a care plan based on physician's orders and the nursing assessment. The activity professional can use the admitting notes, nursing assessment and initial care plans to find out information about a new resident before meeting him/her.

Activity professionals work closely with nursing on a daily basis. Communication needs to be open and frequent. Medical information of residents' needs to be constantly updated and communicated to other activity professionals who have daily or less-than-daily contact with residents on a specific unit. Activity professionals need to keep nursing informed of activities, changes, and new activities as well as residents' motivation, participation, responses to activities, and outcome(s) of activities.

Nursing can assist activity professionals in understanding specific diseases, diagnoses, disabilities, limitations, medication and treatments. Activity professionals can help nurses know about the purpose, goals, objectives, philosophy, scope of programming, activity assessment, activity analysis and universal need for activities (care plan). Activity professionals are residents' advocates in sharing with nursing their interests, preferences, abilities and limitations related to participating in activities, schedules, etc.

Collaboration is a daily entity in planning, scheduling, conducting and evaluating activities. Health education, medication groups, orientation groups and/or discharge planning groups led by nursing are incorporated into the resident's activity schedule. Nursing may be invited to attend resident council meetings at the residents' request. Activity professionals who serve as the liaison for resident council would invite nursing to attend the next meeting.

Certified Nursing Assistants (CNA)

Nursing assistants are certified by the state. They work under the supervision of a licensed practical nurse or a registered nurse. Activity professionals are dependent on CNAs for having residents up, groomed and ready for activities of their choice, as well as assisting in transporting residents to and from activities. Increasingly, CNAs are being trained to assist and/or lead activities seven days per week in special care units for residents with dementia.

Activity professionals collaborate with CNAs by providing supplies and equipment for individuals and/or one-to-one activities for residents in or out of their rooms. CNAs work with activity professionals in co-leading groups, assisting with activities in the facility, outdoors and during outings. In small facilities CNAs may lead activities during an activity professional's absence. CNAs can assist with playing scheduled music, showing videos and introducing entertainers in the absence of activity professionals. In decentralized treatment programs CNAs lead small-group activities while activity professionals conduct one-to-one activities or vice versa.

Communication with CNAs is very important. CNAs and activity professionals spend the most time with residents; thus, sharing of information is pertinent.

Restorative Nursing Assistants (RNA)

Restorative nursing aides are certified nursing assistants with additional training in rehabilitation/restorative care. Restorative nursing aides function under the supervision of a rehabilitative/restorative nurse. They provide direct care for residents, promoting independence in communication, activities of daily living, as well as range of motion, body mechanics, transferring, and posting. Restorative nursing aides assist residents in learning to use and accept adaptive devices and equipment safely. They are also involved in providing exercise programs for residents (individual and group).

Activities professionals and restorative nursing assistants collaborate in conducting exercise programs, and providing cognitive stimulation, sensory stimulation and socialization. Groups can be co-lead or be lead by both professionals, each having a different functional level of programming. Restorative nursing aides assist with pre/post-meal programs with emphasis on physical, cognitive and social stimulation. They also conduct programs for residents with low-cognitive-functioning abilities on units.

Restorative nursing aides assist with outings and special events. Ambulation programming may include walking a resident to the activity area as a part or the plan of care and encouraging residents to be a part of a walking group after they no longer need restorative care. Restorative nursing aides assist with transfers in accordance with a resident's plan of care. Special feeding programs may include stimulation before or after feeding in which the restorative nursing aide is involved.

Residents can have one or multiple goals related to physical, mental and psychosocial functioning. The restorative nursing assistant can utilize activities to assist a resident to achieve his/her goals. The activity professional needs to be creative in assisting restorative nursing aides in determining which activities would be the best for a restorative nursing aide to use in accordance with the resident's needs, abilities, limitations, interests and preferences.

Dietitian (RD)

Dietitians are nationally registered and licensed as required by state regulations. Activity professionals work very closely with dietitians in planning, implementing and evaluating food related activities.

Dietitians can provide training for activity professionals related to good nutrition as well as nutrition problems related to specific diseases, diagnoses and physical limitations. Dietitians can keep activity professionals up-to-date with regulations concerning infection-control procedures related to storing, preparing and serving food.

Activity professionals collaborate with dietitians in planning food activities in advance, ordering food through dietary and scheduling food activities so that they do not interfere with meals. Activity professionals need to communicate with dietitians and nursing in regard to diets and change of residents' diets. Information related to a resident's food preferences are shared with dietary and nursing during the initial assessment and throughout a resident's stay. Activity professionals can assist with nutrition and hydration programs for individual residents through offering a beverage during one-to-one and group activities, and serving nutritious refreshments for parties and special events.

The dietitian and activity professionals collaborate in planning menus for special events (holidays, celebrations, parties, picnics, socials, etc.). A special event such as an Oktoberfest may include a morning coffee hour with strudel and coffee, a German meal for dinner and supper, pretzels and beer for an afternoon fest, and/or Limburger cheese with onions on rye bread for an evening snack.

Activity professionals also collaborate with dietitians in planning and conducting pre/post-meal activities in the dining room for residents who are not involved in other activities. Part of the program may include providing water or juice prior to the meal being served, particularly for residents with low-cognitive abilities who may be hungry/thirsty and unable to express their needs.

Dietitians may lead or co-lead nutrition or specific diet education/support groups; be involved in orientation groups for residents, discharge planning groups, or resident menu planning groups; and/or be invited to attend resident council upon request from residents. Scheduling groups involving the dietitian would be the activity professional's responsibility.

At times it may be necessary for activity professionals to make arrangements to obtain food that is not provided or ordered through the facility's food service providers. Activity professionals need to be aware of the dietary budget and the facility's/agency's philosophy regarding food activities. Activity professionals may need to advocate for residents for food-related activities with dietary and administration.

Social Worker (BSW, MSW, LISW)

Social workers may be licensed social workers or licensed independent social workers. They interview residents, family members or significant others to obtain assessment information and to write a social history. During the assessment process social workers learn about residents' family history (parents and siblings), education, military and work history, marital status and family information, financial management, coping skills, lifestyle, interests and preferences. All of this information is helpful to the activity professional in understanding the resident.

Social workers assist residents with adjustment to placement/illness/disability, coping with illness/ pain/ disability/limitations/death and dying, obtaining personal needs (clothing,), and making arrangements in coordination with nursing for medical/dental/psychological care. Social workers also conduct support groups, participate in orientation groups and health education groups, and provide individual resident counseling and family education, support and/or counseling as needed.

Activity professionals and social workers collaborate in conducting support and/or expressive groups, resident and family councils, and one-to-one activities involving the resident's expression of feelings;

obtaining clothing for outings and special activities; expenditure of money for personal/activity needs and family activities, advocating for residents' rights, etc. Some facilities have psychosocial departments in which activity professionals and social workers have the same department manager.

Social workers may make referrals to a psychologist or mental health agency. Thus, the social worker may be the contact person for community psychological services. Information from the activity professional would be included in communication about the resident for initial assessment, treatment and follow-up to treatment.

Summary

Activity professionals have an awesome responsibility of providing activities in a variety of service settings. Activity professionals need to take care of themselves so that they can care for others. A support system is essential for providing care and support for clients/residents. A variety of models of care and services have been developed over the years. Each activity professional will have to decide which model is best for the clients in each service setting. Communication is basic in providing activity services. Different techniques may be needed for individuals. Participants have a right to their autonomy and often need assistance in connecting with others. New friends can be made through participation in activities.

Chapter 9

Care Planning Practices

Quality of Life

"It's not the number of years but the quality of life that matters"

Quality of life includes one's attitudes and values towards family, friends, religion, health, work, leisure, environment, life style, etc. For one person a good quality of life is family, food, shelter and health services. For another person it may be family, religion, food, shelter, education, work and health. Another person may view a good quality of life as having the best job, the biggest house, the finest car, a boat, electronic equipment, gourmet food, money in the bank, and involvement in community activity in addition to the basic values of family, religion and work.

An older adult's quality of life may continue from middle age or it may change. Living on Social Security and having enough income for the essentials (food, shelter and clothing) may be sufficient. When long-term care is needed the same essentials are provided in an environment that may be the same or above previous living standards. For the person who can afford the best of health care in a long term care facility, the environment must be similar to former standards of living. Expectations of care are high. Individual wants and needs may be perceived as more important than the needs of others.

Long-Term Care

OBRA regulations state, "A facility must care for its residents in a manner and in an environment that promotes maintenance or enhancement of each resident's quality of life" (F240 A) – Quality of Life). Quality of life includes:

Dignity: Staff must treat individual residents with respect, recognizing their individuality. This includes grooming, dressing, and assistance in attending activities of resident's choice, independence and dignity in dining, respect of private space and property, respecting resident's social status (addressing resident by preferred name such as Mr., Mrs., Dr., first name, nick-name prior to becoming a resident) and individual attention when talking with a resident.

Self-Determination: Residents have a right to choose activities, schedules and health care consistent with their interests, assessment and plans of care. Staff needs to make adjustments to allow residents to exercise their individual choices and self-determination. This would include but not be limited to schedules for getting up and going to bed, receiving treatments, visiting, selecting with whom to eat, grooming, clothing, bath or shower, everyday life, participation in care-planning and involvement in activities (individual, one-to-one, groups, family activities, community activities, etc.).

Choices: The resident has the right to make choices about life in a facility that significant to them. Residents must be made aware of a no-smoking policy before they enter a facility. If a policy regarding smoking is made after a resident has entered a facility, the facility must allow residents to smoke in an area that maintains their quality of life.

Resident Groups: Residents have the right to form resident groups (resident council). Space, privacy for meetings and staff support needs to be provided. Staff attendance at meetings is by invitation only.

Family Groups: Families have the right to form family groups and to meet in the facility in a private area. A staff liaison is appointed to assist the group as needed. Staff attends meetings by invitation only. The facility must listen to the concerns and recommendations of family groups.

Other Activities: Residents have a right to participate in social, religious and community activities. Participation in these activities cannot interfere with the rights of other residents in the facility. Staff needs to assist residents in pursuit of involvement in community activities. While the regulations do not state how this is to be done, the most common accommodations include contacting families, staff and/or volunteers for escorting and transporting residents to community events, arranging for individual transportation, or using public transportation.

Accommodation of Needs: Individual needs and preferences are taken into account to maintain independent functioning, dignity, well-being and self-determination. The facility makes adaptations in the facility environment and staff behaviors to accommodate residents without endangering the health and safety of other residents. Accommodation of needs includes bath or shower, change in bath/shower schedule, preferences in the form of a refusal and how staff tries to learn what and why a resident is refusing something, use of adaptive equipment to stand independently, transfer and maintain body symmetry, and to participate in preferred activities. Accommodation also includes freedom in walking in safe areas for residents with dementia, reality-orientation aids (clocks, calendars, pictures, etc.), adaptive equipment for bathing and toileting (grab bars, raised toilet seats, etc.).

Residents with communication impairment need adaptations such as staff getting their attention before attempting verbal communication, talking with residents at eye level so that residents can read lips, amplification of communication, removing a resident from a noisy area, attempting to interpret communication behind a specific behavior for residents with dementia, etc.

Notice of Changes: The residents receive notice before they have a change in room or roommate and preferably some choice in the change.

Activities: The facility must provide for an ongoing program of activities designed to meet, in accordance with the comprehensive assessment, the interests and the physical, mental, and psychosocial well-being of each resident. Activities can occur at anytime and are not limited to formal activities being provided by activity staff; others involved may be any facility staff, volunteers and visitors.

The activities program is correlated with individual resident's comprehensive assessments and care plans. The activities program includes individual, one-to-one and group activities to meet individual residents' needs, interests, preferences, abilities and limitations. Activities are planned to meet the residents' functional levels. There are specific activities for residents who are confined to bed/room or who are unwilling to participate in group activity, as well as structured activities for residents with Alzheimer's disease. Activities are adapted to meet the functional levels of residents (cognitive, physical, emotional, social). Verbal cues and demonstrations are used for residents who are unable to independently follow instructions or suggestions.

The activities program is varied and reflects the residents' interests identified in their individual comprehensive assessments. Cultural and religious interests, as well as seasonal and special events, are reflected in the activities program. Activities appeal to men, women and different age groups. Activities take place in a variety of locations inside and outside the facility and in the community.

Additionally there must be documentation of resident involvement in the assessment and care-planning process, participation in activities, i.e., daily activity participation record, and outcome/ responses to activity participation/ intervention in progress notes.

The activities program must be directed by a qualified activity professional (see end of Chapter One for "Regulations").

Social Services: "The facility must provide medically-related social services to attain or maintain the highest practical physical, mental, and psychosocial well-being of each resident." Social services include arrangements for adaptive equipment, clothing, personal items, maintaining contact with family, referrals to health and community agencies, assistance with legal and financial matters, funeral arrangements, providing or arranging for counseling, discharge-planning and transfer to home or other health-care facilities.

Social services also includes supporting residents in their daily living in a long-term care facility, assisting in the development of relationships between residents and staff, promoting staff care that enhances and maintains residents' individuality, dignity and respect, assisting residents in making health-care decisions and preference of involving others in the decision making process, assisting staff in informing residents and other designated persons of resident's health and/or change of condition. Residents and staff may need assistance in deciding upon options for health care. A social worker tries to help staff understand residents' behavior so that alternative care and services can be utilized versus drug therapy and/or restraints. Social-service staff assists residents with their physical and emotional needs and grieving process. They are able to assist other staff in applying a team approach to meeting residents' needs (physical, cognitive, emotional, social, spiritual, etc.).

Environment: The facility must provide a safe, clean, comfortable and homelike environment, allowing the resident to use his or her personal belongings to the extent possible. Residents are provided the opportunity to use personal belongings to support a homelike environment (pictures, furniture, knick-knacks, etc.). Residents have the housekeeping and maintenance services necessary for a sanitary, orderly and comfortable environment. Bath linens need to be clean and in good condition. Each resident has private closet space. Lighting is adequate and comfortable. Temperatures are safe and comfortable (range of 71°–81° F), including space utilized for activities. Sound levels are comfortable. Sound is amplified as needed (one-to-one and group activities).

Quality of Life Groups

Interdisciplinary team members can meet with multiple small groups of three to six residents on a regular basis to discuss their quality of life. Questions surveyors ask can be a part of the group meeting. Recommendations from multiple small groups can be implemented as feasible. Feedback to the group on accomplishments related to their recommendations empowers residents to speak up so that staff can accommodate their needs and preferences.

Quality of Care

"A caring staff for quality care"

Each resident must receive and the facility must provide the necessary care and services to attain or maintain the highest practical physical, mental, and psychosocial well-being in accordance with the comprehensive assessment and plan of care. Activities potential is a part of the comprehensive assessment. Activities are also included in the resident's individualized plan of care.

Quality of care includes maintaining or improving activities of daily living functional abilities (bathing, dressing, grooming, transfer, ambulation, toileting and eating), tasks segmentation for residents with cognitive impairments, and restorative care. Activities can augment residents' involvement in ADLs and restorative care through exercise programs, ambulation to/from activities, proper body alignment during activities, being sure residents have used the restroom in advance of an activity, use of adaptive equipment for activity pursuits, opportunities for socialization and meeting other needs of residents with disabilities, involvement in education, and support groups.

Residents need opportunities for vision and hearing screening. Activity professionals need to be aware of vision and hearing deficits and adapt activities for residents' highest level of functioning. Print size, placement of objects, lighting, seating arrangements, and position of resident to staff/peers may need to be adapted for individual residents. One-to-one and communication in groups may need to be amplified. Activity staff can assist with a resident's psychosocial adjustment to the facility by providing opportunities for interaction with staff, peers and volunteers as well as activities related to present and former interests, lifestyle and functional abilities.

Involvement in new resident orientation groups, support groups, education groups, expressive groups (with focus of expression of feelings), discussion groups, life review, reminiscing, use of validation techniques, religious/spiritual activities, community activities, family activities, resident councils, etc. allows residents to express their thoughts and feelings and adjust to illness, disabilities and living in a long-term-care facility.

Residents involved in counseling, psychotherapy and/or support groups need supportive and understanding staff. Their need to talk or to remain quiet needs to be respected. Individual residents may need a structured environment. This would include opportunities for structured socialization to prevent or reduce isolation and withdrawal.

Specialized Rehabilitation Services

Specialized rehabilitation may be a part of the resident's total plan of care. Rehabilitation services include physical therapy, occupational therapy, speech/language pathology, and health rehabilitation services for mental illness and mental retardation. Activity staff needs to work closely with therapists and collaborate in designing activities programs that augment therapies. Activity staff may co-facilitate IADL (instrumental activities of daily living). IADLs can include preparing a meal, cleaning, using the telephone, writing, reading, shopping, laundry, gardening, money management, and travel.

Community reintegration is an important aspect of therapy for residents who are going home. Involvement in previous or new leisure interests is important for maintaining a balanced lifestyle. A resident may need leisure education or participate in leisure awareness groups. A resident may be involved in a community based mental health center, workshop or training program. Often these types of services are 6-8 hours per day, five days per week. Individualized activities programs need to be developed with residents to accommodate their need during the time that they are in the facility.

Quality Assurance

Staff in long-term-care facilities must address quality assessment and assurance issues that negatively affect the quality of care and services provided for residents. Problems and/or concerns are identified, and a plan of action is developed and implemented. Expected outcomes can include better or more efficient/effective care and/or services, new systems, policies and procedures, and/or protocols. Activity professionals are responsible for identifying and correcting quality assessment and assurance issues.

The Relationship of Quality of Care to Quality of Life

Quality of life, while individualized is dependent on the perceived and actual quality of care provided on a daily basis in long–term care. How care is provided is what is important to the resident. A kind and loving approach to care is perceived as staff caring and taking good care of the person. A hurried approach is perceived as a task and the resident not feeling cared for. Greeting and calling a resident by his/her preferred name individualizes the initial approach to care. A staff member can prepare a resident for a procedure by explaining the procedure or the steps of the procedure in terms that the resident can understand.

Inviting a resident to a group activity and giving a brief explanation of the activity or referring to past interests or identifying who usually attends, i.e. acquaintances or friends of the resident being invited, helps the resident decide on participation. Having earned a trust relationship helps in motivating a resident to participate in activities of interest and preference. Resident satisfaction is linked to personal involvement in the planning and executing of an activity. This can involve choices, i.e., pattern or material for a craft, a specific game among a variety of choices, prizes for games or the planning of a party, date, time, place, decorations, food, entertainment, etc. In evaluating an activity a resident's satisfaction is from a personal point of view. If needs, interests, preferences are met; it is likely the person will voice satisfaction. Dissatisfaction is often expressed with negative comments, 'Why" questions, i.e. "Why did we have to have_____", shaking of heads

meaning no or disgust. Americans are motivated by food, so if the residents perceive the food at an activity as good, they may voice satisfaction with the activity.

An activity professional needs to listen to participants' comments objectively and not take them personally. There will be times that things happen beyond the activity professional's control, e.g., residents requested ice cream for a party and the order was not delivered, so a substitute of a choice of pudding with whipped topping was provided. Residents will most likely accept the change knowing what happened. They have lived lives of change. The main thing is to include them on the change and still give them a choice of what is available. Some residents may have their heart set on having ice cream particularly if they don't get it as often as they wish because of diet or financial restraints. These residents may be very disappointed and initially voice their dissatisfaction and later come to accept the change. Investigating the non-delivery of the ice cream, may assist in ordering earlier or double checking on the order 1-2 days in advance and telling the residents what has been done to prevent this from happening again. This may change their attitude knowing that staff has tried to prevent the situation from happening again.

It is recommended that activity staff ask residents to evaluate the activities program at least quarterly. Results of the evaluation can be used to improve the program. Progress may be seen or indicated in the next quarterly review.

Accurate Care

"Prepared staff is paramount for accurate care"

Accurate care is based on individualized assessment by all disciplines involved in the care of the resident. Three or more residents may be the same age, sex and have identical diagnosis and medication but each has a different life history, needs, abilities, limitations, interests and preferences. So they must all have a different person-centered treatment plan. The physician, the resident's team leader is dependent upon all professionals from different disciplines to be his eyes and ears when he/she is not in the facility to see a resident's response to treatment, medicine, interaction with family, peers and staff and his/her life within the long-term-care community.

Professionals may differ on their assessment of a resident. The resident may have been more responsive to one professional than another for many reasons including but not limited to: how he/she was feeling physically, mentally, and socially; the professional's approach; time of day; preference to being alone or doing something else versus being interviewed; tired of being asked the same or similar questions; not being able to understand questions being asked because of a cognitive or hearing limitation; not feeling comfortable with a stranger or other reasons.

The interdisciplinary team must listen to each other's information to formulate an accurate treatment or care plan and then implement the treatment/care plan, communicate findings and indicate whether or not the treatment/care plan is working.

Activity professionals like other professionals, need to provide sufficient time to assess a resident accurately and not jump to conclusions about problems, needs, abilities, limitation, interests and preferences. resident may indicate that he enjoyed playing the violin but does not indicate he has not played it for years because he lost his index finger in a work accident. The activity professional did not observe that the resident was missing his index finger. In preparing the resident's care plan the activity professional sets a goal for the resident to resume playing the violin by a certain date. There was no discussion as to why the resident has not played his violin and the activity professional failed to observe the loss of the index finger and she did not read completed assessments by other professionals; thus, missing the diagnosis of a missing index finger. Without input and agreement from the resident, the activity professional's goal to resume playing the violin was inaccurate.

Activity professionals must be good communicators, observers and adept at reading clinical records and interpreting information. These skills are learned over time. Having a mentor assists the activity professional in learning and applying principles of assessment, developing appropriate individualized treatment plans and reporting and interpreting observations of resident reaction to activity care and services.

Interdisciplinary Assessment

"Sharing information and concern is vital"

Long–term care facilities have hand-written or electronic interdisciplinary assessment. The interdisciplinary assessment may be a packet of assessments for each discipline to complete versus having a different assessment with some of the same information on each discipline's assessment. The MDS (Minimum Data Set) is an example of an interdisciplinary assessment. Each discipline is responsible for completing one or more sections of the MDS. Professionals involved in the assessment sign their name or initials indicating what part of the Interdisciplinary

assessment they completed. The activity related assessment might be somewhat shorter or less specific than a multidisciplinary assessment. There is no right or wrong as to which type of assessment, interdisciplinary or multidisciplinary assessment to use. Accuracy is imperative.

A standardized assessment completed by one discipline can be utilized by other disciplines, e.g., depression assessments, mini mental state examination, clock assessment.

Multidisciplinary Assessment

"Know the mental, physical, psychological, social & spiritual condition of the resident"

In a multidisciplinary assessment system, each discipline has its own assessment, i.e. Activity Assessment. Most Activity Assessments contain information that is obtained from other disciplines, e.g., date of birth, age, diagnosis, diet, occupation, armed force services, retirement, religion, etc. The Activity Assessment would include information of a person's abilities and limitations as well as his/her interests and preferences. Three residents may like music. One prefers to listen to classical music while another prefers Rock and Roll and another Country Western. In identifying interests and preferences related to animals, one resident may like cats and dogs and another prefers birds. Obtaining this individualized information helps the activity professional plan individualized care appropriately.

Activities of Daily Living (ADLs)

"Residents should do as much as possible for themselves"

Beers and Berkow (2000) state Activities of Daily Living are self care activities that a person must perform every day, e.g., eating, dressing, bathing, transferring between the bed and a chair, using the toilet, controlling bladder and bowels. Patients unable to perform these activities and obtain adequate nutrition usually require caregiver support 24/7 hours/day.

The 2006 Interpretive Guidelines for Surveyors for Tag # F248, state: "ADL-related activities, such as manicures, pedicures, hair styling and makeovers, may be considered part of the activities program. These activities may be provided by other professionals or volunteers within the state's regulations, i.e., hair styling involving cutting hair would be under the state's regulations for qualified beauticians and barbers.

A nursing assistant would be qualified to cut a person's nails during manicure but an activity professional is not licensed to do this. Residents who are capable can cut/file their own nails independently or with some guidance. It is imperative for anyone cutting/ filing nails to be extremely cautious when providing the service for a resident who has diabetes, to prevent infection.

Pedicures given by a podiatrist are not the same as a pedicure provided by a licensed beautician. Manicures provided by a licensed beautician are not the same as a group of residents meeting at the same time for a manicure. The latter involves more socialization.

For many people manicures and pedicures are a part of their life style that they may choose to continue or discontinue in a long–term-care facility. General nail care is part of ADLs provided by nursing. Activity professionals need to be explicit as to when a manicure is an activity and when a pedicure is an activity versus a treatment by a beautician or a podiatrist. Policies and procedures need to be written after conferring with the medical director, director of nursing, and the person responsible for infection control.

Instrumental Activities of Daily Living

"Living is doing"

Beers and Berkow (2000) indicate that IADLs are activities that enable a person to live independently in a house or apartment, e.g. preparing meals, performing housework, taking drugs, going on errands, managing finances, using a telephone.

Functional Ability

"Challenging activities lead to fulfillment"

Functional ability is the ability to do ADLs and IADLs. Usually in a long-term-care facility nurses complete the ADLs and IADLs assessment or a resident is referred to an Occupational Therapist (OT) for assessment and treatment. An activity professional must be aware of a resident's functional abilities, adaptations and/or adaptive equipment. If a resident uses a magnifying glass for reading, he/she will need it for activities that involve reading, e.g. games, song sheets, written or typed instructions for arts/crafts/needlework. A person who uses a weighted spoon for eating will need it to eat ice cream or other deserts served for parties or special events. A person with hemiopposi, who only sees out of the right side of both eyes would need a plate or activity supply moved to the right so that he/she could see the item in his/her field of vision.

Activity Documentation

"Activity documentation is part of the clinical record."

Overview

Activity documentation is required in all activity settings to some degree. In health-care facilities, specific activity documentation is regulated by city, state and/or federal regulations. State regulations differ from state to state. Activity professionals must keep abreast of required documentation. In completing any type of documentation for participants, it must be individualized, accurate, timely and legible.

Activity documentation includes the following records:

1. Physician's Orders
2. Assessment:
   A. Activity Assessment
   B. MDS (Minimum Data Set, required for certified Medicaid and Medicare facilities)
3. Precautions List
4. Plan of Care (interdisciplinary or multidisciplinary)
5. Participation Records
   A. Daily Activity Participation Records of individual participants
      1. Group attendance/participation
      2. One to one attendance /participation
   B. Total Attendance Records (total number of persons served or statistics)
6. Progress Notes (evaluation)
   A. Incidental Progress Notes
   B. Quarterly Notes
   C. Discharge Notes (unanticipated discharge)
   E. Discharge Summary (anticipated discharge)
7. Post-Discharge Plan of Care.

Activity professionals must be familiar with diseases, diagnoses, medications, treatments, medical terminology, abbreviations and symbols. Training of activity professionals includes some information on medical terms. Terminology is learned on the job, through reading and through continuing education.

Resources

All activity professionals need resources on medical terminology and medication. Knowing and understanding different diseases and diagnoses helps in understanding the needs of participants. Knowing the potential side effects of medications assists the activity professional in identifying changes in a participant's behavior that may be related to medications. Activity professionals must be able to communicate with other health care professionals—orally and in writing

Resources for medical terminology and medications include:

1. Medical Encyclopedia
2. Medical Dictionary
3. Books on Medical Terminology
4. Pamphlets on Diseases and Diagnosis from National, State and Local Associations, e.g., American Heart Association
5. Books on Anatomy and Physiology
6. Websites on terminology and diseases
7. webmd.com

8. Books on Medication, i.e., PDR – Physicians' Desk Reference
9. Books on the normal aging process.

Physicians' Orders

"Comply with physician's orders."

Physicians are responsible for the total health care of their patients. Any physician's order must be signed and dated by a licensed physician to be a legal document giving permission for a patient to participate in activities. Not all community-based programs require a physician's order for participating in activities. Senior citizen centers may require a physician's permission to participate in specific activities such as exercise, aerobics, yoga, etc., but not require a physical exam or a physician's approval to participate in activities to be a member of the center.

Regulations

Adult day-service centers and long-term-care facilities require physician's orders for clients and residents to participate in the activities program. States may mandate physician's orders for participating in the activities program in long-term-care facilities. There is no regulation under the OBRA Law of 1987 (Omnibus Budget Reconciliation Act) requiring a specific physician's order for a resident to participate in activities. The resident has the right to choose activities.

OBRA Regulation 483.15 Quality of Life, Tag #F242 states:

"The resident has the right to - Choose activities, schedules, and health care consistent with his or her interests, assessment, and plan of care..."

There is a regulation related to medical appropriateness if a resident desires to work.

Regulation 483.10 Resident Rights:
Interpretive Guidelines: Tag #F169 (h) (1)-(2)
" ... All resident work, whether of a voluntary or paid nature, must be part of the plan of care. A resident's desire for work is subject to discussion of medical appropriateness. As part of the plan of care, the resident must agree to a therapeutic work assignment. The resident also has the right to refuse such treatment at any time that he or she wishes. At the time of development or review of the plan, voluntary or paid work can be negotiated."

(The entire regulation related to Work is Tag # F 169 of Regulation 483.10 Resident Rights)

Having physician's orders to participate in activities programs has been a standard practice of activity professionals in long-term-care since at least 1974. Whether or not it is a state regulation, adult day-service centers, other community-based programs and long-term-care facilities may require physician's orders for participation in activities in the facility or outdoors, and for trips/outings. In essence, having physician's orders for participation in activities, assures that the person's involvement in activities is not in conflict with the medical treatment plan.

Types of Orders

Activity professionals need to read all physician orders, not just those specific to participation in activities, so as to comply with medical treatment. A participant may have an order for a sunscreen that must be followed when involved in any outdoor activity. Dietary restrictions may affect consumption of specific foods and liquids. An order may be to increase food and/or fluids. Orders may include restriction on bed rest or time out of bed, mobility, range of motion of upper and/or lower extremities or exercise of extremities. Therapies may be ordered or discontinued. Orders for special treatments or medical and psychological consultations can affect the time or amount of time a person can be involved in activities. Restraints can be ordered or discontinued. An order for medication can be PRN (as needed) or a very specific order.

A physician's orders for a resident in a long-term-care facility may have significant impact related to involvement in activities. The activity professional must consider all physicians' orders when developing an activity plan of care in coordination with other health care professionals.

State of the Art of Physician Orders

Today in long-term-care facilities, physician orders are computerized. Frequently they are generated through pharmacies. Physician orders for treatment and medication may be on the same or separate forms. The treatment orders are specific—identifying amount, frequency and duration. Orders can also indicate PRN (as needed). Orders for consultation or evaluation by other health-care professionals are written on the same physician's order form or a separate order form.

Faxed and telephone orders facilitate immediate orders when a physician is not in a facility to write an order. If there has been a change in a resident's condition (decline or improvement) and the order for participation in activities needs to be changed, a charge nurse or other designated nurse can call the physician for a change in the order. The nurse writes in the nursing notes that the physician was called and that the order for participation in the activities program was changed.

A faxed order is signed and dated prior to being faxed to the facility. It is then placed in the physician's order section in the resident's medical record. A telephone order is usually written on a carbon order form. The nurse receiving the order writes the order on the form, signs and dates the order and places the carbon copy in the resident's medical record. The original order is sent to the physician to be signed and dated, or the order is signed and dated when the physician makes his/her next visit.

Physicians' orders in long-term-care facilities are reviewed and updated as needed (or a minimum of monthly) by the attending physician. Physician's progress notes indicate the resident's response to treatment and recommendations. They are written in the designated space below the orders or on a separate page.

Physician Orders Activities

Sample Orders: (Physician would check items or fill in the blank space on the order.) Orders for participation in activities programming are usually listed under ancillary orders.

> May participate in activities program as desired and tolerated:
> __ in the facility ___ outdoors ___ outings/trips
> May have alcoholic beverages: __ Yes __ No
> If yes, amount of consumption allowed is:
> _____
> Limitations: _____

> May participate in individual, one-to-one, group activities per choice and tolerance:
> __ in the facility __ outdoors __ outings/trips
> May have alcoholic beverages: __ Yes __ No
> If yes, amount of consumption allowed is:
> _____
> Limitations: _____

The facility's medical director needs to be consulted when developing or revising physician's orders for residents to participate in specific activities/activities program.

Note: Physician orders stated "Activities as tolerated" mean activities of daily living; thus, they are not orders to participate in specific activities and/or activities program.

Examples of Physicians' Orders
Therapeutic Work Orders

> May participate in therapeutic work activity, per resident's desire, frequency and duration, within normal working hours on a (volunteer) (paid) basis.
> Limitations:
> _____

General Activity Participation Orders

> May participate in therapeutic work activity (name of activity or task) on a volunteer basis, per desire but limited to __ hours per (day), (week).
> Limitations: _____

Activity Assessment

"A positive attitude makes life more enjoyable."

In long term care activity professionals are responsible for two assessments:

1. The RAI (Resident Assessment Instrument) which has two parts:

    a. MDS (Minimum Data Set) Section F Activity Pursuit Patterns – a formal standardized assessment - required by federal law.

    b. CAA(Care Area Assessment)

2. An Activity Assessment – informal Assessment

Computerized

The state of the art is computerized MDSs. There are various software programs. Each program has a system for checking all triggered items and then identifying which CAT (Care Area Trigger) were triggered on the summary form (Care Area Legend).

Care Area Assessment

The MDS includes a CAA Summary. It identifies the twenty core items that have been assessed and which ones actually triggered as a result of the process of completing the CAA. Care-planning decisions (to proceed or not proceed with a care plan) for each CAT is identified. Additionally, the location of information related to care planning is indicated.

A CAA summary includes identification of the problem, complications, other factors to be considered; risk factors, referral to other health professionals; and reason to proceed or not proceed with a new care-plan, a care-plan revision of continuation of a care-plan. This information can be written in any designated place in the resident's medical record. A separate page of CAA Notes (summaries) is one method of recording the required information.

CAA Note

Some facilities use an interdisciplinary CAA Note page. All CAA notes are written on one or more pages. Each note is labeled by the number and name of the CAA, e.g., # 10 Activities. Notes are dated and signed by the writer.

#10 Activities

The purpose of the activities CAA is to identify strategies to assist residents with increasing their involvement in activities that interested and stimulated them in the past and or to help them find satisfying activities to replace activities that are no longer available because of functional or situational loss.

When a CAA is triggered, nursing home staff should follow their facility's protocol for performing the CAA. Each facility may have a different policy/procedure to address CAAs. The MDS 3.0 manual states; no specific tool is mandated as long as the tools are current and founded on evidence-based or expert-endorsed research, clinical practice guidelines and resources. This CAA is triggered when the resident may have indications of decreased involvement in social activities. The information identified from the assessment should be used to identify residents who have either withdrawn or are uneasy joining into activities and social relationships, top identifies resident's interests, and to identify any related possible contributing and risk factors. The next step is to develop a resident-specific care plan based on directly on these conclusions. The focus of the care plan should concentrate on the identified underlying factors, interests, cognitive, physical/functional, and social abilities in order to stimulate and facilitate social engagement. The activities should fulfill the resident's wishes, be adapted to physical and cognitive skills, provide enjoyment, and provide an opportunity for peer interaction.

An example of an activity CAA note:

#10 Activities: Resident has stated that it is important for him to listen to his preference in music (opera) but can't due to no music or player in his room. (B-5) He also stated that it is important, but can't do or no choice to do his favorite activities, attending the opera. (F-5). Resident refuses invitations to music programs because opera is not currently offered. He currently has no means to listen to music independently and misses attending live performances of opera music. He is at risk for social and recreational engagement. He needs CD player and opera CDs for in room engagement and DVDs on opera performance to accommodate his music interest. The activity department will proceed to care plan centered on providing a CD player, CDs and DVDs on opera performance. Will introduce to residents with similar interest to develop relationships and investigate opportunities to attend opera performance in the community.

-Jane Doe, ADC

OBRA Regulations

The April 1992 and the June 1995 Interpretive Guidelines for the OBRA Regulations identify the core items in the minimum data set and the time frames for completing the MDS. It also addresses accuracy, comprehensive care plans, discharge summary, and preadmission screening for mentally ill individuals and individuals with mental retardation.

Precautions

In developing activity care plans and activity programs, activity professionals must consider precautions for individual participants so as to not to cause death, harm, illness, discomfort, or negative emotional reaction. It is also important to know precautions to prevent requesting a participant to do something that he/she is incapable of doing, or that is against medical treatment. Knowing precautions allows the activity professional to make adaptations for individual participants and/or group of participants. Knowing participants' diets allows the activity professional to plan appropriate food-related activities around the participants' diets. If a participant is allergic to metals, i.e., gold or silver, jewelry provided for bingo prizes could include items without these metals. Knowing participants' ambulation abilities and the need for wheelchair, cane, or walker is essential for planning assistance for short and long distances. In planning outings, the activity professional plans for accessibility related to ambulation and to persons with heart or breathing problems. A participant who is unable to speak may be able to communicate with a communication board or perhaps use sign language. Participants' ability to see different sizes of print or the ability and willingness to use a talking book machine is important when developing reading programs.

A person who is forgetful needs reminders to participate in activities. Participants with severe cognitive impairment may need frequent cueing and redirection. Persons with hearing impairments may be able to hear low loud tones or may need hearing aids. Inappropriate behavior may limit a person's involvement in specific activities. These are just some of the precautions to be considered.

PRECAUTIONS

	Bedfast	Cane Walker	G/C W/C	Disoriented	Short-term Memory Loss	Shsort Attention Span	Places objects in Mouth	Wanders	Visual Impairment	Hearing Impairment	Aphasia Non-Verbal	Diabetic	Low Sodium	Soft	SOB	No Alcohol	Sun Sensitive	Incont. Bowel/Bladder
Alice Ater			W							√					√			
Sylvia Baker			W						√			√					√	B
Howard Birch	√								√	√		√				√		
Gary Carson			G	√	√	√	√		√	√	√			√		√		BO
Helen Daniels		C						√					√		√	√		
Gladys Down		W		Allergic to strawberries/chocolate													√	

In the above checklist where there are two related precautions, i.e., Cane, Walker, the first letter of the word is printed in bold. Only the first letter is written in the column to identify the specific precaution.

Additional precautions, i.e. an allergy to strawberries and chocolate, can be written on the form. Symbols such as an asterisk (*) can also be used to identify a specific precaution. The meaning of the asterisk or other symbol would be written on the top or bottom of the form.

Another way to add more individual precautions is to use an asterisk to indicate that there are more precautions written for the participant on the back of the form. The participant's name would be written on the back of the form with the specific precaution(s).

Potential Precautions

Potential precautions related to activities can include but not be limited to the following categories:

Allergies:
- Cosmetics/lotions (identify)
- Fabric (identify)
- Food (identify)
- Metals (identify)
- Pets
- Smoke
- Sun sensitivity

Behavior:
- Agitated
- Anxious
- Banging
- Combative
- Crying
- Demanding
- Destructive with objects
- Hoarding (specify)
- Hostile
- Impatient
- Placing object in mouth
- Sexually abusive
- Sexually inappropriate
- Taking objects
- Verbally abusive
- Wandering
- Yelling

Ambulation
- Bedfast
- Cane
- G/C (geri chair
- Potential for falls
- W/C with assist
- Walker with assist
- Walks with assist

Cognitive:
- Disoriented as to time, place, person, routine

- Forgetful (specify)
- Gives unreliable information
- Hallucinates
- Limited short-term memory
- Paranoid (identify)
- Short attention span
- Suspicious (identify)
- Unable to comprehend
- Unable to follow direction

Communication:
- Aphasic
- Braille
- Foreign language
- Non-verbal
- Points/gestures/signs
- Reads printed word
    - Uses communication board/chart
    - Uses pen/paper
    - Uses switch plate /communication board

Diets:
- Alcohol with supervision
- Diabetic
- Low sodium
- Needs fluids
- N/G tube
- No alcohol
- No caffeine/chocolate
- No spicy food
- N.P.O. (nothing by mouth)
- Pureed diet
- Soft

Physical:
Bowels and bladder
- Incontinent of bladder
    - Uses incontinence pads

- Catheter
- Chokes (liquids, soft)
- Dizziness
- Falls
- Fatigue
- Hearing-impaired
- Hypertension
- Motion sickness (outing)
- Pacemaker
- Pain
- Paralysis
- Paresis
- Restraint (mitts, soft vest, wrist, other)
- Seizures
- Smoking with supervision
- S.O.B. (shortness of breath)
- Swallowing
- Tires easily
- Visually impaired
- Weak

Social:
- Aggressive (verbally)
- No small/large group
- Not accepted by others
- Not considerate of others
- Outspoken
- Prefers to be alone; with family/roommate
- Sexually inappropriate (groups/children)

Other:

Precautions List

Precautions lists assist activity professionals in remembering all the individual participants' precautions. A precautions checklist can be an effective tool. Individual precautions can be recorded on a precautions checklist after the participant's activity assessment is completed. Precautions should be updated on a regular basis. Activity professionals need to be kept abreast of changes, e.g., thickened liquids and adaptive equipment. It is a good practice to review and revise precautions when the participant's care plan or program plan is reviewed and revised as necessary. It is recommended that a precautions checklist be kept up-to-date using a computer or pencil versus a pen.

A precautions checklist can be developed using approximately 20 of the most common precautions of the participants. Additional precautions can be written on the form (horizontally). A more in-depth list can be developed by the use of several forms.

In the checklist on the previous page where there are two related precautions, i.e., Cane, Walker, the first letter of the word is printed in bold. Only the first letter is written in the column to identify the specific precaution.

Additional precautions, i.e., an allergy to strawberries and chocolate, can be written on the form. Symbols such as an asterisk (*) can also be used to identify a specific precaution. The meaning of the asterisk or other symbol would be written on the top or bottom of the form

Another way to add more individual precautions is to use an asterisk to indicate that there are more precautions written on the back of the form. The participant's name would be written on the back of the form with the specific precautions.

The Assessment Process

"Know what is, and then move to what should be"

Activity Assessment:

Definition

Assessment is a systematic process of gathering information about a person in order to make decisions regarding his/her care plan or program plan, i.e., community-based program. It is a continuous process involving the participant, family, friend, significant others (as appropriate), and assessment team.

Assessment Team

The assessment team in a health-care facility and health related adult day-service center would include clinical team members: physician, nurses, nursing assistants, activity professionals, dietician, social worker, rehabilitation professionals, i.e., physical therapist, occupational therapist, speech pathologist, and rehabilitation aides. Assessment also involves non-clinical staff, e.g., admissions coordinator, housekeeping and other staff who have contact with the resident.

The assessment team in a community based program, such as a senior center, would consist primarily of programming staff. Other staff that has contact with a new member could also be involved in the assessment process.

The depth and frequency of assessment is dependent upon the purpose of the agency/organization or facility. Adult day-service centers and senior centers would follow assessment guidelines established by their professional organizations. Long-term-care facilities and hospitals receiving Medicare and/or Medicaid funding must comply with state and federal regulations related to activity assessment.

Each state differs in regard to licensing of group homes, personal care facilities, assisted living facilities and retirement homes. State or federal law may not require an activity assessment. However, it is essential for activity professionals to assess residents in order to develop meaningful activity programs.

Time Frames

There are two time frames for the assessment process: (1) the initial assessment and (2) ongoing assessment. The initial assessment is completed upon admission to a health care-facility or health-related community-based program, or upon membership in a community-based program, i.e., senior center. Ongoing assessment may be for specific intervals. In long-term-care facilities, federal law mandates that residents be assessed a minimum of quarterly.

It is during the initial assessment process that the activity professional begins to establish a trust relationship with the new participant/resident. This is a transition period for the participant, whether it is adjusting to the new involvement in a senior center or adult day-care center, or adjusting to and accepting placement in a long-term-care facility. In all cases it is a new experience. Information gathered during the initial activity assessment process establishes a baseline for activities programming via an activities plan of care or program plan.

The on-going assessment starts immediately following the initial assessment and development of an activities care plan or program plan. Information is continuously gathered and recorded.

The process includes information learned from interaction with the participant; observations of participant; information from other team members, family, friends, significant other(s), as appropriate; medical treatment; consultations; and evaluations.

Recordings of changes (physical, cognitive, emotional, social, spiritual, and activity participation) are reviewed and discussed with the participant, family (as appropriate), and other staff. Information is used to continuously evaluate and update the person's individualized activity plan of care or program plan.

Types of Assessment

There are two types of assessment:
1. Informal assessment – use of a non-standardized assessment instrument (form)
2. Formal assessment – use of a standardized assessment instrument

Activity professionals may use one or both types of assessment. An informal assessment may be used to obtain background information; past, present and future interests; activity lifestyle patterns; personal characteristics; traits; cultural identity; values; motivation; coping skills; and other information to identify the individuality of the participant.

Formal assessment is the utilization of one or more standardized assessments. This type of assessment is used to measure specific functional ability (physical, cognitive, emotional, social), personal concepts, e.g., self esteem, coping skills, stress, interests, barriers to participation, etc. The person administering the standardized assessment needs to be trained so that the assessment is administered, scored and interpreted correctly.

Depending upon the background and training of an activity professional, he/she may be involved in administering, scoring and interpreting the results of a standardized assessment, or may use the interpretation of the results of a standardized assessment administered by another professional, e.g., psychologist. Standardized assessments such as the Short Portable Mental Status Questionnaire (SPMSQ) and the Geriatric Depression Scale are being used in many adult day-care centers and long-term-care facilities. The Minimum Data Set (MDS) or Minimum Data Set Plus (MDS+) is required by federal law for certified Medicare and Medicaid facilities.

Informal Assessment

Information for an informal assessment is gathered through:
1. Interviews
2. Observation
3. Information from other staff
4. Record review

Interview

In a senior center the interview would be with the new participant. In an adult day-care center and a long-term-care facility the interview would be with the client/resident, family, friends or significant other(s).

Purpose

The purpose of the interview is threefold: (1) to obtain information and observe the person in the process, (2) to establish rapport with the participant, and (3) to explain the activities program, identify opportunities to participate in activities related to personal interests, and discuss the participant's preference for current or future participation.

Process

The interview process has three phases:
1. Beginning
2. Working
3. Termination

Beginning Phase

In the beginning phase the activity professional introduces him/herself to the participant and welcomes the participant. In this phase, the activity professional attempts to develop a comfortable environment by establishing eye-contact, asking and using the participant's preferred name, being open with the participant, and showing attention and respect.

The activity professional explains his/her role, the purpose of the interview, and how the information will be utilized. An approximate timeframe for the interview is identified. The interview procedure is explained, i.e., asking the participant questions to complete an activity assessment form.

The participant is informed that the information is confidential. Answering questions and remembering facts can be stressful. The participant needs to be informed that he/she can at any time stop the interview.

The activity professional needs to be extremely observant before and during the interview process. The interview may need to be terminated if the participant is unable or unwilling to provide information.

Working Phase

In the working phase, information is gathered through conversation, questions and answers and/or completion of an assessment form. The technique most frequently used is question and answer (open-ended, yes/no, or choice). Questions are asked systematically in relation to information to be completed on an activity assessment form. Comments, personal recognition, and interest in the participant assist the participant in feeling at ease to answer questions.

It may take more than one interview to complete the activity assessment. If two or more interviews were needed, the activity professional would repeat an introduction and the purpose of the interview. A summary of information gathered through the last interview can be stated, followed by identifying the process that will be used to complete the interview and assessment at the present time.

Termination Phase

The activity professional can identify the number of questions, e.g. "I have two more questions" to be asked prior to completion of the interview, or the remaining amount of time can be stated. This sets the stage for termination.

Upon completion of the interview, information obtained is summarized. Personal recognition related to information can be given. Goals can be established. Presenting a schedule of activities and pointing out or highlighting activities of interest can be effective motivation techniques for participation in the activities program. Explanation of reminders of activities and transportation to/from activities can reduce concerns of not remembering or not being able to independently get to an activity of choice.

Using a personable, warm departure of making eye-contact, extending a hand for a handshake, and thanking the person (using his/her name) for the interview provide personal appreciation and recognition. The activity professional can complete the termination phase by stating when he/she will see the resident again.

Observation

Observation includes what is seen and heard concerning the participant, i.e., interaction with others, behaviors, participation in activities, responses to participation, experiences, etc. For the initial assessment this observation may be from the day of admission in a long-term-care facility until the date the initial activity assessment was completed. This is usually a seven-day period.

What to Observe

The first observation one makes is personal appearance (physical stature, facial expressions, cleanliness, grooming, clothing, posture, movement and coordination). Observation of a participant's involvement in an activity, task or interaction with others can reveal his/her cognitive, physical, emotional and social skills, abilities and limitations. Watching involvement in individual, one-to-one and group activities can identify and correlate interests and preferences with what was obtained during the initial assessment process. Abilities, limitations, adaptations, coping skills, resourcefulness, social comfort level and interactional skills can be identified.

Activity professionals need to listen intently to what is being said, how it is being communicated, and the ease of communication. This provides information on what is important to the individual (needs, fears, wants, wishes, etc.). It also provides information on the person's cognitive and communication skills, abilities and limitations.

Through observation the activity professional has another opportunity to see individualized characteristics of the participant. Observations seen by the activity professional may differ from observations by another professional. Sharing of information related to observations facilitates the assessment process.

Information from Other Staff

Information about the participant can be obtained from other staff. In a long-term-care facility this would include staff from all three shifts. A person may display an interest in watching late night movies. Only nightshift staff could actually verify this information. Responses to treatment, attitudes towards health and family, nutritional intake, orientation to reality, emotional responses, and interaction with others during different times of the day can be learned from other staff.

Record Review

A review of records will provide information on medical history/physical health, diagnosis, allergies, consultations, evaluation, medication, treatment, lab work and outcome, assessment by other disciplines, and legal documents, i.e., advanced directives. Cognitive, physical, emotional, and social history assessment will provide further information about the participant. The information in the records, e.g., medical record, in addition to information learned through interviews, observation and from other team members, give the activity professional an initial, total picture of the participant.

Recording of Information for Informal Activity Assessment

Checklists, fill-in-the-blank forms, and/or a blank page can be used for recording information. Activity professionals most commonly use a combined checklist and fill-in-the-blank type of activity assessment form. The activity assessment form can include the following information, depending upon the setting:

1. Basic information: name, preferred name, sex, date of birth, age, admission date and room number or membership date, i.e., senior center.
2. Background information: Birthplace/hometown, cultural/ethnic background, marital status, number of children, religion/church, education, foreign language, occupation(s), military service and volunteer work. In long-term-care facilities additional information may be obtained related to, for example, being registered to vote and interest in voting. Potential people who will visit may also be identified.
3. Medical and dietary information: diagnosis, allergies and diets.
4. Habits: smoking, alcohol, other.
5. Physical status: vision, hearing, speech, communication, hand-dominance, mo-

bility, physical disabilities, abilities and limitations. Mental Status: alertness, orientation to self/family/staff/time/place/routine/forgetfulness, and cognitive abilities and limitations.
6. Emotional Status: content, pleasant, outgoing, hopeful, withdrawn, anxious, hostile, aggressive, agitated, independent, dependent, or other characteristics as well as emotional abilities and limitations.
7. Social Status: preference to be alone or to socialize on a one-to-one basis and/or in groups, preference for visiting or being visited, and keeping in contact with others through telephone, letters and cards.
8. Leisure Lifestyle/Behavior: leisure lifestyle, membership/leadership in clubs and organizations, identification of interest, i.e., a checklist of past, present, future interests, individual interests, family activities, group activities, identification of activities that would like to be learned, preferred time for activities, favorite items, e.g., color, animal, season, etc., and identification of what would keep the person from participating in activities (per the participant).
9. Additional items if assessment is conducted by a certified therapeutic recreation specialist could include leisure awareness, leisure activity skills, social interactive skills, leisure resources (in the home, neighborhood, community), management, e.g., leisure time, money for leisure time, stress management, leisure barriers, preference for social reintegration and/or community reintegration, initiation of leisure, participant/resident goal, family goal as applicable, and other.
10. Identification of who provided the information for the activity assessment (participant/resident, family, friend, significant other, staff, chart and/or through care conference).

11. Summary of assessment: Abilities and limitations (cognitive, physical, emotional, social), precautions, narrative statement (summary and impressions), and recommendations for activity services.
12. Signature and date.

Formal Assessment

Formal assessments are standardized reproducible assessments. A structured standardized method is used to administer, score and interpret the results of the assessment. This insures that the same information is collected on each person in the same manner. Standardized assessment can include questionnaire, tests and surveys. The advantage of using standardized assessment is that it allows comparison between participants. It clarifies needs and increases accountability.

All standardized assessments must meet three criteria (1) validity, (2) reliability, and (3) usability.

This is accomplished through research. Multiple studies are done until the instrument is standardized.

Validity

Validity means that the assessment instrument measures what it is intended to measure. All activity professionals in long-term-care facilities use the Minimum Data Set (MDS) assessment instrument to measure a resident's preferences for customary routine and activities. If ten activity professionals ask the same resident the questions on the MDS, all ten would record the same responses to the questions.

Reliability

Reliability means that the instrument consistently and accurately examines or measures the stated purpose of the assessment. If the assessment was repeated within a given time frame, the results should be the same. An example would be the administration, scoring and interpretation of the results of the Geriatric Depression Scale. If ten social workers administered the Geriatric Depression Scale to the same resident within 24–48 hours, it is most likely that the social workers would give the resident the same score identifying the degree of depression.

Usability

Usability means that the instructions for using the assessment instrument are easy to understand.

Instructions include guidelines for scoring and interpreting the scores. Usability also means that the assessment instrument is easy to administer and that the assessment was valid and reliable. It would not be useable if the resident gave a number of different answers.

MDS 3.0

MDS 3.0

The Minimum date set (MDS) is a standardized, functionally based assessment. Completing the MDS requires interviews with resident, family, significant others, observation, and information from all clinical team members. The MDS data contributes to quality improvement, a person centered approach to care and supports the culture change movement by creating opportunity for the residents to be involved in providing information and input during assessments and have a role in decision making. The Resident Assessment Instrument (RAI) helps nursing home staff gather definitive information on a resident's strengths and needs for formulating the care plan. Problem identification is identified from the assessment and paired with clinical interventions the care plan becomes the resident's unique path toward achieving or maintaining his highest practical level of well being. Holistically treating residents with thorough assessment promotes quality of care and quality of life.

The content of the RAI for nursing homes consists of three basic components: The Minimum Data set (MDS) version 3.0, the Care Area Assessments (CAA) process and the RAI utilization guidelines. The use of the three components of the RAI yields information about the resident's functional status, strengths, weaknesses and preferences and offering guidelines on further assessment once problems have been identified. Each component flows naturally into the next component.

- Minimum Data Set (MDS) - A core set of screening, clinical and functional status elements, including common definitions and coding categories which forms the foundation of a comprehensive assessment for all residents of nursing homes certified to receive Medicare and Medicaid.

- Care Area Assessment Process (CAA) - This process is designed to assist the assessor to systematically interpret the information recorded on the MDS. Once a care area has been triggered, nursing home providers use current, evidenced-based clinical resources to conduct an assessment of the potential problem and determine whether or not to care plan for it. The CAA process helps the clinician to focus on key issues identified during the assessment process so that decisions as to whether and how to intervene can be explored with the resident. Components of the CAA process include:
    - o Care Are Triggers (CATS) are specific resident responses for one or a combination of MDS elements. The triggers identify residents who have or are at risk for developing specific functional problems and require further assessment.
    - o CAA resources are a list of resources that may be helpful in performing the assessment of a triggered care area. Premade assessments for triggered MDS sections and cue cards for resident interviewing.
    - o CAA Summary Section V of the MDS 3.0 provides a location for documentation of the care area(s) that have triggered from the MDS and the decisions made during the CAA process regarding whether or not to proceed to care planning. Previously known as the resident assessment care summary
- Utilization Guidelines- the Utilization Guidelines provide instructions for when and how to use the RAI. These include instructions for completion of the RAI as well as structured frameworks for synthesizing MDS and other clinical information available from
- http://cms.hhs.gov/manuals/Downloads/som107ap_pp_guidelines_ltcf.pdf

Reimbursement-The MDS primary purpose is as an assessment tool it is also used for the Medicare and Medicaid reimbursement system and monitoring the quality of care provided to nursing home residents. The MDS is also used for hospital swing bed programs for reimbursement under the skilled nursing facility prospective payment system (SNF PPS). The MDS contains items that reflect the acuity level of the resident. The MDS is used as a data collection tool to classify Medicare residents into RUGS. The RUG classification system is used in the PPS SNF, hospital swing bed and in many states Medicaid case mix payments to group residents into similar usage categories for the purpose of reimbursement.

Quality of Care- MDS assessment data is also used to monitor the quality of care in the nation's nursing homes. MDS based quality indicators (QIs) and quality measures (QMs) were developed by researchers to assist: (1). State Survey and Certification staff to identify potential care concerns in N.H. (2.) N.H. providers with efforts in quality improvement activities. (3.) N.H. consumers in understanding the quality of care provided by a N.H. (4) CMS with long term quality monitoring and program planning. CMS is continually evaluating the usefulness of the QI/QMs which may be modified in the future to enhance their effectiveness.

Consumer Access to Nursing Home Information. Consumers are able to access information about every Medicare/Medicaid certified N.H.in the country. The Nursing Home Compare Tool http://www.medicare.gov/nhcompare/home.asp provides public access to N.H. characteristics, staffing and quality of care measures for certified N.H.

Advantages of the MDS 3.0

A 5-year CMS Nursing Home MDS 3.0 Validation Study suggests that the MDS 3.0 has many advantages such as:

- Increased resident's voice
- Increased clinical relevance for assessment
- Increased accuracy, both validity and reliability
- Increased clarity and efficiency
- 45% reduction in the average time for completion
- Supports the movement of items toward future electronic formats.

(See Appendix D for MDS form.)

RAI (Resident Assessment Instrument)

Federal law (OBRA '87) requires long-term care facilities (certified for Medicare and/or Medicaid) to use the resident assessment instrument (RAI) that has been specified by the state. Each state's RAI supplement must be approved by the Center for Medicare Medicaid Services (CMS). The RAI must include at least the MDS (minimum data set of core elements to be used in conducting comprehensive assessments), care area triggers, care area assessments, resident interviews, and utilization guidelines. Some states have added other core items to the MDS. These additional items have to be completed each time an RAI is required (CATs and CAA). See "Excerpts from OBRA Regulations Interpretive Guidelines, November 19, 2004" at the end of this section and refer to specific state regulations.

Quality assessment is the link to comprehensive care planning. The RAI system, composed of the MDS, care area assessments (CAA) and the care area triggers (CAT) is a structured approach to identifying problems, needs, preferences and strengths for care planning. It is also used for classifying residents into homogeneous resource utilization groups for equitable payment, as well as for monitoring systems. States such as Ohio have a Medicaid reimbursement system based on the state's comprehensive assessment.

Care area Assessment Summary

The MDS requires either a check mark (✔) or a numerical response to each of the core items for which the resident is assessed. Predetermined triggers related to the response codes identify when clinical factors are present that may or may not represent a problem, need, preference, or strength that should be care-planned. The triggers indicate additional assessment regardless of eventual care-planning decisions.

A CAA (Care Area Assessment)

The CAA (Care Area Assessment) is an assessment of several MDS core items or sets of items that are defined as triggers, Care Area Triggers (CATs).

There are 20 CATs: Delirium, cognitive loss, visual function, communication, ADLs-functional status, urinary incontinence and indwelling catheter, psychosocial well being, mood state, behavioral symp toms, activities, falls, nutrition status, feeding tube, dehydration/fluid maintenance, dental care, pressure ulcer, psychotropic medication use, physical restraints, pain and return to community referral.

The MDS triggered care areas form a clinical link between MDS and care planning decisions. CAA (Care Area Assessments) cover the majority of problems areas known to be problematic for nursing home residents, however other areas may need assessment as well. A triggered CAA must be assessed but may or may not warrant being addressed by a care plan. The CAA process functions as a decision facilitator, which means it should lead to a move through understanding of the areas of concern that have been triggered for further review. The assessment of the causes and contributing factors will provide the interdisciplinary team (IDT) with a base line of clinical information that is necessary for the development of a comprehensive plan of care. Using the results of the assessment, the IDT and the resident and or resident's family will be able to identify areas of concern.

The MDS 3.0 identifies the actual or potential problem areas and the CAA process each triggered CAA must be assessed further to facilitate care planning decision making, but it may not represent a condition that should be addressed in the care plan. Care Area Triggers (CATs) are a list of items and responses from the MDS that are considered CATs for the issue or condition. The triggers identify those who have or are at risk for developing various concerns/problems in any of the 20 CAAs and direct the staff to evaluate further. The Care Area Resources is a list of resources that may be helpful in performing the assessment of a triggered care area. The Care Area Summary (Section V of the MDS 3.0), provides a location for documentation of the care areas that have triggered from the MDS and the decisions made during the CAA process regarding whether or not to proceed with care planning.

Further documentation for each triggered CAA is required. Documentation for each triggered CAA should describe:

- The nature of the issue, concern or condition
- Causes and contributing factors
- Complications resulting from the triggered area
- Risk factors

- Need for referral or further evaluation by appropriate health care professionals

There are four types of triggers which can change how the CAA is reviewed:
- Potential Problems
- Broad Screening Triggers
- Prevention of Problems
- Rehabilitation Potential

In terms of activities, the purpose of the CAA is to identify strategies to assist the resident in increasing their involvement in meaningful activities that have been of interest to them in the past and to help them find new or adapted activities of interest to accommodate their current level of functioning. The CAA for activities is triggered when there are indications that the resident may have a decrease in involvement in social activities. The information from the assessment should be used to identify residents who may be uneasy in social relationships and activities. In addition, assessment information is to identify resident interests and identify possible causes or risk factors.

One example of a triggered CAA(Care Area Assessment) item on the 2010 MDS 3.0 related to activities is " how important is it to you to do your favorite activities" Further assessment includes reviewing core items on the MDS related to psychosocial wellbeing. This section may be completed by social service, so you must work closely with your interdisciplinary team. Guidelines are also provided to identify why a resident feels that it is important but can't do or no choice. Through the assessment process the activity professional can decide whether or not to proceed with care planning.

Future MDS

MDS 3.0 is current and was implemented in October of 2010. The MDS will continue to change and evolve to meet the resident needs and voice.

Tags

483.20   Resident Assessment.

F-271   *The facility must conduct initially and periodically a comprehensive, accurate, standardized, reproducible assessment of each resident's functional capacity.*

Refer to   **(a) Admission orders.**   At the time each
F272   resident is admitted, the facility must have physician orders for the resident's immediate care.

F-272
483.20

Resident Assessment Instrument

A facility must make a comprehensive assessment of a resident's needs, using the resident assessment instrument (RAI) specified by the state. The assessment must include at least the following:

(i) Identification and demographic information,
(ii)customary routine,

(iii) cognitive patterns,
(iv) communication,
(v) vision,
(vi) mood and behavior pattern,
(vii) psychological well-being,

(viii) physical functioning and structural problems,
(ix) continence,
(x) disease diagnosis and health conditions,
(xi)dental and nutritional status,
(xiii) skin condition,
(xiii) activity pursuit,
(xiv) medications,
(xv) special treatments and procedures,
(xvi) discharge potential,
(xvii) documentation of summary information regarding the additional assessment performed on the care areas triggered by the completion of the Minimum Data Set (MDS),
(xviii) documentation of participation in assessment.

F-273 483.20 (b) (2)

When required, a facility must conduct a comprehensive assessment of a resident as follows:

(i)   Within 14 calendar days after admission, excluding readmission in which there is no significant change in the resident's physical or mental condition. (For the purpose of this

section, "readmission" means a return to the facility following a temporary absence for hospitalization for therapeutic leave.)

F276 483.20(C)
Quarterly Review Assessment

A facility must assess a resident using a the quarterly review instrument specified by the State and approved by CMS not less frequently than once every 3 months.

F286 483.20 (d)
Use

A facility must maintain all resident assessments completed within the previous 15 months in the resident's active record.

F-287 483.20 (f)
Automated Data Processing Requirement
483.20 (f) (1) Encoding Data.

Within 7 days after a facility completes a resident's assessment, a facility must encode the following information for each resident in the facility:

(i)	Admission assessment,
(ii)	Annual assessment updates,
(iii)	Significant change in status
(iv)	assessments.,
(v)	Quarterly review assessments,
(vi)	A subset of items upon a resident's transfer, reentry, discharge and death.
(vii)	Background (face-sheet) in

483.20 (f) (2) *Within 7 days after a facility completes a residents assessment, a facility must be capable of transmitting to the State information for each resident contained in the MDS in a format that conforms to standard record layouts and data dictionaries, and that passes standardized edits defined by CMS and the State.*

483.20 (f) (3)
Monthly transmittal requirements.

A facility must electronically transmit, at least monthly encoded, accurate, completed MDS data to the State for all assessments conducted during the previous month including the following: Admission assessment, annual assessment, significant change in status assessment, significant correction of prior full assessment, significant correction of prior quarterly assessment,

quarterly review, a subset of items upon a resident's transfer, reentry, discharge and death. Background information, for an initial transformation of MDS data on a resident that does not have an admission assessment.

483.20 (f) (4) Data format

The facility must transmit data in the format specified by CMS of for a State which has an alternate RAI approved by CMS, in the format specified by the State and approved by CMS.

F278 483.20 (g) Accuracy of Assessment
The assessment must accurately reflect the resident's status.

483.20 (h) Coordination
A registered nurse must conduct or coordinate each assessment with the appropriate participation of health professionals.

483.20 (h) Interpretive guidelines

*According to the Utilization Guidelines for each State's RAI, the physical, mental, psychosocial condition of the resident determines the appropriate level of involvement of physicians, nurses, rehabilitation therapists, **activities professionals,** medical social workers, dietitians and other professionals, such as a developmental disabilities specialist, in assessing the resident, and in correcting resident assessments. Involvement of other disciplines is dependent upon resident status and needs.*

483.20 (g) (h) Probes

Have appropriate health professionals assessed the resident? For example, has the resident's nutritional status been assessed by someone who is knowledgeable in nutrition and capable of correctly assessing a resident?

483.20 (i) Certification
(1) A registered nurse must sign and certify that the assessment is completed.
Each individual who completes a portion of the assessment must sign and certify the accuracy of that portion of the assessment

(d) Comprehensive care plans.

F279 *(1) The facility must develop a comprehensive care plan for each resident that includes measurable objectives and timetables to meet* a resident's medical, nursing, mental and psychosocial needs that are identified in the comprehensive assessment.

(i) The services that are to be furnished to attain or maintain the resident's highest practicable physical, mental, and psychosocial well-being as required under 483.25; and

(ii) Any services that would otherwise be required under 483.25 but are not provided due to the resident's exercise of rights under 483.10, including the right to refuse treatment under 483.10 (b) (4).

F280 483.20 (d) (3)

The resident has the right to – unless adjudged incompetent or otherwise found to be incapacitated under the laws of the State- participate in planning care and treatment or changes in care and treatment.

F280 (2) A comprehensive care plan must be-

(i) Developed within 7 days after completion of the comprehensive assessment.

(ii) Prepared by an interdisciplinary team, that includes the attending physician, a registered nurse with responsibility for the resident, and other appropriate staff in disciplines as determined by the resident's needs, and to the extent practicable, the participation of the resident, the resident's family or the resident's legal representative; and

(iii) Periodically reviewed and revised by a team of qualified persons after each assessment.

(3) The services provided or arranged by the facility must—

F281 (i) Meet professional standards of quality; and

F282 (ii) Be provided by qualified persons in accordance with each resident's written plan of care.

F-283 Discharge summary. When the facility anticipates discharge, a resident must have a discharge summary that includes-

F283 (1) A recapitulation of the resident's stay;

(2) A final summary of the resident's status to include items in paragraph (b)(2) of this section, at the time of the discharge that is available for release to authorized persons and agencies, with the consent of the resident or legal representative; and

F284 (3) A post-discharge plan of care that is developed with the participation of the resident and his/her family which will assist the resident to adjust to his/her new living environment.

F285 483.20 Coordination

A facility must coordinate assessments with the pre-admission screening and resident review program under Medicaid in part 483, subpart C to the maximum extent practicable to avoid duplicative testing and effort.

Page 200 Interpretive Guidelines: S483.20(K) (3) (1)

Possible reference sources for standards of practice may include:

- Current Manuals or textbooks on nursing, social service, physical therapy, etc.

- Standards published by professional organizations such as American Dietetic association, National Association of Activity Professionals, etc.

- Clinical practice guidelines published by the Agency of Health Care Policy and Research.

- Current Professional journal articles.

F285 (m) Preadmission screening for mentally ill individuals and individuals with mental retardation.

(1) A nursing facility must not admit, on or with—

(i) Mental illness as defined in paragraph (f)(2)(i) of this section, unless the State mental health authority has determined, based on an independent physical and mental evaluation performed by a person or entity other than the State mental health authority. prior to admission,

(A) That, because of the physical and mental condition of the individual, the individual requires the level of *services provided by a nursing facility; and*

(B) If the individual requires such level of services whether the individual requires activity treatment for mental illness; or

(ii)Mental retardation, as defined in paragraph (f)(2)(ii) of this section, unless the State mental retardation or developmental disability authority has determined, prior to admission—

(A) That, because of the physical and mental condition of the individual, the individual requires the level of services provided by a nursing facility; and

(B) If the individual requires such level of services, whether the individual requires active treatment for mental retardation.

(2)Definition. For purposes of this section—

(i) An individual is considered to have "mental illness" if the individual has a serious mental illness as defined in 483.102(b)(1).

(ii) An individual is considered to be "mentally retarded" if the individual is mentally retarded as defined in 483.102(b)(3) or is a person with related condition as described in 42 CFR 435.1009.

Interdisciplinary Care Planning

Interdisciplinary care planning involves all clinical disciplines. Individualized care planning is based on clinical assessments, social history, cultural background and the resident's wants and preferences. Care planning usually takes place during individual resident's care conference. Most facilities care conferences involve a representative from each clinical discipline, the resident, family or significant other, or representative. The initial care plan and review/updating of care plans takes place during the care conference.

The initial care plan is based upon assessments (activity and MDS) and the updated care plans are based on evaluation and new assessments.

Sometimes non-clinical disciplines are involved in the care plan interventions, e.g. maintenance staff may have a resident walk with him during maintenance rounds and check off items that need to be repaired or items that meet safety standards, to help a person feel useful and prevent inappropriate behavior, e.g. going in other people rooms and picking up items.

MDS and the Care Plan Working Together

When residents trigger for activities, the CMS RAI Version 3.0 manual states that the focus of the care plan should be to address the underlying cause(s) and the development of the addition of activity programs that are customized to the resident's interests and his or her abilities. Activities should focus on helping residents carry out their wishes and dreams,

use cognitive skills and provide enjoyment and opportunities for socialization with others. Preferences for Customary Routine and Activities (Section F)

Residents are to be interviewed for their activity interests and routine preferences. The RAI Version 3.0 Manual suggests various ways for the interviewer to phrase the questions, probe for clarification of residents' responses and to utilize adaptive techniques such as cue cards, an interpreter, opportunity to write out answers, etc. The residents are to rate the level of importance by using the following codes:

1. Very important
2. Somewhat important
3. Not very important
4. Not important at all
5. Important, but can't do or no choice

this means the resident finds it important but feel he/she cannot do that at this time because of health or because of nursing home resources or scheduling.

No response or non-responsive (resident, family or significant other refuses to answer or doesn't know, if the resident does not respond to the question 3 times, or provides a nonsensical response. A nonsensical response is defined as, "any unrelated, incomprehensible or incoherent response that is not informative with respect to the item being rated". When coding the activity preferences interview, no look back is provided. The resident is to respond to their current preferences while in the facility. Family members and significant others may be the primary respondent to the interview questions if the resident is unable to do so. In this case, the family member or significant other may have to consider past preferences if they are unsure of current preferences and the resident is unable to communicate. There is a series of questions that relates to the resident's preferences for daily routine such as bathing, bedtime, clothing, etc. Questions connecting to activities include:

- *How important is it to you to have books, newspapers, and magazines to read?*
- *How important is it to you to listen to music you like?*
- *How important is it to you to be around animals such as pets?*
- *How important is it to you to keep up with the news?*
- *How important is it to you to do things with groups of people?*
- *How important is it to you to do your favorite activities?*
- *How important is it to you to go outside to get fresh air when the weather is good?*
- *How important is it to you to participate in religious services or practices?*

For residents who cannot answer the questions and a family member or significant other is not available to answer on behalf of the resident, a staff assessment of activities and daily preferences is conducted. Staff is instructed to observe the resident's response during activity programs. A variety of routine and activity preferences are listed and staff is to check off each item as it applies in the last 7 days. The items listed are as follows:

A. Choosing clothes to wear

B. Caring for personal belongings

C. Receiving tub bath

D. Receiving shower

E. Receiving bed bath

F. Receiving sponge bath

G. Snacks between meals

H. Staying up past 8:00 p.m.

I. Family of significant other involvement in care discussions

J. Use of phone in private

K. Place to lock personal belongings

L. Reading books, newspapers, or magazines

M. Listening to music

N. Being around animals such as pets

O. Keeping up with the news

P. Doing things with groups of people

Q. Participating in favorite activities

R. Spending time away from the nursing home

S. Spending time outdoors

T. Participating in religious activities or practices

U. None of the above

CMS stated a sample of individuals that completed the revised Preferences for Customary Routine and Activities (Section F), findings indicated that:

- 81% rated the interview items as more useful for care planning

- 80% found that the interview changed their impression of resident's wants

- 1% felt that some residents who responded didn't really understand the items

- More likely to report that post-acute residents appreciated being asked

Types of Comprehensive Care Plans:

Two types of care plans are: (1) interdisciplinary care plans and (2) multidisciplinary care plans.

(1) Interdisciplinary care plans:

In the Interdisciplinary Care Plan system, each discipline addresses the same problem (as appropriate) on the same page. The goal may be interdisciplinary or there may be more than one goal. The interdisciplinary team identifies their responsibility for an approach or intervention by indicating their professional discipline after each statement, e.g., Transport to weekly men's craft group (Nsg) NSG means anyone in nursing. Provide 1:1 instruction, cueing and redirection (Act).

Interdisciplinary care plans can be handwritten or electronically processed. Computerized care plans are the state of the art. Most computerized care plans have a library, in which new information can be added for general use or just for a specific resident.

(2) Multidisciplinary care plans:

In the Multidisciplinary Care Plan system, each discipline addresses problems on their identified care plan form. Some facilities use color-coded forms for each discipline. Usually the Multidisciplinary Care Plans are handwritten, typed or computerized by a representative of each professional discipline.

Frequency/Time Frame

A resident's care plan is initiated by nursing within 24 hours after admission. Activity professionals and other interdisciplinary team members initiate care plans within seven days after the completion of the comprehensive assessment, or earlier if needed or required by a facility's policy. Care plans are reviewed and updated quarterly, when there is a significant change, and annually.

Excerpts from OBRA Regulations Interpretive Guidelines November, 2004 (effective November 19, 2004)

F280 483.20 (d) (3)

The resident has the right to – unless adjudged incompetent or otherwise found to be incapacitated under the laws of the State- participate in planning care and treatment or changes in care and treatment.

F280 (2) *A Comprehensive Care Plan must be ... developed within 7 days after the completion of the comprehensive assessment.*

(ii) Prepared by an interdisciplinary team, that includes the attending physician, a registered nurse with responsibility for the resident, and other appropriate staff in disciplines as determined by the resident's needs, and, to the extent practicable, the participation of the resident and the resident's family or the resident's legal representative; and

(vii) Periodically reviewed and revised by a team of qualified persons after each assessment, i.e., quarterly assessment, annual assessment, significant change.

F281 483.20 (k)(3))

(3) The services provided or arranged by the facility must...

(i) Meet professional standards of quality; and

F282 483.20 (k) (3)

(ii) Be provided by qualified persons in accordance with each resident's written plan of care.

Interpretive Guidelines: S483.20(k(3)

*"**Professional standards of quality** means services that are provided according to accepted standards of clinical practice. Standards may apply to care provided by a particular clinical discipline or in a specific clinical situation or setting. Standards regarding quality care practices may be published by a professional organization, licensing board, accreditation body or other regulatory agency. Recommended practices to achieve desired resident outcomes may also be found in clinical literature..."*

483.20 Coordination

A facility must coordinate assessments with the pre-admission screening and resident review program under Medicaid in part 483, subpart C to the maximum extent practicable to avoid duplicative testing and effort.

Page 200 Interpretive Guidelines: S483.20(K) (3) (1)

Possible reference sources for standards of practice may include:

- *Current Manuals or textbooks on nursing, social service, physical therapy, etc.*
- *Standards published by professional organizations such as American Dietetic association, National Association of Activity Professionals, etc.*
- *Clinical practice guidelines published by the Agency of Health Care Policy and Research.*
- *Current Professional journal articles.*

Developing Care Plans

Care plans are individualized; therefore, a care plan can be developed based on a resident's problems, needs, interests, preferences and/or strengths.

Problems

Problems (cognitive, physical, emotional, social, etc.) can be real, actual or potential. The cause or complication related to a problem and/or signs/ symptoms are included in a problem statement. Descriptive words are used to individualize a problem.

Examples:

- Refuses activities in afternoon. Complains of a pain in back, related to (R/T) arthritis.
- Disoriented to time & place R/T Alzheimer's disease – asks, "Where do I get the bus?"
- "I have to get home to make supper."
- Easily distracted, R/T to dementia. Becomes agitated (bangs on G/C table) in large groups or in noisy environment.
- Unable to verbally express self, R/T aphasia.

Needs

A need is related to something that is required, useful or desirable for mental, physical, emotional, social or spiritual well-being. A need statement identifies the specific need followed by the reason for the need.

Examples:

- Needs mental stimulation – to increase awareness. Needs a large-print Bible – to continue former daily practice of reading the Bible
- Needs reminders to attend activities – forgets time of activities, related to (R/T) short-term memory impairment

Strengths

Strengths are related to ability, knowledge, skills, interests, preferences, or a want or wish that the resident has displayed or stated. A strength statement can be written after a problem to indicate a strength related to the problem statement or it can be written as a separate statement.

Examples:

Problem followed by a strength statement:

- Dependent on staff for stimulation R/T dementia.
  Strength: Likes to look at pictures of animals, flowers, and babies/children.

Strength statement:

- Likes to be useful in helping others.
- Prefers to stay in room and do his/her own thing-watch T.V., read, and work crossword puzzles (a lifestyle preference).
- Wants to go on outing when knee heals.

Integration of Problems, Needs, Strengths

Problems, needs and strengths need to be integrated with other disciplines as appropriate. In an interdisciplinary plan of care system, the problems/needs written by other disciplines may be sufficient to cover activity-related problems/needs. If they are not, activity-related problems/needs/ or strengths need to be added to the care plan.

In a multidisciplinary plan of care system, the activity professional would write problems/needs that have been identified by another professional on the activity care plan. The professional discipline(s), which made the assessment, would be identified after the problem statement.

Example:

- *Problem:* Loss of 10 lbs. (per nursing/ dietary). Goals related to loss of weight may be different for nursing, dietary, social service and activities. The activity goal related to weight gain could be stated in a food-related goal, e.g., "Will eat high-calorie snacks during food-related activities (i.e., coffee hours, parties, socials, and special events, minimum of 1 x wk., by 10/31/11".

Goals

Outcomes are written as goals and/or objectives. Long-term-care facilities use one of two methods for writing outcomes. In a two-step system a broad goal is written, followed by measurable objectives. In a one-step system either a measurable goal or objective is written. The term used is whatever is printed on the care plan form. Goals must be resident-centered, measurable, realistic, dated and prioritized.

Resident Centered

Goals are written on an individual resident's plan of care for the resident and not the staff. The word "resident" (Res.) can be omitted from the beginning of the statement unless the facility's policy is to start the goal statement with "Resident" (Res.).

Action Verb:

Goal statements are started with an action verb written in future tense.

Will participate	Will continue
Will lead	Will state
Will complete	Will identify
Will go	Will read
Will watch	Will paint
Will attend	Will express

Examples:

- Will walk with assistance to and from the activity room a min. of 1x per day by 9/30/11
- Will attend a minimum of one special event with family by 12/25/11.
- Will look at picture books (children, animals, flowers) with A.S. assistance 2x per wk. by 11/30/11.

Behavior:

The action verb is followed by a behavior that can be seen or heard.

Examples:

- Will demonstrate ability to bowl from wheelchair in bowling alley 1x by 8/15/11 *(The resident would be seen bowling.)*

- Will verbally express feeling about being in nursing home during orientation group 2 out of 4 sessions by 12/15/11. *(Verbal expression would be heard.)*

Condition:

If there is a condition under which the goal is to be achieved, it is stated, e.g., independently, with assistance, without assistance, with verbal prompt.

Examples:

- Will independently complete one craft project of choice (wood craft, ceramic, holiday decoration) by 2/15/11.
- Will play bingo, with assistance from volunteer, 1x per week by 12/31/11.

Measurement:

Goal statement must be measurable. A goal can include:

Frequency: How often, i.e., # of times such as 3x day, daily, 2x per week, month, year.

Duration: How long, i.e., the amount of time – such as 15 minutes.

Quantity: How much, i.e., 1, 2, 3, 4, etc.

Quality: How accurately, i.e., correctly, accurately, consistently, precisely right, proper, 3 out of 4 tries.

Speed: How fast. e.g., by the end of 2 sessions, within 5 minutes.

Level of participation: Active, passive observer, assistant, leader, volunteer.

With Whom: Alone, peer(s), A.S. (activity staff), family, friend, volunteer.

In What Activity: e.g., Trivia, Sensory Group, Outing

In What Location: In own room, in activity room, in lounge, outside, on an outing.

Examples

- Will remain in sensory group with redirection for a minimum of 10 minutes by 11/30/11.
- Will correctly answer a minimum of 3 questions in Trivia R/T (related to) history, famous quotes, and opposites 1x per week by 6/30/11.
- Will complete one painting in 3 art lessons by 3/30/11.

Time Frame:

A target date for accomplishing a goal is written at the end of a goal statement. Some care plan forms have a column for target date; thus the date is written under the column heading. The specific date includes the month/day/year (12/1/11).

Realistic Time Frame

It is important to be realistic in identifying the amount of time that is needed to accomplish the goal. Items to consider include the resident's abilities, limitations and motivation; availability of resources (staff, volunteers, family, friends, supplies, equipment, transportation); time of year, etc.

The time frame for accomplishing the goal is from the date that the problem, need or strength was written to the target date. It may take 3, 6, 9 or 12 months to reach a goal.

If a problem was written on 3/15/11 and it was thought that the resident would need at least 6 months to achieve the goal, the target date would be 9/30/11. It is recommended that a little extra time is given to accomplish a goal unless the goal is to be accomplished on a specific date, i.e., performing in a talent show on a specific date, voting, or participation in an annual special event.

Words to Use with Target Dates

The words **"by"** or **"through"** are used with target dates. The word **"by"** is used when a desired behavior or action has not been previously achieved ("Will participate in bingo one time by 12/2/11"). The "word through" is used for a maintenance type goal for an action or behavior that is to be continued. The words "Will continue" are used at the beginning of a goal statement. ("Will continue to read newspaper daily through 1/15/11.")

Examples:

By Date

- Will answer yes/no to questions related to (R/T) previous life experience in reminiscing group 3x **by** 12/31/11.

Through Date

- Will continue to reminisce about family, work and experiences during 1:1 interaction with A.P. (activity professional) 1x per week **through** 12/31/11.
- Will continue to participate in scheduled activities of choice daily (i.e. crafts, music, exercises, discussion group, or outing **through** 1/30/11.

Approaches/Interventions

Care plan forms have the word "approaches" or "interventions" or the combined words, printed on the form. The terms "approaches" and "interventions" are used to identify what and when something is to be done as well as whom is responsible related to accomplishing a stated goal. Individualized approaches/interventions are written in sequential (step-by-step) order.

Specific approaches, interventions and/or plans include the following items:

1. Involvement of staff, family, other residents, and/or volunteers.
2. Frequency (number of times – e.g., 3x).
3. Duration (amount of time – e.g., 5–30 Min.).
4. Specific tasks.
5. Specific activities.
   A. Independent, individual, one-to-one and/or group
   B. Specific activity/programs (art, poetry, outing, church)
   C. Specific techniques to use related to activity, e.g., sensory stimulation for smell: perfumes, spices, etc.
6. Specific services, i.e., library service, provision of candy cart, distribution of mail, newspaper, etc.
7. Specific techniques (R.O., redirection, cueing, etc.)
8. Motivation
   A. Prior to Activity (invite, remind, ask, inform, etc.)
   B. During Activity (praise, cue, instruct, redirect, etc.)
   C. Completion of Activity (thank, praise)
   D. Follow-Up
9. Stimulation.
10. Situation, i.e., resident is disruptive.
11. Where (in room, lounge, activity room, chapel, restaurant).
12. Use of adaptive equipment/supplies.
13. Obtainment of needed supplies/equipment.
13. Positioning of resident.
14. Release of restraints.
15. Precautions.
16. Assistance to be provided.
17. Monitoring (When watching—"monitoring"—a specific situation, behavior or action, indicate an alternate plan in case the original plan does not work.)
18. Other.

Integration of Approaches with other Disciplines

In an **"interdisciplinary"** plan of care system, activity professionals indicate their responsibilities for specific approaches, as appropriate, by writing in the letter "**A**" behind each approach. Some approaches will be for just one discipline, i.e., Nursing – "**N**", whereas others may be for two or more disciplines, i.e., dietary – "**D**", Social Service – "**S**". When all disciplines are responsible for following an approach or implementing an intervention/plan, the word "**All**" is used.

Example:

Invite and assist to activity of interest
All
Escort to sensory stimulation group
A, NA

In a "**multidisciplinary**" plan of care system the activity professional needs to be sure that what is written on the Activities of Care related to another clinical discipline (e.g., nursing, social service, dietary) is also written by that discipline on its section of the comprehensive plan of care. In a multidisci-

plinary care plan system; either the staff's initials or department is listed under the column "Responsible." If there is not a separate column to indicate the responsible person(s), the professional writing the care plan identifies the responsible discipline prior to writing interventions.

Example:

l. Remind of activities of interest (church, parties, sing-a-long) 10 minutes prior to act. **Act**.
or
A.P. (Activity Professional) to:
1. Provide monthly activity schedule, discuss and circle activities of interest (current events, word games, entertainment).
2. Invite to all social events (parties, picnics, contests, special events, etc.)
3. Obtain yarn for crocheting.

Record Keeping

The current interpretive guidelines for federal regulation F-248 Activities, addresses activity documentation in regards to Assessment, care planning and care planning revision; it does not address activity attendance/participation records. However some states do not address the attendance/participation record keeping.

It is difficult to write an accurate quarterly progress note without some type of participation record. The most useful type of participation record is an individualized record coordinated with the resident care plan.

The record can include participation in specific activities, behaviors, responses to specific interventions, and duration of involvement, e.g., one-to-one activity as appropriate.

Activity Progress Notes

Definition

Activity progress notes are narrative, antidotal notes and/or summaries of a participant's involvement or lack of participation in activities related to his/her individualized plan of care. The notes are a permanent written record—a part of the participant's medical record or a program record, in non-clinical settings.

Purpose

Activity progress notes are a communication tool. Notes indicate that the participant's plan of care was implemented. Responses, outcomes, behaviors, change in condition, participation and/or behavior, provide valuable information about an individual participant.

The activity care plans with measurable goals establish direction for activities, care and services. Activity progress notes are like mini-chapters/ reports indicating what has or has not happened at different intervals of time.

Frequency

Activity progress notes are written in accordance with the frequency designated by federal, state, and/or city regulations, voluntary regulations agencies, e.g., JCAHO, and/or agency or facility policy. If an agency or facility's policy is more stringent than federal, state or city regulations, then the agency/facility's policy is followed. Quarterly progress notes are the norm in most long-term-care facilities as required by OBRA. In health-care settings with skilled nursing, sub-acute units, and rehabilitation units, progress notes may be written more frequently, i.e., weekly, because of the changing condition of participants and shorter stays.

Activity progress notes must be written on or before a target date for a care plan goal. Notes are written each time the care plan is reviewed/revised. Activity progress notes are also written when there is a change in condition or a significant change in participation and/or behavior. Care conference notes may be a part of the activity progress notes system and thus are identified as "Care Conference Notes" on the Activity Progress Notes. They are usually written immediately after a care conference or as indicated by facility policy. Discharge notes and/or discharge summaries are also a part of the activity progress note record system and are identified as such, i.e., "Discharge Note," "Discharge Summary".

Forms

Forms for activity progress notes can be purchased or developed by the agency/facility. The heading **Activity Progress Notes** indicates the type of note in the medical or program record. It is recommended that the activity progress notes form be separate from the activities assessment form. This separates all assessment information from all progress (evaluation) information. Some organizations/facilities use color-coded forms. This is not essential but helps to easily distinguish the activity progress notes from those of other departments.

An agency/facility may use an interdisciplinary progress note system. Each discipline writes on the same form. The discipline is identified by a subheading and/or signature, title, or department. Subheadings may be simply the identification of the specific notes, i.e., "Activities," "Dietary," "Nursing" and "Social Service".

Placement

In long-term-care and other health care facilities, the activity progress notes are kept in the resident's medical record. Medical records have an index system for placement of information. Activity progress notes are usually placed behind a tab named "Activities" or in an integrated section of the medical record labeled "Progress Notes." The order in which progress notes are placed in the medical record under their designated index tab is dependent upon the facility's policy. When a second page of notes is added, they can be placed on the bottom or the top of the first page, in accordance with the facility's policy. In non-clinical community agency settings, activity progress notes may be kept in a separate file or be a part of a total record.

Format

Activity progress notes are written in ink—usually black ink, but not erasable ink. A narrative format is used. Each statement or sentence can begin with reference to the resident/participant or with a verb. Progress notes are written in past and present tense, i.e., relating back to the care plan [past tense] or what is happening at present [present tense]. Behavioral language (descriptive words) individualizes the progress notes. Residents can be referred to by their last name (Mr. Jones), first name (Frank), or by pronouns (he/she). The activity professional refers to him/ herself in the third person, A.C. (Activity Coordinator), or "This writer." The personal pronoun "I" is not used.

Only facts are written. Personal opinions are omitted. Opinions stated by residents or participants are included if they are pertinent to the content/context of the progress note. Activity progress notes are a communication tool. They need to be written clearly, concisely, accurately, timely, sequentially and logically. They need to be legible for others to read. It is imperative to identify the date the note is written. The date can be written before or after the note. Most forms have a column for the date to the left of the space for the note. A full date is used, i.e., August 1, 2011 or 8/1/11, but not 8/11.

All notes must be signed by the writer, indicating job title or certification initials. Signatures are written immediately after the last word of the note, toward the right side of the page, or beneath the note to the right side of the page. A single line is drawn from the last word of the note to the first letter of the signature. This assures that no one can write in the blank space in the note which the activity professional has signed. Legal signature consists of legal name or first initial and surname. The initials of job title or certification are written after the signature, i.e., Sue Smith, A.C., or Sue Smith, A.C.C.

Using the above system for writing the date and signature gives an easy-to-read format. All dates are listed on the left side of the page, the notes in the middle, and signatures on the right side of the page.

Content of Activity Progress Notes

Information Related to Care Plans

Activity progress notes relate to the resident's or participant's plan of care. The notes identify whether or not the person was involved in his/her own plan of care. If the person was not involved, the reason is identified.

Progress or lack of progress related to the problems, goals and approaches/interventions on the care plans needs to be cited. Responses and outcomes are pertinent. These can include responses related to involvement in activities: requests; instructions; answers to questions (yes/no, open-ended, feeling-type questions); interaction with peer, family/friends, staff and volunteers; and change of condition, attitude and/or participation, family involvement, roommate and/or staff.

Involvement

Identification of the participant's level of involvement in activities, frequency and duration related to the plan of care provides a basis of progress as well as a means for indicating needs. Goal attainment or identification as to "why" goals were not accomplished establishes a point of reference for continuation or revision of the plan of care.

It may be pertinent to identify the condition under which the plan of care was implemented. A condition could include weather/temperature; inside or out-of-doors; in the facility versus in the community; in a small group versus a large group; and whether or not an activity was a self-directed individual activity or a one-to-one activity. A participant's response to going on an outing to a park with wide-open spaces (unlimited boundaries) may be quite different from going on a van ride, particularly if the participant has cognitive impairment.

Observation

Observations of behavior, facial expression, body language, physical appearance, i.e., posture, dress, movements, and attitude need to be recorded if pertinent to the participant. Grimacing during an activity may indicate pain or increased pain. Relaxation of facial muscles and upper torso can indicate relaxation. A change in attitude often affects participation. An avid bingo player who becomes angry with a peer during a game may refuse to participate in bingo and/or other activities in which the peer is involved.

Detail Information for Activity Progress Notes

Pertinent information specifically related to the participant individualizes progress notes. Every progress note will be different because they are written at different intervals of a person's life. No two periods of time in one's life are exactly the same. There are changes of seasons, activities, special events, and involvement with others.

Progress notes can include the following information:

① Attitude

A participant's attitude may change. Changes to be noted can include attitudes towards:
a. Him/herself (participation, performance, competition, individual, one-to-one, group activities, etc.).
b. Illness, disability, ability, limitation (real or perceived).
c. Long-term-care placement or membership in senior center.
d. Family, friends, other residents, staff, and/or volunteers.
e. Interaction/socialization with peers, staff, family and volunteers.

② Interest, Participation and Performance

A participant's interest, as well as participation and performance, may change. A participant may have a new interest, continue former interests, or decide he/she is no longer interested in a specific activity. Exposure to new activities and experiences may elicit a positive or negative response. Changes in level of participation may be noteworthy such as a self-directed, independent participant who now needs assistance or cueing, or shows a change in his/her ability to participate. Change(s) can affect whether a person participates in specific activities. An active participant may choose to become passive and watch others involved in an activity. Increased or decreased frequency or duration of involvement in an activity needs to be observed and noted.

Performance quality may continue or change. This can be related to increase or decrease in physical, cognitive, and social abilities, as well as interests and/or experiences. If pertinent, the continuance or change, and reason for change need to be noted.

Involvement in specific activities related to the plan of care is important to document. If a person refuses to participate in an activity which is a part of his/her plan of care, it is more significant than if a person refuses to participate in another activity. Identifying whether the activity was an individual, one-to-one or group activity, structured, spontaneous, indoor, out-of-doors, or in the community shows different types of involvement and location. Identification of the person(s) with whom the activity took place may be significant. Did the participant do the activity with an activity professional, family member, volunteer or with a peer?

③ Supplies and Equipment

Information related to the provision and/or utilization of supplies and equipment may be pertinent. In a long-term-care facility, a person who is confined to a room may not have a TV, radio or cassette recorder for individual stimulation. Families may be requested to obtain these items. Outcome of the requests affects the participant's participation. A resident's independent involvement in ordering supplies for a specific hobby or activity reinforces his/her independence. Provision of crossword puzzles, magazines, books and responses need to be noted if applicable.

A participant just learning how to use a remote control on the TV may have progressed to independently using a VCR. The participant's attitude when introduced to adaptive equipment will affect his/her response to using the equipment, e.g., Talking Book, cardholder, card-shuffler, large print reading materials, etc. Progress in acceptance/rejection of adaptive equipment needs to be documented.

④ Abilities, Limitations, Behaviors, Responses

Continuance or changes in abilities, limitations, behaviors and responses can be documented related to the three behavioral domains (cognitive, physical, affective) and social/interaction skills. Changes may be slight, significant or permanent.

A. Cognitive

The cognitive domain includes orientation to person, time, place, routine, and expectation; memory (short-term, long-term, remote); ability to follow directions, make decisions, follow through, completion of tasks; appropriate response to questions, statements, conversation; making needs known; recognition and recall; comprehension; reading, writing, mathematics; attention and concentration span; distractibility; and preoccupation and hallucinations (visual, auditory). Responses may be incidental or consistent. A person may be able to respond appropriately to a game requiring long term memory, but not be able to recall the day or date related to cognitive impairment. Over a period of time, these responses may remain consistent and then gradually or suddenly decline. Documentation of this type of information becomes the basis for changing the plan of care.

B. Affective

The affective domain includes attitudes, values, feelings and interests. A person's attitude affects his/her involvement in activities as well as how he/she sees him/herself (independent, needing assistance, feeling helpless). Values based on philosophy of life and activities can be motivating factors related to participation in specific activities and interpersonal relationships. Religious values may affect a person's participation in cards, bingo, dancing and celebration of holidays and/or religious activities.

Expression of feelings is important for emotional stability. Expressive activities (verbal and non-verbal) such as discussion, art, music, poetry, dance, movement, creative writing, etc., allow a person to express feelings. Through expression, the activity professional can identify changes in feelings and whether or not they are congruent. A person may express anger for placement in a long-term-care facility, and then show adjustment and acceptance. When a person can accept a situation, he or she is more apt to participate in activities of choice. A person who cries, withdraws from interactions and/or activities, does not eat even a favorite dessert or snack, may be grieving or showing signs of depression. Documentation of this information may be consistent with what other professionals have seen, thus substantiating a need for treatment or change in treatment. A change in medication may have a positive or negative effect on behaviors. Documentation of change(s) in behaviors and reactions can be utilized by the physician in evaluating/changing medication for a participant.

C. Physical

The normal process of aging includes physical changes. Pathological changes are not normal. The activity professional must be observant and document changes in physical appearance, abilities and responses.

The physical domain includes sensory abilities, ambulation, use of body parts, e.g., upper and lower extremities, ability to sit or stand, coordination, balance, energy level, endurance, etc. Documentation of diet awareness, acceptance and compliance is important. Not following a prescribed diet can lead to other physical, cognitive, emotional and/or social problems. Some medications can cause increased sensitivity to the sun. Documentation of utilization of prescribed sunscreen and reaction to the sun during an outdoor activity is pertinent. If the sunscreen was not effective, treatment will need to be changed. A person may need a different sunscreen and to wear protective clothing to prevent an adverse reaction. Unknown allergies need to be communicated and documented. A person in a reminiscing group may bring up an incident of being allergic to bee stings. He or she may have forgotten about the incident. However this is pertinent information. The physician needs to be notified so that appropriate care can be prescribed to prevent a catastrophic reaction.

A person may respond positively to one or more specific sensory stimulations. In working with a resident with very low-cognitive-functioning abilities, it is important to document both positive and negative responses. Over a period of time the preferred sense can be identified and the plan of care can be revised to reflect the appropriate goals and approaches/interventions.

D. Social/Interaction

In both community settings and health care settings, observation of social interaction skills is important. A person who was a loner may prefer to remain a loner. However, with exposure to other social opportunities, he/she may increase interaction and involvement. Some people prefer individual independent activities and/or one-to-one activities; others may like these as well as group activities.

Social interaction skills include communication (verbal, non-verbal), use of communication devices, sign language, gestures, interaction/socialization with family/friends/peers/staff/visitors, acceptance of others and being accepted, being cooperative or competitive, and liking similar activities as peers. A person may prefer to do individual activities alone or in the presence of others. A change in physical, affective and cognitive abilities and opportunities can affect social and interactive skills and opportunities. Documenting involvement in specific activities can identify social interaction and skills without stating such. Identifying that a person independently participated in working crossword puzzles in his/her private room indicates an individual, independent activity. A person who initiated conversation with a new resident during crafts indicates the person's ability to verbalize and be assertive. Grooming and appearance can have an affect on socialization and acceptance by others. If one does not care about how he/she looks and smells, it could be related to cognitive impairment, physical, and/or emotional problems. Rejection by others can have a negative effect.

Process for Writing Activity Progress Notes
First Progress Note

Review the initial activity assessment and MDS., the plan of care and the daily participation records. Reflect on the participant's adjustment, attitude, participation and responses to activities, or interventions. Determine whether a goal or progress toward goal was made. If not, determine why it was not achieved. Think about changes in the participant or the participant's responses and/or new situations. Organize thoughts. Write down key words to be remembered. Write the note. Review the note, and add any additional pertinent information before signing the note. If something is thought of after the note is signed, an additional note can be added by recording the date, writing the note and signing it.

Updated Progress Note

Review the previous activity progress note, as a point of reference, as well as progress notes from other disciplines. Review the plan of care and daily participation record. Reflect back to what the participant has done or said. Organize thoughts. Write down key words relating to information that needs to be documented. Separate new needs, wishes, wants and preferences from information pertaining to the care plan. Write progress notes. It is not necessary to state what is to be done about new information, as this will be recorded in the plan of care. Progress notes are written in past and present tenses. What is to be done (future tense) is recorded in the care plan. It is important to revise the plan of care as needed after the progress notes have been written. If time does not permit immediate revision of the care plan, the progress notes can be used as a reference for development of a new care plan.

Incidental Progress Notes

A short notation can be written in the progress notes at any time. It is more effective to write a specific note than it is to try to remember an incident when writing quarterly notes. Incidental progress notes usually are immediate recordings of something significant. A participant's first response after many attempts of sensory stimulation would be significant. An unusual involvement or interaction may be noteworthy. Identifying that a specific community resource had been contacted (and the outcome) would be significant, e.g., arranging transportation for a resident in a nursing home to attend a program at the local senior center.

Annual Progress Note

The annual progress note accompanies the annual MDS. This note should include a summary of the resident's progress over the year. Included are resident accomplishments throughout the year,

Discharge Note

A discharge note is written for a non-anticipated discharge, e.g., when a person in a long-term-care facility is admitted to the hospital. The note is identified as a discharge note by using a subheading DISCHARGE NOTE after writing the date and before writing the note. The discharge note first identifies progress or lack of progress related to the care plan. The same process used for writing an updated progress note is used for the discharge note.

The last paragraph or statement indicates that the participant was discharged. The note identifies the date of discharge, reason (if known) and place, e.g., "Resident fell on 7/25/10, discharged to University Medical Center with possible broken hip". If a person expires, the discharge note states that the person expired on a specific date, i.e., "Expired 1/20/11".

Discharge Summary

A discharge summary is written when there is an anticipated discharge, i.e., resident is going home or to another facility. There are four steps to writing a discharge summary. First, the note is identified as a DISCHARGE SUMMARY. Second, a progress note related to the plan of care is written. Third, a paragraph is written that focuses on a recapitulation of the resident's stay from admission through the date of discharge. The fourth step is identifying where the resident was discharged.

Summary

The activity progress notes tell an unfolding story (information) about the resident/participant from admission in a health-care facility or acceptance in a community-based program through discharge from the facility or termination of involvement in a community-based program. The activity professional is responsible for documenting accurate information in a timely manner using correct grammar, spelling, punctuation and legible handwriting.

With electronic technology changing rapidly most facilities are doing some form of documentation on the computer, however some are still writing narrative notes. Both formats require a legal signature. However, a legal signature will still be required.

Post Discharge Plans

OBRA Requirement

OBRA requires post-discharge plans for residents in long-term-care facilities for whom discharge to home or another facility is anticipated. The post-discharge plan is usually written within 7 to 14 days of the anticipated discharge date.

OBRA Regulation 483.20 Resident Assessment

Tag F284 (3) A post-discharge plan of care that is developed with the participation of the resident and his or her family, which will assist the resident to adjust to his or her new living environment.

Post Discharge Plan

Activity professionals can work with a resident and his or her family in preparation for discharge, related to involvement in activities. A resident may need adaptive devices or resources for adaptive devices such as a card-holder, card shuffler, page-turner, large print newspaper, magazine and/or books, needle threader, or lighted magnifying glass. A resident may want to go to a senior center or to return to a senior center but need to have transportation arranged. Families may need to be taught how to adapt activities. A resident may want to continue to have a garden but needs plans and ideas for a raised garden. Families may need to be taught how to place supplies within a person's field of vision.

A list of accessible facilities in the community may be helpful to the resident and family. Opportunities for volunteer work at home or in the community may also be needed.

Often the post-discharge plan is written and coordinated by the social worker with input from activity and other health-care professionals. An activity professional may have to assist with family education and obtaining community resources.

Community Resource Library

In preparation for discharge, activity professionals can develop a community resource library to use with residents and families. The resource library can be developed for specific cities, counties or other areas. It may also include information that is not geographically specific. Information can include specific senior focal points; senior centers/clubs; organizations that arrange travel for senior citizens; specific interest groups (for seniors or those which are intergenerational); volunteer organizations; service organizations (volunteer readers, Friendly Visitors, telephone reassurance programs, AA); accessible recreational facilities and schedules, as well as a list of local merchants who sell activity-related supplies and equipment, e.g., art/craft/needlework stores, hobby shops, garden centers, discount stores, electronic equipment stores, etc. Sample catalogs of supplies and equipment for activities need to be a part of the library's collection.

Most frequently residents need a list of specific transportation services, identifying services, cost and restrictions. A list of contacts for local churches identifying services that are available, e.g., volunteer transportation to church, visitors in the home, opportunities for a prayer group in-home, etc., can provide the impetus for a resident to resume involvement in religious/spiritual activities.

The resources in a resource library can be endless. It takes time to develop a resource library. Assistance from other staff members and volunteers in obtaining information is very valuable. Developing a team approach to developing the library is also a way to educate staff on the importance of working with a resident and/or family on the resident's discharge plans. Once a basic resource library is developed, it needs to be kept up-to-date. Once a year, community resources can be contacted for updated information. New resources are usually announced in newspapers. They can be contacted for information/application. It is best to date all material as a means of keeping all materials/information up-to-date.

Managing Time for Documentation
"Set up a block of time for documentation"

The amount of required activity documentation will differ among agencies, health-care and long-term-care facilities. Regulatory agencies, professional standards of practice, and policies and procedures will determine the amount and frequency of documentation.

All activity professionals must manage their time in completing required documentation accurately and in a timely manner. It is best to schedule the task of documentation when one's energy level allows quick and clear thinking. Morning people may be most effective documenting early in the morning versus late-night people who might do better documenting in the afternoon or late afternoon.

Approximate Time Frames

Interviews with participants for obtaining information for the activity assessment must be conducted when the participant is available. Information needed for part of the assessment can be obtained from the medical record prior to an interview with the participant. The summary part of the assessment can be completed after the interview. It generally takes 30 minutes for an assessment and recording precautions on a precautions form.

In long-term-care facilities, completion of the activity pursuit section on the MDS requires approximately 20 minutes per interview-able resident for an experienced activity professional. Upon completion

of the MDS, the activity CAA needs to be explored if there are any potential triggers (approximately 10 to 15 minutes per resident for an experienced professional). It takes approximately 10 to 15 minutes to complete a CAA Note and CAA Summary.

Development of care plans can require 15 to 60 minutes, depending on whether a team develops the care plans together or the activity professional develops care plans independently. Pre-printed daily activity participation records can be initiated by placing a new participant's name on the form and then keeping the records up to date daily (approximately 30 to 45 minutes per day).

Incidental and quarterly progress notes, and discharge notes and summaries, may require 5 to 45 minutes of time, depending on the amount of information that needs to be recorded. In some agencies progress notes may be weekly. However, weekly notes tend to be shorter than quarterly notes.

A consistent time, with flexibility, needs to be established, i.e., 1 to 2 hour periods. A quiet, uninterrupted area for documenting is ideal. An area away from the office or nurses' station may be the best place for documentation. Phone calls need to be held. A receptionist or other designated person can be asked to take messages to prevent interruptions.

Organization

All needed documentation materials and forms need to be obtained before starting to document. Concentration needs to be on one participant/resident at a time. Stay focused. Refrain from socializing while documenting. Activity professionals need to be assertive in requesting other staff to refrain from interrupting for social purposes.

A record, i.e., Activities Documentation Flow Sheet, of completed documentation and dates of needed documentation helps to keep an activity professional up-to-date. Keeping track of the next review date and target dates for goals can be an effective system. Completed documentation can be recorded in ink; dates for future documentation can be recorded in pencil. When the due date arrives and the documentation is completed, the date can be erased and replaced with the actual date of documentation in ink.

Accepted Medical Abbreviations

ALPHABETICAL LISTING OF ABBREVIATIONS USED IN MEDICAL RECORDS
(Partial List)

Basic abbreviations (not all inclusive) used in medical records are listed below.

&	and	Act. Rm.	Activity room
~	approximately	A.D.	Activity Director
@	at	ADA	American Dietetic Association
º	Degree	ADC	Activivity Director Certified
"	Inch/Inches	ADD	adduction
'	Foot/Feet	ADL	activities of daily living
>	Greater than	ad. lib.	as patient can tolerate
<	Less Than	adm	admission
%	Percent	ADT	alternate day therapy
#	Pound	AEB/aeb	as evidenced by
↑	increase, up, elevate	AF	Atrial Fibrillation
↓	decrease, down, lower	A/I	accident/incident
♂	male	A.K.	above knee
♀	female	AKA	above knee amputation
I	one	A.M.	Ante meridian
II	two	AMA	against medical advice
1º	primarily	amb	ambulation
1:1	one-to-one	amt	amount
2º	secondary to	AP	apical pulse
3D	3 dimensional	appl	applicator
a	*before*	AROM	active range of motion
A	assistance	A.R.T.	Accredited Record Technician
A.A.	Alcoholics Anonymous	ASA	aspirin
A.A.	Activity Assistant	ASAP	as soon as possible
AAROM	active assistive range of motion	ASHD	arteriosclerosis heart disease
ABC	abduction	A&W	alive and well
abn	abnormal	D	dependent
a.c.	before meals		
A.C.	Activity Coordinator	*B.*	*Ball (e.g.basket B.)*
ACF	Acute Care Facility	B & B	bowel and bladder
Act.	Activities	bid	twice a day

bil	bilateral		CRT	controlled release tablet
B.J.M.	bones, joints, muscle		CTG	contact guard
Bk.	Book		CTRS	certified therapeutic recreation specialist
BK	below the knee			
BKA	below the knee amputation		C/S	culture & sensitivity
B.M.	bowel movement		CSF	cerebrospinal fluid
BMR	basal metabolic rate		CV	Cerebrovascular
BP	blood pressure		CVA	cerebral vascular accident (stroke)
BRP	bathroom privilege			
BS	blood sugar		*CVD*	*Cardiovascular Disease*
BSF	benign senilistic forgetfulness		*CVR*	*cardiovascular respiration*
B.U.E.	bilateral upper extremity			
			d	day
$\bar{c}$	with		D/C	discontinue
°c	Celsius		D&C	dilation and curettage
CA	cancer		D.D.	developmental disability
CA-	calcium		DF	dispensed for
cal	calories		Diab. Mell	Diabetes Mellitus
c-5	cervical lesion at the 5th vertebra		diff	differential
Ca	cancer		DIP	distal interphalangeal joint
cap	capsule		disc.	discuss
cath.	catheterize		*disp*	*dispenser*
CBS	chronic brain syndrome		*D.M.*	*Diabetes Mellitus*
c/c	chief complaint		DNR	Do Not Resuscitate
CHF	congestive heart failure		DON	Director of Nursing Services
Ch	church		DOA	dead on arrival
chol.	cholesterol		Dr.	doctor
ck. or	check		D.R.	Dining room
CBC	complete blood count		D.R./Act.Rm.	dining/activity room
c.c.	cubic centimeter		D/S	dextrose and saline
CC	chief complaint		DSS	docusate sodium – colace
chew	chewable		D/T	due to
CHF	Congestive Heart Failure		D.T.'s	delerium tremens
chlor	chloride		dtr	deep tendon reflexes
cl	cloudy		DTR	Dietary Technicain Registered
cm	centimeter		D&V	diarrhea and vomiting
C.N.	cranial nerves		Dx.	diagnosis
CN	Certified Nutritionist			
CNS	central nervous system		ea.	Each
CO2	carbon dioxide		ECG/EKG	electrocardiogram
c/o	complained of		E.C.T.	electroconvulsive
cod	codeine		ed.	Educate/education
cog.	Cognitive		E.E.G.	electroencephalogram
comp	complete		EENT	eye, ear, nose and throat
comm.	Community/communicate		e.g.	for example
Comm.	Communion		EKG	electrocardiogram
conc	concentrate		emot.	Emotional
cont'd	continued		E.R.	emergency room
COPD	Chronic Obstructive Pulmonary Disease		EMR/EMH	educable mentally retarded or handicapped
			ENT	ear, nose and throat
COTA	*Certified Occupational Therapy*		ES.T.	electroshock therapy
C.P.	cerebral palsied		Exp	expectorant

Exp Lap	Exploratory Laparotomy		Hx	history
°F	Fahrenheit		I	independent
F	female		ICU	intensive care unit
F	fasting		ID	intradermal
fac.	facility		I & D	incision & drainage
FBS	fasting blood sugar		i.e.	that is
Fe	iron		I.M.	intramuscular (into the muscle)
FF	force fluids		Imp	impaired
FH	family history		indep.	independent
FL	below functional limits		info	information
freq	frequent		indiv.	individual
F.R.O.M.	full range of motion		I&O	intake & output
ft.	feet		IPPB	intermitten positive pressure
F/U	full upper		intele.	Intellectual
f/u	follow-up		intro.	introduce
FUO	fever of unknown origin		IT	inhalation therapy
F.W.B.	full weight-bearing		I.U.D.	intrauterine device
Fx.	Fracture I&O		I.V.	intravenous (into the vein)
gal	gallon		jt	joint handicapped
G.B.	gallbladder			
GC	gonorrhea		K	kilo
G/C	gerichair		K+	potassium
GDR	generic dispensed of		kg	kilogram
G.I.	gastrointestinal		KUB	kidneys, ureters and bladder
gm	gram		Lab	laboratory
GPN	Graduate Practical Nurse			
gr	grain			
gp/grp.	group			
gran	granules			
GRD	groundGran			
G/R	geri recliner			
GTT	glucose tolerance test			
G.U.	genetourinary			
GYN	gynecological			
h	hour			
H/hm.	home			
Hb	hemoglobin			
hgb	hemoglobin			
hemi	hemiplegia			
H20	water			
H202	hydrogen peroxide			
HHP	hot hydrocollator packs			
HOB	head of bed			
HOH	hand over hand & hard of hearing			
H&P	history & physical			
HRF	health related facility			
h.s.	*hour of sleep*			
HT	hypertension			
ht.	height			

l	liter	M.S.	multiple sclerosis
L	left	multi	multiple
L-5	lumbar lesion at the 5th vertebra		
Lab	laboratory	N	nursing
Lap	Laparotomy	n	normal
lb	# pound	na	Sodium
L.D.	learning disability	NAD	no abnormality detected
LE	lower extremity	N.A.	Nurses Aide
leis.	leisure	N.A.S.	no added salt
leis.ed.	leisure education	NC	nasal cannula
lg.	large	NCA	not clinically anemic
lg.gp./grp.	large group	N.C.S.	no concentrated sweets
lib.	library	neg.	negative
liq	liquid	N.H.	Nursing Home
LKS	liver, kidney, spleen	NKA	no known allergies medication
LLE	left lower extremity	NN	nursing notes
LOA	leave of absence	no.,#	number
LOB	loss of balance	noc	night
LOS	length of stay	NP	neuropsychiatric
LKS	liver, kidney, spleen	NPO	nothing by mouth
LOB	loss of balance	nsg.	nursing
L.P.N.	Licensed Practical Nurse	nsg.hm.	nursing home
L.P.T.	Licensed Physical Therapist	N.S.R.	normal sinus rhythm
LTC	long term care	N/V	nausea & vomiting
LTG	long-term goal	N.W.B.	non weight-bearing
Lytes	electrolytes		
M	male	o	other
mag.	magazine	O2	oxygen
max	maximum	OBS	organic brain syndrome
MBS	modified barium swallow	obst	obstruction
MC	Medicare	od	every day
MCE	Medical Care Evaluation	O.D.	overdose
mcgm	microgram	OD	right eye
MCP	metacarpal phalangeal joint	Oint	ointment
		OOB	out of bed
M.D.	medical doctor, muscular dystrophy	OOF	out of facility
		OOR	out of room
MDR	main dining room	O.R.	operating room
Meds	medication	Ortho	Orthopedics
Meq	milliequivalent	OS	left eye
Mg	milligram	OSOB	on side of bed
M.I.	Myocardial Infarction	O.T.	Occupational Therapy
Min	minute	O.U.	both eyes
MIN	minimum	Oz	ounce
ml	myocardial infarction		
M.L.	midline	p	after
mm	milliliter	p	passive
Mo.	month	P.	pulse
mod	moderate	P&A	percussion and auscultation
mon	month	PAB	partial adaptive bag
MR	Mental Retardation	PBI	protein bound iodine
		p.c.	after meals

part.	participate	q.p.m.	every night
Path	pathology	q.s.	quantity sufficient
p.c.	after meals	qt	quart
PE	physical examination	q.w.	every week
Ped	Podiatrics		
pet t.	pet therapy	R	rectal
pet v.	pet visit	R	respiration
PH	past history	RBC	red blood count
ph I-V	phalanges (1-5 fingers)	Re:	regarding
phys.	physical (as in physical activities)	rec.	recreation
PID	Pelvic Inflammatory Disease	Ref	refill
PIP	proximal interphalangeal Joint	Reg	regular
P/L	partial lower	rel.	religious
P.M.	post meridian	remot.	remotivation
PMH	past medical history	req	requires
P.N.D.	post nasal drip	res.	resident
po	by mouth	resp	respirations
POC	plan of care	RHC	respirations have ceased
POD	plan of discharge	RHD	Rheumatic Heart Disease
pos	positive	RLE	right lower extremity
post op	after surgery	Rm	room
Pow	powder	R.N.	Registered Nurse
P.R.E.	Passive Inflammatory Disease	R. O.	reality orientation
pre op	before surgery; also means pre op	R/O	rule out
prep	prepare for surgery	ROJM	range of joint motion
prev	previous	R.O.M.	range of motion
PRN/p.r.n.	given as needed	R, R, rt.	right
PRO	protein	R.R.S.	radio reading service
prog.	program (as in activity program)	r/t	related to
proj.	project	R.T.	recreation therapy or recreation therapist
PROM	passive range of motion		
Pt.	patient	RWR	reasonable weight range
pt	pint	Rx	prescription/treatment
P.T.	physical therapy	RX no	prescription number
P/U	partial upper		
pub.	public	S	supervision
pub.lib.	public library	s	without
pulv	pulvule	s & s	signs & symptoms
PWB	partial weight bearing	SA	sustained action
		SBA	stand-by assist
		s.c.	subcutaneous
q	every	SCA	Sickle Cell Anemia
Q	Quarterly	sched.	schedule
qam	every morning	SDAT	Senile Dementia Alzheimer's Type
q.d.	every day	Sed rate	sedimentation rate
q2h	every 2 hours	sen.	sensory
QHS	every night at bedtime	sen. stim.	sensory stimulation
q.i.d.	four times a day	Sig:	instructions (when to take drugs)
qns	quantity not sufficient	sl	sublingual
q.o.d.	every other day	SLR	straight leg raise
q.p.m.	every night	sm.	small
q.o.d.	every other day	sm. gp./grp	small group
		S.N.	Student Nurse

SNF	skilled nursing facility		T.R.	therapeutic recreation
S.O.B.	shortness of breath		T.R.S.	Therapeutic Recreation Specialist
Soc.	social		tsp	teaspoon
sol	solution		TTWB	toe-touch weight-bearing
S/P	status post		TIR	Transurethral Resection
spec.	special (e.g., spec.event)		T.V.	television
sp.gr	specific gravity		TX	treatment
SR	sustained release			
SRC	sustained released capsule		U	unit
ss	one half		U/A/	urinalysis
S.S.	Social Services		U.E.	upper extremith
S/S	signs and symptoms		UE	upper extremity
SSA	Social Security Administration		up ad.	allow patient to move around as much as he feels he can
SSE	soapsuds enema		U.R.	utilization review
ST	speech therapy		URI	upper respiratory infection
STG	short term goal		UTI	urinary tract infection
stat	immediately		U/S	ultrasound
str	strength			
strep	Streptococcus		VA	Veteran's Association
sulf	sulfate		Vag	vaginal
supp	suppository		V.C.	verbal cues
surg	surgery		V.D.	venereal disease
susp	suspension		V.D.G.	gonorrhea
SWA	Social Worker Assistant		Vit	vitamin
Syr	syrup		Vol.	volunteer
sx	symptoms		V.S.	vital signs
			v.t.	validation therapy
T	temperature			
T-5	thoracic lesion at the 5th vertebra		w	white
			W/B/	weight bearing
Tach	tachycardia		WBC	white blood count
TB	tuberculin		w/c	wheelchair
T.B.	talking book		W/D	well developed
Tbsp	tablespoon		WFL	within functional limits
T/C	throat cultulre		wk.	week, work
TD	tim,e disintegrate		wk.end	weekend
T.H.R.	total hip replacement		WN	well nourished
t.i.d.	three times a day		WNL	within normal limits
tinct	tincture		W/P	whirlpool
T.O.	telephone order		wt.	weight
tol	tolerated			
T.P.	total protein		x	times (e.g., 3x per day)
TPR	temperature, pulse, respiration		xc	except
tr	trace			
			yr.	year

Standardized Clinical Language

It is imperative that activity professionals use standardized clinical language so that any health care professional reading activity documentation understands the meaning of the language used. Specific activity language may be new to clinicians; thus, it has to be consistent. Health care facilities have an approved list of medical terminology. Activity professionals will need to confer with the director of medical records related to the established procedure for adding terms to the approved list of medical terminology.

SNOMED: Systemized Nomenclature of Medicine

SNOMED was developed by the College of American Pathologists (CAP). SNOMED CT resulted from a merger between SNOMED-RT (Reference Terminology) and the England and Wales National Health Service's clinical terms. SNOMED CT is considered to be the first *international* terminology.

A new international organization, The Health Terminology Standards Development Organization (IHTSDO, also known as SNOMED SDO) acquired ownership of SNOMED Clinical Terms on April 26, 2007 and will be responsible for the future maintenance and development. "

SNOMED CT is the most comprehensive medical terminology developed to date and can be used to support patient data in electronic patient record. There are over 300,000 medical concepts and their relationships. SNOMED CT has been licensed in at least 30 countries. A 5-year renewable license agreement between the CAP and the National Library of Medicine provides free access to the English and Spanish language editions.

In years to come, activity professionals will see more standardization of medical terminology particularly in the physician assessments and physician orders.

National Health Infrastructure

President Bush, in his State of the Union address, January 20, 2004 emphasized the need to computerize health records for three (3) reasons: (1) reduce cost, (2) improve care and (3) lower the risks of medical mistakes. Personal health care records are stored in many locations, e.g. hospitals, nursing homes, physician offices, free standing surgery, radiology, sleep disorder centers. Many of these records are hand written and difficult to read. When a person needs some type of radiology, he/she is often requested to bring reports of former X-rays, MRIs, Mammograms, etc., so that the results of the new radiology reports can be compared. This can be time consuming for the patient; however helpful to the radiologist.

Today there are more physician groups using an electronic medical record system. Each physician in the group can pull up patient information from the other physicians in the system. This reduces time in obtaining information and the patient only needs to update the physician versus having to tell each physician his/her medical history, over and over again. For older adults this is a great relief of stress, as they do not have to remember dates and services, once it is recorded. Physicians can also electronically prescribe medications which are printed out versus hand written for the patient. This prevents pharmacy errors, when the pharmacist is unable to read or misreads a prescription. Additionally, printed care recommendations can be given to the patient to follow. A trip to the doctor is taking less time with the use of electronic health records.

Some long–term-care facilities share a resident's assessment and activity progress notes when a resident is discharged to a new facility. This gives the activity professional background information upon which to build a trust relationship with the new resident and complete an accurate activity assessment including history from the former facility.

The MDS Background (Face Sheet) Information at Admission is sent to the new facility with the resident's other medical records. This is a very useful assessment to obtain demographic information and customary routine.

Electronic health records are the wave of the future. The National Health Information infrastructure seeks to utilize healthcare information technology (HIT) to improve health care and reduce medical errors.

Dr. Yasnoff (2004) the federal government senior advisor for the NHII and former officer of the Oregon Health Division has stated that its over arching goal is "anytime, anywhere access to clinical information with appropriate authorization and authentication will facilitate clinical research to develop evidenced–based practice and improve public health surveillance of emergency disease and other potential threats.

Today's activity professionals will be the pioneers in recording activity information of individual residents in an electronic health records system. Yes, it will take time to learn how to record the information but in the end it will save time and provide more time for activity services.

There are several vendors who have developed electronic activity records system that may be helpful for activity professionals to explore.

See Appendix G for Activity Resources.

Clinical Records

"If it isn't written, it wasn't done."

A resident's clinical record is a legal document. It is also referred to as the medical record. The clinical record is an individualized record of multidisciplinary care and services provided during a resident's stay in a health-care facility.

A clinical record includes but is not limited to the following items:

1. **Admissions Record**

2. **Transfer Form from Transferring Facility, i.e., hospital**

3. **Pre-Admission Screening**

4. **Advance-Directives Information**

5. **Acknowledgment of Resident's Rights**

6. **Physician's Orders**

   a. Medications

   b. Treatment

   c. Diet

   d. Activities (usually listed under Ancillary Orders)

   e. Restorative Services

   f. Appliances, i.e., splints

   g. Restraints

   h. Consultation with other Health-Care Professionals

   i. Level of Care

   j. Order for Discharge/ Transfer/Release of Body

7. **Certification/Recertification (Medicare Program)**

8. **Two-Step Mantoux Test Results**

9. **History and Physical Examination**

10. **Physician's Progress Notes**

11. **Social History**

12. **Comprehensive Resident Assessments**

    a. Assessment by all disciplines (Activities, Dietary, Nursing, Social Service and Rehabilitation Services if ordered)

    b. MDS (Minimum Data Set) and CAA Care Area Assessment

c. Additional Assessments as needed, e.g., falls assessment

13. **Comprehensive Care Plans (Interdisciplinary)**

14. **Nurses' Notes**

15. **Progress Notes (Activity, Dietary, Social Service, and Rehabilitation if services were ordered)**

16. **Medication Record**

17. **Treatment Record**

18. **Behavior Record (if needed)**

19. **Laboratory Reports**

20. **X-Ray, Laboratory and Other Diagnostic Reports**

21. **Consultation Reports**

22. **Discharge Instructions**

23. **Inventory of Personal Items, i.e., clothing**

24. **Miscellaneous**

OBRA Regulation 483.75, Administration Clinical Records Tag Number F514, states:

"(1) Clinical records.
(i) The facility must maintain clinical records on each resident in accordance with accepted professional standards and practices that are:

(i) Complete;
(ii) Accurately documented;
(iii) Readily accessible; and
(iv) Systematically organized."

The Interpretive Guidelines

"A complete clinical record contains an accurate and functional representation of the actual experience of the individual in the facility It must contain enough information to show that the facility knows the status of the individual, has adequate plans of care, and provides sufficient evidence of the effects of the care provided. Documentation should provide a picture of the resident's progress, including response to treatment, change in condition, and changes in treatments."

Under Tag F514 the regulation states

"(5) The clinical record must contain
(i) Sufficient information to identify the resident;
(ii) A record of the resident's assessments;
(iii) The plan of care and services provided;
(iv) The results of any preadmission screening conducted by the state; and
(v) Progress notes."

Confidentiality

All information in a resident's clinical record is confidential. The resident must give permission to have his/her record released for stated purposes. Upon admission a resident signs a release form indicating permission to have his/her medical record released to physicians, transferred to another health care institution, and/or used for other stated purposes (third-party payment)

Entry

All entries must be dated (month/day/year) and signed by the person making the entry. The entry needs to be legible, written in ink, typed or electronically generated. Entries written in ink must be reproducible. Black ink is preferred. Nursing may use different color inks for entries to identify the period of time (day, evening, night) that an entry is made.

Entries must be accurate, factual and written in a professional manner. Personal feelings towards a resident and his/her care are not included in the clinical records. All information needs to be clear and succinct.

Abbreviations

It is permissible to use approved medical and other abbreviations in accordance with facility policies and professional standards of practice.

Correcting an Error

The clinical record is a legal document. Misspelled words, wrong information and errors in dates cannot be erased, scratched out or covered. All errors can be legally corrected. A single line is drawn through an error, i.e., date, a word, phrase, paragraph, or page, with the word "error" written above the mistake. The date of the correction is indicated to the left of the word "error" and the initials of the person correcting the error is identified to the right of the word "error." The correct word is then written. From a legal perspective, the procedure shows that an error was made as well as the correction, yet there was no tampering with the legal document.

Example:

7/23/11 error J.D.
Mr. ~~Jan~~ James Jones

Signature

Legal signatures are required for all clinical records. A legal signature can be a person's full name, or first initial and last name. Activity professionals can use the initials of their job title (AD, Activity Director) or the initials of their certification level (ADC, Activity Director Certified).

Example:

Legal Signature with job title: Jean Jones, ADC

Retention of Clinical Records

Example:

Certification Initials:

Jane Doe, ADC (Activity Director Certified)
Betty Smith, CTRS (Certified Therapeutic Recreation Specialist)

> **Clinical Records must be kept for a minimum of five years under OBRA Law or by state law if it is more stringent.**

Summary

Quality of life is personal. Expected standards differ among older adults. OBRA regulations related to Quality of Life and quality of care provides a frame of references to ensure that residents receive individualized care and services. In long term care, activity professionals are responsible for completing the Preferences for customary routine and activities on the MDS and writing RAP notes if a resident triggered in activities. An activity Assessment is more comprehensive than the Activity Pursuit Patterns section of the MDS. The list of interests can be integrated with other residents interests by recoding the interests on a Tally of Interest .This record will show who is interested in specific activities from which to plan individual, one-to-one and group activities in accordance with information obtained from assessments Activity professionals need to be aware of assessments completed by other health care professionals, including activities of daily living and functional abilities.

Activity professionals need training and experience to complete accurate assessments so that they can work with the health care team in developing care plans.

An interdisciplinary plan of care is the state of the art. All disciplines cooperatively identify problems, state strengths, develop measurable goals and identify specific individualized approaches or interventions. On an interdisciplinary care plan, the discipline responsible for following the interventions is listed along with the initials of the person who agreed to the intervention on the care plan.

Physician orders can be general or specific. A resident must have an order for Therapeutic Recreation as appropriate. Only a therapeutic recreation specialist can follow the order.

It is imperative that activity professionals use standardized clinical language so that any health care professional reading activity documentation understands the meaning of the language. Activity professionals need to know and understand diagnoses, treatments and medical record systems. Electronic medical records are the state of the art. There are activity vendors who can provide specific activity documentation programs.

See Appendix G. Resources for Activities.

Chapter 10

Care Giving Practices
(Service Delivery)
"Don't do for the resident what he/she can do for themselves"

Delivering Activity Care and Services Accurately in the Group Setting

Resident Centered

An activities program is resident centered. The program is based on an accurate individual activity assessment and designed for successful and enjoyable participation. Individual resident's needs, interests, preferences, former lifestyle, abilities, and limitations are considered in developing and /or revision an activities program. To be dynamic, activities programs are constantly changing to meet the changing needs of residents. Activity schedules reflect the residents' interests and preferences. Schedules change with the season, holidays, religious observances and multiple cultural celebrations related to the residents and local community as well as residents preferences for changes in programming.

Adaptive devices and techniques need to be considered for individuals when planning and developing programs so that individuals with specific needs can participate.

Other factors involved in planning successful programming include but are not limited to:

(1) number of potential participants

(2) staffing (training and experience, number of staff, days and hours of work, daily assignments/responsibilities, etc.)

(3) volunteers (expertise, and experience, number of volunteers, days and hours of service, assignments and responsibilities)

(4) interdisciplinary support

(5) space available for programming on and off units, centralized space, i.e., dining room, auditorium, in-doors and out of doors, availability of space, e.g., when dining room is available for programming,

(6) budget,

(7) supplies and equipment,

(8) geographical area (weather, seasons, customs, special events),

(9) available transportation,

(10) community support and

(11) regulations (city, county, state, federal), or national guidelines

1991 Federal Register, Resident Centered and 2006 Guidelines for Surveyors

The federal regulation for activities has remained the same since 1991. Activities are listed as a sub heading under Quality of Life; thus emphasizing activities as a part of an individual's quality of life. The 1991 activity requirements #483.15 (f) (1) Activities was kept the same, when the Interpretive Guidelines for Surveyors were changed in 2006. However, the intent of the requirement was specified along with definitions and specific guidelines for compliance. The definitions explain what is accepted by the terms Activities, ADL –related activities, one-to-One Programming, Person Appropriate and Program of Activities.

Today's emphasis is on Resident Centered Programming for all individuals regardless of their disabilities and limitations. The new interpretive guidelines addresses individuals involved in non-traditional settings, e.g. facilities who have implemented a cultural change model of operation. In a cultural change model residents and staff plan activities daily, more like a home atmosphere including but not limited to simple housekeeping tasks, caring for plant, animals, having breaks for snack an socializing, assisting in preparation for activities, involvement in spontaneous activities etc...

The 2006 Guidelines for surveyors are more specific than in previous documents. The guidelines also give the administrator, activity professionals and other staff guidance in planning and supporting programs (staff, funding, space, equipment and supplies as well as accommodations in schedules)

"Intent: 483.15 (f) (1) Activities

483.15 (f) (1) The facility must provide for an ongoing program of activities designed to meet, in accordance with the comprehensive assessment, the interests and the physical, mental, and psychosocial well-being of each resident.

INTENT: 483.15 (f) (1) Activities

The intent of this requirement is that:

- The facility identifies each resident's interests and needs; and

- The facility involves the resident in an ongoing program of activities that is designed to appeal to his or her interest and to enhance the resident's highest practicable level of physical, mental and psychosocial well-being.

Definitions

Definitions are provided to clarify key terms used in this guidance.

- 'Activities refer to any endeavor, other than routine ADLs in which a resident participates that is intended to enhance his/her sense of well-being and to promote or enhance physical, cognitive and emotional health. These include, but are not limited to, activities that promote self- esteem, pleasure, comfort, education, creativity, success, and independence.

NOTE: ADL-related activities, such as manicures/pedicures, hairstyling and makeovers, may be considered part of the activities program.

- "One-to-One Programming" refers to programming provided to residents who will not, or cannot, effectively plan their own activity pursuits or residents needing specialized or extended programs to enhance their overall daily routine and activity pursuit needs.

- "Person Appropriate" refers to the idea that each resident has a personal identity and history that involves more than just their medial illnesses or functional impairments. Activities should be relevant to the specific needs, interests, culture, background, etc. of the individual for whom they are developed.

- "Program of Activities" includes a combination of large and small group, one-to-one and self-directed activities; and a system that supports the development, implementation and evaluation of the activities provided to the residents in the facility."

An activity professional needs to consider developing three (3) different types of programs to meet participant's needs:

1. Individual self directed programs

2. One-to-One programs

3. Group Programs

   a. Small Groups

   b. Large Groups

Delivering Activity Care to Individuals as Individualized Services

"Rest and Relaxation are enjoyable as change from activities"

Activity care and services must be individualized to be meaningful. Some assisted living and long term care facilities have specialized units for persons with the same or similar diagnosis, i.e., dementia, Alzheimer's type. Today, there is greater emphasis on specialized units in long-term care, to better meet the needs of residents. Staff is specifically trained to provide services; the specialized units function as a separate unit within the total facility. Medical, psychological, nursing, social service and dietary needs for residents on specialized units may be different from other resident needs. Resident available time for participation in activities may vary depending upon their total needs.

Activity professionals need education and training related to the general care and services for residents on specialized units. Understanding disease, diagnosis and related concerns assists the activity professional in developing programs for residents in special care units

Most Clients Need Both Individual and Group Activity Involvement

Assisted and Long-term Care

Residents in assisted and long-term care and participants in adult day service usually need individual and group activity involvement to continue their former leisure life style. Participants formerly involved in independent individual activities may need assistance in starting or completing an activity. A person may no longer be able to see the numbers on a remote control and need assistance with changing TV channels. Many older adults continue to enjoy reading, including the Bible in large print. They may be dependent upon the activity professional to obtain a large print Bible or other materials from the public library. A person may prefer to watch a video in his/her own room or separate area in an adult day service versus with a group of people.

Group activities provide an opportunity for a person to get to know other participants and perhaps develop new friendships. A common interest, geographical location of former residence, former community, and church or community involvement may be the catalyst for developing a friendship. Involvement is seasonal and special events with or with out family or other invited guests may appeal to new participants as well as those who have enjoyed the celebrations in the past. Many older adults see life as a continuous opportunity for learning and like group learning experiences.

Activity professionals may find participants need a little motivation or information before they attempt a group activity. Other participants can assist in giving information and inviting a peer to a group and informing the person that he/she will be in the group. This may facilitate interest and involvement knowing that he/she will know someone in the group. It is important for the activity professional to discuss the person's feelings and experience after involvement in a new group activity to evaluate their perception of the activity and their individual involvement and make changes as needed.

Independent

Residents/clients have the human need for separateness as well as togetherness. Time to be by oneself to think, meditate or pray is important. This need is greater for some persons than for others. In ones own home, apartment, room or a special space, it is important to have a quiet place where the resident/client can retreat to be by him/herself. This can also be a time for relaxing, reflecting, and pondering.

On the other hand human beings need to relate to other humans. Various kinds of group activities provide for this need. Three or more residents/clients gathered can meet this basic need of socialization. Visiting, playing games, listening to music, etc., provide persons an opportunity to share in a social setting. Many of the programmed activities the activity professional plans are group experiences. Choice is the key element which allows residents/clients to be alone or to share with others. A variety of possibilities allows for many choices. An effective activity program provides for these choices.

Basic Group Structure

"Being with others adds feeling and fulfillment"

Types of groups were explained earlier in this chapter. Participants may form their own group based on identified interest/preference, i.e., card group. A group of residents individually making art, crafts or needlework for the annual craft sale is considered an independent/interdependent group. The group members work individually but are dependent upon each other to reach their goal of completing their items in time for the annual sale.

Active and Passive Participation

The terms active and passive participation have been used for centuries regarding participation. Active participation was associated with "doing- being active in an activity, i.e. playing baseball. The players are active throwing, pitching, or catching a ball, batting a ball or running. The audience "watching" the game was considered to be passive since they were not actually involved in the game. The terms are used less to day as a result of behavioral writing that started in the 1980's. Today, goals and objectives are written for activities. The activity goals are broad statements, whereas, the objectives are measurable criteria. A goal for a new participant may be: Hilda will increase socialization. The objective could be Hilda will initiate conversation with other participants a minimum of three times by date. In using a baseball game as an example for a goal and objective, the goal could be "Will increase participation in community events." The objective could be "John will watch a minimum of five innings as evidenced by focusing on the players and the ball, clapping for players, smiling when a play is made by his preferred team. In looking at the stated objectives, John is actively watching the ballgame versus playing in it. So both the players and the watchers are actively involved in the game, one as a player the other as a spectator.

Specific Group Goals
"Activities can be fun, fantastic and fulfilling"

In establishing a group, the purpose and goal need to be well thought out. What is to be achieved by offering a group activity? The goals for the group can be general as they are for all participants and are not measurable, whereas, objectives are measurable and developed with individual residents in mind.

Selection of Group Members
"Matching and motivating for success"

Not all residents/participants will be interested in the same group activities. It is important to establish some type of criteria for selecting group members. Groups can be open to all residents/participants but not all will participate. Selection of group members can be based on:

1. interests and preferences
2. abilities
3. limitations
4. male and/or female
5. needs
6. availability
   a. time of day or evening
7. resident suggested activity
8. other

Size of Group
"Grade and pace activities"

The size of a group will depend somewhat on the number of potential participants. A small organization would have fewer participants in a large group than a large organization. A small group could be 2-3 participants or a mid size group could be 16-50. A large group could be 51 or more depending upon the group and the amount of interaction that is required.

The size of groups will depend on several factors including but not limited to:

1. specific activity and the amount of involvement and/or interaction needed
2. the number or interested participants with the same abilities
3. functional abilities needed
4. knowledge or previous experience related to the group
5. indoor or outdoor, or in the community
6. availability of staff and/or volunteers
7. availability of transportation
8. mobility of participants for outings

Setting of the Group

"Happiness can be found in various settings"

The group setting can be indoors, outside or in the community. Quiet small space is best for intellectual and cognitive activities. A large space would be needed to safely accommodate a large group, i.e., entertainment. A room with a table and ample seating would be needed for a craft group. Reading activities need to be offered in a quiet area.

If only one space is available, i.e., dining/activity room, two quiet activities may take place in opposite sides or corners of the room. Several activities could be provided in one large room with designated areas as long as the activities do not distract or another group in the room. Activities involving increased noise level, i.e., choir, rhythm band, horse racing is best scheduled at times when other activities are not scheduled. Movies can be shown to a small or large group depending upon the participants' cognitive functioning abilities.

There may be a need for several groups based on the same interests but with different functioning levels. They could be conducted simultaneously or at different times. An integrated group of participants with different cognitive levels can be successfully accommodated by the organization of the group. If the group is primarily for participants with high cognitive functioning abilities, in a classroom type or semi circle setting with the participants sitting in rows facing the leader, the participants with the high cognitive functioning skills need to be seated in the first two-three rows with the participants with the low cognitive functioning abilities seated in the back row. If a group is for participants with low cognitive functioning abilities they need to be seated in the first two–three rows with participants with high cognitive functioning abilities seated in the back rows. People in the back rows may get bored or lose interest in the group and leave. If they do, they would not interfere with the group, providing there is easy access to exit the room.

Duration of Meetings

"Plan, prepare and play creatively"

Group activities need to be planned and conducted based on the potential participants' functional abilities. A participant may have high cognitive functioning abilities and have a high desire to participate in a specific activity but may not have the endurance to sit for more than 15 minutes. Other participants may have the physical ability to sit for 15 minutes but not the cognitive ability to stay with the group. The amount of time allotted for a specific group would also depend on the nature of the group. A sensory stimulation group for participants with low cognitive functioning abilities could be 15- 45 minutes depending upon the size of the group and the severity of cognitive impairment. It is usually best to engage participants with low cognitive functioning abilities in a variety of activities for frequent short time periods, whereas participants with high cognitive functioning abilities would have the attention span to be involved in a group for 45- 60 minutes. Sometimes it is trial and error in terms of determining the amount of time for a group activity. It is best to allocate more time than may be needed than to plan for less time.

Transportation of participants needs to be factored into the time frame for a group. If a large number of participants need to be transported, the first persons transported will need to wait until the last participant is transported before the group starts. This affects the first people in attendance in terms of the total time they are waiting for a group to start and the actual involvement in the group. A special event may involve many activities, one after another. Some participants may participate in all the activities and others in one or two of the activities.

The number of staff/volunteers available to lead, colead or assist in leading a group will also affect the amount of time for a planned group activity.

Planning the duration of activities on special units will vary with the total care and services for participants. Participants in a rehabilitation unit may have very limited time for group activity because of their heavy multiple therapies schedules and need to rest/sleep. Group activity for this unit may be mostly in the evenings and involve families. Group activities may be for short duration, less then 45 minutes to prevent fatigue. Participants' willingness to be involved in group activities may not begin until they have adjusted to their therapy schedules and have built up endurance for more involvement in their daily life on the unit. Pre-meal activities may work best as participants are in the dining room waiting for their meal to be served. This could be a 15-minute program such as trivia, musical entertainment, quizzes placed on tables for four people, or other activities based on the participants' interests and preferences. Residents in sub-acute and rehabilitation units have short-term stays, so the activity program and duration of activities are constantly changing.

Importance of Emotional Relationships

"All relationships involve emotions"

A member of any group needs to feel comfortable being with group members. This is enhanced by a new person being welcomed to the group and introduced to the group and leader. Sharing information about the group helps the newcomer feel more at ease about the group.

Interpersonal communication before, during or after the group, depending upon the purpose and structure of the group facilitates socialization and getting to know others in the group. Names may be forgotten but a non verbal recognition helps a person to feel recognized and accepted

The activity professional and/or peers can help eliminate personal negative thoughts such as fear by assisting the participant as needed/wanted, demonstrating how to do something, as well as recognizing the person and his/her accomplishments.

A person may feel wanted and needed when ask to do something within their ability and than thanked and praise.

Self esteem can be fostered through participation in preferred activities or in trying new ones or giving suggestions for the activity or new activities Self esteem can also be promoted by calling a person by name, recognizing absence and welcoming back to the group, praising attempts and accomplishments, giving awards, printing a persons name in newsletter, asking for feed back, asking to assist with tasks, informing other group members of participant's willingness to volunteer, etc.

Group members can have adversarial relationships. The activity professional may need to intervene so that these relationships don't escalate or affect other members in the group. The activity professional can work with the participants or if needed seek assistance from other health care professionals. The ad-versarial relationship may not just be displayed in a group. There may be something else going on, unbeknown to the activity professional; thus, sharing information with other professionals may assist the activity professional in understanding the dynamics and better able to intervene as well as cope with the participants.

The activity professional must be aware of his/her leadership style and its affect on individuals or the group. It is also important to be in touch with personal and professional feelings about the group. A negative attitude is easily assessed by participants. Being ready, prepared and starting a group on time, helps others feel that the leader really cares about group members.

Any group activity must be meaningful for the participants; if not, they will not want to participate. Reasons for absence may need to be explored. This shows the participant that he/she was missed and if needed, negative feeling about the group can be discussed and possibly resolved.

Placing meaning within you activity groups needs to be re-examined. If the resident feels the activity is meaningful and has purpose the outcome is positive and rewarding. Residents in long term care continue to need to contribute to the community and society. Making decorations and polishing silver becomes meaningful if connected to a tea party. Consider how can activities be meaningful for the individual and not "one size fits all"? What would make activities a natural part of living? We normally don't make decorations without a holiday or birthday. People normally don't polish their silverware without an event to prepare for. Activity programming should be about engagement and celebrate individual expression. Activity programs should have a greater social consciousness, a connection to a larger group.

They should be part of something bigger, be purposeful and provide pleasure.

One resident at Otterbein Home said "Activities Keep Me Going"; thus the title of the first book was created. This resident like so many others was expressing her feelings. She had a positive attitude towards activities and was happy to express it.

Emotional relationships have a definite impact on individual participants, the group as well as the Leader and volunteers. The activity professional must stay abreast of members and volunteers as well as his/her own feelings.

Trust Development

"Trust is not an instant experience"

It is important to develop a trust relationship with participants. They need to trust the activity professional as a professional and feel respected as an individual. They need to trust that a planned activity is going to be provided on the day, time as scheduled or if there is a change; participants are notified and offered a substitute activity or given an opportunity to suggest and vote on an activity in place of the cancelled activity. Trust also includes knowing and experiencing that there will be ample space for the activity, sufficient supplies and equipment, ability to hear during the activity and a comfortable environment. Participants must learn to trust the activity professional when he or she states he/she will do something specific to meet the participant's needs, i.e., take the participant back to his/her room or other preferred location after an activity or that the participant can leave the activity to go to the bathroom or leave the activity if he/she doesn't like it. Participants also need to trust that what they say in a group will remain in the group and if an activity professional feels that something needs to be shared with other professionals, he/she will advise the participant.

Personal Interaction within the Group

"Activities give participants a chance to love and live"

The activity professional and volunteers need to have personable and professional interaction within the group. A variety of leadership techniques need to be used to facilitate a group. Leadership techniques are developed over time. Calling participants by their preferred name, giving support, recognizing attempts as well as accomplishments, explaining something in understandable terms, being patient and sincere, treating participants as individuals with dignity are all attributes for developing personal interactions within a group over time.

Activity Leading Skills

"Work is love made visible"

Activity leading skills are developed over time through practice and evaluation. Reading about leadership, observing other leaders is helpful but actually leading an activity is the best learning experience. Critique of leadership skills by an experience leader is an invaluable learning experience.

Leadership skills include but are not limited to:

- Knowledge of activity
- Knowledge of supplies and equipment needed for activity
- Knowledge of safety procedures
- Organization
- Preparedness
- Time management
- Scheduling

- Knowledge of participants interest, preference, abilities and limitations
- Affective Interpersonal Communication
- Ability to establish a therapeutic milieu
- Ability to explain, teach activity
- Ability to adapt activity
- Knowledge of group dynamics
- Ability to motivate others
- Feeling self assured
- Focusing attention on others not self
- Ability to recognize and praise others
- Ability to assess participants participation
- Ability to evaluate program and make changes as needed.
- Ability to take and evaluate criticism, and do something about it, if appropriate
- Continue to learn and explore more about the activity
- Continue to develop skills through reading, classes, observation of others, participating in activity in the community

1. Autocratic Leadership

The autocratic leader is a controller—an "in charge" person. The leader makes all decisions. Little or no group participation is permitted. Direction is given without explanation of reason. Obedience is expected. Dependency is fostered. The leader is the authority and maintains responsibility.

Situations

Autocratic leadership is needed in time of a life/death situation. Someone with knowledge and expertise must take immediate charge directing others in what to do.

In a new department an activity professional is the expert and authority on activities. An agency or organization relies on the activity professional to "take charge" in developing the department. The activity professional is responsible for total development from formulation of a philosophy of operation—based on the philosophy of the organization—to development of policies and procedures, forms for services and documentation, ordering of supplies and equipment, setting up the activity areas, planning, developing, implementing and evaluating the activity program.

A resident with very low-cognitive-functioning abilities who is totally dependent on the activity professional for stimulation and socialization is not able to give input into his/ her care plan and activity program. Thus the activity professional maintains control of which activities are best for the resident.

Autocratic leadership is not effective in day-to-day supervision of an activity department. It fosters dependency on the leader versus the growth and independence of individual staff members. The focus is on tasks—not relationships—in achieving tasks. Staff is not empowered to be creative, take risks, nor voice their opinions, concerns, or solutions to problems. Staff feels unimportant and devalued. Negativism develops. Morale is low. Turnover of staff can be great, which is costly.

2. Democratic Leadership

The democratic leader fosters participation of team members in decision-making. The leader listens to ideas, concerns and solutions. Group members are empowered to get involved. The focus is on teamwork. There is a "we" feeling between the leader and group members. All persons feel valued. There is a high level of positive energy and spirit.

Situations

Democratic leadership is effective in day-to-day supervision of an activity department. Staff has input into the direction of the department and their roles and responsibilities based on changing needs of participants and situations. There is respect for the leader's and team members' knowledge, abilities, skills and experience. The democratic leader fosters creativity, cooperation, personal and professional growth, and risk-taking. Changes are viewed as challenges. Team members support one another. There is an excitement and joy in working together. Accomplishments are celebrated by all.

Empowering residents to give input and recommendations for resident-planned activity meetings is an example of democratic leadership. The residents make the decisions. The activity professional assists in the facilitation of implementing the recommendations. Resident council, food committees, selection of crafts to make for a bazaar or recommendation of places to go on outings is other examples of democratic leadership.

The residents' ideas, suggestions and recommendations are respected. The activity professional fosters choices and independence. Residents feel important and valued.

It is not appropriate to use democratic leadership in some health and safety situations. In a baking/cooking group the leader cannot be democratic in allowing participants to decide if they are going to wear gloves. Washing of hands and wearing gloves for infection control are required.

3. Laissez-Faire Leadership

Laissez-faire leadership fosters participation. Group members participate in solving problems and making decisions. The leader has minimum control and does not exert authority.

Situations

Interdisciplinary care teams, continuous quality-improvement teams, and employee recognition teams are examples of laissez-faire leadership. The administrator or CEO (Chief Executive Officer) identifies a need and develops a team of highly trained, competent employees. The team decides the purpose, goals, and objectives of the team; the roles and responsibilities of team members; the timeframe for accomplishing their mission, and the outcome criteria. The team is accountable for its actions and outcome.

An activity professional practices laissez-faire leadership when interested, competent residents/ participants are given the responsibility to plan and direct evening activity programs. Resident directed resident councils and independent family councils are other examples of laissez-faire leadership. The goal is for the participants to exercise independence. Laissez-faire leadership would be inappropriate for participants/residents who have short-term memory impairments. They need structure and direct leadership to function successfully in groups.

The negative type of laissez-faire leadership is exemplified by a manager who does not give direction and avoids questions, interaction, solving problems or making decisions. Staff is left on their own. The leader is not respected. Staff feels devalued—what they do doesn't matter. Work is a job. Tasks may or may not be completed. Negative attitudes fester and morale is low.

Factors Influencing Leadership Style for Programming

Three factors influencing leadership style are:

1. Leader's personality and ability
2. Abilities and needs of residents
3. Environment

A leader may prefer to work in situations requiring a specific leadership style. The leader's personality and abilities affect leadership style. A person who wants and needs control would most likely prefer autocratic leadership, whereas a laidback person may prefer the democratic or laissez-faire leadership style, allowing group members to have input into decisions or to be on their own to make decisions.

In activities the abilities and needs of residents dictate the leadership style that is needed. Independent high-cognitive-functioning residents need to be empowered to plan and make decisions on their own. A democratic or laissez-faire-style leadership would work best. Residents who are dependent with low-cognitive-functioning abilities need to feel safe and secure. They need to know who is in charge. Autocratic leadership meets their need.

Activities are provided in a variety of environments. There has to be an "in-charge" person for outings so that they are safe and meaningful experiences. However, the leader would use a democratic or laissez-faire style of leadership in the planning and evaluation of the outing. Control is required when a leader is directing the performance of a resident choral group. An activity professional working with independent residents in a retirement village with a wide variety of rooms for activities would foster independent leadership among participants.

Flexibility

Activity professionals must be flexible and be able to change leadership styles to match the needs of residents within a variety of situations and environments. It may be difficult for a person who prefers to be in control to "let go" and practice a participatory leadership style. It can be equally difficult for an activity professional that prefers and is successful in using a democratic or laissez-faire-style to have to switch to an autocratic leadership style.

Group Management Skills

"Achievement is a prime motivator"

The first two management skills for a group activity are planning and preparation. More time will be devoted to planning and preparation than the actual time of the activity. By the time a person becomes an activity professional, he/she has been involved in planning and preparing for some type of special event, i.e., celebration, picnic, party, dinner for family and or friends and can identify with the amount of planning and preparation time versus the actual time for activity. It may take hours, days or weeks for planning and preparing for a special meal for family and friends and it only takes 30- 90 minutes for the meal to be consumed. It is the same with planning and preparing for an activity. Some activities will require more time than others because there are more equipment and supplies involved, some of which have to be purchased. Ample time is needed to purchase supplies and equipment so that they are ready in time for the scheduled activity. Whenever an activity involves other departments, the activity professional needs to learn what time frame the other departments work within, i.e., dietary, how far in advance do they need an order? Are there certain items i.e. food that needs to be frozen verses just stored that need to be ordered in a time frame when there will be room in a freezer for an ordered item. A service organization may have very specific policies and procedures for ordering supplies and names of approved vendors.

Equipment needs to be checked for good working order and, if needed, time for repair. Transportation may need to be obtained, contract signed within a standard period established by the transportation service. Transportation may be provided by the service organization and policies and procedures, including time frames need to be followed in reserving transportation and driver.

An activity professional needs to consider whether or not to place all the needed supplies and equipment in a room before a group or bring them to the group. Either way, the activity professional needs some type of system to know that he/she has everything ready for an activity. A cooking activity would include more supplies than a trivia activity.

The next management skill is the actual provision of supplies and equipment to individual participants and as needed instruction on using the supplies and equipment.

Supervision of participants is essential for safety and successful participation. Group management skills includes supporting, assisting, praising, thanking participants and requesting assistance with clean up, i.e., returning supplies and equipment, counting supplies, cleaning equipment, making note of what needs to be refurbished and/or suggestions for alternate supplies and equipment.

Therapeutic Environment

"Successful therapy brings healing"

A therapeutic environment is a comfortable environment including (1) the physical environment and (2) the social environment.

The physical environment needs to be safe, clean, uncluttered, physically comfortable (not too hot or too cool, without sun glare, no unpleasant odors, ample work and table space and comfortable table height, sufficient and comfortable seating including space for wheelchairs, Geri chairs.

The social environment includes the comfort level between the activity professionals, volunteers and other staff with participants, participants and peers. A part of the social environment is using the appro-priate leadership style for the specific group, that were discussed under the topic "**Activity leading skills**"

An activity professional needs to be able to intervene in a professional caring manner with dignity when there is conflict among participants. The activity professional must be in touch and in control of his/her emotions and present him/herself in a calm respectful manner. When needed the activity professional must feel free to seek backup support from other staff so that the other participants and the group have the least distraction possible.

Vulnerability of Group Members

"Group activities provide for risk"

The activity professional must also be watchful of vulnerable participants. These participants would include participants who are defenseless to physical attempt to harm or actual harm, defenseless to verbal degradation, unaware of personal property or supplies provided for a specific activity, unaware of personal space in relation to another participant's space (resident who gets too close to another resident's inner space), a resident who is unable to see, hear or understand.

The activity professional needs to be alert at all times and attempt to prevent vulnerable participants from negative experiences. Sometimes, seating arrangements can prevent vulnerability, not seating two participants together, who don't get along, keep-ing a participant near the activity professional to allow for a gentle touch on the arm as a reminder to stop negative behavior, i.e., repetitive banging on a wheelchair tray.

Group activity is the most used type of activity in many of the service settings. It requires a lot of knowledge and sometimes research, planning and preparation, a variety of leadership skills, supervision and evaluation. The success of group activity is individualized for participants. An activity professional perception of success needs to be based on the goals and objectives for the group and actual outcomes.

Self-Directed Activities

"Some residents/clients prefer personal activities"

Individual self-directed programs are usually individual and/or family/visitor activities. The person is capable of initiating and participating in the activity with or without assistance such as, turning on and watching TV program of choice, reading (book, magazine, catalog, poetry, Bible, spiritual material, etc.; turning on radio, tape recorder, VCR, DVD, and watching or listening to program of choice; using a computer; using handheld games, playing a musical instrument; art, crafts, needlework, using the telephone/cell phone, writing, caring for plants, caring for pet, making bed, dusting and tidying up room; involvement in service project, i.e. labeling envelopes; praying, studying, learning, etc. A person with low cognitive functioning ability may be involved in meaningful activities of a different kind or level, i.e., puttering in room, interactivity with a doll or stuffed animal: coloring; working large piece puzzles, reading; watching video or TV programs of choice; sorting, matching, folding items; dusting, sweeping; rummaging through dresser drawers; looking and picking up items in memory boxes; interacting with pet; rocking in rocking chair; people watching; walking in safe areas (indoors and outdoors); sitting outside enjoying the fresh air, etc.

A resident may be self-directed in interacting with family, friend, and visitors. These interactions may be conversations; involvement in some type of familiar activity, i.e., playing cards, or going out to eat, shop or for entertainment, etc.

One-to-One Program

"In time attitude changes feelings"

One-to-one activities involve two people. Involvement can be verbal, non-verbal or both. The type and/or intensity of involvement may differ for the two people. Initiation of an activity can be by either person. The experience can be meaningful to both or for one but not the other.

One-to-one activities would include conversation between two people, talking on the telephone, visiting, going some place with some one, dining with one other person, playing a game of chess and/or checkers or working on a jigsaw puzzle with someone.

The interaction involved in listening to music or watching TV with another person can be verbal and non-verbal. The one-to-one activity may start with a discussion and a decision of what to listen to or watch (verbalization), followed by a period of listening or watching (non-verbal), culminating in discussion or exchange of thoughts and feelings about what was heard and/or seen (verbalization).

Providing sensory stimulation for a person who is dependent upon staff for socialization and stimulation may be more meaningful for the recipient than for the provider. Sharing of meaningful moments can be equally meaningful to the two people involved.

Group Programs

"Activities create while inactivity stagnates

In the early 70's, activity program emphasis was on group activities, primarily large group activities. Many administrators based the success of a program on attendance. Large crowds were thought to be a successful activity. There was little thought as to the appropriateness of the activity for individual participants. Over the years, research, training of activity professionals, increased knowledge of disease and diagnosis, emphasis on dignity, quality of life and quality of care has changed the focus from an activity to outcomes for individuals being served.

History shows that older adults are used to functioning within a group, i.e. family, school, work, volunteer, church, community. Thus, participating in activity groups in various service settings is a natural extension of group involvement in later life.

Group Activities

Group activities can be small or large groups. A small group is three to twenty persons. A mid size group can be twenty to less than 100 persons. A large group may be a hundred or more people. It is difficult to identify the largest number for a small group and the smallest number for large groups as the number may overlap in different situations and circumstances.

Generally, in long-term-care facilities, arts, crafts, table games, reality orientation, sensory stimulation groups, educational programs, baking/cooking activities, expressive groups and support groups are usually small groups. Exercise, sing-a-longs, discussions, picnics, current events, as well as other activities can be in small, mid size or large groups. Parties, celebrations, special events, and entertainment tend to be large-group activities, except when they are planned for residents with low-cognitive functioning abilities or by choice of the residents involved.

Other Types of Groups

In addition to the size, a group can be identified further by types such as independent groups, parallel groups, intra-group or cooperative groups, or inter-groups (competitive teams).

Independent groups are self-directed groups. An evening card group, a resident council that functions without the presence of a staff liaison, a TV group which gets together to watch specific shows, or a group that goes outside and watches birds, animals, people, cars, etc. without much exchange between participants.

Parallel groups are non-interactive. Participants are in the presence of others but do not communicate. A scene in a craft room would be participants working on their individual projects. The atmosphere is comfortable. The participants' focus is on the project and not on interaction.

Intra-groups' or cooperative groups' focus is on a common goal. All group members are dependent on one another to accomplish the groups' goal. A newspaper group is dependent upon different members accomplishing their specific task(s) in order to develop, publish and disseminate a newsletter. There is usually some interaction among participants. A team is an intra-group. Team members learn their roles and responsibilities and focus on a team versus individual effort.

Inter-groups or competitive groups involve two or more cooperative or intra-groups. Team A (intra group or cooperative group) plays against Team B (also an intra-group). The two intra-groups must function cohesively in order to compete against each other.

Interpretation of Activities/Activity Program

"Communicate through activities"

The June 1995 draft of interpretive guidelines for activities regulations 483.15 (f) (i), tag F248 states: "Activities can occur at anytime and are not limited to formal activities being provided by activity staff. Others involved may be any facility staff, volunteers and visitors."

Types of Programming in Long-Term-Care Facilities

The types of programming that are offered in long-term-care facilities is dependent upon the needs, interests, preferences, abilities, and limitations of residents as well as the purpose of the facility, staffing, space and programming philosophy. The focus of programming continues to change as the population in a facility changes. In the early years of programming emphasis was on centralized activities. All activities were conducted in a centralized area, i.e., activity room and/or dining/activity room. As residents' needs and abilities changed, so did programming with a greater emphasis on decentralized or unit-based programming, especially for residents with low cognitive functioning abilities.

1. **Centralized programs:** all activities are conducted in a centralized area, i.e., an activity room or dining/activity room.
2. **Decentralized programs:** activities are unit based. This type of programming has increased with the number of low-cognitive functioning residents who do best when programs are brought to them versus having to leave their secure environment (the unit) for activity.
3. **Referral programs:** participants are referred to specific activities based on established criteria for referral, participation and termination. Referral groups would be therapeutic groups (reality-orientation, remotivation, support groups, expressive groups, some educational groups, etc.). The person referred to the group has a choice and must be willing to participate.
4. **Specialized programs:** activities are designed for a specific group by diagnosis, disability and or some other common factor. Specialized groups for residents with dementia continue to

increase with the influx of specialty facilities and units.

5. **Structured programs:** activities are planned and developed in advance and presented in a structured method following pre-planned steps. A remotivation group is one example of a structured program in which specific steps are followed.

6. **Unstructured programs:** activities are planned with no specific steps or format. An informal discussion would be one example. Current events may be discussed in an unstructured manner with the residents determining the topics of discussion versus topics being pre-planned.

7. **Spontaneous programs:** unplanned activities are provided on a spur of the moment. A group talks about a disaster and immediately decides to do something to help. The group decides to collect money and food, and to send clothing. Within a short time there is a bake and rummage sale involving residents and staff, and a collection of clothing from residents, staff and families. Money earned is sent to a local sponsor. Clothing is sorted by gender, sizes and article (sweaters, dresses, underwear, etc.). Boxes are packed, labeled and sent to the local distribution center. Thus the spontaneous activity paved the way for structured follow-up activities.

8. **Indoor programs:** activities take place in a variety of indoor locations.

9. **Outdoor programs:** activities take place out-of-doors—at the facility (cookout, bird watching, gardening, parties, flying kites, walking, bocce) or off the property (picnic in the park, outdoor concert, county fair, parades).

10. **Community program:** activities take place in the community, indoors or outdoors. Outings can include going to the mall, shopping, dining out, museums, places of historical interest, concerts, plays, symphony, ballet, ballgame, boat ride, train trip, going to the park for a picnic and to feed the ducks, going for a ride to see the countryside/ mountains/ lakes/ocean and going for a ride to tour old areas or to see new ones.

Special Units

Aids Units

In the 1980'and 1990's, specialized units were developed for persons with Aids. Before this, residents with Aids, mostly younger residents, were integrated with other residents. Residents with Aids of any age may feel that they are not accepted by others and refuse to participate in small or large groups. Residents with Aids may be embarrassed about their previous life style or angry that they contacted aids through no fault of their own

Residents with Aids may have lived at home and received home care prior to nursing home placement. They go through the normal process of adjusting to nursing home placement, in addition to potentially knowing that they are near or in the last stage of the disease and have to face dying. They may be or feel estranged from family and friends and feel very much alone, depressed and not wanting to be involved in any type of activities.

It is important for the activity professional to work with the hospice team and provide supplies and equipment for preferred activities. A person with Aids may not want to participate in scheduled activities but be more interested in watching TV, listening to preferred music when awake, even if it is 4:00 A.M. Adaptive hearing devices may be needed if the person has a room mate so that the hours of involvement in individual activities does not negatively affect the roommate.

A resident may have his or her own CD's, videos at home and be encouraged to have someone bring them to the facility if there is sufficient space in the resident's room as well as security. A resident may be interested in a support group in or out of the facility.

The activity professional has to work closely with the dietician and nursing, regarding nutrition concerns. A person may or may not be interested in activities involving food. Scrap booking or other types of activities involving legacy may be of interest to the resident as a way of putting his/her life together. A resident may be more interested in working with the social worker in putting his/her affairs together.

Learning and utilizing relaxation techniques may be of interests to individual residents. Developing a trust relationship with staff, i.e., the activity professional may be the greatest need. Conversation on topics initiated by the resident can be fostered and may lead to involvement in another type of activity. Preference for involvement in religious and spiritual activities needs to be explored. A person may want more involvement with a chaplain than a hospice chaplain can provide; thus, the activity professional can arrange for more involvement with other clergy who regularly visit the residents or others in the community.

Pain may be the primary reason a resident with Aids does not want to participate in an agreed upon activity. Communication with nursing about the resident's pain and tolerance will assist the activity professional in knowing when it is best to approach the resident regarding activity. Negative side effects of pain medication, nausea, dithers, sleepiness, disorientation etc. may prevent a resident from participating in a favorite activity.

Dementia/ Alzheimer's Units

The late 1970's and early 1980's was the first time that nursing homes began to see the increase of residents with dementia. Their needs were different from other residents particularly because of their memory loss (short term and long term memory), short attention span and behaviors. In the late 1980's and early 1990's there was extensive development of services for people with Dementia, Alzheimer's type in adult day services, assisted living and long-term-care. Some assisted living facilities were developed as specialized facilities for people with Alzheimer's disease with the philosophy and dedication of caring for residents until the end of life, with the assistance of home health care services, on a fee for service basis, for individual residents as needed. Initially, states did not provide Medicaid funding for care in Assisted Living facilities. Today, some states provide Medicaid funding.

Activity professionals found it challenging to include residents with various degrees of memory loss in the regular activity programs. During the early years of programming for residents with dementia, there was very little written about activities for persons with dementia and there was little information on activity supplies and equipment for this population.

Today, there is a wealth of information on Dementia, specifically, Alzheimer's type. Activity professionals have become very creative over the years developing and adapting activities for participants with Dementia in adult day service, assisted living, retirement homes, nursing homes, and specialized facilities for persons with Dementia.

The term "age appropriate" has been changed to "person appropriate" and is included in the 2006 Interpretive Guidelines for Surveyors. The definition of "Person Appropriate" in the 2006 Interpretive Guidelines for Surveyors is:

"Person Appropriate" refers to the idea that each resident has a personal identity and history that involves more than just their medical illnesses or functional impairments. Activities should be relevant to the specific needs, interests, culture, background, etc. of the individual for whom they are developed."

Obesity - Bariatric Units

Residents with obesity often have other related heath problems, heart, circulatory, breathing, skin, decreased energy, range of motion, inability to walk, kidney problems, etc. A person with obesity may have been confined to bed prior to nursing home placement because he/she did not have the necessary equipment to be lifted in and out of bed or did not have a large wheelchair for mobility. Activity history usually involves individual and family activities that could be accomplished in bed or at the bedside. Socialization is usually decreased and confined to family and friends who can visit, or communicating with others by phone, e-mail, instant messaging and/or text messaging.

Obesity and related health conditions may improve with bariatric surgery. With increased obesity in the US, more bariatric units may be developed to meet the needs of people with obesity. In bariatric units, residents may need to rest to recuperate from surgery before or during initial involvement in therapy (physical therapy, occupational therapy). In time, individualized care plans and bariatric protocols can include educational, self esteem and support groups provided by nursing, dietician, and psychologist. Initial activity involvement may be individual, family and/or one to one activities. Residents needing bariatric care are usually younger than the majority of residents; thus, they may be most interested in continuing their use of a computer and other technological devices, listening to different music, reading different magazines, knowing and playing different types of card games than older residents.

Occupational therapist and activity professionals can co-lead cooking groups emphasizing food preparation and healthy eating. After completion of physical therapy, residents may be involved in structured physical activities, exercise, walking programs, and relaxation, to build strength and endurance, and learn relaxation techniques. It is important for activity professionals to know the resident's diagnosis and limitation so that involvement in physical activities is not too taxing on the person's heart and lungs. Social activities that usually involve food may need to be adapted to reinforce proper diet.

Transporting residents can be a challenge. Activity professionals need to take precaution in transporting a resident in a wheelchair to prevent injury. Increased time to transport residents needs to be planned, as it will take extra time to transport a resident. Community reintegration is important for increasing comfort in community living and gradual increase in walking without undue stress. Nursing personnel will need to assist transporting residents. It may take two nursing personnel working together to transport a resident needing a wheelchair, in and out of a van.

Activity space needs to be large enough to accommodate larger wheelchairs and higher tables for taller residents. Doors need to be wider than the normal 36" doors.

Sub acute Units

Space for activities on specialized units may also differ. There may be less activity space for a sub acute unit, in which a resident may spend more time in bed between meals and therapy. Individual and one-to-one activities take place in the resident's room, with some residents wanting and willing to participate in large group activities in another part of the facility. Programming emphasis for residents on sub acute units is placed on the following order:

Individual, self directed activities
1. Family activities;
2. One-to-One activities with visitors, staff, peers, volunteers
3. Small group activities
4. Large group activities

It is important for residents on sub acute units to experience their preferred leisure activity while recuperating to be sure that they can continue their interest. A resident may need to learn an adaptive technique or use an adaptive device, i.e., card holder, large print reading materials, page turner, weighted writing devices, talking computer etc. Families may need to be involved in learning adapted techniques or resources for adaptive equipment. Activity professionals could benefit from working with occupational therapists in adapting activities and/or learning and using adaptive equipment.

Knowing residents' functional levels is important to planning and implementing appropriate programming. The number of persons with low cognitive functioning abilities in various service settings is increasing.

Cognitive deficits are primarily related to dementia (Alzheimer's disease, Pick's Disease, Multi-Infarct Dementia, etc.). Residents with dementia experience a slow process of mental deterioration. Losses include short-term memory, ability to make decisions, judgment, ability to follow directions, and ability to independently do ADLs. These losses are gradual but can result in total dependency on staff to meet all needs including stimulation and socialization. In 1990 the Alzheimer's disease and Related Disorders Association, Inc. printed the following statistics in a monograph, "Alzheimer's Disease Statistics":

1. Approximately 4 million Americans are afflicted with Alzheimer's disease.
2. An estimated 12 to 14 million Americans will be affected by the year 2040.
3. Approximately 10% of the population over 65 years of age is affected with Alzheimer's disease. The percentage rises to 47.2% in those over age of 85.
4. More than 50% of all nursing home patients are victims of Alzheimer's disease or a related disorder.

Stages of Alzheimer's

Early or First Stage (Approximately 2-4 years prior to and including diagnosis)

Short-term-memory loss affects daily functioning and job performance
Mild confusion
    Gets lost in familiar places
    Arrives at the wrong place, i.e., church, house, work, store
    Loses track of time

Forgets to pay bills, forgets items on grocery list, forgets to get groceries out of car
Mild communication problems (forgets names, words)
Unable to complete familiar tasks
Exercises poor judgment; makes bad decisions; has difficulty handling money
Indecisive
Behavior changes (moody, anxious, overly sensitive, hostile, angry, withdrawn, may isolate self, is slower in doing and/or completing routine chores)
Personality changes (loss of spontaneity, zest for life)
Motivation changes (loss of initiative; can't start anything)

Middle or Second Stage (Approximately 2–10 years; supervision is needed). This is the longest stage.

Short-term-memory loss increases
Confusion increases (may not recognize family members or close friends or may want to go home, or to see mother or father)
Disoriented to time, place; gets days and nights mixed up
Restless, especially in late afternoon and at night
Short attention span
Word-finding problems (makes up stories to fill in the words)
Repetitive questions, statements and/or movements
Difficulty organizing thoughts and with logical thinking.
Problems with reading, writing and numbers
ADLs are difficult to complete. May need cueing and redirection
Grooming becomes poor; may refuse to bathe
Perceptual-motor problems
Behavior problems increase (may be suspicious, paranoid, irritable, fidgety, teary); may hallucinate; may have difficulty sitting down
Denial is prevalent
Occasional muscle twitches or jerks
Change in weight and intake (gains and then loses weight); gradual loss of interest in food or drink, refuses to eat, or forgets to eat.
Impulse control is lessened (may make socially inappropriate comments.)

Late or Third Stage (Approximately 1–3 years; dependent upon staff)

Cognitive abilities continue to decline

Unable to recognize self in mirror

Unable to recognize family members and friends

Unable to communicate with words (grunting, repetitive sounds and agitation)

May put things in mouth or touch everything

Inability to follow directions

Weight loss even with a good diet

Affect is flat; appears far away, distant

Self care is non-existent; totally dependent on staff

Bladder and bowel incontinence

Body systems break down; may have difficulty with infections and swallowing, skin
breakdown, requires more sleep, may not be able to walk, may have seizures

Immune system weakens; eventually another illness may be the cause of death, i.e., dehydration, pneumonia, urinary tract infection, etc.

Most residents with Alzheimer's disease living in long term care facilities are in the second or third stages of the disease. In the early part of the second stage residents may be successfully integrated into activities with residents with higher-cognitive-functioning abilities. Over time a resident may not be able to participate in regular activities/programs and needs to participate in a specialized activities program.

Specialized Activities Program

"Different programs for different needs"

A specialized activities program is designed for residents with different levels of low cognitive functioning abilities. The specialized activities program offers a variety of activities based on individual needs, interests, preferences and abilities. This provides individual residents an opportunity to participate in individual, one-to-one and/or group activities at their highest possible cognitive, physical and psychosocial functional level.

Activities Related to Functional Level

Some residents will be able to successfully participate in integrated groups in which they can remain attentive. As a resident's disease progresses, his/her need for action-oriented activities increases. Passive activities do not hold their attention. They must be involved in the action or watch someone else perform the action.

Residents may not be able to follow an exercise routine even with cueing. However they may hit a balloon, or move a wand or scarf to music. The object is visual; the music and movement are stimulating.

A resident who used to enjoy coloring is no longer able to manipulate a crayon may find enjoyment in using a bingo dauber to daub color onto a print. It is the repetitive motion of daubing and instant color that attracts their attention.

Singing utilizes long-term memory. When a resident is no longer able to sing songs from adolescent or school years, nursery rhymes are often successful, especially if sung three times in succession.

Reading short stories, showing pictures related to the story, and asking simple open ended or yes/no questions facilitate simple response (eye contact, smiles, tracing design in a picture with a finger or hand, appropriate answers to questions, etc.).

Bible stories may need to replace Bible reading. Praying the Lord's Prayer or singing old hymns like "Jesus Loves Me" may elicit a positive response.

As a person declines so does his/her response to sensory stimulation. In the early stages of dementia a person usually responds to stimulation of all five senses (sight, sound, touch, taste and smell). In the middle to latter part of the last stage of Alzheimer's Disease a person may respond to only one or two sensory stimuli, e.g., sound and touch, with a minimum of response (opening of eyes, guttural sound, change in breathing pattern.

Dolls and stuffed animals provide sensory stimulation (something to touch, hug) and comfort. Residents who like dolls and/or stuffed animals usually have a preference for a specific object. Some will prefer large objects; others will like small items that they can hold in one or both hands.

Food or beverage is often a motivation to sit and then participate in an activity. It is also therapeutic in that residents may eat a little throughout the day but not eat a meal.

In small-group activities, one-to-one techniques may need to be used. However, as one person is being stimulated with action-oriented activities, others may watch.

Types of Specialized Programs

1. *Decentralized (unit-based programs)*. Activities programs are conducted on units versus a centralized area, e.g., dining room, which is away from the unit. Programs are scheduled and structured to meet the functional levels of residents. Residents respond better to parties and celebrations on the units, as the group is smaller than at a large centralized party. A decorated unit provides a festive atmosphere. The activities for the party can be planned to meet the needs and interests of the residents. Refreshments can be simple yet appropriate for the celebration.

2. *Small Groups.* Structured small groups of three to ten people usually work well. The groups need to be structured around residents' functional levels—specifically their cognitive levels. The lower the cognitive level, the smaller the group. While it is important to stimulate residents, caution needs to be taken not to overstimulate which may cause adverse reaction (agitation, irritability, anxiousness, etc.).

Specific Activity Groups: Specific activity groups such as art, crafts, coloring, simple needlework, baking, cooking, food-preparation, ball toss, kickball, bean-bag toss, basketball-toss, balloon badminton, parachute, play, music and movement, alphabet word games, singing, dancing, adapted bingo, card bingo, simple card games, outings, pet visits, lively entertainment parties, celebrations, reminiscing, socials with a snack and other activities can be the catalyst for involvement and enjoyment.

Sensory Group: Sensory group focus is on stimulating the five senses unless individuals respond only to specific senses. A variety of media can be used, including but not limited to the following:

Sight: picture books, pictures, photo albums, colorful place mats, and objects;

Touch: objects to touch and/or manipulate, items to match, stack, sort, put together, take apart; items in a bag to feel and identify, or take out of bag and identify; boxes of items to pick up and look at, dolls and stuffed animals; fabrics to feel and/or fold; items to wash, clean, dust;

Sound: music, nature sounds, environmental tapes, stories to listen to, and cassettes to play;

Taste: pudding, popsicle, fruit, cookie, cake, brownie, raw vegetables and dip, cracker, toast and jelly, cinnamon toast, crackers and cheese, small sandwich, etc. to eat and beverages to drink;

Smell: flowers, spices, oils (peppermint, me, aftershave lotion, etc.

3. *Pre-/Post-Meal Groups*. Residents who are not up for morning or afternoon unit activities can possibly participate in pre-meal or post-meal activities on the unit or in the dining room. A variety of individual, one-to-one or small-group activities can be provided during a 30–45 minute period. Not all residents will participate for the entire time. Individual residents are immediately involved in activities after they are brought into the dining room by the CNAs. Residents sitting at a table may be involved in the same activity or in individual activity that meets their needs, interests and functional ability. Physical activities may be possible if space allows. Residents would be placed in a circle versus at a table. Small groups could form a horseshoe for singing, listening to a story or playing a simple group game.

A beverage could be served prior to an activity. This would increase fluid intake and also satisfy the hunger drive. Residents washing their hands would be a part of the pre-/post-meal activity. Individual warm washcloths or commercial wiping cloths could be used. Residents who are totally dependent on staff for ADL's because of cognitive impairment often demonstrate an ability to wash their hands when given a wash cloth (visual image) and instructed to wash their hands (cue as to what to do). Also seeing others wash their hands is an indicator of what to do. Washing hands is a long-term-memory activity.

Music could be played while residents are entering the dining room and/or when residents wash their hands. If a pre-/post-dining room program cannot be started right away, lively music can be played to stimulate residents. Music needs to be turned off during meals so that residents can concentrate on eating.

4. **Individual Activities**: Some residents will do best in participating in individual activities in the presence of others or by themselves. Action-oriented activities involving the resident usually work well. Individual activities may be supervised or unsupervised depending upon the activity.

5. **One-to-One Activities**: Residents who are unable or unwilling to participate in small group activities need one-to-one and/or individual activities. A resident may need cueing and/or redirection to participate. The activity professional and/or volunteer must present the stimulus in an unhurried, caring manner. The activities selected need to be congruent with the resident's interests, needs, functional abilities and response to sensory stimulation. Doing an activity, e.g., puzzle, painting, looking at pictures, etc., with a resident can be effective. The resident feels the presence of the activity professional or volunteer and has someone to watch and model.

6. **Family Activities**: It is often difficult for families to visit when there is little or no recognition of family members and/or little or no response to conversation. Teaching family members one-to-one stimulation techniques is helpful to them and offers another stimulus to the resident. Families need to be shown to look for a change in breathing pattern when there is no other visual response to sensory stimulation for the person who is bedfast and in the end stage of Alzheimer's disease.

Family members may also get involved with activities for other residents on the unit when their loved one is no longer able to participate. It gives them immediate gratification, provides an opportunity to help others and makes their total visit more meaningful.

7. **Resident/Staff Activities**: Planned structured and spontaneous resident/staff activities can be enjoyable for residents and staff. Providing activity supplies and equipment (cassette recorders, music tapes, books, magazines, pictures, items to paint/color, items to manipulate, cards, simple games, etc.) for staff to use facilitates interaction and involvement in activities with residents.

Playing big band music and music from the 50's is a natural stimulus for dancing.

Monthly or quarterly resident/staff/family potluck dinners can entice a resident to eat. Residents can be involved in food preparation as well as table setting and clean up with supervision. A community spirit is enhanced when staff sits, eats and socializes with residents and families.

Involvement of staff in parties, picnics and socials also provides a community spirit. Food is a universal need. Much of American culture is centered on food. Thus food activities— including ethnic food—provide nutrition, hydration and opportunities to continue cultural activities and socialize with familiar people.

8. **Evening Activities**: Long-term-care facilities are usually quieter after dinner than in the daytime. Residents may be unable to participate in self-directed individual activities but can successfully participate in small-group activities. Involvement in activities after dinner reduces wandering provides stimulation and increases enjoyment. A beverage and/or snack fulfill a physiological need, and the energy expended in an activity may be conducive to sleeping.

9. **Outdoor Activities**: A change of environment, fresh air and outdoor stimulation can be very restful and enjoyable. All outdoor activities need to be in a safe area.

10. **Outings**: Some residents will be able to go on an outing to a closed versus open area (i.e., a conservatory to see flowers versus a picnic in a park) because they feel secure within the boundaries. Residents may feel secure staying in a van or bus and just going for a ride. Night outings will be enjoyable for some residents, whereas others would be frightened.

Specialized programs can be developed over a period of time. The activity professional needs to be creative and continuously ready to change activities/programs to meet the changing needs, interests, preferences and abilities of residents with low-cognitive-functioning abilities.

Diversional Activities

"Activities can encourage and inspire"

Increasingly, interdisciplinary teams are using diversional activities for residents who wander or become agitated, anxious, disruptive, etc. Boredom, the need to physically move, wanting something, wanting to go somewhere, needing to go to the bathroom, and being hungry even though one has just eaten can be reasons a person wanders. Being tired or hungry, wanting attention, being bored, being physically aware of feelings yet unable to express them, and medication can cause agitation, anxiousness and disruptive behavior.

Diversional activities need to be individualized. What works one day may not work another day. What works for one person may not work for another.

Understanding Needs

Activity professionals and other interdisciplinary team members need to try to understand the resident's needs. Using Maslow's Theory of Needs is a starting point. Does the resident need his/her physiological needs met? Is he/she hungry, thirsty, tired, or needing to go to the bathroom? Does the resident feel safe and secure? Does the resident want to go back to a familiar place (his/her room) but can't find it? Does the resident need reassurance that someone (specific name) will take care of him/her? Would providing a doll or stuffed animal provide security and comfort? Does the resident need to feel that he/she is loved? Would a hug, back-rub, holding hands and/or stating, "We love you and will take care of you" soothe the resident? Does esteem needs need to be met? Is positive regard and feedback needed? Would talking about interests (people, places, things, work, activities, animals, etc.) enhance esteem? Is recognition of self-actualization needed? Does the resident need a little reminding of his/her many accomplishments in life and an opportunity to talk about them?

Communication

Residents may or may not be able to communicate their needs (verbally or non-verbally). The longer an activity professional works with a resident with cognitive impairment, the easier it is to understand garbled speech and non-verbal communication. A person may not be able to state what it is he or she wants. It is helpful to try to pick up on body language, a word or sound of a word and to ask simple open-ended questions or yes/no questions.

A resident may communicate a need by asking questions such as, "Do your kidneys hurt?" or "Where is the outhouse?" The person wants to go to the bathroom. The response could be, "Do you have to go to the bathroom?"

If a resident asks, "Do you want to eat?" or "Do you want food?" he/she probably wants food. The response would be, "Would you like _____ (name a food that the resident likes)?" or "Are you hungry?" or "Are you thirsty?" or "Do you want something to drink?"

When observing a resident rummaging through items, a response could be, "What are you looking for?" "I'll try to help you find _____." or "_____, (name of person) are you looking for _____ (name of item)?"

A resident going in and out of rooms may be looking for a bathroom or for a person or specific item or food. A person who uses a wheelchair or a Geri-chair and who is non-verbal may start pounding, trying to tear clothes, squirm a lot, or rapidly and repeatedly touch face/shoulder/arms/legs with one or both hands may be tired or has to go to the bathroom. He/she may be uncomfortable, hungry or thirsty. A small snack even after meals can be physically and emotionally satisfying to the resident. Many residents are hungry all the time. They do not have the cognitive skills to know when they have had enough food to eat and or do not eat much at meals. All staff needs to learn and share individual residents' communication attempts, what they mean and what usually works to calm/satisfy the resident.

Diversional Activities to Meet Residents' Needs

Different diversional activities need to be tried with individual residents. Eventually a flexible list of diversional activities can be developed. The list can be developed in a descending order of what to try first versus last. The list could include food/ beverage, giving a hug, providing a doll or stuffed animal, seating the person is a specific spot, giving specific object(s), playing a specific type of music, reading to the person, engaging the person in a one-to-one activity, looking at a photo album together, reminiscing, etc.

Examples of Diversional Activities for Specific Residents

Mr. Jones

Sit and talk (inside/outside)

Walk and talk (inside/outside)

Talk about farming, hunting, wife, brother

Offer beverage (water, juice, milk, no coffee)

Color pictures of animals, trees, etc.

Trace around name printed on paper.

Use crayon

Provide items to fold or stack

Sort playing cards by number

Look at picture books of farms, animals, farm machinery

Ask to assist with simple repetitive tasks, e.g., folding, weaving yarn on basket

Ask resident to rest if he appears tired

Give stuffed bear

Mrs. Boyer

Remove from noisy area

Provide a choice of coffee, juice or water

Conversation (weather, daughter visiting, topic of her choice)

Reminisce about Frank (husband), KY, flower garden, restaurant (she owned)

Play music (religious, big band)

Play music box

Read Bible story or from poetry book in her room.

Look through the photo album.

Mrs. Sleite

Offer milk, juice, water

Offer cookies or crackers

Give large stuffed bear to hold

Try animated stuffed animal

Try Spinoza (stuffed bear with a tape)

Sit by the window to watch cars

Sit in front of aquarium; point out what to watch

The list of diversional activities can be revised during a care conference unless there is a need to review it sooner because of a change in a resident's behavior and/or functional abilities.

Assisted Living Facilities for People with Multiple Sclerosis

Most commonly assisted living provides relatively independent seniors with supervision, assistance and limits health care in an apartment setting. The typical resident in most assisted living facilities is an 82 year old woman who is mobile but needs assistance with one or two personal activities. The typical length of stay is 24 months.

Young and middle aged persons with disabilities have not yet widely used assisted living. However these programs can bridge the gap for people with multiple sclerosis who are able to maintain a fairly high level of independence but also require some assistance due to the demands of the disease. These are individuals who do not yet need comprehensive care and can benefit from community based care that encourages self determination, self management and provides support when needed.

Assisted living is also an option for individuals who are aging with disabilities and are looking to living options that can make life easier and promote continued independence. Therefore, assisted living meets an important need for a segment of the MS population.

Multiple Sclerosis Units in Nursing Homes

Living in a Nursing Home when you are young or middle aged is thought of as a place of last resort. Many progressive providers have begun to recognize this and are putting special units in there facilities to accommodate younger residents with disabilities. These units allow the MS resident to be among other residents with the same physical condition and age. Activities are planned for the younger resident based from their likes. They enjoy different types of music, games, movies, entertainment and food. Providing these comforts allows the resident to live a more enriched life. Skilled care is provided at the level required and often reimbursable by Medicaid. Living on a MS unit can provide unique opportunities to support each other and develop friendships.

Behavior Units

Behavior units were developed from psychiatric care models of treatment in the 1990's and early 2000's. Behavior units use distinct criteria for admission. Most people in a behavior unit have one or more psychiatric diagnosis with unacceptable behavior patterns. Some times residents with Dementia, Alzheimer's type, are placed in this safe type of unit because of their behaviors.

Psycho geriatric Units

In the 1960's many patients were discharged from mental hospitals to nursing homes. They were placed on strong psychotropic medications to control behavior resulting in cognitive impairment, lethargy, uncontrolled movements, delusions (sight, sound), mistrust, and anti social behavior.

Some state and private psychiatric hospitals had geriatric units with little treatment, except for medication. The older patients were housed separate from younger patients. Some of the older patients may have been institutionalized most of their adult years because treatment had not been developed yet to assist them to become functioning adults and because families were unable to care for them. In the early 1940's and 1950's there was a stigma attached to having a family member who was mentally ill. Often the person with a psychiatric diagnosis was sent away to a psychiatric hospital with little or no contact with family.

In the 1980's psycho geriatric programs were started in hospitals and in long-term-care facilities, with a psychiatrist overseeing treatment. A team of psychiatric professionals, psychiatrist, psychologist, psychiatric nurses, psychiatric nurse assistants, psychiatric social workers, occupational therapist, therapeutic recreation specialists, art therapists, music therapist, dance and movement therapists, horticultural therapist and others provided specialized care and treatment. A variety of approaches and treatment were implemented. By the 1990's, the psycho geriatric units often referred to as gero-psy units were highly utilized for evaluating residents in nursing homes who displayed unacceptable behaviors, symptoms of depression, cognitive changes, etc.

The major mental illness among older adults is depression. This can be from a recent event or a continuation of a history of depression. Residents with schizophrenia who were formerly treated in psychiatric hospitals may now live in long-term-care facilities, attend adult day service or be involved in sheltered workshops. They may be younger than other residents/participants and they may have more than one type of mental illness, i.e. dementia from alcohol.

Working With Residents with Mental Illness

"Special units are needed for special persons"

It is important for activity professionals to learn as much as possible about residents with mental illness, i.e., date and age of onset, course of treatment, behaviors, medication, the resident's awareness and reaction to diagnosis as well as social history prior to the onset of a mental illness. In analyzing former interests, it is important to learn if a resident was involved in activities that required interaction with other people or just objects. A person with a long history of depression may have had a very limited activity lifestyle. A resident who became depressed prior to or after admission may have had an active lifestyle, and the loss of that lifestyle may have contributed to the depression. A resident who had found strength in faith may be able to use the same strength to cope with the depression. A person may have over-zealous involvement with prayer, church and redemption, which causes problems. In working with persons with mental illness it is important to meet them at their level. It will take time to develop a trust relationship. Greeting a person daily with or without a response from the resident reinforces that the activity professional cares. Calling a resident by name and establishing eye contact is important. Informing a resident of what is going on allows him/her an opportunity to decide if he/she wants to participate. Residents with schizophrenia usually do not want to participate in groups—even small groups. They are more comfortable doing individual and/or one-to-one activities if they trust the activity professional. They may attend a party by standing in the back of the room watching but not interacting with anyone. They may obtain food and then leave the room to eat, or may eat at a table by themselves.

Collaboration with Other Health Professionals

"Acts of kindness leads to good relationships

Activity professionals need to collaborate with mental heath professionals (psychiatrist, psychologist, social worker, nurse, dietician, occupational therapist, counselor, expressive therapist [art, dance/movement, drama, music, poetry, horticultural, recreation, etc.]) in working with residents with mental illness. An activity professional may have formal training and certification in one of the activity therapy fields and be qualified to lead therapy groups. Activity professionals who are not certified in one of the activity therapy fields need to be trained to work as a co-leader with another mental health professional if they are to conduct therapy groups.

Individual Activities

Providing supplies for individual activities, e.g., cassette recorder, music/inspirational tapes, reading materials, puzzles [crossword, find-the hidden-word, jigsaw], videos, crafts, gives a resident something to do and to think about besides him/herself. Activities selected need to be related to past and/or present interests. A resident who is depressed may need external motivation to participate in individual activities. If a resident is suicidal, caution must be used as to what types of supplies can be used, i.e., no sharp objects such as scissors for crafts.

One-to-One Activities

Daily interaction is needed for residents who are depressed or who do not socialize with others, i.e., a resident with a diagnosis of schizophrenia. As trust builds so may activity involvement with the activity professional. Eating a meal with a resident who refuses involvement and interaction with others may be non-threatening to the resident. Conversation may be minimal. At first the person may not even give eye contact and then gradually respond with eye contact, a change of facial expression and perhaps a verbal reply to yes/no questions. The activity professional needs to be comfortable with silence and ask permission of the resident to eat with him/her.

One-to-one activities can take place in a resident's room, in a quiet place in the facility, outdoors or on an outing. Sometimes sitting outside allows a resident to open up and begin to talk. The same is true about going for a short ride. The first goal is for a resident who is non-verbal is to respond to questions or statements with yes/no or one or more verbal responses. The activity professional must go slowly with interaction so that the resident does not feel pushed to interact verbally. In time it is hoped that the resident will respond to simple, open-ended questions, initiate greetings, initiate interaction with an activity professional, and then gradually express his/her feelings. One never knows what will trigger a verbal response from a person who is mute. An activity professional needs to be aware when a verbal response is made. It shows trust in the activity profession and it can be followed by a simple response or rephrasing of the response to clarify the response.

Involvement in non-verbal activities often provides a comfort level for the resident that eventually results in verbalization with an activity professional. A resident may feel comfortable doing a one-to-one activity with another staff member, family member, volunteer and/or peer. With medication and/or psychotherapy, a resident may respond quickly to interventions by an activity professional. It is important to inform nursing of residents' behaviors, involvement and interaction during one-to-one activities. The information can be relayed to the resident's physician and mental health professionals with whom he/she is involved.

Groups

A resident with severe depression will not want to participate in groups. A physician may give an order for eating meals in the dining room. This gives the resident an opportunity to be with others with or without the expectation of interaction. It provides a change of environment and stimulation. Specific orders for one or more activity therapies (art, music, recreation, etc.) may be given if these therapies are available in the facility or in the community.

Activity professionals need to work with physicians in determining when a resident is ready for small- and large group activities. Group activities involving watching, i.e., entertainment, video, are less threatening than activities that require activity or interaction. Food activities can be motivating. Some residents will attend an activity (party, social), eat the food and leave without interaction with others. This may be a first step towards involvement/interaction.

Involvement in small-group activities for short periods of time related to interests can be successful. The resident's presence needs to be recognized. Introductions of all group members by the leader or participants provide recognition and set the tone for a group.

In a current events, discussion or reminiscing group, a person may show attentiveness by remaining awake, looking at others who are actively participating, nodding his/her head, and/or smiling. Talking about a topic of interest allows a resident to recall memories, share knowledge and share experiences. Asking the resident yes/no and then simple open-ended questions can facilitate interaction in the group. Game activities requiring long-term memory (alphabet game, trivia, make-a-word, crossword puzzle, etc.) provide stimulation in the presence of others. Social games (cards, board games, interactive games [pennies in a pot]) provide interaction with others but not necessarily verbal interaction. Music related to a resident's interest provides stimulation, enjoyment and possibly a change in feelings. Music is very powerful in eliciting emotional responses.

Creative activities such as crafts and needlework can be non-verbal, providing a resident an opportunity to be involved with an object in the presence of others. Craft and needlework activities provide opportunities to make simple decisions such as selection of an object to make, design, color, etc. Individual recognition can be given for involvement and/or accomplishment. Physical activities, i.e., exercise, deep breathing exercises, relaxation exercises, dancing, walking, adapted sports, increase circulation, heart rate, and respiration, and provide opportunities to use range of motion, stretching, bending, etc. Even with a little exercise a person can begin to feel a difference.

Group Therapy

Residents involved in group psychotherapy go through many stages of involvement from attending but not being responsive in any way in the group to listening to others, to sharing a little information, and finally opening up and sharing thoughts and feelings. The final stage may take a long time or may never be achieved. After attending a psychotherapy group with a mental-health professional, a resident may be exhausted, angry, frustrated, sullen,

wanting to be left alone, etc. Activity professionals need to learn when to allow a resident private time and when to try to intervene to let the resident know that he/she is available if the resident wants to be with someone or to talk. Mental-health professionals usually confer with nursing about a resident. Specific questions can be referred to the mental-health professional through nursing if the mental-health professional is not working in the facility.

Support Groups

Activity professionals, social workers and/or nursing may be involved in co-leading support groups. Support groups can be general in nature for persons with depression or they may focus on specific topics such as losses, grief, or a specific diagnosis (cancer, diabetes, etc.). The groups can be open or closed. In an open group, residents can be invited to attend the group at anytime. A closed group is only open to specific residents. When the group is finished, another group can be started. Support groups can be time specific, i.e., 6–12 weeks, or open-ended (ongoing).

Expressive Therapy

Trained expressive activity therapists, i.e., art, dance/movement, music therapist, can provide a wide variety of therapeutic activities for persons with mental illness. They can provide diagnostic evaluation and treatment. The expressive therapist can work one-to-one or in small groups. An expressive therapist may be willing to train an activity professional to assist with a therapy group and/or make recommendations for follow-up activities. Activity professionals not familiar with expressive therapy groups can contact expressive therapists in local psychiatric hospitals for information and possible observation of a group. Activity professionals are cautioned not to think that they can try activities they observed without further training and experience with an expressive activity therapist.

Expressive Groups

Activity professionals may involve residents in expressive activities (art, music, poetry, dance, movement, etc.) to assist residents to express feelings non-verbally and then verbally. The activity professional needs to be very observant and listen carefully to what a resident expresses. A resident can become very upset getting in touch with and/or expressing feelings that he/she may not have expressed before. It is best for an activity professional to work with a social worker or nurse with a psychiatric background in developing and implementing expressive groups.

Criteria for selecting residents for expressive groups needs to be developed with other team members. Activity professionals need another trained professional with whom to process the group and his/her feelings related to the group. Expressive groups can be as emotionally draining for the activity professional as it is for a resident. The activity professional needs to be in touch with his/her own feelings and to remain objective with the group.

Resident Orientation Group

A resident orientation group coordinated by activity professionals or social workers, and lead by several different staff members, can be educational and therapeutic for a resident. An orientation group may be the catalyst for new residents to participate in other activities (individual, one-to-one and group). In an orientation group, feelings related to placement can be discussed. There is a level of comfort knowing that one is not alone in feeling as he/she does. Sharing provides an opportunity to express losses, concerns and feelings. After an orientation group a new resident may want to talk more or be left alone. The activity professional needs to be aware of the resident's feelings and know when to intervene.

Remotivation Group

An activity professional may be trained in remotivation, which can be a very effective small group technique. In basic remotivation only topics of objective nature are used. The group is leader directed using five specific well-planned steps to assist residents to verbalize and interact with one another:

1. A climate of acceptance—welcoming and recognizing residents
2. A bridge to reality—use of "bounce" questions, poetry, and props to introduce the topic
3. Sharing the world we live in—use of thought-provoking questions, props and sharing of experiences
4. Sharing the world of work —questions, props, sharing of experiences about work, jobs, and tasks related to the topic

5. Climate of appreciation—thanking the residents for participating and informing them of the next meeting.

Remotivation groups are closed groups. The group meets for 30–45 minutes for 12 sessions. At the end of the 12 sessions, group members may wish to stay together for advanced remotivation or to disband. After completion of 12 remotivation sessions a resident may be ready to participate in other group activities.

It is important for an activity professional to evaluate group members' progress after each group. It is also important for the activity professional to evaluate his/her own leadership, preparation for the group, facilitation of the group, and personal feelings that may have surfaced during the group. It is beneficial for the activity professional to process the group with another person trained in remotivation or other group therapy techniques.

Animal/Pet Programs

Holding and petting an animal can be a great source of comfort and joy. A facility pet can be talked to and held. A resident who is upset, anxious, or depressed may have an immediate change of affect from a short involvement with an animal. The resident can share feelings, cry, and smile in the presence of an animal but may not be able to do the same with a family member, staff, volunteer or peer. A visiting pet can provide moments of joy and something for which to look forward.

Precautions

Activity professionals have different training and experiential backgrounds; thus, their involvement in providing therapeutic activities will differ. Activity professionals should not attempt therapeutic activities for residents with mental illness unless they have had training and supervision, or are presently working with someone or are under the supervision of someone with training. Confidentiality must be maintained; however, activity professionals need to learn what information is important to share with other health-care professionals. Any indications of suicidal ideas need to be shared immediately with nursing. Suicide precautions need to be followed during all activities and interactions with residents who are suicidal or potentially suicidal.

Working with People with Physical Disabilities

"It takes special activity professionals to work with special people

Physical and Attitudinal Barriers

One way to minimize negative feelings toward disabilities is to encourage and help persons to remain active in whatever way possible. Many persons with disabilities refuse to consider themselves handicapped and will struggle to remain active in spite of difficulties. Yet there are barriers that make participation difficult.

A barrier-free environment is the goal of all agencies concerned for the elderly, many of who have disabilities. Two federal laws, the Rehabilitation Act and Americans with Disability Act (1990), have had significant impact on accessibility. Public buildings must now be accessible to all. Ramps replace steps, restrooms provide spaces for someone to transfer from a wheelchair to a toilet in privacy, telephones and drinking fountains are accessible to persons in wheelchairs, public transportation is becoming more accessible, elevators have Braille instructions, interpreters for people with hearing disabilities are increasing, and proper lighting is more common.

While physical barriers are being reduced, the worst barrier is the attitudinal barrier. Persons with a negative attitude about those with disabilities would rather not have a person in a wheelchair, one who is deaf or visually impaired, or one who has had a stroke participate in "their" group activity. It is easier to walk away from a person with a severe disability than it is to face that person, to deal with one's personal feelings about the condition, and to accept that person as a human being with feelings, needs and potential.

For the person with a disability, it may be less traumatic to accept his/her limitation and to remain isolated from the group than it is to face others who are embarrassed and uneasy in his/her presence.

The greatest challenge for the activity professional is to face squarely his/her feeling about disabilities before relating to persons with disabilities. Among the fears created are the following:

1. Fear that one might someday have to face the same disability (if one doesn't see the problem, one can more easily ignore it.).
2. Fear of doing or saying something offensive.
3. Fear that the person's own limitations may be discovered.
4. Fear of being rejected by others should a disability develop.
5. Fear of not knowing what to do.

Assessing Individual Needs

When planning with persons with disabilities it is necessary to assess the strengths and weaknesses of each individual. Study backgrounds and interests. Plan for activities that will provide successful experiences.

In-group activities it is important to work individually with each person in the group to assure that the activity is not so difficult that it frustrates, or so simple that it lacks challenge. Encouraging a person to participate in activities that are not meaningful, too difficult or too "childish" defeats the therapeutic goals and makes it more difficult to get the person into the program the next time.

A person who has had a stroke, for example, may be extremely sensitive to the fact that he/she cannot function at a former level of performance. To give that person a project to complete which embarrasses him/her in front of peers will be a severe blow to his/her ego and may result in withdrawal from the program.

Participants in group activities need to be given activities through which they may find a degree of satisfaction and immediate reward. At first, periods of involvement may be short to decrease anxiety or avoid exertion. As persons feel more comfortable in a group and are familiar with the activity, less stress occurs, and time periods may be increased.

Because of a disability (physical, emotional or social) it may be necessary to work with an individual on a one-to-one basis only. When it is possible to work with an individual in a positive group setting there seems to be a greater degree of healing. A social setting that provides stimulation and peer recognition becomes a therapeutic experience.

Baking cookies in small groups of three or four has proven to be a successful activity for persons in long-term-care facilities who have very limited ability. Residents select the item to be made. The activity professional or volunteer secures the ingredients and assists in reading the recipe and measuring quantities. The residents may help to mix, make dough into cookies and remove them from the baking pan once it has cooled from the oven. Such an activity draws on past skills of the resident.

Recreation, crafts or activities that provide stimulation are available for persons with varying degrees of competency. With imagination most activities can be adapted to comply with the many needs of the residents. The key is discovering the person's interest and fabricating tools to make the activities possible.

Assembly Line

Crafts may be produced assembly-line fashion with the least able persons performing the simplest tasks toward the completion of an item. Pom-pom creatures are a good example of this process. Residents with various disabilities (arthritis in the hands, use of one arm due to stroke, blindness, impaired hearing) may be able to roll yarn around a disc to make a pom-pom. More able residents may tie the yarn and remove it from the disc, trim it into a round ball or assemble the pom poms into creatures. Facial features, hand embroidery or decorations may be added by more skillful crafts persons.

Special Equipment
"The right equipment for the right task"

Adaptive devices can help persons with physical limitations. Activity professionals can learn to sense special needs and seek assistance in providing adaptive equipment. An occupational therapist can provide immense suggestions, techniques and resources. The activity professional can confer with other skilled people (family members, the maintenance department, other staff, volunteers, as well as organizations for persons with physical disabilities) for ideas and assistance. The important point is that people are not ignored because they have a physical disability. See Appendix I for resources for adaptive supplies and equipment.

Skilled persons may be family members, the maintenance department, volunteers or other interested persons. The important point is that people are not ignored because they have a physical disability.

Adaptive Devices and Equipment*

In an activity program in nursing homes, the main problem in working with persons with use of one arm or limited use of hand(s) is in finding a method of stabilizing their projects. Most of the adaptive devices listed in this chapter are suggestions for solutions to this problem. However, because adaptive devices may be used in various circumstances they should not be specifically limited to people who have had a stroke, but could be used by any residents hoping to improve their performance of a skill or daily task.

Masking Tape – Small loops placed underneath the four corners will hold paper for writing or drawing; cardboard for gluing objects to it; small pieces of wood when sanding or painting; or copper sheets for tooling. Masking tape can be purchased at variety, hardware, paint, or discount stores.

C-Clamps – Clamps are available in various sizes. They can be used to hold larger pieces of wood for gluing or nailing; clipboards for various projects; or to hold wooden looms to Geri-chairs, bed tables, or work surfaces for knitting or weaving. C-clamps are available at hardware stores and in the hardware section of discount stores.

Portable Vise – Heavy-duty stabilizer. Can be used to hold large pieces of wood for sawing or nailing; boxes for sanding, painting, or decorating; and leather pieces for lacing. Available at hardware and discount stores (hardware departments).

Vacu-Vise – Another type of portable vise that implements a suction pressure principal in adhering vise to surface of table. Exceptionally easy to attach and release. Same use as portable vise. Regular size Vacu-vise available from Fred Sammons.

Note: This material on adaptive devices by Marjorie Watkins, O.T.R., Marion, Ohio was used by permission.

Clipboard – May be used to hold thin objects for writing, reading, cutting, sewing, drawing. Examples: writing paper, construction paper, string or twine, material, or magazines. The clipboard may be held in place by a C-Clamp or a piece of Dycem plastic. Purchase at department, variety, discount, office supply or drug stores.

Silly-Putty – Used to hold nails in position when hammering. Play-dough and clay may also be used; however they sometimes leave a greasy spot that the silly-putty will not do. Purchase at variety, discount, office supply or drug store.

Needle-Threader – Simple method of threading needle for those with one hand and/or poor vision. You may need to stabilize threader with C-Clamp or Dycem plastic. Available at fabric stores.

Wrist-Pincushion – Plastic "bracelet" with piece of foam rubber attached to top. An easy method of stabilizing needle when threading it. Available at variety and fabric stores.

Beeswax on Toothpick – A piece of beeswax, when rolled between fingers, will soften enough to permit you to roll it around the end of a toothpick. While in softened state, it will easily pick up sequins and small beads for gluing or sewing on projects. Beeswax is sold in small round discs. Available in fabric or craft stores.

One-Handed Embroidery Hoop – Wooden embroidery hoop on a stand, attaches to table or Geri chair in a similar fashion to the vise. It holds material steady for sewing and will flip over to permit view of back, if desired. Available from Herrschners or needlework stores.

One-Hand Knitting Needle Holder – One knitting needle is held in holder while stitches are made using a second needle. The holder can be mounted on table edges or chair arms. Available from North Coast Medical, Inc.

Card Holder – Playing cards are held between 2 plastic discs by means of a tension spring. One type has a frame that clips onto the table edge while another type is fastened onto a weighted base that stands on the table. Wooden cardholder racks are also available at a slightly higher cost. Available from activity and adaptive equipment supply companies.

Book Rack – A metal frame to hold books for reading. Can be positioned at various angles for bedfast residents. Also will hold cookbooks open. Adjustable prongs permit pages to be turned with one hand. Available at some bookstores, activity and/or adaptive equipment companies.

Built-Up Items – Foam built-up handles on paintbrushes and small rubber built-up triangles on pens and pencils assist persons with limited hand functions to write, draw or paint.

Dycem Pad – Used mainly for dinner plates. Expensive compared to matting, but more durable. Also available through Fred Sammons and local stores that sell aids and appliances for persons with physical disabilities.

Talking Books – Books recorded on records or cassette tapes are available free of charge for persons unable to read because of visual impairment or physical disability that prevents holding a book. Talking Books are available from The Library of Congress (see resources).

Radio Reading Services – The daily newspaper is broadcast daily over a special receiver. When the newspaper (different sections at specific program times) is not being read by a volunteer reader, music is played. In some areas the rosary is broadcast. Information is available from The National Association of Radio Reading Services (see resources).

Visual Aids – Magnifying glasses—hand-held (available in different strengths), lighted magnifiers, over-the-neck magnifiers, i.e., for needlework, crafts, reading, high-intensity magnifier lamp, raised-lined writing paper, signature guide, audio watches, sewing aids, large-print playing cards, and bingo cards as well as games are a few of the many adaptive devices to assist older persons who have visual impairment. Some low vision aids need to be prescribed by a physician, i.e., high-strength magnifying glasses. Visual aids are available from Cleo Living Aids, Foley Low-Vision Aids, Fred Sammons, L&S Group, Maxi Aids and Vis Aids, Inc.

Amplification Devices – Personal and group communication devices assist persons with hearing impairments to hear spoken words during one-to-one conversation and/or in group activities. Clyde Equipment has a one-to-one communicator and a group communicator. Radio Shack (found in many cities) has a variety of amplification devices. See resources for catalogs that carry a variety of adaptive devices for different physical disabilities.

Walker Bag – Cloth bag with pockets to hold personal items. Attaches to walker with snaps or Velcro. Removes easily for washing. Can also be used on bed-rails or adapted to wheelchair. Usually constructed from sturdy washable fabrics such as denim, ticking, etc. A good project for participants or volunteers to make from scraps of material.

Page-Turning Device

Purpose

To be used when patients' hands are not able to function to turn a page or when fixation prevents patient from being able to reach the pages of book.

Spring-type door stop that normally screws into baseboard to stop door.

Length of wooden dowel rod or section of handle off discarded mop, broom, duster or similar item. Cut rod to necessary length for individual patient requirement.

These spring-door stops are readily available at practically any hardware store.

Tips for Working with Persons with Hearing Impairments

1. Sit near the person. If hearing is better in one ear than the other, sit on that side.

2. Do not speak abruptly to a person with a hearing impairment. First attract the person's attention by facing him and looking straight into his eyes, or by touching his hand or shoulder lightly.

3. Face the person so he/she has the benefit of lip movements and facial expression.

4. Speak slowly and distinctly. Lower the tone of voice if a person is unable to hear normal tone of voice.

5. Wait patiently for a response. The person with a hearing impairment will need to focus all his/her attention on what is being said and will not be able to formulate an answer or comment until he/she has had time to process information. (A hearing person is formulating a response simultaneously as the other person speaks.)

6. Give only one directive or ask one question at a time.

7. Use body movements and gestures freely.

8. Pictures and objects may aid in clarifying conversation.

9. Many people with hearing impairments are sensitive about their disability and may pretend to grasp what you have said even though they have not heard. It may be wise to repeat what you have said, using different words.

10. To test whether you have been correctly heard, ask! Or request the listener to repeat to you what he/she has heard you say.

11. Most older persons who are deaf are literate, so communication may be done through writing.

Techniques for Working with Persons with Visual Impairments

1. Speak directly to a person and state your name.

2. When speaking, use directions: right, left, up, down, toward you, away from you.

3. When walking, have the person hold your arm above the elbow.

4. Determine the need for lighting. Some people need more lighting than others. Some have extreme difficulty with glare indoors or out-of-doors.

5. If using natural lighting (seating in front of window), have person sit with back to window to reduce glare.

6. If bright light is needed, use a 100-watt bulb if person is using a lamp. A three-way bulb can be used if the lowest setting is 100-watts.

7. Light needs to shine over the person's shoulder onto the object or paper being seen.

8. If the person is using a magnifying glass, be sure the light doesn't shine through the magnifier that can cause a glare.

9. Seat the person nearest the person or objects that need to be seen.

10. Place objects in field of vision.

11. For eating, sectional plates may be easier to use.

12. Assist as needed with opening items.

13. Use the clock method of identifying items on place: Brownie is at 12 o'clock and cookies are at 6 o'clock, pop is at 2 o'clock.

14. Use felt-tip markers to print large, bold letters. Black on white is best to see. Use contrasting colors to make posters. Keep posters simple, clear, well organized and uncluttered. Do not use pastel colors. Work with residents to determine the colors they can see easiest.

15. Place a color-contrasting piece of paper under objects that are to be painted or glued. Be sure the color contrast is still contrasted once an item is painted. For example, if a white item were to be painted pink, it would be best not to use any shade of pink paper for the contrasting color.

16. When working on ceramic pieces, place a few drops of food coloring in the light color glaze so that it is easy to see contrast between the bisque and the glaze. The color will dissolve during the firing of the ceramic piece.

17. Use trays and /or containers to hold materials.

18. Provide large-print reading materials, Talking Books, and Radio Reading Service.

19. Stress the use of all senses (sight, sound, smell, taste, touch) in activities as appropriate.

20. Hang clocks, calendars, posters, and signs at eye level.

21. Mark a person's room with visual or tactile clues if person has difficulty finding room. Persons who lose a degree of their hearing late in life may still be able to learn to lip-read or sign. Investigate nearby universities with programs in teaching the deaf. They may be able to send students doing their fieldwork into your facility to teach lip reading or signing.

22. Consult with an occupational therapist concerning appropriate use of an adapted visual aide. Suggest a physician's orders for a low-vision evaluation if there is a low vision evaluation center in the area (usually a part of services for the blind).

23. Be aware of the person's fears, e.g., loosing sight, falling, not knowing where things are, not knowing how to get back to room, etc.

24. Always explain procedures in advance.

25. Check and **clean glasses** as needed.

[1]Exercises for Arthritic Hands

Recipe for Theradoh

Theradoh, a clay-like substance made of flour, salt, oil and water, is beneficial for residents with arthritis. The dough is soft and pliable, and offers little resistance when squeezed by hands or fingers. Residents will experience little pain while exercising.

Recipe:
1 ½ cups flour
½ cup salt
3 tablespoons mineral oil
approximately ½ cup water

Process:
Combine flour and salt. Gradually add mineral oil and water to make soft dough. Dust table lightly with baby talcum to prevent sticking when first using dough. (The powder also adds a pleasant scent.) Store dough in a plastic container with a tight lid. When it hardens, make a new batch.

Techniques for Working with Persons in Wheelchairs/Geri Chairs

Courtesy and safety principles need to be used in working with a person who is in a wheelchair or Geri chair.

1. Greet the person face to face before moving him/her.

2. Ask the person for permission to move him/her.

3. Always push a wheelchair or Geri chair **forward**.

4. In entering an elevator, pull the wheelchair/ Geri chair in **backward** and exit elevator pushing the wheelchair/Geri chair **forward**.

5. Always lock the wheelchair/Geri chair once the person is in position.

6. Use seat belts in the vehicle and lock the wheelchairs.

7. When pushing a wheelchair/Geri chair walk at a pace that is comfortable and safe for the rider.

8. On a steep incline, push the wheelchair **up** the hill facing **forward**. In **descending** an incline, guide the wheelchair **backwards**. Be sure to have safe and secure footing and watch for people or obstacles behind.

9. If a resident falls out of wheelchair/Geri chair, seek nursing assistance. If on an outing without nursing personnel, check for injuries, seek assistance with a safe two-man life, or call 911 for assistance. Call facility and report incident.

[1] This article, Exercises for Arthritic Hands, was prepared by Evelyn Rossky, O.T.R., Moss Rehabilitation Hospital, Department of Occupational Therapy, Philadelphia, PA. Used by permission.

Exercises

1. Using hand, shape Theradoh into a log. Roll back and forth to tips of fingers. Fold log double and repeat. DON'T SQUEEZE.

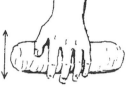

2. Place a small ball of Theradoh between two fingers and bring fingers together. Repeat with each of the other fingers of both hands. Watch your fingers as you exercise them, remembering joint protection principles. ALWAYS use the heel or palm of your hand when pressure is needed whether pushing down on Theradoh or up from a chair. **Work Slowly. Rest Often.**

3. Shape Theradoh into a cone and stick base to a flat surface. Place fingers and thumb over the apex of the cone, resting palm on top. One finger at a time, lift up and away, hard. Then lift all four fingers at once, hard. Relax.

4. Pick up a small ball of Theradoh between thumb and index finger. Touch, tip to tip through the ball, forming an "O" with your fingers; use each joint in every finger if you can. **Don't Pinch.**

5. Shape Theradoh into small balls. Flick each "marble" away, using a different finger, and flexing and extending (bending and straightening) each joint as you "shoot."

Therapy Board

Ask a volunteer to build a "therapy" board for use with persons with limited use of hands.

Attach to the board such things as a button and buttonhole, a zipper, a hook and eye, a door knob, a padlock with a key, a snap, shoestrings, and a slip-lock bolt.

Working with such everyday items can maintain or improve fine-motor movement needed for pushing, twisting, pulling, turning and sliding.

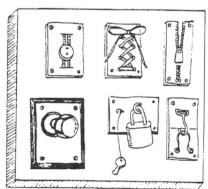

Walker Bag

This easy-to-make walker bag snaps over the cross rod on the walker to hold personal items.

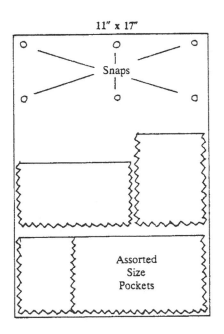

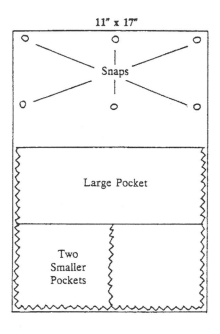

〜〜〜Machine stitched edge.

Activity Programming

"No two programs are alike."

Length of Stay

No two programs are alike because the residents with whom they are planned are different. The purpose of the facility and the length of stay impact the program. Residents in sub-acute and rehabilitation units have a shorter length of stay than do residents in nursing facilities. The length of stay differs for residents in skilled nursing units. Residents needing long-term skilled nursing are usually physically dependent upon staff for their care, i.e., a resident who is comatose or quadriplegic and ventilator-dependent. Residents needing short-term skilled nursing may need IV therapy and assistance with ADLs, and then return home or to a nursing facility.

Planning Activities for Different Lengths of Stay

Planning of activities differs in long-and short-term-care facilities Activities are planned on a monthly basis in long-term-care facilities; activities are planned on a weekly or bi-weekly basis for short-term-care facilities because of the high rate of residents being admitted and discharged.

Specialty Units

The primary focus of sub-acute, short-term skilled nursing and rehabilitation programs is for the resident to return home. A resident's treatment is centered on this goal.

A resident who is involved in multiple therapies one or more times per day may have little time to be involved in activities or is too tired to participate in small-group activities. Individual and one-to-one activities (with staff, families, volunteers and peers) become the focus of their activity program with some daily small-group activities. These activities allow the resident to continue former activities alone or with others, relax and rest the body and increase energy, adjust to using adaptive equipment for leisure activities, and focus on abilities versus limitations.

An activity/dining room can be a focal point of a small specialized unit, i.e., short-term skilled nursing unit, sub acute unit, for meals, small group and parallel group activities. In a parallel group, residents are in the presence of others but are involved in individual activities (reading newspaper, magazine or book; working on a puzzle [crossword, jigsaw or find-a-word], craft or needlework project; listening to music or Talking Books using headphones; being involved in a sensory or multi-sensory activity, a service project, etc.). Parallel groups work well in the midmornings and afternoons. Direct-care staff and/or a therapist responsible for escorting residents to and from therapies can meet or return a resident to the activity/dining room area. The activity professional assists residents in their individual activities as needed and/or conducts or facilitates small-group activities.

Pre- and post-meal programs can be effective. Programs can be conducted thirty to sixty minutes prior to meals (lunch and dinner) in the dining room. This is a good time for small-group activities (cognitive, creative, expressive, social, physical, community service project, religious/spiritual, etc.). Programming such as this allows residents who are only up for meals or who have to rest after therapy an opportunity to be involved in a group activity. Post-meal activities for 15-45 minutes after meals are another effective time for group activities, particularly for those residents who are unable to participate in a pre-meal program. The pre- and post-meal programs can also be designed for different levels of functional abilities.

The facility's philosophy regarding residents eating in the dining room affects the residents' social involvement. Group dining provides opportunities for residents to meet and socialize with peers. Residents are empowered to socialize, express feelings, share experiences, and feel comforted from their involvement and interaction with peers.

A resident's individual plan of care may include involvement in referral groups such as a community reintegration group, instrumental activities of daily living groups (cooking, shopping, cleaning) leisure education group, discharge planning group, or community resource group, etc. These groups may be co-lead by an activity professional or therapeutic recreation specialist and an occupational therapist, physical therapist, respiratory therapist and/or speech pathologist.

Space for Programming

In long-term-care facilities, activities programming can be offered in multiple locations with a variety of small and large group activities in addition to individual and one-to one activities. Activities and programs based on functional levels can be conducted by multiple staff in different areas at different times or simultaneously.

Depending upon the size of a facility, there may be only one dining/activity room or multiple dining/activity areas. Large centralized activities take place in the largest available area. Unit activities and pre/post-meal programs offer opportunities for residents to participate in a variety of activities related to their functional abilities. A pre/post-meal program seven days a week provides an opportunity for residents who are not up for small group activities to participate in parallel or small group activities in the dining room. This increases socialization and stimulation and may reduce the need and/or the frequency for one-to-one programming.

Role of an Activity Professional

An activity professional is responsible for assessing residents and developing an appropriate, dynamic activity program to benefit all residents. The programming model, hours of operation and staffing will all depend upon the needs, interests, preferences, abilities and limitations of the residents, purpose and philosophy of the facility, and residents' length of stay.

Benefits of Activities

The benefit of participation in an activity is individualized. Knowledge of activity assessment and activity analysis assists the activity professional in understanding how a participant could benefit from participating in a specific activity. In setting goals for care plans, the activity professional, the participant, other interdisciplinary team members, family or significant others establish measurable outcomes from activity participation, which are the benefits from participation. A person who is unable to communicate verbally may have a goal of: "Will communicate needs, desires as needed and will communicate with family and friends a minimum of weekly through e-mail." The benefit of using the computer would be increased communication. A part of reaching this goal may have to include teaching a person how to use a computer and set up e-mail. The person would have to have the cognitive skills for learning and the physical skills for typing. Another person may have to use a simple alphabet or picture communication board to communicate by pointing to letters or pictures. The outcome is the same, will communicate needs and desires and will communicate with family friends, staff and peers using a communication board.

Person Centered Puzzle made from a copy of the resident's wedding picture.

J. Krupa

Benefits of Activities (Not all inclusive)

COGNITIVE BENEFITS

Develop/Increase/Maintain:

- ☐ Ability to:
    - ☐ Learn
    - ☐ Make decisions
    - ☐ Plan
    - ☐ Problem solve
    - ☐ Reminisce
- ☐ Alertness
- ☐ Aptitude
- ☐ Attentiveness
- ☐ Identity
- ☐ Independence
- ☐ Insight regarding:_____
  _____
- ☐ Knowledge of:_____
  _____
- ☐ Memory
    - ☐ Short term
    - ☐ Long term
- ☐ Mental Stimulation
- ☐ Orientation to person, time, place, expectation
- ☐ Reality
- ☐ Self image
- ☐ Self-worth
- ☐ Sensory perception

Decrease

- ☐ Confusion
- ☐ Disorientation
- ☐ Distraction
- ☐ Hallucinations
- ☐ Wandering

SOCIAL BENEFITS

Develop/Increase/Maintain:

- ☐ Ability to continue social roles
- ☐ Ability to maintain social skills
- ☐ Autonomy
- ☐ Communication
- ☐ Continuation of life styles
- ☐ Feelings of belonging
- ☐ Interaction with:
    - ☐ Family
    - ☐ Peers
    - ☐ Staff
    - ☐ Volunteers
- ☐ Intergenerational ties
- ☐ Intimacy
- ☐ Opportunity to share
- ☐ Personal feelings of respect
- ☐ Personal appearance
- ☐ Relationships (family, friends, peers, staff, volunteers)
- ☐ Trust relationship
- ☐ Use of telephone and email

Decrease:

- ☐ Isolation
- ☐ Social judgment
- ☐ Withdrawal from activity, family/friends

EMOTIONAL BENEFITS

Develop/Increase/Maintain:

- ☐ Acceptance
- ☐ Adjustment
- ☐ Comfort
- ☐ Control
- ☐ Coping skills
- ☐ Courage
- ☐ Courage
- ☐ Creativity
- ☐ Dignity
- ☐ Empowerment
- ☐ Enjoyment of life and activities
- ☐ Expression of feelings
- ☐ Feeling of being needed/useful
- ☐ Frustration tolerance
- ☐ Fun
- ☐ Hope
- ☐ Humor
- ☐ Imagination
- ☐ Independence
- ☐ Integrity
- ☐ Interests/Preferences
- ☐ Legacy
- ☐ Life satisfaction
- ☐ Optimistic attitude
- ☐ Positive attitude
- ☐ Recognition
- ☐ Safety
- ☐ Security
- ☐ Self actualization
- ☐ Self care
- ☐ Self confidence
- ☐ Self esteem
- ☐ Self expression
- ☐ Self initiated activity
- ☐ Sense of accomplishment

Decrease/Eliminate:

- ☐ Accusatory statements
- ☐ Agitation
- ☐ Anger
- ☐ Anxiety
- ☐ Assultive behavior
- ☐ Depression
- ☐ Guilt feelings
- ☐ Hostility
    - ☐ Verbal
    - ☐ Non verbal
- ☐ Learned helplessness
- ☐ Lethargy
- ☐ Loneliness
- ☐ Mood swings
- ☐ Negative statements
- ☐ Non-acceptance of placement
- ☐ Psychotropic medication
- ☐ Restlessness
- ☐ Stress
- ☐ Worthlessness

Benefits of Activities
(Not all inclusive)

PHYSICAL BENEFITS:

Increase/Improve/Maintain:
- ☐ ADL skills
- ☐ Agility
- ☐ Ambulation
- ☐ Appetite
- ☐ Balance
- ☐ Body awareness
- ☐ Bowel function
- ☐ Breathing function
- ☐ Circulation
- ☐ Coordination:
    - ☐ Eye hand
    - ☐ Eye foot
    - ☐ Hand mouth
- ☐ Energy
- ☐ Flexibility
- ☐ Flexion and extension:
    - ☐ Lower extremities
    - ☐ Upper extremities
- ☐ Hygiene
- ☐ Hydration
- ☐ Mobility
- ☐ Motor movements:
    - ☐ Gross motor
    - ☐ Fine motor
- ☐ Muscle tone
- ☐ Nutrition
- ☐ Posture
- ☐ Range of Motion (ROM)
- ☐ Relaxation
- ☐ Rest
- ☐ Sleep
- ☐ Sleep Pattern
- ☐ Stamina
- ☐ Strength of:_____

- ☐ Use of adaptive equipment and assistive devices
- ☐ Weight
- ☐ Wellness

Decrease:
- ☐ Blood pressure
- ☐ Falls
- ☐ Insomnia
- ☐ Pain
- ☐ Risk of medical problems
- ☐ Sleep
- ☐ Stiffness
- ☐ Tension
- ☐ Weight

SPIRITUAL BENEFITS:

Develop/Increase/Improve/Maintain:
- ☐ Ability to:
    - ☐ Help others
    - ☐ Meditate
    - ☐ Pray
- ☐ Acceptance of life/losses
- ☐ Connection with church, synagogue
- ☐ Coping skills
- ☐ Feeling centered
- ☐ Inner peace
- ☐ Legacies
- ☐ Relationship with higher power
- ☐ Relationship with minister, priest, rabbi
- ☐ Religious/spiritual practices

Experience
- ☐ Life review
- ☐ Reconciliation
- ☐ Reminiscing

Philosophy of Operation

"Positive attitudes lead to positive action"

A philosophical statement is a "belief" statement. Webster's dictionary describes philosophy as "the most general belief, concepts and attitudes of an individual or group..."*

The philosophy of activity operation is derived from and coordinated with the facility's philosophy of care. The philosophy of activities programming indicates beliefs of the activities department and the facility, from which all services and programming are developed and implemented. Goals and objectives for programming and services are derived from the philosophy and resident assessment. Policies and procedures are also based on the philosophy of operation.

A philosophy of operation can be written in the second and/or third persons, i.e., "We believe that _____." "It is the belief of (name of facility) that _____." The philosophy is usually written in one to three short paragraphs with concepts succinctly and clearly identified.

In writing a philosophy of operation, the writer is actually writing the philosophy for the facility, i.e., "We believe that activities are for all residents including those who are confined to their bed/room."

Twenty-One Key Concepts

The following key concepts can be considered in developing a philosophy of activities related to quality of life in a long term-care-facility. These concepts can be adapted or changed for other settings. They are just a guide for developing a philosophy.

1. Individual residents' quality of life is enhanced, fostered or maintained through participation in activities.

2. Residents are treated with dignity and respect. Their right to participate in activities of their choice is respected.

3. Activities are for all residents, including persons confined to bed or room and/or those who are totally dependent upon staff for stimulation and socialization.

4. The activities program is based on an individualized resident assessment: interests (past and present), preferences, former lifestyle; and needs, as well as abilities and limitations.

5. The activities program is related to residents' various social, cultural, economic and religious backgrounds.

6. Residents are empowered to learn, grow, and function at their highest level of physical, mental and psychosocial well-being.

7. Residents are provided opportunities to participate in activities in the morning, afternoon and evening, on weekends, and on holidays.

8. Residents are provided opportunities to participate in a variety of activities in the facility, out-of-doors, and in the community.

9. Residents are provided with opportunities to participate in seasonal, holiday and special event activities.

10. Residents are provided with opportunities for involvement in independent and leader-directed activities.

11. Residents are provided opportunities to recommend, plan, conduct or assist with activities as well as to evaluate activities and programs.

12. Activities are a part of the individual resident's total plan of care.

13. The activities program is creative and dynamic to meet the changing needs of residents (cognitive, physical, social, emotional, creative, spiritual, work/ service and leisure needs).

14. Activities and programs are adapted as needed to empower residents to participate.

15. The activities program creates an environment conducive for interaction and socialization, personal satisfaction, growth, recognition and self-fulfillment.

16. The activities program includes individual, one-to-one and group activities.

17. The activities program involves family, friends and volunteers.

18. Community resources are utilized for programming in the facility as well as in the community.

19. Volunteers are utilized to add dimension to the activities program and to assist residents in activities as needed.

20. The activities program is structured and co-ordinated with other services.

21. The activities program is continuously being evaluated and updated.

Goals and Objectives

"Without goals and objectives there is no direction"

Programming goals and objectives relate to the philosophy of programming, model of operation, age, needs, and length of stay of participants. Goals and objectives will be similar, yet different, in community-based and long-term-care facilities. The goals and objectives establish outcomes and provide a frame of reference for care and services through the provision of activities and programs.

Goals and Objectives for Programming

GOAL #1:

To foster resident's independent, self-care, resumption of normal activities, and continuation of former lifestyle as much as possible, in keeping with interests, preferences, abilities and limitations.

Objective #1:

Residents shall be empowered to:
1. Choose and determine their preference for activities (individual, family, one-to-one, and/or group activities) in/out of facility and in the community.

2. Make decisions regarding activity planning, i.e., individually, through resident council, and resident-planned activity meetings with an activity professional.

3. Care for self at activities as abilities allow, i.e., feed self at parties, wash hands after crafts/pets, put on appropriate clothing for outings.

4. Continue normal activities of interests, e.g., watch T.V., listen to radio/music, write letters, read books/periodicals.

5. Interact with members of the community both inside and outside the facility.

GOAL #2:

To assist individual residents to adjust to illness, disability and/or nursing-home placement.

Objective #2:

Resident shall have an opportunity to:
1. Become familiar with activities staff, department, activities, programs and services as well as activity schedules.

2. Become acquainted with other residents.

3. Express feelings toward illness, disability, nursing home placement and participation in activities.

4. Participate in activities of former interest with adaptations and/or assistive devices as needed.

GOAL #3:

To maintain or improve self-esteem and self-worth through meaningful, goal-oriented activities.

Objective #3:

Resident shall have an opportunity to:
1. Participate in activities that provide a sense of accomplishment, e.g., crafts, cooking, service projects, work activity, resident council, adapted sports, competition, contests and games.

2. Participate in activities that provide opportunities to express self (discussion group, sensory stimulation, religious activities and one-to-one activity with activity staff/volunteers).

GOAL #4:

To provide activities for residents to exercise their cognitive, physical, emotional, and social abilities through a wide variety of activities.

Objective #4:

Resident shall have the opportunity to participate in:

1. Cognitive Activities: Current events, sensory stimulation, reality-orientation, reminiscing, discussions, resident council, games, Bible study, reading.

2. Physical Activities: Exercise, adapted sports (bowling, basketball, ring toss, balloon badminton, etc.), walks, crafts (fine-motor movement).

3. Expressive Activities: Resident council, resident-planned activity meetings, family activities, art, baking/cooking, humor, music, poetry, discussion, reminiscing, life review, orientation group, support group and expressive group.

4. Social Activities: Parties, picnics, celebrations, social hours, special events, family activities, games, men's group, outings, community events, intergenerational programs, visiting, telephoning, correspondence, group games and people watching.

GOAL #5:

To provide activities for residents to fulfill spiritual needs and continue their former spiritual interest and beliefs through religious and spiritual programs.

Objective #5:

1. Residents shall have an opportunity to practice their beliefs and rituals including church services, Mass, Sabbath services, prayer service, communion, rosary, Bible study, inspirational readings, meditations, listening to religious music, and the celebration of religious holidays.

2. Residents shall have an opportunity to visit with clergy of their choice.

GOAL #6:

To provide activities that emphasizes creative expression.

Objective #6:

1. Residents shall have an opportunity to participate in creative activities including arts and crafts, woodworking, ceramics, making decora-

tions, baking, cooking, poetry, music, singing, rhythm band, and creative writing.

GOAL #7:

To provide work/service-type activities to focus on wellness using the abilities that he/she has to do for ones self as well as other persons in the facility/community.

Objective #7:

1. Resident shall have an opportunity to be involved in work/service type activities including assisting with mailings, and newsletters, setting up/cleaning up for activities, serving on committees (welcome, resident council, grievance committee, etc.).

GOAL #8:

To provide activities in which residents can participate with family/friends.

Objective #8:

1. Residents shall have opportunity to visit with families/friends, and to invite family and/or friends to participate in the daily activities programs as well as family-planned activities, e.g., carry-in dinners.

GOAL #9:

To provide diversified activities programs encouraging individual, self-directed activities, independent activities with some assistance, one-to-one activities, as well as small and large-group activities inside and/or outside of facility and in the community.

Objective #9:

Residents shall have an opportunity to participate in the following activities of their choice:

1. Self-directed activities or individual activities with some assistance: Individual crafts/needlework, watching TV, listening to radio/music, reading, listening to Talking Books, writing, reading mail, walking, caring for plants in room, praying, people-watching, bird-watching, and working puzzles and word games.

2. One-to-one activities: Visiting (staff, volunteer, clergy, children and/or pets), reading mail, writing letters, sensory stimulation, games, crafts, decorations, music, religious activities, puzzles, reality orientation, reminiscing, discussions and adapted sports.

3. Small group activities: Sensory stimulation, reminiscing, reality orientation, current events, outside group, outings, cooking, exercise, adapted sports, music/singing, special T.V. viewing, e.g., wrestling, visiting with family and educational programs.

4. Large-group activities: Parties, celebrations, special events, family activities, religious activities, e.g., church service/bingo, bazaars, social hour, etc.

GOAL #10:

To provide activities for all residents (independent, ambulatory, bedfast, chair-bound, and room-bound) in accordance with their interests, preferences, needs abilities and limitations.

Objective #10:

1. Residents shall have assistance/ transportation to and from activity groups as needed.

2. Residents shall be provided personal assistance, and adaptive devices, as needed, i.e., Talking Book machine, magnifier, raised/ enlarged numbers, stabilizing materials, amplification devices, etc.

3. Activities shall be adapted as needed, i.e., adapted sports, one-step activities, non-verbal activities, simplified games, etc.

4. Residents confined to bed or room shall have opportunities to participate in individual and one-to-one activities.

5. Residents in a comatose or semi-comatose state shall have opportunities for one-to-one sensory stimulation and socialization as well as environmental stimulation.

Programming Outcomes

"Meeting resident/client needs brings achievement

The outcome from participation in activities is individualized. Six people participating in planting, growing, and harvesting a garden could have six different personal outcomes. One could feel a sense of accomplishment from having tried something new. The second person could look to working in the garden as a means of maintaining health through physical activity and renewed spirit. The third person could feel a sense of fulfilling responsibility in providing food for the family. The fourth person may enjoy the socialization centered on gardening (as a common interest among friends). The fifth person possibly enjoys researching, planning, and ordering the plants more than the physical activity. A sixth person feeling down may be stimulated by planting, caring for a plant and transferring it outdoors.

Outcomes for individuals may or may not match the goals and objectives established for an activity or program. This is the diversity of programming. Individual needs, desires and experience before, during and after an activity all affect the final outcome of participation. A person who looks forward to a ballgame may meet someone at the game whom he/she has not seen in a long time and learn that the person has recently lost a relative and needs to talk. The focus of conversation is then on the friend's loss. The person feels saddened by the friend's loss, yet satisfied that he/she could be at the ballgame to listen. The friend became more important than the ballgame.

Programming outcomes can be empowerment, maintenance and/or supportive.

Empowerment

A participant feels empowered when he/she has had an opportunity to make choices, take responsibility and or express him/herself and uses the abilities that still remain, the wellness model.

Choices can include determining the type of activities and programs in which one wishes to participate. Given an opportunity to participate in individual, one-to-one and group activities, the person decides which he/she prefers.

Caring for plants, assisting in leading an activity, being an officer of resident council, being an active participant on the newspaper committee, and being a part of the welcoming committee are examples of taking responsibility.

Self-expression is demonstrated through participation in a wide variety of activities including arts, crafts, needlework, cooking/baking, music, poetry, writing, movement, dance, gardening, life review, discussions, reminiscing, support groups, and expressive therapies (art therapy, dance/movement therapy, drama therapy, and poetry therapy lead by qualified therapists).

Maintenance

Through participation in a variety of activities a person can maintain his/her cognitive, physical, emotional and social health.

Cognitive health is enhanced through mentally stimulating activities such as discussions, reminiscing, reading, studying, writing, math, word games, problem solving, puzzles, games involving strategy, memory, recall, reality orientation, etc.

Physical health is fostered through exercise, participation in sports or adapted sports (basketball, balloon badminton, bowling, bean bag toss, horseshoes, and shuffleboard), walking, yoga, relaxation exercises (deep breathing, progressive deep-muscle relaxation, and imagery), water exercise, dance and/or movement. Following diets and getting the proper nutrition affects physical health as well as cognitive, emotional and social health.

Emotional health is nurtured through self-expression, opportunities to help (people, causes, and community events/celebrations), receiving positive feedback from others, opportunities to succeed, celebrations and being recognized as well as involvement in spiritual/religious activities.

Social health can be promoted through personal interactions and involvement in social activities including family gatherings, visiting, birthday/holiday/cultural/seasonal celebrations, parties, picnics, socials, special events and involvement in the community.

Supportive

A person can feel supported from participating in activities that provide stimulation or solace (comfort). Specialized programs for residents with low-cognitive-functioning abilities provide stimulation for those who cannot independently provide their own stimulation. One feels supported when he/she has opportunities to express fears, concerns, disappointment, anger, etc. with a supportive person and in a supportive environment. A person who is dying feels supported in just having someone with him/her, hearing a prayer, having uninterrupted time to express feelings, share experiences and review life.

Involvement in activities produces different outcomes for different people. A person may experience an immediate as well as a long-term outcome from participation in an activity. Outcomes may be simultaneous. A person who is feeling down may have a change of mood after an activity professional plays his/her favorite piece of music. The outcomes are a change in mood and feeling supported by the activity professional.

The real outcome of participation in an activity is determined by the person experiencing the activity—not the professional or volunteer who provided the activity. Activity professionals must be observant and listen to residents talk about their experiences and feelings to begin to understand the complexity of individual outcomes from participation in activities.

Scope of Program
"Too much or too little"

The scope of a program identifies the diversity of the program. It relates to the purpose, philosophy, goals and objectives of the activity program. It is based on the assessment of individual residents and their changing needs, interests, preferences, former lifestyles, abilities, limitations and length of stay. A scope of program can be developed utilizing a categorical listing of activities that are presently available. The scope can list individual, one-to-one and group activities separately or collectively. In a collective list there is no distinction between an activity being provided for an individual or group. The method of service delivery needed for individual participants would determine how the activity is implemented.

COGNITIVE

Book Reviews	*Courses*	*Trivia*	*Spelling*
Current Events	*Demonstrations*	*Entertainment*	*Wheel of Fort.....*
Discussions	*Health Fairs*	*Famous People*	*Word Scramble*
Demonstrations	*Leisure Education*	*Geography*	Life Review
Education	*Community*	*States & Capitals*	Poetry
Adult Education	*Reintegration*	*History*	Puzzles
Classes	*Group*	*Presidents*	Crossword
Courses	Foreign Language	*Historical Events*	Jigsaw
Correspondence	Games	*Math*	Pull-Apart
Courses	*Game Book*	*Science*	Word-Search
Elder Hostel	*Guessing Games*	Word Games	Reminiscing
Instructional Videos	*Group Games*	*Alphabet*	Sensory and Stimulation
Lectures	*Math Games*	*Associations*	Slide Program
Workshops	*Mystery Games*	*Hangman*	Story-Time
Health Education	*Pencil Games*	*Make-a-Word*	Video
Classes	*Price Is Right*		

COMMUNITY

Community Events	Geographical Areas	Movies	Rides
Celebrations	*Beach*	Museums	Senior Center
Cultural	*Lake*	Nature Walk/Hike	Service
Holiday	*Ocean*	Picnic	Group Meetings
Parades	*Mountains*	Race Track	Shopping
Political Events	Library	Religious Services	Sporting Events
Dining Out	Inter-agency/facility	*Church Services*	Swimming
Fishing	events	*Mass*	Trips and Tours
		Sabbath Services	

CREATIVE

Art	Crafts	Food-Related Act.	Needlework
Ceramics	Creative Writing	*Baking*	Poetry
Coloring	Dance/Movement	*Cooking*	Pottery
	Drawing	*Food Preparation*	

EXPRESSIVE

Art	Discussion	Music	Resident Council
Crafts	Drama	*Listening*	Res. Planning Mtg.
Creative Writing	Gardening	*Playing Instrument*	Res. Right Bingo
Dance	Life-Review	Pets	Sing
	Men's Group	Poetry	Women's Group
		Reminiscing	

GROOMING

Hair Care	Nail Care	Make Up Demonstration

INTERGENERATIONAL			
Adopt-a-Grandparent	*East-Egg Hunt*	Journal Exchange	Outings
Audio-Tape Exchange	*Halloween Trick-or-*	Living History	Student Community
Celebrations	*Treat*	Parties	Service
Holiday	Community Events	Pen Pals	Student Internships
Christmas Carolers	Family Events		

PHYSICAL			
Ball Toss	Breathing Exercise	Darts	Nerf-Ball Toss
Balloon Badminton	*Blowing*	Exercise	Parachute
Balloon Bop	*Bubbles*	Fishing	Ring Toss
Balloon Toss	*Kazoo*	Golf	ROM Dance
Basketball	*Pinwheel*	Hockey	Shuffleboard
Bean-Bag Toss	*Deep Breathing*	Horseshoes	Swimming
Bocci	Bumper Pool	Kickball	Volleyball
Bowling	Dancing	Music and Movement	Walking/wheeling

SOCIAL			
Billiards	Nat'l Grandparents	Chess	Intergenerational
Cards	Day	Monopoly	Programs
Bridge	Nat'l. Nursing Home	Casino	Inter-Agency/Facility
500	Week	Dice Games	Programs
Euchre	Older Americans	Horse-racing	Parties
Hearts	Month	Hot Potato	Picnics
Poker	Seasonal	Lucky	Socials
Rummy	Special Events	Pennies-in-the-	Ice Cream
Uno	Games	Pot	Coffee
Celebrations	Bingo	Tic-Tac-Toe	
Birthday	Board Games	Video	
Holiday	Checkers	Nintendo	

SPIRITUAL/RELIGIOUS			
Bible Study/Story	Communion	Meditation	Religious Celebrations
Church	Mass	Prayer Service	Rosary
Clergy Visits			Sabbath Services

THERAPEUTIC			
Animal	Dance Therapy	Life Review	Stress Management
Companionship	Drama Therapy	Music Therapy	Support Groups
Art Therapy	Expressive Group	New Resident	Therapeutic
Community	Group Therapy	Orientation Group	Recreation
Reintegration	Horticultural Therapy	Poetry Therapy	
	Leisure Education		

WORK/SERVICE			
Bird-Feeders	Community Service	Helping Others	Officer of Resident
Clean activity sup-	Projects	(Individual)	Council or
plies and equipment	Crafts for Bazaar	Make Holiday	Committee
		Decorations	Volunteer

Models of Programming

"Models of programming change as needs change."

Models of programming have changed from a medical model in health care settings and a social or recreation model in community-based settings to a variety of models in both types of settings. The model used for programming is dependent upon several factors:

1. Purpose of the Agency or Institution
2. Philosophy of Care and Services
3. Operational Model of Agency or Institution
4. Regulatory Requirements:
   A. Federal, State, City
   B. JCAHO (Joint Commission of Accreditation of Healthcare Organizations)
   C. CARF (Commission on Accreditation of Rehabilitation Facilities)
5. Participants/Residents
   A. Age
   B. Needs, Interests, Preferences of Participants/Residents
   C. Abilities and Limitations (Cognitive, Physical, Emotional, Social) of Participants/Residents
   D. Length of stay in a health care or other institutional setting or frequency of services in a community based program
6. Staffing:
   A. Qualifications
   B. Number
   C. Days and Hours
   D. Roles and Responsibilities
      1. Departmental
      2. Interdisciplinary
      3. Transdisciplinary
7. Volunteers
8. Funding Sources
9. Budget
10. Space
    A. Indoor
    B. Outdoor
11. Other

Models

"Today's model may not work tomorrow"

A model provides a framework for care and services. A facility or community-based program may have one specific model of programming or multiple models of programming. As needs of participants/residents change so do the models of programming. Activity professionals need to be familiar with different models of programming and recommend changes in the models to provide quality care and services. Models can be implemented in their purest form or can be adapted.

Medical Model

The medical model is based on physician prescription or referral. The prescription can be for an evaluation and treatment or a referral to a special program, group or activity. In rehabilitation setting a physician could order a prescription for therapeutic recreation evaluation and treatment by a recreation therapist. A physician could refer a patient to a specific treatment program or therapy such as stress management, leisure counseling, art therapy, music therapy, dance/movement therapy, drama therapy, horticulture therapy and recreation therapy.

In long-term-care, ancillary orders include participation in activities and therapeutic work activities. Orders may be for a specific evaluation or program. The orders for activities may be general or specific in nature.

An order such as "May participate in activities program per preference/choice and as tolerated. Limitations: _____" is a general order allowing the patient to participate in whatever activity is of interest to the patient. The limitations, if any, would be specific to the patient, e.g., no bending, no alcoholic beverages, etc.

Examples of specific orders would be:

- *"Evaluate for meaningful work-type activity"*
- *"May participate in work-type activity of own choice and frequency"*
- *"Level IV Exercise Program"*

- *"Outings per choice"*
- *"Diabetic Education and Support Group"*
- *"Relaxation Group"*
- *"Expressive Group"*
- *"Art Therapy"*

Orders could be for a specific adaptive device for activities. The order could be through an occupational therapist or an activity professional. The way an order is written may be dependent upon whether there is specific reimbursement for the item.

Wellness Model

The focus of a wellness model of programming is on promoting and maintaining good health and a healthy lifestyle. Emphasis is on taking personal responsibility for one's health/wellness. Through education, training and self-determination a person is consciously aware of his/her own body. Steps are taken to improve or maintain physical, mental, emotional and social health.

Health and wellness classes offer opportunities to learn and evaluate one's health/wellness. Medical screening and evaluation provide a baseline from which an individualized wellness program can be developed. Screening can include:

1. Vision
2. Hearing
3. Blood Pressure
4. Heart Rate
5. Respiration
6. Urinalysis
7. Cholesterol
8. Triglycerides
9. Oral/Dental
10. Cancer
11. Blood Sugar
12. Electrolytes
13. Skin
14. Mobility
15. Range of Motion
16. Nutrition
17. Stress
18. Mental Health

A physical would include a medical examination, tests and screenings. Findings are discussed with the physician with recommendations for improving or maintaining health and a healthy lifestyle. This would include diet, nutrition, weight-control, exercise, activity, rest/sleep, stress management, immunizations and lifestyle.

Emotional health is a part of a wellness program. Good self-esteem and self-worth are important. Being assertive, protecting one's rights, having positive self-regard, and respecting others are all a part of mental health. Being loved, loving others, good interpersonal relationships with family, friends, peers, and socialization all affect one's mental/emotional health.

A wellness program can include opportunities for a person to assess his/her assertiveness, self-esteem, communication, relationships and stress management. Programming can include training, support groups, counseling, expressive therapy groups (art therapy, music therapy, dance/movement therapy, drama therapy, horticulture therapy poetry therapy, etc.), coping techniques, and opportunities for socialization.

Stress affects a person physically, mentally, emotionally and socially. Stress management includes diet, nutrition, weight control, exercise, activity, relaxation techniques (massage, meditation, visualization, deep breathing, deep muscle relaxation, yoga, olfactory stimulation, environmental and relaxation music, etc.), rest/sleep, and having a support system. Stress management is individualized.

Holistic Model

A holistic model is an integrated mind/ body/spirit approach to healthy living. It encompasses the wellness model with one added dimension—spiritual well being. A holistic model may be spiritual in nature with all entities centering on spirituality. It can also be an integrated model with all aspects being equally important.

In a religious-sponsored holistic program a member of the clergy would be involved in the spiritual aspects of the program. The clergy could focus on a specific religious denominational approach or a non-denominational approach to spirituality (reading and discussing scripture, inspirational reading, prayer, meditation, listening to religious/inspirational music and/or tapes, etc.). In a non-religious holistic approach, spirituality may or may not include prayer. The focus may be on meditating, centering, reading poetry and/or inspirational readings, listening to music, helping others, etc.

Restorative Model

A restorative model of programming focuses on restoring functional abilities (physical, mental, emotional and social). Emphasis is on structured programs provided by trained, qualified professionals. Programming may be interdisciplinary (two or more disciplines) working on the same goal through different approaches/modalities, or transdiciplinary (two or more disciplines) working in collaboration with a resident to reach a goal.

Interdisciplinary Approach

An interdisciplinary approach for a person to regain physical functioning may include physical therapy, occupational therapy, speech therapy, restorative nursing, social service and activities. Each discipline provides different treatment, care and services with a specified ultimate goal of improved function, i.e., mobility, independent ADL's and instrumental activities of daily living (IADL's, leisure activity, coping, etc. Instrumental activities of daily living (IADL's) include cooking, cleaning, laundry, reading, writing, telephoning, managing money, shopping, managing medication, driving, using public transportation, traveling out of town, climbing stairs, walking outdoors, working outside the home (lawn care, gardening, shoveling snow), paid employment and volunteer work.

Transdisciplinary Approach

In a transdisciplinary approach an activity is developed and co-lead by two or more different disciplines, such as meal preparation in a rehabilitation setting. An occupational therapist and a recreation therapist or activity professional would develop and co-lead the group. Roles and responsibilities of the co-leaders are well defined. In the absence of one the other leads the group. Criteria are established for patient/resident referral to the group, participation in the group and termination from the group.

Assessment

Standardized assessments are used to determine function and needs. These assessments would be administered by trained professionals. Standardized assessments are used for referring a resident to a specific therapeutic group or as a means of further assessment within a group. In a leisure education group, a recreation therapist may use the "Leisure Scope" developed by Leisure Dynamics for individual participants to identify their leisure interests and feelings.

Referral

Referral of a resident to a reality-orientation group would be based on some type of cognitive assessment such as the Mental Status Questionnaire (MSQ), the Short Portable Mental Status Questionnaire (SPMSQ), the Philadelphia Geriatric Mental Status Questionnaire, etc. Referral to an expressive group, group therapy, a support group, or a remotivation group would be based on the Beck Depression Scale, the Geriatric Depression Scale or another standardized assessment.

Social Model

The primary focus of the social model is socialization—being with others, and interaction among and between participants. Social involvement is individualized. One person may feel comfortable and content being around but not necessarily interacting with other people. Another person feels content with one-to-one interaction, whereas others may prefer multiple interactions. A variety of physical, cognitive and social activities provide opportunities for socialization. Activities can be cooperative or competitive (sports, cards, chess, checkers, other games, arts/crafts, poetry, creative-writing contests, music/singing contests, etc.). Travel, trips, tours, dining out, and involvement in senior centers and community organization and events provide opportunities to be involved and to interact with others to the extent one desires. Parties, picnics and birthday/ holiday/seasonal celebrations are natural activities for bringing people together. Interest and participation in specific activities provide an opportunity to meet and get to know others with the same interest. Friendships are often formed through having the same interests and involvement in specific activities. The interest and/or the activity are the catalyst for bringing people together. The type and amount of socialization one prefers and seeks is individualized.

Recreation Model

The recreation model includes fun, enjoyment, and relaxation—alone, or with others (socialization). Participation is intrinsically rewarding—a feeling of satisfaction and well-being. Recreation participation is non-obligatory. Interest and involvement are voluntary and individualized.

Attitude, knowledge, ability, skills, interest and time all affect one's perception of an activity being recreational. Learning a new sport may not be fun or enjoyable at first. However, once one achieves a certain skill level it can meet the individual's criteria of being a recreational pursuit. First a person must learn to read and then be exposed to different types of reading material before he/she can identify a preference for leisure reading.

Leisure values, attitudes, skills and abilities are developed over time from early childhood through older adulthood. In retirement, a person's former paid work time is now leisure time. Homemaking tasks are often lessened because of changes in family responsibility; thus, there is more leisure time.

The way a person utilized his/her leisure time after retirement will have a bearing on how he/she perceives leisure and activity time in an institutional setting (assisted-living, nursing home). Health, abilities, limitations and the person's perception of self will also affect the person's attitude and interest in leisure-time activities alone or with others (one-to-one and groups).

A senior citizen center may refer to its broad scope of programming as leisure or recreational with an emphasis on socialization, as well as having a wellness program incorporated. An assisted-living facility may refer to the evening and weekend activities (other than religious services) as a leisure or recreation program. Emphasis may be on self-directed activities including group activities lead by residents. A rehabilitation center may also refer to evening and weekend programming as leisure or recreation program as there is free choice to participate. The program provides opportunities to participate in activities related to former interests/lifestyle and/or to try new ones.

Therapeutic Recreation Model

Therapeutic recreation specialists usually follow one of two models. Therapeutic recreation following the ATRA definition is used for treatment and recreation. In this model leisure education is a part of treatment.

ATRA *(American Therapeutic Recreation Association)* states:

> "Therapeutic Recreation is the provision of treatment services and the provision of recreation services to persons with illnesses or disabling conditions. The primary purposes of treatment services which are often referred to as recreational therapy are to restore, remediate or rehabilitate in order to improve functioning and independence as well as to reduce or eliminate the effects of illness or disability. The primary purpose of recreation services is to provide recreation resources and opportunities in order to improve health and well-being. Therapeutic recreation is provided by professionals who are trained and certified, registered and/or licensed to provide therapeutic recreation." (ATRA, 1987)

In the leisure ability model—a continuum model developed by Peterson and Gunn—therapeutic recreation is the provision of treatment, leisure education and recreation services. Depending upon the setting and the needs of the clients, a program could offer all three services or just one or two of the services.

Educational Model

Learning is the focus of an educational model of programming. Adult education classes; continuing education programs for older adults sponsored by community organizations, health-care facilities, colleges and universities and Elderhostels are examples of community-based educational opportunities. Some local organizations including health-care, colleges and universities offer educational programs at retirement centers. Educational opportunities are offered in assisted-living facilities and nursing homes. Staff from the facilities or outside speakers provides the training. Educational programs can be anything that interests participants: crafts, sports, politics, retirement, finances, health, wellness, etc.

Long-Term Care

Models of programming in long-term-care facilities are eclectic. The model selected is based on an individualized assessment of each resident; cultural and religious beliefs and practices of individuals, the facility and/or community; NAAP Standards of Practice; federal regulations, i.e., Residents' Rights, Resident Assessment, Resident Behavior and Facility Practices, Quality of Life, Quality of Care, etc.; state and city regulations if they are different from the federal regulations; voluntary regulatory agencies (Joint Commission of Accreditation of Healthcare Organizations, Commission on Accreditation of

Rehabilitation Facilities) as well as other factors specific to the facility, geographical location and/or season.

Wellness/Holistic Model

A wellness model coincides with the OBRA Regulation, 483.15 Quality of Life, and Tag # F248: "The facility must provide for an ongoing program of activities designed to meet, in accordance with the comprehensive assessment, the interests and the physical, mental, and psychosocial well-being of each resident." Through a wide variety of activities adapted to meet the functional ability of residents, the activities program promotes wellness. Religious and spiritual activities add spiritual aspects to mind and body activities thus fostering a holistic program.

Residents are provided choices, have input into programming, and are empowered to function at their highest level of physical, mental and psychosocial well-being. The focus of programming is on improvement, enhancement or maintenance of wellness and spirit. The individual who does not value the spiritual aspect of life can still benefit from other activities that promote wellness.

Health and Activity

Physical Health is promoted through exercise, walking, participation in sports or adapted sports, relaxation techniques and gardening. A feeling of well-being is experienced with the release of endorphins during aerobic exercise. Exercise tones muscles and increases or maintains range of motion. Deep breathing increases lung capacity and relaxes the body. Metabolic rate is increased, thus burning calories and controlling weight.

Mental Health is fostered through cognitive activities. Short-term memory is stimulated through discussions (current events), watching, listening and talking about the news, working on puzzles, involvement in games that require memory of previous moves/cards by opponents, talking on the telephone, visiting, reading, and conversation. Long-term memory is stimulated through reminiscing, life-review, word games, sensory stimulation, etc. Problem-solving and decision-making abilities are fostered through puzzles, needlework, cooking/baking, fund-raising activities, participation in resident council, and involvement in resident-planned activity meetings and committee work.

Reading ability is continued through reading regular or large-print materials. Comprehension is maintained through reading and/or listening to Talking Books, Radio Reading Service or listening to someone else read, as well as through conversations and discussions.

Writing letters, creative writing and participating in writing games utilize writing skills. Math skills are maintained through games, paying for admission fees and meals on outings, fund-raising activities, keeping score for activities, and utilizing money won at activities, e.g., bingo, horse-racing. Educational programs provide opportunities to learn and continue growing.

Emotional Health is enhanced through expression of feelings in discussion groups, expressive groups/therapies (art therapy, music therapy, dance/movement therapy, drama therapy, horticulture therapy, poetry therapy), creative writing, conversations and reminiscing. Practicing stress management techniques reduces tension and anxiety, and fosters a positive attitude and relaxation. Enjoyable experiences, being recognized, feeling that one belongs, opportunities to share knowledge, abilities, skills and experiences all foster emotional health. Intergenerational activities; opportunities to hold, pet and talk to an animal; making new friends; creative experiences; feeding and watching birds; and going for a ride to see the countryside, a lake, mountains and/or the ocean provide something to which to look forward, and provide a sense of enjoyment, contentment and/or renewed interest. Humor programs stimulate laughter, cognition and socialization. Distress is forgotten and new energy is created. Participating in volunteer/service-type activities fosters the feeling of self-worth. Feeling empowered focuses on abilities versus limitations and increases self-esteem.

Social Health is promoted through one-to-one and group activities. Talking on the telephone keeps a person connected to family, friends and the community. Conversations, discussions and sharing involve talking, listening and decreased self-centeredness. Parties, picnics, socials, outings, group games, singing, and entertainment bring people together—an opportunity to share, laugh, have fun and reminisce. Celebrations (birthday, cultural, holiday, seasonal, community) and special events are a means of preserving interest in individual, family, community and cultural activities.

Opportunities for competition meet the competitive drive. Through cooperative activities (resident newsletter, making items for the bazaar, sing-a-longs, rhythm bands, committee work) attention is focused on something other than oneself. A feeling of achievement and mastery are heightened.

Spiritual Health is nourished through participation in individual, one-to-one and group meditation, prayer, spiritual reading and singing, or listening to hymns. Participating in religious services or watching them on TV provides a connection with others.

Reading or listening to the Bible on Talking Books or personally being read or religious/inspirational material provides a means of centering. Saying specific prayers, i.e., the Lord's Prayer, rosary, etc., stimulates long-term memory and feelings. Receiving communion fosters and renews an individual's inner spirit. Celebrating religious holidays continues the cultivation of the meaning of the holiday and provides a connection with others who celebrate the same event.

Seeing a beautiful sunrise or sunset, watching birds/animals, weather and changes of the season, sitting by a lake/ocean or under a tree, listening to music, viewing art and reading poetry, books, articles or inspirational material provide inner peace, joy and/or awe that is often indescribable.

Helping others personally or through specific tasks related to causes provides an inner feeling of peace and contentment. Making a difference in the lives of others is personally rewarding.

Other Models and Systems

Special-Care Units

Under the umbrella of a wellness/holistic model, other models may also be utilized. Special-care units are increasingly using a milieu program model. Direct care staff assigned to the unit is responsible for ADL's and activities (individual, one-to-one and small groups). Certified nursing assistants are trained to plan, develop, conduct and evaluate activities. The activity professional completes activity assessments, develops care plans, writes progress notes, provides staff training, supervises the provision of activities in coordination with the unit director, and is a resource person for the unit.

The program emphasis is on wellness/wholeness within a therapeutic environment. The service is delivered by trained, certified nursing assistants with or without additional programs provided by activity professionals. The activity professional and the unit director evaluate the program based on the outcome of individual residents and input from the direct-care staff providing the program (individual, one-to-one and group activities).

Specialized Program

Specialized programs for residents with low-cognitive-functioning abilities are designed to meet the various levels of cognitive functioning which affect physical, emotional and social functioning.

Using a level system, participants have an opportunity to successfully participate at their highest level of functioning. A person at Level IV may still be able to participate in integrated activities with residents who have high-cognitive functioning abilities (entertainment, sing-a-long, bingo, etc.). A person at Level I is totally dependent upon staff for stimulation and socialization. At this level the person is in the last phase of the end stage of Alzheimer's disease.

Referral Program

Referral programs can include specific activities, therapeutic groups and specific therapies. Activity referral groups are small groups focusing on a specific activity. Residents throughout the facility are referred to the group primarily because of interest and functional ability to participate. Participation is voluntary. Activity referral groups could include a pottery group, computer-training group, photography group, health-education groups (diabetic education, heart disease education, Parkinson's, stroke, etc.).

Activities and Therapeutic Recreation Model

A long-term-care facility with a variety of specialty services may have an activities model and a therapeutic recreation model of programming focusing on wellness. In such a facility, activity professionals may be responsible for activities programming for the skilled-nursing care unit (with long- and short-term lengths of stay), nursing units and special care units, whereas a therapeutic recreation specialist would be responsible for therapeutic recreation for sub acute units, rehabilitation units, geropsychiatry units and outpatient services where the emphasis is on rehabilitation. The therapeutic recreation therapist would provide therapeutic recreation or recreation therapy (treatment) Recreation may be provided by the therapeutic recreation specialist and/or by activity professionals.

Hospitals

Short-Term Hospitalization

In short term hospital settings the program model varies depending upon the philosophy of care, daily census, training of staff, i.e., activity professional, therapeutic recreation specialist, staffing patterns, rehabilitation services (physical therapy, occupational therapy, speech therapy, psychiatry, etc.), specialty services within the hospital, i.e., sleep disorder unit, as well as space for activities and socialization.

Skilled Nursing Units

Skilled-nursing units in hospitals are under the same OBRA regulations as long-term-care facilities. Emphasis is on treatment with the ultimate goal of having a patient return home or to a facility in which he/she can function at his/her highest level.

Some residents will have very little time or energy for participation in activities because of therapy and/or educational schedules, being tired and preference to visit with families. A flexible wellness program model changes with the census. Weekly schedules of activities and services allow more flexibility than a monthly schedule that is used in long-term-care facilities.

Recreation therapy would be a part of the resident's therapy program. This could include a community integration program. The recreation therapist and occupational therapist may use a transdisciplinary approach to instrumental activities of daily living such as shopping, meal preparation, etc.

A social program may focus around meals with residents eating in the dining room and having some type of activity (physical, cognitive, creative, and expressive, etc.) immediately prior to or after the meal. Other social activities would include parties, celebrations (birthday, holiday, cultural, community, seasonal), socials and family activities, and cards and games.

The dining/activity room may be the hub for morning and afternoon activities (individual, one-to-one and small group). Program emphasis is on socialization and activity involvement. Residents who are able are assisted as necessary to the dining/activity room prior to and/or after therapy. A choice of activities is provided reading, listening to music with or without headphones, art, crafts, needlework, horticulture, puzzles (crossword, circle-a-word, jigsaw, mazes, pull apart puzzles, etc.), cards, table games, word games, pet visits, discussion, reminiscing, videos, conversation, etc. A choice of beverage and snack are provided. The activities offered are related to individual resident's interests. Because this is a fast-paced changing population, activities offered are constantly changing.

Religious and spiritual activities are usually provided by the chaplain, ministers, priests, and rabbi and/or volunteers.

Recreation focuses on individual, one-to-one and small-group activities. Resources are provided for in-room activities (individual and one-to-one and/or small family groups).

Educational programs may be a part of a specific treatment program or a referral program within the unit, or, may be conducted by another service in the hospital. A physician may refer a resident to a stress management program conducted by the cardiac rehabilitation program or the department of psychiatry.

Activity Analysis

"Activities can provide meaning"

Peterson* defines activity analysis as: "...a procedure for breaking down and examining an activity to find inherent characteristics that contributes to program objectives."

Participants must have a certain degree of ability to successfully participate in activities. If an activity is too complex or difficult, a person may not want to try or may give up trying. If an activity is not stimulating enough, a person may not get involved or may terminate involvement that had been started.

Activities need to be analyzed to determine what abilities and skills a participant must have to be successful in that activity. Completing analysis, the appropriateness of an activity can be determined (i.e. age, cognitive, physical, social, and emotional appropriateness). Adaptive techniques can be explored so that a participant can have a successful experience. If a person enjoys reading books, has the ability to comprehend, and is able to see print (regular or large), but is unable to physically hold a book, he or she could possibly continue to read independently by using a book-holder on a table and an adaptive mouthpiece for turning pages. The person may enjoy listening to a book being read on a Talking Book machine or cassette player, or listening to someone read to him or her personally.

In the activity assessment process, the activity professional determines a person's background: needs, interests, abilities, limitations and precautions (physical, cognitive, emotional, and social/interaction); activity involvement patterns; time available to participate in activities; and present/future desire to participate in activities. An individualized program plan, care plan or treatment plan is developed with the participant. It is then incorporated into the agency or organization's program plan.

Activity analysis assists in the selection of appropriate activities and interventions such as modifications and use of adaptive techniques and devices. Participants can potentially attain their goals when appropriate success-oriented interventions are utilized.

Activities are analyzed in relation to their physical (sensory motor), cognitive, and affective domains, and the social and interaction skills needed to do an activity successfully. The analysis is applied to the activity and not the participant. **Assessment of the participant** and **analysis of activities** assist the activity professional in providing success-oriented, meaningful activities and programs.

Modification and adaptations of an activity need to be considered related to the purpose of the activity for the participant. If the activity is for leisure/personal enjoyment, does the participant have the skills to participate independently or does he/she need assistance? If the goal is treatment/ rehabilitation in nature, will the activity assist in reaching or maintaining the goal? If the participant wants to learn an activity, what abilities are needed? Does the participant have abilities that can be built upon in learning an activity? Are modification or adaptive techniques and/or devices needed?

Activity analysis can be a very complex task. There are many variables to be considered under the physical, cognitive, and affective behavioral domains, as well as social/interaction skills.

In all programs, activity professional are being challenged to provide activities that meet the cognitive

needs, abilities and interests of participants. What type of memory does a person need, i.e. short-term, long-term or remote memory? Does the activity require the ability to recall information, make decisions, use abstract thinking, and/or use academic skills (reading, writing, and/or math)? How long does the person have to be able to remain attentive or concentrate? Is the ability to strategize and/or verbalize needed? Does the activity require knowledge of language? It is not sufficient to analyze just the cognitive domain. Most activities require other physical, emotional and social/ interactive skills.

A physical activity such as bowling requires cognitive abilities to concentrate, understand the game, know the rules, comprehend scoring/winning/losing, and understand possible tournament play. Physically one has to have eye/hand coordination and the ability to pick up and throw a bowling ball (underhand) weighing 6-16 pounds, stand erect, walk, bend, and transfer weight to one leg/foot. A person must be able to distinguish placement of the bowling ball related to the set-up of the pins and boundaries of the bowling alley, e.g., gutters. Emotionally one has to be able to control impulses, accept winning and losing during competitive play, be a team member and support the team. Socially the game may be played with people of the same or opposite sex and with the same or different age group(s). One must be willing to wait to take a turn, be a cooperative member of a team, and compete with other teams in a socially acceptable manner. If a person does not have these or other needed skills, the activity professional may need to teach specific skills/adaptations or discuss expected appropriate behavior.

Many activities require interaction with others. A person can have specific cognitive and physical skills but may not have the needed social/interactive skills to be successful in doing an activity that involves other people. Interaction skills are hierarchical. If a person cannot get along with other people, it would be difficult for the person to function as a team player. A person who is timid or shy may feel very uncomfortable in any game where he/she becomes an antagonist or an "it", e.g., card game. The hierarchy of interaction skills includes the following interactions, developed by Elliott M. Avedon:*

♦ An **intra-individual** interaction is an activity such as daydreaming or exercising by oneself without the use of objects (equipment, music, video, etc.). The activity takes place in the mind of the individual, i.e. daydreaming, or involves the mind and part(s) of the body (exercise). It does not require involvement with another person or object.

- **Extra-individual** interaction involves an object but not another person. Reading a book, needlework, gardening, painting, and playing an instrument all require an object, i.e. book, needlework, etc., but not another person. These activities are usually referred to as individual activities.

- An **aggregate** is a parallel group. Each person is involved with an object, i.e. crafts, task groups, etc., while in the company of other people but without interaction with others. Everyone does his/her own thing in the same room and persons do not interact with one another.

- **Inter-individual** interaction is competitive interaction between two people. Playing checkers is one example. Each person is competing to win the game.

- **Unilateral** interaction is competition between three or more people, with one person being an antagonist. In the competition, one becomes "it", e.g., card games and board games.

- **Multilateral** interaction is also competition between three or more people, but with no one person being an antagonist, e.g., card games such as poker, euchre and hearts.

- In an **intragroup**, members cooperate in working toward a mutual goal, e.g., playing in a symphony, singing in a group, working on a service project, etc.

Members have positive feelings for one another and try to resolve conflict; thus, there is give-and-take in the group. A team, e.g., baseball team, is an example of an intragroup. All team members have to work and play together to be effective.

- **Intergroup** interaction is competition between two intragroups. Two teams (intragroups) compete against one another, e.g., baseball, hockey, football, basketball.

The interaction skills are learned through participating in a variety of activities from early childhood. If a person is unable to participate in an aggregate (parallel group),

In analyzing activities, the interaction skills are important to consider in terms of skills needed to participate in an activity; however, an individual's participation preferences for interaction must also be considered. A person who is capable of participating in activities involving interaction with others, but does not want to, will either not participate or will participate only for the sake of the leader. Thus, not wanting to participate can affect his/her attitude toward participation and affect the group as a whole.

To facilitate analyzing activities, a sample checklist is being provided. It is suggested that all completed checklists be stored in a binder for future reference.

To complete the checklist, check the appropriate box for each of the skills needed to successfully participate in the activity. As appropriate, identify specific modification and/or adaptive techniques or devices that could be considered.

Summary

Activities programming is resident centered. The program is a based on accurate individual activity .assessment. The new federal interpretive guidelines for Activities emphasizes assessment, individualized care planning and a resident centered program

Group activities can be small or large. There are several types of groups, e.g., Independent groups, parallel, Intra-group, and Inter-group. Each group requires a different level of skills.

In long-term care, programs can include: Centralized, Decentralized, Referral, Specialized, Structured, Unstructured, Spontaneous Indoor and Outdoor.

Activities programs are based on the needs, interests, preferences, lifestyle, abilities and limitations of participants. The philosophy, goals, and objectives provide a frame of reference for programming.

Activity professionals need to collaborate with other health care professionals in designing, developing, implementing and evaluating activities programs for residents who have mental illness. A Trust relationship must be developed between the resident and activity professional. There are a variety of techniques and therapeutic groups that can be used successfully with residents with mental illness. Activity professionals need to be well-trained and needs to have another person, i.e. supervisor with whom he/she can process groups as well as personal and professional feelings.

Activity professionals need to assist residents in overcoming barriers to participation in activities. Adaptive devices, equipment and techniques can be used to meet residents' needs and interests; thus providing successful experiences

Most clients need both individual and group activity involvement to continue their former life style. Group activities provide an opportunity for a person to get to know peers and perhaps develop a friendship. The state of the art is to use behavioral terminology and not refer to clients/residents as being activity or passive in activities.

A philosophy, goals and objectives needs to be well thought out so that programming is successful Criteria needs to be developed for selection of grout members, determining the size of a group, establishing the setting for the group, and the duration of the group.

The activity professional needs to be an award of participants' emotional relationship between the participants and him/herself as well as between peers. Over time and with training, observation and mentoring, an activity professional will increase leading skills and knowing what leadership styles to use with specific groups.

Group management skills are learned over time also.

The activity professional establishes the therapeutic (physical and social) environment for small and large group activity as well as one-to one activities.

A participant needs to feel comfortable physically in the environment as well as socially.

The activity professional must be watchful of vulnerable participants and prevent negative experiences

The success of a group activity is individualized for participants. An activity professional's perception of success needs to be based on the goals and objectives for the group and actual individual and group outcomes

In long term care planning must consider participants different lengths of stay, whether or not residents with the same diagnosis are housed on the same unit, specialized units or are mixed with peers with multiple diagnosis.

Thinking about individual benefits of activities, assist in planning and developing individualized and group goals. Three or more people can participate in the same activity but the benefits will differ.

A Scope of Programming is developed over time. The scope of programming identifies the diversity of the activities program. There are different ways to develop the scope of program. Proving a copy of the Scope of program to peers and families assist them in understanding the breath and depth of the activities program.

With training, experience and mentoring, an activity professional can determines and implement a model for programming.

Activity analysis identifies the skills and abilities a person needs to successfully participate in an activity. Accurately assessing a resident and completing activity analysis related to his/her preferred activity assists in developing appropriate care plans and successful programming.

ACTIVITY ANALYSIS CHECKLIST

_____

Name of Activity

Direction: Check (√) the abilities and skills needed to successfully participate in the specific activity that is being analyzed. Write in recommended modifications of adaptations.

Physical Domain:	YES	NO	MODIFICATION/ADAPTATION

Body Part Involvement:

	YES	NO	
Sit	☐	☐	_____
Stand	☐	☐	_____
Lay	☐	☐	_____

Body part involvement:

Fingers:

Right Hand

	YES	NO	
Thumb	☐	☐	_____
2nd Finger	☐	☐	_____
3rd Finger	☐	☐	_____
4th Finger	☐	☐	_____
5th Finger	☐	☐	_____

Left Hand

	YES	NO	
Thumb	☐	☐	_____
2nd Finger	☐	☐	_____
3rd Finger	☐	☐	_____
4th Finger	☐	☐	_____
5th Finger	☐	☐	_____

Hands:

	YES	NO	
Right	☐	☐	_____
Left	☐	☐	_____

Wrists:

	YES	NO	
Right	☐	☐	_____
Left	☐	☐	_____

Arms:

	YES	NO	
Right	☐	☐	_____
Left	☐	☐	_____

Elbows:

	YES	NO	
Right	☐	☐	_____
Left	☐	☐	_____

Shoulders:

	YES	NO	
Right	☐	☐	_____
Left	☐	☐	_____

		YES	NO	MODIFICATION/ADAPTATION

Neck/Head

Range of Motion:

	YES	NO	MODIFICATION/ADAPTATION
Right Side	☐	☐	_____
Left Side	☐	☐	_____
Down	☐	☐	_____
Up	☐	☐	_____
Back	☐	☐	_____

	YES	NO	
Upper Torso	☐	☐	_____
Lower Torso	☐	☐	_____

Legs:

	YES	NO	
Right	☐	☐	_____
Left	☐	☐	_____

Hips:

	YES	NO	
Right	☐	☐	_____
Left	☐	☐	_____

Knees:

	YES	NO	
Right	☐	☐	_____
Left	☐	☐	_____

Ankles:

	YES	NO	
Right	☐	☐	_____
Left	☐	☐	_____

Feet:

	YES	NO	
Right	☐	☐	_____
Left	☐	☐	_____

Toes:

Right

	YES	NO	
Large Toe	☐	☐	_____
2nd Toe	☐	☐	_____
3rd Toe	☐	☐	_____
4th Toe	☐	☐	_____
5th Toe	☐	☐	_____

Left

	YES	NO	
Large Toe	☐	☐	_____
2nd Toe	☐	☐	_____
3rd Toe	☐	☐	_____
4th Toe	☐	☐	_____
5th Toe	☐	☐	_____

Required Movement:

	YES	NO	
Abduction (movement away from the body)	☐	☐	_____
Adduction (movement toward the body)	☐	☐	_____
Bending	☐	☐	_____

	YES	NO	MODIFICATION/ADAPTATION

Flexion/Extension (identify body part):

	YES	NO	MODIFICATION/ADAPTATION
_____	☐	☐	_____
_____	☐	☐	_____
_____	☐	☐	_____

Stretching:

	YES	NO	
Fingers	☐	☐	_____
Arms	☐	☐	_____

Twisting:

	YES	NO	
To the Right	☐	☐	_____
To the Left	☐	☐	_____

Grasping:

	YES	NO	
Small Item(s)	☐	☐	_____
Large Item(s)	☐	☐	_____
Light Item(s)	☐	☐	_____
Heavy Item(s)	☐	☐	_____
One Hand	☐	☐	_____
Two Hands	☐	☐	_____

Pushing: ☐   ☐   _____

Pulling: ☐   ☐   _____

Reaching:

	YES	NO	
Up	☐	☐	_____
Down	☐	☐	_____
To the Right	☐	☐	_____
To the Left	☐	☐	_____

Punching:
One Hand:

	YES	NO	
Right Hand	☐	☐	_____
Left Hand	☐	☐	_____
Two Hands	☐	☐	_____

Bouncing   ☐   ☐   _____

Catching:

	YES	NO	
Small Object(s)	☐	☐	_____
Large Object(s)	☐	☐	_____
Light Object(s)	☐	☐	_____
Heavy Object(s)	☐	☐	_____

Throwing: List Object(s)

	YES	NO	
_____	☐	☐	_____
_____	☐	☐	_____
_____	☐	☐	_____

Hitting: List Object(s):

	YES	NO	
_____	☐	☐	_____
_____	☐	☐	_____

	YES	NO	MODIFICATION/ADAPTATION
_____	☐	☐	_____
Kicking	☐	☐	_____
Walking	☐	☐	_____
Running	☐	☐	_____
Skipping	☐	☐	_____

Hopping:

	YES	NO	MODIFICATION/ADAPTATION
Right Foot	☐	☐	_____
Left Foot	☐	☐	_____

Sensory Abilities Needed:

	YES	NO	MODIFICATION/ADAPTATION
Sight	☐	☐	_____
Sound	☐	☐	_____
Smell	☐	☐	_____
Taste	☐	☐	_____
Touch	☐	☐	_____

Coordination:

	YES	NO	MODIFICATION/ADAPTATION
Eye/Hand	☐	☐	_____
Hand/Mouth	☐	☐	_____
Eye/Foot	☐	☐	_____

Energy:

	YES	NO	MODIFICATION/ADAPTATION
High	☐	☐	_____
Medium	☐	☐	_____
Low	☐	☐	_____

Endurance:

	YES	NO	MODIFICATION/ADAPTATION
Short Term	☐	☐	_____
Long Term	☐	☐	_____

Speed:

	YES	NO	MODIFICATION/ADAPTATION
Slow	☐	☐	_____
Medium	☐	☐	_____
Fast	☐	☐	_____

	YES	NO	MODIFICATION/ADAPTATION
Flexibility:	☐	☐	_____
Agility:	☐	☐	_____

COGNITIVE DOMAIN: YES   NO   MODIFICATION/ADAPTATION

Memory Needed:

	YES	NO	MODIFICATION/ADAPTATION
Short Term	☐	☐	_____
Long Term	☐	☐	_____
Remote	☐	☐	_____

Ability to:

	YES	NO	MODIFICATION/ADAPTATION
Recognize	☐	☐	_____
Recall	☐	☐	_____
Concentrate:			
__Minutes __Hours	☐	☐	_____

Remain attentive:

	YES	NO	MODIFICATION/ADAPTATION
__Minutes __Hours	☐	☐	_____

	YES	NO	MODIFICATION/ADAPTATION

Comprehend

	YES	NO	MODIFICATION/ADAPTATION
Interpret	☐	☐	_____
Summarize	☐	☐	_____
Follow instructions	☐	☐	_____
Attend to details	☐	☐	_____
Make decisions	☐	☐	_____
Think abstractly	☐	☐	_____
Problem solve	☐	☐	_____
Organize	☐	☐	_____
Sequence	☐	☐	_____
Analyze	☐	☐	_____
Strategize	☐	☐	_____
Verbalize	☐	☐	_____

Use language:

	YES	NO	MODIFICATION/ADAPTATION
(type: _____)	☐	☐	_____
Spell	☐	☐	_____
Read	☐	☐	_____
Write	☐	☐	_____

Do Math:

	YES	NO	MODIFICATION/ADAPTATION
Addition	☐	☐	_____
Subtraction	☐	☐	_____
Multiplication	☐	☐	_____
Division	☐	☐	_____
Percentage	☐	☐	_____
Higher Mathematics:	☐	☐	_____
Use application (utilities materials)	☐	☐	_____
Synthesize (create new from old elements)	☐	☐	_____

Evaluations;

	YES	NO	MODIFICATION/ADAPTATION
Use set criteria to make decisions (e.g. rules for games)	☐	☐	_____
Learn to do new things	☐	☐	_____

Intellectual skills needed:

	YES	NO	MODIFICATION/ADAPTATION
_____	☐	☐	_____
_____	☐	☐	_____
_____	☐	☐	_____

Identification of:

	YES	NO	MODIFICATION/ADAPTATION
Objects	☐	☐	_____
Symbols	☐	☐	_____
Parts	☐	☐	_____
Person	☐	☐	_____

Understanding of:

Direction

	YES	NO	MODIFICATION/ADAPTATION
Up	☐	☐	_____
Down	☐	☐	_____
Right	☐	☐	_____
Left	☐	☐	_____
Diagonal	☐	☐	_____

	YES	NO	
Forward	☐	☐	_____
Backward	☐	☐	_____
Across	☐	☐	_____
Spatial Awareness	☐	☐	_____

AFFECTIVE DOMAIN:	YES	NO	MODIFICATION/ADAPTATION

Activity is consistent with participant's value
System related to:

	YES	NO	
Culture	☐	☐	_____
Family	☐	☐	_____
Money	☐	☐	_____
Religion	☐	☐	_____
Property	☐	☐	_____
Health	☐	☐	_____
Leisure	☐	☐	_____

Ability to:

	YES	NO	
Express self verbally	☐	☐	_____
Express self non-verbally	☐	☐	_____
Accept winning	☐	☐	_____
Accept losing	☐	☐	_____
Control impulses	☐	☐	_____
Be non-assaultive:			
Physically	☐	☐	_____
Verbally	☐	☐	_____
Cope with new situations	☐	☐	_____
Be creative	☐	☐	_____
Share	☐	☐	_____
Be a team member	☐	☐	_____
Listen	☐	☐	_____
Give affection	☐	☐	_____
Receive affection	☐	☐	_____
Use democratic process	☐	☐	_____
Help others	☐	☐	_____
Have fun	☐	☐	_____

Awareness of:

	YES	NO	
Self	☐	☐	_____
Others	☐	☐	_____
Feelings:			
Self	☐	☐	_____
Other	☐	☐	_____
Moods	☐	☐	_____

Motivation:

	YES	NO	
Intrinsic	☐	☐	_____
Extrinsic	☐	☐	_____

Activity can evoke feelings of:

	YES	NO	
Joy	☐	☐	_____
Frustration	☐	☐	_____

Fear	☐	☐	_____
Anger	☐	☐	_____
Guilt	☐	☐	_____

Pain:

Physical	☐	☐	_____
Emotional	☐	☐	_____
Social	☐	☐	_____

SOCIAL SKILLS: YES NO MODIFICATION/ADAPTATION

Activity Requires:

Communication

Verbal	☐	☐	_____
Non-verbal	☐	☐	_____
Cooperation	☐	☐	_____
Competition	☐	☐	_____
Leader	☐	☐	_____
No leader	☐	☐	_____

Interaction with:

Opposite sex	☐	☐	_____
Same sex	☐	☐	_____
Peers	☐	☐	_____
Adults	☐	☐	_____
Adolescents	☐	☐	_____
Children	☐	☐	_____
(age:_____)			
Pre-schoolers	☐	☐	_____
Infants	☐	☐	_____
Animals	☐	☐	_____
(kind:_____)			

Physical contact:

Type(s)_____	☐	☐	_____

_____

Proximity to others:

Approximate amount	☐	☐	_____

Number of participants:

Individual	☐	☐	_____
One-to-One	☐	☐	_____
Small group	☐	☐	_____

Approximate number or range:____

Large group	☐	☐	_____

Approximate number or range:____

INTERACTIVE SKILLS

Intra-individual	☐	☐	_____
Extra-individual	☐	☐	_____
Aggregate	☐	☐	_____

Inter-individual:

Unilateral	☐	☐	_____
Multilateral	☐	☐	_____
Intragroup	☐	☐	_____
Intergroup	☐	☐	_____

Chapter 11

Activity Services: System of Design, Development and Evaluation of Department Services

"Rich lives provide rich memories"

Program Design Is Based on Individual Strengths, Needs, Interests and Functional Ability

Activity programs should be designed around the facility or agency mission. Program in the broadest sense includes all of the activities that are planned for the resident/client. Participation is important whether active participation or passive. Developing a well-rounded program will be designed to consider the participant's strengths, needs, interests and functional abilities. The program is planned and structured to help residents/clients to experience personal meaningful therapeutic events or services. Activities can stimulate personal and group achievements using the current level of ability. Overall programs address a variety of needs among the residents/clients. Specific programs are designed to meet specific needs and interests of individuals or groups. The strength and functional ability of prospective attendees should be considered in planning a specific program, i.e., residents or clients who have limited attention span should not be brought to a lecture program. The scope of program planning should seek to provide spiritual, physical, intellectual, emotional, social elements with a cultural sensitivity.

Activity professionals will design the program to recognize the strengths, weakness, needs, interests and abilities of those they serve. Future programs may be modified depending upon the various needs and interests of the resident/client. Programs that do not achieve the desired goals should be deleted.

Accepted Clinical Practices

The activity professional follows the clinical practices and standards of practice set forth by professional associations.

Clinic practices address the individual assessments of the resident/client. Clinic assessment can identify the ability, the strengths and the limitations of the resident/client. These strengths and limitations need to be considered in planning a given program, i.e., Discussion programs are not appropriate for those who are mentally challenged. Clinic assessments that show low level of mental function need programs that are simple, i.e., pass a ball around the group.

The activity professional will recognize limited cognitive skills in some residents/clients, while others will have strong cognitive skills. The program will be planned for the level of function of persons being served. Residents/clients have different personal characteristics, life styles and preferences. Individual habits play into the response a given person will make to a certain program. Using the personal history and current condition can guide the activity professional to focus on the specific needs of the resident or client. Clinic information is important in planning whether individually or for a group. Strengths and weaknesses are always present factors that need to be considered. The resident/client is the reason for effective planning.

Professional Protocol
"Professionals need the rhythm of movement and rest"

A professional is one who is prepared through training, education and experience in an occupation, being prepared in that field and succeeding in fulfilling that role. Protocol can be defined as a proper and acceptable and correct way of carrying out a role. Activity professionals earn that title by education, training, job performance and successfully leading in an activity role. An activity professional's goal should be skillfully carried out by leading residents/clients in meaningful activities. Activity professionals will bridge the service design through implementing the activities. The task is to meet the needs of the resident/client on an ongoing basis. This means adjusting activities as the level of function changes for the resident/client. Some persons are hard to please, some will misinterpret what is said to them and some will be contrary to what every one plans. Yet, at the end of the day activity professionals who follow the facility or agency's protocol can say they have done their best. Out of shortfalls or mistakes activity professionals can grow and improve. Professionals who love people and enjoy working with them can be effective activity persons. Residents may be challenging, stimulating or troubled persons but all have special needs. Being an activity professional challenges one to be creative and innovative in working with residents/clients.

Policies and Procedures
"Structure in an organization is essential."

Activity department policies must be compatible with the facility or agency policies. The policies are to be consistent with the philosophy, mission and vision for the facility. Departmental policies and procedures are written policies outlining a structure or principles, plans and a course of action for the activity program. These policies guide the planning to deliver accurate care and services. Activity professionals will follow these policies. Policies are needed whether there is only one or several in the activity department. Policies show how the responsibilities are assigned. Each person on the team has a specific role to play to perform the planned care and services. Policies should be general guidelines that give the team members the direction in which the program is to be delivered. Meaningful activities can give residents/clients a reason to get out of bed and do something that is enjoyable, productive and fulfilling. Well-drafted policies give direction and purpose to the day. Activity professionals will respect and follow the adopted policies.

Policies

Policies are designed to meet recurring situations with a consistent pattern of behavior. Policies are broad written statements defining a course of action. They are guidelines for behavior; thus, they state what is to be done.

Policies are written according to an organization's established protocol. They can be written as combined documents with procedures, i.e., policy followed by the procedures, or as separate documents. Policies are not rigid. They can be changed when there is a change in operation, practice and/or regulations.

It is a standard of practice to date all policies, review them annually and update them as needed. Initialing or signing the dated policies may be a part of the organization's protocol.

Procedures

Procedures are derived from policies. They are systematic plans of action for implementing policies. They identify who, when, where, and/or how the policies are to be put into action.

The NAAP and NCCAP Standards of Practice and Codes of Ethics are an essential guide. They are found in Chapter 3.

How to Write Policies and Procedures

I. Policies

A. Determine the format that is to be used for writing all policies and procedures.

1. Determine the format for the heading/title: (a) Name of Facility, Name or Department and Title of Policy and Procedures, or (b) just the Name of the Department and Title or Policy and Procedures, or (c) just the Title of the Policy and Procedures.

2. Use paragraph format for writing policies.

   a. Keep paragraphs short and to the point.
   b. Use language and terms that are easily understood.
   c. Include the name of the policy in the first sentence of the policy statement.
      Example: Bingo shall be scheduled a minimum of one time per week.
   d. Use the legal term shall versus the words "should" or "will" to indicate the intent to implement the policy.

      *Example: An activity assessment **shall** be completed within _____ days of admission.*

      Outings **shall** be scheduled a minimum of two times per month.

II. Procedures

A. Determine the organizational style for writing procedures, particularly when writing activity-related procedures, e.g., Bible study, bowling, exercise, sensory group, singing, etc.

B. Use a step-by-step outline format.

C. Use "command" style—talk directly to the person reading the procedures.

*Example: **Announce** activity on the intercom five minutes before the activity is to start.*

D. Build each statement around a single point.

E. Express ideas in a positive manner.

F. Use terminology and vocabulary that is easily understood by whoever reads it.

G. Be concise and use short sentences.

H. Use correct spelling and grammar.

I. Punctuate carefully. Key words or phrases can be underlined, CAPITALIZED, placed in "quotation marks," or typed in **bold** print.

J. Involve other departments in the writing of policies and procedures that are related to their department. Outings, for example, are interrelated with dietary, nursing, social service, business (financial) and/or other departments.

K. Identify author(s) by signature(s) or initials and the date that the procedures were written in accordance with the facility's protocol.

Example: In the lower right corner of the page, type the initials of the writer and date, i.e., J.B., 2/11 or J.B., 2/15/11

III. Editing Policies and Procedures

A. Request another staff member to read a draft of policies and procedures as they are developed.

1. Ask the reviewer to state the policy and procedure in his/her own words.

2. Listen for the content of what is said. Is it what you intended to write? If not, what needs to be changed/clarified?

3. Request the reviewer to ask questions about the policy and procedure. Questions and answers can help clarify the intent of the document.

IV. Time Management

A. Prepare policies and procedures on a computer, and keep a backup disk.

B. Review the policy and procedures manual annually. Make changes as needed.

C. Add new policies and procedures, as needed, e.g., new regulations, new programs/services.

V. Activities Policies and Procedures

Manual

A. Place all policies and procedures in a loose-leaf book with a title page and table of contents for easy reference. Indicate on the title page the original dates and review/revision dates and signatures of department manager and administrator.

B. Submit policies and procedures manual to administrator for approval.

   1. Make changes per administrator's request.

   2. Resubmit for administrator's approval as needed.

C. Give administrator a copy of the final manual (original or duplicated copy).

D. Place a copy (original or photocopy) of the manual in the activity office.

E. Give other departments copies of **specific** policies and procedures as appropriate:

   1. *Dietary:* Food-related activities, e.g., birthday parties, celebrations [holiday, seasonal, special events, outings, etc.]

Utilization of dining/activity room and ordering food.

   2. *Maintenance:* Room arrangements, moving furniture/large equipment, repairs, safety, other.

   3. *Medical Records:* Assessments (activity assessment and MDS) care plans, progress notes, and physicians' orders for activities program.

   4. *Nursing:* Medical records and infection-control related to activities, outings, food-related activities, escorting residents to/from activities, involvement of certified nursing assistants, restorative aids in activities, in-room activities, etc.

   5. *Personnel:* Job descriptions, activity department's dress code, etc., orientation checklist, performance appraisal form if it is different from that of other departments.

   6. *Social Service:* Scheduling of group activities conducted by social workers (support groups, new resident groups, social groups, unit groups, expressive groups co-led by activity professional). Expenditures of residents' personal funds for personal activity supplies (yarn to make personal items, gifts, etc.), admission to places of interest, outing including a meal, activity equipment, e.g., radio, T.V., DVD.

Activities Policies and Procedures Manual

Content Checklist

I. Introduction to Facility

A. History of Facility

B. Philosophy of Facility

C. Purpose of Facility

D. Organizational Chart of Facility

II. Activities Department

A. History of Activities Department

B. Organization of Department

(Organizational Chart)

C. Staffing and Supervision

D. Hours of Work

E. Job Descriptions
   1. Activity Director/Coordinator
   2. Activity Leaders/Assistant(s)/ Aides
   3. Other Activity Personnel

F. Activity Areas

G. Other

III. Activities Program

A. General Policy Statement Regarding the Activities Program (broad statement related to state and federal regulation per OBRA 6/95) and Joint Commission Accreditation of Healthcare Organizations (JCAHO) or Commission on Accreditation of Rehabilitation Facilities (CARF) if applicable.

B. Activities Policies and Procedures (policy and procedures related to developing, reviewing and revising activities policies and procedures).

C. Purpose Statement of Activities Program

D. Philosophy of Activities Program

E. Goals and Objectives of Activities Program

F. Scope of Program

G. Group Protocols

H. Definitions Related to Activities Program
   1. Activity
   2. Activity Programs
   3. Activity Services
   4. Individual Activities
   5. One-to-One Activity
   6. Group Activities
      a. Small Group
      b. Large Group
      c. Pre-Meal Group/Post-Meal Group
      d. Unit Activities
   7. Activity Areas
      a. Activity Room
      b. Chapel
      c. Dining Room
      d. Lounge
      e. Out-of-doors areas
      f. Other

I. Protocols for Activities

J. Scheduling of Activities (including coordination of activities with other departments)

K. Resident Involvement in Recommending, Planning, Conducting and Evaluating Activities

L. Utilization of Community Resources

M. Other

IV. Activities, Programs and Services

A. Affective Activities:
   1. Adopt-A-Grandparent
   2. Expressive Activities (activities in which feelings are expressed, such as art, dance, drama, music, poetry, writing)
   3. Games, e.g., The Ungame, in which feelings are expressed
   4. Grooming Group
   5. Manicure Group
   6. Intergenerational Programs
   7. Pets
   8. Resident Council
   9. Support Groups
   10. Use of Stuffed Animals and Dolls (for residents with cognitive impairments, as a source of comfort)
   11. Voting and Registration to Vote
   12. Other

B. Cognitive Activities:
   1. Cards
   2. Charades
   3. Computer Activities
   4. Crossword Puzzle Group
   5. Current Events
   6. Discussions
   7. Education Programs
   8. Films/DVDs
   9. Games
   10. Math Quizzes
   11. Music Appreciation
   12. Name That Tune
   13. Newspaper
   14. Old Radio Show (Listening to CDs)
   15. Orientation Group
   16. Pre-/Post-Meal Programs
   17. The Price Is Right
   18. Puzzles
   19. Radio
   20. Radio Reading Service
   21. Reading
   22. Reality Orientation Boards
   23. Reality Orientation (individual and group)
   24. Reminiscing
   25. Spelling

26. Sensory Stimulation (individual and group)
27. Table Games
28. Talking Book
29. Trivia
30. TV
31. Wheel of Fortune
32. Win, Lose or Draw
33. Word Games
34. Other

C. Creative Activities:
1. Art
2. Baking and Cooking
3. Ceramics
4. Coloring, Drawing, Painting
5. Crafts
6. Creative Movement
7. Creative Writing
8. Dancing
9. Decorations/Decorating
10. Drama
11. Flower-Arranging
12. Horticulture
13. Music
14. Needlework
15. Poetry
16. Rhythm Band
17. Wii

D. Physical Activities:
1. Balloon Badminton
2. Basketball
3. Beach Ball
4. Bean-Bag Toss
5. Bocce
6. Bowling
7. Dancing
8. Darts
9. Exercise
10. Fishing
11. Golf (Putt-Putt)
12. Horseshoes
13. Kick Ball
14. Movement and Music
15. Nerf Ball
16. Parachute
17. Relaxation
18. Ring Toss
19. Senior Olympics
20. Shuffle Board

21. Swimming, e.g., Arthritis Swim Program
22. Toss Across
23. Volleyball
24. Walking (individual, 1:1, group)
25. Yoga
26. Other

E. Religious/Spiritual Activities:
1. Bible Study/Reading
2. Church/Synagogue Service
3. Church Service in the Community
4. Church Volunteer Visitors
5. Clergy Visits
6. Communion
7. Hymn-Sing
8. Inspirational Reading
9. Mass
10. Meditation Group
11. Prayer Service
12. Rosary
13. Special Religious Observances (Christian, Jewish, other)
14. Other

F. Social Activities:
1. Bingo
2. Birthday Celebrations (individual/group)
3. Car-Racing
4. Cards
5. Carry-In Dinners (family/staff)
6. Carry-In Dinners - fast food, e.g. McDonald's Night
7. Coffee Hour
8. Entertainment
9. Family Activity/Socials
10. Happy Hour
11. Holiday Celebrations
    a. New Year's Eve
    b. New Year's Day
    c. Valentine's Day
    d. St. Patrick's Day
    e. Easter
    f. Mother's Day
    g. Memorial Day
    h. Father's Day
    i. July 4th
    j. Labor Day

    k. Grandparents' Day
    l. Halloween
    m. Veterans' Day
    n. Thanksgiving
    o. Christmas
    p. Other
12. Horse-Racing
13. Ice-Cream Socials
14. Intergenerational Programs
15. Men's Group
16. One-to-One Activities
17. Outings
18. Parties
19. Picnics
20. Pokeno
21. Popcorn Socials
22. Resocialization Group
23. Shopping
24. Singing, e.g., Community singing
25. Socialization in Lounge
26. Special Events
27. Wine and Cheese Socials
28. Women's Group
29. Other

G. Work/Service Activities:

1. Service Activities
    a. Assisting with Activities
    b. Assisting with the Newsletter
    c. Committee Work
    d. Community Service Project
    e. Book and Magazine Cart
    f. Delivering Mail
    g. Friendly Visiting with Other Residents
    h. Fund Raising Events
    i. Gift Shop or Gift Cart Volunteer
    j. Making Decorations
    k. Officer for Resident Council
    l. Program Planning Committee
    m. Reading Mail to Residents
    n. Teaching Activities
    o. Tele-Care Volunteer
    p. Welcoming Committee
    q. Writing Letters for Other Residents
    r. Other

2. Work Activities
    a. Compensation for Services
    b. Volunteer Services
    c. Other

H. Individual Activities

I. One-to-One Activities (programs)

J. Group Activities (large and small group)

K. Activities Services
  1. Gift Shop/Cart
  2. Music in Room
  3. Public Library Services
  4. Radio Reading Service
  5. Reading Mail for Residents
  6. Shopping
  7. Talking Book
  8. Writing Letters or Recording messages for Residents
  9. Other

V. Budget

A. Annual Budget
B. Donations (accepting donations and soliciting donations)
C. Petty Cash
D. Special Accounts, e.g., resident accounts from fund raising
E. Resident Charges, e.g., craft materials, outings, etc.
F. Purchasing
G. Credit Accounts
H. Fund-Raising
I. Other

VI. Communications

A. Letters
B. Thank-You Letters/Notes
C. Fax
D. Email
E. Invitations
F. Request Forms
G. Intercom
H. Inter-Department Communication
I. Intra-Department Communication
J. Public Address System
K. Posters
L. Bulletin Boards

VII. Community/Public Relations

A. Media Contact/Releases
B. Special Events Sponsored by the Facility for the Community
C. Involvement in Community's Special Events
D. Development/Maintenance of Resident Activities Photo Album and/or Scrapbook
E. Other

VIII. Community Resources

A. General Policy Regarding Utilization of Community Resources
B. Specific Policies and Procedures
   1. Entertainment
   2. Places of Interest, e.g., museums
   3. Volunteer Organizations
   4. Use of Supplies/Equipment, e.g., local schools, service organization, other
   5. Transportation
   6. Other

IX. Documentation: Resident

A. Physician Orders for Activities
B. Therapeutic Work Orders
C. Activities Assessment
D. MDS (assigned activity sections)
E. Activities Precautions List
F. Activities Plan of Care
G. List of Residents to Attend Activities (in accordance with their plans of care) for Nursing
H. Daily Activities Participation Record
I. Total Activities Attendance Record
J. Activities Progress Notes
K. Release Forms (audio/visual, photo, outings, etc.)
L. Other

X. Environment

A. Decorating
B. Movement of Furniture for Activities
C. Storage of Activities Supplies and Equipment
D. Upkeep of Activity Areas
E. Use of Multiple-Purpose Areas, e.g., Activity/Dining Room
F. Noise Level
G. Other

XI. Personnel

A. Utilization of Facility's Personnel Policies and Procedures.
B. Orientation:
   1. Orientation of activity staff to facility.
   2. Orientation of activity staff to activities department (orientation checklist).
   3. Orientation of facility's staff to the activities department.
C. Dress Code for Activities Staff
D. Activity Staff's Work Schedules (including evenings, weekends and holidays).
E. Storage of Activities Staff's personal belongings, i.e., cell phone, purse and coat.
F. Use of Activity Staff's Personal Property for Activities Programs, e.g., records, cds, ipod, dvds, craft materials, game equipment, etc.
G. Professional Development
   1. In-service for activity staff.
   2. Continuing education for activity staff (local/state/national conferences and workshops).
   3. In-service related to activities program for other departments.
H. Other

XII. Quality Assurance/Quality Improvement

A. Quality Assurance/Quality Improvement Program for Activities Department
B. Resident Satisfaction Questionnaire
C. Resident Evaluation of Activities
D. Specific Policies and Procedures for each Quality Assurance (Q.A.) Quality Improvement (Q.I.) Activity
E. Other

XIII. Records and Reports

A. Monthly Department Reports
B. Annual Department Report
C. Program Documentation, i.e., report on a special event, holiday celebrations
D. Incident and Accident Reports (resident/staff fall/injury, property damage)
E. Special Reports

F. Minutes of Meetings
1. Activities department staff meetings
2. Resident council (if an activity staff member is the liaison)
3. Quality assurance/quality improvement
4. Resident evaluation/ recommendations regarding activities programs
G. In-Service Training
H. Other

XIV. Safety

A. MSDS (Material Safety Data Sheet)
B. Restraints (release or use of restraints during activities)
C. Sharps (use of scissors, needles, pins, sharp tools, etc.)
D. Storage of Flammable Materials
E. Supervision of Residents in Activities (indoors, outdoors, outings)
F. Transportation (to and from activities, including outings)
G. Cooking/Baking
H. Use of Electrical Appliances
I. Other

XV. Infection Control

A. Precautions
B. Universal Precautions
C. Storage of Food
D. Baking/Cooking Activities
E. Cleaning of Appliances
F. Washing of Dishes, Silverware, Utensils, Pots, Pans
G. Manicure Supplies
H. Pets

XVI. Supplies, Equipment and

Vehicles

A. Inventory
1. List of All Equipment:
   a. serial Numbers
   b. date of Purchase/warranty
   c. storage area
2. Specific Equipment:
   a. audio/visual Equipment
      1. overhead projector
      2. public address System
      3. 16-mm projector
      4. Radio Reading Service
      5. screen
      6. power point projector
      7. stereo
      8. Ipod, cd player
      9. Talking Book
      10. DVD
      11. other
         a. carts
         b. craft equipment
         c. film
         d. looms
         e. office equipment
      1. computer
      2. copy machine
      3. fax machine
      4. power point projector
      5. lap top computer
      6. other
   g. outdoor equipment
   h. sports equipment
   i. table-top green house
   j. vehicle, i.e., van
   k. other
B. Maintenance
C. Repairs
D. Use of Copy Machine(s)
E. Other

XVII. Volunteers

A. History
B. Philosophy
C. Purpose
D. Goals and Objectives
E. Job Descriptions
F. Recruitment
G. Selection
H. Orientation
I. Training
J. Supervision
K. Performance Appraisal
L. Recognition
M. Termination
N. Specific Policies and Procedures for Volunteers (Individual and Groups)
1. Attendance
2. Communication
3. Completion of forms
4. Confidentiality

5. Do's and don'ts
6. Required medical tests/ examinations
7. Restrictions—communicable diseases
8. Scheduling
9. Shopping for individual residents
10. Signing in and out
11. Use of volunteer's car for outing
12. Other

(SAMPLE)
Activities Department
BINGO

Policy

Bingo shall be conducted by activity staff or volunteers two times per week, including one evening per month in the dining/activity room.

Large print bingo cards and markers (poker chips) shall be used. Residents shall be permitted to play one to two cards per game.

Prizes shall be awarded to winners. The director of activities shall be responsible for obtaining donated or purchased prizes, e.g., jewelry, powder, perfume, after-shave lotion, tissues, note paper, stamps, decorative items, etc. Money shall be awarded one time per month, not to exceed five dollars. Residents involved in bingo shall be asked annually their preference for prizes. Recommendation for prizes shall be implemented as feasible in keeping with the annual budget for bingo.

Activity coordinators assigned to units shall provide nursing with a list of residents who like bingo. Activity and nursing staff shall be responsible for transporting/escorting residents to and from bingo in the dining/activity room.

Procedures

I. Pre-Preparation:

   A. Schedule bingo on monthly activity - schedule a minimum of 2 times per week including 1 evening per month in the dining/activity room.
   B. Submit purchase order for bingo prizes as needed.
   C. Obtain $5.00 of quarters from business office when money is to be used for prizes.

II. Preparation on Day of Activity:

   A. Include bingo and time on Daily Activity Boards on each unit.
   B. Announce bingo as part of the A.M. announcements.
   C. Meet with available volunteers and assign responsibilities approximately 20–30 minutes before the activity.
   D. Set up the dining/activity room.
      1. Place 2 tables together by the south wall for the caller—one table for the bingo cage and master bingo board and the 2nd table for the prizes.
      2. Place 6 tables in pairs so that there are 3 tables with space to seat 6 residents at each table.
      3. Place one table by entrance for bingo cards.
      4. Leave the rest of the tables in their original space.
   E. Obtain bingo supplies and prizes from the storage closet on the south unit.
   F. Place the bingo cage, master card and prizes on the caller's table.
   G. Place bingo cards on table by entrance.
   H. Place a bag of chips (poker chips) for each person on the table. Place extra bags of poker chips on the caller's table.
   I. Announce bingo 15 minutes prior to event.

III. Escort/transport residents to the dining/activity room.

   A. Allow residents to choose where they want to sit as feasible.
      1. As needed, place residents with hearing impairments near the caller.
   B. Assign activity staff/volunteers to stay in the dining/activity room and talk with individual residents while additional residents are being escorted.

IV. Request activity staff/volunteers to assist residents who have visual, hearing, small gross motor movement and/or cognitive impairments.

V. Welcome residents/volunteers.

VI. Request residents to select their bingo cards from the cards placed on the table if they have not already done so.

VII. Provide extra packages of bingo markers as needed.

VIII. Proceed with the game:
  A. Announce what games will be played.
  B. Play 4 games of bingo (straight line, horizontal, vertical, diagonal).
  C. Call numbers twice - repeat as necessary.
  D. When bingo is called, ask resident to identify his/her letters and numbers.
  E. Instruct residents when to clear boards.
  F. Award winner(s) choice of prize - if money is used, give winner(s) a quarter.
  G. Clear leader's board after bingo has been verified.
  H. Return balls to basket.
  I. Play 4 corners for the 5th game.
  J. Instruct residents not to clear cards after bingo has been verified.
  K. Announce cover-all is the last game.
  L. Continue to call numbers until resident(s) call bingo.
  M. When bingo is called, ask resident to identify his/her letters and numbers.
  N. Announce winner(s).
  O. Congratulate all bingo winners.

IX. Thank residents for participating.

X. Escort residents back to their room/lounge or preferred area as needed.

XI. Thank nursing assistants and volunteers for their assistance with escorting/transporting residents.

XII. Clean Up:
  A. Return bingo supplies and unused prizes to storage closet on south unit.
  B. Return tables chairs to their original positions.

XIII. Thank volunteers for their assistance. Ask what they observed and answer questions.

XIV. Document individual resident participation on the Daily Activity Participation Record.

XV. Complete the Total Activities Attendance Record form.

(SAMPLE)

XYZ Long-Term Care
Activities Department
*(Note this policy and procedure has
the name of the facility as a part of the heading.)*

Resident-Planned Activities

Policy

A resident's activity planning meeting shall be scheduled during the second week of each month in the dining room. The meeting shall be used for residents to plan a minimum of four group activities including evening and weekend activities for the next month. Residents shall be able to suggest activities and/or be provided with a list of possible activities (related to residents' interests, season, holiday, special event, national, state, and/or local upcoming events, etc.) from which they can choose.

The Director of Activities or assigned activity staff member shall be responsible for leading or assisting a resident to conduct the Resident Activity Planning Meeting. Residents shall be informed of dates available for their planned activities. Any recommended activity involving food, transportation, new supplies/equipment, money, families, or community shall be discussed and approved by department managers and/or administrator as appropriate. Approved activities shall be scheduled for the upcoming month. If an approved activity cannot be scheduled for the upcoming month, it shall be scheduled at a later date. The resident planned activity shall be indicated as such on the monthly activity schedule.

Residents shall have an opportunity to evaluate their planned activities at the end of each activity and/or at the monthly resident activity planning meeting.

Procedures

I. Pre-Preparation:

   A. Schedule the resident activity planning meeting on Monday, Tuesday or Thursday, at 3:00 P.M. during the second week of the month, so that recommended activities can be scheduled for the upcoming month.

      1. Determine the best day/dates to schedule resident-planned activities for the upcoming month.

      2. Prepare a list of potential activities from which the residents can choose, in case they don't have any recommendations.

II. Preparation on Day of the Activity:

   A. Set up the dining room to allow residents to sit in a horseshoe, facing the leader. Place the white board, portable microphone and speaker in front of the horseshoe where the leader will sit/stand.

   B. Announce the activity on the intercom 15 minutes prior to the meeting and then again within five minutes of the meeting.

III. Personally invite individual residents to the meeting. Explain the purpose of the meeting prior to or after the invitation.

IV. Escort residents to the dining room with the assistance of nurse aides. Place residents with visual and/or hearing impairment in front of the room.

V. Conduct the meeting:

   A. Introduce self and welcome participants or have a resident lead the meeting with staff assistance as needed.

   B. Explain the purpose of the resident activity planning meeting.

   C. Review resident-planned activities that have taken place since the last resident activity planning meeting.

   D. Review residents' evaluation and recommendations related to the planned activities that they have experienced since the last meeting.

   E. Inform participants of the days/dates for resident planned activities for the upcoming month.

   F. Ask for recommendations for the upcoming month.

      1. Write residents' suggestions on the white board. Discuss the ideas and their feasibility. Clarify what residents want to do. Write ideas for activities on the white board if residents are unable to give suggestions.

      2. Inform residents if approval is needed by other departments and/or administrator prior to scheduling an activity, if more time is needed to plan the activity for the upcoming month.

   G. Ask residents to vote on suggested activities for the specified dates and/or for future months. Write the number of votes for each activity on the white board. Identify the top four activities to be planned.

   H. Thank the residents for their participation.

VI. Escort residents back to their rooms or preferred areas.

VII. Rearrange the room to the original setting. Store the microphone and speaker.

VIII. Record residents' participation on the resident's individual Daily Activities Participation Record.

IX. Complete the Total Activities Attendance Record form.

X. Follow up with planning activities with activity staff and other department managers/administrator.

XI. Schedule the recommended activities on the monthly schedule indicating the specific activity.

XII. Keep a record of resident planning activity meetings, planned activities, and planned evaluations (date, attendance, recommendation, dates activities were conducted and resident evaluation of the activities).

Schedule of Activity Services (Calendar)

One of the important displays prepared by the activity profession on a monthly basis is the activity schedule of events. In designing the calendar care needs to be taken to have the information on the calendar for each day. Readability is essential.

There are various ways announcements of activities can be communicated to the residents/clients. Newsletters, information sheets and verbal announcements can keep the resident/client informed. Color is important on the calendar and large plain lettering may be highlighted with different colors. Residents/clients with limited eyesight need to be considered when preparing the calendar. The placement of the calendar should be in a high traffic area where residents or clients frequently pass and where other department employees will see it.

As the activity professional plans the program for each month he/she will need to consider the regular as well as special programs being planned by other departments. While some events are repeated from week to week and month to month other activities being planned for special days will need special attention. To call attention to different activities, designing the calendar in new ways each month will be helpful.

Program Evaluation

"Utilize a team approach for evaluation"

The program is the overall plan of activities being offered. To evaluate is to judge or determine the value in relation to recent activities. Such evaluations can be done after some special programs. Or an overall evaluation can be made annually. The activity department and staff need periodic evaluations. The question needs to be raised: How effective are specific programs as well as the regular programs? Staff needs to gather data and feedback in order to evaluate what was done and seek to improve future programs. New programs need to be designed and planned to attract and hold the interest of attendees.

Evaluation can be formal or informal. The formal process might involve a survey to secure a response from those who attend the activity. This type of evaluation can quantify the interest and value of one program or a series of programs for a period of time. Informal evaluations can occur when individual residents/clients are asked how they like a given program. The purpose of evaluations is to improve future programs determining which are the most meaningful. Community resources should be used when appropriate. The activity person is always seeking to design the activities to meet the interest and satisfaction of the resident/client.

Evaluation of Activities/Programs

Evaluation of activities and/or programs can be multi dimensional. Participants, staff, administration, volunteers, families and community groups can be involved in various phases of the evaluation process. Activities/programs are for participants. Thus participants need to have significant involvement in the evaluative process.

Participants' Evaluation

Participant evaluation can include evaluating an activity immediately after an activity/program; during resident council; during resident activity planning meetings; through resident interest and/or evaluation surveys; and through one-to-one interviews. The focus of evaluation could center on participants' feelings toward the activity (liking/enjoying it, feeling it was beneficial, etc.); time (the time of day the activity is scheduled; the amount of time allotted for the activity—30,45,60,90 minutes, the number of times per week/month the activity is conducted); place (activity room, dining/activity room, chapel, lounge, outdoors, in the community); environment (heat, air conditioning, lighting, ventilation, space, acoustics); and supplies and equipment (type, amount and condition).

Family Evaluation

Family and significant others are concerned with the total health and welfare of their loved one or person entrusted to overseeing their care. Involvement in evaluating activities/programs and activities services differ among individual family members, significant others or a power of attorney. The most significant evaluation of participants is in terms of outcomes seen or heard by family members. This information may be shared directly with an activity professional, through the administrator, or through other staff members.

Family Council

A family council, even though small, is one group that can be requested to evaluate activities/programs and services. Families involved in the council often sponsor activities and are a part of the evaluation process.

Surveys

Surveys related to outcome and satisfaction with participants' care could be effective tools. A survey related to activities/programs can be a focused survey or part of a broader survey of total care and services.

Informal Family Evaluation

Informed families evaluate the availability of activities as a part of their criteria for selecting community-based programs or facilities for care and services. Recommendations through word of mouth to other families seeking care and services are a type of informal evaluation. Activity professionals and administrators do not always hear about these evaluations unless families are asked how they selected the specific community-based program or facility.

Administrator's Evaluation

The administrator is responsible for total quality of care and is concerned with the delivery of services in the most efficient and effective manner. The residents' evaluation of activities /programs is a part of the facility's continuous quality improvement program. The administrator may actively participate in various participant evaluations such as being present during an evaluation after a special event, attending a resident council meeting at the participants' request and listening to the participants comments about activities, and/or con-ducting a part of a total facility one-to-one survey on resident interest or satisfaction with activities/programs. The administrator may work with the activity department, other staff and interested residents in designing a survey.

Review of Records and Reports

A review of a variety of records and reports provides the administrator an ongoing evaluation of activities, programs and services. The use of a coded census sheet to identify resident participation in activities by service delivery mode (independent individual, one-to-one, group activities) and functional abilities provides a quick graphic view of the number of residents in each category and the services needed, which are constantly changing. A review of individual daily activity participation records indicates the specific activities and frequency of participation. Quality assurance and quality improvement studies identify whether standards are being met and problems/concerns are being acted upon and resolved. A summary of surveys provides recommended activities and changes. Monthly activity department reports written by the managing activity professional indicate the accomplishments for the month, the goals for the next month, and problems/concerns and potential solutions (recommendations).

Cost and Effectiveness

The total cost and effectiveness of the activities department have to be evaluated from a cost perspective. Staffing is the largest cost. The administrator has to evaluate the activity staff's qualifications, roles and responsibilities as well as productivity in meeting the needs and interests of participants. Continuing education of the activity staff is essential. The activity professional's knowledge and skills have a direct effect on participant outcomes. Additional staff may be needed, roles and responsibilities may need to be redefined, or support staff may be needed or team effort improved to provide better services. Supplies and equipment are continuously being sought. New products provide better supplies/equipment to meet the interests and functional abilities of resident/client. The cost of activity services has to be evaluated in relation to the total cost of operation and reimbursement of the agency or facility.

Regulatory and Voluntary Surveys

The results of mock surveys, quality assurance standards reviews, and state and federal surveys and JCAHO (Joint Commission Accreditation Health Care Organizations) or CARF (Commission on Accreditation of Rehabilitation Facilities) surveys (if applicable) are other types of evaluation of the activity program. Correction of deficiencies is a joint effort of the activity professionals and administrator. Correction may involve residents, families, staff and/or volunteers.

Activity Professional's Evaluation

Activity professionals continuously evaluate activities, programs and services. Evaluation can be informal or formal (completion of an evaluation form or some type of standardized evaluation). Activity professionals informally evaluate activities/programs immediately upon completion when they review the activity/program (who, attended, the dynamics of individuals/group, participants outcome, organization, timing, place, environment, supplies and equipment, cost, etc.). Documenting participation and writing progress notes is part of the evaluation process related to individual participants. The information is then utilized to update individual participant's plans of care.

Informal Activity Professionals' Evaluation

Informal conversations and discussions with participants, family members, volunteers and staff provide personal and professional approach to evaluation. Information needs to be recorded. Recommendations need to be acted upon if feasible. Feedback on outcome of evaluation and recommendations need to be given to individuals/groups. Open communication, respect for the opinions and suggestions of others, and a concerted effort to make change(s) foster a belief that one's input into the quality of programming will be heard and acted upon.

Records and Reports

A program report includes evaluation of the program and recommendations for the next time the program is provided. The focus is on the quality of planning, preparation and implementation, and evaluation by participants, staff, volunteers and families as appropriate.

Review of records and reports (daily participation records, total activity participation records, e.g., number of participants, number of participants served through one-to-one activities, small groups and large groups, activity schedules, one-to-one schedules, the number of activities for various resident functional levels related to the scope of the program, quality assurance/quality improvement reports, resident-planned activities records, etc.) provide activity professionals with a sizeable amount of evaluation. The findings from all the evaluations can culminate in realistic recommendations for continuing, changing or improving activities, programs and services.

Program Operation

Annual review of purpose, philosophy, goals and objectives, program model and design, and policies and procedures—as well as staffing—provides a focused evaluation on the administrative aspects of the activity department that ultimately affects the quality of programming. A proactive review (annual, six-month or quarterly) of compliance with city, state, federal regulations, agency or corporate standards as well as JCAHO and CARF standards (if applicable) assures compliance. Deficiencies can be corrected. Anxiety is reduced related to passing a survey.

On-going evaluation of the activities department and its services assists in maintaining a dynamic activities program that meets the needs, interests, preferences and functional abilities of all residents/participants.

Staff Evaluation

Direct care staff has opportunities to be directly or indirectly involved with activities/programs. Staff knows residents/participants and is involved in informing them of daily or upcoming activities as well as encouraging them to participate in activities related to their interest. They see participants before and after activities and some see participants during activities. They hear residents' comments and reactions to activities/programs. Direct staff has an overall picture of the resident/participant during their assigned time of care. They are continuously evaluating the persons to whom they are assigned.

Individual and Team Evaluation

Informal individual evaluation of activities/programs related to specific participants/residents can be very effective through one-to-one conversations or in preparation for care conferences or during care conferences with direct-care staff. Team meetings related to organization and delivery of care and services for a specific unit is another approach to evaluation. The team's focus is primarily on participants/residents of the unit; thus, attention is not for the entire agency or facility.

Staff directly involved in activities need to be a part of the total evaluation process (planning, scheduling, preparation, implementation and outcome for participants). Everyone may see the experience from a different point of view, resulting in giving a broad evaluation. The bottom line is that the people involved care and want the best for the participants/residents.

The management team can evaluate activities/programs in relation to outcomes for participants as well as organization, scheduling, team approach, cooperation, etc. in relation to overall care and services. Managers and/or staff can be involved in quality assurance/quality improvement studies and plans related to activities, programs and services.

Staff Surveys

Staff can be surveyed in relation to the effectiveness of activities and programs in general or for specific participants. Surveys on the effectiveness of activities during different times of the day, evening, weekends and holidays give a broader staff perspective than those that are given to just one shift of staff.

State Surveyors

State Surveyors will be asking residents about the quality of life they are experiencing. The activity professional can help prepare the resident ahead of the survey using the following survey form. Residents will respond based on how they feel but the preliminary survey helps them understand the process, e.g., Are there enough activities on weekends?" This might be done once or twice a year.

Activity Satisfaction Survey

1. **What kinds of activities do you like to do?** <u>Poke no, Bingo, Music, Art, Crafts, Sports, Bowling, Rides on the</u> <u>Van, and word Games</u>
    How frequently do you participate in these activities? *(Check one)*
    ☐ many activities everyday ☐ about 1-2 activities / day ☐ a few times a week
    ☐ less than 2 times per week ☐ rarely ☐ never

2. What kinds of activities are available to you? <u>Many different kinds are available.</u> Do these activities meet your needs? ☐ yes ☐ no   If no, please explain why not:_____

    Are these activities similar to the kinds of things you were interested in before you came here?
    ☐ yes   ☐ no **If no, please explain why not:**_____

.   **How satisfied are you with the following:**

    A.   **the number of activities offered Monday through Friday in the morning?**
    ☐ very satisfied ☐ satisfied ☐ unsatisfied ☐ very unsatisfied

    B.   **The number of activities offered Monday through Friday in the afternoon?**
    ☐ very satisfied ☐ satisfied ☐ unsatisfied ☐ very unsatisfied

    C.   **The number of evening activities?**
    ☐ Very satisfied ☐ satisfied ☐ unsatisfied ☐ very unsatisfied

    D.   **The number of activities offered on Saturday and Sunday?**
    ☐ Very satisfied ☐ satisfied ☐ unsatisfied ☐ very unsatisfied

    E.   **The variety of activities offered?**
    ☐ very satisfied ☐ satisfied ☐ unsatisfied ☐ very unsatisfied

    F.   **A community resource is either people coming into the nursing home from the outside (such as an entertainer, pet therapy or volunteers) or residents going outside the nursing home, (such as on field trips). How satisfied are you with the use of community resources both inside and outside the facility?** ☐ very satisfied ☐ satisfied ☐ unsatisfied ☐ very unsatisfied

    G.   **How satisfied are you with the assistance that you are provided? (for example, turning on the tape recorder, having activity supplies put within your reach, having things read out loud when you can't see them, etc.)?**
    ☐ Very satisfied ☐ satisfied ☐ unsatisfied ☐ very unsatisfied

    H.   **People that have difficulty seeing may need a special adaptation such as large print books. People that do not have use of one arm may need a special adaptation to play cards to hold the cards. Which (if any) of the following adaptations do you need?**
    ☐ one to one attention ☐ large print books ☐ book holder ☐ talking books
    ☐ card holder ☐ large print bingo cards ☐ head phone for a tape recorder
    ☐ List any other adaptations you need: <u>Card shuffler</u>

4. | | | |
    |---|---|---|
    | **Do you enjoy the activities that you take part in?** | ☐ yes | ☐ no |
    | **Are the activities that you go to fun?** | ☐ yes | ☐ no |
    | **Do the activities help you make new friends?** | ☐ yes | ☐ no |
    | **Do the activities help you feel good about yourself?** | ☐ yes | ☐ no |

Additional Comments: Resident quotes: "More trivia games would be fun, word games, and more eve and weekend activities." "With activities you feel you're part of something." "I'm satisfied with everything here" "There is too much to do here" "I like to be alone"

Volunteer Management

"Volunteers are a great human resource"

A volunteer may be defined as one who freely makes him/herself available to share time and talent with the residents/clients. Volunteers serve without compensation and can greatly enhance the personal services to the resident/client. Most organizations choose to recognize volunteers at least annually with a lunch, dinner or special tea. Volunteer hours are reported and certificates may be awarded. Recognition and appreciation are the rewards the volunteer receives and enjoys.

One activity professional is assigned the management of the volunteer program. Volunteers need to be orientated, trained, assigned specific responsibilities and motivated. The relationship of the volunteer to the resident/client is of utmost importance. Learning to know what the volunteers' special interest and gifts are will help the volunteer coordinator to match the volunteer with the resident/client. A printed guide or job description will help the volunteer understand his/her role.

A check-in station and time card can help the volunteer feel a sense of belonging, and record time served on each visit. It also guides activity staff persons in knowing which volunteers are serving on a given day in order that appropriate greetings, directions and appreciation is offered each time the volunteer visits. A frequent statement by volunteers is "I get so much more out of this than I give!"

Volunteers – The Basics of a Successful Program

Agencies that are for people realize that one of their best resources for humanizing care and helping people attain their highest potential is the volunteer. When caring for the physical needs of a resident once was viewed as the epitome of good care, in more recent years the emotional, psychological and social components of care are seen as equally important.

Few agencies have sufficient funds to employ enough staff to meet the individual needs of each person in their care. That is where the unpaid volunteer becomes a significant part of the health care team.

The Role of the Administrator

The volunteer program does not just happen. It begins with the enthusiastic support of the administrator whose responsibility is to "sell" the program to the rest of the staff so that they will accept the volunteer as one who may assist in making their tasks easier rather than one who is there to do their "dirty" work or compete for the affection of the client.

He/she must be prepared to add sufficient funds to be budget to add a coordinator to the staff and pay other costs necessary to the satisfactory functioning of the program.

The Volunteer Coordinator

A person with specialized training in working with people is a must. A background in social work, psychology, therapy, or education is preferred. He/she must be pleasant, self-confident, patient, poised, diplomatic, businesslike, flexible, understanding and have organizational ability. He/she will be a liaison between the staff and the volunteer and must be respected by both.

Job Description – A job description for the coordinator will take into consideration such things as:

- The persons ability to recruit, interview, train, assign and supervise volunteers
- Setting up special workshops and training programs
- Planning for annual recognition of volunteers
- Keeping adequate records, making evaluations and reporting progress of the program
- Ability to stay within budgetary guidelines.

The Volunteer

The volunteer who said, "I want to be of some small help. I come home exhausted and have never felt better" possessed the most important trait a volunteer can have … a big heart which expressed itself in a sincere desire to help another person.

A helpful way to discover and evaluate the intentions and goals of one who offers to be a volunteer is to set up a personal interview. In the initial interview and other periods of intentional or spontaneous encounter with a prospective volunteer the coordinator will discover some of the strengths and weaknesses of the volunteer. The coordinator will begin to know the prospective volunteer and be able to consider where the volunteer will best be able to serve. Such questions as the following will come to light:

- How tolerant is he/she of persons who may be slow, forgetful, unkempt, disagreeable or confused?
- What is his/her attitude about his/her own aging?
- Does his/her educational background fit the needs of the client with whom he/she will work?
- Is he/she willing to be a team member taking guidance and suggestions or moving to a different area of service where needed?
- Is he/she willing to take advantage of training opportunities or available reading materials?
- Is he/she willing to work with rather than for a client, to accept clients as they are, to give time regularly, to abide by the rules of the agency and to keep records of time spent as requested?

Roles of the Volunteer

Staff persons who will be directing volunteers will be invited to make suggestions to the coordinator for specific volunteers to fill specific roles. They will complete job descriptions defining the role, the time commitment, dos and don'ts of the specific job, the area of the agency where they volunteer will be working and any other specifications or limitations. Prospective volunteers will be introduced to their staff director who will in turn make the volunteer feel a part of the team.

Recruiting

Recruiting of volunteers for specific responsibilities as determined by staff that will be working with them is a continuous responsibility for the coordinator. Volunteers come from many backgrounds and possess a great variety of diverse skills. They may be found among friends of the agency. They may be senior citizens, recently retired who wish to continue making a contribution to society. They may be independent active residents of the agency. They may be young people. They may be family members of an employee. They may be involved in a community church or civic group looking for a way to serve.

The wise coordinator will become familiar with the community in which the agency is located and will keep a file of persons and groups, along with their respective leaders for reference when searching for volunteers with specific skills.

Orientation Sessions

Orientation for individuals or small groups of volunteers is designed to familiarize the volunteer with the agency and to put the recruit at ease when performing volunteer services. One or more sessions may be needed to complete this important step. The session may be held at the time of the original interview or scheduled for a later time. The following aspects of the program should be covered"

- A historical sketch and philosophy of the agency
- A basic understanding of the aging process and the level of care provided for residents with whom the volunteer will be working
- Goals of the volunteer program
- Service opportunities available. Job descriptions, training opportunities and rewards for the volunteer.
- Code of ethics: dress, grooming, conduct, job efficiency, etc.
- Mechanics of the program such as parking space, use of phone, lounge areas, personal space, meals, restrooms, elevator use
- Relationship of the volunteer to the resident
- Relationship of the volunteer to the staff
- Relationship of the volunteer to the community

Supervision and Support

Volunteer programs are most likely to fail where either training or supervision and support are inadequate. On-the-job supervision with periodic evaluation sessions and special workshops or conferences is essential to the effectiveness of the ongoing program.

Workshops may be designed to develop new skills, to assist the volunteers in understanding the client and his/her needs and/or to interpret techniques designed to meet specific needs.

When assigning workshop leaders, consider using staff members who will be directing certain volunteer activities, community persons who work with or have deep relationships with the elderly or instructors in nearby colleges who have knowledge on the subject being discussed.

Supervision. A variety of persons within the agency may be responsible for supervising volunteers. Generally, the supervisor will be one of the following: the volunteer coordinator, the administrator, a department head or other designated staff person in the area where the volunteer serves or an advanced, well-trained volunteer.

People want to succeed. The supervisor is the main person responsible to see that this happens. In addition to personal observation the supervisor may schedule periodic personal conferences. A friendly informal session may be successful over a lunchtime meeting or when the volunteers first arrives on a daily assignment or is preparing to leave at the close of the day.

Handing more difficult issues may require a set time interview. Problems may occur because of misunderstandings, because of insufficient training for the job, because of differences of opinion between staff and volunteer, or possibly because the volunteer has been place in the wrong job. In some cases, it may be advisable to have a separate session with the staff person who directs the volunteer.

The effective coordinator must be approachable and non-judgmental, willing to listen to both sides of an issue and acting promptly when a problem surfaces.

Recognition

The testimony of the volunteer, "I get so much more out of this than I give" expresses the reward that the volunteer feels for an opportunity to serve. Yet, not enough can be said about the importance of the agency staff expressing appreciation for the service of the volunteer. The ways to say "thank you" are myriad.

In addition to the psychological wages of good feelings felt for sacrificial service, try the following:

- Write a personal note
- Put an article in the local paper. It may or may not mention individuals but can be a general letter of appreciation to the community for support.
- Plan an afternoon tea or an evening program when volunteers and supervising staff members can mingle and get to know one another.
- Award certificates or pins for different increments of service.
- Develop a permanent plaque to hang in a main lobby listing names of those who have reached a set level of hours of service.
- Compile an "Honor Roll" listing names of all volunteers with their length and times of service.

Agency, State and National Regulations

One of the primary tasks of caregivers is to be aware of the "resident's rights." Each agency has rules and regulations that govern what can and cannot be done within an agency. These regulations may be unique to the agency or may be mandated by state and government regulations. The volunteer coordinator must be knowledgeable about such rules and pass them on to volunteers working within the facility. Begin by discussing them with the administrator. He/she may, in turn, refer the coordinator to certain state or national regs with which the coordinator should become familiar.

An example of a state regulation is the Ohio code 3701-17-07 which relates to the requirement for volunteers to be tested for tuberculosis under certain conditions.

Volunteer Evaluation

Volunteer evaluation of activities, programs and/or services is most effective immediately after their individual involvement. Volunteers are involved in activities/programs on a periodic or regular basis. Some volunteers may only be involved in a singular program such as providing assistance for a large special event. Regular activities volunteers may not be interested in completing an evaluation survey, whereas others would be interested.

Informal Volunteers' Evaluation

Activity professionals need to listen to unsolicited volunteers' comments that are evaluative in nature.

Volunteers have a commitment to the participant/residents if only for one time. They are also a link to the greater community. Their evaluation of activities/programs and services is heard by others. Volunteers give another perspective and dimension to the total evaluation process. Additional information and/or training may be needed to assist volunteers in understanding, conducting or assisting with activities as well as evaluating activities.

Person Centered Weaving Cards; made from copies of pictures of the resident's family and pets.

J. Krupa

Bibliography

Abrignani, Catherine, A., Messenger, Bill, *Alzheimer's Disease: Activities that Work*, M & H Publishing Company, Inc., P.O. Box 268, LaGrange, TX 78945-0268.

Alzheimer's Association: (1991). *Steps to Selecting Activities for the Person with Alzheimer's Disease*: Alzheimer's Association, 919 North Michigan Ave., Suite 1000, Chicago, IL 60611-1676.
Barton, J., Grudzen, M., and Zielske,R.. (2003). *Vital Connections in Long –Term Care*, Spiritual Resources for Staff and Residents, Health Professionals Press, Inc., P.O.Box 1062, Baltimore, Maryland 21285-0624.

Beers, M.H. and Berkow, R., Editors. (2000). *Merck Manual of Geriatrics, Third Edition.* Whitehouse Station, NJ: Merck Research Laboratories.

Bernstein, Gail, S. and Halasyn, Judith, A. (1989), *Human services? " That must be so rewarding",* Paul H. Brooks Publishing Co., Inc.
Post Office Box 10624
Baltimore, Maryland 21285-0624.

Bowlby, Carol,. 1993. *Therapeutic Activities with Persons Disabled by Alzheimer's Disease and Related Disorders.* An Aspen Publication, Aspen Publishers, Inc., Gaithersburg, MD 20878.

Brown, Diane L., (editor), MDS 2.0 User's Manual (2004)

Consultant, Idyll Arbor, Inc., Ravensdale 1996.

Creative Forecasting, Inc. P.O. Box 7789, Colorado Springs, CO 80933-7789.

Ciolfi, D.H., Dearing, A.Z., Summers, D., Wasserman, L.A. 1987. *Sensory Stimulation Manual,* Jewish Center for the Aged, c/o Joe Ann Summers, RMT-BC, 13190 South Outer Forty Road, Chesterfield, MO 63017.

Coons, D.H., Metzelaar, L., Robenson, A., Spencer, B. 1986. *Better Life: Helping Family Members, Volunteers and Staff Improve The Quality of Life of Nursing Home Residents Suffering from Alzheimer's Disease and Related Disorders.* The Source for Nursing Home Literature, P.O. Box 1092, Columbus, OH 43216.

Dezan, Nancy, 1992. *Barbers, Cars, and Cigars:Activities Programming for Older Men*, available from Mary E. Miller & Associates, P.O. Box 53182, Cincinnati, OH 45253.

D'Antonio-Nocera, Ann, Nancy DeBolt, Nadine Touhey, Ed., The Professional Activity Manager and Consultant, Idyll Arbor, Inc., Ravensdale 1996.

Edinberg, Mark A. (1985). *Mental Health Practice with the Elderly*. Englewood Cliffs, NJ: Prentice-Hall, Inc.

Exercises for Arthritic Hands, Evelyn Rossky, O.T.R., Moss Rehabilitation Hospital, Department of Occupational Therapy, Philadelphia, PA.

Feder, Elaine & Bernard. (1981). *The Expressive Arts Therapies.* Englewood Cliffs, NJ: Prentice-Hall, Inc.

Feil, Naomi. (1989). *V/F Validation :The Feil Method.* Cleveland, OH: Edward Feil Productions. Freeman, S. 1987. *Activities and Approaches for Alzheimer's.* P.O. Box 1817, St. Simons Island, GA 31522.

Frye, Virginia, Peters, Martha, Therapeutic Recreation: its theory, philosophy, and practice, Stackpole Books, Harrisburg, Pa 17105, 1972.

Haber, Judith, Leach, Anita M., Schudy, Sylvia M. & Sideleau, Barbara Flynn. (1976). *Comprehensive Psychiatric Nursing.* New York, NY: McGraw-Hill Book Company.

Hastings, Linda Emerson. (1981). Complete Handbook of Activities and Recreational Programs for Nursing Homes. *Englewood Cliffs, NJ: Prentice-Hall, Inc.*

Hersh, E., M.D..Anytime, Anywhere Medical Records the National Health Information Infrastructure (NHII), Forum. Spring, 2004

Hitt, William, Ethics and Leadership: Putting Theory into Practice, Batelle Press, Columbus 1990.

Hitt, William D., The Leader-Manager: Guidelines for Action, Batelle Press, Columbus 1988
Laker, Mark. (1980). *Nursing Home Activities for the Handicapped.* Springfield, IL: Charles C. Thomas.
Lanza, Susan E., Essentials for the Activity Professional in Long-Term Care, Delmar, Albany 1997.

Mayer, Richard J., Conflict Management: The Courage to Confront, Second Edition, Batelle Press, Columbus 1995.

Merrill, Toni, M.A., 1974. *Discussion Topics for Oldsters in Nursing Homes: 365 Things to Talk About.* Springfield, IL: Charles C. Thomas

Miller, M.E. , 1994. *Activities Programs for Residents with Low-Cognitive-Functional Abilities,Individual, One-to-One and Group Activities* (Monograph). Mary E. Miller & Associates, Cincinnati, Ohio.

"Modular Education Program for Activity Professionals: Administrative Manual, 2nd Edition", NCCAP 2004.

Modular Education Program For Activity Professionals. Advanced Management Teacher Manual. (1992) Washington, DC. NAAP-NCCAP

O'Morrow, Gerald, S., Therapeutic Recreation A Helping Profession, Reston Publishing Company, Inc., Reston, Virginia, 1976.

Perschbacher, Ruth (1993)Assessment: The Cornerstone of Activity Programs. State College, PA: Venture Publishing.

Peterson, Carol Ann & Gunn, Scout Lee. *Therapeutic Recreation Program Design.* Englewood Cliffs, NJ: Prentice-Hall, Inc. 1984.

Provider Magazine American Health Care Association, 1201 L St., Washington, D.C. 2005, December.

Quadagno, Jill, *Aging and the Life Course*

Sander, P. 1987. *Wake Up!: A Sensory Stimulation Program for Nursing Home Residents*, M & H Publishing Company, Inc., P.O. Box 35752, Houston, TX 77235.

Sheridan, C. 1987. *Failure-Free Activities for the Alzheimer's Patient*, Cottage Books, 2419 13th Avenue, Oakland, CA 94606.

Spring 2004 Oregon's Future. Anytime, Anywhere Medical Records. The National Health Information. Infrastructure (NH11) by William Hersh, M.D.

Ten Points to Listening by Pat Beeman, taken from *A guide to community Membership for Older Adults with Disabilities,* University Affiliated Program of Indiana, Training Resource Network, St. Augustine, FL (866) 823-9800, www.trninc.com

Thompson, June M., McFarland, Gertrude K., Hirsch, Jane E. & Tucker, Susan M. (1993). *Mosby's Clinical Nursing.* St. Louis, MO: Mosby's Year Books, Inc.

Watkins, Marjorie, O.T.R., Marion, Ohio

Weisberg, Nadia, & Wilder, Rosilyn. (1985). *Creative Arts with Older Adults.* New York, NY: Human Sciences Press, Inc.

Wiener, Jerry M.,Editor (1990) Behavioral Science, Second Ed. Baltimore: Williams and Wilkins

"Winds of Change", American Hospital Association, 840, North Lake Shore Drive, Chicago, IL, 1971.

Zimmerman, Bill. (1987). *Make Beliefs*. New York, NY. Guarionex Press, Ltd.

Zgola, J.M., (1987). *Doing Things: A Guide to Programming Activities for Persons with Alzheimer's Disease and Related Disorders*. The Johns Hopkins' University Press, 701 West 40th Street, Baltimore, MD 21211.

END NOTES – Chapter 3

[1] Miller, M. E., Peckham, C.W., & Peckham, A. B. (1998). Activities keep me going and going (pp.217-224). Lebanon, OH: Otterbein Homes.

[2] Alzheimer's Association (n.d.). Activity based Alzheimer care: Building a therapeutic program. Training presentation made 1998.

[3] Thomas, W. H. (2003). Evolution of Eden. In A. S. Weiner & J. L. Ronch (Eds.), Culture change in long-term care (pp. 146-157). New York: Haworth Press.

[4] Bowman, C. S. (2005). Living Life to the Fullest: A match made in OBRA '87. Milwaukee, WI: Action Pact, Inc.

[5] Glantz, C. G., & Richman, N. (2001). Leisure activities. In Occupational therapy: Practice skills for physical dysfunction. St. Louis: Mosby.

[6] Glantz, C. G., & Richman, N. (1996). Evaluation and intervention for leisure activities, ROTE: Role of Occupational Therapy for the Elderly (2nd ed., p. 728). Bethesda, MD.: American Occupational Therapy Association.

[7] Glantz, C. G., & Richman, N. (1998). Creative methods, materials and models for training trainers in Alzheimer's education (pp. 156-159). Riverwoods, IL: Glantz/Richman Rehabilitation Assoc.

[8] Hellen, C. (1992). Alzheimer's disease: Activity-focused care (pp.128-130). Boston, MA: Andover.

[9] American Occupational Therapy Association. (2002). Occupational therapy practice framework: domain & process. American Journal of Occupational Therapy, 56(6), 616-617. Bethesda, MD: American Occupational Therapy Association.

[10] Henderson, A., Cermak, S., Costner, W., Murray, E., Trombly, C., & Tickle-Gegnen, L. (1991). The issue is: Occupational science is multidimensional. American Journal of Occupational Therapy, 45, 370-372. Bethesda, MD: American Occupational Therapy Association.

[11] Pedretti, L. W. (1996). Occupational performance: A model for practice in physical dysfunction. In L. W. Pedretti (Ed.), Occupational therapy: Practice skills for physical dysfunction (4th ed., pp. 3-11). St. Louis: Mosby-Year Book

[12] Christenson, M. A. (1996). Environmental design, modification, and adaptation, ROTE: Role of occupational therapy for the elderly (2nd ed., pp. 380-408). Bethesda, MD: American Occupational Therapy Association.

[13] Coppard, B. M., Higgins, T., & Harvey, K.D. (2004). Working with elders who have orthopedic conditions. In S. Byers-Connon, H.L. Lohman, and R. L. Padilla (Eds.), Occupational therapy with elders: Strategies for the COTA (2nd ed., p. 293). St. Louis, MO: Elservier Mosby.

[14] Glantz, C. G., & Richman, N. (1992). Activity programming for the resident with mental illness (pp. 53-76). Riverwoods, IL: Glantz/Richman Rehabilitation Associates.

[15] Day, K., & Calkins, M. P. (2002). Design and dementia. In R. B. Bechtel & A. Churchman (Eds.), Handbook of environmental psychology (pp. 374-393). New York: Wiley.

[16] Barrick, A. L., Rader, J., Hoeffer, B., & Sloane, P. (2002). Bathing without a battle: Personal care of individuals with dementia (p. 4). New York: Springer.

Talking Books – Contact your local library for information on the nearest source of these remarkable resources for those with vision problems. A majority of books in print are available on records or tapes. The program, including the tape and cassette machine, is free.

Books:

Activities for the Aged and Infirm: A Handbook for The Untrained Worker. Toni Merrill, M.A.. Charles C. Thomas Publisher, 301-327 East Lawrence Ave., Springfield, IL, 1972.

Activities for the Frail Aged. Cornish, Patricia. Potentials Developments, Inc., 40 Hazelwood Dr., Suite 101, Amherst, NY 14228

Choice Magazine Listening, 14 Maple Street, Port Washington, NY 11050.

Choice is an audio anthology of the best writing from printed periodicals on record. It includes fiction, poetry and the best articles chosen from over 50 current periodicals and read by professional voices on record.

Complete Handbook of Activities and Recreation Programs for Nursing Homes. (1981) Linda Emerson Hastings. Englewood Cliffs, NJ: Prentice-Hall, Inc.

American Printing House for the Blind, Inc., P.O. Box 8635, Louisville, Kentucky 40206 (for information on Newsweek Talking Magazine)

Nursing Home Activities for the Handicapped, Laker, Mark. Charles C. Thomas Publisher, 301-327 East Lawrence Ave., Springfield, IL, 1980.

Recreation for Disabled Persons, Elizabeth Ogg. Write for Public Affairs Pamphlet No. 571, 381 Park Ave. South, New York, NY10016

Webster's Ninth New Collegiate Dictionary. (1991). Massachusetts: Merriam-Webster Inc.

APPENDIX

A. Activity Documentation Forms
  1. Activity Assessment
        i. Short Term Assessment
        ii. Extended Stay Assessment

  2. Outcome/Participation Records
        i. Individual
        ii. Group
        iii. Outcome Notes
        iv. One to One Activity Participation

B. Cognitive Assessment and Depression Scale Forms
  1. Mini Mental Status Exam
  2. Short Portable Mental Status Questionnaire (SPMQ)
  3. The Cornell Scale for Depression

C. Federal Activity Regulations
  1. F-248 Activities Program
  2. F-249 Activity Qualifications
  3. F-243 Interpretive Guidelines
  4. F-244 Resident Groups/Council
  5. F-281 Professional Standards of Quality
  6. F-245 Participation in Other Activities
  7. F-169 Work

D. Resident Assessment Instrument (RAI)
  1. MDS 3.0
  2. Section F Preference for Customary Routine
  3. Care Area Triggers (CAT) Legend
  4. Daily Preferences Response Codes

E. Sample Activity Calendars and Program Marketing Materials
  1. Boyd Life Assisted Living Calendar – Wesleyan Village, Elyria, Ohio
  2. Beacon House Assisted Living Calendar – Wesleyan Village, Elyria, Ohio
  3. Assisted Living Calendar – Wellington Manor, North Olmsted, Ohio
  4. Skilled Care Calendar – Wellington Manor, North Olmsted, Ohio
  5. Skilled Care Calendar – Broadway Care Center, Oakwood
  6. Assisted Living/Independent Living Calendar – Shurmer Place
  7. Skilled Care Calendar – Eliza Bryant Village, Cleveland, Ohio
  8. Alzheimer's/Dementia Calendar - Lori Presser

F. Drug List

G. Activity Resources

    1. Activity Supplies and Equipment
    2. Addresses for Activity Programming
    3. Professional and Certification/Registration Organizations
    4. Resources - Aging

H. NCCAP (National Certification Council for Activity Professional Certification)

    1. NCCAP Certification Standards
    2. Application
    3. Certification Specialization

I. NAAP (National Association of Activity Professionals)
    1. Membership Application

J. GLOSSARY

Activity Assessment Profile

Short-term anticipated stay

Background / Factual Information

Name_____Birth date_____Admission Date_____

Birthplace_____Marital Status_____Years Married/Date_____

Living arrangements prior to Admission_____

Veteran_____Military Branch_____No. of Children_____Former Occupations_____

Religion_____Diagnosis _____

Daily Preferences   F0400

*Coding: 1. Very important 2. Somewhat important 3. Not very important 4. Not important at all
5. Important, but can't do or no choice 9. No response or non-responsive.*

A. how important is it to you to **choose what clothes to wear?** ☐

B. how important is it to you to **take care of your personal belongings or things?** ☐

C. how important is it to you to **choose between a tub bath, shower, bed bath, or sponge bath?** ☐

D. how important is it to you to **have snacks available between meals .** ☐

E. how important is it to you to **choose your own bedtime?** ☐

F. how important is it to you to **have your family or a close friend involved in discussions about your care?** ☐

G. how important is it to you to **be able to use the phone in private?** ☐

H. how important is it to you to **have a place to lock your things to keep them safe?** ☐

Activity Preferences   F0500

A. how important is it to you to **have books, newspapers, and magazines to read?** ☐

B. how important is it to you to **listen to music you like?** ☐

C. how important is it to you to **be around animals such as pets?** ☐

D. how important is it to you to **keep up with the news?** ☐

E. how important is it to you to **do things with groups of people?** ☐

F. how important is it to you to **do your favorite activities?** ☐

G. how important is it to you to **go outside to get fresh air when the weather is good?** ☐

H. how important is it to you to **participate in religious services or practices?** ☐

Primary Respondent F0600

☐ **Resident**   ☐ **Family or significant other** *(close friend or other representative)*

☐ **Interview could not be completed by resident or family/significant other**
("No response" to 3 or more items)

Activity Pursuit Patterns (P=Past, C=Current, N=No Interest)

P	C	N		P	C	N	
☐	☐	☐	Educational	☐	☐	☐	Spiritual / Religious
☐	☐	☐	Cards / Games	☐	☐	☐	Computers / Technology
☐	☐	☐	Crafts / Arts	☐	☐	☐	Watching TV / Movies
☐	☐	☐	Exercise / Sports	☐	☐	☐	Gardening / Plants
☐	☐	☐	Parties / Social	☐	☐	☐	Talking / Conversing
☐	☐	☐	Music	☐	☐	☐	Community / Volunteer

Adaptations / Precautions

Diet _____ Hearing _____ Mobility _____

Communications _____ Vision _____

Dietary _____

Precautions _____

Comforts from Home

Favorite food/meal/snack/beverage _____

Interest in pet programs ☐ _____ Other _____

Doctors Orders Requested

☐ Participation in Activity Program   ☐ Outings   ☐ Alcohol   ☐ Work / Service

CAA or Additional Notes

_____

_____

_____

_____

_____

_____

_____

_____

_____

_____

_____

_____

_____

_____

_____

_____

_____

_____

_____

_____

_____

Completed by _____ Date _____ ☐ initial ☐ annual ☐ revise

Activity Assessment Profile

Extended Stay

Background / Factual Information

ame_____ Birth date_____ Admission Date_____

irthplace_____Marital Status_____Years Married/Date_____

iving arrangements prior to Admission _____

eteran _____Military Branch_____No. of Children_____Former Occupations_____

egistered Voter _____Interested in Voting_____Religion_____

iagnosis _____

Daily Preferences   F0400

Coding: 1. Very important 2. Somewhat important 3. Not very important 4. Not important at all
5. Important, but can't do or no choice 9. No response or non-responsive

. *how important is it to you to* **choose what clothes to wear?** ☐

. *how important is it to you to* **take care of your personal belongings or things?** ☐

. *how important is it to you to* **choose between a tub bath, shower, bed bath, or sponge bath?** ☐

. *how important is it to you to* **have snacks available between meals .** ☐

. *how important is it to you to* **choose your own bedtime?** ☐

. *how important is it to you to* **have your family or a close friend involved in discussions about your care?** ☐

. *how important is it to you to* **be able to use the phone in private?** ☐

H .*how important is it to you to* **have a place to lock your things to keep them safe?** ☐

Activity Preferences   F0500

. *how important is it to you to* **have books, newspapers, and magazines to read?** ☐

. *how important is it to you to* **listen to music you like?** ☐

. *how important is it to you to* **be around animals such as pets?** ☐

. *how important is it to you to* **keep up with the news?** ☐

. *how important is it to you to* **do things with groups of people?** ☐

. *how important is it to you to* **do your favorite activities?** ☐

. *how important is it to you to* **go outside to get fresh air when the weather is good?** ☐

. *how important is it to you to* **participate in religious services or practices?** ☐

Primary Respondent F0600

☐ . **Resident** ☐ **Family or significant other** (close friend or other
representative)

☐ **Interview could not be completed** by resident or family/significant other ("No response" to 3 or more
items")

Krupa – Revised February 2011

Activity Pursuit Patterns (P=Past, C=Current, N=No Interest)

P	C	N		P	C	N	
☐	☐	☐	Educational	☐	☐	☐	Spiritual / Religious
☐	☐	☐	Cards / Games	☐	☐	☐	Computers / Technology
☐	☐	☐	Crafts / Arts	☐	☐	☐	Watching TV / Movies
☐	☐	☐	Exercise / Sports	☐	☐	☐	Gardening / Plants
☐	☐	☐	Parties / Social	☐	☐	☐	Talking / Conversing
☐	☐	☐	Music	☐	☐	☐	Community / Volunteer

Adaptations

Diet _____ Hearing _____ Mobility _____

Communications _____ Vision _____

Dietary _____

Precautions

Special Precautions / Limitations/ Considerations

☐ Diabetic   ☐ Restraints _____   ☐ Alcohol Limitations   ☐ Seizures   ☐ Heart Problems

☐ Combative   ☐ No cigarettes   ☐ Swallow Precaution   ☐ Sexually Aggressive   ☐ Wanders

Food Allergies _____   ☐ Ambulation

Comforts From Home

Favorite Food / Meal _____   Favorite Snack _____

Favorite Beverage _____   Flowers / Aroma _____

Interest in Pet Programs _____   Other _____

Doctors Orders Requested

☐ Participation in Activity Program   ☐ Outings   ☐ Alcohol   ☐ Work / Service

CAA or Additional Notes

_____

_____

_____

_____

_____

_____

_____

_____

_____

_____

_____

_____

Completed by _____ Date _____ ☐ initial ☐ annual ☐ revised

Individual Activity Engagement Record

(9)
-Accepted with Contribution 9-Accepted

8-Refused   I-III   G-Resident attended a group

Resident:

Room #:   **Month:**

Activity	1	2	3	4	5	6	7	8	9	10	11	12	13	14	15	16	17	18	19	20	21	22	23	24	25	26	27	28	29	30	31
Art Therapy/Crafts																															
Bible Study/Reading																															
Button Sort+ Match																															
Classic Radio																															
Computer																															
Discovery Apron/Vest																															
Discussion/Conversing																															
Exercise/Sports																															
Games/ Puzzles																															
Memory Box/Guided Imagery																															
Music Listening/Playing																															
Matching Activity																															
Object Identifying/Matching																															
Parties/ Specials/Social																															
People Watching																															
Pet Therapy Visit																															
Picture Identifying/Cuing																															
Reality Orientation/Cuing																															
Reminiscing/Journaling																															
Remotivation																															
Rolling Library/Reading																															
Sensory Game/Identifying																															
Sensory Stimulation Box/Kit																															
Solace/Support																															
Spinoza/Comfort Item																															
Spiritual/ Communion/Visit																															
Strolling Music																															
Tactile/ Touch Feel																															
Talking Books/CDS																															
Time Slips																															
TV/DVD/Classic Movies																															

317

JKrupa – Revised February 2011

GroupActivity Engagement Record

Legend: –Attended with Contribution 9-Attended 8-Refused I-Ill R-Individual 1:1Activity

Resident: _____ Room #: _____ Month: _____

Activity	1	2	3	4	5	6	7	8	9	10	11	12	13	14	15	16	17	18	19	20	21	22	23	24	25	26	27	28	29	30	31
Arts/Crafts/Ceramics																															
Banko/Card Groups																															
Bell Choir																															
Bible Study																															
Bingo/Po-ke-no/Games																															
Computer																															
Community Outings																															
Cooking/Baking																															
Current Events/AM News																															
Discussion Activities																															
Educational																															
Exercise/Yoga/Bowling																															
Happy Hour																															
Intergenerational Activities																															
Matinee/Drama																															
Men's Club/Activities																															
Music/Entertainment																															
Music Movement/Band/Sing																															
Nature/Gardening/Hort.																															
Parties/Specials																															
Pet Therapy																															
People Watch/Socializing																															
Puzzles/Table Games																															
Religion/Spiritual																															
Reminisce/Journaling																															
Resident Council/Wk. Service																															
Resident Right Ed. Act																															
Rolling Library/Comfort Cart																															
Young At Heart Club																															
Volunteering																															
TV/DVD/Classic Movies																															
Outdoors/Patio/Walking																															

JKrupa – Revised February 2011

9

Activity Engagement Outcome Notes

PATIENT'S NAME   ROOM #

NOTES SHOULD BE SIGNED AND DATED

Care Center

ONE TO ONE ACTIVITY PROGRAM PARTICIPATION RECORD AND RESPONSE

Name:_____**Room #**_____

Reason for 1:1 Activity Program: ☐ Resident Preference ☐ Confined to bed
☐ Confined to Room ☐ Inability to participate in Group Activity, reason _____

☐ Needs Additional Attention/ Stimulation, reason _____

Frequency and Duration of One-to-One Activity Program: _____ x per _____ for _____ minutes
Goals:_____
_____

Specific Activities:_____

Date	Record	INT
	Activity, Length of Activity and Resident Responses/Outcomes to Activity and/or Interventions	

APPENDIX B: COGNITIVE ASSESSMENT AND DEPRESSION SCALE FORM

Name: _____

Date: _____

MINI-MENTAL STATE EXAMINATION (MMSE)

The Folstein Mini-Mental Status Examination is a tool for assessing the mental status of older adults who have suspected cognitive impairment. Ask the person to follow a series of simple commands that test the resident's ability to understand and perform cognitive functions. A designated point value is assigned for successful completion of each instruction. The total scores determine the person's mental status. Scores of 26-30 indicates normal range; 22 to 25 mild impairment and less than significant impairment.

	Maximum Score	Score

ORIENTATION

What is the (year) (season) (date) (day) (month)?   5   _____

Where are we: (state)(country) (town or city) (floor, unit, hospital)?   5   _____

(Score one point for each correct response)

REGISTRATION

Name 3 common objects (e.g. "apple", "table", "penny"):   3   _____

(Take 1 second to say each. Then ask the person to repeat all 3 after you have said them.

Give 1 point for each correct answer. Then repeat them until the person learns all 3. Count trials

and record trial : _____).

ATTENTION AND CALCULATION

Spell "world" backwards. The score is the number of letters in correct order

(D __ L __ R __ O __ W __).   5   _____

RECALL

Ask for the 3 objects repeated above.   3

_____

(Give 1 point for each correct answer. (Note: Recall cannot be tested if all 3 objects were not

remembered during registration.)

LANGUAGE

Name a "pencil", and "watch" (Score 1 point for each correct response)   2   _____

Repeat the following: "No ifs, ands, or buts." (Score 1 point for correct response)   1   _____

Follow a 3-stage command: (Score 1 point for each correct response to the 3 part command)   3   _____

"Take a paper in your hand,
    fold it in half, and
    put it on the floor"

Read and obey the following: (Score 1 point for correct response)   1   _____
    Close your eyes.

Write a sentence. (Score 1 point for correct response)   1   _____

Copy the following design: (Score 1 point for correct response)   1   _____

Total Score   _____

Adapted from Folstein MF, Folstein SE, Mc Hugh PR "Mini-Mental State": a practical method for grading the cognitive state of patients for the clinician. **J Psychiatr Res** 1975; 12:196-198, and Cockrell JR, Forlstein MF. Mini-Mental State Examination (MMSE)

Interviewer: _____

assess.30

THE SHORT PORTABLE MENTAL STATUS QUESTIONAIRE (SPMSQ)

RESIDENT'S INITIALS:_____

DATE:_____

THE SHORT PORTABLE MENTAL STATUS QUESTIONAIRE (SPMSQ)		
Scoring	+	-
1. What is today's date?		
2. What day of the week is it?		
3. What is the name of this place?		
4. What is your telephone number?		
4a. What is your street address?		
5. How old are you?		
6. When were you born?		
7. Who is President of the U.S. now?		
8. Who was President just before him?		
9. What was your mother's maiden name?		
10. Subtract 3 from 20 and keep subtracting 3 from each new number, all the		
Total # of Errors		

Mental Status:_____

INSTRUCTIONS: Ask questions 1 through 10 in this list and record all answers.
Ask questions 4a only if resident does not have a telephone.
Record total number of errors based on ten questions.
Allow one more error if subject had only grade school education.
Allow one fewer errors if subject has had education beyond high school

SCORING: 1 –2 errors #_____   Intact mental function
3 – 4 errors #_____   Mild intellectual function
5 – 7 errors #_____   Moderate intellectual impairme
8 – 10 errors #_____   Sever intellectual impairment

assess.30

Cornell Scale for Depression in Dementia

NAME:_____   AGE:___ SEX:_____DATE:_____

WING:_____ _____   ROOM:_____

PHYSICIAN:_____

Ratings should be based on symptoms and signs occurring during the week before interview.
No score should be given if symptoms result from physical disability or illness.

SCORING SYSTEM

A = Unable to evaluate

0 = Absent

1 = Mild to Intermittent

2 = Severe

Score greater than 12 = Probable Depression

MOOD – RELATED SIGNS

	a	0	1	2
1. Anxiety; anxious expression, rumination, worrying				
2. Sadness; sad expression, sad voice, tearfulness				
3. Lack of reaction to pleasant events				
4. Irritability; annoyed, short termed				

BEHAVIORAL DISTSURBANCE

	a	0	1	2
5. Agitation; restlessness, hand wringing, hair pulling				
6. Retardation; slow movement, slow speech, slow reactions				
7. Multiple physical complaints *(score 0 if gastrointestinal symptoms only)*				
8. Loss of interests; less involve in usual activities *(score only if change occurred acutely, i.e., in less than one month)*				

PHYSICAL SIGNS

	A	0	1	2
9. Appetite loss; eating less than usual				
10. Weight loss *(score 2 if greater than 5 pounds in one month)*				
11. Lack of energy; fatigues easily, unable to sustain activities				

CYCLIC FUNCTIONS

12. Diurnal variation of mood; symptoms worse in morning				
13. Difficulty falling asleep; later than usual for this individual				
14. Multiple awakening during sleep				
15. Early morning awaking, earlier than usual for this individual				

IDEATIONAL DISTURBANCE

16. Suicidal; feels life is not worth living				
17. Poor self-esteem; self-blame, self-depreciation, feelings of failure				
18. Pessimism; anticipation of the worst				
19. Mood congruent delusions; delusions of poverty, illness or loss				

NOTES/CURRENT MEDICATIONS:_____

_____

SCORE

ASSESSOR:_____

assess.30

F-TAG #	REGULATION	GUIDANCE TO SURVEYORS
F248	§483.15(f) Activities	(Issued: 6-1-2006, Effective 6-1-06, Implementation: 6-1-06)
	§483.15(f)(1)	**INTENT: §483.15(f)(1) Activities**
	The facility must provide for an ongoing program of activities designed to meet, in accordance with the comprehensive assessment, the interests and the physical, mental, and psychosocial well-being of each resident.	The intent of this requirement is that:
		• The facility identifies each resident's interests and needs; and
		• The facility involves the resident in an ongoing program of activities that is designed to appeal to his or her interests and to enhance the resident's highest practicable level of physical, mental, and psychosocial well-being.
		DEFINITIONS
		Definitions are provided to clarify key terms used in this guidance.
		• **"Activities"** refer to any endeavor, other than routine ADLs, in which a resident participates that is intended to enhance her/his sense of well-being and to promote or enhance physical, cognitive, and emotional health. These include, but are not limited to, activities that promote self-esteem, pleasure, comfort, education, creativity, success, and independence.
		NOTE: ADL-related activities, such as manicures/pedicures, hair styling, and makeovers, may be considered part of the activities program.
		• **"One-to-One Programming"** refers to programming provided to residents who will not, or cannot, effectively plan their own activity pursuits, or residents needing specialized or extended programs to enhance their overall daily routine and activity pursuit needs.
		• **"Person Appropriate"** refers to the idea that each resident has a personal identity and history that involves more than just their medical illnesses or functional impairments. Activities should be relevant to the specific needs, interests, culture, background, etc. of the individual for whom they are developed.

APPENDIX C: FEDERAL ACTIVITY REGULATIONS

F-TAG #	REGULATION	GUIDANCE TO SURVEYORS
F248 cont.		• **"Program of Activities"** includes a combination of large and small group, one-to-one, and self-directed activities; and a system that supports the development, implementation, and evaluation of the activities provided to the residents in the facility.[1]
		## OVERVIEW
		In long term care, an ongoing program of activities refers to the provision of activities in accordance with and based upon an individual resident's comprehensive assessment. The Institute of Medicine (IOM)'s 1986 report, "Improving the Quality of Care in Nursing Homes," became the basis for the "Nursing Home Reform" part of OBRA '87 and the current OBRA long term care regulations. The IOM Report identified the need for residents in nursing homes to receive care and/or services to maximize their highest practicable quality of life. However, defining "quality of life" has been difficult, as it is subjective for each person. Thus, it is important for the facility to conduct an individualized assessment of each resident to provide additional opportunities to help enhance a resident's self-esteem and dignity.
		Research findings and the observations of positive resident outcomes confirm that activities are an integral component of residents' lives. Residents have indicated that daily life and involvement should be meaningful. Activities are meaningful when they reflect a person's interests and lifestyle, are enjoyable to the person, help the person to feel useful, and provide a sense of belonging.[2]
		## Residents' Views on Activities
		Activities are relevant and valuable to residents' quality of life. In a large-scale study commissioned by CMS, 160 residents in 40 nursing homes were interviewed about what quality of life meant to them. The study found that residents "overwhelmingly assigned priority to dignity, although they labeled this concern in many ways." The researchers determined that the two main components of dignity, in the words of these residents, were "independence" and

F-TAG #	REGULATION	GUIDANCE TO SURVEYORS
F248 cont.		"positive self-image." Residents listed, under the categories of independence and positive self-image, the elements of "choice of activities" and "activities that amount to something," such as those that produce or teach something; activities using skills from residents' former work; religious activities; and activities that contribute to the nursing home.
		The report stated that, "Residents not only discussed particular activities that gave them a sense of purpose but also indicated that a lack of appropriate activities contributes to having no sense of purpose." "Residents rarely mentioned participating in activities as a way to just 'keep busy,' or just to socialize. . .The relevance of the activities to the residents' lives must be considered."
		According to the study, residents wanted a variety of activities, including those that are not childish, require thinking (such as word games), are gender-specific, produce something useful, relate to previous work of residents, allow for socializing with visitors and participating in community events, and are physically active. The study found that the above concepts were relevant to both interviewable and non-interviewable residents. Researchers observed that non-interviewable residents appeared "happier" and "less agitated" in homes with many planned activities for them.
		Non-traditional Approaches to Activities
		Surveyors need to be aware that some facilities may take a non-traditional approach to activities. In neighborhoods/households, all staff may be trained as nurse aides and are responsible to provide activities, and activities may resemble those of a private home.[3] Residents, staff, and families may interact in ways that reflect daily life, instead of in formal activities programs. Residents may be more involved in the ongoing activities in their living area, such as care-planned approaches including chores, preparing foods, meeting with other residents to choose spontaneous activities, and leading an activity. It has been reported that, "some culture changed homes might not have a traditional activities calendar, and instead focus on community life to include activities. Instead of an "activities director," some homes have a Community Life Coordinator, a Community Developer, or other title for the individual directing the activities program.[4]

F-TAG #	REGULATION	GUIDANCE TO SURVEYORS
F248 cont.		For more information on activities in homes changing to a resident-directed culture, the following websites are available as resources: www.pioneernetwork.net; www.culturechangenow.com; www.qualitypartnersri.org (click on nursing homes); and www.edenalt.com.
		## ASSESSMENT
		The information gathered through the assessment process should be used to develop the **activities component of the comprehensive care plan. The ongoing program of activities should** match the skills, abilities, needs, and preferences of each resident with the demands of the activity and the characteristics of the physical, social and cultural environments.[5]
		In order to develop individualized-care planning goals and approaches, the facility should obtain sufficient, detailed information (even if the Activities RAP is not triggered) to determine what activities the resident prefers and what adaptations, if any, are needed.[6]
		(Rev 66, Issued: 10-01-10; Effective: 10-01-10; Implementation: 10-01-10) **NOTE:** RAPs have been replaced by CAAs. The above reference to the use of the RAP is interchangeable with the use of the CAA.
		The facility may use, but need not duplicate, information from other sources, such as the RAI, including the CAAs, assessments by other disciplines, observation, and resident and family interviews. Other sources of relevant information include the resident's lifelong interests, spirituality, life roles, goals, strengths, needs and activity pursuit patterns and preferences.[7] This assessment should be completed by or under the supervision of a qualified professional (see F249 for definition of qualified professional).
		NOTE: Some residents may be independently capable of pursuing their own activities without intervention from the facility. This information should be noted in the assessment and identified in the plan of care.

F-TAG #	REGULATION	GUIDANCE TO SURVEYORS
F248 cont.		## CARE PLANNING Care planning involves identification of the resident's interests, preferences, and abilities; and any issues, concerns, problems, or needs affecting the resident's involvement/engagement in activities.[8] In addition to the activities component of the comprehensive care plan, information may also be found in a separate activity plan, on a CNA flow sheet, in a progress note, etc. Activity goals related to the comprehensive care plan should be based on measurable objectives and focused on desired outcomes (e.g., engagement in an activity that matches the resident's ability, maintaining attention to the activity for a specified period of time, expressing satisfaction with the activity verbally or non-verbally), not merely on attendance at a certain number of activities per week. **NOTE:** For residents with no discernable response, service provision is still expected and may include one-to-one activities such as talking to the resident, reading to the resident about prior interests, or applying lotion while stroking the resident's hands or feet. Activities can occur at any time, are not limited to formal activities being provided only by activities staff, and can include activities provided by other facility staff, volunteers, visitors, residents, and family members. All relevant departments should collaborate to develop and implement an individualized activities program for each resident. Some medications, such as diuretics, or conditions such as pain, incontinence, etc. may affect the resident's participation in activities. Therefore, additional steps may be needed to facilitate the resident's participation in activities, such as: If not contraindicated, timing the administration of medications, to the extent possible, to avoid interfering with the resident's ability to participate or to remain at a scheduled activity; or If not contraindicated, modifying the administration time of pain medication to allow the medication to take effect prior to an activity the resident enjoys.

F-TAG #	REGULATION	GUIDANCE TO SURVEYORS
F248 cont.		The care plan should also identify the discipline(s) that will carry out the approaches. For example:
		• Notifying residents of preferred activities;
		• **Transporting residents who need assistance to and from activities (including indoor, outdoor, and outings);**
		• Providing needed functional assistance (such as toileting and eating assistance); and
		• Providing needed supplies or adaptations, such as obtaining and returning audio books, setting up adaptive equipment, etc.
		Concepts the facility should have considered in the development of the activities component of the resident's comprehensive care plan include the following, as applicable to the resident:
		• A continuation of life roles, consistent with resident preferences and functional capacity (e.g., to continue work or hobbies such as cooking, table setting, repairing small appliances);[9]
		• Encouraging and supporting the development of new interests, hobbies, and skills (e.g., training on using the Internet); and
		• Connecting with the community, such as places of worship, veterans' groups, volunteer **groups, support groups, wellness groups, athletic or educational connections (via outings or** invitations to outside groups to visit the facility).
		The facility may need to consider accommodations in schedules, supplies and timing in order to optimize a resident's ability to participate in an activity of choice. Examples of accommodations may include, but are not limited to:

F-TAG #	REGULATION	GUIDANCE TO SURVEYORS
F248 cont.		• Altering a therapy or a bath/shower schedule to make it possible for a resident to attend a desired activity that occurs at the same time as the therapy session or bath;
		• Assisting residents, as needed, to get to and participate in desired activities (e.g., dressing, toileting, transportation);
		• Providing supplies (e.g., books/magazines, music, craft projects, cards, sorting materials) for activities, and assistance when needed, for residents' use (e.g., during weekends, nights, holidays, evenings, or when the activities staff are unavailable); and
		• Providing a late breakfast to allow a resident to continue a lifelong pattern of attending religious services before eating.
		INTERVENTIONS
		The concept of individualized intervention has evolved over the years. Many activity professionals have abandoned generic interventions such as "reality orientation" and large-group activities that include residents with different levels of strengths and needs. In their place, individualized interventions have been developed based upon the assessment of the resident's history, preferences, strengths, and needs. These interventions have changed from the idea of "age-appropriate" activities to promoting "person-appropriate" activities. For example, one person may care for a doll or stroke a stuffed animal, another person may be inclined to reminisce about dolls or stuffed animals they once had, while someone else may enjoy petting a dog but will not be interested in inanimate objects. The surveyor observing these interventions should determine if the facility selected them in response to the resident's history and preferences. Many activities can be adapted in various ways to accommodate the resident's change in functioning due to physical or cognitive limitations.
		Some Possible Adaptations that May be Made by the Facility [10, 11]

F-TAG #	REGULATION	GUIDANCE TO SURVEYORS
F248 cont.		When evaluating the provision of activities, it is important for the surveyor to identify whether the resident has conditions and/or issues for which staff should have provided adaptations. Examples of adaptations for specific conditions include, but are not limited to the following:
		• For the resident with visual impairments: higher levels of lighting without glare; magnifying glasses, light-filtering lenses, telescopic glasses; use of "clock method" to describe where items are located; description of sizes, shapes, colors; large print items including playing cards, newsprint, books; audio books;
		• For the resident with hearing impairments: small group activities; placement of resident near speaker/activity leader; use of amplifiers or headphones; decreased background noise; written instructions; use of gestures or sign language to enhance verbal communication; adapted TV (closed captioning, magnified screen, earphones);
		• For the resident who has physical limitations, the use of adaptive equipment, proper seating and positioning, placement of supplies and materials[12] (based on clinical assessment and referral as appropriate) to enhance:
		○ Visual interaction and to compensate for loss of visual field (hemianopsia);
		○ Upper extremity function and range of motion (reach);
		○ Hand dexterity (e.g., adapted size of items such as larger handles for cooking and woodworking equipment, built-up paintbrush handles, large needles for crocheting);
		○ The ability to manipulate an item based upon the item's weight, such as lighter weight for residents with muscle weakness;[13]
		• For the resident who has the use of only one hand: holders for kitchen items, magazines/books, playing cards; items (e.g., art work, bingo card, nail file) taped to the table; c-clamp or suction vise to hold wood for sanding;

F-TAG #	REGULATION	GUIDANCE TO SURVEYORS
F248 cont.		• For the resident with cognitive impairment: task segmentation and simplification; programs using retained long-term memory, rather than short-term memory; length of activities based on attention span; settings that recreate past experiences or increase/decrease stimulation; smaller groups without interruption; one-to-one activities;
		NOTE: The length, duration, and content of specific one-to-one activities are determined by the specific needs of the individual resident, such as several short interventions (rather than a few longer activities) if someone has extremely low tolerance, or if there are behavioral issues. Examples of one-to-one activities may include any of the following:
		○ Sensory stimulation or cognitive therapy (e.g., touch/visual/auditory stimulation, reminiscence, or validation therapy) such as special stimulus rooms or equipment; alerting/upbeat music and using alerting aromas or providing fabrics or other materials of varying textures;
		○ Social engagement (e.g., directed conversation, initiating a resident to resident conversation, pleasure walk or coffee visit);
		○ Spiritual support, nurturing (e.g., daily devotion, Bible reading, or prayer with or for resident per religious requests/desires);
		○ Creative, task-oriented activities (e.g., music or pet activities/therapy, letter writing, word puzzles); or
		○ Support of self-directed activity (e.g., delivering of library books, craft material to rooms, setting up talking book service).
		• For the resident with a language barrier: translation tools; translators; or publications and/or audio/video materials in the resident's language;

APPENDIX C: FEDERAL ACTIVITY REGULATIONS

F-TAG #	REGULATION	GUIDANCE TO SURVEYORS
F248 cont.		• For residents who are terminally ill: life review; quality time with chosen relatives, friends, staff, and/or other residents; spiritual support; touch; massage; music; and/or reading to the resident;[8] NOTE: Some residents may prefer to spend their time alone and introspectively. Their refusal of activities does not necessarily constitute noncompliance. • For the resident with pain: spiritual support, relaxation programs, music, massage, aromatherapy, pet therapy/pet visits, and/or touch; • For the resident who prefers to stay in her/his own room or is unable to leave her/his room: in-room visits by staff/other residents/volunteers with similar interests/hobbies; touch and sensory activities such as massage or aromatherapy; access to art/craft materials, cards, games, reading materials; access to technology of interest (computer, DVD, hand held video games, preferred radio programs/stations, audio books); and/or visits from spiritual counselors;[14] • For the resident with varying sleep patterns, activities are available during awake time. Some facilities use a variety of options when activities staff are not available for a particular resident: nursing staff reads a newspaper with resident; dietary staff makes finger foods available; CNA works puzzle with the resident; maintenance staff take the resident on night rounds; and/or early morning delivery of coffee/juice to residents; • For the resident who has recently moved-in: welcoming activities and/or orientation activities; • For the short-stay resident: "a la carte activities" are available, such as books, magazines, cards, word puzzles, newspapers, CDs, movies, and handheld games; interesting/ contemporary group activities are offered, such as dominoes, bridge, Pinochle, poker, video games, movies, and travelogues; and/or individual activities designed to match the goals of therapy, such as jigsaw puzzles to enhance fine motor skills;

APPENDIX C: FEDERAL ACTIVITY REGULATIONS

F-TAG #	REGULATION	GUIDANCE TO SURVEYORS
F248 cont.		• For the younger resident: individual and group music offerings that fit the resident's taste and era; magazines, books and movies that fit the resident's taste and era; computer and Internet access; and/or contemporary group activities, such as video games, and the opportunity to play musical instruments, card and board games, and sports; and
		• For residents from diverse ethnic or cultural backgrounds: special events that include meals, decorations, celebrations, or music; visits from spiritual leaders and other individuals of the same ethnic background; printed materials (newspapers, magazines) about the resident's culture; and/or opportunities for the resident and family to share information about their culture with other residents, families, and staff.
		## Activity Approaches for Residents with Behavioral Symptoms[15, 7]
		When the surveyor is evaluating the activities provided to a resident who has behavioral symptoms, they may observe that many behaviors take place at about the same time every day (e.g., before lunch or mid-afternoon). The facility may have identified a resident's pattern of behavior symptoms and may offer activity interventions, whenever possible, prior to the behavior occurring. Once a behavior escalates, activities may be less effective or may even cause further stress to the resident (some behaviors may be appropriate reactions to feelings of discomfort, pain, or embarrassment, such as aggressive behaviors exhibited by some residents with dementia during bathing).[16] Examples of activities-related interventions that a facility may provide to try to minimize distressed behavior may include, but are not limited to the following:
		For the resident who is constantly walking:
		• Providing a space and environmental cues that encourages physical exercise, decreases exit behavior and reduces extraneous stimulation (such as seating areas spaced along a walking path or garden; a setting in which the resident may manipulate objects; or a room with a calming atmosphere, for example, using music, light, and rocking chairs);

F-TAG #	REGULATION	GUIDANCE TO SURVEYORS
F248 cont.		• Providing aroma(s)/aromatherapy that is/are pleasing and calming to the resident; and
		• Validating the resident's feelings and words; engaging the resident in conversation about who or what they are seeking; and using one-to-one activities, such as reading to the resident or looking at familiar pictures and photo albums.
		For the resident who engages in name-calling, hitting, kicking, yelling, biting, sexual behavior, or compulsive behavior:
		• Providing a calm, non-rushed environment, with structured, familiar activities such as folding, sorting, and matching; using one-to-one activities or small group activities that comfort the resident, such as their preferred music, walking quietly with the staff, a family member, or a friend; eating a favorite snack; looking at familiar pictures;
		• Engaging in exercise and movement activities; and
		• Exchanging self-stimulatory activity for a more socially-appropriate activity that uses the hands, if in a public space.
		For the resident who disrupts group activities with behaviors such as talking loudly and being demanding, or the resident who has catastrophic reactions such as uncontrolled crying or anger, or the resident who is sensitive to too much stimulation:
		• Offering activities in which the resident can succeed, that are broken into simple steps, that involve small groups or are one-to-one activities such as using the computer, that are short and repetitive, and that are stopped if the resident becomes overwhelmed (reducing excessive noise such as from the television);
		• Involving in familiar occupation-related activities. (A resident, if they desire, can do paid or volunteer work and the type of work would be included in the resident's plan of care, such as working outside the facility, sorting supplies, delivering resident mail, passing juice and snacks, refer to F169, Work);

APPENDIX C: FEDERAL ACTIVITY REGULATIONS

F-TAG #	REGULATION	GUIDANCE TO SURVEYORS
F248 cont.		• Involving in physical activities such as walking, exercise or dancing, games or projects requiring strategy, planning, and concentration, such as model building, and creative programs such as music, art, dance or physically resistive activities, such as kneading clay, hammering, scrubbing, sanding, using a punching bag, using stretch bands, or lifting weights; and
		• Slow exercises (e.g., slow tapping, clapping or drumming); rocking or swinging motions (including a rocking chair).
		For the resident who goes through others' belongings:
		• Using normalizing activities such as stacking canned food onto shelves, folding laundry; offering sorting activities (e.g., sorting socks, ties or buttons); involving in organizing tasks (e.g., putting activity supplies away); providing rummage areas in plain sight, such as a dresser; and
		• Using non-entry cues, such as "Do not disturb" signs or removable sashes, at the doors of other residents' rooms; providing locks to secure other resident's belongings (if requested).
		For the resident who has withdrawn from previous activity interests/customary routines and isolates self in room/bed most of the day:
		• Providing activities just before or after meal time and where the meal is being served (out of the room);
		• Providing in-room volunteer visits, music, or videos of choice;
		• Encouraging volunteer-type work that begins in the room and needs to be completed outside of the room, or a small group activity in the resident's room, if the resident agrees; working on failure-free activities, such as simple structured crafts or other activity with a friend; having the resident assist another person;

F-TAG #	REGULATION	GUIDANCE TO SURVEYORS
F248 cont.		• Inviting to special events with a trusted peer or family/friend;
		• Engaging in activities that give the resident a sense of value (e.g., intergenerational activities that emphasize the resident's oral history knowledge);
		• Inviting resident to participate on facility committees;
		• Inviting the resident outdoors; and
		• Involving in gross motor exercises (e.g., aerobics, light weight training) to increase energy and uplift mood.
		For the resident who excessively seeks attention from staff and/or peers: Including in social programs, small group activities, service projects, with opportunities for leadership.
		For the resident who lacks awareness of personal safety, such as putting foreign objects in her/his mouth or who is self-destructive and tries to harm self by cutting or hitting self, head banging, or causing other injuries to self:
		• Observing closely during activities, taking precautions with materials (e.g., avoiding sharp objects and small items that can be put into the mouth);
		• Involving in smaller groups or one-to-one activities that use the hands (e.g., folding towels, putting together PVC tubing);
		• Focusing attention on activities that are emotionally soothing, such as listening to music or talking about personal strengths and skills, followed by participation in related activities; and
		• Focusing attention on physical activities, such as exercise.
		For the resident who has delusional and hallucinatory behavior that is stressful to her/him:

APPENDIX C: FEDERAL ACTIVITY REGULATIONS

F-TAG #	REGULATION	GUIDANCE TO SURVEYORS
F248 cont.		• Focusing the resident on activities that decrease stress and increase awareness of actual surroundings, such as familiar activities and physical activities; offering verbal reassurance, especially in terms of keeping the resident safe; and acknowledging that the resident's experience is real to her/him. The outcome for the resident, the decrease or elimination of the behavior, either validates the activity intervention or suggests the need for a new approach. **ENDNOTES** 1 Miller, M. E., Peckham, C. W., & Peckham, A. B. (1998). Activities keep me going and going (pp. 217-224). Lebanon, OH: Otterbein Homes. 2 Alzheimer's Association (n.d.). Activity based Alzheimer care: Building a therapeutic program. Training presentation made 1998. 3 Thomas, W. H. (2003). Evolution of Eden. In A. S. Weiner & J. L. Ronch (Eds.), Culture change in long-term care (pp. 146-157). New York: Haworth Press. 4 Bowman, C. S. (2005). Living Life to the Fullest: A match made in OBRA '87. Milwaukee, WI: Action Pact, Inc. 5 Glantz, C. G., & Richman, N. (2001). Leisure activities. In Occupational therapy: Practice skills for physical dysfunction. St Louis: Mosby. 6 Glantz, C. G., & Richman, N. (1996). Evaluation and intervention for leisure activities, ROTE: Role of Occupational Therapy for the Elderly (2nd ed., p. 728). Bethesda, MD.: American Occupational Therapy Association. 7 Glantz, C.G., & Richman, N. (1998). Creative methods, materials and models for training trainers in alzheimer's education (pp. 156-159). Riverwoods, IL: Glantz/Richman Rehabilitation Associates.

F-TAG #	REGULATION	GUIDANCE TO SURVEYORS
F248 cont.		8 Hellen, C. (1992). Alzheimer's disease: Activity-focused care (pp. 128-130). Boston, MA: Andover.
		9 American Occupational Therapy Association. (2002). Occupational therapy practice framework: domain & process. American Journal of Occupational Therapy, 56(6), 616–617. Bethesda, MD: American Occupational Therapy Association.
		10 Henderson, A., Cermak, S., Costner, W., Murray, E., Trombly, C., & Tickle-Gegnen, L. (1991). The issue is: Occupational science is multidimensional. American Journal of Occupational Therapy, 45, 370-372, Bethesda, MD: American Occupational Therapy Association.
		11 Pedretti, L. W. (1996). Occupational performance: A model for practice in physical dysfunction. In L.W. Pedretti (Ed.), Occupational therapy: Practice skills for physical dysfunction (4th ed., pp. 3-11). St. Louis: Mosby-Year Book
		12 Christenson, M. A. (1996). Environmental design, modification, and adaptation, ROTE: Role of occupational therapy for the elderly (2nd ed., pp. 380-408). Bethesda, MD: American Occupational Therapy Association.
		13 Coppard, B. M., Higgins, T., & Harvey, K.D. (2004). Working with elders who have orthopedic conditions. In S. Byers-Connon, H.L. Lohman, and R.L. Padilla (Eds.), Occupational therapy with elders: Strategies for the COTA (2nd ed., p. 293). St. Louis, MO: Elsevier Mosby.
		14 Glantz, C. G., & Richman, N. (1992). Activity programming for the resident with mental illness (pp. 53-76). Riverwoods, IL: Glantz/Richman Rehabilitation Associates.
		15 Day, K., & Calkins, M. P. (2002). Design and dementia. In R. B. Bechtel & A. Churchman (Eds.), Handbook of environmental psychology (pp. 374-393). New York: Wiley.
		16 Barrick, A. L., Rader, J., Hoeffer, B., & Sloane, P. (2002). Bathing without a battle: Personal care of individuals with dementia (p. 4). New York: Springer.

F-TAG #	REGULATION	GUIDANCE TO SURVEYORS
F248 cont.		# INVESTIGATIVE PROTOCOL

ACTIVITIES

Objective

To determine if the facility has provided an ongoing program of activities designed to accommodate the individual resident's interests and help enhance her/his physical, mental, and psychosocial well-being, according to her/his comprehensive resident assessment.

Use

Use this procedure for each sampled resident to determine through interview, observation and record review whether the facility is in compliance with the regulation.

Procedures

Briefly review the comprehensive assessment and interdisciplinary care plan to guide observations to be made.

1. OBSERVATIONS

Observe during various shifts in order to determine if staff are consistently implementing those portions of the comprehensive plan of care related to activities. Determine if staff take into account the resident's food preferences and restrictions for activities that involve food, and provide ADL assistance and adaptive equipment as needed during activities programs. For a resident with personal assistive devices such as glasses or hearing aides, determine if these devices are in place, glasses are clean, and assistive devices are functional.

F-TAG #	REGULATION	GUIDANCE TO SURVEYORS
F248 cont.		For a resident whose care plan includes group activities, observe if staff inform the resident of the activities program schedule and provide timely transportation, if needed, for the resident to attend in-facility activities and help the resident access transportation to out-of-facility and community activities.
		Determine whether the facility provides activities that are compatible with the resident's known interests, needs, abilities and preferences. If the resident is in group activity programs, note if the resident is making attempts to leave, or is expressing displeasure with, or sleeping through, an activity program. If so, determine if staff attempted to identify the reason the resident is attempting to leave, and if they addressed the resident's needs. Determine whether the group activity has been adapted for the resident as needed and whether it is "person appropriate."
		NOTE: If you observe an activity that you believe would be age inappropriate for most residents, investigate further to determine the reason the resident and staff selected this activity. The National Alzheimer's Association has changed from endorsing the idea of "age-appropriate" activities to promoting "person-appropriate" activities. In general, surveyors should not expect to see the facility providing dolls or stuffed animals for most residents, but some residents are attached to these items and should be able to continue having them available if they prefer.
		Regarding group activities in common areas, determine if the activities are occurring in rooms that have sufficient space, light, ventilation, equipment, and supplies. Sufficient space includes enough space for residents to participate in the activity and space for a resident to enter and leave the room without having to move several other residents. Determine if the room is sufficiently free of extraneous noise, such as environmental noises from mechanical equipment and staff interruptions.
		For a resident who is involved in individual activities in her/his room, observe if staff have provided needed assistance, equipment and supplies. Observe if the room has sufficient light and space for the resident to complete the activity.

F-TAG #	REGULATION	GUIDANCE TO SURVEYORS
F248 cont.		## 2. INTERVIEWS **Resident/Representative Interview** Interview the resident, family or resident representative as appropriate to identify their involvement in care plan development, defining the approaches and goals that reflect the resident's preferences and choices. Determine: • What assistance, if any, the facility should be providing to facilitate participation in activities of choice and whether or not the assistance is being provided; • Whether the resident is participating in chosen activities on a regular basis, and if not, why not; • Whether the resident is notified of activities opportunities and is offered transportation assistance as needed to the activity location within the facility or access to transportation, where available and feasible, to outside activities; • Whether the facility tried, to the extent possible, to accommodate the resident's choices regarding her/his schedule, so that service provision (for example, bathing and therapy services) does not routinely conflict with desired activities; • Whether planned activity programs usually occur as scheduled (instead of being cancelled repeatedly); and • Whether the resident desires activities that the facility does not provide. If the resident has expressed any concerns, determine if the resident has discussed these with staff and, if so, what was the staff's response.

F-TAG #	REGULATION	GUIDANCE TO SURVEYORS
F248 cont.		**Activity Staff Interview** Interview activities staff as necessary to determine: • The resident's program of activities and related goals; • What assistance/adaptations they provide in group activities according to the resident's care plan; • How regularly the resident participates; if not participating, what is the reason(s); • How they assure the resident is informed of, and transported to, group activities of choice; • How special dietary needs and restrictions are handled during activities involving food; • What assistance they provide if the resident participates in any individual (non-group) activities; and • How they assure the resident has sufficient supplies, lighting, and space for individual activities. **CNA Interview** Interview CNAs as necessary to determine what assistance, if needed, the CNA provides to help the resident participate in desired group and individual activities, specifically: • Their role in ensuring the resident is out of bed, dressed, and ready to participate in chosen group activities, and in providing transportation if needed; • Their role in providing any needed ADL assistance to the resident while she/he is participating in group activities;

343

F-TAG #	REGULATION	GUIDANCE TO SURVEYORS
F248 cont.		• Their role in helping the resident to participate in individual activities (if the resident's plan includes these), for example, setup of equipment/supplies, positioning assistance, providing enough lighting and space; and
		• How activities are provided for the resident at times when activities staff are not available to provide care planned activities.
		Social Services Staff Interview
		Interview the social services staff member as necessary to determine how they help facilitate resident participation in desired activities; specifically, how the social services staff member:
		• Addresses the resident's psychosocial needs that impact on the resident's ability to participate in desired activities;
		• Obtains equipment and/or supplies that the resident needs in order to participate in desired activities (for example, obtaining audio books, helping the resident replace inadequate glasses or a hearing aid); and
		• Helps the resident access his/her funds in order to participate in desired activities that require money, such as attending concerts, plays, or restaurant dining events.
		Nurse Interview
		Interview a nurse who supervises CNAs who work with the resident to determine how nursing staff:
		• Assist the resident in participating in activities of choice by:
		○ Coordinating schedules for ADLs, medications, and therapies, to the extent possible, to maximize the resident's ability to participate;

APPENDIX C: FEDERAL ACTIVITY REGULATIONS

F-TAG #	REGULATION	GUIDANCE TO SURVEYORS
F248 cont.		○ Making nursing staff available to assist with activities in and out of the facility;
		• If the resident is refusing to participate in activities, how they try to identify and address the reasons; and
		• Coordinate the resident's activities participation when activities staff are not available to provide care planned activities.
		3. RECORD REVIEW
		Assessment
		Review the RAI, activity documentation/notes, social history, discharge information from a previous setting, and other interdisciplinary documentation that may contain information regarding the resident's activity interests, preferences and needed adaptations.
		Compare information obtained by observation of the resident and interviews with staff and the resident/responsible party (as possible), to the information in the resident's record, to help determine if the assessment accurately and comprehensively reflects the resident's status. Determine whether staff have identified:
		• Longstanding interests and customary routine, and how the resident's current physical, mental, and psychosocial health status affects her/his choice of activities and her/his ability to participate;
		• Specific information about how the resident prefers to participate in activities of interest (for example, if music is an interest, what kinds of music; does the resident play an instrument; does the resident have access to music to which she/he likes to listen; and can the resident participate independently, such as inserting a CD into a player);

F-TAG #	REGULATION	GUIDANCE TO SURVEYORS
F248 cont.		• Any significant changes in activity patterns before or after admission;
		• The resident's current needs for special adaptations in order to participate in desired activities (e.g., auditory enhancement or equipment to help compensate for physical difficulties such as use of only one hand);
		• The resident's needs, if any, for time-limited participation, such as a short attention span or an illness that permits only limited time out of bed;
		• The resident's desired daily routine and availability for activities; and
		• The resident's choices for group, one-to-one, and self-directed activities.
		Comprehensive Care Planning
		Review the comprehensive care plan to determine if that portion of the plan related to activities is based upon the goals, interests, and preferences of the resident and reflects the comprehensive assessment. Determine if the resident's care plan:
		• Includes participation of the resident (if able) or the resident's representative;
		• Considers a continuation of life roles, consistent with resident preferences and functional capacity;
		• Encourages and supports the development of new interests, hobbies, and skills;
		• Identifies activities in the community, if appropriate;
		• Includes needed adaptations that address resident conditions and issues affecting activities participation; and

APPENDIX C: FEDERAL ACTIVITY REGULATIONS

F-TAG #	REGULATION	GUIDANCE TO SURVEYORS
F248 cont.		• Identifies how the facility will provide activities to help the resident reach the goal(s) and who is responsible for implementation (e.g., activity staff, CNAs, dietary staff). If care plan concerns are noted, interview staff responsible for care planning regarding the rationale for the current plan of care. **Care Plan Revision** Determine if the staff have evaluated the effectiveness of the care plan related to activities and made revisions, if necessary, based upon the following: • Changes in the resident's abilities, interests, or health; • A determination that some aspects of the current care plan were unsuccessful (e.g., goals were not being met); • The resident refuses, resists, or complains about some chosen activities; • Changes in time of year have made some activities no longer possible (e.g., gardening outside in winter) and other activities have become available; and • New activity offerings have been added to the facility's available activity choices. For the resident who refused some or all activities, determine if the facility worked with the resident (or representative, as appropriate) to identify and address underlying reasons and offer alternatives.

Section V—Guidance to Surveyors **PP-113**

347

APPENDIX C: FEDERAL ACTIVITY REGULATIONS

F-TAG #	REGULATION	GUIDANCE TO SURVEYORS
F248 cont.		## DETERMINATION OF COMPLIANCE (Task 6, Appendix P) ### Synopsis of Regulation (F248) This requirement stipulates that the facility's program of activities should accommodate the interests and well-being of each resident. In order to fulfill this requirement, it is necessary for the facility to gain awareness of each resident's activity preferences as well as any current limitations that require adaptation in order to accommodate these preferences. ### Criteria for Compliance The facility is in compliance with this requirement if they: • Recognized and assessed for preferences, choices, specific conditions, causes and/or problems, needs and behaviors; • Defined and implemented activities in accordance with resident needs and goals; • Monitored and evaluated the resident's response; and • Revised the approaches as appropriate. If not, cite at F248. ### Noncompliance for Tag F248 After completing the Investigative Protocol, analyze the information gained in order to determine whether noncompliance with the regulation exists. Activities (F248) is an outcome-oriented requirement in that compliance is determined separately for each resident sampled.

F-TAG #	REGULATION	GUIDANCE TO SURVEYORS

F248 cont.		The survey team's review of the facility's activities program is conducted through a review of the individualization of activities to meet each resident's needs and preferences. For each sampled resident for whom activities participation was reviewed, the facility is in compliance if they have provided activities that are individualized to that resident's needs and preferences, and they have provided necessary adaptations to facilitate the resident's participation. Non compliance with F248 may look like, but is not limited to the following:
		
		The facility does not have an activity program and does not offer any activities to the resident;
		
		• A resident with special needs does not receive adaptations needed to participate in individualized activities;
		
		• Planned activities were not conducted or designed to meet the resident's care plan;
		
		Potential Tags for Additional Investigation
		
		During the investigation of the provision of care and services related to activities, the surveyor may have identified concerns with related outcome, process and/or structure requirements. The surveyor is cautioned to investigate these related requirements before determining whether noncompliance may be present. Some examples of requirements that should be considered include the following (not all inclusive):
		
		• **42 CFR 483.10(e), F164, Privacy and Confidentiality**
		
		  o Determine if the facility has accommodated the resident's need for privacy for visiting with family, friends, and others, as desired by the resident.
		
		• **42 CFR 483.10(j)(1) and (2), F172, Access and Visitation Rights**
		
		  o Determine if the facility has accommodated the resident's family and/or other visitors (as approved by the resident) to be present with the resident as much as desired, even round-the-clock.

APPENDIX C: FEDERAL ACTIVITY REGULATIONS

F-TAG #	REGULATION	GUIDANCE TO SURVEYORS
F248 cont.		• **42 CFR 483.15(b), F242, Self-Determination and Participation** 　○ Determine if the facility has provided the resident with choices about aspects of her/his life in the facility that are significant to the resident. • **42 CFR 483.15(e)(1), F246, Accommodation of Needs** 　○ Determine if the facility has provided reasonable accommodation to the resident's physical environment (room, bathroom, furniture, etc.) to accommodate the resident's individual needs in relation to the pursuit of individual activities, if any. • **42 CFR 483.15(f)(2), F249, Qualifications of the Activities Director** 　○ Determine if a qualified activities director is directing the activities program. • **42 CFR 483.15(g)(1), F250, Social Services** 　○ Determine if the facility is providing medically-related social services related to assisting with obtaining supplies/equipment for individual activities (if any), and assisting in meeting the resident's psychosocial needs related to activity choices. • **43 CFR 483.20(b)(1), F272, Comprehensive Assessment** 　○ Determine if the facility assessed the resident's activity needs, preferences, and interests specifically enough so that an individualized care plan could be developed. • **43 CFR 483.20(k)(1), F279, Comprehensive Care Plan** 　○ Determine if the facility developed specific and individualized activities goals and approaches as part of the comprehensive care plan, unless the resident is independent in providing for her/his activities without facility intervention.

APPENDIX C: FEDERAL ACTIVITY REGULATIONS

F-TAG #	REGULATION	GUIDANCE TO SURVEYORS
F248 cont.		• **43 CFR 483.20(k)(2), F280, Care Plan Revision** ◦ Determine whether the facility revised the plan of care as needed with input of the resident (or representative, as appropriate). • **43 CFR 483.30(a), F353, Sufficient Staff** ◦ Determine if the facility had qualified staff in sufficient numbers to assure the resident was provided activities based upon the comprehensive assessment and care plan. • **43 CFR 483.70(g), F464, Dining and Activities Rooms** ◦ Determine if the facility has provided sufficient space to accommodate the activities and the needs of participating residents and that space is well lighted, ventilated, and adequately furnished. • **43 CFR 483.75(g), F499, Staff Qualifications** ◦ Determine if the facility has employed sufficient qualified professional staff to assess residents and to develop and implement the activities approaches of their comprehensive care plans. **V. DEFICIENCY CATEGORIZATION (Part V, Appendix P)** Deficiencies at F248 are most likely to have psychosocial outcomes. The survey team should compare their findings to the various levels of severity on the Psychosocial Outcome Severity Guide at Appendix P, Part V.

APPENDIX C: FEDERAL ACTIVITY REGULATIONS

F-TAG #	REGULATION	GUIDANCE TO SURVEYORS
F249	**§483.15(f)(2) The activities program must be directed by a qualified professional who—** (i) Is a qualified therapeutic recreation specialist or an activities professional who— (A) Is licensed or registered, if applicable, by the State in which practicing; and (B) Is eligible for certification as a therapeutic recreation specialist or as an activities professional by a recognized accrediting body on or after October 1, 1990; or (ii) Has 2 years of experience in a social or recreational program within the last 5 years, 1 of which was full-time in a patient activities program in a health care setting; or (iii) Is a qualified occupational therapist or occupational therapy assistant; or (iv) Has completed a training course approved by the State.	(Issued: 6-1-2006, Effective 6-1-06, Implementation: 6-1-06) **INTENT §483.15(f)(2) Activities Director** The intent of this regulation is to ensure that the activities program is directed by a qualified professional. **DEFINITIONS** **"Recognized accrediting body"** refers to those organizations that certify, register, or license therapeutic recreation specialists, activity professionals, or occupational therapists. **ACTIVITIES DIRECTOR RESPONSIBILITIES** An activity director is responsible for directing the development, implementation, supervision and ongoing evaluation of the activities program. This includes the completion and/or directing/delegating the completion of the activities component of the comprehensive assessment; and contributing to and/or directing/delegating the contribution to the comprehensive care plan goals and approaches that are individualized to match the skills, abilities, and interests/preferences of each resident. Directing the activity program includes scheduling of activities, both individual and groups, implementing and/or delegating the implementation of the programs, monitoring the response and/or reviewing/evaluating the response to the programs to determine if the activities meet the assessed needs of the resident, and making revisions as necessary. **NOTE:** Review the qualifications of the activities director if there are concerns with the facility's compliance with the activities requirement at §483.15(f)(1), F248, or if there are concerns with the direction of the activity programs.

F-TAG #	REGULATION	GUIDANCE TO SURVEYORS
F249 cont.		A person is a qualified professional under this regulatory tag if they meet any one of the qualifications listed under 483.15(f)(2). **DETERMINATION OF COMPLIANCE (Task 6, Appendix P)** **Synopsis of Regulation (F249)** This requirement stipulates that the facility's program of activities be directed by a qualified professional. **Criteria for Compliance** The facility is in compliance with this requirement if they: • Have employed a qualified professional to provide direction in the development and implementation of activities in accordance with resident needs and goals, and the director: ○ Has completed or delegated the completion of the activities component of the comprehensive assessment; ○ Contributed or directed the contribution to the comprehensive care plan of activity goals and approaches that are individualized to match the skills, abilities, and interests/preferences of each resident; ○ Has monitored and evaluated the resident's response to activities and revised the approaches as appropriate; and ○ Has developed, implemented, supervised, and evaluated the activities program. If not, cite at F249.

APPENDIX C: FEDERAL ACTIVITY REGULATIONS

F-TAG #	REGULATION	GUIDANCE TO SURVEYORS
F249 cont.		## Noncompliance for F249

Tag F249 is a tag that is absolute, which means the facility must have a qualified activities professional to direct the provision of activities to the residents. Thus, it is cited if the facility is non-compliant with the regulation, whether or not there have been any negative outcomes to residents.

Noncompliance for F249 may include (but is not limited to) one or more of the following, including:

* Lack of a qualified activity director; or

* Lack of providing direction for the provision of an activity program;

V. DEFICIENCY CATEGORIZATION (Part V, Appendix P)

Once the team has completed its investigation, reviewed the regulatory requirements, and determined that noncompliance exists, the team must determine the severity of each deficiency, based on the resultant effect or potential for harm to the resident. The key elements for severity determination for F249 are as follows:

1. Presence of harm/negative outcome(s) or potential for negative outcomes due to a lack of an activities director or failure of the director to oversee, implement and/or provide activities programming.

* Lack of the activity director's involvement in coordinating/directing activities; or

* Lack of a qualified activity director.

APPENDIX C: FEDERAL ACTIVITY REGULATIONS

F-TAG #	REGULATION	GUIDANCE TO SURVEYORS
F249 cont.		**2. Degree of harm (actual or potential) related to the noncompliance.** Identify how the facility practices caused, resulted in, allowed or contributed to the actual or potential for harm: • If harm has occurred, determine level of harm; and • If harm has not yet occurred, determine the potential for discomfort to occur to the resident. **3. The immediacy of correction required.** Determine whether the noncompliance requires immediate correction in order to prevent serious injury, harm, impairment, or death to one or more residents. **Severity Level 4 Considerations: Immediate Jeopardy to Resident Health or Safety** Immediate jeopardy is not likely to be issued as it is unlikely that noncompliance with F249 could place a resident or residents into a situation with potential to sustain serious harm, injury, or death. **Severity Level 3 Considerations: Actual Harm that is not Immediate Jeopardy** Level 3 indicates noncompliance that results in actual harm, and may include, but is not limited to the resident's inability to maintain and/or reach his/her highest practicable well-being. In order to cite actual harm at this tag, the surveyor must be able to identify a relationship between noncompliance cited at Tag F248 (Activities) and failure of the provision

F-TAG #	REGULATION	GUIDANCE TO SURVEYORS
F249 cont.		and/or direction of the activity program by the activity director. For Severity Level 3, both of the following must be present:
		1. Findings of noncompliance at Severity Level 3 at Tag F248; and
		2. There is no activity director; or the facility failed to assure the activity director was responsible for directing the activity program in the assessment, development, implementation, and/or revision of an individualized activity program for an individual resident; and/or the activity director failed to assure that the facility's activity program was implemented.
		NOTE: If Severity Level 3 (actual harm that is not immediate jeopardy) has been ruled out based upon the evidence, then evaluate as to whether Level 2 (no actual harm with the potential for more than minimal harm) exists.
		Severity Level 2 Considerations: No Actual Harm with Potential for more than Minimal Harm that is not Immediate Jeopardy
		Level 2 indicates noncompliance that results in a resident outcome of no more than minimal discomfort and/or has the potential to compromise the resident's ability to maintain or reach his or her highest practicable level of well being. The potential exists for greater harm to occur if interventions are not provided. In order to cite Level 2 at Tag F249, the surveyor must be able to identify a relationship between noncompliance cited at Level 2 at Tag F248 (Activities) and failure of the provision and/or direction of activity program by the activity director. For Severity Level 2 at Tag F249, both of the following must be present:
		1. Findings of noncompliance at Severity Level 2 at Tag F248; and
		2. There is no activity director; or the facility failed to involve the activity director in the assessment, development, implementation, and/or revision of an individualized activity program for an individual resident; and/or the activity director failed to assure that the facility's activity program was implemented.

APPENDIX C: FEDERAL ACTIVITY REGULATIONS

F-TAG #	REGULATION	GUIDANCE TO SURVEYORS
F249 cont.		**Severity Level 1 Considerations: No Actual Harm with Potential for Minimal Harm** In order to cite Level 1, no actual harm with potential for minimal harm at this tag, the surveyor must be able to identify that: There is no activity director and/or the activity director is not qualified, however: • Tag F248 was not cited; • The activity systems associated with the responsibilities of the activity director are in place; • There has been a relatively short duration of time without an activity director; and • The facility is actively seeking a qualified activity director.

F-TAG #	REGULATION	GUIDANCE TO SURVEYORS
		sleep, and whether this is the resident's preferred time. Also determine whether the facility is honoring the resident's preferences regarding the timing (morning, afternoon, evening and how many times a week) for bathing and also the method (shower, bath, in-bed bathing). Obtain further information as necessary from observations and staff interviews. If the resident is unaware of the right to make such choices, determine whether the facility has actively sought information from the resident and/or family (for a resident unable to express choices) regarding preferences and whether these choices have been made known to caregivers.
F243	**§483.15(c) Participation in Resident and Family Groups** (1) A resident has the right to organize and participate in resident groups in the facility; (2) A resident's family has the right to meet in the facility with the families of other residents in the facility; (3) The facility must provide a resident or family group, if one exists, with private space; (4) Staff or visitors may attend meetings at the group's invitation; (5) The facility must provide a designated staff person responsible for providing assistance and responding to written requests that result form group meetings;	See Interpretive Guidance for §483.15(c) at Tag F244.

F-TAG #	REGULATION	GUIDANCE TO SURVEYORS

F244	§483.15(c)(6)
	
	When a resident or family group exists, the facility must listen to the views and act upon the grievances and recommendations of residents and families concerning proposed policy and operational decisions affecting resident care and life in the facility.
		Interpretive Guidelines §483.15(c)
		
		This requirement does not require that residents' organize a residents or family group. However, whenever residents or their families wish to organize, facilities must allow them to do so without interference. The facility must provide the group with space, privacy for meetings, and staff support. Normally, the designated staff person responsible for assistance and liaison between the group and the facility's administration and any other staff members attend the meeting only if requested.
		
		• "A resident's or family group" is defined as a group that meets regularly to:
		
		   ○ Discuss and offer suggestions about facility policies and procedures affecting residents' care, treatment, and quality of life;
		
		   ○ Support each other;
		
		   ○ Plan resident and family activities;
		
		   ○ Participate in educational activities; or
		
		   ○ For any other purpose.
		
		The facility is required to listen to resident and family group recommendations and grievances. Acting upon these issues does not mean that the facility must accede to all group recommendations, but the facility must seriously consider the group's recommendations and must attempt to accommodate those recommendations, to the extent practicable, in developing and changing facility policies affecting resident care and life in the facility. The facility should communicate its decisions to the resident and/or family group.
		
		Procedures §483.15(c)
		
		If no organized group exists, determine if residents have attempted to form one and have been unsuccessful, and, if so, why.

APPENDIX C: FEDERAL ACTIVITY REGULATIONS

F-TAG #	REGULATION	GUIDANCE TO SURVEYORS
F281	§483.20(k)(3)	**Intent §483.20(k)(3)(i)**
	(3) The services provided or arranged by the facility must—	The intent of this regulation is to assure that services being provided meet professional standards of quality (in accordance with the definition provided below) and are provided by appropriate qualified persons (e.g., licensed, certified).
	(i) Meet professional standards of quality and;	**Interpretive Guidelines §483.20(k)(3)(i)**
		"**Professional standards of quality**" means services that are provided according to accepted standards of clinical practice. Standards may apply to care provided by a particular clinical discipline or in a specific clinical situation or setting. Standards regarding quality care practices may be published by a professional organization, licensing board, accreditation body or other regulatory agency. Recommended practices to achieve desired resident outcomes may also be found in clinical literature. Possible reference sources for standards of practice include:
		• Current manuals or textbooks on nursing, social work, physical therapy, etc.
		• Standards published by professional organizations such as the American Dietetic Association, American Medical Association, American Medical Directors Association, American Nurses Association, National Association of Activity Professionals, National Association of Social Work, etc.
		• Clinical practice guidelines published by the Agency of Health Care Policy and Research.
		• Current professional journal articles.
		If a negative resident outcome is determined to be related to the facility's failure to meet professional standards, and the team determines a deficiency has occurred, it should be cited under the appropriate quality of care or other relevant requirement.

APPENDIX C: FEDERAL ACTIVITY REGULATIONS

F-TAG #	REGULATION	GUIDANCE TO SURVEYORS
F245	**§483.15(d) Participation in Other Activities** A resident has the right to participate in social, religious, and community activities that do not interfere with the rights of other residents in the facility.	**Interpretive Guidelines §483.15(d)** The facility, to the extent possible, should accommodate an individual's needs and choices for how he/she spends time, both inside and outside the facility. Ask the social worker or other appropriate staff how they help residents pursue activities outside the facility.
F246	**§483.15(e) Accommodation of Needs** A resident has a right to — **§483.15(e)(1)** Reside and receive services in the facility with reasonable accommodations of individual needs and preferences, except when the health or safety of the individual or other residents would be endangered; and	(Rev. 48; Issued: 06-12-09; Effective/Implementation Date: 06-12-09) **Interpretive Guidelines: §483.15(e)(1)** **"Reasonable accommodations of individual needs and preferences,"** means the facility's efforts to individualize the resident's physical environment. This includes the physical environment of the resident's bedroom and bathroom, as well as individualizing as much as feasible the facility's common living areas. The facility's physical environment and staff behaviors should be directed toward assisting the resident in maintaining and/or achieving independent functioning, dignity, and well-being to the extent possible in accordance with the resident's own needs and preferences. **NOTE:** For issues regarding the psychosocial environment experienced by the resident, such as being ignored by staff, being made to feel unwelcome or that their care needs are burdensome to staff, refer to §483.15(a), Tag F241, Dignity. The facility is responsible for evaluating each resident's unique needs and preferences and ensuring that the environment accommodates the resident to the extent reasonable and does not endanger the health or safety of individuals or other residents. This includes making adaptations of the resident's bedroom and bathroom furniture and fixtures, as necessary to ensure that the resident can (if able):

F-TAG #	REGULATION	GUIDANCE TO SURVEYORS
F169	**§483.10(h) Work** The resident has the right to— (1) Refuse to perform services for the facility; (2) Perform services for the facility, if he or she chooses, when— (i) The facility has documented the need or desire for work in the plan of care; (ii) The plan specifies the nature of the services performed and whether the services are voluntary or paid; (iii) Compensation for paid services is at or above prevailing rates; and (iv) The resident agrees to the work arrangement described in the plan of care	**Interpretive Guidelines §483.10(h)(1)-(2)** **"Prevailing rate"** is the wage paid to workers in the community surrounding the facility for essentially the same type, quality, and quantity of work requiring comparable skills. All resident work, whether of a voluntary or paid nature, must be part of the plan of care. A resident's desire for work is subject to discussion of medical appropriateness. As part of the plan of care, a therapeutic work assignment must be agreed to by the resident. The resident also has the right to refuse such treatment at any time that he or she wishes. At the time of development or review of the plan, voluntary or paid work can be negotiated. **Procedures §483.10(h)(1)-(2)** Are residents engaged in what may be paid or volunteer work (e.g., doing housekeeping, doing laundry, preparing meals)? Pay special attention to the possible work activities of residents with mental retardation or mental illness. If you observe such a situation, determine if the resident is in fact performing work and, if so, is this work, whether voluntary or paid, described in the plan of care?
	§483.10(i) Mail The resident has the right to privacy in written communications, including the right to—	
F170	**§483.10(i)(1)** Send and promptly receive mail that is unopened; and	See Guidance under Tag 171.

Resident _____ Identifier _____ Date _____

MINIMUM DATA SET (MDS) – Version 3.0
RESIDENT ASSESSMENT AND CARE SCREENING
Nursing Home Comprehensive (NC) Item Set

Section A	Identification Information

A0100. Facility Provider Numbers

A. National Provider Identifier (NPI):

☐☐☐☐☐☐☐☐☐☐

B. CMS Certification Number (CCN):

☐☐☐☐☐☐☐☐☐☐☐☐

C. State Provider Number:

☐☐☐☐☐☐☐☐☐☐☐☐☐☐

A0200. Type of Provider

Enter Code ☐	**Type of provider** 1. **Nursing home (SNF/NF)** 2. **Swing Bed**

A0310. Type of Assessment

Enter Code ☐☐	**A. Federal OBRA Reason for Assessment** 01. **Admission** assessment (required by day 14) 02. **Quarterly** review assessment 03. **Annual** assessment 04. **Significant change in status** assessment 05. **Significant correction** to **prior comprehensive** assessment 06. **Significant correction** to **prior quarterly** assessment 99. **Not OBRA required** assessment
Enter Code ☐☐	**B. PPS Assessment** **PPS Scheduled Assessments for a Medicare Part A Stay** 01. **5-day** scheduled assessment 02. **14-day** scheduled assessment 03. **30-day** scheduled assessment 04. **60-day** scheduled assessment 05. **90-day** scheduled assessment 06. **Readmission/return** assessment **PPS Unscheduled Assessments for a Medicare Part A Stay** 07. **Unscheduled assessment used for PPS** (OMRA, significant or clinical change, or significant correction assessment) **Not PPS Assessment** 99. **Not PPS** assessment
Enter Code ☐	**C. PPS Other Medicare Required Assessment - OMRA** 0. **No** 1. **Start of therapy** assessment 2. **End of therapy** assessment 3. **Both Start and End of therapy** assessment
Enter Code ☐	**D. Is this a Swing Bed clinical change assessment?** Complete only if A0200 = 2 0. **No** 1. **Yes**
Enter Code ☐	**E. Is this assessment the first assessment** (OBRA, PPS, or Discharge) **since the most recent admission?** 0. **No** 1. **Yes**
Enter Code ☐☐	**F. Entry/discharge reporting** 01. **Entry** record 10. **Discharge** assessment-**return not anticipated** 11. **Discharge** assessment-**return anticipated** 12. **Death in facility** record 99. **Not entry/discharge** record

Resident _____ Identifier _____ Date _____

Section A — Identification Information

A0410. Submission Requirement

Enter Code [ ]
1. **Neither federal nor state required submission**
2. **State but not federal required submission** (FOR NURSING HOMES ONLY)
3. **Federal required submission**

A0500. Legal Name of Resident

A. **First name:**
[ ][ ][ ][ ][ ][ ][ ][ ][ ][ ][ ][ ][ ][ ]

B. **Middle initial:**
[ ]

C. **Last name:**
[ ][ ][ ][ ][ ][ ][ ][ ][ ][ ][ ][ ][ ][ ][ ][ ][ ]

D. **Suffix:**
[ ][ ][ ]

A0600. Social Security and Medicare Numbers

A. **Social Security Number:**
[ ][ ][ ] – [ ][ ] – [ ][ ][ ][ ]

B. **Medicare number** (or comparable railroad insurance number):
[ ][ ][ ][ ][ ][ ][ ][ ][ ][ ][ ][ ]

A0700. Medicaid Number - Enter "+" if pending, "N" if not a Medicaid recipient

[ ][ ][ ][ ][ ][ ][ ][ ][ ][ ][ ][ ][ ][ ]

A0800. Gender

Enter Code [ ]
1. **Male**
2. **Female**

A0900. Birth Date

[ ][ ] – [ ][ ] – [ ][ ][ ][ ]
Month   Day   Year

A1000. Race/Ethnicity

↓ Check all that apply

[ ] A. **American Indian or Alaska Native**

[ ] B. **Asian**

[ ] C. **Black or African American**

[ ] D. **Hispanic or Latino**

[ ] E. **Native Hawaiian or Other Pacific Islander**

[ ] F. **White**

A1100. Language

Enter Code [ ]
A. **Does the resident need or want an interpreter to communicate with a doctor or health care staff?**
0. **No**
1. **Yes** → Specify in A1100B, Preferred language
9. **Unable to determine**

B. **Preferred language:**
[ ][ ][ ][ ][ ][ ][ ][ ][ ][ ][ ][ ][ ][ ][ ][ ]

Resident _____ Identifier _____ Date _____

Section A   Identification Information

A1200. Marital Status

Enter Code [ ]
1. **Never married**
2. **Married**
3. **Widowed**
4. **Separated**
5. **Divorced**

A1300. Optional Resident Items

A. **Medical record number:**

[ ][ ][ ][ ][ ][ ][ ][ ][ ][ ][ ][ ]

B. **Room number:**

[ ][ ][ ][ ][ ][ ][ ][ ]

C. **Name by which resident prefers to be addressed:**

[ ]

D. **Lifetime occupation(s) - put "/" between two occupations:**

[ ]

A1500. Preadmission Screening and Resident Review (PASRR)

Complete only if A0310A = 01

Enter Code [ ]
Has the resident been evaluated by Level II PASRR and determined to have a serious mental illness and/or mental retardation or a related condition?
0. **No**
1. **Yes**
9. **Not a Medicaid certified unit**

A1550. Conditions Related to MR/DD Status

If the resident is 22 years of age or older, complete only if A0310A = 01

If the resident is 21 years of age or younger, complete only if A0310A = 01, 03, 04, or 05

↓ **Check all conditions that are related to MR/DD status** that were manifested before age 22, and are likely to continue indefinitely

	MR/DD With Organic Condition
[ ]	A. **Down syndrome**
[ ]	B. **Autism**
[ ]	C. **Epilepsy**
[ ]	D. **Other organic condition related to MR/DD**
	MR/DD Without Organic Condition
[ ]	E. **MR/DD with no organic condition**
	No MR/DD
[ ]	Z. **None of the above**

A1600. Entry Date (date of this admission/reentry into the facility)

[ ][ ] - [ ][ ] - [ ][ ][ ][ ]
Month   Day   Year

A1700. Type of Entry

Enter Code [ ]
1. **Admission**
2. **Reentry**

Resident _____ Identifier _____ Date _____

Section A	Identification Information

A1800. Entered From

Enter Code ☐☐
- 01. **Community** (private home/apt., board/care, assisted living, group home)
- 02. **Another nursing home or swing bed**
- 03. **Acute hospital**
- 04. **Psychiatric hospital**
- 05. **Inpatient rehabilitation facility**
- 06. **MR/DD facility**
- 07. **Hospice**
- 99. **Other**

A2000. Discharge Date

Complete only if A0310F = 10, 11, or 12

☐☐ – ☐☐ – ☐☐☐☐
Month   Day   Year

A2100. Discharge Status

Complete only if A0310F = 10, 11, or 12

Enter Code ☐☐
- 01. **Community** (private home/apt., board/care, assisted living, group home)
- 02. **Another nursing home or swing bed**
- 03. **Acute hospital**
- 04. **Psychiatric hospital**
- 05. **Inpatient rehabilitation facility**
- 06. **MR/DD facility**
- 07. **Hospice**
- 08. **Deceased**
- 99. **Other**

A2200. Previous Assessment Reference Date for Significant Correction

Complete only if A0310A = 05 or 06

☐☐ – ☐☐ – ☐☐☐☐
Month   Day   Year

A2300. Assessment Reference Date

Observation end date:

☐☐ – ☐☐ – ☐☐☐☐
Month   Day   Year

A2400. Medicare Stay

Enter Code ☐
A. Has the resident had a Medicare-covered stay since the most recent entry?
- 0. **No** → Skip to B0100, Comatose
- 1. **Yes** → Continue to A2400B, Start date of most recent Medicare stay

B. Start date of most recent Medicare stay:

☐☐ – ☐☐ – ☐☐☐☐
Month   Day   Year

C. End date of most recent Medicare stay - Enter dashes if stay is ongoing:

☐☐ – ☐☐ – ☐☐☐☐
Month   Day   Year

Resident _____ Identifier _____ Date _____

Look back period for all items is 7 days unless another time frame is indicated

Section B	Hearing, Speech, and Vision

B0100. Comatose

Enter Code [ ]

Persistent vegetative state/no discernible consciousness
- 0. **No** → Continue to B0200, Hearing
- 1. **Yes** → Skip to G0110, Activities of Daily Living (ADL) Assistance

B0200. Hearing

Enter Code [ ]

Ability to hear (with hearing aid or hearing appliances if normally used)
- 0. **Adequate** - no difficulty in normal conversation, social interaction, listening to TV
- 1. **Minimal difficulty** - difficulty in some environments (e.g., when person speaks softly or setting is noisy)
- 2. **Moderate difficulty** - speaker has to increase volume and speak distinctly
- 3. **Highly impaired** - absence of useful hearing

B0300. Hearing Aid

Enter Code [ ]

Hearing aid or other hearing appliance used in completing B0200, Hearing
- 0. **No**
- 1. **Yes**

B0600. Speech Clarity

Enter Code [ ]

Select best description of speech pattern
- 0. **Clear speech** - distinct intelligible words
- 1. **Unclear speech** - slurred or mumbled words
- 2. **No speech** - absence of spoken words

B0700. Makes Self Understood

Enter Code [ ]

Ability to express ideas and wants, consider both verbal and non-verbal expression
- 0. **Understood**
- 1. **Usually understood** - difficulty communicating some words or finishing thoughts **but** is able if prompted or given time
- 2. **Sometimes understood** - ability is limited to making concrete requests
- 3. **Rarely/never understood**

B0800. Ability To Understand Others

Enter Code [ ]

Understanding verbal content, however able (with hearing aid or device if used)
- 0. **Understands** - clear comprehension
- 1. **Usually understands** - misses some part/intent of message **but** comprehends most conversation
- 2. **Sometimes understands** - responds adequately to simple, direct communication only
- 3. **Rarely/never understands**

B1000. Vision

Enter Code [ ]

Ability to see in adequate light (with glasses or other visual appliances)
- 0. **Adequate** - sees fine detail, including regular print in newspapers/books
- 1. **Impaired** - sees large print, but not regular print in newspapers/books
- 2. **Moderately impaired** - limited vision; not able to see newspaper headlines but can identify objects
- 3. **Highly impaired** - object identification in question, but eyes appear to follow objects
- 4. **Severely impaired** - no vision or sees only light, colors or shapes; eyes do not appear to follow objects

B1200. Corrective Lenses

Enter Code [ ]

Corrective lenses (contacts, glasses, or magnifying glass) used in completing B1000, Vision
- 0. **No**
- 1. **Yes**

Resident _____   Identifier _____   Date _____

Section C — Cognitive Patterns

C0100. Should Brief Interview for Mental Status (C0200-C0500) be Conducted?
Attempt to conduct interview with all residents

Enter Code ☐
  0. **No** (resident is rarely/never understood) → Skip to and complete C0700-C1000, Staff Assessment for Mental Status
  1. **Yes** → Continue to C0200, Repetition of Three Words

Brief Interview for Mental Status (BIMS)

C0200. Repetition of Three Words

Enter Code ☐

Ask resident: *"I am going to say three words for you to remember. Please repeat the words after I have said all three. The words are: **sock, blue, and bed.** Now tell me the three words."*
Number of words repeated after first attempt
  0. **None**
  1. **One**
  2. **Two**
  3. **Three**
After the resident's first attempt, repeat the words using cues ("*sock, something to wear; blue, a color; bed, a piece of furniture*"). You may repeat the words up to two more times.

C0300. Temporal Orientation (orientation to year, month, and day)

Enter Code ☐

Ask resident: *"Please tell me what year it is right now."*
A. Able to report correct year
  0. **Missed by > 5 years** or no answer
  1. **Missed by 2-5 years**
  2. **Missed by 1 year**
  3. **Correct**

Enter Code ☐

Ask resident: *"What month are we in right now?"*
B. Able to report correct month
  0. **Missed by > 1 month** or no answer
  1. **Missed by 6 days to 1 month**
  2. **Accurate within 5 days**

Enter Code ☐

Ask resident: *"What day of the week is today?"*
C. Able to report correct day of the week
  0. **Incorrect** or no answer
  1. **Correct**

C0400. Recall

Ask resident: *"Let's go back to an earlier question. What were those three words that I asked you to repeat?"*
If unable to remember a word, give cue (something to wear; a color; a piece of furniture) for that word.

Enter Code ☐
A. Able to recall "sock"
  0. **No** - could not recall
  1. **Yes, after cueing** ("something to wear")
  2. **Yes, no cue required**

Enter Code ☐
B. Able to recall "blue"
  0. **No** - could not recall
  1. **Yes, after cueing** ("a color")
  2. **Yes, no cue required**

Enter Code ☐
C. Able to recall "bed"
  0. **No** - could not recall
  1. **Yes, after cueing** ("a piece of furniture")
  2. **Yes, no cue required**

C0500. Summary Score

Enter Score ☐☐
Add scores for questions C0200-C0400 and fill in total score (00-15)
Enter 99 if the resident was unable to complete the interview

Resident _____ Identifier _____ Date _____

Section C — Cognitive Patterns

C0600. Should the Staff Assessment for Mental Status (C0700 - C1000) be Conducted?

Enter Code ☐
- 0. **No** (resident was able to complete interview) → Skip to C1300, Signs and Symptoms of Delirium
- 1. **Yes** (resident was unable to complete interview) → Continue to C0700, Short-term Memory OK

Staff Assessment for Mental Status

Do not conduct if Brief Interview for Mental Status (C0200-C0500) was completed

C0700. Short-term Memory OK

Enter Code ☐

Seems or appears to recall after 5 minutes
- 0. **Memory OK**
- 1. **Memory problem**

C0800. Long-term Memory OK

Enter Code ☐

Seems or appears to recall long past
- 0. **Memory OK**
- 1. **Memory problem**

C0900. Memory/Recall Ability

↓ Check all that the resident was normally able to recall

☐	A. **Current season**
☐	B. **Location of own room**
☐	C. **Staff names and faces**
☐	D. **That he or she is in a nursing home**
☐	Z. **None of the above** were recalled

C1000. Cognitive Skills for Daily Decision Making

Enter Code ☐

Made decisions regarding tasks of daily life
- 0. **Independent** - decisions consistent/reasonable
- 1. **Modified independence** - some difficulty in new situations only
- 2. **Moderately impaired** - decisions poor; cues/supervision required
- 3. **Severely impaired** - never/rarely made decisions

Delirium

C1300. Signs and Symptoms of Delirium (from CAM©)

Code **after completing** Brief Interview for Mental Status or Staff Assessment, and reviewing medical record

↓ Enter Codes in Boxes

Coding:
- 0. **Behavior not present**
- 1. **Behavior continuously present, does not fluctuate**
- 2. **Behavior present, fluctuates** (comes and goes, changes in severity)

☐	A. **Inattention** - Did the resident have difficulty focusing attention (easily distracted, out of touch or difficulty following what was said)?
☐	B. **Disorganized thinking** - Was the resident's thinking disorganized or incoherent (rambling or irrelevant conversation, unclear or illogical flow of ideas, or unpredictable switching from subject to subject)?
☐	C. **Altered level of consciousness** - Did the resident have altered level of consciousness (e.g., **vigilant** - startled easily to any sound or touch; **lethargic** - repeatedly dozed off when being asked questions, but responded to voice or touch; **stuporous** - very difficult to arouse and keep aroused for the interview; **comatose** - could not be aroused)?
☐	D. **Psychomotor retardation** - Did the resident have an unusually decreased level of activity such as sluggishness, staring into space, staying in one position, moving very slowly?

C1600. Acute Onset Mental Status Change

Enter Code ☐

Is there evidence of an acute change in mental status from the resident's baseline?
- 0. **No**
- 1. **Yes**

Resident _____ Identifier _____ Date _____

Section D — Mood

D0100. Should Resident Mood Interview be Conducted? - Attempt to conduct interview with all residents

Enter Code [ ]

0. **No** (resident is rarely/never understood) → Skip to and complete D0500-D0600, Staff Assessment of Resident Mood (PHQ-9-OV)
1. **Yes** → Continue to D0200, Resident Mood Interview (PHQ-9©)

D0200. Resident Mood Interview (PHQ-9©)

Say to resident: **"Over the last 2 weeks, have you been bothered by any of the following problems?"**

If symptom is present, enter 1 (yes) in column 1, Symptom Presence.
If yes in column 1, then ask the resident: "About **how often** have you been bothered by this?"
Read and show the resident a card with the symptom frequency choices. Indicate response in column 2, Symptom Frequency.

1. **Symptom Presence**
   0. **No** (enter 0 in column 2)
   1. **Yes** (enter 0-3 in column 2)
   9. **No response** (leave column 2 blank)

2. **Symptom Frequency**
   0. **Never or 1 day**
   1. **2-6 days** (several days)
   2. **7-11 days** (half or more of the days)
   3. **12-14 days** (nearly every day)

	1. Symptom Presence	2. Symptom Frequency
	↓ Enter Scores in Boxes ↓	
A. Little interest or pleasure in doing things	[ ]	[ ]
B. Feeling down, depressed, or hopeless	[ ]	[ ]
C. Trouble falling or staying asleep, or sleeping too much	[ ]	[ ]
D. Feeling tired or having little energy	[ ]	[ ]
E. Poor appetite or overeating	[ ]	[ ]
F. Feeling bad about yourself - or that you are a failure or have let yourself or your family down	[ ]	[ ]
G. Trouble concentrating on things, such as reading the newspaper or watching television	[ ]	[ ]
H. Moving or speaking so slowly that other people could have noticed. Or the opposite - being so fidgety or restless that you have been moving around a lot more than usual	[ ]	[ ]
I. Thoughts that you would be better off dead, or of hurting yourself in some way	[ ]	[ ]

D0300. Total Severity Score

Enter Score [ ]

Add scores for all frequency responses in Column 2, Symptom Frequency. Total score must be between 00 and 27. Enter 99 if unable to complete interview (i.e., Symptom Frequency is blank for 3 or more items).

D0350. Safety Notification - Complete only if D0200I1 = 1 indicating possibility of resident self harm

Enter Code [ ]

Was responsible staff or provider informed that there is a potential for resident self harm?
0. **No**
1. **Yes**

Resident _____ Identifier _____ Date _____

Section D	Mood

D0500. Staff Assessment of Resident Mood (PHQ-9-OV*)

Do not conduct if Resident Mood Interview (D0200-D0300) was completed

Over the last 2 weeks, did the resident have any of the following problems or behaviors?

If symptom is present, enter 1 (yes) in column 1, Symptom Presence.
Then move to column 2, Symptom Frequency, and indicate symptom frequency.

1. **Symptom Presence**
   - 0. **No** (enter 0 in column 2)
   - 1. **Yes** (enter 0-3 in column 2)

2. **Symptom Frequency**
   - 0. **Never or 1 day**
   - 1. **2-6 days** (several days)
   - 2. **7-11 days** (half or more of the days)
   - 3. **12-14 days** (nearly every day)

	1. Symptom Presence	2. Symptom Frequency
	↓ Enter Scores in Boxes ↓	
A. Little interest or pleasure in doing things	☐	☐
B. Feeling or appearing down, depressed, or hopeless	☐	☐
C. Trouble falling or staying asleep, or sleeping too much	☐	☐
D. Feeling tired or having little energy	☐	☐
E. Poor appetite or overeating	☐	☐
F. Indicating that s/he feels bad about self, is a failure, or has let self or family down	☐	☐
G. Trouble concentrating on things, such as reading the newspaper or watching television	☐	☐
H. Moving or speaking so slowly that other people have noticed. Or the opposite - being so fidgety or restless that s/he has been moving around a lot more than usual	☐	☐
I. States that life isn't worth living, wishes for death, or attempts to harm self	☐	☐
J. Being short-tempered, easily annoyed	☐	☐

D0600. Total Severity Score

☐ **Enter Score** Add scores for all frequency responses in Column 2, Symptom Frequency. Total score must be between 00 and 30.

D0650. Safety Notification - Complete only if D0500I1 = 1 indicating possibility of resident self harm

Enter Code ☐ Was responsible staff or provider informed that there is a potential for resident self harm?
   - 0. **No**
   - 1. **Yes**

Resident _____ Identifier _____ Date _____

Section E — Behavior

E0100. Psychosis

↓ Check all that apply

- [ ] A. **Hallucinations** (perceptual experiences in the absence of real external sensory stimuli)
- [ ] B. **Delusions** (misconceptions or beliefs that are firmly held, contrary to reality)
- [ ] Z. **None of the above**

Behavioral Symptoms

E0200. Behavioral Symptom - Presence & Frequency

Note presence of symptoms and their frequency

Coding:
0. **Behavior not exhibited**
1. **Behavior of this type occurred 1 to 3 days**
2. **Behavior of this type occurred 4 to 6 days,** but less than daily
3. **Behavior of this type occurred daily**

↓ Enter Codes in Boxes

- [ ] A. **Physical behavioral symptoms directed toward others** (e.g., hitting, kicking, pushing, scratching, grabbing, abusing others sexually)
- [ ] B. **Verbal behavioral symptoms directed toward others** (e.g., threatening others, screaming at others, cursing at others)
- [ ] C. **Other behavioral symptoms not directed toward others** (e.g., physical symptoms such as hitting or scratching self, pacing, rummaging, public sexual acts, disrobing in public, throwing or smearing food or bodily wastes, or verbal/vocal symptoms like screaming, disruptive sounds)

E0300. Overall Presence of Behavioral Symptoms

Enter Code [ ] Were any behavioral symptoms in questions E0200 coded 1, 2, or 3?
0. **No** → Skip to E0800, Rejection of Care
1. **Yes** → Considering all of E0200, Behavioral Symptoms, answer E0500 and E0600 below

E0500. Impact on Resident

Did any of the identified symptom(s):

Enter Code [ ] A. **Put the resident at significant risk for physical illness or injury?**
0. No
1. Yes

Enter Code [ ] B. **Significantly interfere with the resident's care?**
0. No
1. Yes

Enter Code [ ] C. **Significantly interfere with the resident's participation in activities or social interactions?**
0. No
1. Yes

E0600. Impact on Others

Did any of the identified symptom(s):

Enter Code [ ] A. **Put others at significant risk for physical injury?**
0. No
1. Yes

Enter Code [ ] B. **Significantly intrude on the privacy or activity of others?**
0. No
1. Yes

Enter Code [ ] C. **Significantly disrupt care or living environment?**
0. No
1. Yes

E0800. Rejection of Care - Presence & Frequency

Enter Code [ ] Did the resident reject evaluation or care (e.g., bloodwork, taking medications, ADL assistance) **that is necessary to achieve the resident's goals for health and well-being?** Do not include behaviors that have already been addressed (e.g., by discussion or care planning with the resident or family), and/or determined to be consistent with resident values, preferences, or goals.
0. **Behavior not exhibited**
1. **Behavior of this type occurred 1 to 3 days**
2. **Behavior of this type occurred 4 to 6 days,** but less than daily
3. **Behavior of this type occurred daily**

Resident _____ Identifier _____ Date _____

Section E	Behavior

E0900. Wandering - Presence & Frequency

Enter Code [ ]

Has the resident wandered?
- 0. **Behavior not exhibited** → Skip to E1100, Change in Behavioral or Other Symptoms
- 1. **Behavior of this type occurred 1 to 3 days**
- 2. **Behavior of this type occurred 4 to 6 days,** but less than daily
- 3. **Behavior of this type occurred daily**

E1000. Wandering - Impact

Enter Code [ ]

A. **Does the wandering place the resident at significant risk of getting to a potentially dangerous place** (e.g., stairs, outside of the facility)?
- 0. **No**
- 1. **Yes**

Enter Code [ ]

B. **Does the wandering significantly intrude on the privacy or activities of others?**
- 0. **No**
- 1. **Yes**

E1100. Change in Behavior or Other Symptoms

Consider all of the symptoms assessed in items E0100 through E1000

Enter Code [ ]

How does resident's current behavior status, care rejection, or wandering **compare to prior assessment (OBRA or PPS)?**
- 0. **Same**
- 1. **Improved**
- 2. **Worse**
- 3. **N/A** because no prior MDS assessment

Resident _____ Identifier _____ Date _____

Section F — Preferences for Customary Routine and Activities

F0300. Should Interview for Daily and Activity Preferences be Conducted? - Attempt to interview all residents able to communicate. If resident is unable to complete, attempt to complete interview with family member or significant other

Enter Code [ ]
- 0. **No** (resident is rarely/never understood **and** family/significant other not available) → Skip to and complete F0800, Staff Assessment of Daily and Activity Preferences
- 1. **Yes** → Continue to F0400, Interview for Daily Preferences

---

F0400. Interview for Daily Preferences

Show resident the response options and say: **"While you are in this facility..."**

↓ Enter Codes in Boxes

Coding:
1. **Very important**
2. **Somewhat important**
3. **Not very important**
4. **Not important at all**
5. **Important, but can't do or no choice**
9. **No response or non-responsive**

[ ]	A. how important is it to you to **choose what clothes to wear?**
[ ]	B. how important is it to you to **take care of your personal belongings or things?**
[ ]	C. how important is it to you to **choose between a tub bath, shower, bed bath, or sponge bath?**
[ ]	D. how important is it to you to **have snacks available between meals?**
[ ]	E. how important is it to you to **choose your own bedtime?**
[ ]	F. how important is it to you to **have your family or a close friend involved in discussions about your care?**
[ ]	G. how important is it to you to **be able to use the phone in private?**
[ ]	H. how important is it to you to **have a place to lock your things to keep them safe?**

F0500. Interview for Activity Preferences

Show resident the response options and say: **"While you are in this facility..."**

↓ Enter Codes in Boxes

Coding:
1. **Very important**
2. **Somewhat important**
3. **Not very important**
4. **Not important at all**
5. **Important, but can't do or no choice**
9. **No response or non-responsive**

[ ]	A. how important is it to you to **have books, newspapers, and magazines to read?**
[ ]	B. how important is it to you to **listen to music you like?**
[ ]	C. how important is it to you to **be around animals such as pets?**
[ ]	D. how important is it to you to **keep up with the news?**
[ ]	E. how important is it to you to **do things with groups of people?**
[ ]	F. how important is it to you to **do your favorite activities?**
[ ]	G. how important is it to you to **go outside to get fresh air when the weather is good?**
[ ]	H. how important is it to you to **participate in religious services or practices?**

F0600. Daily and Activity Preferences Primary Respondent

Enter Code [ ]

Indicate primary respondent for Daily and Activity Preferences (F0400 and F0500)
1. **Resident**
2. **Family or significant other** (close friend or other representative)
9. **Interview could not be completed** by resident or family/significant other ("No response" to 3 or more items)

Resident _____ Identifier _____ Date _____

Section F — Preferences for Customary Routine and Activities

F0700. Should the Staff Assessment of Daily and Activity Preferences be Conducted?

Enter Code ☐

0. **No** (because Interview for Daily and Activity Preferences (F0400 and F0500) was completed by resident or family/significant other) → Skip to and complete G0110, Activities of Daily Living (ADL) Assistance
1. **Yes** (because 3 or more items in Interview for Daily and Activity Preferences (F0400 and F0500) were not completed by resident or family/significant other) → Continue to F0800, Staff Assessment of Daily and Activity Preferences

F0800. Staff Assessment of Daily and Activity Preferences

Do not conduct if Interview for Daily and Activity Preferences (F0400-F0500) was completed

Resident Prefers:

↓ Check all that apply

☐ A. Choosing clothes to wear
☐ B. Caring for personal belongings
☐ C. Receiving tub bath
☐ D. Receiving shower
☐ E. Receiving bed bath
☐ F. Receiving sponge bath
☐ G. Snacks between meals
☐ H. Staying up past 8:00 p.m.
☐ I. Family or significant other involvement in care discussions
☐ J. Use of phone in private
☐ K. Place to lock personal belongings
☐ L. Reading books, newspapers, or magazines
☐ M. Listening to music
☐ N. Being around animals such as pets
☐ O. Keeping up with the news
☐ P. Doing things with groups of people
☐ Q. Participating in favorite activities
☐ R. Spending time away from the nursing home
☐ S. Spending time outdoors
☐ T. Participating in religious activities or practices
☐ Z. None of the above

Resident _____ Identifier _____ Date _____

Section G	Functional Status

G0110. Activities of Daily Living (ADL) Assistance
Refer to the ADL flow chart in the RAI manual to facilitate accurate coding

Instructions for Rule of 3
- When an activity occurs three times at any one given level, code that level.
- When an activity occurs three times at multiple levels, code the most dependent, exceptions are total dependence (4), activity must require full assist every time, and activity did not occur (8), activity must not have occurred at all. Example, three times extensive assistance (3) and three times limited assistance (2), code extensive assistance (3).
- When an activity occurs at various levels, but not three times at any given level, apply the following:
  ○ When there is a combination of full staff performance, and extensive assistance, code extensive assistance.
  ○ When there is a combination of full staff performance, weight bearing assistance and/or non-weight bearing assistance code limited assistance (2).
  If none of the above are met, code supervision.

1. ADL Self-Performance
Code for **resident's performance** over all shifts - not including setup. If the ADL activity occurred 3 or more times at various levels of assistance, code the most dependent - except for total dependence, which requires full staff performance every time

Coding:

    Activity Occurred 3 or More Times
0. **Independent** - no help or staff oversight at any time
1. **Supervision** - oversight, encouragement or cueing
2. **Limited assistance** - resident highly involved in activity; staff provide guided maneuvering of limbs or other non-weight-bearing assistance
3. **Extensive assistance** - resident involved in activity, staff provide weight-bearing support
4. **Total dependence** - full staff performance every time during entire 7-day period

    Activity Occurred 2 or Fewer Times
7. **Activity occurred only once or twice** - activity did occur but only once or twice
8. **Activity did not occur** - activity (or any part of the ADL) was not performed by resident or staff at all over the entire 7-day period

2. ADL Support Provided
Code for **most support provided** over all shifts; code regardless of resident's self-performance classification

Coding:
0. **No** setup or physical help from staff
1. **Setup** help only
2. **One** person physical assist
3. **Two+** persons physical assist
8. ADL activity itself **did not occur** during entire period

	1. Self-Performance	2. Support
	↓ Enter Codes in Boxes ↓	
A. Bed mobility - how resident moves to and from lying position, turns side to side, and positions body while in bed or alternate sleep furniture	☐	☐
B. Transfer - how resident moves between surfaces including to or from: bed, chair, wheelchair, standing position (**excludes** to/from bath/toilet)	☐	☐
C. Walk in room - how resident walks between locations in his/her room	☐	☐
D. Walk in corridor - how resident walks in corridor on unit	☐	☐
E. Locomotion on unit - how resident moves between locations in his/her room and adjacent corridor on same floor. If in wheelchair, self-sufficiency once in chair	☐	☐
F. Locomotion off unit - how resident moves to and returns from off-unit locations (e.g., areas set aside for dining, activities or treatments). **If facility has only one floor**, how resident moves to and from distant areas on the floor. If in wheelchair, self-sufficiency once in chair	☐	☐
G. Dressing - how resident puts on, fastens and takes off all items of clothing, including donning/removing a prosthesis or TED hose. Dressing includes putting on and changing pajamas and housedresses	☐	☐
H. Eating - how resident eats and drinks, regardless of skill. Do not include eating/drinking during medication pass. Includes intake of nourishment by other means (e.g., tube feeding, total parenteral nutrition, IV fluids administered for nutrition or hydration)	☐	☐
I. Toilet use - how resident uses the toilet room, commode, bedpan, or urinal; transfers on/off toilet; cleanses self after elimination; changes pad; manages ostomy or catheter; and adjusts clothes. Do not include emptying of bedpan, urinal, bedside commode, catheter bag or ostomy bag	☐	☐
J. Personal hygiene - how resident maintains personal hygiene, including combing hair, brushing teeth, shaving, applying makeup, washing/drying face and hands (**excludes** baths and showers)	☐	☐

Resident	Identifier	Date

Section G   Functional Status

G0120. Bathing

How resident takes full-body bath/shower, sponge bath, and transfers in/out of tub/shower (**excludes** washing of back and hair). Code for **most dependent** in self-performance and support

Enter Code [ ]
A. Self-performance
- 0. **Independent** - no help provided
- 1. **Supervision** - oversight help only
- 2. **Physical help limited to transfer only**
- 3. **Physical help in part of bathing activity**
- 4. **Total dependence**
- 8. **Activity itself did not occur** during the entire period

Enter Code [ ]
B. Support provided
(Bathing support codes are as defined in item **G0110 column 2, ADL Support Provided**, above)

G0300. Balance During Transitions and Walking

After observing the resident, **code the following walking and transition items for most dependent**

↓ **Enter Codes in Boxes**

Coding:
- 0. **Steady at all times**
- 1. **Not steady, but able to stabilize without human assistance**
- 2. **Not steady, only able to stabilize with human assistance**
- 8. **Activity did not occur**

[ ] A. **Moving from seated to standing position**
[ ] B. **Walking** (with assistive device if used)
[ ] C. **Turning around** and facing the opposite direction while walking
[ ] D. **Moving on and off toilet**
[ ] E. **Surface-to-surface transfer** (transfer between bed and chair or wheelchair)

G0400. Functional Limitation in Range of Motion

Code for limitation that interfered with daily functions or placed resident at risk of injury

↓ **Enter Codes in Boxes**

Coding:
- 0. **No impairment**
- 1. **Impairment on one side**
- 2. **Impairment on both sides**

[ ] A. **Upper extremity** (shoulder, elbow, wrist, hand)
[ ] B. **Lower extremity** (hip, knee, ankle, foot)

G0600. Mobility Devices

↓ **Check all that were normally used**

[ ] A. **Cane/crutch**
[ ] B. **Walker**
[ ] C. **Wheelchair** (manual or electric)
[ ] D. **Limb prosthesis**
[ ] Z. **None of the above** were used

G0900. Functional Rehabilitation Potential
Complete only if A0310A = 01

Enter Code [ ]
A. **Resident believes he or she is capable of increased independence** in at least some ADLs
- 0. **No**
- 1. **Yes**
- 9. **Unable to determine**

Enter Code [ ]
B. **Direct care staff believe resident is capable of increased independence** in at least some ADLs
- 0. **No**
- 1. **Yes**

Resident _____ Identifier _____ Date _____

Section H — Bladder and Bowel

H0100. Appliances

↓ Check all that apply

- [ ] A. **Indwelling catheter** (including suprapubic catheter and nephrostomy tube)
- [ ] B. **External catheter**
- [ ] C. **Ostomy** (including urostomy, ileostomy, and colostomy)
- [ ] D. **Intermittent catheterization**
- [ ] Z. **None of the above**

H0200. Urinary Toileting Program

Enter Code ☐
A. **Has a trial of a toileting program (e.g., scheduled toileting, prompted voiding, or bladder training)** been attempted on admission/reentry or since urinary incontinence was noted in this facility?
- 0. **No** → Skip to H0300, Urinary Continence
- 1. **Yes** → Continue to H0200B, Response
- 9. **Unable to determine** → Skip to H0200C, Current toileting program or trial

Enter Code ☐
B. **Response** - What was the resident's response to the trial program?
- 0. **No improvement**
- 1. **Decreased wetness**
- 2. **Completely dry** (continent)
- 9. **Unable to determine** or trial in progress

Enter Code ☐
C. **Current toileting program or trial** - Is a toileting program (e.g., scheduled toileting, prompted voiding, or bladder training) currently being used to manage the resident's urinary continence?
- 0. **No**
- 1. **Yes**

H0300. Urinary Continence

Enter Code ☐
Urinary continence - Select the one category that best describes the resident
- 0. **Always continent**
- 1. **Occasionally incontinent** (less than 7 episodes of incontinence)
- 2. **Frequently incontinent** (7 or more episodes of urinary incontinence, but at least one episode of continent voiding)
- 3. **Always incontinent** (no episodes of continent voiding)
- 9. **Not rated,** resident had a catheter (indwelling, condom), urinary ostomy, or no urine output for the entire 7 days

H0400. Bowel Continence

Enter Code ☐
Bowel continence - Select the one category that best describes the resident
- 0. **Always continent**
- 1. **Occasionally incontinent** (one episode of bowel incontinence)
- 2. **Frequently incontinent** (2 or more episodes of bowel incontinence, but at least one continent bowel movement)
- 3. **Always incontinent** (no episodes of continent bowel movements)
- 9. **Not rated,** resident had an ostomy or did not have a bowel movement for the entire 7 days

H0500. Bowel Toileting Program

Enter Code ☐
Is a toileting program currently being used to manage the resident's bowel continence?
- 0. **No**
- 1. **Yes**

H0600. Bowel Patterns

Enter Code ☐
Constipation present?
- 0. **No**
- 1. **Yes**

Resident _____ Identifier _____ Date _____

Section I — Active Diagnoses

Active Diagnoses in the last 7 days - Check all that apply
Diagnoses listed in parentheses are provided as examples and should not be considered as all-inclusive lists

Cancer
- [ ] I0100. **Cancer** (with or without metastasis)

Heart/Circulation
- [ ] I0200. **Anemia** (e.g., aplastic, iron deficiency, pernicious, and sickle cell)
- [ ] I0300. **Atrial Fibrillation or Other Dysrhythmias** (e.g., bradycardias and tachycardias)
- [ ] I0400. **Coronary Artery Disease (CAD)** (e.g., angina, myocardial infarction, and atherosclerotic heart disease (ASHD))
- [ ] I0500. **Deep Venous Thrombosis (DVT), Pulmonary Embolus (PE), or Pulmonary Thrombo-Embolism (PTE)**
- [ ] I0600. **Heart Failure** (e.g., congestive heart failure (CHF) and pulmonary edema)
- [ ] I0700. **Hypertension**
- [ ] I0800. **Orthostatic Hypotension**
- [ ] I0900. **Peripheral Vascular Disease (PVD) or Peripheral Arterial Disease (PAD)**

Gastrointestinal
- [ ] I1100. **Cirrhosis**
- [ ] I1200. **Gastroesophageal Reflux Disease (GERD) or Ulcer** (e.g., esophageal, gastric, and peptic ulcers)
- [ ] I1300. **Ulcerative Colitis, Crohn's Disease, or Inflammatory Bowel Disease**

Genitourinary
- [ ] I1400. **Benign Prostatic Hyperplasia (BPH)**
- [ ] I1500. **Renal Insufficiency, Renal Failure, or End-Stage Renal Disease (ESRD)**
- [ ] I1550. **Neurogenic Bladder**
- [ ] I1650. **Obstructive Uropathy**

Infections
- [ ] I1700. **Multidrug-Resistant Organism (MDRO)**
- [ ] I2000. **Pneumonia**
- [ ] I2100. **Septicemia**
- [ ] I2200. **Tuberculosis**
- [ ] I2300. **Urinary Tract Infection (UTI) (LAST 30 DAYS)**
- [ ] I2400. **Viral Hepatitis** (e.g., Hepatitis A, B, C, D, and E)
- [ ] I2500. **Wound Infection** (other than foot)

Metabolic
- [ ] I2900. **Diabetes Mellitus (DM)** (e.g., diabetic retinopathy, nephropathy, and neuropathy)
- [ ] I3100. **Hyponatremia**
- [ ] I3200. **Hyperkalemia**
- [ ] I3300. **Hyperlipidemia** (e.g., hypercholesterolemia)
- [ ] I3400. **Thyroid Disorder** (e.g., hypothyroidism, hyperthyroidism, and Hashimoto's thyroiditis)

Musculoskeletal
- [ ] I3700. **Arthritis** (e.g., degenerative joint disease (DJD), osteoarthritis, and rheumatoid arthritis (RA))
- [ ] I3800. **Osteoporosis**
- [ ] I3900. **Hip Fracture** - any hip fracture that has a relationship to current status, treatments, monitoring (e.g., sub-capital fractures, and fractures of the trochanter and femoral neck)
- [ ] I4000. **Other Fracture**

Neurological
- [ ] I4200. **Alzheimer's Disease**
- [ ] I4300. **Aphasia**
- [ ] I4400. **Cerebral Palsy**
- [ ] I4500. **Cerebrovascular Accident (CVA), Transient Ischemic Attack (TIA), or Stroke**
- [ ] I4800. **Dementia** (e.g. Non-Alzheimer's dementia such as vascular or multi-infarct dementia; mixed dementia; frontotemporal dementia such as Pick's disease; and dementia related to stroke, Parkinson's or Creutzfeldt-Jakob diseases)

Neurological Diagnoses continued on next page

Resident _____ Identifier _____ Date _____

| Section I | Active Diagnoses |

Active Diagnoses in the last 7 days - Check all that apply
Diagnoses listed in parentheses are provided as examples and should not be considered as all-inclusive lists

Neurological - Continued

- ☐ I4900. **Hemiplegia or Hemiparesis**
- ☐ I5000. **Paraplegia**
- ☐ I5100. **Quadriplegia**
- ☐ I5200. **Multiple Sclerosis (MS)**
- ☐ I5250. **Huntington's Disease**
- ☐ I5300. **Parkinson's Disease**
- ☐ I5350. **Tourette's Syndrome**
- ☐ I5400. **Seizure Disorder or Epilepsy**
- ☐ I5500. **Traumatic Brain Injury (TBI)**

Nutritional

- ☐ I5600. **Malnutrition** (protein or calorie) or at risk for malnutrition

Psychiatric/Mood Disorder

- ☐ I5700. **Anxiety Disorder**
- ☐ I5800. **Depression** (other than bipolar)
- ☐ I5900. **Manic Depression** (bipolar disease)
- ☐ I5950. **Psychotic Disorder** (other than schizophrenia)
- ☐ I6000. **Schizophrenia** (e.g., schizoaffective and schizophreniform disorders)
- ☐ I6100. **Post Traumatic Stress Disorder (PTSD)**

Pulmonary

- ☐ I6200. **Asthma, Chronic Obstructive Pulmonary Disease (COPD), or Chronic Lung Disease** (e.g., chronic bronchitis and restrictive lung diseases such as asbestosis)
- ☐ I6300. **Respiratory Failure**

Vision

- ☐ I6500. **Cataracts, Glaucoma, or Macular Degeneration**

None of Above

- ☐ I7900. **None of the above active diagnoses** within the last 7 days

Other

- ☐ I8000. **Additional active diagnoses**
  Enter diagnosis on line and ICD code in boxes. Include the decimal for the code in the appropriate box.

  A. _____ ☐☐☐☐☐☐☐☐

  B. _____ ☐☐☐☐☐☐☐☐

  C. _____ ☐☐☐☐☐☐☐☐

  D. _____ ☐☐☐☐☐☐☐☐

  E. _____ ☐☐☐☐☐☐☐☐

  F. _____ ☐☐☐☐☐☐☐☐

  G. _____ ☐☐☐☐☐☐☐☐

  H. _____ ☐☐☐☐☐☐☐☐

  I. _____ ☐☐☐☐☐☐☐☐

  J. _____ ☐☐☐☐☐☐☐☐

Resident _____   Identifier _____   Date _____

Section J — Health Conditions

J0100. Pain Management - Complete for all residents, regardless of current pain level

At any time in the last **5 days**, has the resident:

Enter Code [ ] **A. Been on a scheduled pain medication regimen?**
  0. No
  1. Yes

Enter Code [ ] **B. Received PRN pain medications?**
  0. No
  1. Yes

Enter Code [ ] **C. Received non-medication intervention for pain?**
  0. No
  1. Yes

J0200. Should Pain Assessment Interview be Conducted?

Attempt to conduct interview with all residents. If resident is comatose, skip to J1100, Shortness of Breath (dyspnea)

Enter Code [ ]
  0. **No** (resident is rarely/never understood) → Skip to and complete J0800, Indicators of Pain or Possible Pain
  1. **Yes** → Continue to J0300, Pain Presence

Pain Assessment Interview

J0300. Pain Presence

Enter Code [ ] Ask resident: **"Have you had pain or hurting at any time** in the last 5 days?"
  0. **No** → Skip to J1100, Shortness of Breath
  1. **Yes** → Continue to J0400, Pain Frequency
  9. **Unable to answer** → Skip to J0800, Indicators of Pain or Possible Pain

J0400. Pain Frequency

Enter Code [ ] Ask resident: **"How much of the time have you experienced pain or hurting** over the last 5 days?"
  1. **Almost constantly**
  2. **Frequently**
  3. **Occasionally**
  4. **Rarely**
  9. **Unable to answer**

J0500. Pain Effect on Function

Enter Code [ ] **A.** Ask resident: "Over the past 5 days, **has pain made it hard for you to sleep at night**?"
  0. **No**
  1. **Yes**
  9. **Unable to answer**

Enter Code [ ] **B.** Ask resident: "Over the past 5 days, **have you limited your day-to-day activities because of pain?**"
  0. **No**
  1. **Yes**
  9. **Unable to answer**

J0600. Pain Intensity - Administer ONLY ONE of the following pain intensity questions (A or B)

Enter Rating [ ][ ] **A. Numeric Rating Scale (00-10)**
  Ask resident: *"Please rate your worst pain over the last 5 days on a zero to ten scale, with zero being no pain and ten as the worst pain you can imagine."* (Show resident 00-10 pain scale)
  Enter two-digit response. Enter 99 if unable to answer.

Enter Code [ ] **B. Verbal Descriptor Scale**
  Ask resident: *"Please rate the intensity of your worst pain over the last 5 days."* (Show resident verbal scale)
  1. **Mild**
  2. **Moderate**
  3. **Severe**
  4. **Very severe, horrible**
  9. **Unable to answer**

Resident _____ Identifier _____ Date _____

Section J — Health Conditions

J0700. Should the Staff Assessment for Pain be Conducted?

Enter Code ☐
- 0. **No** (J0400 = 1 thru 4) → Skip to J1100, Shortness of Breath (dyspnea)
- 1. **Yes** (J0400 = 9) → Continue to J0800, Indicators of Pain or Possible Pain

Staff Assessment for Pain

J0800. Indicators of Pain or Possible Pain in the last 5 days

↓ Check all that apply

- ☐ A. **Non-verbal sounds** (e.g., crying, whining, gasping, moaning, or groaning)
- ☐ B. **Vocal complaints of pain** (e.g., that hurts, ouch, stop)
- ☐ C. **Facial expressions** (e.g., grimaces, winces, wrinkled forehead, furrowed brow, clenched teeth or jaw)
- ☐ D. **Protective body movements or postures** (e.g., bracing, guarding, rubbing or massaging a body part/area, clutching or holding a body part during movement)
- ☐ Z. **None of these signs observed or documented** → If checked, skip to J1100, Shortness of Breath (dyspnea)

J0850. Frequency of Indicator of Pain or Possible Pain in the last 5 days

Enter Code ☐
Frequency with which resident complains or shows evidence of pain or possible pain
- 1. **Indicators of pain** or possible pain observed **1 to 2 days**
- 2. **Indicators of pain** or possible pain observed **3 to 4 days**
- 3. **Indicators of pain** or possible pain observed **daily**

Other Health Conditions

J1100. Shortness of Breath (dyspnea)

↓ Check all that apply

- ☐ A. **Shortness of breath** or trouble breathing **with exertion** (e.g., walking, bathing, transferring)
- ☐ B. **Shortness of breath** or trouble breathing **when sitting at rest**
- ☐ C. **Shortness of breath** or trouble breathing **when lying flat**
- ☐ Z. **None of the above**

J1300. Current Tobacco Use

Enter Code ☐
Tobacco use
- 0. **No**
- 1. **Yes**

J1400. Prognosis

Enter Code ☐
Does the resident have a condition or chronic disease that may result in a **life expectancy of less than 6 months?** (Requires physician documentation)
- 0. **No**
- 1. **Yes**

J1550. Problem Conditions

↓ Check all that apply

- ☐ A. **Fever**
- ☐ B. **Vomiting**
- ☐ C. **Dehydrated**
- ☐ D. **Internal bleeding**
- ☐ Z. **None of the above**

Resident _____   Identifier _____   Date _____

Section J	Health Conditions

J1700. Fall History on Admission
Complete only if A0310A = 01 or A0310E = 1

Enter Code [ ] A. Did the resident have a fall any time in the **last month** prior to admission?
    0. **No**
    1. **Yes**
    9. **Unable to determine**

Enter Code [ ] B. Did the resident have a fall any time in the **last 2-6 months** prior to admission?
    0. **No**
    1. **Yes**
    9. **Unable to determine**

Enter Code [ ] C. Did the resident have any **fracture related to a fall in the 6 months** prior to admission?
    0. **No**
    1. **Yes**
    9. **Unable to determine**

J1800. Any Falls Since Admission or Prior Assessment (OBRA, PPS, or Discharge), whichever is more recent

Enter Code [ ] Has the resident **had any falls since admission or the prior assessment** (OBRA, PPS, or Discharge), whichever is more recent?
    0. **No** → Skip to K0100, Swallowing Disorder
    1. **Yes** → Continue to J1900, Number of Falls Since Admission or Prior Assessment (OBRA, PPS, or Discharge)

J1900. Number of Falls Since Admission or Prior Assessment (OBRA, PPS, or Discharge), whichever is more recent

↓ **Enter Codes in Boxes**

Coding:
  0. **None**
  1. **One**
  2. **Two or more**

[ ] A. **No injury** - no evidence of any injury is noted on physical assessment by the nurse or primary care clinician; no complaints of pain or injury by the resident; no change in the resident's behavior is noted after the fall

[ ] B. **Injury (except major)** - skin tears, abrasions, lacerations, superficial bruises, hematomas and sprains; or any fall-related injury that causes the resident to complain of pain

[ ] C. **Major injury** - bone fractures, joint dislocations, closed head injuries with altered consciousness, subdural hematoma

Resident _____ Identifier _____ Date _____

Section K — Swallowing/Nutritional Status

K0100. Swallowing Disorder

Signs and symptoms of possible swallowing disorder

↓ Check all that apply

☐	A. Loss of liquids/solids from mouth when eating or drinking
☐	B. Holding food in mouth/cheeks or residual food in mouth after meals
☐	C. Coughing or choking during meals or when swallowing medications
☐	D. Complaints of difficulty or pain with swallowing
☐	Z. None of the above

K0200. Height and Weight - While measuring, if the number is X.1 - X.4 round down; X.5 or greater round up

☐☐ inches	A. **Height** (in inches). Record most recent height measure since admission
☐☐☐ pounds	B. **Weight** (in pounds). Base weight on most recent measure in last 30 days; measure weight consistently, according to standard facility practice (e.g., in a.m. after voiding, before meal, with shoes off, etc.)

K0300. Weight Loss

Enter Code ☐	Loss of 5% or more in the last month or loss of 10% or more in last 6 months 0. **No** or unknown 1. **Yes, on** physician-prescribed weight-loss regimen 2. **Yes, not on** physician-prescribed weight-loss regimen

K0500. Nutritional Approaches

↓ Check all that apply

☐	A. Parenteral/IV feeding
☐	B. Feeding tube - nasogastric or abdominal (PEG)
☐	C. Mechanically altered diet - require change in texture of food or liquids (e.g., pureed food, thickened liquids)
☐	D. Therapeutic diet (e.g., low salt, diabetic, low cholesterol)
☐	Z. None of the above

K0700. Percent Intake by Artificial Route - Complete K0700 only if K0500A or K0500B is checked

Enter Code ☐	A. **Proportion of total calories the resident received through parenteral or tube feeding** 1. **25% or less** 2. **26-50%** 3. **51% or more**
Enter Code ☐	B. **Average fluid intake per day by IV or tube feeding** 1. **500 cc/day or less** 2. **501 cc/day or more**

Section L — Oral/Dental Status

L0200. Dental

↓ Check all that apply

☐	A. Broken or loosely fitting full or partial denture (chipped, cracked, uncleanable, or loose)
☐	B. No natural teeth or tooth fragment(s) (edentulous)
☐	C. Abnormal mouth tissue (ulcers, masses, oral lesions, including under denture or partial if one is worn)
☐	D. Obvious or likely cavity or broken natural teeth
☐	E. Inflamed or bleeding gums or loose natural teeth
☐	F. Mouth or facial pain, discomfort or difficulty with chewing
☐	G. Unable to examine
☐	Z. None of the above were present

Resident _____ Identifier _____ Date _____

Section M	Skin Conditions

Report based on highest stage of existing ulcer(s) at its worst; do not "reverse" stage

M0100. Determination of Pressure Ulcer Risk

↓ Check all that apply

- [ ] A. Resident has a stage 1 or greater, a scar over bony prominence, or a non-removable dressing/device
- [ ] B. Formal assessment instrument/tool (e.g., Braden, Norton, or other)
- [ ] C. Clinical assessment
- [ ] Z. None of the above

M0150. Risk of Pressure Ulcers

Enter Code [ ] Is this resident at risk of developing pressure ulcers?
  0. No
  1. Yes

M0210. Unhealed Pressure Ulcer(s)

Enter Code [ ] Does this resident have one or more unhealed pressure ulcer(s) at Stage 1 or higher?
  0. No → Skip to M0900, Healed Pressure Ulcers
  1. Yes → Continue to M0300, Current Number of Unhealed (non-epithelialized) Pressure Ulcers at Each Stage

M0300. Current Number of Unhealed (non-epithelialized) Pressure Ulcers at Each Stage

Enter Number [ ] A. Number of Stage 1 pressure ulcers
  Stage 1: Intact skin with non-blanchable redness of a localized area usually over a bony prominence. Darkly pigmented skin may not have a visible blanching; in dark skin tones only it may appear with persistent blue or purple hues

B. **Stage 2:** Partial thickness loss of dermis presenting as a shallow open ulcer with a red or pink wound bed, without slough. May also present as an intact or open/ruptured blister

Enter Number [ ] 1. Number of Stage 2 pressure ulcers - If 0 → Skip to M0300C, Stage 3

Enter Number [ ] 2. Number of these Stage 2 pressure ulcers that were present upon admission/reentry - enter how many were noted at the time of admission

3. Date of oldest Stage 2 pressure ulcer - Enter dashes if date is unknown:

[ ] [ ] – [ ] [ ] – [ ] [ ] [ ] [ ]
Month   Day   Year

C. **Stage 3:** Full thickness tissue loss. Subcutaneous fat may be visible but bone, tendon or muscle is not exposed. Slough may be present but does not obscure the depth of tissue loss. May include undermining and tunneling

Enter Number [ ] 1. Number of Stage 3 pressure ulcers - If 0 → Skip to M0300D, Stage 4

Enter Number [ ] 2. Number of these Stage 3 pressure ulcers that were present upon admission/reentry - enter how many were noted at the time of admission

D. **Stage 4:** Full thickness tissue loss with exposed bone, tendon or muscle. Slough or eschar may be present on some parts of the wound bed. Often includes undermining and tunneling

Enter Number [ ] 1. Number of Stage 4 pressure ulcers - If 0 → Skip to M0300E, Unstageable: Non-removable dressing

Enter Number [ ] 2. Number of these Stage 4 pressure ulcers that were present upon admission/reentry - enter how many were noted at the time of admission

M0300 continued on next page

Resident _____ Identifier _____ Date _____

| **Section M** | **Skin Conditions** |

M0300. Current Number of Unhealed (non-epithelialized) **Pressure Ulcers at Each Stage** - Continued

---

	E. **Unstageable - Non-removable dressing:** Known but not stageable due to non-removable dressing/device
Enter Number □	1. **Number of unstageable pressure ulcers due to non-removable dressing/device** - If 0 → Skip to M0300F, Unstageable: Slough and/or eschar
Enter Number □	2. **Number of these unstageable pressure ulcers that were present upon admission/reentry** - enter how many were noted at the time of admission

	F. **Unstageable - Slough and/or eschar:** Known but not stageable due to coverage of wound bed by slough and/or eschar
Enter Number □	1. **Number of unstageable pressure ulcers due to coverage of wound bed by slough and/or eschar** - If 0 → Skip to M0300G, Unstageable: Deep tissue
Enter Number □	2. **Number of these unstageable pressure ulcers that were present upon admission/reentry** - enter how many were noted at the time of admission

	G. **Unstageable - Deep tissue:** Suspected deep tissue injury in evolution
Enter Number □	1. **Number of unstageable pressure ulcers with suspected deep tissue injury in evolution** - If 0 → Skip to M0610, Dimension of Unhealed Stage 3 or 4 Pressure Ulcers or Eschar
Enter Number □	2. **Number of these unstageable pressure ulcers that were present upon admission/reentry** - enter how many were noted at the time of admission

---

M0610. Dimensions of Unhealed Stage 3 or 4 Pressure Ulcers or Eschar
Complete only if M0300C1, M0300D1 or M0300F1 is greater than 0

If the resident has one or more unhealed (non-epithelialized) Stage 3 or 4 pressure ulcers or an unstageable pressure ulcer due to slough or eschar, identify the pressure ulcer with the largest surface area (length x width) and record in centimeters:

□□.□ cm	A. **Pressure ulcer length:** Longest length from head to toe
□□.□ cm	B. **Pressure ulcer width:** Widest width of the same pressure ulcer, side-to-side perpendicular (90-degree angle) to length
□□.□ cm	C. **Pressure ulcer depth:** Depth of the same pressure ulcer from the visible surface to the deepest area (if depth is unknown, enter a dash in each box)

M0700. Most Severe Tissue Type for Any Pressure Ulcer

Enter Code □	Select the best description of the most severe type of tissue present in any pressure ulcer bed
	1. **Epithelial tissue** - new skin growing in superficial ulcer. It can be light pink and shiny, even in persons with darkly pigmented skin
	2. **Granulation tissue** - pink or red tissue with shiny, moist, granular appearance
	3. **Slough** - yellow or white tissue that adheres to the ulcer bed in strings or thick clumps, or is mucinous
	4. **Necrotic tissue (Eschar)** - black, brown, or tan tissue that adheres firmly to the wound bed or ulcer edges, may be softer or harder than surrounding skin

---

M0800. Worsening in Pressure Ulcer Status Since Prior Assessment (OBRA, PPS, or Discharge)
Complete only if A0310E = 0

Indicate the number of current pressure ulcers that were **not present or were at a lesser stage** on prior assessment (OBRA, PPS, or Discharge). If no current pressure ulcer at a given stage, enter 0

Enter Number □	A. **Stage 2**
Enter Number □	B. **Stage 3**
Enter Number □	C. **Stage 4**

ANTMANT

start

Resident _____ Identifier _____ Date _____

Section M — Skin Conditions

M0900. Healed Pressure Ulcers
Complete only if A0310E = 0

Enter Code ☐   **A. Were pressure ulcers present on the prior assessment (OBRA, PPS, or Discharge)?**
- 0. **No** → Skip to M1030, Number of Venous and Arterial Ulcers
- 1. **Yes** → Continue to M0900B, Stage 2

Indicate the number of pressure ulcers that were noted on the prior assessment (OBRA, PPS, or Discharge) that have completely closed (resurfaced with epithelium). If no healed pressure ulcer at a given stage since the prior assessment (OBRA, PPS, or Discharge), enter 0

Enter Number ☐   **B. Stage 2**

Enter Number ☐   **C. Stage 3**

Enter Number ☐   **D. Stage 4**

M1030. Number of Venous and Arterial Ulcers

Enter Number ☐   **Enter the total number of venous and arterial ulcers present**

M1040. Other Ulcers, Wounds and Skin Problems
↓ Check all that apply

Foot Problems
- ☐ A. **Infection of the foot** (e.g., cellulitis, purulent drainage)
- ☐ B. **Diabetic foot ulcer(s)**
- ☐ C. **Other open lesion(s) on the foot**

Other Problems
- ☐ D. **Open lesion(s) other than ulcers, rashes, cuts** (e.g., cancer lesion)
- ☐ E. **Surgical wound(s)**
- ☐ F. **Burn(s)** (second or third degree)

None of the Above
- ☐ Z. **None of the above** were present

M1200. Skin and Ulcer Treatments
↓ Check all that apply
- ☐ A. **Pressure reducing device for chair**
- ☐ B. **Pressure reducing device for bed**
- ☐ C. **Turning/repositioning program**
- ☐ D. **Nutrition or hydration intervention** to manage skin problems
- ☐ E. **Ulcer care**
- ☐ F. **Surgical wound care**
- ☐ G. **Application of nonsurgical dressings** (with or without topical medications) other than to feet
- ☐ H. **Applications of ointments/medications** other than to feet
- ☐ I. **Application of dressings to feet** (with or without topical medications)
- ☐ Z. **None of the above** were provided

Resident _____ Identifier _____ Date _____

Section N — Medications

N0300. Injections

Enter Days	Record the number of days that **injections of any type** were received during the last 7 days or since admission/reentry if less than 7 days. If 0 → Skip to N0400, Medications Received
☐	

N0350. Insulin

Enter Days	
☐	A. **Insulin injections - Record the number of days that insulin injections** were received during the last 7 days or since admission/reentry if less than 7 days
☐	B. **Orders for insulin - Record the number of days the physician (or authorized assistant or practitioner) changed the resident's insulin orders** during the last 7 days or since admission/reentry if less than 7 days

N0400. Medications Received

↓ Check all medications the resident received at any time during the last 7 days or since admission/reentry if less than 7 days

☐	A. **Antipsychotic**
☐	B. **Antianxiety**
☐	C. **Antidepressant**
☐	D. **Hypnotic**
☐	E. **Anticoagulant** (warfarin, heparin, or low-molecular weight heparin)
☐	F. **Antibiotic**
☐	G. **Diuretic**
☐	Z. **None of the above were received**

Resident _____   Identifier _____   Date _____

Section O	Special Treatments, Procedures, and Programs

O0100. Special Treatments, Procedures, and Programs

Check all of the following treatments, procedures, and programs that were performed during the last **14 days**

	1. While NOT a Resident	2. While a Resident
1. While NOT a Resident Performed *while NOT a resident* of this facility and within the *last 14 days*. Only check column 1 if resident entered (admission or reentry) IN THE LAST 14 DAYS. If resident last entered 14 or more days ago, leave column 1 blank **2. While a Resident** Performed *while a resident* of this facility and within the *last 14 days*	1. While NOT a Resident	2. While a Resident
	↓ Check all that apply ↓	
Cancer Treatments		
A. Chemotherapy	☐	☐
B. Radiation	☐	☐
Respiratory Treatments		
C. Oxygen therapy	☐	☐
D. Suctioning	☐	☐
E. Tracheostomy care	☐	☐
F. Ventilator or respirator	☐	☐
G. BiPAP/CPAP	☐	☐
Other		
H. IV medications	☐	☐
I. Transfusions	☐	☐
J. Dialysis	☐	☐
K. Hospice care	☐	☐
L. Respite care	■	☐
M. Isolation or quarantine for active infectious disease (does not include standard body/fluid precautions)	☐	☐
None of the Above		
Z. None of the above	☐	☐

O0250. Influenza Vaccine - Refer to current version of RAI manual for current flu season and reporting period

Enter Code [ ]	A. Did the **resident receive the influenza vaccine in this facility** for this year's Influenza season?
	    0. **No** → Skip to O0250C, If Influenza vaccine not received, state reason
	    1. **Yes** → Continue to O0250B, Date vaccine received

	B. Date vaccine received → Complete date and skip to O0300A, Is the resident's Pneumococcal vaccination up to date? [ ][ ] – [ ][ ] – [ ][ ][ ][ ] Month Day Year

Enter Code [ ]	C. If Influenza vaccine not received, state reason:
	    1. **Resident not in facility** during this year's flu season
	    2. **Received outside of this facility**
	    3. **Not eligible** - medical contraindication
	    4. **Offered and declined**
	    5. **Not offered**
	    6. **Inability to obtain vaccine** due to a declared shortage
	    9. **None of the above**

O0300. Pneumococcal Vaccine

Enter Code [ ]	A. Is the resident's Pneumococcal vaccination up to date?
	    0. **No** → Continue to O0300B, If Pneumococcal vaccine not received, state reason
	    1. **Yes** → Skip to O0400, Therapies

Enter Code [ ]	B. If Pneumococcal vaccine not received, state reason:
	    1. **Not eligible** - medical contraindication
	    2. **Offered and declined**
	    3. **Not offered**

Resident _____   Identifier _____   Date _____

Section O — Special Treatments, Procedures, and Programs

O0400. Therapies

A. Speech-Language Pathology and Audiology Services

Enter Number of Minutes

1. **Individual minutes** - record the total number of minutes this therapy was administered to the resident **individually** in the last 7 days

Enter Number of Minutes

2. **Concurrent minutes** - record the total number of minutes this therapy was administered to the resident **concurrently with one other resident** in the last 7 days

Enter Number of Minutes

3. **Group minutes** - record the total number of minutes this therapy was administered to the resident as **part of a group of residents** in the last 7 days

If the sum of individual, concurrent, and group minutes is zero, → skip to O0400B, Occupational Therapy

Enter Number of Days

4. **Days** - record the **number of days** this therapy was administered for **at least 15 minutes** a day in the last 7 days

5. **Therapy start date** - record the date the most recent therapy regimen (since the most recent entry) started

   Month — Day — Year

6. **Therapy end date** - record the date the most recent therapy regimen (since the most recent entry) ended - enter dashes if therapy is ongoing

   Month — Day — Year

B. Occupational Therapy

Enter Number of Minutes

1. **Individual minutes** - record the total number of minutes this therapy was administered to the resident **individually** in the last 7 days

Enter Number of Minutes

2. **Concurrent minutes** - record the total number of minutes this therapy was administered to the resident **concurrently with one other resident** in the last 7 days

Enter Number of Minutes

3. **Group minutes** - record the total number of minutes this therapy was administered to the resident as **part of a group of residents** in the last 7 days

If the sum of individual, concurrent, and group minutes is zero, → skip to O0400C, Physical Therapy

Enter Number of Days

4. **Days** - record the **number of days** this therapy was administered for **at least 15 minutes** a day in the last 7 days

5. **Therapy start date** - record the date the most recent therapy regimen (since the most recent entry) started

   Month — Day — Year

6. **Therapy end date** - record the date the most recent therapy regimen (since the most recent entry) ended - enter dashes if therapy is ongoing

   Month — Day — Year

C. Physical Therapy

Enter Number of Minutes

1. **Individual minutes** - record the total number of minutes this therapy was administered to the resident **individually** in the last 7 days

Enter Number of Minutes

2. **Concurrent minutes** - record the total number of minutes this therapy was administered to the resident **concurrently with one other resident** in the last 7 days

Enter Number of Minutes

3. **Group minutes** - record the total number of minutes this therapy was administered to the resident as **part of a group of residents** in the last 7 days

If the sum of individual, concurrent, and group minutes is zero, → skip to O0400D, Respiratory Therapy

Enter Number of Days

4. **Days** - record the **number of days** this therapy was administered for **at least 15 minutes** a day in the last 7 days

5. **Therapy start date** - record the date the most recent therapy regimen (since the most recent entry) started

   Month — Day — Year

6. **Therapy end date** - record the date the most recent therapy regimen (since the most recent entry) ended - enter dashes if therapy is ongoing

   Month — Day — Year

O0400 continued on next page

Resident _____ Identifier _____ Date _____

Section O — Special Treatments, Procedures, and Programs

O0400. Therapies - Continued

Enter Number of Minutes ☐☐☐☐ **Enter Number of Days** ☐	**D. Respiratory Therapy**	
	1. Total minutes - record the total number of minutes this therapy was administered to the resident in the last 7 days If zero, → skip to O0400E, Psychological Therapy	
	2. Days - record the **number of days** this therapy was administered for **at least 15 minutes** a day in the last 7 days	
Enter Number of Minutes ☐☐☐☐ **Enter Number of Days** ☐	**E. Psychological Therapy** (by any licensed mental health professional)	
	1. Total minutes - record the total number of minutes this therapy was administered to the resident in the last 7 days If zero, → skip to O0400F, Recreational Therapy	
	2. Days - record the **number of days** this therapy was administered for **at least 15 minutes** a day in the last 7 days	
Enter Number of Minutes ☐☐☐☐ **Enter Number of Days** ☐	**F. Recreational Therapy** (includes recreational and music therapy)	
	1. Total minutes - record the total number of minutes this therapy was administered to the resident in the last 7 days If zero, → skip to O0500, Restorative Nursing Programs	
	2. Days - record the **number of days** this therapy was administered for **at least 15 minutes** a day in the last 7 days	

O0500. Restorative Nursing Programs

Record the **number of days** each of the following restorative programs was performed (for at least 15 minutes a day) in the last 7 calendar days (enter 0 if none or less than 15 minutes daily)

Number of Days	Technique
☐	**A. Range of motion (passive)**
☐	**B. Range of motion (active)**
☐	**C. Splint or brace assistance**

Number of Days	Training and Skill Practice In:
☐	**D. Bed mobility**
☐	**E. Transfer**
☐	**F. Walking**
☐	**G. Dressing and/or grooming**
☐	**H. Eating and/or swallowing**
☐	**I. Amputation/prostheses care**
☐	**J. Communication**

O0600. Physician Examinations

Enter Days ☐☐ Over the last 14 days, **on how many days did the physician (or authorized assistant or practitioner) examine the resident?**

O0700. Physician Orders

Enter Days ☐☐ Over the last 14 days, **on how many days did the physician (or authorized assistant or practitioner) change the resident's orders?**

Resident _____   Identifier _____   Date _____

Section P   Restraints

P0100. Physical Restraints

Physical restraints are any manual method or physical or mechanical device, material or equipment attached or adjacent to the resident's body that the individual cannot remove easily which restricts freedom of movement or normal access to one's body

	↓ Enter Codes in Boxes
	Used in Bed
☐	A. Bed rail
☐	B. Trunk restraint
☐	C. Limb restraint
☐	D. Other
	Used in Chair or Out of Bed
☐	E. Trunk restraint
☐	F. Limb restraint
☐	G. Chair prevents rising
☐	H. Other

Coding:
0. Not used
1. Used less than daily
2. Used daily

Resident _____ Identifier _____ Date _____

Section Q   Participation in Assessment and Goal Setting

Q0100. Participation in Assessment

Enter Code	A. Resident participated in assessment
	  0. No
	  1. Yes

Enter Code	B. Family or significant other participated in assessment
	  0. No
	  1. Yes
	  9. No family or significant other

Enter Code	C. Guardian or legally authorized representative participated in assessment
	  0. No
	  1. Yes
	  9. No guardian or legally authorized representative

Q0300. Resident's Overall Expectation
Complete only if A0310E = 1

Enter Code	A. Resident's overall goal established during assessment process
	  1. Expects to be **discharged to the community**
	  2. Expects to **remain in this facility**
	  3. Expects to be **discharged to another facility/institution**
	  9. **Unknown or uncertain**

Enter Code	B. Indicate information source for Q0300A
	  1. **Resident**
	  2. If not resident, then **family or significant other**
	  3. If not resident, family, or significant other, then **guardian or legally authorized representative**
	  9. **None of the above**

Q0400. Discharge Plan

Enter Code	A. Is there an active discharge plan in place for the resident to return to the community?
	  0. No
	  1. Yes → Skip to Q0600, Referral

Enter Code	B. What determination was made by the resident and the care planning team regarding discharge to the community?
	  0. **Determination not made**
	  1. **Discharge to community determined to be feasible** → Skip to Q0600, Referral
	  2. **Discharge to community determined to be not feasible** → Skip to next active section (V or X)

Q0500. Return to Community

Enter Code	A. Has the resident been asked about returning to the community?
	  0. No
	  1. Yes - previous response was **"no"**
	  2. Yes - previous response was **"yes"** → Skip to Q0600, Referral
	  3. Yes - previous response was **"unknown"**

Enter Code	B. Ask the resident (or family or significant other if resident is unable to respond): **"Do you want to talk to someone about the possibility of returning to the community?"**
	  0. No
	  1. Yes
	  9. Unknown or uncertain

Q0600. Referral

Enter Code	Has a referral been made to the local contact agency?
	  0. **No** - determination has been made by the resident and the care planning team that contact is not required
	  1. **No** - referral not made
	  2. **Yes**

Resident _____ Identifier _____ Date _____

| **Section V** | **Care Area Assessment (CAA) Summary** |

V0100. Items From the Most Recent Prior OBRA or Scheduled PPS Assessment
Complete only if A0310E = 0 and if the following is true for the **prior assessment:** A0310A = 01- 06 or A0310B = 01- 06

Enter Code [ ][ ]	**A. Prior Assessment Federal OBRA Reason for Assessment** (A0310A value from prior assessment) 01. **Admission** assessment (required by day 14) 02. **Quarterly** review assessment 03. **Annual** assessment 04. **Significant change in status** assessment 05. **Significant correction** to **prior comprehensive** assessment 06. **Significant correction** to **prior quarterly** assessment 99. **Not OBRA required** assessment
Enter Code [ ][ ]	**B. Prior Assessment PPS Reason for Assessment** (A0310B value from prior assessment) 01. **5-day** scheduled assessment 02. **14-day** scheduled assessment 03. **30-day** scheduled assessment 04. **60-day** scheduled assessment 05. **90-day** scheduled assessment 06. **Readmission/return** assessment 07. **Unscheduled assessment used for PPS** (OMRA, significant or clinical change, or significant correction assessment) 99. **Not PPS** assessment
	C. Prior Assessment Reference Date (A2300 value from prior assessment) [ ][ ] – [ ][ ] – [ ][ ][ ][ ] Month Day Year
Enter Score [ ][ ]	**D. Prior Assessment Brief Interview for Mental Status (BIMS) Summary Score** (C0500 value from prior assessment)
Enter Score [ ][ ]	**E. Prior Assessment Resident Mood Interview (PHQ-9©) Total Severity Score** (D0300 value from prior assessment)
Enter Score [ ][ ]	**F. Prior Assessment Staff Assessment of Resident Mood (PHQ-9-OV) Total Severity Score** (D0600 value from prior assessment)

Resident _____ Identifier _____ Date _____

Section V — Care Area Assessment (CAA) Summary

V0200. CAAs and Care Planning

1. Check column A if Care Area is triggered.
2. For each triggered Care Area, indicate whether a new care plan, care plan revision, or continuation of current care plan is necessary to address the problem(s) identified in your assessment of the care area. The Addressed in Care Plan column must be completed within 7 days of completing the RAI (MDS and CAA(s)). Check column B if the triggered care area is addressed in the care plan.
3. Indicate in the Location and Date of CAA Information column where information related to the CAA can be found. CAA documentation should include information on the complicating factors, risks, and any referrals for this resident for this care area.

A. CAA Results

Care Area	A. Care Area Triggered	B. Addressed in Care Plan	Location and Date of CAA Information
	↓ Check all that apply ↓		
01. Delirium	☐	☐	
02. Cognitive Loss/Dementia	☐	☐	
03. Visual Function	☐	☐	
04. Communication	☐	☐	
05. ADL Functional/Rehabilitation Potential	☐	☐	
06. Urinary Incontinence and Indwelling Catheter	☐	☐	
07. Psychosocial Well-Being	☐	☐	
08. Mood State	☐	☐	
09. Behavioral Symptoms	☐	☐	
10. Activities	☐	☐	
11. Falls	☐	☐	
12. Nutritional Status	☐	☐	
13. Feeding Tube	☐	☐	
14. Dehydration/Fluid Maintenance	☐	☐	
15. Dental Care	☐	☐	
16. Pressure Ulcer	☐	☐	
17. Psychotropic Drug Use	☐	☐	
18. Physical Restraints	☐	☐	
19. Pain	☐	☐	
20. Return to Community Referral	☐	☐	

B. Signature of RN Coordinator for CAA Process and Date Signed

1. Signature
2. Date ☐☐ - ☐☐ - ☐☐☐☐ (Month / Day / Year)

C. Signature of Person Completing Care Plan and Date Signed

1. Signature
2. Date ☐☐ - ☐☐ - ☐☐☐☐ (Month / Day / Year)

Resident _____ Identifier _____ Date _____

Section X — Correction Request

X0100. Type of Record

Enter Code [ ]
1. **Add new record** → Skip to Z0100, Medicare Part A Billing
2. **Modify existing record** → Continue to X0150, Type of Provider
3. **Inactivate existing record** → Continue to X0150, Type of Provider

Identification of Record to be Modified/Inactivated - The following items identify the existing assessment record that is in error. In this section, reproduce the information EXACTLY as it appeared on the existing erroneous record, even if the information is incorrect. This information is necessary to locate the existing record in the National MDS Database.

X0150. Type of Provider

Enter Code [ ]
Type of provider
1. **Nursing home (SNF/NF)**
2. **Swing Bed**

X0200. Name of Resident on existing record to be modified/inactivated

A. **First name:**
[ ][ ][ ][ ][ ][ ][ ][ ][ ][ ][ ][ ][ ][ ]

C. **Last name:**
[ ][ ][ ][ ][ ][ ][ ][ ][ ][ ][ ][ ][ ][ ][ ][ ][ ][ ]

X0300. Gender on existing record to be modified/inactivated

Enter Code [ ]
1. **Male**
2. **Female**

X0400. Birth Date on existing record to be modified/inactivated

[ ][ ] – [ ][ ] – [ ][ ][ ][ ]
Month   Day   Year

X0500. Social Security Number on existing record to be modified/inactivated

[ ][ ][ ] – [ ][ ] – [ ][ ][ ][ ]

X0600. Type of Assessment on existing record to be modified/inactivated

Enter Code [ ][ ]
A. **Federal OBRA Reason for Assessment**
01. **Admission** assessment (required by day 14)
02. **Quarterly** review assessment
03. **Annual** assessment
04. **Significant change in status** assessment
05. **Significant correction** to **prior comprehensive** assessment
06. **Significant correction** to **prior quarterly** assessment
99. **Not OBRA required** assessment

Enter Code [ ][ ]
B. **PPS Assessment**
PPS Scheduled Assessments for a Medicare Part A Stay
01. **5-day** scheduled assessment
02. **14-day** scheduled assessment
03. **30-day** scheduled assessment
04. **60-day** scheduled assessment
05. **90-day** scheduled assessment
06. **Readmission/return** assessment
PPS Unscheduled Assessments for a Medicare Part A Stay
07. **Unscheduled assessment used for PPS** (OMRA, significant or clinical change, or significant correction assessment)
Not PPS Assessment
99. **Not PPS** assessment

Enter Code [ ]
C. **PPS Other Medicare Required Assessment - OMRA**
0. **No**
1. **Start of therapy** assessment
2. **End of therapy** assessment
3. **Both Start and End of therapy** assessment

X0600 continued on next page

Resident _____ Identifier _____ Date _____

Section X — Correction Request

X0600. Type of Assessment - Continued

Enter Code [ ]
D. Is this a Swing Bed clinical change assessment? Complete only if X0200 = 2
0. **No**
1. **Yes**

Enter Code [ ][ ]
F. Entry/discharge reporting
01. **Entry** record
10. **Discharge** assessment-**return not anticipated**
11. **Discharge** assessment-**return anticipated**
12. **Death in facility** record
99. **Not entry/discharge** record

X0700. Date on existing record to be modified/inactivated - Complete one only

A. Assessment Reference Date - Complete only if X0600F = 99
[ ][ ] – [ ][ ] – [ ][ ][ ][ ]
Month — Day — Year

B. Discharge Date - Complete only if X0600F = 10, 11, or 12
[ ][ ] – [ ][ ] – [ ][ ][ ][ ]
Month — Day — Year

C. Entry Date - Complete only if X0600F = 01
[ ][ ] – [ ][ ] – [ ][ ][ ][ ]
Month — Day — Year

Correction Attestation Section - Complete this section to explain and attest to the modification/inactivation request

X0800. Correction Number

Enter Number [ ][ ]
Enter the number of correction requests to modify/inactivate the existing record, including the present one

X0900. Reasons for Modification - Complete only if Type of Record is to modify a record in error (X0100 = 2)

↓ Check all that apply

[ ] A. **Transcription error**
[ ] B. **Data entry error**
[ ] C. **Software product error**
[ ] D. **Item coding error**
[ ] Z. **Other error requiring modification**
If "Other" checked, please specify: _____

X1050. Reasons for Inactivation - Complete only if Type of Record is to inactivate a record in error (X0100 = 3)

↓ Check all that apply

[ ] A. **Event did not occur**
[ ] Z. **Other error requiring inactivation**
If "Other" checked, please specify: _____

Resident _____   Identifier _____   Date _____

Section X	Correction Request

X1100. RN Assessment Coordinator Attestation of Completion

A. Attesting individual's first name:

B. Attesting individual's last name:

C. Attesting individual's title:

D. Signature

E. Attestation date

		–			–				

Month   Day   Year

Resident _____ Identifier _____ Date _____

Section Z	**Assessment Administration**

Z0100. Medicare Part A Billing

A. Medicare Part A HIPPS code (RUG group followed by assessment type indicator):

☐☐☐☐☐

B. RUG version code:

☐☐☐☐☐☐☐☐☐☐

Enter Code ☐

C. Is this a Medicare Short Stay assessment?
0. No
1. Yes

Z0150. Medicare Part A Non-Therapy Billing

A. Medicare Part A non-therapy HIPPS code (RUG group followed by assessment type indicator):

☐☐☐☐☐

B. RUG version code:

☐☐☐☐☐☐☐☐☐☐

Z0200. State Medicaid Billing (if required by the state)

A. RUG Case Mix group:

☐☐☐☐☐☐☐☐☐☐

B. RUG version code:

☐☐☐☐☐☐☐☐☐☐

Z0250. Alternate State Medicaid Billing (if required by the state)

A. RUG Case Mix group:

☐☐☐☐☐☐☐☐☐☐

B. RUG version code:

☐☐☐☐☐☐☐☐☐☐

Z0300. Insurance Billing

A. RUG Case Mix group:

☐☐☐☐☐☐☐☐☐☐

B. RUG version code:

☐☐☐☐☐☐☐☐☐☐

Resident _____ Identifier _____ Date _____

Section Z — Assessment Administration

Z0400. Signature of Persons Completing the Assessment or Entry/Death Reporting

I certify that the accompanying information accurately reflects resident assessment information for this resident and that I collected or coordinated collection of this information on the dates specified. To the best of my knowledge, this information was collected in accordance with applicable Medicare and Medicaid requirements. I understand that this information is used as a basis for ensuring that residents receive appropriate and quality care, and as a basis for payment from federal funds. I further understand that payment of such federal funds and continued participation in the government-funded health care programs is conditioned on the accuracy and truthfulness of this information, and that I may be personally subject to or may subject my organization to substantial criminal, civil, and/or administrative penalties for submitting false information. I also certify that I am authorized to submit this information by this facility on its behalf.

Signature	Title	Sections	Date Section Completed
A.			
B.			
C.			
D.			
E.			
F.			
G.			
H.			
I.			
J.			
K.			
L.			

Z0500. Signature of RN Assessment Coordinator Verifying Assessment Completion

A. Signature: _____

B. Date RN Assessment Coordinator signed assessment as complete:

☐☐ – ☐☐ – ☐☐☐☐
Month — Day — Year

SECTION F: PREFERENCES FOR CUSTOMARY ROUTINE AND ACTIVITIES

Intent: The intent of items in this section is to obtain information regarding the resident's preferences for his or her daily routine and activities. This is best accomplished when the information is obtained directly from the resident or through family or significant other, or staff interviews if the resident cannot report preferences.

F0300: Should Interview for Daily and Activity Preferences Be Conducted?

F0300. Should Interview for Daily and Activity Preferences be Conducted? - Attempt to interview all residents able to communicate. If resident is unable to complete, attempt to complete interview with family member or significant other
Enter Code ☐   0. **No** (resident is rarely/never understood <u>and</u> family/significant other not available) → Skip to and complete F0800, Staff Assessment of Daily and Activity Preferences 1. **Yes** → Continue to F0400, Interview for Daily Preferences

Item Rationale

Health-related Quality of Life

- Most residents capable of communicating can answer questions about what they like.
- Obtaining information about preferences directly from the resident, sometimes called "hearing the resident's voice," is the most reliable and accurate way of identifying preferences.
- If a resident cannot communicate, then family or significant other who knows the resident well may be able to provide useful information about preferences.

Planning for Care

- Quality of life can be greatly enhanced when care respects the resident's choice regarding anything that is important to the resident.
- Interviews allow the resident's voice to be reflected in the care plan.
- Information about preferences that comes directly from the resident provides specific information for individualized daily care and activity planning.

Steps for Assessment

1. Review **Makes Self Understood** item (B0700) to determine whether or not resident is understood at least sometimes (B0700 = 0, 1 or 2).
2. Review **Language** item (A1100) to determine whether or not the resident needs or wants an interpreter.

   - If the resident needs or wants an interpreter, complete the interview with an interpreter.

3. The resident interview should be conducted if the resident can respond:

   - verbally,
   - by pointing to their answers on the cue card, <u>OR</u>
   - by writing out their answers.

F0300: Should Interview for Daily and Activity Preferences Be Conducted? (cont.)

Coding Instructions

Record whether the resident preference interview should be attempted.

- **Code 0, no:** if the interview should not be attempted with the resident. This option should be selected for residents who are rarely/never understood (B0700 = 3), who need an interpreter but one was not available, and who do not have a family member or significant other available for interview. Skip to F0800, (Staff Assessment of Daily and Activity Preferences).

- **Code 1, yes:** if the resident interview should be attempted. This option should be selected for residents who are always, usually or at least sometimes understood (B0700 = 0, 1, or 2), for whom an interpreter is not needed or is present, or who have a family member or significant other available for interview. Continue to F0400 (Interview for Daily Preferences) and F0500 (Interview for Activity Preferences).

Coding Tips and Special Populations

- If the resident needs an interpreter, every effort should be made to have an interpreter present for the MDS clinical interview. If it is not possible for a needed interpreter to be present on the day of the interview, **and** a family member or significant other is not available for interview, **code F0300 = 0** to indicate interview not attempted, and complete the Staff Assessment of Daily and Activity Preferences (F0800) instead of the interview with the resident (F0400 and F0500).

F0400: Interview for Daily Preferences

F0400. Interview for Daily Preferences	
Show resident the response options and say: **"While you are in this facility..."**	
	↓ Enter Codes in Boxes
Coding: 1. **Very important** 2. **Somewhat important** 3. **Not very important** 4. **Not important at all** 5. **Important, but can't do or no choice** 9. **No response or non-responsive**	☐ **A.** how important is it to you to **choose what clothes to wear?**
	☐ **B.** how important is it to you to **take care of your personal belongings or things?**
	☐ **C.** how important is it to you to **choose between a tub bath, shower, bed bath, or sponge bath?**
	☐ **D.** how important is it to you to **have snacks available between meals?**
	☐ **E.** how important is it to you to **choose your own bedtime?**
	☐ **F.** how important is it to you to **have your family or a close friend involved in discussions about your care?**
	☐ **G.** how important is it to you to **be able to use the phone in private?**
	☐ **H.** how important is it to you to **have a place to lock your things to keep them safe?**

F0400: Interview for Daily Preferences (cont.)

Item Rationale

Health-related Quality of Life

- Individuals who live in nursing homes continue to have distinct lifestyle preferences.
- A lack of attention to lifestyle preferences can contribute to depressed mood and increased behavior symptoms.
- Resident responses that something is important but that they can't do it or have no choice can provide clues for understanding pain, perceived functional limitations, and perceived environmental barriers.

Planning for Care

- Care planning should be individualized and based on the resident's preferences.
- Care planning and care practices that are based on resident preferences can lead to
  - improved mood,
  - enhanced dignity, and
  - increased involvement in daily routines and activities.
- Incorporating resident preferences into care planning is a dynamic, collaborative process. Because residents may adjust their preferences in response to events and changes in status, the preference assessment tool is intended as a first step in an ongoing dialogue between care providers and the residents. Care plans should be updated as residents' preferences change, paying special attention to preferences that residents state are important.

Steps for Assessment: Interview Instructions

1. Interview any resident not screened out by the **Should Interview for Daily and Activity Preferences Be Conducted?** item (F0300).
2. Conduct the interview in a private setting.
3. Sit so that the resident can see your face. Minimize glare by directing light sources away from the resident's face.
4. Be sure the resident can hear you.

   - Residents with hearing impairment should be interviewed using their usual communication devices/techniques, as applicable.
   - Try an external assistive device (headphones or hearing amplifier) if you have any doubt about hearing ability.
   - Minimize background noise.

5. Explain the reason for the interview before beginning.

   Suggested language: "I'd like to ask you a few questions about your daily routines. The reason I'm asking you these questions is that the staff here would like to know what's important to you. This helps us plan your care around your preferences so that you can have a comfortable stay with us. Even if you're only going to be here for a few days, we want to make your stay as personal as possible."

F0400: Interview for Daily Preferences (cont.)

6. Explain the interview response choices. While explaining, also show the resident a clearly written list of the response options, for example a cue card.

   Suggested language: "I am going to ask you how important various activities and routines are to you **while you are in this home.** I will ask you to answer using the choices you see on this card [read the answers while pointing to cue card]: 'Very Important,' 'Somewhat important,' 'Not very important,' 'Not important at all,' or 'Important, but can't do or no choice.'"

   Explain the "Important, but can't do or no choice" response option.

   Suggested language: "Let me explain the 'Important, but can't do or no choice' answer. You can select this answer if something would be important to you, but because of your health or because of what's available in this nursing home, you might not be able to do it. So, if I ask you about something that is important to you, but you don't think you're able to do it now, answer 'Important, but can't do or no choice.' If you choose this option, it will help us to think about ways we might be able to help you do those things."

7. Residents may respond to questions

   • verbally,

   • by pointing to their answers on the cue card, <u>OR</u>

   • by writing out their answers.

8. If resident cannot report preferences, then interview family or significant others.

Coding Instructions

> **DEFINITIONS**
>
> **NONSENSICAL RESPONSE**
> Any unrelated, incomprehensible, or incoherent response that is not informative with respect to the item being rated.

   • **Code 1, very important:** if resident, family, or significant other indicates that the topic is "very important."

   • **Code 2, somewhat important:** if resident, family, or significant other indicates that the topic is "somewhat important."

   • **Code 3, not very important:** if resident, family, or significant other indicates that the topic is "not very important."

   • **Code 4, not important at all:** if resident, family, or significant other indicates that the topic is "not important at all."

   • **Code 5, important, but can't do or no choice:** if resident, family, or significant other indicates that the topic is "important," but that he or she is physically unable to participate, or has no choice about participating while staying in nursing home because of nursing home resources or scheduling.

F0400: Interview for Daily Preferences (cont.)

- **Code 9, no response or non-responsive:**
  — If resident, family, or significant other refuses to answer or says he or she does not know.
  — If resident does not give an answer to the question for several seconds and does not appear to be formulating an answer.
  — If resident provides an incoherent or nonsensical answer that does not correspond to the question.

Coding Tips and Special Populations

- Stop the interview and skip to Item F0700 if
  — the resident has given 3 nonsensical responses to 3 questions, OR
  — the resident has not responded to 3 of the questions.
- No look-back is provided for resident; he or she is being asked about current preferences while in the nursing home. Family or significant others are also responding to current preferences, but may have to consider past preferences if the resident is unable to communicate.

Interviewing Tips and Techniques

- Sometimes respondents give long or indirect answers to interview items. To narrow the answer to the response choices available, it can be useful to summarize their longer answer and then ask them which response option best applies. This is known as echoing.
- For these questions, it is appropriate to explore residents' answers and try to understand the reason.

Examples for F0400A, How Important Is It to You to Choose What Clothes to Wear (including hospital gowns or other garments provided by the facility)?

1. Resident answers, "It's very important. I've always paid attention to my appearance."

   Coding: F0400A would be **coded 1, very important**.

2. Resident replies, "I leave that up to the nurse. You have to wear what you can handle if you have a stiff leg."

   Interviewer echoes, "You leave it up to the nurses. Would you say that, while you are here, choosing what clothes to wear is [pointing to cue card] very important, somewhat important, not very important, not important at all, or that it's important, but you can't do it because of your leg?"

   Resident responds, "Well, it would be important to me, but I just can't do it."

   Coding: F0400A would be **coded 5, important, but can't do or no choice**.

F0400: Interview for Daily Preferences (cont.)

Examples for F0400B, How Important Is It to You to Take Care of Your Personal Belongings or Things?

1. Resident answers, "It's somewhat important. I'm not a perfectionist, but I don't want to have to look for things."

    Coding: F0400B would be **coded 2, somewhat important**.

2. Resident answers, "All my important things are at home."

    Interviewer clarifies, "Your most important things are at home. Do you have any other things while you're here that you think are important to take care of yourself?"

    Resident responds, "Well, my son brought me this CD player so that I can listen to music. It is very important to me to take care of that."

    Coding: F0400B would be **coded 1, very important.**

> **DEFINITIONS**
>
> **PERSONAL BELONGINGS OR THINGS** Possessions such as eyeglasses, hearing aids, clothing, jewelry, books, toiletries, knickknacks, pictures.

Examples for F0400C, How Important Is It to You to Choose between a Tub Bath, Shower, Bed Bath, or Sponge Bath?

1. Resident answers, "I like showers."

    Interviewer clarifies, "You like showers. Would you say that choosing a shower instead of other types of bathing is very important, somewhat important, not very important, not important at all, or that it's important, but you can't do it or have no choice?"

    The resident responds, "It's very important."

    Coding: F0400C would be **coded 1, very important.**

2. Resident answers, "I don't have a choice. I like only sponge baths, but I have to take shower two times a week."

    The interviewer says, "So how important is it to you to be able to choose to have a sponge bath while you're here?"

    The resident responds, "Well, it is very important, but I don't always have a choice because that's the rule."

    Coding: F0400C would be **coded 5, important, but can't do or no choice.**

F0400: Interview for Daily Preferences (cont.)

Example for F0400D, How Important Is It to You to Have Snacks Available between Meals?

1. Resident answers, "I'm a diabetic, so it's very important that I get snacks."

> **Coding:** F0400D would be **coded 1, very important.**

Example for F0400E, How Important Is It to You to Choose Your Own Bedtime?

1. Resident answers, "At home I used to stay up and watch TV. But here I'm usually in bed by 8. That's because they get me up so early."

Interviewer echoes and clarifies, "You used to stay up later, but now you go to bed before 8 because you get up so early. Would you say it's [pointing to cue card] very important, somewhat important, not very important, not important at all, or that it's important, but you don't have a choice about your bedtime?"

Resident responds, "I guess it would be important, but I can't do it because they wake me up so early in the morning for therapy and by 8 o'clock at night, I'm tired."

> **Coding:** F0400E would be **coded 5, important, but can't do or no choice**.

Example for F0400F, How Important Is It to You to Have Your Family or a Close Friend Involved in Discussions about Your Care?

1. Resident responds, "They're not involved. They live in the city. They've got to take care of their own families."

Interviewer replies, "You said that your family and close friends aren't involved right now. When you think about what you would prefer, would you say that it's very important, somewhat important, not very important, not important at all, or that it is important but you have no choice or can't have them involved in decisions about your care?"

Resident responds, "It's somewhat important."

> **Coding:** F0400F would be **coded 2, somewhat important**.

DEFINITIONS

BED BATH
Bath taken in bed using washcloths and water basin or other method in bed.

SHOWER
Bath taken standing or using gurney or shower chair in a shower room or stall.

SPONGE BATH
Bath taken sitting or standing at sink.

TUB BATH
Bath taken in bathtub.

SNACK
Food available between meals, including between dinner and breakfast.

F0400: Interview for Daily Preferences (cont.)

Example for F0400G, How Important Is It to You to Be Able to Use the Phone in Private?

1. Resident answers "That's not a problem for me, because I have my own room. If I want to make a phone call, I just shut the door."

    Interviewer echoes and clarifies, "So, you can shut your door to make a phone call. If you had to rate how important it is to be able to use the phone in private, would you say it's very important, somewhat important, not very important, or not important at all?"

    Resident responds, "Oh, it's very important."

    Coding: F0400G would be **coded 1, very important**.

Example for F0400H, How Important Is It to You to Have a Place to Lock Your Things to Keep Them Safe?

1. Resident answers, "I have a safe deposit box at my bank, and that's where I keep family heirlooms and personal documents."

    Interviewer says, "That sounds like a good service. While you are staying here, how important is it to you to have a drawer or locker here?"

    Resident responds, "It's not very important. I'm fine with keeping all my valuables at the bank."

    Coding: F0400H would be **coded 3, not very important**.

F0500: Interview for Activity Preferences

F0500. Interview for Activity Preferences	
Show resident the response options and say: **"While you are in this facility..."**	

Coding:
1. Very important
2. Somewhat important
3. Not very important
4. Not important at all
5. Important, but can't do or no choice
9. No response or non-responsive

↓ Enter Codes in Boxes

☐	**A.** how important is it to you to **have books, newspapers, and magazines to read?**
☐	**B.** how important is it to you to **listen to music you like?**
☐	**C.** how important is it to you to **be around animals such as pets?**
☐	**D.** how important is it to you to **keep up with the news?**
☐	**E.** how important is it to you to **do things with groups of people?**
☐	**F.** how important is it to you to **do your favorite activities?**
☐	**G.** how important is it to you to **go outside to get fresh air when the weather is good?**
☐	**H.** how important is it to you to **participate in religious services or practices?**

F0500: Interview for Activity Preferences (cont.)

Item Rationale

Health-related Quality of Life

- Activities are a way for individuals to establish meaning in their lives, and the need for enjoyable activities and pastimes does not change on admission to a nursing home.

- A lack of opportunity to engage in meaningful and enjoyable activities can result in boredom, depression, and behavior disturbances.

- Individuals vary in the activities they prefer, reflecting unique personalities, past interests, perceived environmental constraints, religious and cultural background, and changing physical and mental abilities.

Planning for Care

- These questions will be useful for designing individualized care plans that facilitate residents' participation in activities they find meaningful.

- Preferences may change over time and extend beyond those included here. Therefore, the assessment of activity preferences is intended as a first step in an ongoing informal dialogue between the care provider and resident.

- As with daily routines, responses may provide insights into perceived functional, emotional, and sensory support needs.

Coding Instructions

- **See Coding Instructions on page F-5.**
  Coding approach is identical to that for daily preferences.

Coding Tips and Special Populations

- **See Coding Tips on page F-5.**
  Coding tips include those for daily preferences.

- Include Braille and or audio recorded material when coding items in F0500A.

Interviewing Tips and Techniques

- **See Interview Tips and Techniques on page F-5.**
  Coding tips and techniques are identical to those for daily preferences.

DEFINITIONS

READ
Script, Braille, or audio recorded written material.

NEWS
News about local, state, national, or international current events.

KEEP UP WITH THE NEWS
Stay informed by reading, watching, or listening.

NEWSPAPERS AND MAGAZINES
Any type, such as journalistic, professional, and trade publications in script, Braille, or audio recorded format.

F0500: Interview for Activity Preferences (cont.)

Examples for F0500A, How Important Is It to You to Have Books (Including Braille and Audio-recorded Format), Newspapers, and Magazines to Read?

1. Resident answers, "Reading is very important to me."

   Coding: F0500A would be **coded 1, very important**.

2. Resident answers, "They make the print so small these days. I guess they are just trying to save money."

   Interviewer replies, "The print is small. Would you say that having books, newspapers, and magazines to read is very important, somewhat important, not very important, not important at all, or that it is important but you can't do it because the print is so small?"

   Resident answers: "It would be important, but I can't do it because of the print."

   Coding: F0500A would be **coded 5, important, but can't do or no choice.**

Example for F0500B, How Important Is It to You to Listen to Music You Like?

1. Resident answers, "It's not important, because all we have in here is TV. They keep it blaring all day long."

   Interviewer echoes, "You've told me it's not important because all you have is a TV. Would you say it's not very important or not important at all to you to listen to music you like while you are here? Or are you saying that it's important, but you can't do it because you don't have a radio or CD player?"

   Resident responds, "Yeah. I'd enjoy listening to some jazz if I could get a radio."

   Coding: F0500B would be **coded 5, important, but can't do or no choice.**

Examples for F0500C, How Important Is It to You to Be Around Animals Such as Pets?

1. Resident answers, "It's very important for me NOT to be around animals. You get hair all around and I might inhale it."

   Coding: F0500C would be **coded 4, not important at all.**

2. Resident answers, "I'd love to go home and be around my own animals. I've taken care of them for years and they really need me."

   Interviewer probes, "You said you'd love to be at home with your own animals. How important is it to you to be around pets while you're staying here? Would you say it is [points to card] very important, somewhat important, not very important, not important at all, or is it important, but you can't do it or don't have a choice about it."

   Resident responds, "Well, it's important to me to be around my own dogs, but I can't be around them. I'd say important but can't do."

   Coding: F0500C would be **coded 5, Important, but can't do or no choice.**

   Rationale: Although the resident has access to therapeutic dogs brought to the nursing home, he does not have access to the type of pet that is important to him.

F0500: Interview for Activity Preferences (cont.)

Example for F0500D, How Important Is It to You to Keep Up with the News?

1. Resident answers, "Well, they are all so liberal these days, but it's important to hear what they are up to."

   Interviewer clarifies, "You think it is important to hear the news. Would you say it is [points to card] very important, somewhat important, or it's important but you can't do it or have no choice?"

   Resident responds, "I guess you can mark me somewhat important on that one."

   Coding: F0500D would be **coded 2, somewhat important.**

Example for F0500E, How Important Is It to You to Do Things with Groups of People?

1. Resident answers, "I've never really liked groups of people. They make me nervous."

   Interviewer echoes and clarifies, "You've never liked groups. To help us plan your activities, would you say that while you're here, doing things with groups of people is very important, somewhat important, not very important, not important at all, or would it be important to you but you can't do it because you feel nervous about it?"

   Resident responds, "At this point I'd say it's not very important."

   Coding: F0500E would be **coded 3, not very important.**

Examples for F0500F, How Important Is It to You to Do Your Favorite Activities?

1. Resident answers, "Well, it's very important, but I can't really do my favorite activities while I'm here. At home, I used to like to play board games, but you need people to play and make it interesting. I also like to sketch, but I don't have the supplies I need to do that here. I'd say important but no choice."

   Coding: F0500F would be **coded 5, important, but can't do or no choice.**

2. Resident answers, "I like to play bridge with my bridge club."

   Interviewer probes, "Oh, you like to play bridge with your bridge club. How important is it to you to play bridge while you are here in the nursing home?"

   Resident responds, "Well, I'm just here for a few weeks to finish my rehabilitation. It's not very important."

   Coding: F0500F would be **coded 3, not very important**.
   Coding: F0500G would be **coded 1, very important.**

F0500: Interview for Activity Preferences (cont.)

Example for F0500G, How Important Is It to You to Go Outside to Get Fresh Air When the Weather Is Good (Includes Less Temperate Weather if Resident Has Appropriate Clothing)?

1. Resident answers, "They have such a nice garden here. It's very important to me to go out there."

Examples for F0500H, How Important Is It to You to Participate in Religious Services or Practices?

1. Resident answers, "I'm Jewish. I'm Orthodox, but they have Reform services here. So I guess it's not important."

   Interviewer clarifies, "You're Orthodox, but the services offered here are Reform. While you are here, how important would it be to you to be able to participate in religious services? Would you say it is very important, somewhat important, not very important, not important at all, or would it be important to you but you can't or have no choice because they don't offer Orthodox services."

   Resident responds, "It's important for me to go to Orthodox services if they were offered, but they aren't. So, can't do or no choice."

   Coding: F0500I would be **coded 5, important, but can't do or no choice.**

2. Resident answers "My pastor sends taped services to me that I listen to in my room on Sundays. I don't participate in the services here."

   Interviewer probes, "You said your pastor sends you taped services. Would you say that it is very important, somewhat important, not very important, or not important at all, to you that you are able to listen to those tapes from your pastor?"

   Resident responds, "Oh, that's very important."

   Coding: F0500I would be **coded 1, very important**.

> **DEFINITIONS**
>
> **OUTSIDE**
> Any outdoor area in the proximity of the facility, including patio, porch, balcony, sidewalk, courtyard, or garden.
>
> **PARTICIPATE IN RELIGIOUS SERVICES**
> Any means of taking part in religious services or practices, such as listening to services on the radio or television, attending services in the facility or in the community, or private prayer or religious study.
>
> **RELIGIOUS PRACTICES**
> Rituals associated with various religious traditions or faiths, such as washing rituals in preparation for prayer, following kosher dietary laws, honoring holidays and religious festivals, and participating in communion or confession.

F0600: Daily and Activity Preferences Primary Respondent

	F0600. Daily and Activity Preferences Primary Respondent
Enter Code ☐	Indicate **primary respondent** for Daily and Activity Preferences (F0400 and F0500) 1. **Resident** 2. **Family or significant other** (close friend or other representative) 9. **Interview could not be completed** by resident or family/significant other ("No response" to 3 or more items")

Item Rationale

- This item establishes the source of the information regarding the resident's preferences.

Coding Instructions

- **Code 1, resident**: if resident was the primary source for the preference questions in F0400 and F0500.

- **Code 2, family or significant other:** if a family member or significant other was the primary source of information for F0400 and F0500.

- **Code 9, interview could not be completed:** if F0400 and F0500 could not be completed by the resident, a family member, or a representative of the resident.

F0700: Should the Staff Assessment of Daily and Activity Preferences Be Conducted?

	F0700. Should the Staff Assessment of Daily and Activity Preferences be Conducted?
Enter Code ☐	0. **No** (because Interview for Daily and Activity Preferences (F0400 and F0500) was completed by resident or family/significant other) → Skip to and complete G0110, Activities of Daily Living (ADL) Assistance 1. **Yes** (because 3 or more items in Interview for Daily and Activity Preferences (F0400 and F0500) were not completed by resident or family/significant other) → Continue to F0800, Staff Assessment of Daily and Activity Preferences

Item Rationale

Health-related Quality of Life

- Resident interview is preferred as it most accurately reflects what the resident views as important. However, a small percentage of residents are unable or unwilling to complete the interview for Daily and Activity Preferences.

- Persons unable to complete the preference interview should still have preferences evaluated and considered.

Planning for Care

- Even though the resident was unable to complete the interview, important insights may be gained from the responses that were obtained, observing behaviors, and observing the resident's affect during the interview.

Steps for Assessment

- Review resident, family, or significant other responses to F0400A-H and F0500A-H.

F0700: Should the Staff Assessment of Daily and Activity Preferences Be Conducted? (cont.)

Coding Instructions

- **Code 0, no:** if **Interview for Daily and Activity Preferences** items (F0400 and F0500) was completed by resident, family or significant other. Skip to Section G, Functional Status.

- **Code 1, yes:** if **Interview for Daily and Activity Preferences** items (F0400 and F0500) was not completed because the resident, family, or significant other was unable to answer 3 or more items in either section (3 or more items coded as **9** in F0400 or F0500).

Coding Tips and Special Populations

- A resident may have up to 2 items coded as **9** in F0400 and 2 items coded as **9** in F0500, and the interview is considered complete. Some interviews, therefore, will be coded complete even with a total of 4 missing responses when F0400 and F0500 are considered together.

F0800: Staff Assessment of Daily and Activity Preferences

	F0800. Staff Assessment of Daily and Activity Preferences
	Do not conduct if Interview for Daily and Activity Preferences (F0400-F0500) was completed
	Resident Prefers:
	↓ Check all that apply
☐	A. Choosing clothes to wear
☐	B. Caring for personal belongings
☐	C. Receiving tub bath
☐	D. Receiving shower
☐	E. Receiving bed bath
☐	F. Receiving sponge bath
☐	G. Snacks between meals
☐	H. Staying up past 8:00 p.m.
☐	I. Family or significant other involvement in care discussions
☐	J. Use of phone in private
☐	K. Place to lock personal belongings
☐	L. Reading books, newspapers, or magazines
☐	M. Listening to music
☐	N. Being around animals such as pets
☐	O. Keeping up with the news
☐	P. Doing things with groups of people
☐	Q. Participating in favorite activities
☐	R. Spending time away from the nursing home
☐	S. Spending time outdoors
☐	T. Participating in religious activities or practices
☐	Z. None of the above

F0800: Staff Assessment of Daily and Activity Preferences (cont.)

Item Rationale

Health-related Quality of Life

- Alternate means of assessing preferences must be used for residents who cannot communicate. This ensures that information about their preferences is not overlooked.
- Activities allow residents to establish meaning in their lives. A lack of meaningful and enjoyable activities can result in boredom, depression, and behavioral symptoms.

Planning for Care

- Caregiving staff should use observations of resident behaviors to understand resident likes and dislikes in cases where the resident, family, or significant other cannot report the resident's preferences. This allows care plans to be individualized to each resident.

Steps for Assessment

1. Observe the resident when the care, routines, and activities specified in these items are made available to the resident.
2. Observations should be made by staff across all shifts and departments and others with close contact with the resident.
3. If the resident appears happy or content (e.g., is involved, pays attention, smiles) during an activity listed in **Staff Assessment of Daily and Activity Preferences** item (F0800), then that item should be checked.

   If the resident seems to resist or withdraw when these are made available, then do not check that item.

Coding Instructions

Check all that apply in the last 7 days based on staff observation of resident preferences.

- **F0800A.** Choosing clothes to wear
- **F0800B.** Caring for personal belongings
- **F0800C.** Receiving tub bath
- **F0800D.** Receiving shower
- **F0800E.** Receiving bed bath
- **F0800F.** Receiving sponge bath
- **F0800G.** Snacks between meals
- **F0800H.** Staying up past 8:00 p.m.
- **F0800I.** Family or significant other involvement in care discussions
- **F0800J.** Use of phone in private
- **F0800K.** Place to lock personal belongings

F0800: Staff Assessment of Daily and Activity Preferences (cont.)

- **F0800L.** Reading books, newspapers, or magazines
- **F0800M.** Listening to music
- **F0800N.** Being around animals such as pets
- **F0800O.** Keeping up with the news
- **F0800P.** Doing things with groups of people
- **F0800Q.** Participating in favorite activities
- **F0800R.** Spending time away from the nursing home
- **F0800S.** Spending time outdoors
- **F0800T.** Participating in religious activities or practices
- **F0800Z.** None of the above

CAT LEGEND (for MDS Version 3.0)

Key: ● = One item required to trigger   ❷ = Two items required to trigger   * = Three or more items required to trigger
Proceed to RAP Review once triggered

Item	Item Description	Code	CAA 1	CAA 2	CAA 3	CAA 4	CAA 5	CAA 6	CAA 7	CAA 8	CAA 9	CAA 10	CAA 11	CAA 12	CAA 13	CAA 14	CAA 15	CAA 16	CAA 17	CAA 18	CAA 19	CAA 20	Item
A0310A	Federal OBRA reason for assessment	3,4,5	❷							❷			❷										A0310A
B0200	Hearing	1,2,3				●																	B0200
B0700	Makes self understood	1,2,3				●																	B0700
B0800	Ability to understand others	1,2,3				●																	B0800
B1000	Vision	1,2,3,4			●																		B1000
C0500	BIMS resident interview: summary score	00-15	❷	●			❷																C0500
C0700	Staff assessment mental status: short-term memory OK	1		●																			C0700
C0800	Staff assessment mental status: long term memory OK	1		●																			C0800
C1000	Cognitive skills for daily decision making	1,2,3		●			❷																C1000
C1300A	Signs of delirium: inattention	1,2		●																			C1300A
C1300B	Signs of delirium: disorganized thinking	1,2		●																			C1300B
C1300C	Signs of delirium: altered level of consciousness	1,2		●																			C1300C

(continued)

CAT LEGEND (for MDS Version 3.0) (con't)

Key: ● = One item required to trigger   ❷ = Two items required to trigger   * = Three or more items required to trigger

Proceed to RAP Review once triggered

Item	Item Description	Code	CAA1	CAA2	CAA3	CAA4	CAA5	CAA6	CAA7	CAA8	CAA9	CAA10	CAA11	CAA12	CAA13	CAA14	CAA15	CAA16	CAA17	CAA18	CAA19	CAA20	Item
C1300D	Signs of delirium: psychomotor retardation	1,2		●																			C1300D
C1600	Acute mental status change	1	●																				C1600
D0200A1	PHQ resident mood interview: little interest or pleasure in doing things - presence	1							●			●											D0200A1
D0200I1	PHQ resident mood interview: thoughts better off dead - presence	1								●													D0200I1
D0300	PHQ resident mood interview: total mood severity score	00-27								●❷*													D0300
D0500A1	PHQ staff assessment of resident mood: little interest or pleasure in doing things - presence	1							●			●											D0500A1
D0500I1	PHQ staff assessment: thoughts better off dead - presence	1								●													D0500I1
D0600	PHQ staff assessment: total mood score	00-30								●*													D0600
E0200A	Physical behavioral symptoms directed toward others	1,2,3		●					*														E0200A

(continued)

CAT LEGEND (for MDS Version 3.0) (con't)

Key: ● = One item required to trigger   ❷ = Two items required to trigger   * = Three or more items required to trigger

Proceed to RAP Review once triggered

Item	Item Description	Code	CAA 1	CAA 2	CAA 3	CAA 4	CAA 5	CAA 6	CAA 7	CAA 8	CAA 9	CAA 10	CAA 11	CAA 12	CAA 13	CAA 14	CAA 15	CAA 16	CAA 17	CAA 18	CAA 19	CAA 20	Item
E0200B	Verbal behavioral symptoms directed toward others	1,2,3		●					*														E0200B
E0200C	Other behavioral symptoms not directed toward others	1,2,3		●																			E0200C
E0300	Overall presence of behavioral symptoms	1									●												E0300
E0800	Rejection of care: presence and frequency	1,2,3		●							●												E0800
E0900	Wandering: presence and frequency	1,2,3		●							●		●										E0900
E1100	Change in behavioral or other symptoms	2									●												E1100
F0500A	Resident interview: how important is it to you to have books, newspaper, magazines to read	4,5							*			*											F0500A
F0500B	Resident interview: how important is it to you to listen to music	4,5							*			*											F0500B
F0500C	Resident interview: how important is it to you to be around animals/pets	4,5							*			*											F0500C
F0500D	Resident interview: how important is it to you to keep up with news	4,5							*			*											F0500D

(continued)

CAT LEGEND (for MDS Version 3.0) (con't)

Key: ● = One item required to trigger　❷ = Two items required to trigger　✱ = Three or more items required to trigger
Proceed to RAP Review once triggered

Item	Item Description	Code	CAA 1	CAA 2	CAA 3	CAA 4	CAA 5	CAA 6	CAA 7	CAA 8	CAA 9	CAA 10	CAA 11	CAA 12	CAA 13	CAA 14	CAA 15	CAA 16	CAA 17	CAA 18	CAA 19	CAA 20	Item
F0500E	Resident interview: how important is it to you to do things with groups of people	4,5							✱			✱												F0500E
F0500F	Resident interview: how important is it to you to do your favorite activities	3,4,5						●	✱			✱												F0500F
F0500G	Resident interview: how important is it to you to go outside in good weather	4,5							✱			✱												F0500G
F0500H	Resident interview: how important is it to you to participate in religious practices	4,5							✱			✱												F0500H
F0600	Primary respondent: daily/activities preferences	1							✱															F0600
F0800L	Staff assessment: reading books, newspapers, magazines	Not ✓										✱												F0800L
F0800M	Staff assessment: listening to music	Not ✓										✱												F0800M
F0800N	Staff assessment: being around animals/pets	Not ✓										✱												F0800N
F0800O	Staff assessment: keeping up with news	Not ✓										✱												F0800O

(continued)

CAT LEGEND (for MDS Version 3.0) (con't)

Key: ● = One item required to trigger   ❷ = Two items required to trigger   * = Three or more items required to trigger

Proceed to RAP Review once triggered

Item	Item Description	Code	CAA 1	CAA 2	CAA 3	CAA 4	CAA 5	CAA 6	CAA 7	CAA 8	CAA 9	CAA 10	CAA 11	CAA 12	CAA 13	CAA 14	CAA 15	CAA 16	CAA 17	CAA 18	CAA 19	CAA 20	Item
F0800P	Staff assessment: doing things with groups	Not ✓										*											F0800P
F0800Q	Staff assessment: participating in favorite activities	Not ✓							●			*											F0800Q
F0800R	Staff assessment: spend time away from nursing home	Not ✓										*											F0800R
F0800S	Staff assessment: spend time outdoors	Not ✓										*											F0800S
F0800T	Staff assessment: participate religious activities	Not ✓										*											F0800T
G0110A1	ADL: bed mobility: self-performance	1,2,3,4,7,8					❷											●					G0110A1
G0110B1	ADL: transfer: self-performance	1,2,3,4					❷																G0110B1
G0110C1	ADL: walk in room: self-performance	1,2,3,4					❷																G0110C1
G0110D1	ADL: walk in corridor: self-performance	1,2,3,4					❷																G0110D1
G0110E1	ADL: locomotion on unit: self-performance	1,2,3,4					❷																G0110E1
G0110F1	ADL: locomotion off unit: self-performance	1,2,3,4					❷																G0110F1

(continued)

CAT LEGEND (for MDS Version 3.0) (con't)

Key: ● = One item required to trigger   ❷ = Two items required to trigger   ✱ = Three or more items required to trigger

Proceed to RAP Review once triggered

Item	Item Description	Code	CAA 1	CAA 2	CAA 3	CAA 4	CAA 5	CAA 6	CAA 7	CAA 8	CAA 9	CAA 10	CAA 11	CAA 12	CAA 13	CAA 14	CAA 15	CAA 16	CAA 17	CAA 18	CAA 19	CAA 20	Item
G0110G1	ADL: dressing: self-performance	1,2,3,4					❷																G0110G1
G0110H1	ADL: eating: self-performance	1,2,3,4					❷																G0110H1
G0110I1	ADL: toilet: self-performance	1,2,3,4.					❷	●															G0110I1
G0110J1	ADL: personal hygiene: self-performance	1,2,3,4					❷																G0110J1
G0120A	ADL: bathing: self-performance	1,2,3,4					❷																G0120A
G0300A	Balance: moving from seated to standing position	1,2					●						●										G0300A
G0300B	Balance: walking (with assistive device if used)	1,2					●						●										G0300B
G0300C	Balance: turning around while walking	1,2					●						●										G0300C
G0300D	Balance: moving on and off toilet	1,2					●						●										G0300D
G0300E	Balance: surface to surface transfer	1,2					❷						●										G0300E
G0900A	Resident believes capable of increased independence	1					❷																G0900A

(continued)

CAT LEGEND (for MDS Version 3.0) (con't)

Key: ● = One item required to trigger　❷ = Two items required to trigger　✱ = Three or more items required to trigger

Proceed to RAP Review once triggered

Item	Item Description	Code	CAA 1	CAA 2	CAA 3	CAA 4	CAA 5	CAA 6	CAA 7	CAA 8	CAA 9	CAA 10	CAA 11	CAA 12	CAA 13	CAA 14	CAA 15	CAA 16	CAA 17	CAA 18	CAA 19	CAA 20
G0900B	Staff believes resident capable of increased independence	1					❷															
H0100A	Appliances: indwelling bladder catheter	1						●														
H0100B	Appliances: external (condom) catheter	1						●														
H0100D	Appliances: intermittent catheterization	1						●														
H0300	Urinary continence	1,2,3						●										●				
H0400	Bowel continence	2,3																●				
H0600	Constipation	1														●						
I1700	MRSA/VRE/clostridium diff. infection/colonization	✓														●						
I2000	Pneumonia	✓														●						
I2100	Septicemia	✓														●						
I2200	Tuberculosis	✓														●						
I2300	Urinary tract infection (UTI)	✓														●						
I2400	Viral hepatitis (includes type A, B, C, D, and E)	✓														●						
I2500	Wound infection (other than foot)	✓														●						

(continued)

CAT LEGEND (for MDS Version 3.0) (con't)

Key: ● = One item required to trigger   ❷ = Two items required to trigger   * = Three or more items required to trigger

Proceed to RAP Review once triggered

Item	Item Description	Code	CAA 1	CAA 2	CAA 3	CAA 4	CAA 5	CAA 6	CAA 7	CAA 8	CAA 9	CAA 10	CAA 11	CAA 12	CAA 13	CAA 14	CAA 15	CAA 16	CAA 17	CAA 18	CAA 19	CAA 20	Item
I4200	Alzheimer's disease	✓, Not ✓							*														I4200
I4800	Dementia	✓, Not ✓							*														I4800
I6500	Cataracts, glaucoma, or macular degeneration	✓			●																		I6500
J0400	Resident pain interview: frequency	1,2																			❷		J0400
J0500A	Resident pain interview: made it hard to sleep	1																			●		J0500A
J0500B	Resident pain interview: limited daily activities	1																			●		J0500B
J0600A	Resident pain interview: pain numeric intensity rating scale	4-10,7-10																			❷ ●		J0600A
J0600B	Resident pain interview: pain verbal descriptor scale	2,3,4																			❷ ●		J0600B
J0800A	Staff pain assessment: non-verbal sounds	1																			●		J0800A
J0800B	Staff pain assessment: vocal complaints of pain	1																			●		J0800B
J0800C	Staff pain assessment: facial expressions	1																			●		J0800C
J0800D	Staff pain assessment: protective movements/postures	1																			●		J0800D

(continued)

CAT LEGEND (for MDS Version 3.0) (con't)

Key: ● = One item required to trigger ❷ = Two items required to trigger ✱ = Three or more items required to trigger
Proceed to RAP Review once triggered

Item	Item Description	Code	CAA 1	CAA 2	CAA 3	CAA 4	CAA 5	CAA 6	CAA 7	CAA 8	CAA 9	CAA 10	CAA 11	CAA 12	CAA 13	CAA 14	CAA 15	CAA 16	CAA 17	CAA 18	CAA 19	CAA 20	Item
J1550A	Problem conditions: fever	✓														●							J1550A
J1550B	Problem conditions: vomiting	✓														●							J1550B
J1550C	Problem conditions: dehydrated	✓												●		●							J1550C
J1550D	Problem conditions: internal bleeding	✓														●							J1550D
J1700A	Fall history: fall during month before entry	1											❷										J1700A
J1700B	Fall history: fall 2 to 6 months before entry	1											❷										J1700B
J1800	Falls since admit/prior assessment: any falls	1											●										J1800
K0200A	Height	BMI (18.5-24.9)												❷									K0200A
K0200B	Weight	BMI (18.5-24.9)												❷									K0200B
K0300	Weight loss	1,2												●				●					K0300
K0500A	Nutritional approaches: parenteral/IV feeding	1												●		●							K0500A
K0500B	Nutritional approaches: feeding tube	1													●	●							K0500B
K0500C	Nutritional approaches: mechanically altered diet	1												●									K0500C

(continued)

CAT LEGEND (for MDS Version 3.0) (con't)

Key: ● = One item required to trigger   ❷ = Two items required to trigger   ✱ = Three or more items required to trigger
Proceed to RAP Review once triggered

Item	Item Description	Code	CAA 1	CAA 2	CAA 3	CAA 4	CAA 5	CAA 6	CAA 7	CAA 8	CAA 9	CAA 10	CAA 11	CAA 12	CAA 13	CAA 14	CAA 15	CAA 16	CAA 17	CAA 18	CAA 19	CAA 20	Item
K0500D	Nutritional approaches: therapeutic diet	1												●									K0500D
L0200A	Dental: broken or loosely fitting denture	✓															●						L0200A
L0200B	Dental: no natural teeth or tooth fragment(s)	✓															●						L0200B
L0200C	Dental: abnormal mouth tissue	✓															●						L0200C
L0200D	Dental: cavity or broken natural teeth	✓															●						L0200D
L0200E	Dental: inflamed/bleeding gums or loose teeth	✓															●						L0200E
L0200F	Dental: pain, discomfort, difficulty chewing	✓															●						L0200F
M0150	Is resident at risk of developing pressure ulcer	1																●					M0150
M0300A	Number of Stage 1 pressure ulcers	0-9																●					M0300A
M0300B1	Number of Stage 2 pressure ulcers	0-9												●				●					M0300B1
M0300C1	Number of Stage 3 pressure ulcers	0-9												●				●					M0300C1

(continued)

CAT LEGEND (for MDS Version 3.0) (con't)

Key: ● = One item required to trigger　❷ = Two items required to trigger　✱ = Three or more items required to trigger

Proceed to RAP Review once triggered

Item	Item Description	Code	CAA 1	CAA 2	CAA 3	CAA 4	CAA 5	CAA 6	CAA 7	CAA 8	CAA 9	CAA 10	CAA 11	CAA 12	CAA 13	CAA 14	CAA 15	CAA 16	CAA 17	CAA 18	CAA 19	CAA 20	Item
M0300D1	Number of Stage 4 pressure ulcers	0-9												●				●					M0300D1
M0300E1	Number of un-staged pressure ulcers due to dressing	0-9												●				●					M0300E1
M0300F1	Number of pressure ulcers un-staged due to slough/eschar	0-9												●				●					M0300F1
M0300G1	Number of pressure ulcers un-staged – deep tissue	0-9												●				●					M0300G1
M0800A	Worsened since prior assessment: Stage 2 pressure ulcers	0-9																●					M0800A
M0800B	Worsened since prior assessment: Stage 3 pressure ulcers	0-9																●					M0800B
M0800C	Worsened since prior assessment: Stage 4 pressure ulcers	0-9																●					M0800C
M1040A	Other skin problems: other foot/lower extremity	1														●							M1040A
N0400A	Medications: antipsychotic	1																	●				N0400A
N0400B	Medications: antianxiety	1											●						●				N0400B

(continued)

CAT LEGEND (for MDS Version 3.0) (con't)

Key: ● = One item required to trigger ❷ = Two items required to trigger ✱ = Three or more items required to trigger
Proceed to RAP Review once triggered

Item	Item Description	Code	CAA 1	CAA 2	CAA 3	CAA 4	CAA 5	CAA 6	CAA 7	CAA 8	CAA 9	CAA 10	CAA 11	CAA 12	CAA 13	CAA 14	CAA 15	CAA 16	CAA 17	CAA 18	CAA 19	CAA 20	Item
N0400C	Medications: antidepressant	1											●						●				N0400C
N0400D	Medications: hypnotic	1																	●				N0400D
P0100A	Restraints used in bed: bed rail (any type)	1,2																		●			P0100A
P0100B	Restraints used in bed: trunk restraint	1,2											●						●		●			P0100B
P0100C	Restraints used in bed: limb restraint	1,2																		●			P0100C
P0100D	Restraints used in bed: other	1,2																		●			P0100D
P0100E	Restraints in chair/out of bed: trunk restraint	1,2											●						●		●			P0100E
P0100F	Restraints in chair/out of bed: limb restraint	1,2																		●			P0100F
P0100G	Restraints in chair/out of bed: chair stops rising	1,2																		●			P0100G
P0100H	Restraints in chair/out of bed: other	1,2																		●			P0100H
Q0400A	Active discharge plan for return to community	0																				✱	Q0400A
Q0400B	Determination regarding discharge to community	1																				✱	Q0400B

(continued)

CAT LEGEND (for MDS Version 3.0) (con't)

Key: ● = One item required to trigger   ② = Two items required to trigger   * = Three or more items required to trigger

Proceed to RAP Review once triggered

Item	Item Description	Code	CAA 1	CAA 2	CAA 3	CAA 4	CAA 5	CAA 6	CAA 7	CAA 8	CAA 9	CAA 10	CAA 11	CAA 12	CAA 13	CAA 14	CAA 15	CAA 16	CAA 17	CAA 18	CAA 19	CAA 20	Item
Q0500B	Resident response about returning to community	1																				*	Q0500B
V0100D	BIMS resident interview: summary score (prior assessment)	00-15	②																				V0100D
V0100E	PHQ resident mood interview: total mood severity score (prior assessment)	00-27								●													V0100E
V0100F	PHQ staff assessment: total mood score (prior assessment)	00-30								*													V0100F

Very important

Somewhat important

Not very important

Not very important at all

Important, but can't do or no choice

APPENDIX E: Sample Activity Calendar: ASSISTED LIVING CALENDAR – Wesleyan Village

February 2011 — Activities for Assisted Living (Boyd Life Enrichment Room)

Sunday	Monday	Tuesday	Wednesday	Thursday	Friday	Saturday
		1 9:45 Sittercise; 10:30 Linden School/Toddlers Chinese New Year; 11:00 Today In…; 11:30 Announcements & Dev.; 1:15 Rhone Pet Visit/Arts & Crafts w/ Peggy –AOPHA Project; 3:30 Pot-Pour-Ri	**2** *Groundhog Day* 9:45 Sittercise; 10:30 Linden School/Infant II; 11:00 Punxsutawney Phil; 1:30 Animal Talk – Animal Idioms; 2:30 Bingo; 3:30 Pot-Pour-Ri	**3** *Chinese New Year Year of the Rabbit* 9:30 **Ladies Breakfast/RR**; 9:45 Sittercise; 10:30 Linden School/ Toddlers Chinese New Year cont.; 1:30 Megan Sings Gospel; 1:30 Pet Visit - APL; 2:30 Word within a Word; 3:30 Pot-Pour-Ri	**4** 9:45 Sittercise; 11:00 Lyrics & Limericks; 11:30 Announcements & Dev.; 1:30 Music Variety; 2:00 **Catholic Mass/C**; 2:30 Super Bowl Party; 3:30 Pot-Pour-Ri	**5** 9:45 **In the News/Poe**; 1:30 Saturday Afternoon Matinee; 7:00 **Saturday Nite Out/CH**; Activity Supplies set out for your enjoyment throughout the day.
6 *Super Bowl Sunday* 10:30 Coffee w/ Don; 3:30 **Chapel Service/C**; Activity Supplies set out for your enjoyment throughout the day.	**7** 9:45 Sittercise; 10:30 Expressions & Expectations; 11:30 Announcements & Dev.; 1:30 **2nd Wind Dreams Celebration/CH**; 2:30 Bible Study; 3:30 Pot-Pour-Ri	**8** 9:45 Sittercise; 10:30 Linden School/Toddlers; 11:00 Today In…; 11:30 Announcements & Dev.; 1:15 Rhone Pet Visit/Arts & Crafts w/ Peggy –AOPHA Project; 3:30 Pot-Pour-Ri	**9** 9:45 Sittercise; 10:15 Linden School/Infant II; 11:00 A Chocolate Story; 12:00 **Valentine Lunch & Dance/CH**; 2:30 Bingo; 3:30 Pot-Pour-Ri	**10** 9:00 **Men's Breakfast/RR**; 9:45 Sittercise; 10:00 **Buckeye Room – Van Outing**; 1:30 Megan Sings Gospel; 2:30 Word within a Word; 3:30 Pot-Pour-Ri	**11** 9:45 Sittercise; 10:30 Things I Love; 11:00 Lyrics & Limericks; 11:30 Announcements & Dev.; 1:30 Lincoln: A Presidential Essay; 2:45 Bingo; 3:30 Pot-Pour-Ri	**12** *Lincoln's Birthday* 9:45 **In the News/Poe**; 1:30 Saturday Matinee Matinee; 2:30 **Valentine's Ladies Tea/ Bridge & Falls Rooms**; Activity Supplies set out for your enjoyment throughout the day.
13 10:30 Coffee w/ Don; 3:30 **Chapel Service/C**; Activity Supplies set out for your enjoyment throughout the day.	**14** *Valentine's Day* 9:45 Sittercise; 10:30 Valentine Trivia Famous Couples; 11:00 Linden School/Blue Room; 11:30 Announcements/Dev.; 1:30 Bible Study; 2:30 How I Met My Spouse; 3:30 Pot-Pour-Ri	**15** 9:45 Sittercise; 10:30 Linden School/Toddlers; 11:00 Today In…; 11:30 Announcements & Dev.; 1:15 Rhone Pet Visit/Arts & Crafts w/ Peggy –AOPHA Project; 3:30 Pot-Pour-Ri	**16** 9:45 Sittercise; 10:30 **Good News Messengers/CH**; 1:30 Honoring Famous African Americans; 2:30 Bingo; 3:30 Pot-Pour-Ri; 4:30 **Birthday**	**17** 9:45 Sittercise; 9:45 **Tennyson School Outing**; 10:30 Baking Cinnamon Rolls; 11:30 Announcements & Dev.; 1:30 Megan Sings Gospel; 3:00 **Dalton Love/BH**	**18** 9:45 Sittercise; 10:15 Balloon Badminton; 11:00 Lyrics & Limericks; 11:30 Announcements & Dev.; 1:30 Music Variety; 2:45 Bingo; 3:30 Pot-Pour-Ri	**19** 9:45 **In the News/Poe**; 1:30 Saturday Matinee; 7:00 **Saturday Nite Out/CH**; Activity Supplies set out for your enjoyment throughout the day.

PLEASE NOTE: BOLD PRINT DENOTES ACTIVITY TAKES PLACE OUTSIDE OF THE BOYD LIFE ENRICHMENT ROOM OR OFF CAMPUS.

CH = Cascade Hall, RR = Rose Room Dining Room, BH = Beacon House, C - Chapel

APPENDIX E: Sample Activity Calendar: ASSISTED LIVING CALENDAR – Wesleyan Village

SUNDAY	MONDAY	TUESDAY	WEDNESDAY	THURSDAY	FRIDAY	SATURDAY
20 10:30 Coffee w/ Don 3:30 **Chapel Service/C** Activity Supplies set out for your enjoyment throughout the day.	**21 President's Day** 9:45 Sittercise 10:30 Presidential Facts 11:30 Announcements/Dev. 1:30 Bible Study 2:30 Presenting the Presidents 3:30 Pot-Pour-Ri	**22 *Washington's Birthday*** 9:45 Sittercise 10:30 Linden School/Toddlers 11:00 Today In…...Washington 11:30 Announcements/Dev. 1:15 Rhone Pet Visit/ Arts & Crafts w/ Peggy –AOPHA Project 3:30 Pot-Pour-Ri	**23** 9:45 Sittercise 10:15 Linden School/Infants II 11:30 Announcements/Dev. 1:30 **John Kowalski/CH** 2:30 Bingo. 3:30 Pot-Pour-Ri	**24** 9:45 Sittercise 10:30 Today In 11:00 Jarts 11:30 Announcements/Dev 1:30 Word within a Word 1:30 Megan Sings Gospel 2:30 **Resident Quarterly Meeting/CH** 3:30 Pot Pour Ri	**25** 9:45 Sittercise 10:30 **Resident Forum/CH** 11:00 Lyrics & Limericks 11:30 Announcements/ Dev. 1:30 Music Variety 2:45 Bingo 3:30 Pot-Pour-Ri	**26** 9:45 **In the News/Poe** 1:30 Saturday Matinee 3:30 **Book Sharing/Mill** Activity Supplies set out for your enjoyment throughout the day.
27 10:30 Coffee w/ Don 3:30 **Chapel Service/C** Activity Supplies set out for your enjoyment throughout the day.	**28** 9:45 Sittercise 10:30 Linden School/ Blue Rm. 11:00 Balloon Badminton 11:30 Announcements 1:30 Bible Study 2:30 Bowling 3:30 Pot-Pour-Ri	JVS OUTING FEB. 10 IS FULL!		**Scheduled Times for Activities:** **Monday – Friday** **9:45 – 11:30 AM &** **1:30 – 4:00 PM**		

Assisted Living Activities

Our Support Groups meet to provide education, offer information on new resources available, and to share experiences.

Memory Support Grp.
2nd **Wednesday of Month**
Location: Poe Conf.Rm
Time: 9:45 a.m.
Facilitator: Judy Wakefield, LPN

Cardia/Stroke Support
2nd **Tuesday of Month**
Location: Poe Conf. Rm.
Time: 9:45 a.m.
Facilitator: Judy Wakefield, LPN

Hearing Loss Support Group
4th Tuesday Every Other Month
Location: Poe Conf. Room
Time: 1:00 p.m.
Facilitator: Donna Gibbons, LPN

TOPS Weight Loss
Every Thursday
Location: Falk Room
Time: 9:00 a.m.
Facilitator: Donna Gibbons, LPN

Diabetic Support Group
1st **Thursday of Month**
Locatin: Poe Conf. Rm.
Time: 2:00 p.m.
Facilitator: Pat Hornbebck, RN

Alzheimer's Support
2nd **Thursday of Month**
Location: Reeder Lounge
Time: 1:00 p.m.
Facilitator: Ginney Tinney

Low Vision Support
3rd **Thursday**
Every other Month
Location: Poe Conf. Room
Time: 2:00 p.m.
Facilitator: Pat Hornbeck, RN

*PLEASE NOTE: BOLD PRINT DENOTES ACTIVITY TAKES PLACE OUTSIDE OF THE BOYD LIFE ENRICHMENT ROOM OR OFF CAMPUS.
CH = Cascade Hall, RR = Rose Room Dining Room, BH = Beacon House, C - Chapel

APPENDIX E: Sample Activity Calendar: 2. Beacon House ASSISTED LIVING – Wesleyan Village

Beacon House Assisted Living Program Calendar February 2011

Sunday	Monday	Tuesday	Wednesday	Thursday	Friday	Saturday
		1 10:00 Gathering Time to Plan Activities for the Day; 10:00 Lee & Marilyn Poetry; 2:00 **Stronger Seniors/CH** Project	**2** *Groundhog Day* 10:00 Gathering Time to Plan Activities for the Day; 11:00 Expressions & Expectations; 1:30 Groundhog Day Trivia	**3** *Chinese New Year Year of the Rabbit* 10:00 Gathering Time to Plan Activities; 10:00 Linden School / Infants; 11:00 Worship w/ Rev. McKee; 1:30 **Megan Sings Gospel/AL**; 2:00 **Stronger Seniors/CH**; 3:00 Chinese New Year Trivia	**4** 10:00 Gathering Time to Plan Activities for the Day; 2:00 **Catholic Mass/Chapel**	**5** 10:00 Gathering Time to Plan Activities for the Day; 11:00 Bird Aviary for the Day; 1:30 Valentine's Party/LR (Hedricks); 7:00 **Saturday Nite Out/CH**
6 *Super Bowl Sunday* 10:00 Gathering Time to Plan Activities; 3:30 **Chapel Service/C** (also channel 19)	**7** 10:00 Gathering Time to Plan Activities for the Day; 1:30 **2nd Wind Dreams Celebration/CH**; 1:30 **Bible Study/AL**	**8** 10:00 Gathering Time to Plan Activities for the Day; 10:00 Lee & Marilyn Poetry; 2:00 **Stronger Seniors/CH**	**9** 10:00 Gathering Time to Plan Activities for the Day; 12:00 **Valentine's Lunch & Dance/CH**	**10** 10:00 Gathering Time to Plan Activities for the Day; 10:00 Linden School / Infants; 11:00 Worship w/ Rev. McKee; 1:30 **Megan Sings Gospel/AL**; 2:00 **Stronger Seniors/CH**	**11** 10:00 Gathering Time to Plan Activities; 10:00 Linden School/ Infants; 11:00 Worship w/ Rev. McKee; 1:30 **Megan Sings Gospel/AL**; 2:00 **Stronger Seniors/CH**	**12** *Lincoln's Birthday* 10:00 Gathering Time to Plan Activities for the Day
13 10:00 Gathering Time to Plan Activities; 3:30 **Chapel Service/C** (also channel 19)	**14** *Valentine's Day* 10:00 Gathering Time to Plan Activities for the Day; 11:00 Valentine's Trivia; 1:30 **Bible Study/AL**; 3:00 Valentine's Word Game	**15** 9:45 Sittercise; 10:00 Gathering Time to Plan Activities /; 10:00 Lee & Marilyn Poetry; 2:00 **Stronger Seniors/CH**	**16** 10:00 Gathering Time to Plan Activities; 10:00 Lee & Marilyn Poetry; 2:00 **Stronger Seniors/CH**	**17** 9:45 **Tennyson School Outing**; 10:00 Gathering Time to Plan Activities; 10:00 Linden School /Infants; 11:00 Worship w/ Rev. McKee; 1:30 **Megan Sings Gospel/AL**; 2:00 **Stronger Sr/CH**; 3:00 Dalton Love	**18** 10:00 Gathering Time to Plan Activities; 11:00 Bird Aviary Care; 1:30 **Music Variety/ AL**	**19** 10:00 Gathering Time to Plan Activities for the Day; 7:00 **Saturday Nite Out/CH**

*PLEASE NOTE BOLD PRINT DENOTES ACTIVITY TAKES PLACE OUTSIDE OF BEACON HOUSE OR OFF-CAMPUS

APPENDIX E: Sample Activity Calendar: 2. Beacon House ASSISTED LIVING – Wesleyan Village

SUNDAY	MONDAY	TUESDAY	WEDNESDAY	THURSDAY	FRIDAY	SATURDAY
20 10:00 Gathering Time to Plan Activities 3:30 **Chapel Service/C** (also channel 19)	**21** *President's Day* 10:00 Gathering Time to Plan Activities 11:00 President's Day Trivia 1:30 **Bible Study/AL** 3:00 President's Day Puzzles & Games	**22** *Washington's Birthday* 10:00 Gathering Time to Plan Activities 10:00 Lee & Marilyn Poetry 2:00 **Stronger Seniors/CH**	**23** 10:00 Gathering Time to Plan Activities 10:00 Lee & Marilyn Poetry 2:00 **Stronger Seniors/CH**	**24** 10:00 Gathering Time to Plan Activities 10:00 Linden School /Infants 11:00 Worship w/ Rev. McKee 1:30 **Megan Sings Gospel/AL** 2:00 **Stronger Seniors/CH**	**25** 10:00 Gathering Time to Plan Activities 11:00 Bird Aviary Care 1:30 **Music Variety/ AL**	**26** 10:00 Gathering Time to Plan Activities throughout the day.
27 10:00 Gathering Time to Plan Activities 3:30 **Chapel Service/C** (also channel 19)	**28** 10:00 Gathering Time to Plan Activities 1:30 **Bible Study/AL**		LEGEND

AL = Assisted Living
CH = Cascade Hall
C = Chapel
PR = Park Room | | **Birthdays**

Betty Faro   10th | |

Beacon House Activities

February Violet

Our Support Groups meet to provide education, offer information on new resources available, and to share experiences.

Memory Support Grp.
2ⁿᵈ **Wednesday of Month**
Location: Poe Conf.Rm
Time: 9:45 a.m.
Facilitator: Judy Wakefield,   LPN

Cardia/Stroke Support
2ⁿᵈ **Tuesday of Month**
Location: Poe Conf. Rm.
Time: 9:45 a.m.
Facilitator: Judy Wakefield, LPN

Hearing Loss Support Group
4ᵗʰ Tuesday Every Other Month
Location: Poe Conf. Room
Time: 1:00 p.m.
Facilitator: Donna Gibbons, LPN

TOPS Weight Loss
Every Thursday
Location: Falk Room
Time: 9:00 a.m.
Facilitator: Donna Gibbons, LPN

Diabetic Support Group
1ˢᵗ **Thursday of Month**
Locatin: Poe Conf. Rm.
Time: 2:00 p.m.
Facilitator: Pat Hornbebck, RN

Alzheimer's Support
2ⁿᵈ **Thursday of Month**
Location: Reeder Lounge
Time: 1:00 p.m.
Facilitator: Ginney Tinney

Low Vision Support
3ʳᵈ **Thursday**
Every other Month
Location: Poe Conf. Room
Time: 2:00 p.m.
Facilitator: Pat Hornbeck, RN

*PLEASE NOTE BOLD PRINT DENOTES ACTIVITY TAKES PLACE OUTSIDE OF BEACON HOUSE OR OFF-CAMPUS

March 2011 — ASSISTED LIVING

Sunday	Monday	Tuesday	Wednesday	Thursday	Friday	Saturday
		1 10:00 EXERCISE -3CR 10:45 MENS CLUB – 2WW 2:00 BALLOON VOLLEYBALL-3CR 3:45 DRAMA CLUB -3CR 6:30 SKIPBO CARD GAME – 3CR	**2** 10:00 EXERCISE -3CR 1:30 NEW HOPE CHURCH -3WW 3:30 CURRENT EVENTS – 3CR DINNER MUSIC WITH DAN ELISH 6:30 NICKEL BINGO -3CR	**3** 10:00 EXERCISE-3CR 12:00 OUTING TO REGAL MOVIE THEATRE: **THE KINGS SPEECH** 1:30 MOVIE MATINEE - CHANNEL 2 6:30 124TH ANNUAL WORLD DAY OF PRAYER -3WW	**4** COMMUNION 10:00 EXERCISE -3CR 2:00 NICKEL BINGO -3CR	**5** 9:30 EXERCISE -3CR 1:30 CARNIVAL -3CR 6:30 MOVIE NIGHT -3CR
6 1:30 BOWLING -3CR	**7** 10:00 EXERCISE – 3CR 11:00 BOOKWORMS -3CR 2:00 SONG CATCHERS SPRING CONCERT -3CR	**8** 10:00 EXERCISE -3CR 10:30 ROSARY-3CR 2:00 MARIO ROMANO ENTERTAINS -3CR 3:45 DRAMA CLUB -3CR 6:30 DOMINOES -3CR	**9** 10:00 EXERCISE -3CR 2:00 YAHTZEE DICE GAME -3CR 3:30 CURRENT EVENTS – 3CR 6:30 NICKEL BINGO -3CR	**10** 10:00 EXERCISE-3CR 1:30 MOVIE MATINEE - CHANNEL 2 2:00 SHOPPING AT MARC'S 3:15 BIBLE STUDY – 3WW 6:30 PINOCHLE & GAMES – 2WW STORE OPEN	**11** 10:00 EXERCISE -3CR 10:30 MASS -3CR 2:00 CRAFT-3CR	**12** 9:30 EXERCISE -3CR 10:30 BAKING CLUB -2WW 2:00 BAKING CLUB SAMPLES -2WW 6:30 MOVIE MATINEE- 3CR
13 DON'T FORGET TO CHANGE YOUR CLOCK ONE HOUR AHEAD Daylight Savings Time Begins	**14** 10:00 EXERCISE – 3CR 11:00 BOOKWORMS - 3CR 11:00 LUNCH AT THE ORGINAL PANCAKE HOUSE 1:30 MOVIE MATINEE - CHANNEL 2 2:00 BOCCE BALL-3CR	**15** *Mardi Gras* 10:00 EXERCISE-3CR 10:45 MEN'S CLUB: MARCH MADNESS TRIVIA -2WW 2:30 BLACK BEAR CALEDONIA PIPE BAND -3CR 6:30 NICKEL POKENO – 3CR	**16** 10:00 EXERCISE – 3CR 1:30 NEW HOPE CHURCH -3WW 3:30 CURRENT EVENTS – 3CR 6:30 NICKEL BINGO -3CR	**17** 10:00 EXERCISE-3CR 2:00 ST. PATRICK'S DAY SOCIAL -3CR 6:30 ST PATRICK'S DAY 20 QUESTIONS – 2WW *St. Patrick's Day*	**18** COMMUNION 10:00 EXERCISE -3CR 1:30 NICKEL BINGO -3CR 3:30 GERMAN AMERICAN CULTURAL CENTER FISH FRY DINNER OUTING	**19** 9:30 EXERCISE -3CR 2:00 MUSICAL BINGO -3WW 6:30 MOVIE MATINEE- 3CR
20 1:30 BAKING CLUB: HAMANTASCHEN & THE STORY OF PURIUM-3WW Spring Begins Purim	**21** 10:00 EXERCISE – 3CR 10:45 EYEGLASS CLEANING & ADJUSTMENTS -3WW 11:00 BOOKWORMS-3CR 1:30 MOVIE MATINEE - CHANNEL 2 2:00 SHOPPING AT WALMART	**22** 10:00 EXERCISE – 3CR 10:30 ROSARY-3CR 2:00 GROUP CROSSWORD PUZZLE – 3CR 3:45 DRAMA CLUB -3CR 6:30 YAHTZEE DICE GAME -3CR	**23** 10:00 EXERCISE -3CR 11:00 BROWN BAG CONCERT @ TRINITY CATHEDRAL: ORGAN RECITAL WITH LUDWIG RUCKDESCHEL OF PASSAU, GERMANY 3:30 CURRENT EVENTS – 3CR 6:30 NICKEL BINGO -3CR	**24** 10:00 EXERCISE-3CR 1:30 MOVIE MATINEE - CHANNEL 2 1:30 SHOPPING AT KOHL'S 3:15 BIBLE STUDY -3WW 6:30 PINOCHLE & GAMES – 2WW	**25** COMMUNION 10:00 EXERCISE -3CR 2:00 NICKEL BINGO -3CR STORE OPEN	**26** 9:30 EXERCISE -3CR 2:00 POTATOE CHIP DAY -3WW 6:30 MOVIE MATINEE- 3CR
27 SPRING IS HERE!? CHECK TO SEE WHO CAN FIND THE FIRST CROCUS' OF THE SEASON	**28** 10:00 EXERCISE – 3CR 11:00 BOOKWORMS -3CR 2:00 SKIPBO CARD GAME -3CR	**29** 10:00 EXERCISE -3CR 10:45 MENS CLUB – 2WW 2:00 HORSERACING GAME -3CR 3:45 DRAMA CLUB -3CR 6:30 NAMETHAT TUNE-3CR	**30** 10:00 EXERCISE-3CR 11:00 BROWN BAG CONCERT @ TRINITY CATHEDRAL: TRINITY CHAMBER PLAYERS, WIND INSTRUMENTS 2:00 RESIDENT COUNCIL – 3CR 3:30 CURRENT EVENTS – 3CR 6:30 NICKEL BINGO-3CR	**31** 10:00 EXERCISE - 3CR 1:30 MOVIE MATINEE - CHANNEL 2 2:00 CORN HOLE -3CR 6:30 "SCHOOL HOUSE ROCK LIVE" PERFORMANCE AT ST. RICHARDS SCHOOL	ALL ACTIVITIES ARE SUBJECT TO CHANGE **STORE HOURS** 11:00-11:30AM & 1:30PM – 2:00PM	

KEY: 3CR = 3RD FLOOR COMMUNITY ROOM; 3WW = 3RD FLOOR WEST WING; 2WW = 2ND FLOOR WEST WING

March 2011 — SKILLED & LTC

Sunday	Monday	Tuesday	Wednesday	Thursday	Friday	Saturday
		1 10:00 EXERCISE; 10:45 MEN'S CLUB; 1:00 "IN THE MOOD" WATER COLORS WITH MARY LOU; 6:30 CORN HOLE	**2** 10:00 EXERCISE; 10:45 AROUND THE KITCHEN TABLE; 1:30 NEW HOPE CHURCH -3WW; 6:30 NICKEL BINGO	**3** 10:00 EXERCISE; 10:45 BOOKWORMS: **ALWAYS LOOKING UP** BY MICHAEL J. FOX; 1:30 MOVIE MATINEE - CHANNEL 2; 2:30 JEOPARDY; 6:30 124TH ANNUAL WORLD DAY OF PRAYER-3WW	**4** COMMUNION; 10:00 EXERCISE; 10:45 GOOD DEEDS: COUPON CUTTING; 1:00 LOVING HANDS; 2:30 NICKEL BINGO	**5** 10:30 EXERCISE; 1:30 CARNIVAL-3CR; 6:30 MOVIE NIGHT
6 1:30 BALLOON VOLLEYBALL	**7** 10:00 EXERCISE; 10:45 JEWELRY MAKING: MARDI GRAS BEADS; 1:00 DINNING ROOM CENTER PIECES; 2:00 SONG CATCHERS-3CR	**8** 10:00 EXERCISE; 10:45 BOB'S CORNER; 11:00 ROSARY; 1:00 KNITTING & CROCHETTING; 2:00 MARIO ROMANO ENTERTAINS – 3CR; 6:30 BOCCE BALL *Mardi Gras*	**9** 10:00 EXERCISE; 10:45 AROUND THE KITCHEN TABLE; 2:30 WORDS WITH "ASH" PUZZLE; 6:30 NICKEL BINGO	**10** 10:00 EXERCISE; 10:45 BOOKWORMS: **ALWAYS LOOKING UP** BY MICHAEL J. FOX; 1:30 MOVIE MATINEE - CHANNEL 2; 2:30 MUSICAL BINGO; 3:15 BIBLE STUDY – 3WW; 6:30 PINOCHLE & GAMES	**11** 10:00 EXERCISE; 10:30 MASS -3CR; 2:00 CANDY MAKING	**12** 10:30 BAKING CLUB; 2:00 BAKING CLUB SAMPLES; 6:30 MOVIE NIGHT
13 DON'T FORGET TO CHANGE YOUR CLOCK ONE HOUR AHEAD *Daylight Savings Time Begins*	**14** 10:00 EXERCISE; 10:45 NATIONAL POTATOE CHIP DAY; 1:00 CRAFT; 2:30 BOWLING	**15** 10:00 EXERCISE; 10:45 MEN'S CLUB: MARCH MADNESS TRIVIA; 1:00 WHO'S WHO IN FOOD: FAMOUS ICONS; 2:30 BLACK BEAR CALEDONIA PIPER BAND-3CR; 6:30 CORN HOLE	**16** 10:00 EXERCISE; 10:45 AROUND THE KITCHEN TABLE; 1:30 NEW HOPE CHURCH -3WW; 3:15 FAMOUS IRISH-AMERICAN TRIVIA; 6:30 NICKEL BINGO	**17** 10:00 EXERCISE; 10:45 BOOKWORMS: **ALWAYS LOOKING UP** BY MICHAEL J. FOX; 2:00 ST. PATRICK'S DAY CELEBRATION; 6:30 HELP YOUR NEIGHBOR CARD GAME *St. Patrick's Day*	**18** COMMUNION; 10:00 EXERCISE; 10:45 GOOD DEEDS: COUPON CUTTING; 1:00 LOVING HANDS; 2:30 NICKEL BINGO	**19** 10:30 EXERCISE; 2:00 BOCCE BALL; 6:30 MOVIE NIGHT
20 1:30 ROOT BEER FLOATS *Spring Begins Purim*	**21** 10:00 EXERCISE; 10:45 EYEGLASS CLEANING & ADJUSTMENTS -3WW; 1:00 SPRING DOUBLES BOWLING; 2:30 BOWLING	**22** 10:00 EXERCISE; 10:45 BOB'S CORNER; 11:00 ROSARY; 1:00 KNITTING & CROCHETTING; 2:30 GROUP CROSSWORD PUZZLE	**23** 10:00 EXERCISE; 10:45 AROUND THE KITCHEN TABLE; 11:00 BROWN BAG CONCERT @ TRINITY CATHEDRAL: ORGAN RECITAL WITH LUDWIG RUCKDESCHEL OF PASSAU, GERMANY; 2:00 SPRING CRAFT; 6:30 NICKEL BINGO	**24** 10:00 EXERCISE; 10:45 BOOKWORMS: **ALWAYS LOOKING UP** BY MICHAEL J. FOX; 1:00 BAKING CLUB; 1:30 MOVIE MATINEE - CHANNEL 2; 3:15 BIBLE STUDY – 3WW; 6:30 PINOCHLE & GAMES	**25** COMMUNION; 10:00 EXERCISE; 10:45 GOOD DEEDS: COUPON CUTTING; 2:30 RESIDENT'S MONTHLY BIRTHDAY PARTY	**26** 10:30 EXERCISE; 2:00 BALLOON VOLLEYBALL; 6:30 MOVIE NIGHT
27 SPRING IS HERE!? CHECK TO SEE WHO CAN FIND THE FIRST CROCUS' OF THE SEASON	**28** 10:00 EXERCISE; 10:45 READING ROUNDTABLE: A FIZZ HEARD 'ROUND THE WORLD' COCA-COLA; 1:00 HORSERACE GAME; 2:30 BOWLING; DINNER MUSIC WITH NORM TISCHLER	**29** 10:00 EXERCISE; 10:45 MEN'S CLUB; 1:00 WHO AM I?; 2:00 RESIDENT COUNCIL; 6:30 CORN HOLE	**30** 10:00 EXERCISE; 10:45 AROUND THE KITCHEN TABLE; 11:00 BROWN BAG CONCERT @ TRINITY CATHEDRAL: TRINITY CHAMBER PLAYERS, MUSIC FOR WIND INSTRUMENTS; 2:30 JEOPARDY; 6:30 NICKEL BINGO	**31** 10:00 EXERCISE; 10:45 BOOKWORMS: **ALWAYS LOOKING UP** BY MICHAEL J. FOX; 1:30 MOVIE MATINEE - CHANNEL 2; 1:30 THANK YOUR LUCKY STAR GAME; 2:30 GROUP CROSSWORD PUZZLE; 6:30 TRIPOLY		

ALL ACTIVITIES TAKE PLACE IN THE ACTIVITY CENTER ON THE SECOND FLOOR UNLESS OTHERWISE NOTED

KEY: 3CR = 3RD FLOOR COMMUNITY ROOM, 3WW, 3RD FLOOR WEST WING

Calendar of Events
Broadway CareCenter
December 2010

Sunday	Monday	Tuesday	Wednesday	Thursday	Friday	Saturday
			1 10:15 - Morning Visits 10:30 - St.Monica's 11:00 - Sing Along 1:00 - TV/Room Visits 2:30 - Bingo	**2** 10:30 - Coffee Social 1:00 - TV/Room Visits 2:00 - Ball Toss 3:15 - Music w/Sam 6:30 - Movie Night/Uno	**3** 10:30 - Fitness 11:00 - Trivia 1:00 - TV/Room Visits 2:30 - Warrensville Church 6:30 - Horseracing	**4** 10:00 - Brother Nick 10:30 - Manicures 1:00 - TV/Room Visits 3:00 - Girl Scouts
5 9:00 - Church Group 10:30 - Coffee Social 11:00 - News 1:00 - Browns Game 2:30 - Witness Light	**6** 10:30 - Stretching 11:00 - This & That 1:00 - TV/Room Visits 2:30 - Ice Cream Social	**7** 10:15 - Morning Visits 10:30 - Bible Study 1:00 - TV/Room Visits 2:30 - Dollar Bingo 7:00 - Rev. Miller	**8** 10:30 - St. Monica's 11:00 - Noodle Ball 1:00 - TV/Room Visits 2:00 - New Home Church 2:30 - Arts & Crafts	**9** 10:30 - Pet Visits 1:00 - TV/Room Visits 2:30 - Church 3:00 - Ball Toss 6:30 - Movie Night	**10** 10:30-2:00 - Bake Sale 1:00 - TV/Room Visits 2:30 - Popcorn Friday 6:30 - Auction	**11** 10:15 - Morning Visit 11:00 - Spelling Bee 1:00 - TV/Room Visits 2:30 - Bingo (Stuffed Animals)
12 10:15 - Morning Visit 10:30 - Coffee Social 11:00 - News 1:00 - Browns Game 2:00 - Board Games	**13** 10:30 - Stretching 11:00 - Call Answers 1:00 - TV/Room Visits 2:30 - Ice Cream Social	**14** 10:15 - Morning Visits 10:30 - Bible Study 1:00 - TV/Room Visits 2:30 - Bingo 7:00 - Gospel House	**15** 10:30 - St. Monica's 11:00 - Hangman 1:00 - TV/Room Visits 2:30 - Bingo 7:00 - Mt. Moriah	**16** 10:30 - Coffee Social 1:00 - TV/Room Visits 2:30 - Resident Council 6:00 - CHRISTMAS WITH FAMILIES	**17** 10:30 - Fitness 11:00 - Trivia 1:00 - TV/Room Visits 2:30 - Popcorn Friday 6:30 - Happy Hour/ Benny	**18** 10:15 - Morning Visit 10:30 - Manicures 1:00 - TV/Room Visits 2:30 - Zion Chapel
19 9:00 - Church Group 10:30 - Coffee Social 1:00 - Browns Game 2:00 - Singing Angels 2:30 - Witness Light	**20** 10:30 - Stretching 11:00 - This & That 1:00 - TV/Room Visits 2:30 - Ice Cream/Shane 7:00 - Rev. Miller	**21** 10:15 - Morning Visits 10:30 - Bible Study 1:00 - TV/Room Visits 2:30 - Cooking 6:30 - Word Church	**22** 10:30 - St. Monica's 11:00 - Rosary 1:00 - TV/Room Visits 1:30 - Embassy Buddies 2:30 - Bingo	**23** 10:15 - Morning Visits 10:30 - Pet Visits 1:00 - TV/Room Visits 2:30 - AARP Birthday Party 6:30 - Movies/Uno	**24** 10:15 - Morning Visits 10:30 - Fitness 11:00 - Trivia 1:00 - TV/Room Visits 2:30 - Popcorn Friday	**25** 10:15 - Morning Visits 11:00 - Spelling Bee 1:00 - TV/Room Visits 2:30 - Snack Bingo *MERRY CHRISTMAS*
26 10:15 - Morning Visits 10:30 - Coffee Social 11:00 - News 1:00 - Browns Game 2:00 - Card Games	**27** 10:30 - Stretching 11:00 - Call Answers 1:00 - TV/Room Visits 2:30 - Ice Cream Social 6:30 - Church/Joanne	**28** 10:15 - Morning Visits 10:30 - Bible Study 1:00 - TV/Room Visits 2:30 - Bingo	**29** 10:15 - Morning Visits 10:30 - St. Monica's 11:00 - Hangman 1:00 - TV/Room Visits 2:30 - Penny Ante	**30** 10:15 - Morning Visits 10:30 - Coffee Social 1:00 - TV/Room Visits 2:30 - Jewelry Making 6:30 - Movies/Uno	**31** 10:15 - Morning Visits 10:30 - Fitness 11:00 - Trivia 1:00 - TV/Room Visits 2:30 - Popcorn Friday *NEW YEARS EVE*	

February 2011

ASSISTED LIVING/ INDEPENDENT LIVING — Shurmer Place

Sunday	Monday	Tuesday	Wednesday	Thursday	Friday	Saturday
		1 9:30 Muscles in Motion 10:00 Companion Radio 11:00 Intro to Black History Month 2:00 Dominoes 2:30 Arts-N-Crafts 3:30 Music – 2nd FL	**2 GROUND HOG DAY** 9:30 Muscles in Motion 10:30 BINGO 10:00 Companion Radio 10:30 Yarn Club – CR 11:00 Tai Chi – 3rd FL 2:30 Groundhog Program (CR) 2:30 Horticulture 3:30 1:1 Visits 3:30 Pet Visits	**3** 9:30 Muscles in Motion 10:30 Bible Study 11:00 Companion Radio 1:45 Trip to Tooties 2:30 Choir (CR) 3:30 1:1 Visits	**4** 9:00 – 2:00 pm Clothing Sale with Sunshine Brothers- CR 10:30 Worship Service – 2nd FL 10:30 Companion Radio 2:00 Movie CH 13 2:30 Peter Tavens 2nd FL 6:45 Movie CH 13 7:00 Drive In Movie - CR	**5** 10:30 Bingo 2:00 Movie Ch 13 3:00 Trivia w/ Tamara 7:30 Movie Ch. 13
6 11:00 Rev. Hull – 2nd Fl 2:00 Movie Ch 13 2:30 Arts-n-Crafts 6:00 SUPER BOWL --Party – 3rd Floor	**7** 9:30 Muscles in Motion 10:45 Mass – Chapel 10:00 Companion Radio 2:30 African American History- L.V.C. w/ Malek Vodanoff - CR 3:30 1:1 Visits	**8** 10:00 Companion Radio 10:30 Hug-A-Bear 2:00 Dominoes 2:30 Arts-N-Crafts 3:30 Music – 2nd FL	**9** 9:30 Muscles in Motion 10:30 BINGO 10:30 Companion Radio 10:30 Yarn Club – CR 11:00 Tai Chi – 2nd FL 2:30 Horticulture 3:30 1:1 Visits 3:30 Pet Visits	**10** 9:30 Muscles in Motion 10:00 Companion Radio 10:30 Bible Study 1:45 Trip to Tooties 2:30 Choir (CR) 3:30 1:1 Visits	**11** 10:30 Worship Service – 2nd FL 10:30 Companion Radio 2:00 Movie Ch 13 2:30 Entertainment 4:00 Home School Troop 6:45 Movie CH 13	**12** 10:30 Bingo 2:00 Movie Ch 13 3:00 Music w/Sam Fosh (CR) 7:30 Movie Ch.13
13 10:30 Cookies & Coffee 1:30 Dean Guy - Music 2:00 Movie – Ch 13 3:00 Moses Free Spirit Baptist Church – 2nd Fl 7:30 Movie – Ch 13	**14** 9:30 Muscles in Motion 10:00 Communion – Chapel 10:00 Companion Radio 2:30 Baking Valentine Cookies with Renard 3:30 1:1 Visits	**15** 9:30 Muscles in Motion 10:00 Companion Radio 11:00 Current Events 2:00 Dominoes 2:30 Nail Care 2:30 Tuskegee Airmen Movie/Social 3:30 Music – 2nd FL 7:00 Valentine Concert, Townsmen Orchestra (CR)	**16** 9:30 Muscles in Motion 10:30 BINGO 10:00 Companion Radio 10:30 Yarn Club – CR 11:00 Tai Chi – 2nd FL 2:30 Flower Arranging 3:30 1:1 Visits 3:30 Pet Visits	**17** 10:30 Bible Study 10:30 Harold Wyant Music 2:30 Choir (CR) 3:30 1:1 Visits	**18** 9:30 Muscles in Motion 10:30 Worship Service – 2nd FL 10:30 Companion Radio 2:00 Movie Ch 13 2:30 Tuskegee Airmen- Roy Richardson - CR 6:45 Movie CH 13	**19** 10:30 Bingo 2:00 Movie Ch 13 2:30 Hangman 7:30 Movie Ch.13
20 11:00 Worship with Rev Hull – 2nd FL 2:00 Movie – Ch 13 2:30 Current Events 7:30 Movie – Ch	**21** 9:30 Muscles in Motion 10:00 Communion – Chapel 10:00 Companion Radio 2:30 Glory the movie Social 3:30 1:1 Visits	**22** 9:30 Muscles in Motion 10:00 Companion Radio 2:00 Dominoes 2:30 Men's Club – CR 3:30 Music – 2nd FL	**23** 9:30 Muscles in Motion 10:30 BINGO 10:00 Companion Radio 10:30 Yarn Club – CR 11:00 Tai Chi – 2nd FL 1:30 Horticulture 2:30 Birthday Bash - CR	**24 FLAG DAY** 9:30 Muscles in Motion 10:00 Companion Radio 10:30 Bible Study 1:45 Trip to Tooties 2:30 Choir (CR) 3:30 1:1 Visits	**25** 9:30 Muscles in Motion 10:30 Worship Service – 2nd FL 10:30 Companion Radio 2:00 Movie Ch 13 2:30 Annual Black History Program - CR 6:45 Movie CH 13	**26** 10:30 Bingo 2:00 Movie Ch 13 3:45 Sherry Hour – 2nd FL 7:30 Movie Ch.13
27 10:30 Sunday School Visits – 2nd Fl 2:00 Movie – Ch 13 3:00 Greater Cleveland Pan Hellenic Choir - CR 7:30 Movie – Ch 13	**28** 10:00 Communion – Chapel 10:00 Companion Radio 2:30 Resident Council 3:15 Dining Committee 3:30 1:1 Visits					

Tooties Tea Room Open Monday-Friday 8 a.m. – 3:00 p.m

Companion Radio Stations
Reminiscence 87.9 – 1
Imagination 99.9 –
Serenity 101.7 –
Potpourri 107.1

Movies of the Week Channel 13
Friday @ 6:45/9:30 pm
Saturday @ 2:00/7:30 pm
Sunday @ 2:00/7:30 pm

BIRTHDAYS
Margaret Bernaky – 1st
John Bricker – 4th
Gloria Wyant – 4th
Berendette Denninger – 11th
Wilma Gundersen – 11th
Harry Robinson - 20th

Eliza Bryant Village   February 2011

Black History Month

Sun	Mon	Tue	Wed	Thu	Fri	Sat
MP= Multi-Purpose Room VE1= 1st Floor Activity Room-LTC		1	2	3 11:00am-MP Mr. Brown: Reflections	4 10:00am&11:00am African Drum Making-MP	5
6	7	8	9 Black Heritage Tribute Day! Dress in Traditional African Attire.	10	11 10:00am&11:00am African Drum Making-MP	12 2:30pm Gospel Music: Brown /Jones-MP
13	14 11:00am Mr. Bibb, Sr. Speaker-MP	15	16 Soul Day Celebration Food and Fun!	17 11:00am Foluke Arts Presentation-MP	18 10:00am&11:00am African Drum Making-MP	19 2:30pm Gospel Piano-VE1
20 3:00pm The sounds of Catron-MP	21 11:00am-MP Karamu Dancers 3:00 MP Safiri Dancers	22 11:00am-MP Birthday Party MLK / R. Parks	23 10:30am -MP Story Tellers: "One House"	24 MOTOWN DAY Music and More	25 10:00am&11:00am African Drum Making-MP	26
27	28 11:00am-MP Black History Month Celebra-					

ELIZA BRYANT VILLAGE BLACK HISTORY MONTH

Additional Programs scheduled this month.

(Dates to be announced.)

Tri-C Black Caucus
CSU, Black Studies
Mt. Zion Congregational Church
The Voices OF Hope Mass Choir
Kingdom of God Girl Scouts
EBV Choir

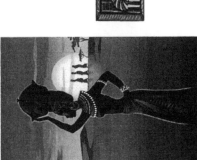

SPRING GARDEN
JULY

Mail Delivery Daily

All Activities on Spring Garden unless marked

Sunday	Monday	Tuesday	Wednesday	Thursday	Friday	Saturday
		1 10:00 Walking Club 10:20 Drumming Circle 11:15 Finish The Phrase 1:30 Walking Club 2:30 Digging For Gold 4:00 Sound Therapy 7:00 Comedy Movies	**2** 10:00 Walking Club 10:20 Bingo 11:15 Balloon Volleyball 1:30 Walking Club 2:30 Gardening on the Patio 4:00 Resident Chat 7:00 Lawrence Welk	**3** 10: 00 Walking Club 10:20 Let's Get Cookin 11:15 Music & Motion 1:30 Walking Club 2:30 Sports Games 4:00 Aromatherapy 7:00 Little Rascals	**4** 10:00 Patriotic Social w/Linda Hamski MDR 11:15 Sentimental Singalong 1:30 Walking Club 2:30 Timeslips Stories 4:00 Rosary 7:00 I Love Lucy	**5** 10:00 Catholic Mass MDR 10:00 Coffee/& Daily News 11:15 Rhythm Band 1:30 Walking Club 2:30 Bingo 4:00 Art Expression 7:00 Classic Movies
6 10:00 Walking Club 10:20 Shake loose Memory 11:15 Colors in Motion 1:30 Walking Club 2:00 Doodle Le Do MDR 4:00 Laughter Therapy 4:30 Puzzle Time 7:00 Adventure Movie	**7** 10:00 Singalong w/ Brenda 11:15 Balloon Volleyball 1:30 Walking Club 2:30 Bowling 4:00 Reiki 4:30 Soothing Sounds 7:00 Travel Adventures 7:00 Bingo ADR	**8** 10:00 Walking Club 10:20 Drumming Circle 11:15 Clue Trivia 1:30 Walking Club 2:30 Gardening on the Patio 4:00 Tai Chi 4:30 Magazine Search 7:00 "Who Done It" Movie	**9** 10:00 Walking Club 10:20 Bingo 11:15 Music & Motion 1:30 Walking Club 2:30 A Day at the Races 4:00 Sound Therapy 4:30 Crossword Search 7:00 Armchair Vacation	**10** 10:00 Walking Club 10:20 Let's Get Cookin' 11:15 Reminisce Dice 1:30 Walking Club 2:30 Penny Ante 4:00 Reading Roundtable 4:30 Finish The Phrase 7:00 Lawrence Welk	**11** Bus Trip 10:00 Walking Club 10:20 A Spiritual Connection 11:15 Movin & Groovin 1:30 Walking Club 2:30 Paper Projects 4:00 Rosary 4:30 Sentimental Singalong 7:00 I Love Lucy	**12** 10:00 Walking Club 10:20 Manicures & Music 11:15 Colors in Motion 1:30 Walking Club 2:30 Bingo 4:00 Art Expression 7:00 John Wayne Film
13 10:00 Catholic Comm. MDR 10:00 Finish The Phrase 11:15 Rhythm Band 1:30 Walking Club 2:30 Watermelon on Patio 4:00 Judge & Jury 4:30 Bead Making 7:00 Suspense Movie	**14** 10:00 Music Ministry 11:15 Music & Motion 1:30 Walking Club 2:30 Art Expression 4:00 Polarity Energy 4:30 Mystery Hour 7:00 Movie Musical	**15** 10:00 Walking Club 10:20 Drumming Circle 11:15 Tip o Tongue Trivia 1:30 Walking Club 2:30 Birthday Party MDR 4:00 Lotion/Aromatherapy 7:00 Western Movie	**16** 10:00 Walking Club 10:20 Bingo 11:15 Colors in Motion 1:30 Walking Club 2:30 Kickin' It w/Joel 4:00 Nurturing Touch 7:00 Armchair Travels	**17** 10:00 Walking Club 10:20 Let's Get Cookin' 11:15 Parachute 1:30 Walking Club 2:30 Gardening on Patio 4:00 Sound Therapy 7:00 Lawrence Welk Hour	**18** Bus Trip 10:00 Walking Club 10:20 Spiritual Connection 11:15 Movin & Groovin 1:30 Walking Club 2:30 Art Expression 4:00 Rosary 7:00 I Love Lucy	**19** 10:00 Walking Club 10:15 Manicures & Music 11:15 Balloon Volleyball 1:30 Walking Club 2:30 Bingo 4:00 Table Games 7:00 Movie Musicals
20 Family Day 10:00 Catholic Comm. MDR 10:00 Coffee & the News 11:15 Music & Motion 1:30 Walking Club 2:00 Family Day w/ Ray 4:00 Reading Roundtable 7:00 Comedy Classics	**21** 10:00 Golden Oldies w/John Thayer 11:15 Colors in Motion 1:30 Walking Club 2:30 Memories In Music 4:00 Aromatherapy 7:00 Lawrence Welk	**22** 10:00 Walking Club 10:20 Drumming Circle 11:15 Finishing Lines 1:30 Walking Club 2:30 Shake Loose a Taste 4:00 Patio Social 7:00 A "Who Done It?" Movie	**23** 10:00 Walking Club 10:20 Bingo 11:15 Singalong 1:30 Walking Club 2:30 Taboo 4:00 Laughter Therapy 7:00 Comedy Classics 7:00 Golden TV Shows	**24** 10: 00 Walking Club 10:20 Cooking Time 11:15 Music & Motion 1:30 Walking Club 2:00 Polkas with Ted MDR 4:00 Nurturing Touch 7:00 Lawrence Welk	**25** 10:00 Walking Club 10:20 A Spiritual Connection 11:15 Rhythm Band 1:30 Walking Club 2:30 Art Expression 4:00 Rosary 7:00 I Love Lucy	**26** 10:00 Walking Club 10:15 Manicures & Music 11:15 Movin & Groovin 1:30 Walking Club 2:00 Bingo 4:00 Variety Time 7:00 Comic Classics
27 10:00 Catholic Comm MDR 10:00 Sunday News 11:15 Balloon Volleyball 1:30 Walking Club 2:30 Spelling Bee 4:00 Timeslips Stories 7:00 Variety Time	**28** 10:00 Walking Club 10:20 Gardening on Patio 11:15 Music & Motion 1:30 Walking Club 2:30 Digging For Gold 4:00 Judge & Jury 7:00 Travel Adventures	**29** 10:00 Walking Club 10:20 Drumming Circle 11:15 Memory Lane 1:30 Walking Club 2:00 50's Sock Hop MDR 4:00 Aromatherapy 7:00 Movie Classics	**30** 10:00 Walking Club 10:20 Bingo 11:15 Colors in Motion 1:30 Walking Club 2:30 Resident Welcome 4:00 Sound Therapy 7:00 Lawrence Welk	**31** 10:00 Walking Club 10:20 Let's Get Cookin 11:15 Music & Motion 1:30 Walking Club 2:30 Bowling 4:00 Reiki 7:00 Comedy Classics		

Activity Room Key
ADR-Activity Dining Room
MDR– Main Dining Room
ACR–Arts & Crafts Room
ALA–Activity Lounge Area
GHP-Greenhouse Patio
AL–Autumn Lane
SG–Spring Garden
U5-Unit 5 Dining Room

Common Drug Abbreviations

Warning: Drug abbreviations are not standardized. Use professional judgment.

Abbreviation	Meaning	Abbreviation	Meaning
APAP	acetaminophen	MSO4	morphine sulfate (careful)
ASA	aspirin	MOM	milk of magnesia
BC	birth control	MTX	methotrexate (careful)
Ca, Ca++	calcium	MVI	multivitamin
CHF	congestive heart failure	Na, Na+	sodium
Cl	chloride, chlorine	NaCl 0.9%	normal saline
Cod	codeine	NS, NSS	normal saline
CR	controlled release	NSAID	non-steroidal anti-inflammatory drug
DM	dextromethorphan		
DCN,	Darvocet N-100	NTG	nitroglycerin
DN100	doxycycline	OC	oral contraceptive
doxy	enteric coated	ORS	oral rehydration solution
EC	enteric coated aspirin	PB	phenobarbital
EC ASA	extended release	PCN	penicillin
ER	(ethyl) alcohol	PNV	prenatal vitamin
EtOH	iron	PTU	propylthiouracil
Fe, FE++	ferrous sulfate (iron)	SMX/TMP	sulfamethoxazole and trimethoprim
FeSO4	hydrocortisone		
HC	hydrocortisone or	SMZ/TMP	sulfamethoxazole and trimethoprim
HCT	hydrochlorothiazide (careful)		
HCO3	bicarbonate	SR	slow release or sustained release
HCTZ	hydrochlorothiazide	TAC	triamcinolone
HS	half strength	TCN	tetracycline
INH	isoniazid	TMP/SMX	sulfamethoxazole and trimethoprim
K, K+	potassium		
LA	long acting (time released)	TMP/SMZ	sulfamethoxazole and trimethoprim
Mg, Mg++	magnesium		
MgSO4	magnesium sulfate (careful)	TR	time release
		XL	extended release
		XR	extended release
		Zn, Zn++	zinc
		ZnSO4	zinc sulfate

ACTIVITY RESOURCES for ACTIVITIES SUPPLIES AND EQUIPMENT

ACTIVITIES

Briggs Corp., Life Enrichment & Activities
Cross Creek Recreation Products Inc.
Elderbooks
Eldergames
Eldersong
Pickett Enterprises
Sea Bay Game Co.

ADAPTED CLOTHING, REGULAR CLOTHING & PERSONAL ITEMS

American Heritage Apparel
Dr. Leonard's
Foot Smart
Support Plus/Fashion Able
Vocational Guidance and Rehabilitation
    Services
Wardrobe Wagon

ADAPTED SUPPLIES & EQUIPMENT

Access With Ease

Adapt Ability
American Foundation for the Blind, (Products
    For People With Vision Problems)
American Printing House for the Blind
Choice Magazine
Dr. Leonard's
Fred Sammons (Be OK - Self Help Aid) Health
Care
Gold Violin
Harriet Carter
Large-Print Pub. Co. (Crossword, Circle Word,
    Puzzles
Books, Trivia, Quizzes)
Library of Congress (Talking Books)
Lighthouse International, Inc.
LS&S Learning, (sight& sound made easier)
FLAG House

ARTS/CRAFTS/NEEDLEWORK

American Handicrafts/Merribee Needlecrafts
Briggs Life Enrichment & Activities
Curriculum Resources
J & A Handy-Crafts, Inc.
Gold Times
Nasco Activity Therapy
Nasco Arts & Crafts

S & S Arts & Crafts
Triarco Arts & Crafts

BALLOONS

Pioneer Balloon Company

BIRTHDAYS

Pickett Enterprises
Presidential Greeting
Sea Bay Game Co.
The White House, Washington, D.C.

CALENDARS

Briggs Corp. Life Enrichment & Activities
Pickett Enterprises
Sea Bay Games Co.

CLIP ART/ILLUSTRATION

Artmaster
Dover Publications, Inc.
Wilco Publishing Co.

DECORATIONS/PARTIES/SPECIAL EVENTS

Hubert
M & N International, Inc.
Oriental Trading Co., Inc.
Paradise Products, Inc.
Pickett Enterprises
Pioneer Balloon Company
Positive Promotions
The Promotion Planner, Paper World

DISCUSSIONS

Bi-fokal Productions Inc.
Good Old Days - Special Issue
Ideals Magazine
Professional Printing & Publishing, Inc.
Reminisce
Women's History Project

EXERCISE AND ADAPTIVE SPORTS EQUIPMENT

Flaghouse Inc.
Hammatt Senior Products
Pickett Enterprises
Snitz Manufacturing Co.
Sportime Senior Products

FOOD (Snacks)

Gold Medal Products (popcorn)
Ottis Spunkmeyer (cookie dough)

GAMES

"A Nite at the Races" Inc.
Bingo King
Cross Creek
Eldergames
Eldersongs
Flaghouse, Inc.
Large Print Pub. Co.
NASCO
Pickett Enterprises
Residents' Rights Bingo
Sea Bay Game Co.
Snitz Manufacturing Co.
Things From Bell
3 Score 10
World Wide Games

HORTICULTURE

Breck's
Geo. W. Park Seed Co., Inc.
Schoolmaster Science - (Table Top Greenhouse)
Stark Bros.
The Wayside Gardens

MUSIC

Credence Cassettes (Catholic hymns/rosary
    tapes)
Educational Record Sales
Eldersong Publication, Inc.
Hal Leonard Publishing
Heartwarmers
Kimbo Educational
MMMB Music, Inc.
Music For All to Hear
Music In Motion
Music is Elementary
Pickett Enterprises
Professional Printing & Publishing, Inc.
Recordings for Recovery
Rhythm Band, Inc.
West Music Company

NEWSLETTERS FOR ACTIVITY PROFESSIONS

A New Day (Magazine)
Activity Director's Guide (Eyemann
Publications, Inc.)
The Anderson Planner
Creative Forecasting, Inc.
Activityconnection.com

PETS

Pets Are Wonderful Council
AKC Canine Good Citizen
Delta Society

POSTERS

Giant Photos, Inc.
Pickett Enterprises Presidential
Presentation Vantage
Communications, Inc.
Time Slips

REALITY ORIENTATION

Concepts du Sablier
NASCO Activity Therapy

RELIGIOUS

American Bible Society
Bible Alliance
Choice Magazine Listening
Daily Word
Elder Source
Guideposts
John Milton Magazine
Radio Bible Class
The Source for Everything Jewish (Jewish
    Music)
Xavier Society for the Blind

SENSORY STIMULATION

Eldersong Publications, Inc.
Nasco, Activity Therapy
Special Populations, Flag House
Spinoza

SOUND SYSTEM
Anchor Audio, Inc.

VOLUNTEERS

Positive Promotions

ADDRESSES FOR ACTIVITIES PROGRAMMING

1. Activity Connections.Com, LLC, 818 SQ 3rd Ave., #222, Portland, OR 97204

2. Activity Director's Guide, Box 3577, Remo NV 89505 (Newsletter)

3. Adapt Ability, P.O. Box 515, Colchester, CT 06415-0515

4. Alzheimer's Store, 12633 159th Court North, Jupiter, FL 33478 1- (800) 752-3238
   www.alzstore.com

5. American Bible Society, 1865 Broadway, New York, NY 10023

6. American Foundation for the Blind, 11 Penn Plaza, Suite 300 New York, NY 10001 (Products for people with vision problems)

7. American Handicrafts/Merribee Needlecrafts, P.O. Box 791, Fort Worth, TX 76101

8. Anchor Audio, Inc., 913 West 223nd St., Torrance, CA 90502

9. A New Day, Gary Grimm & Associates, 82 S Madison Street, Carthage, IL 62321

10. American Printing House for the Blind, Inc. 1839 Frankfort Ave, Louisville, KY 40206-3152

11. Ames & Rollinson, Inc, 215 Park Ave South, New York, N.Y.10003 (212)-473-7000

12. Artmaster, 550 N. Claremont Blvd., Calremont, CA 91711

13. Balloon World, Inc., Paige Alexander, 205, W IRS Court, Andover, KS 67002

14. Bible Alliance, Inc., P.O. Box 1549, Bradenton, FL 34206

15. Bi-Folkal Productions, Inc., 911 Williamson St. Madison WI 53703-3549

16. Bingo King, P.O. Box 2499, Littleton, CO 80161

17. Boin Arts & Crafts Co., Box 659, Morristown, NJ 07960

18. Breck's, U.S. Reservation Center, 6523 N. Galena Rd., Peoria, IL 61632

19. Briggs Corporation, P.O. Box 1698, Des Moines, IA 50306

20. Brown Industries, 101 South Chester Rd, Swartmore, PA 19081-1998 1-800-522-7696

21. Caring Concepts, 315 Tucapau Rd. Duncan, SC 29334

22. Carter, Harriet, Dept 37, North Wales, PA 19455, www.harrietcarter.com

23. Concepts du Sablier, 49 St-Joseph, Warwick, Qc. Canada JOA 1MO 1-(800) 888-907-6878
   www.sablier.com

24. Creative Forecasting, Inc. 2607 Farragut Circle, Colorado Springs, CO 80907 (Newsletter)

25. Credence Cassettes, 115 E. Armour Blvd., Box 414291, Kansas City, MO 64141-4291

26. Crestwood Company, 6625 N. Sidney Place, Milwaukee WI 53204-0606

27. Cross Creek, Recreational Products, Inc., P.O. Box 289, Millbrook, NY 12545

28. Curriculum Resources, Inc., P.O. Box 923, 2 Post Rd., Fairfield, CT 06430

29. Daily Word, Unity Village, MO 64065-0001

30. Discount School Supply File No.73847 P.O. Box 60000, San Francisco, CA 94160-3847
   1-(800) 627- 2829 www.DiscountSchoolSupply.com

31. Dover Publications, Inc. 180 Varick Street, New York, NY 10014

32. Dr. Leonard's HEALTHCARE CATALOG, 100 Nixon Lane, P.O. Box 7821, Edison, NJ -8818-7821

33 Educational Record Sales, 157 Chambers St., New York, NY 10007

34. Elder Source Senior Ministries, PO Box 4848, Greenville, SC 29608, 1-(800)827-2710
    www.eldersouceinfo.org

35. Elderbooks, 731 Treat Avenue, San Francisco, CA 94110

36. Eldergames/USHC, 1331 H. Street, NW, Suite 500, Washington, DC 20005-4706

37. ElderSong Publications, Inc. P.O. Box 74, Mt. Airy, MD 21771

38. Eyemann Publications, Inc., P.O. Box 3577, Reno, NV 89505

39. Flaghouse SPECIAL POPULATIONS, 601 FlagHouse Dr., Hasbrouck Hts., NJ07604-3116
    (800) 793-7900 www.FlagHouse.com

40. Fred Sammons, Inc. Box 32, Brookfield, IL 60513

41. George W. Park Seed Co., Inc., P.O. Box 31, Greenwood, SC 29646

42. Geriatric Resources, P.O. Box 239, Radium Springs, NM 88054-0239

43. Giant Photos, Inc., Box 406, Rockford, IL 61106

44. Gold Metal Products, 10700 Medallion Dr., Cincinnati, OH 45214

45. Gold Timers (A Division of Incentives for Learning, Inc.) 1ll Center Ave., Suite 1, Pacheco, CA
    94553

46. Gold Violin, 1717-2B Allied St, Suite 1, Charlottesville, VA 22903 1-(877) 648-8400
    www.goldviolin.com

47. *Guidepost* Good Old Days, House of White Birches, 306 E Parr Rd., Berne, IN 46711,
    Carmel NY 10512

48. HEALTH PROFESSIONS PRESS, A division of Brookes Publishing Co. P.O.Box 10624,
    Baltimore, MD 21285-0624 1-(888) 337-8808 www.healthpropress.com

49. Heartwarmers, GN Box 534, Glendale Rd., Medinah, IL 60157 1-888-256-7322 then dial pin
    #0437, www.heartwarmers.org

50. Idyll Arbor,Inc., PO Box 720, Ravendale, WA 98051 (360) 825-7797 www.IDYLLArbor.com

51. Innovative Caregiving Resources. 5370 E. Lake creek Rd Heber City, UT 84031
    1 (800) 249-5600, WWW.videorespite.com

52. Ideals Magazine, Ideals Publishing Corp., P.O Box 148000 Nashville, TN 37214-9988

53. J & A Handy-Crafts, Inc., 210 Front St., Hempstead, NY 1155062.

54. John Milton Magazine, John Milton Society for the Blind, 475 Riverside Dr. Room 832, New York,
    N.Y.10115

55. Kimbo Educational, P.O. Box 477, Long Branch, NJ 00740

56. Lancaster Bingo Co. 200 Quarry Rd, Lancaster, OH 43130

57. LARGE-PRINT Pub. Co., 103 Forest Glen, West Springfield, MA 01089, 1-(800) 810-2777

58. The Lighthouse International, 111 East 59th St, 12 Floor, New York, NY 10022-1202
   1-(800)-829-0500 www.lighthouse.org

59. Let Freedom Ring, Pennsylvania Society of Sons of the Revolution, 121 South Broad Street,
   Suite 1910, Philadelphia, PA19107

60. Large Print Pub. Co., 103 Forest Glen, West Springfield, MA 01089

61. Library of Congress, Div. for the Blind & Physically Handicapped, Washington, D.C. 20542

62. Lighthouse International, 111 East 59th St. 12th Fl., New York NY 10022-1202

63. Maddoak, Inc., Subsidiary of Bel-Art Products, Pequanock, NJ 07440

64. Make-Aids, 42 Executive Blvd., P.O. Box 3209, Farmingdale, NJ 11735

65. MB Music, Inc., P.O. Box 32410, 10370 Page Industrial Blvd., St. Louis, MO 63132

66. M & N International, Inc., P.O. Box 64784, St. Paul, MN 55164-0784

67. Mobility Works, 810 Moe Dr, Akron, OH 44398-1073

68. Music For All To Hear, Inc., P.O. Box 6347, Evanston, IL 60204

69. Music In Motion, 109 Spanish Village, Suite 645, Dallas, TX 75248

70. Music Is Elementary, P.O. Box 24263, Cleveland, OH 44124

71. NASCO Senior Activities, 901 Janesville Ave., P.O. Box 901, Fort Atkinson, WI
   53538-0901 www.eNasco.com

72. National Women's History Project, 7738 Bell Rd. Windsor, CA 95492-8518

73. NCR Credence Cassettes, 115 E. Armour Blvd., P.O. Box 419491, Kansas City, MO 64141
   (Catholic Hymns and Rosary on cassette tapes)

74. Old Favorites Sing-A-Long, Inc., P.O. Box 1006, Harrisonburg, VA 22801

75. Oriental Trading Ct., Inc., 4206 South 108th St., Omaha NE 68137-1215

76. Otis Spunkmeyer, 14490 Catalina St., San Lendro, CA 94577 510-357-9836

77. Paper Projects, 184 Sunflower Dr. Brunswick, OH 42212

78. Pickett Enterprises, P.O. Box 11000, Prescott, AZ 86304

79 Pioneer Balloon Company, 5000 E.29th St. North, Wichita, KA 67220-211,
   1-(800) 880-6118, (Canada 1-(905) 560-6534)

80. Pioneer Network, P.O. Box 18648, Rochester, N.Y. 14618, 1-585-271-7570.
   www.PioneerNetwork.net

81. Positive Promotions, 40-01 168th St., Flushing, NY 11358

82. Professional Printing & Publishing, Inc., 601 Bardsdale Blvd., P.O. Box 5758, Bossier City, LA 71171

83. The Promotion Planner, Paper World, 30 Prescott St., Worcester, ME 01605

84. Radio Bible Class, Box 22, Grand Rapids, MI 49555

85. Recordings for Recovery, Michael Hoy, Exec Dir, 413 Cherry, Midland, MI 48640 (Free
   loan of cassette tapes music)).

86. Reminisce, 5927 Memory Lane, P.O. Box 3088, Milwaukee, WI 53201-3088

87. Residents' Rights Bingo, The Legal Center, 455 Sherman St. #130, Denver, CO 80203

88. Rhythm Band, Inc., P.O. Box 126, Ft. Worth, TX 76101

89. S & S Arts & Crafts, Colchester, CT 06415

90. Schoolmasters Science, 745 State Circle, P.O. Box 1941, Ann Arbor, MI 48106

91. Sea Bay Game Co., 77 Cliffwood Ave Ste. 1 D, Cliffwood, NJ 07721, 1-(800) 568- 0188, www.seabaygame.com

92. Senior Shopping Service, Inc., 319 Anderson Rd., Chesterfield, IN 46017. 1-(800) -334-2897 www.seniorshoppingservice.com

93. Sentimental Productions, 1620 Harrison Ave., Suite 100, Cincinnati, OH 45214

94. Spring Hill Nursery, 110 West Elm St., Tipp City, Oh 45371-1699, (513) 354-1509 www.SpringHill Nursery.com

95. The Source For Everything Jewish, Hamakor Judaica, Inc., P.O. Box 59453, Chicago, IL 60659

96. Spinoza, 287 East 6th Street, St. Paul, MN 55101

97. Stark Brothers, Nurseries & Orchard Co., Louisiana, MO 63353-0010

98. Triarco Arts & Crafts, 14650 28th Ave. N., Plymouth, MN 55441

99. U.S. Toy Co., Inc., 5314 W. Lincoln Ave., Skokie, IL 60077

100. Vocational Guidance & Rehabilitation Services, 2239 E. 55th St., Cleveland, OH 44103

101. Wardrobe Wagon, Inc., 2846 Valcor Ct., Reynoldsburg, OH 43068

102. West Music Co., P.O. Box 5521, 1212 5th St. Coralville, IA 52241

103. The White House, Presidential Greetings Office, The White House, 1600 Pennsylvania Ave. Washington, DC 20500 www.whitehouse.gov/contact/

104. Xavier Society for the Blind, 154 East 23rd St., New York, NY 10010,

ACTIVITY RESOURCES

Professional and Certification/Registration Organizations

NAAP (National Association of Activity Professionals), P.O. Box 5530, Severiville TN
37864-5530, 1- (865) 429-0717, www.thenaap.com

NCCAP (National Certification Council for Activity Professionals), P.O. Box 62689,
Virginia Beach, VA 23466, 1-(757) 552-0653, www.nccap.org

AATA (American Art Therapy Association, Inc.), 225 North Fairfax Street, Alexandria, VA 22304,
www.arththerapy.org

ADTA (American Dance Therapy Association) adta.org

AHTA (American Horticulture Therapy Association), www.ahta.org

AMTA (American Music Therapy Association, Inc.), 8455 Colesville Rd. Suite 1000,
Silver Springs, MD 20910, 1 9301) 58903300, www.musictherapy.org

APTA (Americn Physical Therapy Association), 1111 North Fairax St, Alenandria, VA
22314-1488, 1-(800) 999-2782, www.apta.org

ASHA (American Speech-Language-Hearing Association), 10801 Rockville, Maryland,
20852, 1- 301-897-5700

ATRA (American Therapeutic Recreation Association), 1414 Prince St Suite 204,
Alexandria, VA 22314, 1-703) 683-9420, www.ata-tr.org

NADT (National Association for Drama Therapy), www.NADT.org

NAPT (National Association of Poetry Therapy), www.poetrytherapy.org

NCTRC (National Council for Therapeutic Recreation Certification), 7 Elmwood Drive,
New City, New York 10956 1-(845)639-1439, www.nctrc.org

NTRS (National Therapeutic Recreation and Parks Association) 22377 Belmont Ridge Rd., Ashburn, VA
20148, 1-800-626-6772, NTRSNRPA@NRPA.org

NCCDP (Certification Council for Dementia Practitioners) NCCDP.org

RESOURCES

Aging

AARP (American Association of Retired Persons**)**, 601 E. St. NW, Washington, DC20049, 888-687-2277, www.aarp.org

Alliance for Aging Research, www.agingresearch.org

AAHSA (American Association of Homes and Services for the Aging), 2519 Connecticut Ave. NW, Washington, DC 20008, 1- (202) 783-2242, www.aahsa.org

AGS (American Geriatrics Society), The Empire State Building, 350 5th Ave. Suite 801, New York, New York 10118, 1- (212)308-1414, www.americangeriatrics.org

AHCA (American Health Care Association), 1201 L St. NW, Washington, DC 20005, 1-(202)842-4444, www.ahca.org

American Seniors Housing Association, 5222 Wisconsin Ave. NW, Suite 502,

Washington, DC 20016, (202)-885-5563, www.seniorhousing.org

Assisted Living Federation of America, 11200 Waples Mill Rd. Suite 150, Fairfax, VA 22030, 1- (703) 691-8100, www.alfa.org

Center for Aging Services Technologies, 2519 Connecticut Ave. NW, Washington, DC 20008-1520, 1- (202) 508-9463, www.agingtech.org

Center for Economics and Demography of Aging, University of California, Berkley, 2232 Piedmont Ave., Berkeley, CA 94720, 1-(510) 642-9800, www.ceda.berkeley.edu

Leading Age, 600 Maryland Ave. SW Suite 550, Washington, DC 20024, 1-(202) 484-5261, www.leadingage.org

National Certification Council for Activity Professionals

Certification Standards

National Certification Council for Activity Professionals

NATIONAL OFFICE
P.O. Box 62589
Virginia Beach, VA 23466-2589
Tel: 757-552-0653
Fax: 757-552-0491
E--Mail Address: info@nccap.org
http://www.nccap.org

GENERAL
Standard Information

Each profession has its own professional standards. The following are the National Certification Council for Activity Professionals, NCCAP's, standards. These standards must be met to become a NCCAP Certified Activity Professional. It is the wish of the NCCAP Board of Directors and administration that you join our ranks as a Certified Activity Professional. We also wish to help you in any way we can to facilitate your process of becoming certified. Do not hesitate to write, call or e-mail the office or a Board member when you have need of assistance. We look forward to serving you.

The National Certification Council for Activity Professionals (NCCAP), is one of the Certifying Bodies recognized by Federal law, and incorporated in many state regulations. NCCAP is the ONLY national organization that exclusively certifies activity pro- fessionals who work with the elderly.

Certified Activity Professionals receive the following benefits:

- Enhanced professional recognition and development
- Collaboration at the national level with other long-term health care associations
- Four newsletters annually
- Inclusion in the national registry of Certified Activity Professionals

Why Become NCCAP Certified?

Federal Law, OBRA, states that an activity department must be directed by a "qualified professional." One of the ways to become qualified is to become a Certified Activity Professional.

NCCAP certification is recognized by CMS (Formerly Health Care Financing Administration) as an organization that certifies activity professionals who work specifically with the elderly.

NCCAP certification assures administrators and surveyors that you have met certain professional standards to become certified.

Many administrators will only hire activity professionals who are certified.

Some administrators offer a higher salary to a certified professional.

Become NCCAP certified so others will know that you are nationally qualified and offering quality activity service to your residents/clients.

Table of Contents

NCCAP Certification Standards

Welcome to the NCCAP certification process!

NCCAP Certifies On Three Levels:
1. Activity Assistant Certified - AAC
2. Activity Director Certified - ADC
3. Activity Consultant Certified - ACC

Each of these levels has differing TRACKS to help you obtain your certification.

Each of these TRACKS has, at minimum, four qualifying components:
- A. Academic Education
- B. Activity Experience.
- C. Continuing Education
- D. The MEPAP
- E. Consulting Experience. (ACC level only)

A. ACADEMIC EDUCATION
May derive from a wide variety of curriculums: Social Work, Recreation, Education, Science, and Business degrees. These are a few of the educational backgrounds that represent our certified members. **Refer to page 5** for more detailed information.

B. ACTIVITY EXPERIENCE
Activity work experience (within past 5 years) with elderly popu-lations, where at least 50% are 55+ years of age. Some volunteer work with elderly clients may be applied. **Refer to page 5** for more detailed information.

C. CONTINUING EDUCATION
Current continuing education (within past 5 years): workshops, seminars, college courses that keep the activity professional abreast of present trends. NCCAP's Body of Knowledge contains 28 areas of education with many subheadings that are applicable. **Refer to page 6** for more detailed information.

D. The MEPAP
2nd edition is 180 hours of educational learning and 180 hours of ex-periential learning (practicum), and is required for NCCAP certification. The MEPAP 2nd edition is (generally presented/taught) divided into 2 teaching portions of 90 hours each.

Part 1 prepares students for the basic functions and duties of an activity professional: to design, deliver and evaluate activity services for older adults across the continuum of care.

Part 2 prepares students to apply principles of management in their role as activity professional: to provide service through leadership, using principles of planning, organizing, staffing, directing and controlling.

E. CONSULTING EXPERIENCE
May include: advising a group, working one to one, teaching a class, conducting workshops, publishing professional articles, supervising students and/or managing 5 or more activity staff persons. **Refer to page 7** for more detailed information.

LEVELS of Certification

Activity Assistant Certified - AAC

One who meets NCCAP standards to assist, with supervision, in carrying out an activity program.

Track 1

A. ACADEMIC EDUCATION
30 college semester credits (must include an English **PLUS** 1 other course from B, C, and D of the required coursework areas).

AND

B. ACTIVITY EXPERIENCE
2000 hours within past 5 years.

AND

C. CONTINUING EDUCATION
20 clock hours (Body of Knowledge) within past 5 years.

Track 2

A. ACADEMIC EDUCATION
High school diploma or GED, **PLUS** 6 college credits (must include an English and 1 other course from the required coursework areas).

AND

B. ACTIVITY EXPERIENCE
4000 hours within past 5 years.

AND

C. CONTINUING EDUCATION
20 clock hours (Body of Knowledge) within past 5 years.

Track 3

A. ACADEMIC EDUCATION
High school diploma or GED, plus the 90-Hour Modular Education Program for Activity Professionals Part 1. (C.C.1-11)

AND

B. ACTIVITY EXPERIENCE
2000 hours within past 5 years.

AND

C. CONTINUING EDUCATION
20 clock hours (Body of Knowledge) within past 5 years.

FEES The cost of being certified initially ranges from $60 to $80 depending upon the level. Renewal is required every two years with 20–40 hours of continuing education and a fee of $50. **Refertopage7** for more detailed information.

Activity Director Certified - ADC

One who meets NCCAP standards to direct an activity staff and program.

Track 1

A. ACADEMIC EDUCATION
Bachelor's Degree (or higher) must include an English **PLUS** 7 other courses with at least one course from B, C, and D of the required coursework areas.

AND

B. ACTIVITY EXPERIENCE
4000 hours within past 5 years.

AND

C. CONTINUING EDUCATION
30 clock hours (Body of Knowledge) within past 5 years.

AND

D. MEPAP
Modular Education Program for Activity Professionals (MEPAP)

Track 2

A. ACADEMIC EDUCATION
Associates Degree (including English PLUS 5 other courses, with at least 1 course from B, C, and D of the required coursework areas).

AND

B. ACTIVITY EXPERIENCE
6000 hours within past 5 years.

AND

C. CONTINUING EDUCATION
30 clock hours (Body of Knowledge) within past 5 years.

AND

D. MEPAP
Modular Education Program for Activity Professionals (MEPAP)

Track 3

A. ACADEMIC EDUCATION
60+ college semester credits (must include an English PLUS 5 other courses, with at least 1 course from B, C, and D of the required coursework areas).

AND

B. ACTIVITY EXPERIENCE
6000 hours within past 5 years.

AND

C. CONTINUING EDUCATION
30 clock hours (Body of Knowledge) within past 5 years.

AND

D. MEPAP
Modular Education Program for Activity Professionals (MEPAP)

Continued on pa...

Track 4

ACADEMIC EDUCATION

1. 90-Hour Modular Education Program for Activity Professionals Part 1 (C.C. 1-11) and the 90-Hour Practicum (Basic Education Course). *

2. 90 Hour Modular Education Program for Activity Professionals Part 2 (C.C. 12-20) and 90-Hour Practicum (Advanced Management Course). *

3. 12 semester college credits - cannot include #1 and #2 (must include an English **PLUS** 1 other required coursework area). *

AND

ACTIVITY EXPERIENCE

4. 6000 hours within past 5 years.

AND

CONTINUING EDUCATION

5. 30 clock hours (Body of Knowledge) within the past 5 years.

* MEPAP 2nd Edition is core content 1-20.

Activity Director Provisionally Certified - ADPC

The Activity Director Provisionally Certified is one who is work- ing towards requirements to meet NCCAP standards for ADC certifi- on. Certification is provisional for 6 years, and nonrenewable after t time. To maintain provisional certification it must be renewed ry 2 years during the 6 years with 30 clock hours. By the end of 6-year period all 5 components must have been met to be ADC ck 4 (or meet ADC certification standards from Track 1, 2 or 3).

this level can only be applied for one time.
The ADPC must meet three of the five standards in Track 4.)

Activity Consultant Certified - ACC

One who meets NCCAP standards to be a consultant or educator an activity program, staff, or department.

Track 1

ACADEMIC EDUCATION

Master's Degree (must include an English PLUS 7 other coursework reas with at least 1 course from areas B, C, and D).

AND

ACTIVITY EXPERIENCE

2000 hours activity experience within the last 5 years.

AND

CONTINUING EDUCATION

40 clock hours (Body of Knowledge) within the past 5 years.

AND

D. CONSULTING EXPERIENCE

200 hours of activity consulting experience within the past 3 years.

AND

E. MEPAP

Modular Education Program for Activity Professionals (MEPAP)

Track 2

A. ACADEMIC EDUCATION

Bachelor's Degree (must include an English PLUS 7 other course-work areas with at least 1 course from areas B, C, and D).

AND

B. ACTIVITY EXPERIENCE

4000 hours activity experience within the last 5 years.

AND

C. CONTINUING EDUCATION

40 clock hours (Body of Knowledge) within the past 5 years.

AND

D. CONSULTING EXPERIENCE

200 hours of activity consulting experience within the past 3 years.

AND

E. MEPAP

Modular Education Program for Activity Professionals (MEPAP)

Track 3

A. ACADEMIC EDUCATION

Bachelor's Degree (must include an English PLUS 7 other coursework areas with at least 1 course from areas B, C, and D).

AND

B. ACTIVITY EXPERIENCE

4000 hours activity experience within the last 5 years.

AND

C. CONTINUING EDUCATION

40 clock hours (Body of Knowledge) within the past 5 years.

AND

D. CONSULTING EXPERIENCE

(Arranged with the Track 3 Consultant Review Committee).

AND

E. MEPAP

Modular Education Program for Activity Professionals (MEPAP)

The candidate for certification will complete an independent study pro-gram with TheProfessionalActivityManagerandConsultant . Successfully completing this book and a project is the consulting experience requirement for this track. Request a ACC, Track 3 packet for more specific information.

DEFINITIONS of NCCAP Certification Standards

A. Academic Education Standards

1. High School Diploma or GED

2. Academic Degrees or College Credits for AAC (Track 1 & 2), ADC, ACC:

a. from an accredited college or university, acredited by the US Department of Education

b. a variety of degrees and college courses are accepted, provided the course content areas are met

c. no time limit for college degree or credits

d. required course work areas must be a grade of "C" or better

e. nursing schools, technical credits, and foreign transcripts must be accompanied by an official evaluation from an accredited US College, University or Independent Agency.

f. see applicable course work areas below #3

3. Numbers and Areas of Applicable Course Work

A — English

1 English Composition
2 Report Writing
3 Technical Writing

B — Art / Recreation / Programming

4 Modular Education Program for Activity Professionals & 90-Hour Practicum Part I
(Taken from NCCAP pre-approved instructor)(C.C. 1–11)

5 Modular Education Program for Activity Professionals & 90-Hour Practicum Part II
(Taken from NCCAP pre-approved instructor)(C.C. 12–20)

6 Speech, Drama, Languages, Non-Verbal Communication
7 Art Appreciation & Theory, Creative Arts
8 Music Appreciation & Theory, Performing Arts
9 Spirituality, Religion, Theology
10 Leisure Education
11 Literature, Creative Writing

C — Sciences

12 Gerontology, Aging
13 Psychology, Human Development, Counseling
14 Sociology, Death & Dying
15 Health Services, Public Health, Non-Traditional Health, Pharmacology
16 Wellness, Fitness, Movement, Dance, PE
17 Therapies (Occupational, Recreational, Dance, Music, Speech, Physical)
18 Biological Sciences (Anatomy, Physiology, Biology of Aging)
19 Human Services (Behavior Management, Stress Management, Family Services)

D — Management

20 Communication Arts, Graphics, Journalism, Media
21 Leadership, Group Dynamics, Interpersonal Relationships
22 Professional Development, Ethics
23 Administrative Practices, Personnel, Marketing, Statistics
24 Community Relations, Public Relations, Public Speaking
25 Education Theory & Practice, Adult Learning, Curriculum Development

26 Computer Science, Software Development, Data Entry
27 Budget, Math, Finance
28 Western Civilization, American Government, World Histo

4. Amount of required course work needed (depending on track chosen):

All tracks requiring college credit contain a requirement an English course. See each track for specific information

5. Comparing semester to quarter credits/units:

One semester credit/unit = 1.5 quarter credit/units

6. Activity courses, other than the MEPAP, may only app toward continuing education for certification.

7. Documentation needed to verify academic education

a. copy of High School Diploma or GED

b. **OFFICIAL** transcript from each college or university refer to in your application (Student copies are not acceptable) Foreign transcripts and credits received from technical ir tutions or nursing schools **must** be accompanied by an c cial evaluation from an accredited US and Canadian Colle University or Independent Agency.

c. certificate of satisfactory completion of Modular Educa Program for Activity Professionals Parts I & II and 90 H Practicums Parts I & II (MEPAP *C.C. 1–20*).

B. Activity Experience Standards

1. Applicable activity work experience:

a. directly working with activity programming/ documentation 50% of the time

b. 50% or more of residents/clients are 55 yrs. old and over

c. 20% of this experience can be overtime

d. 20% of this experience can be volunteer work

e. internship if not included in academic credits

2. Activity experience dates:

AAC, ACC, ADC, and ADPC within past 5 years

3. Documentation of activity experience (sample letter format enclosed on page 11)

a. on facility or program letterhead

b. verify each aspect used, from B. 1-2 above

c. letter must verify:

1) employee title

2) dates of beginning and end of employment (within last 5 years only for AAC, ADC, ADPC, & ACC)

3) defines type of population served

4) states **actual total** hours of activity experience to dat letter (Be specific and state the number of hours worked. Example: 20 hours a week. Stating full time part time is not acceptable.)

d. letter signed by administrator, program director or supervis

Continued on pa

Continuing Education Standards

Time when continuing education was taken:

for initial certification, completed within previous 5 years; this includes college or university course work

for renewal of certification, completed within previous 2 years; this includes college or university coursework

Qualifying continuing education:

has not been used for academic education requirement

content from:
1) Body of Knowledge (see page 8)
2) Modular Education Program for Activity Professionals (MEPAP)
3) Applicable course work
   (see A. 3. page 5 or Body of Knowledge, page 8)

conditions to meet continuing education standards:
1) at least 60 minutes in length
   (consistent with IACET standards)
2) taken in a group setting with leader and discussion or has NCCAP pre-approval.
3) when CEU's are received, one (.1) CEU=1 actual 60 minute clock hour

Types of applicable continuing education
1) healthcare related courses up to 20% of total (CNA, CDL, Transfer Training, transporting, first aid, CPR, etc.)
2) mandatory work place in-service, at least 30 minutes in length, can be up to 20% of total continuing education required:
3) 20% of CE hours per level =
   - AAC = 4
   - ADPC = 6
   - ADC = 6
   - ACC = 8
4) 30% CE, taken in a facility that is a subscriber to Primedia, (Silver Chair and other such companies, see website for complete list) acceptable, provided the certificate of attendance has the information listed in 4.b (1-7) or a NCCAP pre-approval #.
   30% of CE hours per level
   - AAC = 6 hours
   - ADC = 9 hours
   - ADPC = 9 hours
   - ACC = 12 hours
5) facility tours, when part of state or national activity conventions and with prior NCCAP approval
6) Distance/Advanced Technology must be pre-approved by NCCAP (internet, correspondence, home study courses, etc.)
7) activity related adult education, workshops, seminars, and educational sessions at professional meetings
8) additional college courses not used for the Academic requirement:
   a) taken from accredited college or university
   b) one college credit 10 clock hours
9) Modular Education Program for Activity Professionals (MEPAP) may be used if not used to meet D. For initial certification
10) activity courses other than MEPAP can be used only for continuing education
11) college or university independent study or correspondence study courses that meet required content standards as C. 2. b. above

12) educational articles published in state or national professional publications or online written by the applicant
   a) count 1 hour for each 400-600 words
   b) include a copy of published material with application
   c) up to 20% of total CE Hours
13) speeches given and workshops, inservices, and courses presented:
   a) meet standards C. 2. a, b, and c above
   b) count double the actual presentation time to account for preparation time
   c) count only initial presentation if repeated
   d) only 20% of CE's can come from presenting courses, workshops, and inservices or giving speeches
14) workplace inservices **ONLY** can be a minimum of 30 minutes in length, up to 20% of total CE's required

3. Items that do not meet NCCAP standards for continuing education:
a. entertainment, reading, travel
b. business and committee meetings
c. self-taught courses
d. any home study, internet, advanced technology (i.e.: video and audio tapes) not preapproved by NCCAP
e. activity experience does not constitute education

4. Documentation of continuing education (sample certificate enclosed on page 11).
a. verification of CEU's being awarded from a college or University or other accrediting body OR
b. a copy (retain original) of certificate of attendance (original may be requested by NCCAP office) that includes:
   1) name of the attendee
   2) title of the educational session
   3) date of the session — *Sessions/workshops over 8 hours need to include a time outline verifying the number of hours attended*
   4) clock hours spent in the session
   5) instructor's name and credentials
   6) signature of instructor **or** sponsor
   7) sponsoring agency
c. if the certificate does not include the content above, attach to the certificate a copy of advertisement brochure or explanation that contains the missing information
d. copy of transcripts from each college or university from which you took course work including independent study and correspondence courses (include title of course, outline/syllabus or course description) grade report not accepted
e. for articles published include a copy of the article with indication of how many words article contains
f. for speeches given, workshops and courses presented send proof that the presentation did occur (proof consists of verification on letterhead and signed by the sponsor or a copy of the participant sign-in sheet and/or a signed letter)
g. for facility in-service a copy of the sample certificate of attendance or verification including all of C. 4. b. above and the in-service director's signature

Continued on page 7

DEFINITIONS
of NCCAP Certification Standards,
Continued from page 6

D. Consulting Experience

1. Applicable activity consultant experience must meet criteria on page 5. B. 1. a-d and may be a combination of:
  a. one-to-one activity consultation
  b. teaching a class and workshop of at least one hour
     1) count the actual teaching time of presentation only the first time it is given
     2) content from:
        a) applicable course work (see page 5, A. 3. above)
        b) Modular Education Program for Activity Professionals (MEPAP).
        c) Body of Knowledge (see page 8)
  c. articles published in state or national publications
     1) count 1 hour of consulting for each 400-600 words up to 20%
     2) include a copy of published materials with application
  d. may count up to 40 hours direct on-site supervision of activities related practicum
  e. may count hours managing an activity staff of 5 or more persons at the rate of 6 hours per month up to 100 hours
  f. at least 40 hours of consulting must occur outside place of current employment
  g. at least 40 hours of consultation must be direct activity consultation
  h. Activity Consultant Track 3 Candidate contact NCCAP office to obtain details about Track 3 requirements

2. Consulting Experience Dates: 200 hours consulting experience must be from within the last 3 years.

3. Documentation of consulting experience
  a. on facility or program letterhead (sample letter format enclosed on page 11)
  b. verify each aspect used, from D. 1 above
  c. letter(s) also verifies:
     1) employee title
     2) dates of beginning and end of employment (within the last 3 years only)
     3) states **actual total hours** of experience to date of letter
  d. letter signed by administrator, program director, or supervisor
  e. for all teaching submit a copy of advertising document, a copy of certificate of attendance, and verification that the session was presented (see C.4.f) including:
     1) title of educational offering
     2) date and time of day offered (3-15-96, 1:00–3:00)
     3) place of presentation
     4) presenter's name and qualification for teaching: degree, or certification #, or experience

What Are The Certification Fees?

Activity Consultant Certified, ACC .... $80.
Activity Director Certified, ADC................................... $70.
Activity Director Provisionally Certified, ADPC .... $65.
Activity Assistant Certified, AAC................................... $60

A nonrefundable processing fee of $40 will be charged new applications, renewals, and level changes. The processing f included in the certification fees listed above. Returned checks be assessed a $40 fee. Applications will not be processed with receipt of payment. It is the policy of NCCAP to deposit ch upon receipt. **Thisdoesnotmeanthatcertificationhasb granted.** Refunds will be processed based on NCCAP polici stated in these standards.

Is There A Renewal Required

1. Renewal is required every two years.

2. To renew you need to acquire continuing education during the two years after initial certification.
   a. AAC — 20 hours continuing education
   b. ADC or ADPC — 30 hours continuing education
   c. ACC — 40 hours continuing education

3. Applicable continuing education see page 6

4. For all levels of certification the renewal fee is $50.00

5. The renewal process must be completed (applied for and approved) by the expiration date on the Renewal Form or a late renewal fee of $55.00 will be added- This will need to be paid addition to the renewal fee of $50.00 (total of $105.00)

6. Expiration of Renewal is not based on receipt of payment, but remains constant with the date issued at the time of certification.

Level Change

Activity Professionals seeking a level change need to c plete a new application. This application will be merged the one on file for review. It is not necessary to duplicate in mation already on file with the first application. Applicants need to add the additional information obtained. The fee is $ Expiration date will remain the same.

NCCAP Pre-Approval Numbe For Educational Offerings

As a service to instructors and security for participants, CAP offers course and workshop pre-approval numbers that ca part of a marketing brochure and the certificate of attendance. ucators and instructors can contact the NCCAP office for Pre proval Application forms. Activity professionals can forward na and addresses of continuing education providers to the NCC office and in turn, a pre-approval packet will be forwarded.

Body of Knowledge. Topics for Continuing Education
CURRICULUM CONTENT FOR ACTIVITY PROFESSIONALS

WORKING WITH PARTICIPANTS CLIENTS

) Human Development and Late Adult Years
- Life Span Potential
- Theories of Aging

) Human Development and Aging
- Human Behavior and Aging
- Potential and Creativity
- Wellness and Self-Esteem

) Spirituality of Aging
- Reminiscing
- Tasks of Life Review
- Worship — Religion
- Death — Dying
- Palliative Care
- Journaling
- Ethics
- Tasks of Vital Aging
- Prayer — Scripture
- Personal Growth
- Wisdom in Aging
- Comparative Religions

4) Biology of Aging
- Changes — Physical & Sensory
- Sexuality
- Medications
- Nutrition
- Healthy Aging
- Illness and Dysfunction
- Bariatric Issues
- Behavioral Interventions
- Pain Management

5) Sociology of Aging
- Involvement — Isolation
- Dependence/Independence
- Living Alone — Social Networks
- Cultural Attitudes
- Social Histories
- Long Term Care/Aging/Social Needs
- Living Arrangements — Retirement Housing, Elder Communities, Long-Term Care, Adult Day Services, Assisted Living, Mental Health, Sub-Acute, Independent Living, Home Health, Aging in Place, Senior Centers
- Culture Change in the Continuum of Care
- Baby Boomers
- Sign Language
- Foreign Language
- Elder Abuse

6) Psychology of Aging
- Leisure & Aging
- Psychological Choices — Depression, Anxiety, Fears
- Drugs & Alcohol
- Security
- Successful adaptations

- Hospice
- Counseling Techniques
- Stereotypes — Myths
- Confusion/Disorientation
- Institutionalization
- Aging in Place
- Memory Care

7) Leisure and Aging
- Recreation — Definition, Types, Philosophy
- Lifestyles
- Retirement Living
- Attitudes — Motivation
- Analysis of Leisure Time
- Client Interests
- Client Rights — Different Categories
- Volunteerism
- Creativity in Aging
- Leisure Education
- Barriers to Leisure
- Person Centered Programming

8) Basic Health
- First Aid
- Health Precautions
- Personal Health Issues
- Geriatric Medications/Contra-Indications in the Activities Delivery systems
- Nutritional Issues/Diabetes

9) Group Instruction/Leadership
- Adult Learning Modes
- Instruction Methods — Lecture, Handouts, Videos
- Demonstrations, Samples, Slides, Discussion, Participation, Survey, Sharing Experience
- Teaching Materials — Tools, Resources
- Group Dynamics/Leadership
- In-Service
- Leader Listening
- Esteem Building
- Build Group Support

10) Therapy for the Disabled Aging
- Overview of P.T., O.T., Speech Therapy, Art Therapy, Recreation Therapy, Dance Therapy, Music Therapy, Drama Therapy, Validation, Poetry Therapy, Reality Orientation, Remotivation, Horticulture Therapy, etc.
- Restorative Programs — Feeding Training, ADL Skills, etc.
- Patient Physical Transfer Techniques
- Therapeutic Approach — Meaningful, Purposeful, How it Helps
- Therapeutic Feeding Techniques
- Aroma Therapy
- Massage Therapy
- Therapeutic Swimming

Continued on page 9

11) With Residents & Staff
- Types of Communication
- Listening Skills
- Responding Skills
- Communication with Frail
- Communication with Confused
- Intercultural Concerns
- Morale Building
- Dealing with Difficult Situations

12) Public Speaking
- Professional Image
- Leading Meetings
- Business Etiquette

13) Public Relations
- The Written Message
- Media Use — Press releases, P.S.A., T.V., Radio
- Publicity — News
- Letters of Appreciation
- Volunteer Programs
- Fund Raising
- Marketing Activity Importance letters, Bulletin Boards, Posters, Graphic Techniques
- Community Marketing of Facility and Activities Delivery Systems

14) Interpersonal Relationships
- Staff Team Approach — Working Together
- Coordination of Services — Staff, Families, Volunteers, etc.
- Peer Relationships — Staff, Residents
- Family Relationships — Various Age Needs and Attitudes
- Empowerment/Managing Relationships/ Personality Evaluation
- Staff/Client Relationships
- Consultant Relationships
- Organizational Relationships
- Organizational Structures in Different Levels of Care
- Conflict Resolution
- Dealing with Difficult People
- Assertiveness Training

15) Motivation
- Of Clients, Families, Staff, Volunteers
- Professional Improvement
- Motivational Techniques

16) Community Services/Support/Relations
- Recreation Resources
- Service Clubs
- Religious Resources
- Mainstreaming
- Adult Health Services — Alzheimer's, MS, Ostomy Clubs, Parkinsons, Arthritis, Amputee, Cancer
- Business — Chamber of Commerce
- Family Open Houses
- Library Resources

17) Regulations
- State & Federal Activities, Regulations & Standards — OSHA, ADA & Professional Standards
- Survey Process
- Plan of Corrections
- Legislative Updating
- JCAHO, CARF, Specialty Standards
- Assisted Living Regulations/Memory Care/ Enhanced Assisted Living Regulations
- Medical Adult Day Health Regulations
- Mental Health Adult Day Health Regulations/ Adult Day Habilitation (MR/DD)
- Adult Home Regulations/ Personal Care and Boarding

PROGRAMMING

18) Individualized Care Planning
- Assessment — MDS & RAP
- Interdisciplinary Team
- Care Planning, Approach, Progress Notes
- Professional Standards
- Legal — Ethical Issues
- Medical Terms
- Charting — Confidentiality
- Patient — Resident Involvement
- For Participant Learning
- Quality Indicators
- Individualized Service Plans
- Person Centered Care Planning/"I" Care Plans

19) Program Management
- Philosophy of Operation
- Expressive/Creative Program Scope — Physical, Mental, Social, Emotional, Community, Spiritual, Educational
- Program Planning — Resident Centered
- Organization — Calendar
- Program Implementation — Conducting Activities
- Evaluation Techniques
- Operating Audio—Visual Equipment
- Equipment & Supplies — Control, Safety Precautions, Resource Materials, Ordering
- Modes of Programming
- Operating Facility Vehicles

20) Computer Skills
- Word Processing
- Database
- Charting
- Desktop Publishing
- Games
- Participant Learning
- Internet

21) Program Types -- Theory and Practice
- Supportive
- Maintenance
- Empowerment

Continued on page 16

Body of Knowledge. Topics for Continuing Education *(continuation)*

- Exercise — General, Volleyball, e.g., Wheelchair, Reike, Tae Kwon Do, Yoga, etc.
- Social — e.g., Parties
- Outdoor — e.g., Barbecues, Games, Walks
- Away from the Facility — e.g., Visits to Community Places of Interest
- Religious — e.g., Bible Study, Services
- Creative — e.g., Crafts, Drama, Writing, Journaling, Scrapbooking,
- Educational — e.g., Current Events, Alzheimer's Group, Adult Learning
- Residents with special needs — e.g., AIDS, DDs, MRs, MS et al.
- Resident Planned — e.g., Resident Council or Any Activity
- In-Room — e.g., Adapt Out-of-Room Activities
- Sensory — e.g., Braille Materials, Any Sensory Stimulation, Pet, Food Related, Snozelen™, Meditation, Massage, Reflexology
- Reality Awareness e.g., with Other Programs
- Entertainment — e.g., Games, Entertainer Resources
- Self Help — e.g., Nail Polishing Group, Independent Activities
- Music — Basic & Adaptive Techniques
  1. Accompaniment Instrument-Chord Structure, Ear Training
  2. Recreational — Rhythm Instruments, Musical Games, Movement, Literature for the Aged
- Community Oriented e.g., Intergenerational, Community Groups in the Facility
- Computer Based
- Lesson Planning
- Technological Advancements
- Wii
- Outings/Policies and Procedures
- Recreational/Leisure Vehicle Training
- Bar Tending/Mixology/Wine Tasting
- Proper Food Handling

MANAGEMENT/PERSONNEL, LEGAL AND ETHICAL ISSUES

22) Personal Employment
- Recruitment, Interviewing, Hiring, Termination, Development, Recognition, Evaluation, — Staff and Volunteers
- Job Search — Resume Writing, Interview Preparation

23) Management Leadership
- Interdisciplinary Care Plan Team
- Leadership Styles
- Program Management
- Program Evaluation
- Supervision Philosophies and Techniques
- Delegating — Enabling Staff Ability
- Self Analysis
- Time Management

- Activity Staff In-Service
- How to Conduct Meetings: Staff, Association
- Problem Solving
- Resident Council and Family Council
- Record Keeping
- Dealing with Challenging People
- Stress Management
- Memory Improvement
- Violence in the Workplace
- Controlling
- Advocacy/ Ombudsman
- Universal Worker Concepts
- Culture Change/ Greenhouse Concepts
- Management and Management Techniques
- Generational Diversity/Gender Issues
- Quality Assurance, CQI, TQM, etc.
- Association Management/Conference
- Committee Development
- Customer Service

24) Management Writing Skills
- Documentation Chart Auditing
- Job Descriptions
- Policies and Procedures Manuals
- Incident Records/Reports
- Letters of Request — Direct Mail
- Grant Writing
- Public Relations
- E-mail and Internet Etiquette
- Form Development

25) Financial Management
- Reimbursement
- Budget Writing
- Record Keeping
- Expense Control
- Establishing Non-Profit Status
- Fund raising
- Establishing Budgets
- Donation Management

26) Professional Development
- Certification
- Professional Attitude Toward Residents
- Professional Associations
- Business Expectations
- Professional Standards — Ethics
- Professional Affiliations
- Professionalism

27) Consulting
- Consultant's Role, Goals, Knowledge
- Consultant's Education

28) Resources
- How to Work with Volunteers
- How to Work with Supervisors
- How to Work with Consultants
- How to Work as Middle Management
- Intra-departmental Skills
- How to work with Vendors

Verification of Activity Experience

Name of Applicant_____Date of Letter: _____

Name of Agency _____

Telephone Number:_____

Applicant's Title _____

Agency Address_____

Name and Title of_____
Supervisor

Activity Employment Dates: From _____To _____

Please check: 50% (do not average) of the residents/participants are 55 years or older: ❑ Yes ❑ No

Number of Hours worked in activities per week _ Total

of Activity Hours worked since hire _____

Number of Activity Hours worked within the last 5 years _____

Summarize the duties specific to the _____
position: _____

_____

Signature of Supervisor: _____

This is a sample forma
assist with employn
verification. The letter n
be on the original fac
letterhead and signed
the supervisor.

*This sample is provided as a courtesy of NCCAP to assist wit the documentation/verification of CE

This information is provided to assist you with the needed requirements to document at- tendance of NCCAP acceptable workshops, seminars, or classes. This may also be used in cases where certificates are not issued at the conclusion of a program. It is imperative that a representative of the sponsoring agency/or the instructor sign the certificate as verification of your attendance.

1. _____
Name of Sponsor/Sponsoring Association

Certificate Of Attendance

This is to document that

2. _____
(Name of Participant)

3. _____
(Title of Education Session)

for 4. _____clock hours on 5. __at 6. _____(Date)
(City and State)

Presented by:

7. _____, _____
(Instructor's name)   (Instructor's credentials)

8. Signature of sponsor **OR** instructor: _____

9. NCCAP Pre-Approval # (if applicable)

a. if the certificate does not include the content in the sample certificate above, attach to the certifica a copy of advertisement brochure or explanation that contains the missing information
b. for speeches, workshops and courses presented, send verification that the presentation did occur
c. for facility in-service, send a copy of the sample certificate above with the in-service director's sign ture) or a sign-in sheet with all required information

AAPC (Activity Assistant Provisional Certified)

1. Completion of the MEPAP (Part 1 Core Content 1-11)
2. 50 volunteer hours (can be the practical/or other volunteer hours)
3. 20 CE's (can include honors classes, AP classes may be accepted)

ADC Track 5

1. High school diploma.
2. A Basic Activity Course (MUST have been completed between (1991-2001)-verified by submitting a certificate of completion, signed by the instructor
3. 6 years (12,000 hours) of current activity experience- within the past 10 years
4. 30 hours of continuing education must include (20% = 6 hours) of documentation

ACC Track 3

For those that are ADC Track 2. The 200 hours of consulting and completion of the 2 year Activity Professional Manager & Consultant curriculum, with the qualified mentor, are eligible to apply for a level change to ACC Track 3.

NCCAP Specialization Options

For each desired designation, the individual must submit evidence showing 10 CE's from the Specialization Body of Knowledge ic areas, which are listed on the www.nccap.org site.

If an individual will be requesting their initial specialization at the same time as their renewal, they would submit the required mber of CE's and fee for their renewal PLUS the additional 10 CE's and $25.00 PER each specialization they are requesting. person will only be requesting the specialization not in conjunction with their renewal they would simply send the 10 CE's and 5.00 fee for each specialization they are requesting.

Verification that the CE's come from the designated specialization track is the responsibility of the applicant. Initial specializations go back 5 years for their CE's, and renewal specializations can go back 2 years, in keeping with the NCCAP standards.

ADC for example:

A Specialization in Assisted Living would be ADC/ALF

A Specialization in Memory Care would be ADC/MC

A Specialization in Adult Day Programs would be ADC/AD

A Specialization in Educating would be ADC/EDU

AAC would be AAC/ALF, AAC/MC, AAC/AD, etc.

ACC would be ACC/ALF, etc.

Specialization Fees:

Initial specialization costs $25.00 per specialization. Renewal is required every two years with 10 hours of continuing education that Specialization Body of Knowledge and a fee of $10.00 per specialization.

NCCAP
Application

P.O. Box 62589, Virginia Beach, VA 23466-2589 • www.nccap.org • Fax 757-552-0491 • Phone 757-552-065

The following information shall be kept in the **confidential** files of the National Certification Council for Activity Professiona It shall be available to the Certification Review Committee and the Appeals Committee unless otherwise specified by the applicant.

Name _____ Today's Date _____
 Last   First   Former or Maiden

Name as it should appear on Certificate/Card _____

Mailing Address _____

City _____ State _____ Zip _____ Home Telephone(_____) _____

Name of Agency/Facility _____ Address _____

City _____ State _____ Zip _____ Office Telephone(_____) _____

Social Security # _____ Fax Number:(_____) _____ E-Mail _____

I prefer mail sent to: My home address ❑   My work address ❑

LEVEL OF CERTIFICATION REQUESTED (Check level and track):

Activity Assistant Certified	Activity Director Certified	Activity Consultant Certified
Track 1	Track 1 Track 4	Track 1
Track 2	Track 2 Track 5	Track 2
Track 3	Track 3	Track 3

❑ Activity Director Provisionally Certified (Check which THREE components you are submitting):
  ❑ Modular Education Program for Activity Professionals (MEPAP) & 90-Hour Practicum, Part 1
  ❑ Modular Education Program for Activity Professionals (MEPAP) & 90-Hour Practicum, Part 2
  ❑ 12 Semester College Credits
  ❑ 6000 Hours Work Experience
  ❑ 30 Hours Continuing Education

I will accept certification at another level if the level indicated above cannot be granted   ❑ Yes ❑ No

REASON FOR APPLICATION REQUEST (Check one):

❑ First request for certification

❑ Level change (NCCAP level and certification number):_____

❑ Level change and recertification (NCCAP level and certification number):_____

❑ Specialization: _____Asst _____MC _____AD _____EDU

❑ **Check here if you do not wish your name published in the Certification Registry**

I have been an activity professional for _____years.

I have the following academic preparation: (Please indicate the highest level)
  ❑ (GED)   ❑ High School Diploma   ❑ Some College Credits (Enter number on Line)_____
  ❑ Associate's Degree   ❑ Bachelor's Degree   ❑ Master's Degree   ❑ Doctorate

Concentration of College Work: (e.g.. Social Work, Recreation) _____

REFERRED BY (Person) _____
ASSOCIATION _____

ACADEMIC
Education

Complete the portions of this page that apply to your level and track

gh School _____

            name   city, state   graduation or GED date

(Send verification of High School Graduation or GED for any level)

DLLEGE/UNIVERSITY	STATE	DATES ATTENDED	MAJOR	DEGREE AWARDED AND DATE
_____	_____	____to____ month/yr month/yr	_____	_____
_____	_____	____to____ month/yr month/yr	_____	_____
_____	_____	____to____ month/yr month/yr	_____	_____
_____	_____	____to____ month/yr month/yr	_____	_____

TOTAL CREDITS: [_____]   *This must be completed*

For college credits that apply to this application...

e course from each of the required areas:

OURSE TITLE m College Transcript) *not repeat courses)*	COURSE NUMBER From College Transcript *(Do not repeat courses)*	REQUIRED AREA From NCCAP Definitions of Standards *(Do not repeat areas of coursework)*	COLLEGE/UNIVERSITY
x. *English Composition*	*Eng. 101*	*A-1*	*XYZ University*
_____	_____	*English*	_____
1 _____	_____	*Art/Recreation/Programming*	_____
2 _____	_____	*Sciences*	_____
3 _____	_____	*Management*	_____
_____	_____	_____	_____
_____	_____	_____	_____

official copy of your transcript(s) must accompany your application. Enclose the **official** transcripts with your application. Some lleges/universities will not send students/graduates an official transcript. In this case enclose a copy of your letter to the college uesting that your transcript be mailed to NCCAP. Please note that you may need to request a student copy to adequately complete s portion of the application.

HOUR NCCAP MODULAR EDUCATION PROGRAM FOR ACTIVITY PROFESSIONALS (MEPAP) PART 1 AND 90-HOUR PRACTICUM (BEC)

_____   _____   _____
tes Completed   Instructor & Credentials   pre-approval #

HOUR NCCAP MODULAR EDUCATION PROGRAM FOR ACTIVITY PROFESSIONALS (MEPAP) PART 2 AND 90-HOUR PRACTICUM (AMC)

_____   _____   _____
tes Completed   Instructor & Credentials   pre-approval #

Copy of Certificate of Completion must accompany your application.

- -

ACTIVITY
Experience

ALL APPLICANTS - Complete as many sections of this page as necessary to support the amount of activity experien required for your level and track of certification. If you need more space, make a copy of this page first.

DOCUMENTATION must accompany this application that verifies your activity experience. Submit your letter letters:

1. **On official facility or agency letterhead stating:**
   a. your work title
   b. dates of beginning and end of activity employment within the last 5 years only
   c. that at least 50% of residents/clients are 55+ years of age
      (Population must be based on the percentage and not the average number of residents.)
   d. State <u>actualtotal</u> hours of activity experience to date of letter. (Be specific and state the number of hours worked. Example: 20 hours a week. Stating full time or part time is not acceptable.)
2. Signed by the administrator, program director or supervisor

Please note that the sample letter format found in the Certification Standards is designed to help you with this process

A. Agency _____ Telephone (____) _____

Applicant's Title _____

Agency Address_____City _____State _Zip _____ Name and Title

Supervisor _____

Employment: From _____to _____
                        Month   Day   Year   Month   Day   Year

Please Check: 50% of resident/clients are 55+ years _____yes _____no

Check: ❏ Full-time   _____Number of Hours per week   **TOTAL HOURS WITHIN LAS**

Check: ❏ Part-time   _____Number of Hours per week   **5 YEARS_____**

Practice Setting: _____Asst _____MC _____AD _____SNF

B. Agency _____ Telephone (____) _____

Applicant's Title _____

Agency Address_____City _____State _Zip _____ Name and Title

Supervisor _____

Employment: From _____to _____
                        Month   Day   Year   Month   Day   Year

Please Check: 50% of resident/clients are 55+ years _____yes _____no

Check: ❏ Full-time   _____Number of Hours per week   **TOTAL HOURS WITHIN LAS**

Check: ❏ Part-time   _____Number of Hours per week   **5 YEARS_____**

Practice Setting: _____Asst _____MC _____AD _____SNF

GRAND TOTAL HOURS of activity experience listed within the last 5 years.   **# of Hours** _____

This must completed

CONTINUING Education

tach documentation for the required number of clock hours appropriate to the level of certification for which you are applying. is not necessary to submit all clock hours obtained, but only the amount required. **DO NOT SEND ORIGINAL DOCUMENTS OF OUR CONTINUING EDUCATION. SEND COPIES ONLY! THEY WILL NOT BE RETURNED OR KEPT ON FILE!** Arrange rtificates in the same order as you listed them below.

ease refer to the sample certificate in the certification standards to help you with this process. If certificates awarded to you for ontinuing education do not contain the required information, attach additional documentation to verify the missing components the certificates.

you attend a conference/seminar/symposium, simply write # of total hours received and submit proper verification of INDIVIDUAL ssions attended.

ITLE FROM CERTIFICATE/TRANSCRIPT	DATE	CLOCK HOURS	BODY OF KNOWLEDGE *(TOPIC #FROM PAGE 8)*
Ex. NCCAP Symposium	*6/5/09 - 6/6/09*	*14 hours*	
Ex. Mandatory Facility Inservices	*2008 - 2009*	*6 hours*	

SPECIALIZATION: _____ASST   ____MC   ____AD   ____EDU

SPECIALIZATION: _____ASST   ____MC   ____AD   ____EDU

Total of clock hours within the past five years. | # Hours | *This must be completed*

CONSULTING Experience

This page is to be completed by persons applying for consultant level certification. Applicable experience is defined in Definitions. All columns must be completed for each type of consulting. You may consolidate appropriate hours and dates. Examples:

1) 5/1/06-5/1/07	XYZ Corporation (312-555-5555)	40 hours/week 2080 hrs. total	Central Div. Act. Advisor to 40 facilities
2) 4/1/06-8/1/07	Illinois Dept of Health (312-222-2222)	90 Hours	Taught the MEPAP Course
3) 8/1/07-8/1/08	XYZ Facility (312-999-9999)	4 hours/month 48 hrs. total	Provided consultation for activity staff

If you need more space, make a copy of this page first.

DATE/S OF SERVICE OR PUBLICATION DATE PRESENTATION DATE	EMPLOYER NAME (FACILITY) & PHONE NUMBER OR SPONSOR'S NAME	HOURS OF CONSULTING NUMBER OF WORDS LENGTH OF PRESENTATION	DESCRIBE DUTIES

SEE DEFINITIONS FOR DOCUMENTATION OF CONSULTING EXPERIENCE.

TOTAL HOURS OF CONSULTING EXPERIENCE
(within last 3 years)   *This must be completed*

LETTERS, ARTICLES, BROCHURES ETC.,
VERIFYING CONSULTING EXPERIENCE MUST ACCOMPANY THIS APPLICATION

- -

Disclaimer

These standards and it's certification program have been developed by NCCAP after years of surveying and research. By applying for certification, applicant tacitly agrees to the standards. By applying for certification, applicant expressly waives any right of law for redress or compensation due to failure to obtain certification by NCCAP. (Applicant acknowledges NCCAP certification as voluntary and that applicant's failure to obtain certification does not effect his or her right to obtain gainful employment.)

Declaration

I acknowledge that it is my responsibility:

1. **To keep the NCCAP office informed of any name or address change**
2. To keep my certification current by renewing every two years before the expiration date.

I further understand that NCCAP will remind me of my need to send in my completed renewal form, documentation and fee. Then have:

1. At least 60 days in which to submit my form and fee and if I am delinquent in my response NCCAP has the following policy:
    a. My file will be kept for one calendar year past the expiration date. During this reinstatement period I am not permitted to use my certification, title or claim, to be certified with NCCAP.
    b. My certification will be suspended after the expiration date and my name removed from the NCCAP registry.
    c. At the end of the reinstatement period my file will be destroyed.
    d. If I fail to respond within the year past my date for renewal and want to become a Certified Activity Professional after this point, I must begin the initial process of certification under the current certification standards and fees.

I acknowledge that falsification or misrepresentation of information or supporting documentation at any time during the certification process can lead to NCCAP's refusal to certify me. By signing below, I consent to NCCAP checking references, verifying information, and obtaining any other reports it may deem necessary to evaluate my application. I agree that by signing this declaration, I will hold NCCAP harmless from any result of such reference checks.

Applicant's Signature _____ Date _____

Notarization of NCCAP Application

I, _____, a Notary Public, hereby certify that on the _____ day of _____, 20_____ personally appeared before me _____, who signed the foregoing document as the applicant, and declared that the statements contained therein are true.

_____
Notary Public

_____
Commission expires

(for notarization seal)

Fees

Activity Consultant Certified (ACC)...................$80.00
Activity Director Certified (ADC)...................$70.00
Activity Director Provisionally Certified (ADPC)...................$65.00
Activity Assistant Certified (AAC)...................$60.00
Level Change $45.00
Specialization...................$25.00 each

Persons 65 years and older should submit proof of age to receive a $10.00 discount.
If your check is returned for insufficient funds, an additional fee will be charged of $40

PAYABLE TO: **National Certification Council for Activity Professionals, or NCCAP**
SEND: **Check, Money Order, No cash.**
MAIL WITH APPLICATION TO: **NCCAP**
P.O. Box 62589, Virginia Beach, VA 23466-2589

For assistance call **(757) 552-0653 or email info@nccap.org**

**PLEASE NOTE: Checks are deposited upon receipt. This does not mean certification has been granted.
If you are not successful, your certification fee minus the $40 processing fee may be refunded by written request only.**

APPLICATION Checklist

Please make a copy of your application and all attachments for your files.

❑ Is application **completely**, **legibly** (neatly) and **accurately** filled out?

Have you included:

❑ pages 1-6 of application (**typed** or **printed** legibly and intact.) (You must complete each applicable section on the application form. Answering "see attached" is NOTACCEPTABLE. Your application will be returned.)

❑ documentation of CE? (Copies only-originals will not be returned.)

❑ high school diploma or GED for any level. (Copies only-originals will not be returned)

❑ official transcripts or copy of letter requesting transcripts enclosed.

❑ verification letter(s) of activity employment experience? (The original on letterhead.)

❑ verification letter(s) of consulting experience? (The original on letterhead), brochures, articles.

❑ notarization?

❑ check or money order?

MAINTAIN A COMPLETE COPY OF THIS APPLICATION, ALL CERTIFICATION STANDARDS AND ALL ATTACHMENTS IN YOUR FILES!

CERTIFICATION Review Process

You may opt to mail the application by certified mail (return receipt requested) to assure it has been received. Sending applications overnight will not expedite the review process.

When an Application is received at the NCCAP office, The staff will:

* Determine if the application documentation is complete:
* Send application file to the Certification Review Committee (CRC). The CRC is a team of Activity Consultants Certified who: carefully review every aspect of the application, grant or deny certification based upon NCCAP standards. CRC return the application file to the NCCAP office with a decision.
* If application and supporting documentation is not accurate, complete or legible, it will be returned requesting more information.
* The NCCAP office notifies you of CRC's decision (usually within 12 weeks).
* Approved applicants will receive a certificate, certification card, Bylaws, Code of Ethics, pin order form, and a welcome letter.

If certification is denied, a letter is sent stating the reason for denial. There are two recourses for you, the applicant:

1. Meet the standards by:
    a. obtaining academic education, or proof of such
    b. obtaining activity **and/or** consulting experience, or proof of such
    c. obtain MEPAP course
    d. obtaining continuing education or proof of such and then re-apply
    OR
2. Prepare a typed appeal within 60 days of receipt of the denial of certification. This appeal should be mailed to the NCCAP office. The Appeals Committee will review appeals and render a decision.

Pending or denied applications will be maintained on file for 6 months. The application fee minus the $40 processing fee will be refunded by request only.

NCCAP Certification Specialization

Specialization in Assisted Living
Specialization in Memory Care
Specialization in Adult Day Programs
Specialization in Educating

For each desired designation, the individual must submit evidence showing 10 CE's from the Specialization Body of Knowledge topic areas.

If an individual will be requesting their initial specialization at the same time as their renewal, they would submit the required number of CE's and fee for their renewal PLUS the additional 10 CE's and $25.00 PER each specialization they are requesting.

If a person will only be requesting the specialization not in conjunction with their renewal they would simply send the 10 CE's and $25.00 fee for each specialization they are requesting.

Verification that the CE's come from the designated specialization track is the responsibility of the applicant. Initial specializations can go back 5 years for their CE's, and renewal specializations can go back 2 years, in keeping with the NCCAP standards.

ADC title example -
A Specialization in Assisted Living would be ADC/ALF
A Specialization in Memory Care would be ADC/MC
A Specialization in Adult Day Programs would be ADC/AD
A Specialization in Educating would be ADC/EDU

AAC would be AAC/ALF, AAC/MC, AAC/AD, etc.
ACC would be ACC/ALF, etc.

Specialization Fees:

Initial specialization costs $25.00 per specialization. Renewal is required every two years with 10 hours of continuing education and a fee of $10.00 per specialization.

NAAP   Membership Application   2011

Please Type or Print Clearly: (Incomplete form will delay the processing of your membership)   ☐ New
Check Appropriate Box ☐ New Address ☐ Name Change ☐ Facility Change   ☐ Renewal   ☐ Reinstate

Mail to be sent to:
Name: _____ Credentials: _____ Previous Name: _____
Address: _____
City: _____
State/Province: _____ Zip: _____
Phone # Home (   ) _____ Phone # Work (   ) _____
Fax #   (   ) _____ Email _____

Facility Address:
Name: _____
Address: _____
City/State/Province: _____
Zip: _____ Phone # (   ) _____
Fax # (   ) _____ Email _____

Check work setting
☐ Long-Term Care Facility   ☐ Adult Day Care Service   ☐ Senior Center
☐ Retirement Home   ☐ Assisted Living Center   ☐ Alzheimer's Dementia Unit
☐ Sub-Acute Unit   ☐ Senior Service Center   ☐ Other _____
☐ Activity Consultant and/or Educator in the field of activities whose primary focus is on geriatric population.

National Certification   ☐ None ☐ NCCAP   ☐ NCTRC   ☐ RMT   ☐ OT   ☐ Other _____
(Although you do not have to be Nationally Certified to be a NAAP Member, NAAP strongly encourages and supports the certification process)

Length of Experience: Number of years _____ ☐ Full time ☐ Part time   ☐ Volunteer

Education: _____ Advanced Studies: _____

Amount Enclosed: ☐   **Active Membership**   **59.00 (USD)**
                       ☐   **Associate/Retired Membership**   **39.00 (USD)**
                       ☐   **International Membership(outside U.S.)**   **39.00 (USD)**
                       ☐   **Student Membership**   **49.00 (USD)**
                       ☐   **Corporate Rate- eleven or more members**   **49.00 (USD)**
                       A Corporate Employee participants list must accompany the application to be eligible.

☐ I do not want my name included in the membership list sold.

Credit Card Payment   ☐ Visa   Credit Card # _____
                          ☐ Master Card   Expiration Date: _____
                          ☐ AMX   Signature: _____
                          ☐ Discover Card

Send checks, money orders or credit card to: **NAAP**
                                              PO Box 5530
                                              Sevierville, TN 37864   Phone # (865) 429-0717
                                              Federal I. D. #36-3253020   Fax #   (865) 453-9914

For NAAP Office Use Only:
Date Received: _____ Amount Paid: _____ Check # _____
Date Mailed: _____ Membership Number: _____

GLOSSARY

Active listening A type of listening in which the listener responds both to the message and the feelings of the sender.

Authority The right or power to act, to decide, and to command others.

Budget A plan expressed in numerical terms – so much money for each category of expenditure for a specified period of time, usually one year.

Case mix A system of reimbursement based on the cost of providing care for a particular disorder.

Chart of organization A diagram that shows all levels of management and the lines of authority and communication within an organization.

CNA Registry A central registry that each state must maintain that includes information on all certified nurse aides in that state.

Communication The exchange or interchange of ideas, information, feelings, etc., with mutual understanding of what has been transmitted.

Consultant A contractual employee who brings expertise in a given area and who advises, recommends, teaches, and problem-solves.

Controlling The management function of measuring work performance against original plans and correcting work errors.

Coordination The art of getting people to work together toward a common goal in spite of their differences in interest, effort, speed, work, or attitudes, etc.

COI Continuous quality improvement that occurs when TQM is used effectively.

Decentralization of authority The tendency to disperse decision-making authority in an organization structure so that departments or units make decisions whenever possible.

Delegation Giving a portion of one's authority to a subordinate(s) who then makes certain decisions.

Departmentalization Setting up units of assigned activities and delegating authority to a supervisor (department head) responsible for performance.

Directing The management function that involves all methods a supervisor uses to ensure that employees perform how and when they have been instructed.

Duties Tasks or work activities that are assigned to an employee.

E-mail A system within World Wide Web whereby one computer sends a message to another computer.

Executive staff Usually the top manager and 3 to 5 assistants, found especially in larger organizations.

Fax (facsimile) A machine or a function on a copy machine that sends and receives exact copies of correspondence, drawings, and the like, by means of telephone transmission.

Feedback Securing information from an employee that indicates whether or not instructions have been received with understanding.

Formal organization The organizational structure approved by the governing body of an organization.

Goal The end result toward which all effort and activity are directed, sometimes referred to as an objective.

Governing body An individual or group with full legal authority to operate a facility.

Guidelines A term often used interchangeably with standards. Both are all-inclusive terms referring to the plan of operations.

Hardware The tangible parts of a computer which includes such peripheral devices as a printer and storage device that can be attached to the computer.

Informal organization Cliques, grapevines and other loosely organized unofficial groups within an organization.

Internet A huge, rich resource of information stored at many different sites and available only via a series of computer interfaces.

Leadership The process of influencing employees to work willingly and enthusiastically toward accomplishment of group goals whether the leader is present or not.

Levels of Management Top, middle and line management comprise the management hierarchy.

Line authority An authority relationship in which one person directs, controls, and is responsible for the work of another person(s).

Malpractice Errors in treatment, mistreatment, neglect, and so on that are harmful to a resident can be classed as malpractice.

Management Getting work done with and through people. Using knowledge and skill to direct employees' effort toward group goals.

MBWA Management by Walking Around. A style of management in which the administrator daily visits each department of the facility observing the work that is being done and the work environment.

MBO Management by Objectives is a style of management in which objectives are clearly stated, plans established, time limits set, and progress continuously measured.

MDS Minimum Data Set is a form used in doing an assessment of a resident's functioning in the five ADLs.

Mission (or purpose) The basic task assigned to an enterprise by society.

Modem A peripheral device that connects computers to each other for sending communication via the telephone line. The modem modulates the digital data of the computer into analog signals to send over the telephone line, then demodulates back into digital signals to be read by the computer on the other end; thus the name modem for modulation/demodulation.

Need Hierarchy Maslow's theory that basic human needs exist in an ascending order of importance and that once a lower level need is satisfied, it ceases to motivate a person.

Nonverbal communication Expressions, tone of voice, body movements, and gestures used when one communicates.

Open door policy One in which the manager allows any employee at any organizational level to bring problems directly to him.

Organizing The management function of grouping activities and employees, assigning roles, and delegating authority to supervisors in a manner that prevents friction and helps to attain goals.

Participative management A management style in which employees participate in planning and decision making; they have input on how their work should be done.

Planning The act of deciding what is to be done (goals) and developing guidelines (policies, procedures, rules and budgets) to attain the goals.

Policy A broad general statement that primarily guides thinking, decision making, and to some extent, action governing activities required to accomplish a goal.

Positive reinforcement The reinforcement of positive behaviors by some type of reward, as praise, recognition and approval in order to promote better morale and employee effort.

Principle of the economy of action When a higher paid employee is making a decision that a lesser paid employee can do as well or better, it is wasting money.

Principle of reciprocal action A management principle that says no change may be made in any unit of an enterprise that does not affect all other units directly or indirectly.

PRN Pro re nata A physician's order for a medication to be administered as needed.

Problem solving The process of examining a problem situation and helping those involved to select and carry out the best course of action for them.

Procedure A step-by-step guide to action that spells out how activities will be carried out in order to attain a goal.

Program A summation of goals, policies, procedures, rules, work assignments, schedules, etc., to be used to execute an overall plan.

RAI Resident assessment instrument is a form used to assess a resident's condition when they have a special problem, e.g., incontinence.

Rapport Harmony and accord between management and employees.

Reinforcement theory Skinner's theory that behavior that goes unrewarded tends to extinguish itself.

Representing The art of interpreting employee desires, actions, and needs to others, especially to upper management levels.

Respondent superior The legal term for the facility being responsible for acts of its employees while they are on duty.

Responsibility Response to the duties assigned and the authority delegated. It cannot be assigned or delegated, it is exacted.

Risk Management A program that reduces occurrences that may lead to action that damages the facility's reputation or results in economic loss.

Rule A specific guide to specific action that has no exception. It states that certain action shall or shall not be taken.

Scalar chain A method of organizing that shows several levels of management from the governing board down to the line workers.

Site A location where information is stored and accessible via computer.

Software The instructions, called programs given to a computer that enable it to do things such as locating a web site that contains desired information.

Span of management The number of employees a manager can effectively supervise (direct and control).

Staff authority A relationship in which one person gives advice, counsel and/or recommendations to another person but cannot enforce decisions.

Staffing The management function of selecting, training, promoting, demoting, terminating, retiring, etc., employees.

Standards Another term for the goals, policies, procedures, rules and other plans used to guide employee behavior and performance.

Strategies General plan of action that focuses largely on long-range goals.

Superior/subordinate relationship The relationship that occurs between the supervisor and his employees in which the supervisor has authority to direct and monitor employee performance.

TQM Total Quality Management. A type of management that involves staff in group problem solving with a focus on improving work quality and promoting employee knowledge and skills.
Two-factor theory Herzberg's theory that factors producing job satisfaction are entirely separate from factors producing job dissatisfaction.

Unity of command Insofar as possible an employee has one supervisor who gives him direction and supervises his work.

Voice response system An automated telephone answering system designed to forward telephone calls, to record messages, or to provide information to the caller.

World Wide Web A convergence of computation and concepts for presenting and linking information dispersed across an Internet in an easily accessible way.

(Winborn E. Davis, et al)

INDEX